THE CHALLENGES OF TAX REFORM IN A GLOBAL ECONOMY

THE CHALLENGES OF TAX REFORM IN A GLOBAL ECONOMY

edited by

James Alm, Jorge Martinez-Vazquez, and Mark Rider
Andrew Young School of Policy Studies,
Georgia State University, Atlanta, USA

Springer

Library of Congress Control Number: 2005934721

ISBN:10: 0-387-29912-2 e-ISBN-10: 0-387-29914-9
ISBN-13: 978-0387-29912-9 e-ISBN-13: 978-0387-29914-3

Printed on acid-free paper.

Printed in the United States of America.

9 8 7 6 5 4 3 2 1

springeronline.com

Contents

Contributing Authors

James Alm Department of Economics, Andrew Young School of Policy Studies, Georgia State University

Rosanne Altshuler Rutgers University

Roy Bahl Department of Economics, Andrew Young School of Policy Studies, Georgia State University

Richard M. Bird University of Toronto, Canada

Robert S. Chirinko Emory University and CESifo

Arindum Das-Gupta Goa Institute of Management, India

Dagney Faulk Indiana University Southeast

Timothy Goodspeed Department of Economics, Hunter College and CUNY Graduate Center

Elizabeth Gugl Department of Economics, University of Victoria, Victoria, British Columbia, Canada

Arnold C. Harberger University of California, Los Angelos

Walter Hettich Department of Economics, California State University at Fullerton, CA.

Janet Holtzblatt Office of Tax Analysis, U.S. Department of the Treasury

Jane Malme Lincoln Institute of Land Policy, Cambridge, Massachusetts

Jorge Martinez-Vazquez Department of Economics, Andrew Young School of Policy Studies, Georgia State University

William McCarten World Bank

Charles E. McLure, Jr. Hoover Institution, Stanford University

Jack M. Mintz C. D. Howe Institute, University of Toronto

Luc Noiset Department of Economics, Kennesaw State University

Michael Rushton Department of Public Adminsitration, Andrew Young School of Policy Studies, Georgia State University

Benno Torgler Yale Center for International and Area Studies, Leitner Program in International and Comparative Political Economy, and Center for Research in Economics, Management and the Arts (CREMA) Switzerland

Sally Wallace Department of Economics, Andrew Young School of Policy Studies, Georgia State University

John Douglas Wilson Department of Economics, Michigan State University East Lansing

Stanley L. Winer Canada Research Chair Professor, School of Public Policy and Department of Economics, Carleton University, Ottawa, Canada

Joan Youngman Lincoln Institute of Land Policy, Cambridge, Massachusetts

George R. Zodrow Baker Institute for Public Policy, Rice University

1

INTRODUCTION

Chapter 1

THINKING ABOUT TAX REFORM IN THE EMERGING GLOBAL ECONOMY

JAMES ALM, JORGE MARTINEZ-VAZQUEZ, AND MARK RIDER
Andrew Young School of Policy Studies, Georgia State University

The last several decades have seen a dizzying array of different tax reforms around the world. Major tax reforms have been undertaken in a number of countries with such diverse backgrounds as China, Colombia, Indonesia, Jamaica, Russia, Spain, the United States, and elsewhere. Even when the entire tax system has not been reformed, many countries have pursued narrower, more specific reforms of individual taxes, especially the value-added tax and income taxes. However, despite the enormous amount of time and resources invested in these reform efforts, the lessons from all of this work have been very unevenly disseminated. There are clearly many unresolved issues, and it seems unlikely that these issues are going to go away. With the steady advance of globalization, regional integration, and technology, it seems more likely that, if anything, the issues of adapting tax systems to new economic environments and reforming specific taxes will become even more pressing in the near future for many countries.

This volume is a collection of original essays that highlight the state of knowledge of tax reform, present new thinking about this issue, and analyze useful policy options. These essays were presented at a conference held in Atlanta in May 2004, and sponsored by the Andrew Young School of Policy Studies at Georgia State University, entitled "The Challenges of Tax Reform in a Global Economy". It is our hope that the essays in this volume will deepen our understanding of the current challenges that tax reforms must address in the emerging global economy, and will allow us to assess the directions that "successful" tax reforms are likely to take in the future.

There are several specific themes in this collection of essays: how to deal with distributional concerns, how to tax capital income, how to design specific taxes (e.g., the income tax, the value-added tax, the property tax), how to think about the political and administrative aspects of tax reform, and how to put all of these separate insights together in a comprehensive reform of a tax system. Each of these themes represents a section in this volume.

The first set of essays in part 2 examines taxation and distribution. The essay by Arnold Harberger surveys much of the literature on how government tax and expenditure policies are distributed across income classes and how these policies in turn affect the underlying distribution of income. Of course, Harberger's own work on the incidence of taxation has had a profound effect on this area of research. He concludes that the distribution of the burden of taxes and the benefits of government spending is considerably more amenable to the influence of government policy than the distribution of income itself. Indeed, Harberger believes that the evidence across many countries is that government has remarkably little ability to affect the underlying distribution of income per se, either from the tax side or from the expenditure side. However, this "counsel of despair," as Harberger puts it, does not mean that government cannot redistribute income via its policies. Indeed, he concludes in particular that government has a greater scope to improve the status of the poor, by raising their incomes and improving their educational attainments, and it is on these areas that government should focus its distributional efforts.

Janet Holtzblatt focuses more on poverty, using the experiences of the United States and the United Kingdom. Countries face some difficult tradeoffs in designing transfers to the poor. Universal benefits can be quite expensive. Instead, benefits can be targeted to meet various goals, such as increasing horizontal and vertical equity, making work more attractive, and lifting families out of poverty, without spending as much as under a system of universal benefits. However, targeting can also increase the complexity of the transfer system, and the higher marginal tax rates required to target benefits on the poor can also worsen work and family incentives. Holtzblatt examines U.S. and U.K. policies over the last several decades, especially the use in these countries of the tax system to provide low-income support. She concludes that providing targeted assistance to individuals via the income tax system (e.g., the U.S. earned income tax credit, the U.K. working families' tax credit) may often be the most appropriate policy.

Dagney Faulk's comments complete the first section, integrating the insights of both essays.

Part 3 makes more explicit some of the international dimensions of tax reform. Charles McLure details the intricacies of transfer pricing and tax havens. Both practices, individually and together, adversely affect the ability of countries – especially less developed countries and countries in transition from socialism – to raise revenues because both practices lead to the avoidance of corporate and individual income taxes. McLure weaves his way through the labyrinth of laws and practices that define the international tax "system," and then details the many ways in which these laws and practices generate revenue losses. He outlines a variety of possible solutions that may help mend the "tears" in the revenue net, including such things as the establishment of transfer pricing guidelines, anti-deferral rules, and anti-tax competition measures. Given the complexity of transfer pricing and tax havens, however, McLure is not very optimistic that these methods will help less developed and transition countries mend their revenue nets.

Timothy Goodspeed focuses on the ways in which tax incentives affect foreign direct investment (FDI), looking specifically at the complicated ways in which FDI incentives can be affected by the international tax system of home and host countries. In his essay, Goodspeed presents some intriguing recent information on the importance of FDI in a sample of countries, and he discusses a number of FDI incentives that operate through the tax system, including lower tax rates on FDI, tax exemptions and holidays, investment incentives, accelerated depreciation, exemption of import duties and/or value-added taxation on input purchases, and subsidized loans. Goodspeed demonstrates that these incentives affect both investment decisions and (as in McLure's earlier analysis) income shifting. Goodspeed concludes that the challenges facing developed countries in their use of tax incentives are considerably different than those facing developing countries. He argues that developing countries are likely to be in a no-win situation in the use of incentives. Such incentives seem unlikely to outweigh the importance of investment fundamentals in attracting FDI and thus will most likely lead to a revenue loss without attracting additional FDI.

The next three papers in this section build on the essays by McLure and Goodspeed by examining different aspects of tax incentives in a world with mobile international capital. Jack Mintz reviews the tax regimes of 15 developing countries that have been the most successful in attracting FDI over the last part of the 1990s, to investigate the common practices of these countries. Like Goodspeed, Mintz finds evidence that these tax incentives (e.g., lower corporate tax rates, tax holidays, capital cost incentives, special financing regimes) have in fact been very successful in attracting investment, and that the more recent practice has emphasized reduced corporate tax rates rather than tax holidays or other incentives. He also constructs a simple theoretical model that demonstrates rate reductions are in most circumstances likely to be the preferred policy of a small open economy; that is, he finds that greater income-shifting via debt finance by multinational firms tends to lower the corporate income tax rate and to reduce the incentive to use investment tax credits to attract FDI. Mintz concludes that both theory and evidence indicate that government incentive policies should focus mainly on reducing tax rates than on providing other types of tax incentives.

Elisabeth Gugl and George Zodrow develop a theoretical model to examine the optimal choice of tax incentives by the government of a small open economy. In their model, there are two types of capital, one type that is mobile and another type that is immobile. The country is a small open economy, taking the world price of all traded outputs and inputs as given, and the government perceives that unilaterally imposing a tax on mobile factors will increase the price of these factors in its own country compared to the rest of the world, leading to some outflow of perfectly and imperfectly mobile capital and thereby lowering the productivity of local factors. They also assume a uniform tax rate on all types of capital, and allow for tax incentives that can lower the effective tax rate on perfectly mobile capital, relative to the effective tax rate of the less mobile capital. Government is assumed to maximize residents' utility subject to firms' profit maximization conditions. Gugl and Zodrow demonstrate that, if head taxes can be imposed by government, then tax incentives should be enacted to leave perfectly mobile capital untaxed, a standard result. However, they also show that, if head taxes cannot be imposed in the efficient amount, tax incentives may help by decreasing the amount of under provision of public services that results from international tax competition facing the small open economy, although these incentives will be less generous than when head taxes are present.

John Douglas Wilson also examines the use of tax incentives by a country facing tax competition from another open economy. Wilson constructs a model in which there are two countries competing for mobile capital in a simultaneous-move game, and he solves for the mixed strategy equilibrium of the game. In particular, he investigates whether a preferential or non-preferential tax regime raises more revenue when one base is perfectly mobile, given that a mixed strategy is played in the non-preferential case. Somewhat surprisingly, Wilson's analysis demonstrates that preferential treatment of a highly mobile tax base can in fact sometimes generate greater expected revenue than in the non-preferential regime.

Rosanne Altshuler discusses the first two essays, and presents some recent empirical evidence that complements their results. Robert Chirinko discusses the next three essays, and places their results in the perspective of the broader tax competition literature.

Part 4 examines some of the more important specific taxes that have been the object of tax reform efforts around the world. James Alm and Sally Wallace look at the practice of taxing individual income in developing countries. The individual income tax is used in many all countries around the world, and is often a significant source of revenues for the government. However, they argue in their essay that it is unlikely – and increasingly so – that a developing country can actually administer a broad-based "global" income tax, in which income from all sources is aggregated and subject to a single rate structure, after adjustments for personal exemptions and deductions. Instead, they make the case that the most suitable form of individual income tax that most developing countries are likely to be able to achieve is one characterized by a "schedular" approach to income taxation, in which each of the main types of income flows (e.g., wages and salaries, dividends, interest, rent) are subject to separate rate schedules that are typically not graduated. Alm and Wallace find evidence for this by focusing on Jamaica. The Government of Jamaica has worked hard to reform its individual income tax, and has made significant progress in improving its structure and performance. Even so, the positive achievements in reforming the Jamaican individual income tax have come largely as a result of a move toward a more schedular approach to income taxation. More generally, Alm and Wallace conclude that the individual income tax should remain in most developing countries' tax portfolios, but that a schedular approach to income taxation is likely to be the most appropriate path for developing countries to travel, especially given the emerging forces that continue to reduce the ability of governments to collect income taxes.

Kelly Edmiston and William Fox look at the value-added tax (VAT). The major initiative in tax reform in the last quarter century has been the worldwide introduction of the VAT, and this tax is now one of the main workhorses in the tax systems of many countries. Edmiston and Fox survey the practice of value-added taxation, and identify some of the key VAT policy issues that have arisen in the implementation of this tax. They examine four main issues that are in need of tax reform efforts: what threshold level should be established for firm registration under the VAT, how does value-added taxation affect trade flows, how should financial services be taxed in a VAT, and how should revenues of a subnational VAT be distributed to subnational governments. They contend that these four issues will be at the center of VAT reform efforts in coming years.

As with the VAT, there have been efforts in many countries to reform the property tax. Jane Malme and Joan Youngmann examine these efforts, in countries as diverse as Indonesia, Japan, Kenya, the Netherlands, Russia, and the United Kingdom. They identify several dominant trends in recent years, including political and economic integration, the impact of political decentralization, the changing importance of property rights and property taxes, and the emerging evidence of the effect of property taxation on land use. They examine the implications of these trends for reform of the property tax. Malme and Youngmann contend that the property tax must remain an important feature of tax systems but also that its reform must reflect the demands of market economies and democratic institutions.

Richard Bird, Jorge Martinez-Vazquez, and Benno Torgler take a somewhat broader perspective, by examining the overall level of tax effort in developing countries. There is a considerable body of empirical work that examines the level of taxes (as a percent of gross domestic product). Most of this work concludes that many countries have the "capacity" to tax that exceeds the "effort" that they make; that is, these countries have "tax handles" that allow them to tax, but they do not seem able to utilize these handles fully. The problem thus seems obvious: poor countries need to tax more if they want to provide the basic services that will allow them to be less poor. The solution is not so obvious, but it seems to lie in changing political institutions. The emphasis in earlier empirical analysis of factors such as tax handles remains important in explaining what countries actually do, but telling a country that wants to raise its tax level to find oil and minerals may not be particularly helpful. Bird, Martinez-Vazquez, and Torgler suggest that institutions might be seen as an indicator of the extent to which citizens feel they have a meaningful "voice" in influencing the state; at the same time, however, the level of taxation can also be expected to be related to the availability of what may be called the "exit option" of the so-called "shadow economy." In their essay, they explore these broad questions. They focus on an empirical examination of the determinants of tax levels across a broad sample of developing and transition countries. They take into account not only "supply factors" like tax handles, but also "demand factors" such as institutions, the size of the shadow economy, wealth inequality, and "tax morale" (e.g., the intrinsic motivation by citizens to pay taxes or their attitude toward the state). Their empirical results suggest that institutions play a significant role in the determination of the level of tax effort of developing and transition countries. Demand factors thus matter, though the conventional supply factors continue to play a robust and significant role throughout the estimations. They conclude that a more legitimate and responsive state is likely an essential precondition for a more adequate level of tax effort in developing countries.

Michael Rushton provides a summary of these essays.

The political and administrative dimensions of tax reform are the subject of part 5. Walter Hettich and Stanley Winer suggest that a formal analysis of tax "reform" as tax change is possible and desirable. They then outline a descriptive model distinguishing different responses to shocks, speculate about the effects of globalization and international institutions, consider the influence of different electoral systems, and examine another approach – another explicit calculation of political feasibility. Their conclusion is that tax reform can be studied as a positive enterprise, in which a tax change is the natural outcome of political and economic shocks. The consideration of information and coordination problems in political equilibrium suggests ways of discussing tax change, and political feasibility can be assessed using formal models of political equilibrium.

Arindam Das-Gupta looks more precisely at the role of tax administration. He argues that we know very little about tax administration: there is no "one size fits all" policy; "the devil is in the details", implementation is as important as design and political will, support, and non-interference in operations are indispensable prerequisites for successful reform of tax administrations. He believes that the key technical administrative insights are that tax designs that economize on information requirements are least costly to administer, and he recommends a tax system with as few taxes as possible, a limited number of rates for each tax, limited exemptions, and a broad base as one that has proven much easier to administer and results in higher compliance levels than more complex tax systems.

William McCarten also examines the administrative aspects of tax reforms. The typical components of tax administration reform strategies include such elements as improving management and organizational structures, modernizing taxpayer registration, strengthening return processing and payment systems, improving collection enforcement, developing effective audit programs, developing better taxpayer services, improving appeals, automating and establishing unique taxpayer identifications, and, especially, establishing large taxpayer units (LTUs). McCarten characterizes the classic LTU as one involving the monitoring of large taxpayers exclusively through registration, tax accounting, collections, auditing, and taxpayer service provision covering more than one type of tax. He presents evidence that LTUs have facilitated major tax policy reforms, such as adoption of a VAT and the reform of administrative procedures like the implementation of self-assessment, modern auditing, electronic filing of tax statements, and the functional organization of work. Overall, McCarten presents evidence that these LTUs have had positive effects in a range of dimensions, such as improved compliance, fewer abuses of transfer pricing, the introduction of new organizational structures and procedures, better management of arrears, and the provision of better services to large taxpayers. He also recognizes that there are some risks involved with LTU establishment, including the creation of a "parallel" tax administration, the lack of modernization of procedures for medium and small taxpayers, the political interference in LTU's day-to-day operations, and the over-emphasis on control of large taxpayers. McCarten concludes that the long-term effectiveness of LTUs depends on its incorporation into a broader tax administration reform.

Luc Noiset invokes his own experiences in his discussion of these papers.

Roy Bahl synthesizes the general themes of the essays in the final section (part 6) of the volume. Whether tax reform is partial or comprehensive, he contends that careful study ought to precede recommendation for action. Bahl asks whether the current environment for tax reform means that "careful study" means something different in the emerging global economy. Should countries be advised to design their comprehensive reform studies in different ways in the global economy? Should international advisors think differently about how to structure their advice? Should there be some universal "rules" that might guide the next round of comprehensive tax reform efforts in developing countries? Bahl argues that the new setting for comprehensive tax reform may cause different thinking about the options for tax reform. In this new context, he suggests that some of the longstanding ideas about the best route to tax reform might be rethought and possibly some priorities might be changed. He proposes six propositions for this rethinking:

- A comprehensive reform can succeed even in the context of a fiscal crisis
- Comprehensive tax reform should be designed as big-bang as opposed to piecemeal
- The objective of vertical equity cannot drive a comprehensive tax reform
- The effects of taxes on economic decisions play a more important role in the design of comprehensive reform than in the past
- Reform should emphasize first policy and then administration
- Fiscal reform is probably better than tax reform.

As Bahl concludes, the challenge facing many governments is to get its comprehensive reform plan from the bookshelf to implementation, and he suggests four main guidelines for implementation of a comprehensive reform program. First, the government must see the project as its own and not that of a donor or even that of a technical assistance research team. Second, the technical assistance team should have the right mix of skills and experience, and above all, should have expert credentials. Third, tax reform should not be hurried: it takes time to get the technical proposals properly in place, and the public debate needs time. Finally, education about tax reform is important.

In summary, it is our hope that the essays in this volume will provide guidance to policy makers charged with the reform of tax systems, and will deepen our understanding of the relevant problems and issues of tax reform.

2

TAXATION AND DISTRIBUTION

Chapter 2

TAXATION AND INCOME DISTRIBUTION: MYTH AND REALITIES

ARNOLD C. HARBERGER
University of California, Los Angelos

1. INTRODUCTION

In this paper I first explore some evidence from existing studies of the impact of taxes on the income distribution of a country. The main point of such studies is that the tax systems in question do not stray much from the line of proportionality—i.e. from total tax payments that are approximately proportional to the incomes of taxpayers. This evidence suggests that the tax systems in question have little effect upon the income distribution in their countries.

At this point we suggest that it would be more relevant to pose the question of how the costs of government are shared by different segments of the population, especially by different income groups. This way of framing the question has much less potential for demagoguery and sensationalism than statements with respect to the income distribution. In particular it does not accept or imply that the government in power is in some sense "responsible" for whatever happens to the nation's income distribution during its tenure. When the question is put this way, the same studies referred to earlier take on a different flavor. When one says that a tax system doesn't affect the income distribution, it sounds as if that system lacks the potency to do something that it should be doing. When one describes the same system by saying that the top quintile pays 40 to 50 percent of the total tax bill, while the bottom quintile pays 4 or 5 percent, the impression one garners is quite different. Now it carries no connotation of impotence, nor, for most people, of inequity.

Of course, the above tells only part of the story. Public finance economists have long said that the progressivity or regressivity of any individual tax is a matter of little interest or relevance; If one is interested in how the tax burden is shared, one has to look to the progressivity or regressivity of the entire tax system. That part is certainly true, but note that it also invites the further question of how different income groups are affected by the expenditure side of the government's budget. Thinking along this line has led to studies in which the authors tried to calculate the impact of "taxes and transfers" or of "taxes and government spending" on different segments of the income distribution. Such studies have typically found that expenditures are more evenly spread among the income groups than are taxes, with the result that the lowest income groups receive significant net subsides, while the taxes of the highest income groups amply exceed the value of the benefits they receive from government expenditures.

We are in substantial accord with the idea of measuring the total impact of government (through the combined effects of taxes and expenditures). And in that vein we would like to suggest a new benchmark measure—not to preclude the now-standard metric of progressivity and regressivity, but rather to supplement it with an additional metric that conveys a lot of useful and interesting information in a very concise form. This benchmark asks the question, how would different income groups be affected if the tax burden were distributed in proportion to income, while the allocable expenditures of government were distributed in proportion to population (i.e. an equal amount per capita)? One can reach this way of thinking by many different routes, but I would like to focus on just one of them. Starting in the mid-1970s, the government of Chile, largely under the aegis of its dynamic planning minister, Miguel Kast, embarked on a program of focalizacion, which in that case represented the targeting of the "social expenditures" of government toward the bottom 20 percent of the population. This approach was widely hailed by international organizations and by humanitarian groups. And in my opinion it was pursued with considerable vigor, not only by Miguel Kast's ministry, but by successor Chilean governments up to the present day. Yet it is arguable that even with all this direct concentration and sincere effort, the bottom 20 percent of Chilean households may not even today receive more than 20 percent of the allocable expenditures of the Chilean government. There are number of reasons for this, not least of which is the fact that just about everywhere, the main beneficiaries of government subsidies to university education are in the higher income groups. But beyond this rather obvious fact there is another one that is equally or even more important. It derives from the "political economy" attributes of government spending and focuses on the three middle quintiles of the income distribution. The proposition is that these three quintiles are typically willing to accept that the lowest groups should receive benefits like free education or free or subsidized medical care. But they are not willing to support such benefits unless they (the three middle quintiles) receive them as well. The political economy forces deriving from this stance of the middle quintiles of the population lead to a situation in which the major social expenditures of most governments (particularly in developing countries) come in the form of entitlements that in principle apply to everybody, but in practice tend to cover at least the bottom four quintiles and often the top one as well.

If one takes the above proposition as "social science truth", then the idea of bringing the lowest quintile "up to par" makes a great deal of sense, but the idea of having a heavy concentration of social expenditures on just the bottom group, to the exclusion of the great bulk of the population, appears illusory. This also renders more meaningful the idea of treating as a sort of benchmark the case in which allocable expenditures are distributed equally among the different segments of the income distribution. Readers please note: I am not trying to give moral overtones to the target of equal per capita distribution of allocable expenditures. But I would say that it is worth noting when a government (or a society) that claims to be concentrating its expenditures on the poor turns out to fall short even of an equal-per-capita standard.

The last part of this paper is devoted to a little-recognized—one might even suggest unrecognized—methodological issue. This concerns the way in which the incidence of taxes is typically measured. The standard methodology entails the "assignment" of tax revenues to specific groups of taxpayers (typically income groups). If a tax raises $100 million, it is that $100 million that is distributed across the population groups. Thus a value added tax might be distributed among families in accordance with their consumption expenditures; alcohol and tobacco taxes might be distributed in accordance with the different groups' expenditures on these items, etc.

Finally, the corporation income tax might be distributed among households in accordance with their dividend receipts (implementing the notion that the tax is borne by shareholders); or in accordance with their consumption expenditures (implementing the idea that the tax is shifted forward to consumers); or it might be split into two parts, assuming part is borne by shareholders and the rest shifted to consumers.

There are many reasons to complain about this approach, but we will focus on just one main line of reasoning—a line that is sufficiently far-reaching to encompass multiple methodological issues. The key element of this line of reasoning is the idea that some groups can easily end up bearing <u>more than the full burden</u> of a tax. That is, a particular group can suffer costs that amply exceed the amount that the government collects from a particular tax. Some readers may here think of the standard triangles that measure the efficiency costs or "excess burdens" of taxes. But our complaint does not refer specifically to these, which are sometimes referred to as second-order effects. Rather our complaint focuses mainly on the direct, first-order effects of taxes upon the distribution of costs and benefits across population groups. Import duties are the simplest example of a particular group bearing costs that exceed what the government collects from a tax. So long as the tariff is a protective one; that is, so long as there are domestic producers who are "protected" by the tariff, the burden borne by users of the product includes not only the higher price paid on actual imports (which is the amount collected by the government), but also the higher price paid on the domestically produced items that are protected by the very same tariff. Students of international trade and of public finance have long been taught that an import tariff is equivalent to a tax on the whole domestic consumption of the item in question (regardless of whether it is imported or domestically produced), together with an equivalent subsidy to the domestic producers of the same item. Thus, if domestic production amounts to twice the amount imported, the burden borne by consumers of the item will be three times the tariff revenue collected by the government, while the implicit subsidy to domestic producers will equal twice the amount of government revenue. Following our line of reasoning, the proper assignment of the distributive effects of the tariff should assign three times the tariff receipts to consumers of the item (as a cost), and up to twice the amount of those receipts to the relevant producer groups (as a benefit).[1]

Tariffs were presented here as a simple and easily understandable example of a particular group bearing significantly more than what the government collects. But they are probably not the most important example. That distinction almost certainly belongs to the corporation income tax, at least in any economy that can be regarded as reasonably "open" to the world market. The key to the incidence of the corporation income tax in such an economy is the manufacturing sector—more specifically, the corporate tradables sector. Here the intuitive vision is that the corporation income tax represents a "wedge" inserted between the price of the final product and the various elements of its cost. In an open-economy setting, the international price of the item is thought of as being set in the world market; it therefore cannot rise to reflect the corporate income tax. At the same time, with capital being internationally mobile, its rate of return (including an appropriate allowance for "country risk") has to be basically the same (net of tax) in the presence of the tax as it was in its absence. The gross-of-tax rate of return therefore has to rise to reflect the tax. The only way to compensate this rise, compatible with a product price that <u>does not change</u> as a result of the tax, is for the wages of labor to fall in the affected activities. But if there is a functioning labor market in the country, the wage cannot fall just in the corporate tradables sector; it has to fall in every sector.

The simplest analysis of this type segments the economy into four sectors—corporate tradables (manufacturing), corporate non-tradables (public utilities and transport), non-corporate tradables (agriculture), and non-corporate non-tradables (services). If wages do not fall to reflect the tax, the manufacturing sector simply goes out of business. If wages do fall, the reduction in wages spreads throughout the economy. Labor everywhere thus shares in the burden of the tax. Lower wages in agriculture are matched by a benefit to landowners, as agricultural prices are basically determined in the world marketplace. Lower wages in services are reflected in a benefit to the users of those services. In public utilities and transport, lower wages absorb all or part of the corporation tax paid by these sectors, but the part that is not thus absorbed is passed on to consumers in the form of higher prices (which can rise as needed because these non-tradables prices are not set in the world market). The first result, then, is that the incidence of the corporation income tax in an open economy falls on labor, but the further result states that labor bears significantly more than what the government collects, with labor's additional cost being reflected principally in benefits to the owners of agricultural land and to the consumers of non-tradable services.

We strongly urge our colleagues to try to pursue this line of thinking in direct studies of incidence for specific countries. Just to signal how big a difference it might make, we have explored (in the final sections of this paper) a simulation experiment with a Cobb-Douglas economy—(where the production functions in every sector are Cobb-Douglas, and where also the demand functions take the form (of constant expenditure shares for each sector) that would follow from a Cobb-Douglas utility function. Some subtleties are involved in interpreting the results of this simulation, which will be explained in the full exposition. We can, however, summarize the key result here—that taking into account the features we have just analyzed causes there to be a much greater burden on labor, and leads to the tax system as a whole being significantly less progressive (or more regressive) than would have been revealed by the traditional methodology of simply allocating tax revenues across income groups in the standard way.

After correcting the methodology, we must still conclude that government does not have a very substantial impact on the distribution of income and welfare across income groups. It also renders even more unrealistic the notion that the distribution of income in a country is something that should be regarded as a major responsibility of government and that the government can "improve" at will, if it only tries.

2. RESULTS OF PREVIOUS STUDIES—THE U.S. CASE

Joseph A. Pechman, longtime director of economic studies at the Brookings Institution, was the major figure in the evolution of tax incidence studies in the United States. His work is aptly summarized in two publications. Who Bears The Tax Burden? (with Benjamin Okner, 1974) and Who Paid The Taxes 1966-85? (1985); both studies lead to the same conclusion, that the US tax system does not deviate much from proportionality with respect to income.

Table 1 shows the distribution of family income before and after tax as calculated by Pechman and Okner for the year 1966. In all, they pursued eight different packages of assumptions. In all of them, the individual income tax was regarded as being borne by the taxpayers themselves (with zero shifting to others). Also in all of them, sales and excise taxes were allocated on the basis of the consumption of the taxed commodities. The main differences among the variants arose from different allocations of the corporation income tax and of the property tax. For example, in different variants the corporation income tax was allocated all in proportion to dividend income, all in proportion to total property income, half and half between these two allocations, half and half between property income and consumption, and finally half in proportion to dividends, a quarter in proportion to consumption and a quarter in proportion to wage income. Similarly there were two allocations of taxes on property income from land (to landowners and to property income in general) and three allocations of taxes on property income from structures (according to expenditures on shelter and consumption, or to property income, or split between these two).

The most progressive variant (1c) assigns the corporation income tax half to dividends and half to property income in general, and assigns property taxes to property income in general. The least progressive variant (3b) assigns half the corporation income tax to consumption and assigns the full property tax on structures in accordance with expenditures on shelter and consumption.

As can be seen in Table 1, there is very little difference in the incidence implications, even of these extreme variants. The after-tax Gini coefficients are almost identical, and the change from before-tax to after-tax is minor in both cases.

Table 1. Distribution[1] of Family Income, Before and After Tax

Decile	Most Progressive Variant[2]			Least Progressive Variant[3]		
	Before Tax	After Tax	Net Change	Before Tax	After Tax	Net Change
1	1.21	1.33	0.12	1.25	1.27	0.02
2	2.67	3.01	0.34	2.73	2.81	0.08
3	4.25	4.46	0.21	4.31	4.37	0.06
4	5.79	5.85	0.06	5.86	5.77	-0.09
5	7.24	7.50	0.26	7.41	7.43	0.02
6	9.06	8.88	-0.18	9.29	8.83	-0.46
7	9.80	10.59	0.79	10.16	10.58	0.42
8	12.27	12.69	0.42	12.43	12.63	0.20
9	15.16	15.20	0.04	15.48	15.26	-0.22
10	32.55	30.49	-2.06	31.08	31.05	-0.03

Source: Pechman and Okner (1974), Table 4-6, p. 56.

[1] Data refer to Federal, State and Local Taxes in the United States for the year 1966.
[2] Pechman and Okner's variant 1c
[3] Pechman and Okner's variant 3d

(Variants differ due to different assumptions used in distributing tax burdens across income groups).

Gini Coefficients: 0.4367 0.4158 -2.09 0.4252 0.4240 -0.0012

Tables 2 and 3 are derived from Pechman's later volume (1985) and show how attributes of the tax system changed over the years. It would be better to say, in this case, how they didn't change over the years. For example the after-tax share of the top decile floated over the years between 45.7 and 48.0 percent under the most progressive variant, and between 46.3 and 48.8 percent under the least progressive variant. At the other extreme all the figures for the after-tax share of the bottom decile lie between 4.1 and 4.8 percent. (see Table 3)

These results should give readers a sense of how it came about that most public finance specialists came to regard proportionality as a good description of the U.S. tax system, in spite of the ostensible progressiveness of its rate structure and its relatively heavy taxation of income from capital.

Table 2. Effective Rates of Federal, State, and Local Taxes By Population Decile. Selected Years, 1966-85

Population Decile	1966	1970	1975	1980	1983
Most Progressive Variant					
1[1]	16.8	18.8	21.2	20.6	21.9
2	18.9	19.5	19.9	20.4	21.3
3	21.7	20.8	20.5	20.6	21.4
4	22.6	23.2	22.0	21.9	22.5
5	22.8	24.0	23.0	22.8	23.1
6	22.7	24.1	23.3	23.3	23.5
7	22.7	24.3	23.6	23.6	23.7
8	23.1	24.6	24.4	25.0	24.6
9	23.3	25.0	25.3	25.7	25.1
10	30.1	30.7	27.1	27.3	25.3
All Deciles					
Least Progressive Variant					
1	27.5	25.8	29.6	28.9	28.2
2	24.8	24.2	24.2	25.7	25.6
3	26.0	24.2	23.4	24.6	24.6
4	25.9	25.9	24.6	25.2	25.2
5	25.8	26.4	25.3	25.8	25.3
6	25.6	26.2	25.3	25.9	25.6
7	25.5	26.2	25.5	26.0	25.4
8	25.5	26.4	26.0	27.1	26.3
9	25.2	26.1	26.3	27.2	26.1
10	25.9	27.8	24.2	24.9	23.3
All Deciles[2]	25.9	26.7	25.5	26.3	25.3

Source: Pechman (1985), p. 68.

[1] Includes only units to the sixth to tenth percentiles.
[2] Includes negative incomes not shown separately.

Table 3. Distribution of Adjusted Family Income, Before and After Federal, State, and Local Taxes. Selected Years, 1966-85

Population Quintile	1966	1970	1973	1980	1985
		Most Progressive Variant			
Before Tax					
First	3.9	4.1	4.6	4.1	4.2
Second	10.0	10.1	10.2	9.7	10.0
Third	16.3	16.2	15.6	15.4	15.8
Fourth	22.0	23.0	21.8	21.9	23.3
Fifth	47.7	46.5	47.9	48.9	47.7
After Tax					
First	4.3	n.a.	4.8	4.3	4.4
Second	10.3	n.a.	10.5	10.1	10.2
Third	16.4	n.a.	15.8	15.6	15.8
Fourth	23.3	n.a.	22.0	22.0	22.4
Fifth	45.7	n.a.	46.8	48.0	47.3
		Least Progressive Variant			
Before Tax					
First	4.0	4.1	4.6	4.1	4.2
Second	10.2	10.2	10.3	9.8	10.0
Third	16.7	16.5	15.8	15.6	15.9
Fourth	22.6	23.5	22.1	22.1	22.5
Fifth	46.6	45.7	47.2	48.4	47.3
After Tax					
First	4.1	n.a	4.6	4.1	4.2
Second	10.1	n.a	10.4	9.9	10.0
Third	16.3	n.a	15.7	15.4	15.6
Fourth	23.2	n.a	21.9	21.8	22.2
Fifth	46.3	n.a	47.5	48.8	48.0

Source: Pechman (1985), p. 74.

2.1 Results of Previous Studies—The Chilean Case

Chile is a good example of a developing country with a relatively modern tax system and a quite effective tax administration. Its income tax is quite progressive, with maximum rates of around 45%. Yet in spite of this, an allocation of tax revenues following a methodology similar to Pechman's produces a similar result. Table 4 shows virtually no change in the Gini coefficient (indeed, a slight increase—meaning a slightly more unequal distribution after taxes than before taxes)

Table 5 reports on a series of experiments in which different hypothetical modifications of the tax system are assumed. Once again, this panoply of potential changes leads to virtually zero change in the Gini coefficient. Zero change, of course, is precisely what would happen if the tax system were strictly proportional.

Table 4. Taxes and Income Distribution in Chile, 1996

Income Decile	Income Share Before Tax	Income Share After Tax	Taxes as % of Group Income	Taxes as % of Total Income[1]
	(1)	(2)	(3)	(4)
1	1.45	1.40	14.4	0.21
2	2.74	2.63	16.0	0.44
3	3.77	3.62	15.8	0.60
4	4.73	4.59	15.2	0.72
5	5.56	5.47	15.0	0.84
6	6.76	6.64	14.3	0.97
7	8.22	8.21	13.8	1.13
8	10.60	10.61	13.1	1.40
9	15.42	15.75	12.2	1.88
10	40.75	41.09	11.8	4.81
Total	100.00	100.00		13.0
Average Gini Coef.	0.4883	0.4961		

Source: Engel, Galetovich and Raddatz (1999), Table 5, p. 172.

[1] Calculated from Col. (1) x Col (5)

3. THE IMPACT OF TRANSFER PAYMENTS

It was pointed out on the introduction to this paper that the distribution of tax burdens is only part of the story—the expenditure side can be equally or even mere important. Both of the studies cited previously delve a bit into the expenditure side, by providing data on the distribution of transfer payments across income groups. These results are presented in Tables 6 and 7.

Table 5. Distribution of Income in Chile (1996) Under Alternative Assumption

Case Description	**Gini Coefficient**	**Income of Top Decile ÷ Income of Bottom Decile**
1. Actual Distribution Before Taxes	0.4883	13.41
2. Actual Distribution After Taxes	0.4961	14.12
3. Case # 2, With Allowances Eliminated	0.4954	14.07
4. Case # 2, Eliminating Both Allowances and Underreporting of Income	0.4837	13.37
5. Case # 2, Increasing VAT from 18% to 25%	0.5003	14.44
6. Case # 2, Eliminating Import Tariffs	0.4906	13.64
7. Case # 2, Doubling Excise Tax on Gasoline	0.4958	14.08
8. Case # 2, Replacing Personal Income Tax by a Flat Tax With High Exemption Level	0.4995	14.35
9. Case # 4, Replacing Personal Income Tax By a Flat Tax With high Exemption Level	0.4925	13.92

Source: Engel, Galetovich and Raddatz (1999), Table 5 - 9, pp. 172-176.

Table 6 reveals a highly progressive distribution of transfer payments in the U.S., with such payments accounting for large fractions of total income in the lower deciles, and quite small fractions in the higher deciles. The second column of the table presents the transfers received by each group as a fraction of the overall income of all groups taken together. Thus, if transfers were distributed on an equal basis per capita, all the figures in this second column would be equal. As it stands, the shares going to the different deciles hover around 1.1 percent of total income, with the lower deciles having a somewhat larger share, and the higher deciles and somewhat smaller share.

For the case of Chile, the paper by Engel, et al.did not give an allocation of transfers by income group, but it was possible to fill this gap making use of data provided by Schkolnik (1995). These data are presented in the third column of Table 7. This column also shows the lower income quintiles receiving higher total transfers than the higher quintiles.

Table 6. U.S. Transfer Payments By Income Decile, 1980

Decile	Transfers as % of Family Income[1]	Transfers as % of Total Income[2]	Taxes as % of Total Income
1	99.8	1.3	1.3
2	56.5	1.6	2.8
3	34.7	1.5	4.2
4	23.7	1.3	5.6
5	15.5	1.1	7.1
6	10.7	0.9	8.5
7	7.7	0.8	10.1
8	5.6	0.7	12.0
9	4.3	0.7	15.3
10	2.6	0.9	33.1
			100.0

Source: Pechman (1985), Tables 4.6 and 4.7, pp. 52-53.

[1] The percentages in this column are the averages of the percentages given by Pechman in Table 4.7 for transfers under his variants 1c and 3b. They show transfers received by each group as a percentage of the income of that group.
[2] The percentages given in this column are the averages of those in Table 4.7 for Pechman's variants 1c and 3b. These show transfers received by each group as percentages of the total income of all the groups (deciles) taken together.

In spite of the apparent strong progressivity of transfers as shown in Tables 6 and 7, their impact on the final distribution of income is relatively modest. Pechman reports that transfers by themselves reduce the Gini coefficient from .480 to .443, while taxes and transfers taken together bring it to .440.[2] The Chilean exercise of Table 7 shows that taxes and transfers taken together bring the Gini coefficient from .455 to .416.

Table 7. Taxes, Transfers and Income Distribution in Chile, 1996

Income Quintile	Income Share Before Taxes and Transfers[1]	Quintile Taxes As % of Total Income[2]	Quintile Transfers As % of Total Income[3]	Income Shares After Taxes and Transfers
1	4.19	0.65	2.25	5.96
2	8.50	1.32	1.68	9.54
3	12.32	1.81	1.17	12.60
4	18.82	2.53	0.71	18.35
5	56.17	6.69	0.19	53.55
Sum	100.00	13.00	6.00	100.00
Gini Coef.	0.4552	-	-	0.4158

Source: Engel, Galetovich and Raddatz (1999).

[1] Based on Table 4, Column (1).
[2] Based on Table 4, Column (4).
[3] Total Transfers (6.00) equal to 0.374 times Total Taxes (13.00). Distributed across quintiles by fractions specified in Schkolnik (1993).

4. A NOTE ON TRANSFERS AND ALLOCABLE EXPENDITURES

Transfer payments, of course, represent only a part of total government expenditures. In general, they include items that end up being counted as money income by taxpayers and as personal income in the national accounts. They accordingly do not incorporate items like free or subsidized public schooling, medical care, housing and the like.

I like to make a distinction between expenditures of these kinds on the one hand, and general government expenditures on items like administration, defense, police, the justice system, etc. on the other. The term I use in making this distinction is "allocable"—the concept being that certain classes of expenditures (like those on schooling, medical care and housing, plus, of course, direct transfers) can readily he allocated across population groups, while others (administration, defense, etc.) cannot.

I believe we can be quite sure that when all allocable expenditures are taken into account, their distribution across deciles will show less of a preference for the lower income groups than we find, taking into account transfers alone. That is, the final distribution of allocable expenditures would probably end up being relatively more equal across income groups, perhaps even skewed toward the middle quintiles rather than toward the bottom.

As an exercise, I present in Table 8 the case of a hypothetical income distribution, in which the successive quintiles receive, respectively, 5, 10, 15, 20 and 50 percent of the overall income pie. This distribution is similar to those of some developing countries, but typically their distributions are more unequal than this one. This means that the present example is a somewhat "conservative" representative of the typical third world country. Interestingly, this hypothetical exercise gives us a reduction of .03 in the Gini coefficient, whereas the empiral results for the U.S. and Chile gave us a reduction of about .04. But note that we have reason to expect a smaller reduction in this exercise, because we are in principle taking account of all allocable expenditures, rather than just explicit transfers.

Table 8. Distribution Effects of Taxes and Expenditures

Income Quintile	**Group Income Before Taxes and Alloc. Expend.**	**Taxes (=20% of Group Income)**	**Allocable Expenditures**	**Group Income after taxes and Alloc. Expend.**
1	100	20	40	120
2	200	40	40	200
3	300	60	40	280
4	400	80	40	360
5	1000	200	40	840
Total	2000	400	200	1800
Gini	0.4			0.37

Note: Allocable expenditures are assumed to equal ½ of total tax revenues, and to be equally distributed across income groups.

5. NOW, SOME SERIOUS DOUBTS ABOUT METHODOLOGY

In our reporting on the U.S. and Chilean studies, we implicitly accepted at face value the authors' approach to the measurement of tax incidence. Here we question that approach, arguing along the lines set out in the introductory section of this paper. As argued there, we are troubled by the fact that no allowance was made in these studies (nor, to our knowledge, in incidence studies in general) for the phenomenon of particular groups ending up bearing more than the full burden (i.e., more than the government collects) of particular types of taxes, while other groups end up being important net beneficiaries of the same taxes. We mentioned in the introduction the cases of protective import tariffs (where the protected domestic producers are the beneficiaries) and of the corporation income tax in an open economy setting

(where the owners of agricultural land and the consumers of non-tradable services are the groups that gain as a consequence of the tax)

While the case of import tariffs deserves attention on its own merits, it is not clear that making the necessary adjustment would affect the country's income distribution in any predictable or pronounced way. For that reason, we have here concentrated on the case of the corporation income tax in an open economy.

As indicated in the introduction, our model consists of four sectors—two (manufacturing and agriculture) producing tradables and two ("public utilities and transport" and services) producing non-tradables. In each of these categories the first-named sector is considered to be corporate in form, thus having to pay the corporation income tax (CIT) on its income. Agriculture and services are considered to be predominantly non-corporate in form, thus not being liable for the CIT.

In each of the sectors, the production process is described by a Cobb-Douglas production function. The factors of production are labor and land in the case of agriculture, and labor and capital in the cases of the other three sectors. Of these, public utilities and transport is the most capital-intensive, and services the most labor-intensive. Total expenditures in this economy are initially assumed to equal total income, and to be divided among the sectors as follows—40% to manufactures, 30% to services, 20% to public utilities and transport and 10% to agriculture.

Table 9 summarizes this allocation in the initial (no-tax) equilibrium. Given the earnings of capital shown there, we can work back to the implied capital stock by considering a certain equilibrium rate of return (here 10%). In this way we derive the initial capital stock of 4500.

Table 9. The Four-Sector Model: No taxes (Units are Equilibrium Monetary Flows)

Sector	**Value of Product**	**Return to capital**	**Earnings of Labor**	**Return to Farmland**
Manufacturing	400	200	200	0
Agriculture	100	0	50	50
Pub. Util. & Transp.	200	150	50	0
Services	300	100	200	0
Total	1000	450	500	50

Note: Implied total capital stock = 4500 (assuming, equilibrium rate of return = 10%)

Pm = Pa = Pput = Ps = Pfl = W = 1

From Table 9 it can be inferred that the shares of capital and labor are 75-25 in public utilities and transport, 50-50 in manufacturing and 33-67 in services. Also, land and labor share equally in the income generated by agriculture. Equilibrium of trade is assumed. This is fully compatible with some manufactures being exported while others are imported, and similarly for agricultural products. In the initial equilibrium, however, we additionally assume that trade is balanced within each of these tradables sectors. This is needed for total demand for manufactures to end up equaling total supply, and similarly for agricultural products.

We now assume a new "tax wedge" is thrust into this placid scene. The government is now going to take 30 percent of the income earned by capital that is occupied in manufacturing and in public utilities and transport. To keep macroeconomic balance, the government has to spend this money. We assume it to be spent on the products of the four sectors in the same proportions (.4, .3, .2, .1) as apply to private sector spending. This is the simplest possible assumption we can make concerning government demand.

The insertion of the 30% tax wedge wreaks all kinds of havoc. Capital, not being able to earn its market rate of return in the two tradables sectors, flees the country. With the same labor force now collaborating with a smaller capital stock, wages go down. The prices of agricultural and manufactured products cannot change (being set in the international marketplace). In the end, the fall in wages in manufacturing has to be sufficient to absorb the impact of the new tax wedge, thus permitting both that product price should remain the same and that the after-tax return to capital is restored to its equilibrium level of 10 percent.

In this process the output of agriculture increases, while that of the other sectors decreases. Landowners benefit from a 42 percent rise in the return on land; buyers of services benefit from a fall of 21 percent in their price. Buyers from the public utilities and transport sector, on the other hand, suffer a price rise of 19.5 percent. The biggest part of the story, however, is that a) GDP falls by 30 percent b) wages fall by 30 percent and c) the domestic capital stock falls by 52 percent, from 4500 to 2160.

The above effects are shown in Table 10, where the assumption is made that trade is balanced. Perhaps better put, it is assumed that when capital leaves the country as a result of the insertion of the tax wedge, there are no further repercussions. The income yielded by that capital simply does not appear in the post-tax scenario.

Table 11 differs from Table 10 precisely by taking explicitly into account the income from this outward flight capital. The equilibrium of Table 11 is found by the country's having an excess of expenditures over production that is precisely equal to the earnings (227) from the capital that moved abroad.

Note that product and factor prices are no different as between Tables 10 and 11. The key to everything is price formation in the manufacturing sector. Its Cobb-Douglas production function has a mathematical twin, or "dual", expressing the relationship of factor and product prices. This is $P_m = P_{kg}^{\ 1/2} w^{\ 1/2}$, where P_{kg} is the gross-of-tax rental price of capital services. If all initial values are set at 1, we have that P_{kg} must go up to 1.428 in order for the net price to stay at 1.0. Since P_m must also stay at 1.0, w must fall to 0.7, independent of what happens to the earnings of the capital that moves out of the country.

Table 10. The Four-Sector Model: CIT – 30% (Units are Equilibrium Monetary Flows)

Sector	**Domestic Demand**	**Value of Product**	**Return to Capital**	**Earnings of Labor**	**Return to Farmland**
Manufacturing	280	207.15	103.57	103.57	0
Agriculture	70	142.85	0	71.43	71.42
Pub. Util. & Transp.	140	140	105	35	0
Services	210	210	70	140	0
Total	**700**	**700**	**278.57**	**350**	**71.42**

Note:

Taxes (CIT) = 0.3 x (103.57 + 105)	62.57
Cap Return (net)	216
Capital Stock (@ 10% net rate of return)	2160

Pm=Pa=1
Ps= 0.79
Pfl=1.43
Pput=1.195
w=0.70

	Manufacturing	Agriculture
Domestic Demand	280.00	70.00
Domestic Supply	207.15	142.85
Import	72.85	
Export		72.85

The big difference between Tables 10 and 11 is with respect to the allocation of resources. Whereas in Table 10, the supply of goods is divided 50-50 between tradables and non-tradables, that division becomes 34-66. Recall that in Table 11 aggregate demand is 927 compared with an aggregate supply of 700. Our demand conditions require that half of the aggregate demand must go to services and public utilities and transport. That amounts to 463.5, and since we are talking here of non-tradables, local resources must be present in the non-tradables sector to accommodate this demand. This leaves only 236.5 of resources to produce tradables. The excess of demand for tradables (463.5) over their local production of 236.5 over their local production of 236.5 is precisely 227, which represents the income stemming from the 2270 of capital that moved abroad as a result of the tax.[3]

Table 11. The Four-Sector Model: CIT – 30%; Equilibrium Trade Deficit = 227

Sector	**Domestic Demand**	**Domestic Supply**	**Return to Capital**	**Earnings of Labor**	**Return to Farmland**
Manufacturing	370.80	93.64	46.82	46.82	-
Agriculture	92.70	142.86		71.43	71.43
Pub. Util. & Transp.	185.40	185.40	139.05	46.35	
Services	278.10	278.10	92.70	185.40	
Total	927.00	700.00	278.57	350.00	71.43

Note:
Tax on Capital = (0.3 x 185.87) = 55.76
Net Earnings in Capital at Home = 222.81
Net Earnings in Capital Abroad = 227.19
Total Earnings from Capital = 450.00

Trade Deficit = Total Demand – Total Supply = 227
Trade Deficit = Tradables Demand – Tradables Supply
Trade Deficit = Income from Capital Abroad
Product and Factor Prices = Same as table 10

6. RELAXING THE ASSUMPTIONS: THE U.S. CASE

International trade economists have long experience with the "small country hypothesis", which postulates that the country in question is a price-taker for its imports, for its exports, and in the world capital market. This is precisely, the assumption we have used in our exercises up to this point.

It is hard to exaggerate the power of the small country hypothesis in enabling us to deal simply with what might otherwise be problems of brain-wracking complexity.

However, this assumption introduces its own rigidities, and it is always useful to inquirewhether one's conclusions are reasonably robust, in cases where the small-country assumption is relaxed. This is what we attempt to do in Table 12. I label it the U.S. case, because of the high relative weight of the United States in the world capital market. It is perfectly reasonable to expect that a fall in world interest rates (or other returns to capital) would surely result if, as a consequence of a tax (or some other disturbances) we were to observe an outward movement of an important fraction of the U.S. capital stock.

This sort of scenario is simulated in Table 12, where the resulting fall in world rates of return is taken to be one percentage point. Table 12 is like Table 11, in that the country is assumed to be spending the income of the capital that went abroad as a result of the tax wedge. It differs in that the country's total net income from capital, which was assumed to be 450 both in the no-tax situation (Table 9) and in the post-tax equilibrium of Table 11, is now taken (in Table 12) to be 405, representing a 9% return rather than one of 10%. The 9% rate is to be thought of as the new market-clearing rate.throughout the world capital market, not as anything that is "special" for U.S-owned capital assets.

Table 12. The Four-Sector Model: The U.S. Case Return to Capital Falls to 9% CIT – 30%; Equilibrium Trade Deficit = 150 (Units are Equilibrium Monetary Flows)

Sector	Domestic Demand	Domestic Supply	Return to Capital	Earnings of Labor	Return to Farmland
Manufacturing	37.1	185.3	92.6	92.7	-
Agriculture	92.8	128.6		64.3	64.3
PU & T	185.6	185.6	139.2	91.4	
Services	278.3	278.3	92.8	185.5	
Total	**927.8**	**777.8**	**324.6**	**388.9**	**64.3**

Note:
Tax in Capital = 0.3 x (92.6 + 139.2) = 69.5
Net Earnings in Capital at Home = 255.1
Net Earnings in Capital Abroad = 149.9
Total Earnings from Capital = 405.0 (= 9% x 4500)

Trade Deficit = Total Demand – Total Supply = 150
Trade Deficit = Tradables Demand – Tradables Supply = 150
Trade Deficit = Income from Capital Abroad = 149.9

Pm = Pa = 1; w = 0.778; Pfl = 1.286
Pput = 1.134; Ps = 0.82

One byproduct of this scenario is that foreign owners of capital suffer a similar one point reduction in their rate of return, simply as a consequence of the U.S. CIT. The beneficiaries of this reduction would presumably be the workers of those foreign countries. If manufacturing in those countries also was described by a Cobb-Douglas production function with a 50-50 split between labor and capital, then a drop of capital's return from 10% to 9% would cause the wage rate to rise in inverse proportion, from index 100 to index 111.

The results of Table 12 are interesting but not surprising. It is perfectly reasonable that more of the capital stock should stay in the country when the required rate of return is 12.857 percent (which yields 9% after tax) in the corporate sector, than when it is 14.286 percent (which yields 10% after tax). Similarity more capital should stay in the non-corporate sector when the required rate of return there is 9% than when it is 10%. So instead of 2228 of capital staying in the country (in the case of Table 11) we have 2834 units staying at home in the case of Table 12. The larger stock, collaborating with the same labor force, generates a higher real wage (0.778 instead of 0.700) in the local economy. Since there is less capital abroad, and since it is earning at a lower rate, it should come as no surprise that the trade deficit would have to be lower (150 rather than 227), because in the exercises of Tables 11 and 12 the only source of financing for this deficit is the earnings of the capital that went abroad as a consequence of the tax.

The relaxation of the small country assumption thus brings us no surprise, and I believe it is fair to say that the broad picture that emerged from Table 11 holds up very well as we move to Table 12. All movements are in the same direction, but smaller in magnitude.

We did not attempt at this point to modify the price taker assumptions with respect to the country's import and export goods. This possibility is taken up in Harberger (1995), where it is demonstrated that these assumptions can also be relaxed without changing the fundamental analytical skeleton we have been working with.

7. IMPLICATIONS FOR INCOME DISTRIBUTION

We now embark on a series of exercises in which we try to extract the implications of the preceding scenarios, with respect to the distribution of income of the country.

For calculating the effects of the corporation income tax on the distribution of income we start by assuming how the incomes from capital, labor and farmland would be distributed in the absence of any tax. Table 13 shows this assumed distribution, which is the same as the one shown in Table 8. Its Gini coefficient, as before, is 0.40.

The effects of a CIT of 30% under standard open-economy assumptions all stem from the requirement of price equilibrium in the manufacturing sector. The "dual" expression for pricing of manufactures would be $P_m = w^{1/2} P_{kg}^{1/2}$ where P_{kg} is the gross of tax rental price of capital and P_m the price of manufactures. We know that P_{kg} must rise from 1 to (1/0.7); hence w must fall from 1 to 0.7 in order for P_m to stay at 1.0

Since the corresponding "dual" for agricultural prices is $P_a = w^{1/2} P_{fl}^{1/2}$, we see that in order for P_a to stay at 1.0, P_{fl}, the rental price of farmland, must rise to 1.4286 (=1/0.7). These results are embodied in Tables 14 and 15.

Table 13. Distribution of Income by Quantities (Base Cases: No Taxes)

	Total	**Quintiles**				
Income From		**1**	**2**	**3**	**4**	**5**
Labor	500	50	75	100	150	125
Land	50	-	-	-	-	50
Capital	450	-	25	50	50	325
Total	1000	50	100	150	200	500

Note:
Gini Coefficient = 0.40

Labor's Wage = 1.00
Rent of Land = 1.00
Return to Capital = 10%

Capital Stock (Domestic = Total) = 4500

This case corresponds to the situation depicted in Table 9

Comparing Tables 14 and 15 we see how one can quite "naturally" get a wrong impression, simply by measuring the distribution only of the income that is generated domestically. Looking at it that way, it appears that the CIT actually "improves" the distribution of income (if only very slightly), with the Gini coefficient dropping from 0.40 to 0.394. In contrast the true situation is shown in Table 14, where the Gini coefficient turns out to be 0.446.[4]

In Table 16 we pursue the scenario of the U.S. case, as derived in Table 12. In this case we pursue the effects of the CIT on the earnings of the capital assets employed domestically, but not of the part that left the country as a result of the tax. This leads to just a very modest change in the Gini coefficient, in spite of the fall in the rate of return from 10% to 9%. This result stems from the fact that the reduced rate of return leads to more capital remaining in the country. The influences of these two forces tend to offset each other in the calculation of the Gini coefficient.

Table 14. Distribution of Income by Quantities; CIT = 30%, All Capital Income Counted

	Total	**Quintiles**				
Income From		**1**	**2**	**3**	**4**	**5**
Labor	350.00	35	52.5	70	105	87.5
Land	71.43	-	-	-	-	71.43
Capital (net)	450.00	-	25.0	50.0	50.0	325.0
Total	871.43	35.0	77.5	120.0	155.0	483.93

Note:
Gini Coefficient = 0.448

Labor's Wage = 0.70
Rent of Land = 1.4286
Return to Capita = 10%

This case corresponds to the situations depicted in Tables 10 and 11. They are the same with respect to income earned by factors of production. They differ in that, in Table 10, the income earned by capital outside the country is thought of as also being spent abroad. In Table 11, this income is thought to be repatriated and spent at home.

Table 17 follows the same general scenario as Table 16, except that in this case the calculation now counts the income earned abroad on the capital that left the country. This adjustment makes clear that the actual effect of the corporation income tax is to make the distribution of income somewhat more unequal. The move in the direction of greater inequality is, however, not as marked as that shown in Table 14. This is because a) the return on capital is 9% rather than 10%, and b) the wage falls, as a consequence of the tax, only to 0.778 rather than to 0.700 as in Table 14.

The exercises depicted in Table 10-17 represent a departure from common practice in empirical studies of tax incidence, in that they quite clearly take account of the fact that a given group (in this case labor) can end up bearing a burden that is much greater than what the government collects. In the case of Table 11, whose distributional consequences are laid out in Table 14, labor's earnings fall by a full 300, while the government's collections from the CIT amount to only 55.78.

Table 15. Distribution of Income by Quantities; CIT = 30%, Income from Abroad Not Counted

	Total	**Quintiles**				
Income From		**1**	**2**	**3**	**4**	**5**
Labor	350.00	35.00	52.50	70.00	105	87.50
Land	71.43	-	-	-	-	71.43
Capital	222.81	-	12.38	24.77	24.77	160.89
Total	644.24	35.00	64.88	94.77	129.77	319.82

Note:
Gini Coefficient = 0.394

Labor's Wage = 0.70
Rent of Land = 1.4286
Return to Capital = 10%

Capital Used Domestically = 2227
Capital Held Abroad = 2273

(This case corresponds to the situation depicted in Table 11, but not counting the income earned by capital located outside the country).

Table 16. Distribution of Income by Quantities; CIT = 30%, Income from Abroad Not Counted

	Total	**Quintiles**				
Income From		**1**	**2**	**3**	**4**	**5**
Labor	388.90	38.89	58.34	77.78	116.67	97.22
Land	64.30	-	-	-	-	64.30
Capital	255.10	-	14.17	28.34	28.35	184.24
Total	708.30	38.89	72.51	106.12	145.02	345.76

Note:
Gini Coefficient = 0.388

Labor's Wage = 0.778
Rent of Land = 1.286
Return to Capital = 9%

Capital Used Domestically = 2833
Capital Held Abroad = 1667

(This case corresponds to the situation depicted in Table 12, but not counting the income from capital located outside the country).

Table 17. Distribution of Income by Quantities; CIT = 30%, Income from Abroad is Counted (the U.S. Case-Return to Capital Falls to 9%)

Income From	Total	Quintiles 1	2	3	4	5
Labor	388.90	38.89	58.34	77.78	116.67	97.20
Land	64.30	-	-	-	-	64.30
Capital	405.00	-	22.50	45.00	45.00	292.50
Total	858.20	38.89	80.84	122.78	161.67	454.02

Note:
Gini Coefficient = 0.425

Labor's Wage = 0.778
Rent of Land = 1.286
Return to Capital = 9%

Capital Used Domestically = 2833
Capital Held Abroad = 1667

(This case corresponds to the situation depicted in Table 12, but in this case counting the income from capital located outside the country).

In the case of Table 12, whose distributional results are shown in Table 17, labor's earnings fall by 222, while government receipts from the tax amount to only 69.5.

It would be wonderful if, in a real-world empirical study, we could obtain reasonably accurate data on what would be a country's stock of capital, both in the presence and in the absence of a given tax (or of a whole set of taxes). Unfortunately, there is little hope of achieving such a goal, so we will probably have to be content with simulations like the ones presented here. They should be linked to empirical data, of course, by calibrating them to the actual distributions of demand and of production by sector, and to the actual shares of the different factors in the total product of each sector. In such exercises, Cobb-Douglas assumptions can serve as a convenient starting point, but the aim should be to achieve as good an approximation as one can to the actual production relationships that prevail in any given real-world case. Where the data cannot be mobilized to give us strong evidence on production and demand relationships, the best strategy is probably to explore the results of different "packages" of assumptions, spanning a plausible range[5], in the hope that some "robust" conclusions will emerge.

In conclusion I would emphasize that it is much more sensible to focus studies of this type on the direct effects of taxes (or better, of taxes plus allocable expenditures) on the costs and benefits accruing to particular groups, than to concentrate attention on the distribution of income (or a measure of it like the Gini coefficient). In our oversimplified case, is it not more relevant to say that labor's burden is over 5 times (Table 14) or over 3 times (Table 17) government receipts from the corporation income tax than it is to say that the CIT by itself shifts to the Gini coefficient from 0.4 to 0.446 (Table 14) or to 0.425 (Table 17)?

Notes

1. In the case of an item which would not be produced domestically in the absence of the tariff, the implicit subsidy can be largely eaten up in the higher resource costs of domestic production. In this case it is still correct to assign a cost equal to three times the tariff revenue to the consumers of the product, but the offsetting benefit to producers would be significantly less than twice the tariff revenue, and could end up being negligible.
2. Pechman (1985), Table 4-8, pages 55. The figures in the text are averages of the reported results in Pechman's most and least progressive varrants.
3. Since the amount of capital that moves abroad is different for different levels of domestic demand, one has to find the solution of the system by a process of iteration
4. These calculations do not attempt to allow for changes in the price levels of services and of public utilities and transport. Our assumption is that these changes affect all 5 quintiles equally, hence do not influence the relative income distribution.
5. For example, one might replace Cobb-Douglas assumptions (which imply a generalized elasticity of substitution equal to one) with constant-elasticity-of-substitution assumptions, using one-half as a plausible alternative generalized elasticity of substitution.

References

Engel, M.R.A., Alexander Galetovich, and Claudio E. Raddatz (1999), "Taxes and Income Distribution in Chile: Some Unpleasant Redistributions Arithmetic", *Journal of Development Economics*, Vol. 59, p. 172.

Pechman, Joseph A. and Benjamin A. Okber (1974), *Who Bears the Tax Burden?*, Washington, D.C.: The Brookings Institution.

Pechman, Joseph A. (1985), *Who Paid the Taxes, 1966-85?*, Washington, D.C.: The Brookings Institution.

Chapter 3

TRADE-OFFS BETWEEN TARGETING AND SIMPLICITY: LESSONS FROM THE U.S. AND BRITISH EXPERIENCES WITH REFUNDABLE TAX CREDITS

JANET HOLTZBLATT[1]
Office of Tax Analysis, U.S. Department of the Treasury

1. INTRODUCTION

In the United Kingdom and many other European countries, every child receives a cash benefit. Eligibility for the benefit, as well as the benefit amount, is determined without regard to the parents' income or asset holdings or marital status. As automated data systems become more sophisticated and unique identifiers (e.g., the social security number in the United States) become more prevalent, universal benefits could be as easy to distribute as voter registration or library cards.[2]

However, policymakers have other goals in addition to making the job of program administrators easier. These goals may include removing families from poverty, encouraging work, and restraining budgetary costs. In the United States, the earned income tax credit (EITC) was expanded in 1993 both to make work pay and to lift more full-time minimum wage workers out of poverty. To achieve this goal, the maximum credit rate for families with two or more children was increased from 25 percent to 40 percent of earnings and the maximum credit was increased by nearly $1,400. Eligibility for the maximum credit rate was limited to families with incomes below $8,425, and families with incomes above $27,000 were ineligible for any credit.[3] Achieving certain other goals of the 1993 legislation – namely deficit reduction – would not have been possible had similar size benefits been provided to all families.

Thus, policymakers – in the United States, but also increasingly in the United Kingdom – rely on targeting to provide benefits to the neediest families without breaking the bank. But targeting can also increase compliance burdens and administrative costs. Targeting may require trade-offs with other tax and social policy goals. Distinguishing among families based on differences in ability to pay can achieve horizontal equity goals, but codifying these distinctions may be difficult and result in complicated laws. Taxpayers (and administrators, as well) may be confused by subtle distinctions, leading to unintentional errors. Phasing out benefits to provide assistance to those with the greatest need may achieve vertical equity goals, but can also result in high marginal tax rates and marriage penalties. High marginal tax rates and marriage penalties may adversely affect labor supply and family formation decisions. They may also encourage applicants to misreport income and family status (such as number of children and filing status) to obtain more benefits.

Short of eliminating targeting, policymakers can strive to make the eligibility rules simple to understand and easy to administer. But simplification may go only so far. If policymakers choose to target benefits, then they must address the question of which government agency can best reach out to the targeted population and administer the program well.

In several earlier papers (Holtzblatt, 2000; Holtzblatt and McCubbin, 2004), I have suggested that in the United States assistance to at least some low-income individuals can best be done through the individual income tax system. In particular, there are three features of the U.S. tax-transfer system that favor this approach. First, the income tax already collects information on income and family characteristics, which may also be used to target benefits. Little or no additional information may be required for a targeted benefit. Second, many low-income workers file tax returns, even if they owe no income taxes. Third, many low-income workers do not receive federally-funded assistance from other government agencies, such as state welfare offices. Providing assistance through the tax system may be the most effective method of reaching the working poor.

These arguments, however, do not necessarily extend to other countries and other tax systems. For example, the unit of taxation in the United Kingdom is the individual, so the tax authorities know little about a family's composition or well-being. Second, the United Kingdom has an exact withholding tax system, in which about two-thirds of taxpayers are exempted from filing returns. In addition, the United Kingdom has a universal child benefit that every parent is entitled to receive. The child benefit has – until recently – been administered by the U.K.'s Department of Social Security. These factors would seem to suggest that the United Kingdom should rely on the transfer system to provide further assistance to low-income families.

Yet, the last decade has seen an explosion of targeted tax credits in the United Kingdom. Tax credits have been created for families with children, low-income workers, disabled individuals, and older reentrants into the labor market. The British experience demonstrates that there can be other administrative and political reasons for using the tax system to deliver targeted benefits.

2. U.S. TAX-TRANSFER SYSTEM

2.1 Benefits of Using Income Tax System to Deliver Targeted Benefits

Over the past two decades, the income tax threshold in the United States has gradually risen. Expansions of child-related tax benefits have increased the income tax threshold for families with children to roughly twice the poverty level. For unmarried individuals without children, the income tax thresholds have also increased but at a much slower pace. In 2004, a single filer with no children is exempted from income tax if his or her income is less than the poverty level.

Because many low-income families are exempt from income taxation, the income tax system might not seem the obvious way to provide them with additional assistance. However, there are several other factors to consider. First, the U.S. income tax system already collects information that be used to distinguish among families based on ability-to-pay criteria. Second, the tax system requires many individuals to file even if they do not have an income tax liability. Third, many low-income filers have little or no contact with other government agencies. For them, the point of contact with the federal government is the tax system.

Assistance to low-income families can be provided through refundable tax credits, which entitle recipients to the full amount of the credit even if they have little or no income tax liability.[4] Currently, in the United States, there are three refundable tax credits: the EITC, the refundable portion of the child tax credit (known as the "additional child tax credit"), and the health coverage tax credit. To be eligible for the first two credits, an individual must have earned income. The newer health coverage credit is available only to certain dislocated workers[5] and, as Table 1 demonstrates, is a very small program relative to the other two refundable tax credits.

<u>Distinguishing among families</u>. In the U.S. income tax, the unit of taxation is the individual or, if married, the couple. The definition of income is fairly broad, although means-tested government benefits and certain interest income are exempt from taxation. The income tax adjusts for

ability-to-pay based, in part, on family composition, with the taxpayer receiving additional exemptions for children and other dependents. In addition, taxpayers are eligible for a standard deduction, which size varies based on marital status or, if unmarried, the care of children and other dependents.

Table 1. Costs of Refundable Tax Credits (Millions)

Tax Credit	**Fiscal Years**						
	2003	**2004**	**2005**	**2006**	**2007**	**2008**	**2009**
Earned Income Tax Credit (EITC)							
Receipts	5,099	4,884	5,006	5,477	5,515	5,603	5,780
Outlays	31,961	33,551	34,148	34,488	34,388	34,539	35,161
Total	37,060	38,435	39,154	39,965	39,903	40,142	40,941
Child Tax Credit							
Receipts	37,970	24,340	29,860	24,810	24,680	24,480	25,430
Outlays (Additional Child Tax Credit)	6,435	7,447	11,486	8,440	8,237	7,956	7,909
Total	44,405	31,787	41,346	33,250	32,917	32,436	33,339
Health Coverage Tax Credit (HCTC)							
Receipts	-	50	60	60	70	70	80
Outlays	-	60	90	100	120	130	140
Total	-	110	150	160	190	200	220

Source: U.S. Office of Management and Budget (2004). Table 18-2.

As a result, taxpayers already provide information on the first page of the tax return that would also be required to target benefits to families. Taxpayer-reported information is supplemented by independent information reports about individuals' income – from wages to interest and dividends – from third-party payers. Third-party information provides a check on taxpayers' reports and also includes data on people who do not file returns. The IRS receives more than one billion information returns, including several hundred million wage reports, each year (U.S. Treasury Department, 2003).

What has been missing from IRS data files until recently has been independent data on family relationships. Although the tax system differentiates between taxpayers based on marital status (joint filing), living arrangements (head of household filing status), and family composition (dependents), the IRS did not systemically verify these requirements for many years outside of an audit environment. This has been gradually changing since 1986 and has been partly driven by efforts to improve the administration of refundable tax credits.

The first step in this effort was a requirement in the 1986 Tax Reform Act that taxpayers report a unique identifier (typically, the social security number) for each child over four claimed as a dependent or EITC qualifying child. While this effort was motivated by IRS reports that the number of claimed dependents exceeded reasonable expectations, subsequent efforts were driven by concerns about administering the EITC. Within a decade, a social security number was required for every dependent from birth. In 1996, the IRS was authorized to use expeditious processes to deny both dependency exemptions and the EITC unless taxpayers provided valid social security numbers. Once the IRS could validate social security numbers upfront during processing, the agency began to mount an effort to check for duplicate claims of EITC qualifying children as well as dependent exemptions.

The Tax Relief Act of 1997 gave the IRS access to two new data files that can be linked to IRS files through social security numbers. The first file is the Federal Case Registry of Child Support Orders (FCR) that contains information on custodial arrangements for children whose parents are divorced or separated. The FCR is maintained by the Office of Child Support Enforcement in the Department of Health and Human Services. The second is Kidlink, a Social Security Administration file linking the names and social security numbers of children and their parents. Together, these two data files allow the IRS to check for questionable claims of provisions based on a child's source of support, living arrangements, and relationships.

Currently, the IRS is using both files in a limited manner. The Treasury Department is evaluating the quality of information provided by states for tax enforcement purposes. Kidlink contains information for children who received social security numbers since 1998, meaning that the file will not contain information on a complete cohort of potential child dependents and EITC qualifying children for at least another decade. Still, the files contain sufficient information to be used to help select returns for audits and other enforcement activities.

Independent information on filing status is still scanty. Many states and localities do not have automated registries of marriages and divorce, making it impossible at this time for the IRS to obtain direct access to third-party data on marital status. The IRS is currently testing various commercial data sets that contain information on the names of individuals cohabiting in the same residence. This test is being done in conjunction with an EITC compliance initiative to determine if such data can be useful in detecting questionable claims of marital status.

Most of the family-related activities are aimed at questionable EITC claims, but the IRS has the authority to use this information for non-EITC issues as well, including claims of dependency exemptions and filing status. A key lesson from the past decade is that the inclusion of the family-related credits in the IRS creates synergy. Just as the income related information reported to the IRS helps in the administration of the targeted benefits, the administration of refundable tax credits has made the IRS seek out data on non-income eligibility criteria that may have broader consequences for tax administration.

Filing Requirements. Individuals are required to file a tax return when their gross income equals or exceeds the sum of the taxpayer's personal exemption and the standard deduction (the "filing threshold"). Single individuals without children generally incur income tax liabilities as soon as their gross income exceeds the filing threshold. Thus, it is unlikely that such individuals would be required to file a tax return unless they owe income taxes. In contrast, many individuals with dependents are required to file returns even when they have no positive income tax liability. In effect, they must file returns to identify the dependents who, by making them eligible for dependent exemptions and certain tax credits, also wipe out their income tax liability.

As Figure 1 demonstrates, the gap between the filing and income tax thresholds has widened, particularly for working families with children, in recent years. By 2004, a married couple with two children does not incur any tax liability until their income exceeds 213 percent of poverty. However, they are required to file a tax return with income about 84 percent of poverty. Beginning in 1994, the gap between filing and tax thresholds also increased for childless workers, as a result of an extension of a small EITC to very low-income workers who do not reside with children. In 2004, they are required to file a return when their income is about 82 percent of poverty and pay taxes when their income is about 98 percent of poverty.

Figure 1. Filing and Tax Thresholds Relative to Threshold for Individuals with Earnings

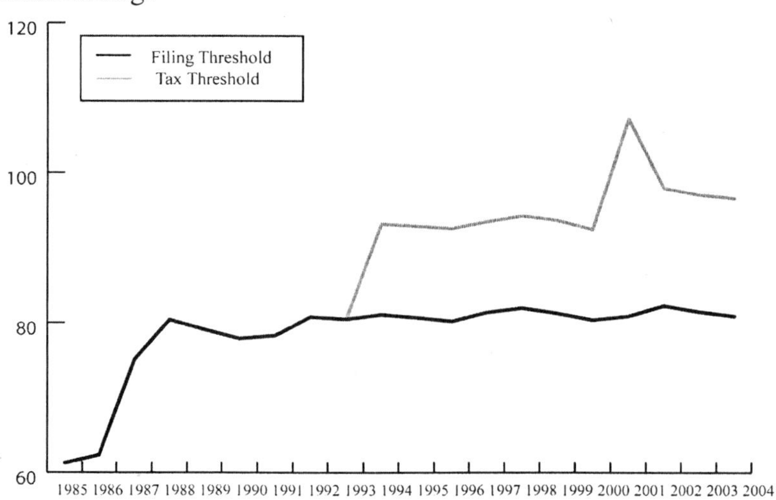

Figure 1a. Single with No Children

Figure 1. Filing and Tax Thresholds Relative to Threshold for Individuals with Earnings (continued)

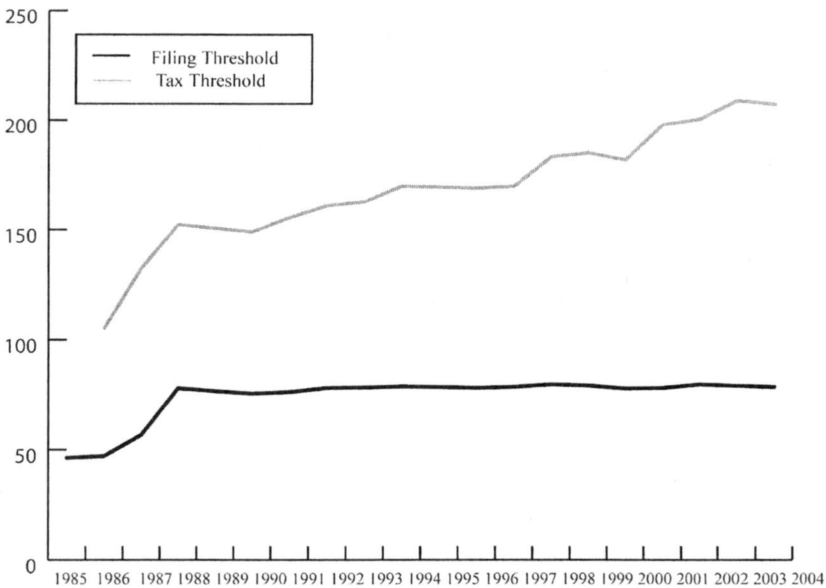

Figure 1b. Head of Household with 1 Child

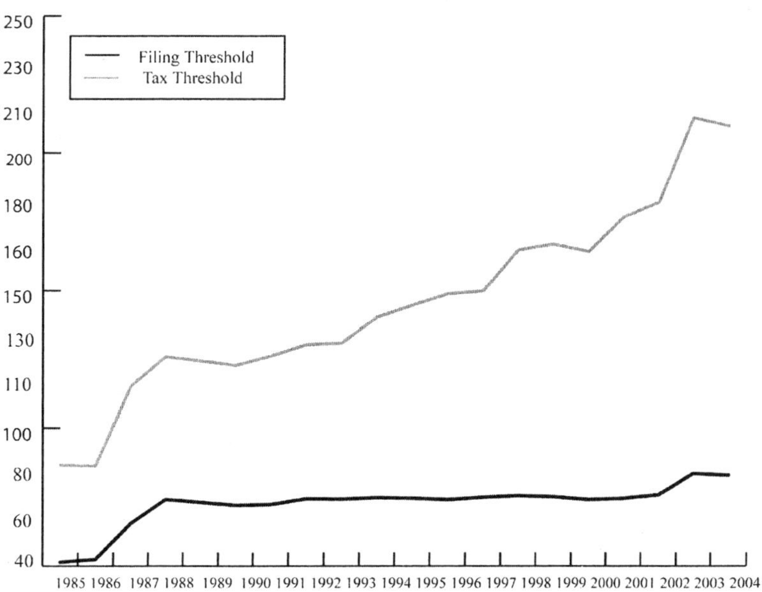

Figure 1c. Married Couple with 2 Children

As Table 2 shows, nearly 90 percent of filers are required to file a tax return. Most of the remainder file to obtain refunds of income taxes that were overwithheld during the year. This is true even of low-income filers. Among taxpayers with adjusted gross income below $30,000, about 79 percent are required to file a tax return and an additional 16 percent file to obtain refunds of overwithheld income taxes. And among those who file to claim either the EITC or the additional child tax credit, nearly 96 percent are required to file and another 3 percent file to obtain refunds of overpaid taxes. Less than 2 percent file solely to obtain refundable tax credits.

Table 2. Reason for Filling a Tax Return in Tax Year 2001

Characteristics of Filers	**Total**	**Adjusted Gross Income Under $30,000**	**Claims EITC or Additional Child Tax Credit**
		Percent of Total	
Required to File			
Positive Income Tax Liability Before EITC	80.0	64.7	59.3
Self-Employment Taxes or Special Taxes	3.1	6.7	9.5
Income Above the Filing Threshold	3.4	7.4	26.8
Required to File Return for Other Reasons	0.1	0.2	*
Subtotal: Required to File	86.7	79.0	95.6
Other Reason to File			
Refund of Overwithheld Taxes	10.6	15.8	2.7
EITC or Additional Child Tax Credit	0.6	1.4	1.7
Subtotal: Other Reason to File	11.2	17.2	4.4
Subtotal: Required or Reason to File	97.9	96.3	100.0
No Apparent Reason to File			
Not in Any of Preceding Categories	2.1	3.7	0.0
Total	100.0	100.0	100.0

Source: Author's calculations using 2001 Statistics of Income.

Notes:
* Fewer than 50,000 fillers or less than .05 percent
Returns with AGI under $30,000 do not include dependent fillers

Point of Contact. Many low-income individuals who have contact with the income tax system do not appear to have regular interactions with other government agencies. Because they are able-bodied and work, they may not be eligible for some forms of assistance such as supplemental security income (SSI). Income and asset tests may limit assistance to the most needy individuals and families. For example, a household with income above 133 percent of poverty and $2,000 of assets is not eligible for food stamp benefits.

Even if they meet the eligibility criteria, many low-income individuals – particularly the working poor – do not the claim the benefits to which they are entitled. Only about 52 percent of eligible households claimed food stamps in 2001. Among eligible households with earnings, the food stamp participation rate was 44 percent (Cunnyngham, 2003). Applying for food stamp benefits imposes significant compliance burdens on individuals, particularly the working poor who often must take time off from work to apply for benefits in-person. (See Ponza, 1999; GAO, 1999.) Some low-income individuals may steer away from applying for certain types of low-income assistance due to stigma concerns.

Thus, it is not surprising to find that relatively few filing units eligible for the EITC report receiving cash transfers. Among low-income workers eligible for the EITC in 2000, only about one in four reported claiming one of the major low-income benefits administered by state welfare agencies or the Social Security Administration in 2000. (See Table 3.)

Table 3. Overlap Between EITC and Transfer System in 2000

Transfer	**% of EITC-Eligible Filing Units Reporting Receipts of Transfers**
Temporary Assistance for Needy Families (TANF)	5
Supplemental Security Income (SSI)	3
Food Stamps	16
Medicaid	17
Any of Above	24

Source: Author's calculations based on March 2001 Current Population Survey.

2.2 Drawbacks of Using the Tax System to Deliver Targeted Benefits

As the preceding discussion suggests, there are compelling arguments as to why the tax system can be used to provide benefits to low-income individuals. But there also are reasons why the tax system may not be the best approach. First, the annual accounting framework of the tax system makes it difficult to time payments to coincide with a family's needs. Second, the U.S. income tax is a self-assessment system, meaning that taxpayers are often either on their own when completing tax returns or paying others to help them. Third, the IRS has many responsibilities and must balance many priorities. The danger is two-sided: a slight nudge in either direction can disturb this delicate balancing act, causing the IRS to devote too many or too few resources to the task of administering refundable tax credits.

Timing of Payments. In the United States, the accounting period for determining income tax liabilities is the tax year (which generally coincides with the calendar year). Thus, income is measured on an annual basis in the income tax. Tax returns are filed between January and April after the end of the tax year. An annual accounting system, combined with end-of-year reconciliation, makes it difficult to time receipt of benefits to coincide with the taxpayer's need. Taxpayers typically do not receive their tax credits until they file returns at the end of the year. However, some low-income workers may need assistance earlier during the tax year.

While it is difficult to change the end-of-year reconciliation system, there have been at least two attempts to accelerate payments of credits. Since 1978, EITC claimants have had the option of requesting advance payments of the EITC from their employers throughout the year.[6] Employers offset the costs of the advance payments by reducing their payments of withheld income and employment taxes. After the tax year is over, the employer notifies the IRS of individuals' receipts of advance payments. When they file their tax returns, credit claimants must reconcile advance payments received during the year with the amount of credit for which they were actually eligible. If they receive too little, they can receive the remaining amount when they file their tax return at the end of the year; conversely, if they receive too much, they must repay the overpayment with their tax return.

While the advance payment option provides a mechanism to receive payments on a timely basis, only a small number of EITC claimants have ever claimed the credit in advance. During tax year 2002, 130,924 taxpayers – less than one percent of EITC claimants with children – claimed the EITC in advance. The reasons for the low utilization rate are not fully known. One popular explanation is that workers simply do not know that they have the option of claiming the credit in advance. A General Accounting Office study (1992) provided some support for this theory when investigators found widespread ignorance about the advance payment option among low-income workers. To remedy ignorance, the Omnibus Budget Reconciliation Act of 1993 required the IRS to test the effectiveness of sending notices informing EITC recipients about the advance payment option. The IRS (1999) found that notices increased participation in the advance payment option by a statistically significant, but small, amount. With its benefits small relative to its costs, the notification program was dropped after a two-year trial.

There may be other barriers to participation in the advance payment option. The GAO study also found that once informed, many workers stated that they would prefer to receive the EITC in a lump-sum payment. While some workers might simply prefer the forced savings provided by receipt of a lump-sum payment at the end of the year, others may not claim the EITC in advance for fear of being forced to repay a sizable overpayment at the end of the year if their income or family status changes during the course of the year.[7] Workers might also be reluctant to ask their employers for advanced payments of the EITC.

Another mechanism to accelerate the payment of credits was used in 2001 and again in 2003, but in neither year was this mechanism applied specifically to target relief to low-income families in a more timely fashion. Instead, the motivation behind advancing payments of the rate reduction credit in 2001 and the child tax credit (including the refundable portion) in 2003 was economic stimulation. Thus when the child tax credit was increased by $400 for tax year 2003 in the Jobs and Growth Tax Relief Reconciliation Act, policymakers also wanted taxpayers to begin spending their tax cuts as quickly as possible. The tax act was enacted in May, and taxpayers began to receive checks for the increase in the child tax credit within two months. Eligibility for the advance payments was based on income and family characteristics as reported on the taxpayer's 2002 tax return. If there was a change in filing status or income during 2003 that was in the taxpayer's favor, he or she could claim the remaining amount when they filed their 2003 tax returns. However, unlike the EITC advance payments, taxpayers were not required to repay overpayments of the advance credits if the change in circumstances was not in their favor. Policymakers were willing to trade-off some loss in targeting precision for administrative ease. Notably, neither the advance payments of the rate reduction credits or the child tax credits were done on a permanent basis.

Other studies suggest that concern with the timeliness of payments (for reasons other than economic simulation) may be misplaced. Three different types of studies find evidence that low-income working families do not rely on the lump-sum EITC payment solely for current consumption. Surveying a sample of individuals claiming the EITC in free tax preparation clinics in Chicago, Smeeding et al (2001) find that they plan to use the credit for savings, car purchases, tuition payments, and moving expenses. Using the Consumer Expenditure Survey, Barrow and McGranahan (2001) estimate that consumption rises, particularly for durable goods, in the months in which EITC refunds are received. Based on interviews of credit claimants in an ethnographic study of the New Hope Project in Milwaukee, Romich and

Weisner (2001) conclude that families view lump-sum payments of the EITC as a form of forced savings. These studies would support a view that low-income working families are able to smooth consumption over the year to account for the receipt of large lump-sum payments.

Self-assessment System. The tax system relies on self-assessment, which means that filers either prepare their own returns (sometimes with the help of special software packages) or they pay others to help them. Taxpayers may also turn to IRS assistance centers or IRS-sponsored volunteer sites for help with tax returns, but the limited availability of free assistance locations can mean long lines and long waits for such services.

Low-income filers face two hurdles in dealing with a self-assessment system. First, they are often poorly educated. Among filers with incomes below 200 percent of poverty, more than a quarter lack a high school diploma (Holtzblatt and McCubbin, 2004). For many, English is not their native tongue. Nearly 20 percent were born in countries where English was neither the official or primary language (Holtzblatt and McCubbin, 2004). While a few forms and publications are available in Spanish, most are available only in English.

A second hurdle is the complexity of the eligibility rules used to target assistance. As I (with Janet McCubbin) have detailed in earlier papers (2003, 2004), the rules governing programs for low-income filers are complicated, sometimes mirroring the complexity in claimants' lives. For example, the additional child tax credit requires proof that the taxpayer provided most of a child's support. However, proving support requires retention of receipts throughout the year on shelter, food, clothing, child care, education, etc. It may be particularly difficult for taxpayers to demonstrate (or prove) compliance with this test when the taxpayer receives outside support from the government or others in addition to his own earnings. The EITC requires proof that the taxpayer lived with her child for over half the year, but parents who share custody of a child may be hard pressed to prove with whom the child resided for 188 days.

Further adding to the confusion is the fact that taxpayer may be eligible for both the EITC and the additional child tax credit, but the credits' eligibility criteria – while similar – differ in subtle ways. In 2005, an estimated 22 million taxpayers – including 16 million filers with children – will claim the EITC. Eleven million filers are estimated to receive the additional child tax credit. Not surprisingly, there is significant overlap between these two populations – with about 8 million (or 75 percent of additional child tax credit claimants) expected to claim both credits. Yet, as Table 4 demonstrates, each credit uses somewhat different rules to target income and family size and composition. Tax experts, themselves, are challenged at trying to explain the difference in the two credits' definitions of earned income.[8]

Table 4. Comparison of EITC and Additional Child Tax Credit in 2004

Eligibility Criteria	EITC	Additional Child Tax Credit
Income Tests		
1. Earnings	Yes	Yes
Minimum Amount	No minimum	Greater than $10,750
Maximum Amount	$35,458 (if married with two children)	No maximum
Definition	Sum of wages, salaries, tips, other taxable employee compensation, self-employment income	Same as EITC except earned must be included in computing taxable income
2. Adjusted Gross Income	Yes	Yes
Maximum Amount	$35,458 (if married with two children)	$150,000 (if married with two children)
Definition	Same as AGI for regular tax	Modified to include amounts earned abroad or in certain possession
3. Investment Income	Yes	No
Maximum Amount	$2,650	N.A.
Definition	Sum of interest (including tax-exempt), dividends, capital gains, rents, royalties, and certain passive income	N.A.
Family Status		
1. Children	Affects size of Credit	Must have to qualify
Number	Two	No limit
Age	Under 19 Under 24 if full-time student No age-cut if disabled	Under 17
Relationship	Son, daughter, grandchild, sibling, niece, or nephew if cared for as if taxpayer's own Foster child if cared for as if taxpayers own	Same as EITC
Residency	More than six months	Residency test applies only to foster children, who must reside with taxpayer for 12 months
Support	No support requirement	Must provide over half child's support
2. Marital Status		
Unmarried	Yes	Yes
Married	Must file jointly	No restrictions

The educational deficiencies of credit recipients, combined with the complexity of the credits' rules, may contribute to the increasing number of EITC claimants who are turning to paid preparers. In 2002, about 56 percent of all taxpayers used paid preparers. Use of paid preparers was higher among EITC claimants, with about 67 percent paying someone else to prepare their return.[9] But it is also possible that EITC claimants turned to preparers for other reasons. They may turn to paid preparers to file electronically, which enables them to receive refunds more quickly. Refundable tax credits have increased substantially in recent years, and recipients may be trading off income for more leisure.

Conflicting Priorities in the IRS. To state the obvious, administering low-income benefits is not the sole task of the IRS. The IRS is responsible for administrating both individual and corporate income taxes, the estate tax (while it continues), and various excise taxes. It also has a role in the administration of pensions and tax-exempt agencies. The IRS processes over 135 million individual and corporate income tax returns a year as well as over a billion information returns from employers and other third-parties. In total, the IRS collects roughly a trillion dollars in taxes each year, while it pays out about $40 billion in refundable credits annually. To achieve these tasks, the IRS receives a budget of nearly $10 billion – of which only a few hundred million dollars is devoted to administering refundable tax credits.

Within its $10 billion budget, the IRS must balance all of these competing priorities. On the one hand, the relative size of refundable tax credits subject to the rest of the IRS's concerns means other issues may (and perhaps) should dominate. On the other hand, political sensitivities surrounding refundable tax credits can sometimes give more weight to its concerns. In the past decade, the IRS has conducted four EITC compliance studies but no comparable studies were done on other provisions in the income tax system – a problem that will be remedied soon with the completion of the National Research Program, a comprehensive study of compliance among individual income taxpayers in 2001. The downside of four EITC compliance studies, with none of other tax provisions, is a pervasive view that the credit is the IRS's largest compliance problem. Evidence of this concern is the higher audit rate for EITC claimants than for all taxpayers (Holtzblatt and McCubbin, 2004) and the fact that the Administration's FY 2005 Budget contains three separate performance goals (one still to be determined) for the EITC out of a total of 54 goals for the entire IRS (OMB, 2004). Until more comprehensive compliance data become available, one cannot judge if this emphasis is too much or too little.

2.3 How Well Do Refundable Tax Credits Do in Meeting Their Goals?

In deciding between refundable tax credits and other approaches, clearly an important consideration is how well the former do in achieving policy and administrative goals. Much of the evidence to date is about the EITC, which is not surprising since it has been in existence far longer than the other refundable credits.

There is some evidence to support the view that the EITC achieves its policy objectives, in large part due to the recent expansions of the credit. In 1991 (the first year for which such data exist), the EITC lifted 1.9 million people out of poverty. Largely as a consequence of the expansions in the Omnibus Budget Reconciliation Acts of 1990 and 1993, expenditures on the EITC have more than doubled since then, increasing from $13 billion in 1991 to over $32 billion in 2002. Similarly, the number of people lifted out of poverty by the EITC has more than doubled over the same period. In 2002, the EITC lifted 4.6 people out of poverty, including 2.5 million children under the age of 18.[10]

Several recent studies have found that the EITC encourages work, as well as alleviate poverty. Comparing the effects of time limits, the EITC, and other policy changes on welfare participation, labor supply, and income, Grogger (2003) concludes that the EITC may be the "single most important" policy parameter for explaining recent declines in welfare and increases in work and earnings among female-headed families. Meyer and Rosenbaum (2001) find that more than 60 percent of a nine percentage point increase in the employment of single mothers between 1984 and 1986 was due to expansions of the EITC. Dickert, Houser, and Scholz (1995) estimated that expansions of the EITC between 1993 and 1996 would induce more than half a million families to move from welfare to work. Eissa and Liebman (1996) find that the EITC expansion in the Tax Reform Act of 1986 significantly increases labor force participation among single mothers, especially less educated women.

The story is more mixed on the administrative side. The good news is that most people who are eligible for the EITC claim the credit. Between 75 and 86 percent of those eligible for the EITC claim the credit (Scholz, 1994, GAO, 2001, Treasury, 2002b). As noted earlier, participation rates for the food stamp program, particularly among the working poor, are notably lower. On the other hand, noncompliance among EITC claimants is high. A study conducted by the IRS of compliance among EITC claimants in tax year 1999 found that between $9.7 billion and $11.1 billion of EITC claims were erroneous.[11] IRS enforcement activities prevented or recovered about $1.2 billion in erroneous claims. Thus, between $8.5 and $9.9 billion in

EITC claims – or between 27.0 and 31.7 percent of total EITC claims – was erroneously paid to taxpayers for tax year 1999 (Treasury, 2002a).[12]

As Table 5 shows, errors are primarily associated with the targeting criteria that are difficult for the IRS to verify. The largest source of EITC errors in 1999 was the failure to claim a child who met the qualifications for the credit. Typically, taxpayers failed to demonstrate that they resided with a qualifying child for the required amount of time. Many taxpayers also misstated their relationship to the child claimed for the EITC at the same time that they misreported how long the child resided with them.

Table 5. EITC Overclaims by Type of Error (1999)

Error	**Amount of Overclaim ($ in millions)**[1]
Family Issues	
Qualifying Child	3,284
Residency	2,698
Relationship	1,447
SSN not Valid for Employment	421
Age	206
Filing Status	2,724
AGI Tiebreaker	1,984
Income	1,710
Underreported Income	1,494
Business Income	854
Other Income	640
Earned Income Overreported	171
Income Recategorized (Total Unchanged)	45
Other Errors	437
Errors Corrected in Processing	939
Did Not Appear for Audit	2,226
Total	11,118

Source: Holtzblat and McCubbin (2004).

Notes:
[1] Sum of this column exceeds total because returns with more than one error appear in more than one row.

Misreporting of filing status was the second largest source of errors. Many taxpayers claimed to be single or head-of-household filers when they were, in fact, still legally married and required to file either jointly with their spouse or "married filing separately." About $2.1 billion in EITC overclaims was attributable to cases where the taxpayers filing status was changed to married filing separately, either alone or in combination with other errors. In addition, over $600 million in overclaims was attributable to couples who should have filed joint returns. In these cases, the EITC was reduced or eliminated when the income of the two spouses was combined.

About $1.7 billion in EITC overclaims occurred on returns with income reporting errors. Farm and non-farm business income – much of which is not reported independently to the IRS – accounted for 57 percent of the unreported income.

The tiebreaker rule accounted for a substantial portion of EITC overclaims. At the time of the study, only the taxpayer with the highest adjusted gross income could claim the child in an extended-family household. The IRS study counted nearly $2 billion of EITC claims by the lower-income taxpayers as errors, without any adjustment for the amount that should have been claimed by other adults in the household. Since the study was conducted, the AGI tiebreaker was simplified, so that it now only applies when more than one taxpayer actually claims the same child. Had this provision been in effect in 1999, about $1.4 billion of EITC overclaims would have been eliminated. If in addition other simplification and enforcement provisions that were enacted in 2001 had been in effect in 1999, EITC overclaims would have been reduced by roughly $2 billion (Holtzblatt and McCubbin, 2004).

2.4 Comparing Spending Programs and Refundable Tax Credits

Lacking data on overall taxpayer compliance, we cannot answer the critical question of how EITC error rates compare to compliance rates for the rest of the income tax. Nor can we answer the fundamental question of whether the EITC causes noncompliance or if the noncompliance we observe among EITC claimants is symptomatic of more pervasive problems throughout the tax system. The EITC error rate can be (and is often) compared to noncompliance rates in means-tested programs administered by non-tax agencies. This is a valid comparison, if the question is whether a benefit should be provided through the tax system or through an expenditure system. Even if the decision is to keep the credit in the tax system (perhaps because eligible individuals have little interaction with the agencies that run welfare programs), the comparison may shed light on whether there are better administrative practices that could be adopted by the IRS.

In past papers (2000, 2004), I have compared the EITC error rate to that of the food stamp program. One of the reasons to compare the food stamp program to the EITC is that both – unlike many other programs targeted to low-income families – are available to people attached to the work force. Both programs have requirements regarding income, assets, household composition, and citizenship. Despite these similarities, the food stamp overpayment error rate is substantially lower than that of the EITC: 6.16 percent (Rosenbaum, 2003). One possible explanation for differences in the error rates is the dissimilarities in how the two benefits are administered.[13]

First, the food stamp application typically requires more information than the taxpayer is required to provide on the Schedule EIC attached to the tax return. In part, this is due to the fact that the taxpayer provides much of the necessary information elsewhere on the tax return. The Schedule EIC asks only for information not available elsewhere on the tax return or through independent data sources: the child's name, social security number, and number of months of residency in the taxpayer's home. Food stamp applications vary by state, but typically require extensive information on income, assets, and household composition. Second, the food stamp program is not a self-assessment program. With few exceptions for the elderly and disabled, food stamp applicants are required to visit a state office to apply for benefits. A personal interview with a state caseworker is required. Most state offices, however, are opened only during working hours, requiring applicants to take time off from their own jobs in order to apply for benefits (Ponza et al., 1999).

A third difference between the two programs is the timing and source of third-party verification. Administrators in both programs recognize the need for third-party verification. With the exception of the W-2 required from all filers with earnings, no documentation is required of EITC claimants at the time of application. As discussed earlier, the IRS has developed several automated data systems that can be matched against tax returns during processing in order to identify questionable claims. When anomalous EITC claims are detected, the taxpayer may be asked to supply documentation in support of their claim. State food stamp programs typically require applicants to provide much more documentation at the time of application. Massachusetts, for example, requires documentation of identity, residence, utility bills, bank accounts, pay stubs, dependent care expenses, unearned income, self-employment income, rental income, medical expenses, etc.[14]

Collecting this information is not without cost. Combined federal and state administrative costs for the food stamp program are about $4 billion – roughly 40 percent of the IRS total budget for a program that serves far fewer units (about 9 million food stamp households compared to over 135 million returns). As discussed earlier, food stamp participation rates are low, with less than half of eligible working households claiming the benefits to which they are entitled.

Another reason for the apparent disparities in the EITC and food stamp error rates may be differences in how compliance is measured in the two programs. To some extent the comparison between the EITC and food stamp error rates can both understate and overstate the differences between the two programs. While both error rates include erroneous payments in the numerator, the denominator for the EITC is the amount claimed while the denominator for food stamps is the amount paid. The EITC error rate would be larger if the denominator was the amount paid, while the food stamp error rate would be smaller if its denominator was the amount claimed.

On the other hand, the IRS may measure erroneous payments (the numerator) more stringently than is done in the food stamp program. In the typical EITC compliance study, every aspect of EITC eligibility is scrutinized. While no one would want to be the subject of a food stamp quality control study, USDA investigators may be less intense than their IRS counterparts. Food stamp quality control manuals make no mention of investigating whether the household actually purchases and prepares meals together. (Some of the state food stamp manuals explicitly state that this is too difficult to measure.[15]) Fluctuations in earnings that occur over the six-month certification period do not affect food stamp benefit amounts. To verify self-employment income, quality control examiners often rely on tax returns, which would be the beginning – not the end – of an IRS audit. Testimony of neighbors and friends is accepted in a food stamp interview, while IRS investigators may discount such information.[16]

The food stamp program offers two lessons. More up-front requirements may be a contributory factor in keeping error rates down, but they also increase administrative costs and may lower participation. The other lesson is that some reasonable expectations about what can be administered can be built into compliance measures.

3. BRITISH TAX-TRANSFER SYSTEM

3.1 Features of the British Income Tax-Transfer System

The British income tax system offers an interesting contrast to the U.S. income tax system. It is an exact withholding system, in which the full amount of income tax liability is withheld at source. As a result, taxpayers are not required to file returns at the end of the year to obtain refunds or to pay a balance due. Exact withholding systems, like the United Kingdom, typically apply a PAYE ("pay-as-you-earn") tax withholding plan for wage income. About two-thirds of British taxpayers are not required to file tax returns. Those who are required to file include taxpayers with significant amounts of asset income and/or capital gains. Taxpayers in the highest rate bracket and those with self-employment income or who are directors of companies are also required to file returns.

Relative to the U.S. income tax system, the British tax system does little to differentiate among taxpayers based on family needs. The unit of taxation is the individual, rather than the marital unit as in the United States. Until recently, there were allowances for married individuals and single parents – similar in concept to our standard deductions for married couples and heads of households – but there was no differential rate treatment based on marital status or deductions and credits for children.[17] Compared to the U.S. income tax, the British tax system has fewer deductions, tax credits, and other preferences.

Instead, the British provided assistance to families with children, particularly low-income working families, through the social security system. Since 1977, the linchpin of this assistance network was the child benefit, available to all families with children, regardless of their income or assets. The universal child benefit was supplemented by other assistance programs, including benefits for low-income working families. In 1971 (four years before the enactment in the United States of the EITC), the United Kingdom introduced the family income supplement (FIS), which provided an earnings supplement for families with at least one full-time worker. In 1988, the FIS was expanded and renamed the family credit (FC). The FC, like the child benefit, was administered by the U.K. Department of Social Security.

Since coming into office in 1997, the Labour Government has implemented major reforms to tax, transfer, and regulatory systems. Many of these reforms were motivated by goals that mirror those behind the recent EITC expansions: making work pay and eliminating child poverty.[18] As part of these reforms, a minimum wage was implemented, and benefits for families with children – particularly low-wage workers – were expanded.

For the Labour Party, these reforms also represented a shift in philosophy towards distributional goals. Brewer et al (2002) note that the Labour Party traditionally favored social insurance programs over targeted assistance, sensing greater political support for universal benefits. As recently as 1993, Labour Party officials were calling for the end of means-testing in some programs. But by 1998, the Labour Government was firmly behind the expansion and reform of targeted assistance as a way to meet certain social policy goals while controlling budgetary costs. Particularly noteworthy was the increasing reliance on the tax system to provide targeted benefits. The reforms to the tax system occurred in two phases.

In the first phase, the Labour government retained the basic structure of certain social security benefit programs, but expanded them and shifted administrative responsibility to Inland Revenue. In 1999, the United Kingdom replaced the FC with the working family tax credit (WFTC). Relative to the FC, the WFTC was more generous, particularly for families with children. By extending the plateau for maximum benefits and by reducing the phase-out rate, the Labour Government also extended eligibility for the WFTC to more families. Shifting administrative authority for the WFTC from the Department of Social Security to Inland Revenue enabled the government to build on the existing PAYE system to pay the credit through employers (pay-via-employer, or PVE) rather than through more traditional means.

But in other key respects, the FC was grafted onto the tax system with little modification. Like the FC, the WFTC was based on the couple's combined earnings, total assets, the number of hours worked, and the number of children in the family. For both the FC and WFTC, eligibility was based on the applicant's earnings and income for a month or two prior to application, rather than the annual income concept used to determine tax liabilities. Losing a job did not affect receipt of the WFTC during the six month period – just as it had not affected eligibility for the FC. And despite the shift of administrative responsibilities, WFTC applicants followed the same steps to apply for benefits as they had when the FC was run by DSS. WFTC claimants were not required to file an end-of-year tax return. Instead, claimants were sent a form (similar to the application form that had been used for the FC) directly to Inland Revenue with information on family composition, family income, and assets.

Over the next several years, other tax credits were added to the British tax system. Notably, the allowances for married couples and single parents were repealed and replaced with a new nonrefundable Children's Tax Credit in April 2001. The Children's Tax Credit was equal to 520 pounds for taxpayers with one or more children under the age of 16. As new tax credits were added, the British system became more complicated because each credit used subtly different criteria (see Table 6) to reach many of the same families. In this respect, the British experience was not unlike that of the United States.

Even as the children's tax credit was being implemented, the British government was laying the groundwork for the next phase of reforms. In 2000, the U.K. Treasury Department announced that further reform was necessitated by the earlier reforms. According to the British Treasury:

Table 6. Comparison of WFTC and Children's Tax Credit

Eligibility Criteria	WFTC	Children's Tax Credit
Refundable	Yes	No
Income and Asset Tests		
1. Earnings	Yes	No
Minimum Amount	No minimum but must work at least 16 hours a week	Not applicable
Definition	Sum of wages, salaries, tips, housing allowances, self-employment income. Net of taxes (including children's tax credit), National Insurance contributions, and one-half pension contributions	Not applicable
2. Income	Yes	Yes
Definition	Couple's combined cash income after taxes	Gross income. Phases out on higher earner's income if he or she is in higher tax rate bracket
3. Assets	Yes	No
Maximum Amount	8,000 pounds	Not applicable
Family Status	Must have to qualify	Must have to qualify
1. Children	No limit	No limit
Number	Under 16 at time of application	Under 16 at start of tax year
Age	Under 19 if full-time student at time of application	
Relationship	Not applicable	Own child (including adopted and step) or a child supported by taxpayer
Residency	Child must normally reside with claimant as member of family	Child must live with taxpayer for some part of tax year
Support	No support required	Applicable if child is not taxpayer's own
2. Marital Status		
Unmarried	If living alone, file separately; if cohabiting with partner, file jointly	Same as WFTC
Married	Must file jointly	Same as WFTC

> Using one system to achieve two objectives – in the case of the Working Families' Tax Credit, better work incentives and increased family support – can give rise to tensions. At the same time, using several different instruments to contribute towards a single goal – increased family support in Income Support, the Working Families Tax Credit and the Children's Tax Credit – can mean a duplication of effort (2000, pg. 22).

Thus, the Labour Government proposed to separate the child support and work incentives functions of the various tax credits. In April 2003, the WFTC, disabled person's tax credit, and children tax credit were replaced by two credits: the child tax credit and the working tax credit. Eligibility for the child tax credit does not depend on work status, and eligibility for the working tax credit is not limited to workers with children. Both are refundable tax credits and use the same definition and unit of income. Like the FC and WFTC, eligibility is based on the combined income of two married couples or cohabitants. But in other respects, eligibility for the new credits is based on criteria more similar to those used throughout the income tax system. Thus, the assets test has been eliminated, and an annual measure of income is used. Table 7 describes the eligibility criteria for the child tax credit and working tax credit.

While the child tax credit is available to nonworkers and the working tax credit is available only to workers (including those without children), a common application is used to apply for either credit. The individual (and his or her partner) must provide address, date of birth, and national insurance number, as well as their children's names and the family's child benefit reference number. The application also asks about child care expenses, hours worked, and income. So, in many respects, the credit application looks like a U.S. income tax return. But after the first year, the applicant does not need to complete another application. Inland Revenue will send each family an annual review, in which they will be asked to verify that their income and circumstances as recorded are correct.

The credits are paid in advance in weekly or monthly increments throughout the year. The working tax credit is paid through the employer (who subtracts credit payments from tax payments), while the child tax credit is paid to the individual's account at a bank, building society, or post office. During the payment period, the credits are based on prior year's income. At the end of the year, the amount paid is reconciled with the recipient's actual income and family circumstances during the year. Should there be a change in circumstances, credit recipients may have to repay the excess to Inland Revenue at the end of the year. However, no repayment is necessary if the change in income is less than 2,500 pounds.

Table 7. Description of Child and Working Tax Credits

Common eligibility rules

1. Claimant must be at least 16 years old and normally living in the United Kingdom.

2. Eligibility is based on gross income. If the individual is married or cohabiting, then eligibility is based on the couple's gross income.

3. Credits are initially based on prior year's income. If income during tax year exceeds prior year's income by £2,500, the recipient will have to repay a portion or all of the credit.

Child Tax Credit

Who is eligible? To be eligible for the child tax credit, an individual (or the couple, if married or cohabiting) must be responsible for one or more qualifying children. In 2003-04, eligibility was extended to families with incomes of to £58,000 a year.

Definition of child. Children must be under the age of 16 or 19 if a full-time student. The applicant must be responsible for the child. Deciding who has the main responsibility for the child is based on facts and circumstances, such as the child's residency with the applicant.

Amount of credit. The child tax credit consists of two basic components: the family element (one per family) and the child element (one per each child). In 2003-04, the maximum amounts of the family and child elements were, respectively, £545 per family and £1,445 per child. The family element is doubled for families with children under the age of one. There are also supplements to the child element for disabled children.

Phase-out. In 2003-04, families with annual gross income below £13,230 were entitled to the full credit. The child elements were phased-out for incomes above £13,230, so that a family with one child and £17,135 would receive only the family element. The family element is phase-out between £50,000 and £58,134 (£66,269 if the family has a child under the age of one).

Working Tax Credit

Who is eligible? Working Tax Credit is for people who are employed or self-employed (either on their own or in partnerships), who usually work 16 hours or more a week, are paid for that work, and expect to work for at least 4 weeks. Applicants must work at least 16 hours a week. Applicants must be at least 16 years old and either is responsible for at least one child or is disabled. Able-bodied workers without children are eligible if they are at least 25 years old and work a minimum of 30 hours a week.

Amount of credit: In 2003-04, the maximum credit was £1,525 for unmarried individuals without children and £3,025 for couples (with or without children) and single parents. Workers with children who work 30 or more hours a week were entitled to an additional £620. There were also supplemental amounts for if workers incurred child care expenses, were disabled, or were over 50 and reentrants into the workforce.

Phase-out. Applicants with annual gross income below £5,060 were entitled to the full amount. As income exceeds £5,060, the credit is phased-out. The credit was reduced to zero at £10,857 for single workers without children and income about £10,857, at £13,237 for part-time workers with children, and £14,911 for full-time workers with children.

The second phase of reform was marked by two other shifts in administrative responsibilities. First, the consolidation of child-related benefits does not end at the tax system. When fully implemented this year, the child tax credit will also include amounts for children previously paid in Income Support and income-based Jobseeker's Allowance. This change – combined with the fact that the refundable child tax credit is not tied to earnings – means that individuals who typically do not have contact with Inland Revenue are being brought into the tax system solely to obtain refundable tax credits. The initial plan is to have information collected by the agencies that these individuals would typically deal with. The information would then be forwarded to Inland Revenue, who would then dispense checks to the eligible individuals.

Second, the administration of the universal child benefit was shifted from the Department of Social Security to Inland Revenue. However, the child benefit has not been reclassified as a tax credit. The application process for the child benefit remains separate from that of the targeted child tax credit. To apply for the child benefit, applicants must provide the child's birth or adoption certificate.

3.2 How Well Do British Refundable Tax credits Do in Meeting Their Goals?

As with the EITC in the United States, the WFTC has been the subject of several evaluations to determine how well it succeeds in meeting its goals. Using micro-data from before and after implementation of the WFTC, Brewer et al (2003) finds that the WFTC increased labor supply of single mothers by 4.6 percentage points, slightly reduced the labor supply of women in couples by .2 percentage points, and increased the labor supply of men in couples by .8 percentage points. The number of children in poverty fell by 800,000 between 1998/1999 and 2002/2003, though the extent to which this drop is attributable to the expansion of the WFTC has not been quantified. (Hussain, 2004)

And as with the EITC, there is mixed news as to the WFTC's administrative performance. One of the goals of the WFTC was to increase participation relative to the FC, which had been received by only 66 to 70 percent of eligible families in 1998-99. However, the WFTC participation rate actually fell to 62 to 65 percent in 2000-01. Participation did increase among WFTC recipients who had been eligible for FC. Among this group, participation rates under the WFTC increased to 75 to 81 (Inland Revenue, 2002).

Noncompliance is a problem, but does not appear to be as large a problem as in the United States. A recent Inland Revenue study (2003) found that between 10 to 14 percent of WFTC awarded in tax year 2000-2001 was paid in error. Most of the errors were attributable to understatement of income or capital assets. Another large source of errors – as in the United States – was misreporting of filing status, with about 14 percent of erroneous claimants stating that they were unmarried or living alone when in fact they should have reported the income of a spouse or cohabitating partner.

There is one dramatic difference between the U.S. and U.K. compliance experiences with refundable tax credits. Inland Revenue reports fewer errors attributable to taxpayers claiming children who do not meet the qualifying criteria, and child residency errors – the largest source of erroneous claims of the EITC – are not identified at all. It is possible that the WFTC had fewer child-related errors because of differences in eligibility criteria. For example, taxpayers remained eligible for the WFTC for the full six month certification period, even if the child changed residency over the period. (If this is true, then the new child tax credit may present new compliance challenges for Inland Revenue, since changes in the child's living arrangements during the year may affect eligibility.) But differences in tax administration between the two countries may have also accounted for the apparent absence of child-related errors.[19]

3.3 Arguments For and Against Using the British Tax System to Deliver Targeted Benefits

Reforms since 1997 have made the British tax system – at least with respect to working families and children – look more like the U.S. income tax system. However, there is a key difference between the two countries because most EITC claimants are required to file a tax return, while most U.K. tax credits recipients are not. In the United Kingdom, the working parent had contact with both the Department of Social Security (in order to apply for the universal child benefit) and Inland Revenue (often through his or her employer), but he or she would not normally provide either agency with all of the information (such as total family income or assets) necessary to determine eligibility for the child tax credit if the credit did not exist. Thus, a major advantage of administering subsidies through the tax system – an application for benefits that follows directly from an activity that the worker must undertake anyway – is not present in the U.K. system.

In both the first and second phases of reform, the Labour government has offered several reasons for using the tax system to deliver targeted benefits. One argument is that shifting the FC (and later other expenditure programs) into the tax system would allow for better integration of the tax and transfer system by simplifying and streamlining the administration of various programs. Closer coordination of tax and transfer policies would also focus attention on high marginal tax rates; in both phases, reforms have been accompanied with expansions of assistance to families, thus reducing the marginal tax rates on lower income families (while increasing them on families higher up the income scale who previously were ineligible for such benefits). (Taylor, 1998, U.K. HM Treasury, 2000, Brewer et al, 2001, Brewer et al, 2003) Further, with the most recent consolidation of credits, the patchwork of eligibility rules that characterized the first phase has been replaced with simpler uniform rules. These arguments make a compelling case for consolidation of assistance programs, but they could support placement of the new credits in either the tax or transfer system.

There are several other arguments – some made by the Labour government, some not – in support of using the tax system to provide targeted assistance. First, payment of the working tax credit builds on the PAYE system, in which taxes are withheld by the employer. The working tax credit operates as a reverse-PAYE in a manner similar to the EITC advance payment option. As with the advance payment option, the worker must repay any amount that is overpaid during the year, but the British limit the risk of repayments (at minimal loss of targeting precision) by ignoring increases in income of less than 2,500 pounds. Paying the credit through the paycheck was viewed as important to reinforce the distinction between the "rewards of work and remaining on welfare" (Taylor, 1998).

A second consideration was stigma. Administering benefits through the tax system, rather than the welfare system, was expected to reduce the stigma associated with claiming the FC and thus lead to an increase in program participation (Taylor, 1998).[20] The evidence is mixed as to whether the shift to the tax system has reduced stigma and increased participation among those eligible for the credits. As noted earlier, overall participation fell after the shift to Inland Revenue, but participation did increase among those who previously had been eligible for the FC. The higher participation rates among those who were eligible under both credits might be attributable to a reduction in stigma, but it also might result from the increased credit amounts or greater outreach efforts. One study finds that the WFTC has lower participation costs than the FC, but the authors cannot distinguish between stigma, transactions costs, or information costs (Brewer et al, 2003). By making the credit payable through a third-party (the employers), the WFTC actually could have increased stigma. However, a survey of WFTC applicants found that only 4 percent said that contact with their employer regarding the credit made them less likely to apply for the credit in the future (McKay, 2003).

A tax credit was thought to be politically more acceptable than social security benefits to most claimants and taxpayers as a whole. The Taylor report (1998) concluded that operating the FC through the tax system "would ensure greater acceptability to both the claimants and taxpayers." The report went on to note, "It is noticeable that the US Administration has secured widespread political support for the EITC at a time when the US welfare budget more generally has been under remorseless attack."

There is one argument that could have been made in defense of the shifting responsibilities, but which was not discussed in the Labour Government reports. Inland Revenue is presumably in a better position to verify eligibility for targeted benefits because of the amount of information on income reported to Inland Revenue in an exact withholding system. The most recent reforms to the system of refundable tax credits were in part motivated to build on the extensive annual income reporting system: thus, eligibility for the child tax credit and working tax credit are based on the same annual accounting system used to determine tax liabilities.

What was lacking in the British system (as in the U.S. income tax system) was independent information on family relationships. This shortfall was partly rectified by the transfer of the administration of the child benefit to Inland Revenue. With this new responsibility presumably came access to data file containing names of parents linked to their children and authenticated by receipt, at application, with the child's birth or adoption certificate. Because applicants for the child tax credit must provide both their National Insurance number and a child benefit reference number, Inland Revenue has the capability to link data from the two programs in order to verify claims. In effect, Inland Revenue – through the universal child benefit – gained access to the counterpart of Kidlink in the United States, without having to wait a generation for the completion of the file. From an organizational perspective, it may have been easier to shift the existing files on children and parents to Inland Revenue rather than to provide the Department of Social Security with all the income information collected in the tax system. The British experience also raises the question of whether a universal benefit may be a way to obtain family data that would not be otherwise easily accessible and which can be used to help target other benefits.

The British experience demonstrates that it is possible to have both a return-free tax system with exact withholding and refundable tax credits, but this achievement comes at some cost to applicants and the tax authorities. While about two-thirds of taxpayers do not file tax returns, about 90 percent of taxpayers with children must file an application that looks very much like a tax return in order to provide the information necessary to demonstrate eligibility for the child tax credit. Brewer (2003) suggests that the new tax credits signal the Labour Government's frustration with individual taxation and PAYE as ways to target resources on the basis of household need. However, as in the United States, it is not obvious that the costs of providing such benefits to both low- and middle-income taxpayers would be significantly less expensive through other agencies.

4. CONCLUSIONS

Providing targeted assistance to low-income individuals through the income tax system may be appropriate under certain circumstances. Under the current tax system in the United States, many low-income working individuals would file income tax returns even if there were no refundable tax credits. Information on their earnings and other income is regularly reported to the IRS. Many of them are either ineligible for needs-based benefits provided by other agencies, or they choose – either because of high transactions costs or concerns with stigma – not to claim those benefits. Thus, for low-income working individuals, the point of contact with the federal government is often the IRS.

The experience of Great Britain demonstrates that even when these conditions do not hold, policymakers may still find it advantageous to use the tax system as a delivery mechanism. One argument, stated by politicians in the U.K., is political: they (and possibly their U.S. counterparts) find that providing benefits through the tax system is more acceptable than expanding spending programs. But the British experience suggests that there may be other considerations. The British, for example, use their exact withholding system in reverse to pay work-related tax credits to workers in a timely fashion. Concern that the stigma of applying for benefits through a "welfare" agency may cut participation also motivates interest in using the tax system. And possibly the most obvious argument in support of using the tax system to provide targeted benefits is the one seldom mentioned: the income tax system in the United Kingdom, as in the United States, has the best access to independent information on income.

Yet as the U.S. experience demonstrates, operating targeted benefit programs through the tax system is fraught with difficulties. Key among them is the fact that the tax system lacks complete data on family composition and needs. Limited resources, relative to other priorities, may limit the IRS's ability to prevent payments of questionable claims. As a result, noncompliance may be higher than in spending programs that rely on more labor-intensive (and more expensive) enforcement techniques.

Reducing noncompliance among EITC claimants remains one of the biggest challenges for the IRS. This year, the IRS is piloting a small program in which 25,000 EITC claimants were asked to provide documentation at the time they filed their tax return demonstrating that they resided with their qualifying children for the required length of time. Without ceding control of the tax credit, the IRS is instead testing the adoption of one of the practices used commonly by other agencies in the administration of targeted benefits. This pilot will be carefully evaluated, to determine the effect of the additional documentation requirement on both compliance and participation.

The British experience also suggests that much simplification can be achieved by consolidating assistance programs. In the United States, several analysts have suggested that child-related tax benefits could be consolidated into one tax credit (Ellwood and Liebman, 2001, Sawicky and Cherry, 2001, Carasso, Rohaly, and Steuerle, 2003). In recent years, the Department of the Treasury has made a number of proposals that would simplify the current targeting rules for the EITC and the additional child tax credit. Some of these proposals conform the eligibility rules for the EITC and the additional child tax credit more closely by, for example, defining a child and earned income in the same way and by eliminating the EITC investment income test. These proposals also lay the groundwork for a consideration of the consolidation of the two credits.

Notes

1. Views and opinions in this paper are those of the author and do not necessarily represent the policies or positions of the Treasury Department
2. Even with universal benefits, there will be problems for administrators to sort through. Keeping accurate and timely records on births and deaths is one hurdle. Administrators may also have to settle competing claims when more than one "guardian" claims benefits on behalf of a minor child or disabled adult.
3. 1996 law in 1994 dollars.
4. The amount payable in excess of income tax liability is scored as an outlay in the federal budget accounts.
5. Eligible individuals include people who receive a Trade Readjustment Allowance (TRA), workers who are 50 or older and who receive a certain percentage of the wage differential between the wages of their previous, adversely-affected employment and their new full-time employment, and pension benefit recipients of the Pension Benefit Guaranty Corporation (PBGC).
6. Neither the self-employed nor childless individuals can avail themselves of this option.
7. To limit the risk of overpayments, Congress constrained the advance payment to 60 percent of the maximum credit for which a worker with one child would be entitled in 1993.
8. Both credits define earned income to include only taxable compensation. But the additional child tax credit further restricts earned income to compensation included in taxable income. For example, some ministers add parsonage allowances to self-employment income when computing self-employment income taxes and the EITC. However, such allowances are excluded from taxable income for purposes of the regular income tax and the additional child tax credit.
9. Unpublished IRS data.
10. Author's computations based on Census data (www.census.gov/hhes/poverty/poverty02/r&dtable5.html).
11. See U.S. Department of the Treasury, Internal Revenue Service, February 28, 2002b. The study was based on audits of 3,457 randomly selected tax year 1999 returns filed during 2000 and claiming the EITC. The sample represents a population of 18.8 million tax returns and about $31.3 billion in EITC claims. The EITC errors identified in the study include both intentional noncompliance and unintentional reporting mistakes, and the two types of errors are not readily distinguishable in the data. Returns were selected

before mathematical and clerical errors were corrected as part of routine IRS processing. Therefore simple computational errors are also counted as noncompliance in this study.

12. The difference between the upper- and lower-bound estimates is attributable to alternative treatments of taxpayers who failed to appear for an audit. Unless otherwise noted, the estimates in this paper are based on the upper-bound set of estimates and on the amount of overclaims prior to any IRS enforcement activities.
13. There are other differences between the two programs that may contribute to the discrepancy. First, food stamp benefits are in-kind benefits, which may reduce their appeal to those not eligible for assistance. However, food stamps benefits are often categorized as near-cash because of its fungible nature. To prevent fraud, the Department of Agriculture maintains an anti-trafficking program.. Second, marginal tax rates are higher in the food stamp program (which could contribute to increased noncompliance). However, the higher marginal tax rates generally apply over a shorter income range than is the case for the EITC.
14. See the Massachusetts application for food stamps benefits at http://www.gettingfoodstamps.org/fsa-pjb.pdf
15. For example, the Florida Economic Self-Sufficiency (ESS) Public Assistance Policy Manual states "...due to the difficulty in verifying whether or not a group of individuals customarily purchases and prepares meals together and, therefore, constitutes an SFU [standard filing unit], the ESS will generally accept the SFU's statement regarding food preparation and purchasing." http://www5.myflorida.com/cf_web/myflorida2/healthhuman/publications/esspolicymanual/pa2200.pdf
16. The IRS is currently evaluating the results of a small pilot in which taxpayers are allowed to provide documentation of an EITC qualifying child's residency from anyone, including neighbors and family, with personal knowledge of the child's whereabouts.
17. Married couples were entitled to a "married couple" allowance. In 1999, the amount was equal to 1,970 pounds ($3,140) if both spouses are under 65. For all eligible taxpayers, the value of the allowance is equal to 10 percent of 1,970 pounds. The couple could elect to divide the married couple allowance between them equally or to allocate it wholly to either spouse. Except for taxpayers aged 65 or older, the married couple allowance was repealed after April 2000. Unmarried individuals who live with a child under age 18 were entitled to an additional personal allowance equal to the married couple allowance. This additional personal allowance was also repealed after April 2000.
18. Intermediate goals were to reduce child poverty by at least a quarter by 2004/2005 from 1998/1999 levels and to halve child poverty over a ten-year period. Unlike the United States, poverty in the United Kingdom is not measured relative to an absolute threshold. Instead, poverty is defined as being a member of a household with income below sixty percent of the median household income. (Brewer et al, 2002).
19. Based on public documents, it is difficult to determine if administrative factors explain the different compliance results in the United Kingdom and the United States. It is important to note that the different results from the compliance studies do not conclusively demonstrate that Inland Revenue has the relative advantage in preventing erroneous claims of children. While Inland Revenue may simply be better than the IRS at detecting erroneous child claims before payment is made, the results are also consistent with the theory that Inland Revenue was worse off because the British agency did not have the ability to detect such errors, even in a compliance study.
20. From an outsider's perspective, the amount of attention paid to stigma concerns in the United Kingdom is interesting and raises the question of what constitutes stigma. In the United States, traditional welfare programs are perceived as stigmatizing because applicants have to meet in person with caseworkers to review their application. Benefit programs are also viewed as stigmatizing when payments are made through third parties (e.g., through employers receiving subsidies for hiring disadvantaged workers or grocery

stores accepting vouchers for food assistance). Verifying eligibility criteria with employers, bankers, and neighbors may also add to stigma. In these three instances, stigma is caused by the involvement of a third-party in the benefit delivery process. By comparison, the FC was administered in ways that should have minimized such effects. Low-income families did not have to go to a state office to apply for the FC but instead could deal with the Department of Social Security through the mail. The FC could be paid directly to the individual through direct deposits into accounts at banks or building societies. Applicants' employers were contacted to verify earnings generally only if payslips were not attached to the application.

References

Brewer, Mike (2003), *The New Tax Credits, Institute for Fiscal Studies Briefing Note No. 35.*

Brewer, Mike, Tom Clark, and Michal Myck (2001), *Credit Where It's Due? An Assessment of the New Tax Credits, Institute for Fiscal Studies Commentary No. 86.*

Brewer, Mike, Alan Duncan, Andrew Shephard, and Maria Jose Suarez (2003), "*Did Working Families' Tax Credit Work? An Impact of In-Work Support on Labour Supply and Programme Participation*",

Barrow, Lisa and Leslie McGranahan (2001), "The Effects of the Earned Income Tax Credit on the Seasonality of Household Expenditures", in: Bruce Meyer and Douglas Holtz-Eakin, editors, *Making Work Pay*, Russell Sage Foundation.

Carasso, Adam, Jeff Roahly, and C. Eugene Steuerle (2003), *Tax Reform for Families: An Earned Income Child Credit, Brookings Institution Policy Brief: Welfare Reform & Beyond No. 26.*

Cunnyngham, Karen (2003), *Trends in Food Stamp Participation Rates: 1994 to 2001, Report submitted to U.S. Department of Agriculture, Food and Nutrition Services,* Washington, D.C.: Mathematica Policy Research, Inc.

Dickert, Stacy, Scott Hauser, and John Karl Scholz (1995), "The Earned Income Tax Credit and Transfer Programs: A Study of Labor Market and Program Participation", in: *Tax Policy and the Economy Vol. 9,* Cambridge, MS: MIT Press.

Eissa, Nada and Jeffrey Liebman (1996), "Labor Supply Response and the Earned Income Tax Credit", *Quarterly Journal of Economics,* Vol. 111(2).

Elwood, David T. and Jeffrey B. Liebman (2001), "The Middle Class Parent Penalty: Child Benefits in the U.S. Tax Code", in: *Tax Policy and the Economy Vol. 15*, Cambridge, MS: MIT Press.

Grogger, Jeffrey (2003), "The Effects of Time Limits, the EITC, and Other Policy Changes on Welfare Use, Work, and Income Among Female-Headed Families", *The Review of Economics and Statistics,*Vol. 85(2), pp.

Holtzblatt, Janet (2000), "Choosing Between Refundable Tax Credits and Spending Programs", in: *Proceedings of the Ninety-third Annual Conference on Taxation*, Washington D.C.: National Tax Association.

Holtzblatt, Janet and Jeffrey L. Liebman (1999), "The Earned Income Tax Credit Abroad: Implications of the British Working Families Tax Credit for Pay-As-You-Earn Administration", *Proceedings of the Ninety-first Annual Conference on Taxation*, Washington, D.C.: National Tax Association.

Holtzblatt, Janet and Janet McCubbin (2004), "Issues Affecting Low-Income Filers", in: Henry Aaron and Joel Slemrod, editors, *The Crisis in Tax Administration,* Washington, D.C.: Brookings Institution Press.

Holtzblatt, Janet and Janet McCubbin (2003), "Whose Child is It Anyway? Simplifying the Definition of a Child", *National Tax Journal,* Vol. 56(3), pp.

Hussain, Medhi (2004), *Tax Credits: The UK Perspective, Paper presented at IRS Research Conference*, Washington D.C.

Liebman, Jeffrey (1997), *Lessons from Tax-Benefit Integration from the U.S. Earned Income Tax Credit Experience,* York: Joseph Rowntree Foundation.

McKay, Stephen (2003), *Working Families Tax Credit, United Kingdom Department of Work and Pensions Research Report No. 181.*

Meyer, Bruce and Dan Rosenbaum (2001), "Making Single Mothers Work: Recent Tax and Welfare Policy and It's Effects", in: Bruce Meyer and Douglas Holtz-Eakin, editors, *Making Work Pay*, Russell Sage Foundation.

Ponza, Michael, James C. Ohls, Lorenzo Moreno, Amy Zambrowski, and Rhonda Cohen (1999), *Customer Service in the Food Stamp Program, Report submitted to U.S. Department of Agriculture, Food and Nutrition Services,* Washington, D.C.: Mathematica Policy Research, Inc.

Rosenbaum, Dottie (2003), *Food Stamp Overpayment Error Rate Hits Record Low,* Center for Budget and Policy Priorities.

Romich, Jennifer L. and Thomas S. Weisner (2001), "How Families View and Use the Earned Income Tax Credit: Advance Payment Versus Lump-Sum Delivery", in: Bruce Meyer and Douglas Holtz-Eakin, editors, *Making Work Pay*, Russell Sage Foundation.

Sawicky, Max C. and Robert Cherry (2001), *Making Work Pay With Tax Reform, Economic Policy Institute Issue Brief No.172.*

Scholz, John Karl (1994), "The Earned Income Tax Credit: Participation, Compliance, and Antipoverty Effectiveness", *National Tax Journal,* Vol. 47(1), pp. 63-85.

Smeeding, Timothy, Katherin Ross Phillips, and Michael A. O'Connor (2001), "The Earned Income Tax Credit: Expectation, Knowledge, Use, and Economic and Social Mobility", in: Bruce Meyer and Douglas Holtz-Eakin, editors, *Making Work Pay*, Russell Sage Foundation.

Taylor, Martin (1998), *Work Incentives, A Report to HM Treasury*, London.

U.K. Inland Revenue (2003), "New Tax Credits – Ensuring Compliance." November.

U.K. Inland Revenue (2002), Analysis and Research, Working Families' Tax Credit: Estimates of Take-up Rates in 2000-01.

U.K. HM Treasury (2000), "Tackling Poverty and Making Work Pay – Tax Credits for the 21st Century." March.

U.S. Department of the Treasury, Internal Revenue Service (1999), "Advance Earned Income Tax Credit: 1994 and 1997 Notice Study." August.

U.S. Department of the Treasury, Internal Revenue Service (2002a), "Compliance Estimates for Earned Income Tax Credit Claimed on 1999 Returns." February.

U.S. Department of the Treasury, Internal Revenue Service (2002b), "Participation in the Earned Income Tax Credit Program for Tax Year 1996." January.

U.S. Department of the Treasury (2003), "Report to the Congress on Return-Free Tax Systems: Tax Simplification Is a Prerequisite." December.

U.S. General Accounting Office, *Earned Income Tax Credit: Advance Payment Option Is Not Widely Known or Understood by the Public*, Washington, D.C.: U.S. General Accounting Office,1992, GAO/GGD-92-26.

U.S. General Accounting Office, *Food Stamp Program: Various Factors Have Led to Declining Participation*, Washington, D.C.: U.S. General Accounting Office, 1999, GAO/RCED-99-185.

U.S. General Accounting Office, *Earned Income Tax Credit: Eligibility and Participation*, Washington, D.C.: U.S. General Accounting Office, 2001, GAO-02-0290R.

U.S. Office of Management and Budget (2004), "Appendix to Budget of the U.S. Government, Fiscal Year 2005." February.

DISCUSSANT COMMENTS

DAGNEY FAULK
Indiana University Southeast

HARBERGER AND HOLTZBLATT

The papers by Harberger and Holtzblatt contribute in different ways to the understanding of the relationship between income taxation and distribution. Each of these papers provides information and analysis that is useful to policymakers. Harberger's papers reflect on several related themes: He begins with the argument that government tax and expenditure policy have little effect on the distribution of income in a country. The way that the government structures the tax system can have more effect on the tax distribution (rather than the income distribution) and the inherent tax burdens of various income groups. Finally, he argues that government resources are better spent targeting poverty by providing education, opportunities for upward mobility, and basic health care for the needy. Harberger makes several suggestions on how to make a relatively proportional system more progressive and key insights into how to determine who bears the burden of the corporate income tax.

The paper by Holtzblatt focuses primarily on structural aspects of the tax system. Holtzblatt examines a specific tax policy, refundable tax credits, focusing primarily of the Earned Income Tax Credit (EITC), the most widely utilized U.S. tax credit, (limited information on the Child Tax Credit and Health Coverage Tax Credit are also included in the analysis) and Britain's Child Tax Credit and Working Tax Credit. She provides an analysis of the advantages and disadvantages of the U.S. and British approach to using the national tax systems, and refundable tax credits in particular, to target assistance to needy families. The analysis is primarily from an administrative perspective.

Distribution issues play a key role in determining tax and transfer policies. The EITC in the U.S. and the Child Tax Credit and Working Tax Credit in Great Britain reduce the tax liability of low income households and households with children thereby lowering the tax burden of these groups and reducing the portion of tax revenue paid by these groups. To know the effectiveness of these types of credits we need to quantify how these credits affect the distribution of taxes among low-income families and families with children. What is the magnitude of the credit in terms of the average credit per family, female-headed households, etc.? This sort of analysis would good next step. In addition, several U.S. states have adopted state EITCs that piggyback on the federal credit. Has there been a similar response among subnational governments in Britain? An analysis of national and subnational policies will provide the true picture of how these types of credits affect the distribution of tax burdens.

Concerning the many points that Harberger made in his papers, I would like to focus on distributional issues concerning the corporate income tax. While much of Harberger's work has focused on who bears the burden in terms of capital and labor. Recent empirical analysis, which has received substantial mass media coverage, has focused on a more general point: the decline in corporate tax collections. For example, a recent report issued by the U.S. General Accounting Office found that a majority of all corporations filing corporate income tax returns in the U.S. reported no tax liability during the 1996-2000 period. This report and others have documented that in the U.S. a large portion of corporate income tax collections are paid by a small number of corporations, and most firms have no or low corporate income tax liability. Aggressive tax planning including the use of tax shelters and loopholes is credited with the dramatic reduction in the corporate tax burden in the U.S. over the past few decades. Corporations have strategically shifted income to low or no tax jurisdictions. What are the implications for the Harberger analysis of who bears the burden of the corporate income tax?

The tax distribution can be measured in various ways: the distribution of tax liability, tax burden as measured by the ratio of tax liability to income, tax burden as measured by effective tax rates, the gini coefficient measured before and after tax changes, etc. While the Harberger analysis includes measures of the distribution of the tax burden, Holtzblatt focuses on policies that change the distribution. One of the recurrent points in these papers is that, while various measures of the tax distribution are readily available, current data on income and tax liability needed to analyze the distribution often is not. Much of the Harberger analysis of tax burdens relies on data from the 1970s. Undoubtedly, access to reliable and current data is one of the major challenges of tax reform.

3

THE INTERNATIONAL DIMENSION AND THE ROLE OF TAX INCENTIVES

Chapter 4

TRANSFER PRICING AND TAX HAVENS: MENDING THE REVENUE NETS OF DEVELOPING AND TRANSITION COUNTRIES

CHARLES E. McLURE, Jr.[1]
Hoover Institution, Stanford University

1. INTRODUCTION

Manipulation of transfer pricing[2] and tax havens,[3] individually and in combination, adversely affect the ability of many countries to raise tax revenues.[4] The loss of revenues caused by evasion of individual income taxes and avoidance (and perhaps evasion) of corporate income taxes[5] are especially severe in developing countries and in countries in transition from socialism,[6] which I will generally lump together and designate as developing and transition countries or DTCs. DTCs are more limited than developed countries in what they can do to mend their revenue nets, *inter alia*, because of the complexity of the administrative problems involved and their lack of administrative resources. Developed countries may, however, assist DTCs, either because they choose to do so or as a byproduct of measures they take to protect their own tax bases.[7]

This paper describes how transfer pricing and tax havens can tear revenue nets and examines, somewhat speculatively, whether the recent Organisation for Economic Co-Operation and Development (OECD) initiative to combat harmful tax competition may indirectly benefit DTCs. The next two sections provide a bare-bones description of the international tax "system" and the revenue implications of tax havens and transfer pricing. Sections 4 and 5, respectively, examine two ways to combat abuse, monitoring transfer pricing and enforcing anti-deferral legislation. Section 6 discusses the OECD initiatives on harmful tax competition, concluding that they will do little to mend the revenue nets of DTCs. Section 7 concludes.

It will be useful to consider three broad classes of countries: tax havens, developed countries, and (non-haven) DTCs.[8] For some purposes it will be useful to distinguish between the least developed and more advanced DTCs. (Most of the former are developing countries.) Since the paper is mostly concerned with the fiscal plight of DTCs, it considers the situation of developed countries primarily as models for what DTCs might do and to understand the likelihood that assistance for DTCs will be forthcoming, perhaps as a collateral benefit of policies developed countries adopt for their own reasons.

The paper considers both the use of tax havens by wealthy individuals to evade taxes in their countries of residence and the use of transfer pricing by multinational enterprises to avoid source-country taxes and the use of tax havens to avoid or defer corporate taxes levied by countries of residence. It does not consider preferential tax treatment for selected non-financial sectors, perhaps limited to foreign investors, in order to attract real (non-financial) activities. Such countries are not ordinarily called tax havens,[9] and these policies – and the possibility that transfer prices are manipulated to shift domestic-source income from taxed activities to activities that benefit from domestic tax incentives – are best treated in a paper on tax incentives.[10] Nor does it consider headquarters havens, except in the context of the OECD initiative and in passing in the brief discussion of corporate inversions. Finally, it does not examine empirical analyses of income shifting; for summaries of that analysis, see US Department of the Treasury (2000, Appendix D), Altshuler (2004), and Hines (2004) and references provided there.

It may be useful to indicate some of the other related topics the paper does not cover, some of which I have discussed elsewhere. First, it does not discuss whether or not having a corporate income tax is a good idea for a small open economy or the related question of whether an individual country should levy such a tax at a rate above zero on income foreigners earn in the country. As Hines notes, economic theory suggests that "countries that ... persist in taxing income earned by foreign investors will have lower incomes than those that do not. (On this topic, see Gordon, 1986, Sadka and Razin, 1991, Gordon and Mac-Kie Mason, 1995, and Gugl and Zodrow, 2004.) The paper is premised on the proposition that a DTC wishes to collect the taxes it has enacted and is not interested in using lax tax administration (e.g., of transfer pricing rules) as a surrogate for explicit tax incentives intended to attract investment.[11]

Second, the paper does not discuss whether taxation should be designed to promote either capital export neutrality or capital import neutrality.[12] Thus, it does not enter into the current debate (raging, for example, in the

United States) over whether or not to either end deferral or move to a more territorial system.

Third, it does not consider whether or how the basic rules that govern taxation of international flows of income, contained in model treaties should be changed to accommodate the development of electronic-commerce (e-commerce).[13]

Fourth, it does not consider whether formula apportionment should replace separate accounting and the arm's length standard as a way to solve the problems identified here related to corporate use of tax havens and transfer prices. (On this, see McLure, 2002, and literature cited there. For a quite different view, see McIntyre, 2004.)

Fifth, the paper does not discuss the tax implications of derivatives and other modern financial instruments, despite their role in greatly complicating efforts to deal with tax havens and other abuses. (See, however, Thuronyi, 2001, and references provided there.)

Finally, it does not consider whether a World Tax Organization, which has been proposed, *inter alia*, by Tanzi (1999) and the UN's Zedillo Commission (UN, 2001), is needed to address the problems described here.

2. THE INTERNATIONAL TAX "SYSTEM"

In principle, all income that crosses international borders could be taxed by the country where it originates (the source or host country) or by the country of residence of the recipients of the income (the residence or home country).[14] If both countries were to tax such income, with no relief for the taxes paid to the other country, double taxation would occur.[15] Both domestic laws and bilateral tax treaties, especially among developed countries, contain provisions intended to prevent double taxation, generally through either exemptions for foreign-source income or credits for foreign taxes. Treaties also provide for exchange of information between the tax administrators of source and residence countries that is intended to prevent undertaxation. Most treaties between developed countries, as well as some between developed countries and DTCs, are based on the OECD Model Treaty. Although developing countries may prefer to follow the UN Model Treaty, which is generally more favorable to source countries, they often lack the political clout to prevail in treaty negotiations with developed countries.

Under these treaties, income is taxed differently, depending on how it is characterized. Source countries ordinarily tax business income on a net basis (that is, they tax income net of deductions for expenses of earning the income), but only if it is earned by a "permanent establishment" (PE) in the country.[16] By comparison, source countries tax interest, dividends, and royalties, if at all, on a gross basis (that is, with no deductions for expenses of earning the income), commonly via withholding taxes, which are generally reduced, sometimes to zero, under treaties. It may thus be necessary for source countries to determine a) whether income is business income or some other kind of income, b) whether or not business income is earned by a PE, c) the geographic source of the income, and d) the amount of income that is taxable. It is also necessary for countries taxing worldwide income to determine the geographic source and amount of income, in order to calculate the limits on foreign tax credits mentioned below and to implement the anti-abuse rules discussed in Section 5.

Residence countries generally either exempt foreign-source income or tax it as part of the taxpayer's worldwide income and allow credits for tax paid to source countries, up to the amount of domestic tax on the income. Countries such as France that tax business income on the basis of source may, none-the-less tax foreign-source passive income of their residents. Subject to limitations to be described in Section 5 below, residence countries generally respect the legal identity of separate corporations; this implies, in practice, that residence country tax on foreign-source income earned by foreign subsidiaries, but not that earned by foreign branches (PEs), is "deferred" until it is repatriated.

A country's tax regime applicable to in-bound or outbound transactions, in combination with the tax systems of other countries, may create incentives to shift income from high-tax to low-tax jurisdictions. Table 1 summarizes the conditions under which incentives exist to shift income from a parent in a high-tax jurisdiction to a subsidiary in a low-tax jurisdiction[17] Incentives to shift income exist if the home country exempts foreign-source income. If the home country taxes worldwide income, such incentives can exist if distribution – and thus residence-country tax – is deferred. Even if income is distributed, incentives for income shifting can arise if the parent has "excess foreign tax credits," perhaps because it has accumulated credits for high foreign taxes that it could not utilize previously.[18] Only if income is to be distributed to a parent that is resident in a country that taxes worldwide income and has a "deficit of foreign tax credits" (the situation where all credits can be utilized currently, because foreign-source income has been taxed at rates below the domestic rate) will there be no incentive to shift income to low-tax jurisdictions. Also, only in this case does the home country of the parent receive any current tax revenue from income earned abroad.

In what follows we examine how transfer pricing and tax havens produce tears in this system and whether and how these tears can be mended. Wealthy individuals in both DTCs and developed countries employ tax havens to evade residence-based taxes on income from passive investments. By comparison, the tears in the corporate revenue net that DTCs and developed countries experience are often not the same. In the former case, the primary risk is to source-based taxation, that is, taxation of corporate income having its source within the country. (See, however, the expositional convention mentioned in footnote 4.) By comparison, developed countries are likely to be concerned about residence-based taxation of corporate income, as well as source-based taxation. An important focus of the paper is to discern whether actions taken by developed countries to protect their tax bases can also help protect those of developing countries, if only indirectly.

Table 1. Conditions for Taxation by Parent's Country of Residence to Offset Source-country Tax

	Territorial Taxation	Worldwide taxation, With foreign tax credits		
	(A)	Income retained abroad	Income distributed to parent	
			Excess FTC (C)	Deficit of FTC (D)
Does current taxation by parent's country of residence offset source-country tax?	No	No	No	Yes
Does parent's country of residence receive revenue currently?	No	No	No	Yes

3. TEARS IN THE SYSTEM

Tax havens and manipulation of transfer pricing create tears in the revenue system.[19] To simplify exposition, this section initially considers the use of tax havens simply to defer, avoid, and evade taxes, ignoring manipulation of transfer prices. It then considers the effects of manipulating transfer prices, in the absence of tax havens. Finally, it considers the realistic case in which tax havens and manipulation of transfer prices occur together. The discussion abstracts from the effects of legislation and administrative techniques intended to prevent tax minimization associated with transfer pricing and tax havens; these are discussed in the next two sections.

3.1 Deferral, Tax Avoidance, and Evasion in "Simple" Tax Haven Cases

Tax havens may arise for several reasons that do not involve manipulation of transfer prices. These generally, but not always, involve wealthy individuals or corporate parents that are residents of a country that taxes worldwide income, rather than exempting foreign-source income. The following brief descriptions will help understand the purpose of the anti-deferral legislation discussed in Section 5 and the OECD project on harmful tax competition discussed in Section 6.

1. Passive investment: deferral and avoidance of corporate taxes and evasion of individual taxes

First, a corporation may use a tax haven subsidiary (or a trust) to make passive investments and accumulate income therefrom, thereby postponing home-country tax that the parent would owe if it received the income currently. In the absence of effective anti-abuse legislation, such as the CFC legislation discussed below, income from income from passive investments in the residence country of the parent might be channeled to the tax haven, thereby allowing the parent to achieve deferral of tax even on domestic-sourcc incomc.[20]

Wealthy individuals (perhaps operating via closely held corporations or trusts) may also engage in this type of tax haven activity, but they are more likely never to pay tax to their country of residence, thus evading tax, rather than merely deferring it.[21] The success of tax evasion may depend on confidentiality provided by the tax haven, in particular on the absence of exchange of information between the tax haven and the residence country, without which it is difficult for tax administrators to track such investments. Easson (2004a, p. 1071) writes, "... pure tax havens are normally associated more with passive investment than with direct investment. Their principal attractions, to passive investors, are nominal or zero tax, together with strict bank secrecy and the absence of effective exchange of information. In other words, *they invite tax evasion*." (Emphasis added) See also Blum *et al.* (1998) and Vann (1998, pp. 759-761.)

In part because of the success of the anti-deferral legislation considered below in curbing corporate abuses, this form of evasion is probably more important than corporate use of tax havens to achieve deferral of tax on passive income and has been characterized as "the weakest point in the entire world fiscal system." (See Kudrle and Eden, 2003, p. 53.) The authors of a 1998 report prepared for the UN (Blum *et al.* p. 110) state:

> What started as a business to service the needs of a privileged few has become an enormous hole in the international legal and fiscal system. We estimate that there are now more than one million anonymous corporations. Consultants for the offshore banking centers say that the centers are home to more than $5 trillion in assets – one trillion in bank deposits and four trillion held in the form of stock, bonds, real estate and commodities.[22]

2. Active investment

Corporate tax haven activity is, of course, not limited to passive investments; controlled foreign corporations (CFCs) can also be used to defer residence-country taxation of business income. Blessing (2000, p. 18:2) describes the following "paradigm for structuring operations with respect to a traditional manufacturing-distributing enterprise" to achieve "the objective of unbundling functions and placing them in jurisdictions that are compatible with tax reductions."

- First, a CFC ("Principal"), resident in a low-tax jurisdiction owns relevant intangibles; is the hub that arranges the manufacturing, distribution, and other functions; owns the goods; and derives residual profits.
- An affiliated or unaffiliated toll manufacturer ... or contract manufacturer manufactures the goods on behalf of the CFC for a modest fee.[23]
- An affiliated commissionaire (a sale agent that acts in its own name for a modest commission) or a stripped buy-sell distributor (a distributor that acquires ownership and resells the goods, incurring relatively little risk, for a modest profit) sells the goods in the local market.
- One or more affiliated service entities might perform procurement, invoicing shipping, and other back-office functions for Principal for a modest fee.

In these scenarios (and others), unbundling functions and interposing a tax haven between them is advantageous, even if income is not shifted between countries, because repatriation and current taxation by the country of residence is deferred.[24] These tax haven activities would not be attractive if foreign-source income were taxed currently, without deferral (and, of course, without evasion of the residence-country tax).

3.2 Income Shifting in "Simple" Transfer Pricing Cases

When affiliated parts of a multinational enterprise (MNE) engage in transactions with each other, it is necessary to specify "transfer prices" to be used to value the transactions. As noted earlier, there is often an incentive to choose transfer prices that shift income from high-tax to low-tax jurisdictions or shift expenses from low-tax to high-tax jurisdictions.

It is instructive to construct a simple example to illustrate the benefits of manipulating transfer prices. Suppose that a parent corporation resident in nation R develops technology that it licenses to a production subsidiary in nation P, which in turn markets its product through a sister subsidiary in nation M. Suppose alternatively that nation R exempts foreign-source income or that it taxes worldwide income and allows a credit for foreign taxes, but repatriation can be postponed. Suppose further that R has the highest tax rate of the three countries and P has the lowest rate, perhaps because of a tax holiday. There is an incentive to manipulate transfer prices, including the terms of the licensing agreement, to shift income from both the parent and the marketing subsidiary to the production subsidiary, and thus from countries R and M to country P, where it will be subject to the lowest tax rate.

The facts assumed in constructing this example are deliberately simple, involving only transfer prices for technology and a finished product. In fact, the world is much more complex, and it is also necessary to establish transfer prices for a wide range of other transactions, among them intermediate products, other intangible assets and products, financial products, services, and technical assistance.[25]

3.3 Combining Tax Havens and Transfer Pricing

A key feature of the "simple" transfer pricing scenario considered above is that the benefits of manipulating transfer prices for a MNE depend on differences in tax rates in countries where real economic activity occurs. Once transfer pricing and tax havens are combined, the benefits of manipulating transfer prices increase dramatically and depend on differences in tax rates in such countries and in tax havens (assumed for simplicity to be zero), where there may be little or no economic activity.

To see the difference in these two situations, the previous example is modified so that a holding company H resident in a tax haven acquires the rights to the technology from its parent in R and owns not only the production and manufacturing subsidiaries, but also a tax-haven subsidiary that buys from the production subsidiary and sells to the marketing subsidiary.[26] In the absence of effective anti-abuse legislation, income attributed to the holding company (or its tax-haven subsidiary) via the manipulation of transfer prices will be subject to little or no taxation as long as it is not repatriated. The most important transfer price in this example is that for the initial transfer of technology; manipulating it shifts income from the country where the technology is developed (usually the parent's country of residence) to the tax haven.[27] (If the marketing subsidiary is located in the country of residence of the parent, transfer pricing can be used to shift income to the tax heaven and thereby avoid current source-based R-country taxation). This incentives exists, even if all three (non-haven) tax rates are the same. And, because the incentives depend on the level of the three tax rates, rather than their differences, the stakes in the transfer pricing are substantially greater than in either of the "simple" cases described earlier.

4. MENDING THE TEARS: TRANSFER PRICING

All countries with inward or outward foreign trade – which is just about all countries – face the need to monitor transfer prices. It will be convenient to begin by ignoring the existence of tax havens and examine solutions to "simple" problems of transfer pricing.[28]

4.1 Transfer Pricing Guidelines

Most developed countries specify rules to be used in establishing and monitoring transfer prices. In general, the objective is to approximate prices that would be charged in arm's length transactions with an unrelated party (e.g., an unrelated buyer, seller, borrower, or lender).

Traditional methods. The United States, which has the most elaborate rules, initially specified three methods of calculating transfer prices (plus unspecified "other" methods): comparable uncontrolled price (CUP), cost plus a margin, and resale price minus a margin. The OECD's *Transfer Pricing Guidelines* (1995), based on guidelines first issued in 1979, envisages use of similar "traditional" methods when possible. The OECD *Guidelines* greatly influence international practice,

Non-traditional methods. Since it may sometimes be difficult to implement any of the traditional rules, especially when intangible assets are involved, in 1994 the United States added two non-traditional methods. Similarly, the OECD *Transfer Pricing Guidelines* includes two additional methods, called "transactional profit methods," but, "as a general matter," discourages their use.[29]

Profit-split methods. Under one of these non-traditional methods, the profit split method, profits (either total or residual) are divided among members of the controlled group. Under the OECD approach the way total profits are split depends on the functions performed and the risks assumed. The US allows the comparable profit split method to be used only when data on profitability of similar activities of uncontrolled taxpayers are available.

The residual profit method is used when there are profits that cannot be explained by traditional methods, because of factors such as economies of scale or the existence of unique assets. Li (2003, p. 111) has noted that the US practice of attributing residual profits to the place where intangible assets have been developed (because cost of development is used as the value of intangibles) is favorable to the United States.[30] Fox and McIntyre (2003) note that, by comparison, "... the cost-plus method and the resale price method allowed them [MNEs] to shift all of their profits, aside from some modest amount, to tax havens" because they "allow the residual profits that a MNE derives from the exploitation of intangible property to be shifted to the country where the owner of the intangible property is resident. By design the place of residency is often a tax haven. In the bulk of cases, the bulk of the profits derived by MNEs come from the exploitation of intangible property."

Profit-comparison methods. The other non-traditional method examines profit margins. Its OECD variant, called the transactional net margin method, examines the profitability of transactions, relative to a base such as costs, sales, or assets and thus operates in a manner similar to the cost plus and resale price methods. The OECD views it as a "last resort." By comparison, in the US the comparable profit method (CPM) looks at operating profits and may be chosen as the "best method." Indeed, Rosenbloom (2000, p. 35.9, n. 10) indicates that "CPM is probably the most common approach used today in applying the arm's-length method in the United States."

Advance Pricing Agreements. Some developed countries have procedures whereby taxpayers and the tax administration agree in advance on the methodology to be used to establish transfer prices. In some cases the tax administration of foreign countries may be party to the agreement; generally this is true only if a tax treaty exists between the two countries.[31]

4.2 Transfer Pricing in DTCs: Problems

DTCs face several layers of overwhelming problems in the area of transfer pricing, in addition to those that a developed country would face.[32] First, their legal framework may not deal adequately with the issue. While

DTCs generally have rules that allow adjustment of transfer prices, many lack detailed administrative guidance on how to implement these rules.[33] (The importance of transfer pricing may not have been fully appreciated until recently. The Appendix surveys what selected tax reform missions to developing countries have had to say about transfer pricing over the years.)

Second – and probably vastly more important – even where a legal framework for monitoring transfer pricing exists (for example, because the country has adopted the OECD Guidelines by administrative ruling), a DTC may lack the administrative capacity, including specially trained economists, to deal with the problem, which is one of the most complex in the entire area of tax administration and compliance;[34] by comparison, MNEs have teams of experts who are occupied with nothing else and may hire away skilled tax administrators.[35] Carl Shoup observed in 1985 (p. 297), based on his experience a decade earlier as a UN adviser, "I was impressed by the disparity in technical resources for handling transfer pricing problems as between the developing country's tax administration and the MNE." Given that transactions between corporate affiliates have increased substantially in number and complexity since then, there is little reason to think this disparity has narrowed appreciably, if at all; indeed, it has probably widened. This problem is compounded by the corruption that is found and apparently tolerated in many DTCs.

Third, comparable uncontrolled transactions and relevant evidence on profitability are even less likely to exist and be accessible to tax administrators in DTCs than in developed countries. Mo (2003, p. 129) observes that the use of data on profitability of non-Mexican companies, such as US parents, is suspect, because the risks (e.g., exchange rate risk, credit risk, political risks, and interest rate risk) may be quite different Moreover, where an entity in a DTC is selling to its parent in an advanced country the tax administration may not have access to the resale price data of the parent that it needs to implement the resale price method; see McCarten (1995, p. 224) and Shoup (1985, p. 297).

Fourth, the typically long period that elapses before transfer pricing cases are settled, as well as the uncertainty of favorable outcomes, may make cash-strapped DTCs relatively uninterested in pursuing them.

All these problems are likely to be more serious in low-income developing countries than in those with higher incomes. Transition countries, having recently benefitted from foreign technical assistance, may have more satisfactory legal structures, but lack administrative capacity.

Ikeda (1992), at the end of an IMF survey that focuses on experience in six developed countries, concludes:

> A transfer pricing policy is an important issue for developing as well as developed countries. Since taxation of

> foreign-related businesses often represents a substantial part of total tax revenue in developing countries, it is not just a matter of tax equity but also one of economic necessity to be able to tap the tax potential of multinational, enterprises. On the other hand, these countries are seriously beset by practical difficulties in applying transfer pricing rules, because their administrations in most cases have only limited resources to cope with complicated international tax issues.

A UN survey reveals that, of developing countries with enough evidence to make a judgment, 61 percent estimated that domestic multinational enterprises were engaged in income shifting and 84 percent believed that foreign enterprises were doing so; 70 percent and 87 percent, respectively, of these countries thought the problem to be significant.[36] Mo (2003) provides illustrative examples of manipulation of transfer prices and steps taken to combat it in China (pp. 80-82; 36-37 and 93-99), India (pp. 48 and 112-13), Brazil (pp. 116; 59-60 and 121-22), and Mexico (71 and 127-29).

Because of differences in laws, regulations, and their interpretation, as well as because of weaknesses in tax administration and the uncertainties inherent in setting transfer prices, corporations may not report the same transfer prices for a given transaction in all countries. (IFA, 2001a, reports differences in transfer pricing policies applied to electronic commerce.) Thus income flowing across international borders may be undertaxed (or overtaxed). Adoption of international standards for transfer pricing, such as those in the OECD Model Treaty and *Transfer Pricing Guidelines*, helps to alleviate – but does not eliminate – problems caused by diverse legal frameworks, but not those caused by inadequate administration.

If all countries used the same transfer pricing rules, interpreted them in the same way, and were totally effective in enforcing those rules, undertaxation (and also overtaxation) caused by inconsistency could not occur. But universal implementation of uniform transfer pricing rules would require unprecedented international cooperation in tax administration, as well as in legislation. Administrative cooperation could take several forms, including arbitration. At the very least there would be exchange of information on transfer pricing, to assure that the same transfer prices were being reported to all countries. Since exchange of information ordinarily occurs only in the context of a tax treaty, and there are relatively few treaties between developed countries and developing countries, there is little such cooperation. (The historical paucity of treaties between developed and developing countries is changing.) Perhaps as important, even where treaties exist, implementing effective exchange of information entails enormous practical problems, especially the lack of administrative resources in DCTs.

This problem is aggravated by the interposition of tax havens between source and residence countries, since tax havens enter into few tax treaties and have little interest in exchanging information.

Even if a multinational corporation does report on a uniform basis everywhere, a transfer pricing adjustment by one country will not necessarily result in an offsetting adjustment elsewhere. In theory mutual agreement procedures (MAPs), arbitration, and multilateral advance pricing agreements could be used to prevent this. (Under most tax treaties, if the competent authority in one country makes a transfer pricing adjustment, the competent authority in the other country is to make a correlative adjustment to ensure that double taxation does not arise.) But, again, lack of treaties, as well as the fact that MAPs take a long time and generally are not binding on competent authorities (tax administrators), stands in the way.[37] Moreover, domestic laws of developed countries or the OECD model treaty and transfer pricing guidelines may attribute to DTCs less income than some believe is appropriate. As noted above, US interpretation of the residual profit split method would attribute the lion's share of income from intangibles developed in the US to the United States, leaving little to market jurisdictions. Also, application of the standard transfer pricing methodology would attribute little e-commerce income to market states.[38] Finally, MNEs may "over-comply" with US transfer pricing rules – and thus "under-comply" with those of DTCs, because the US rules are stricter and their administration is more vigilant.[39]

Many developing countries, when faced with the specter of undercapitalization (and thus excessive use of debt) and payment of excessive interest rates and fees for technical services by local subsidiaries, have resorted to measures such as thin capitalization rules, disallowance of full deduction for certain categories of expenses, and withholding taxes on certain payments to limit abuses. Such "meat ax" rules avoid the difficulty of monitoring transfer prices to limit abuse, but may encounter objections from treaty partners unless carefully structured. (See Oldman, Rosenbloom, and Youngman (1991, p. 393-94).) Detailed discussion of such techniques is beyond the scope of this paper, although Section 6 discusses them in passing.

Low-tax source countries are less likely than high-tax countries to experience transfer pricing problems in the simple case where there are no tax havens, as there is an incentive to shift income to such countries, not from them. This implies that the first line of defense against income shifting is to impose low tax rates, as do many DTCs. This defense may not be adequate, however, once a tax haven is interposed, as in the next part of this section.

4.3 Combining Transfer Pricing and Tax Havens

Combating problems created by the combination of transfer pricing and tax havens, described in the last part of the previous section, poses even greater problems than transfer pricing or tax havens alone. Cooperation between source and residence countries (or between source countries) to prevent inconsistent reporting of transfer prices on the same transaction would be ineffective in preventing revenue cracks, since, from a legal point of view, the tax haven is interposed between the interested countries and it would likely not be a party to such cooperation. Stanley Surrey, writing in 1978, described the problem as follows:

> [T]he United States considered that its parent companies were not charging interest, not being paid for services, not requiring royalties, and not charging proper prices for good sold. Yet it is the developing countries who are most vocal in asserting that they are being imposed on by parent companies of international enterprises. Thus it is asserted that the subsidiary companies in the developing countries are being charged excessive interest rates, being overcharged excessive interest rates, being overcharged for unneeded services, being charged excessive royalties, and being overcharged for goods purchased. (Surrey, 1978, p. 431)

After writing, "Clearly the two images cannot be describing the same transactions," Surrey adds the following in a footnote:

> The two images cannot be describing the same *direct* transaction. But such differing images can coexist as to *indirect* transactions, involving a tax haven. The parent company could *undercharge* on the transaction between it and the tax haven subsidiary and the subsidiary could *overcharge* on the related transaction between it and the subsidiary in the developing country, so that a larger profit will reside in the tax haven. Hence, one tax administrator could see an undercharge and the other an overcharge as respects the basic transaction. (Surrey, 1978, p. 431, n. 52; emphasis in original)

Vann (1998, p. 797) summarizes the situation as follows: "Because of the sophistication of international tax planning and its frequent combination of domestic law, tax havens, and tax treaties, the taxation of nonresident direct investors by developing and transition countries is not an easy task." Mo (2003, p. 116) notes that in 1993 the central bank of Brazil, which had no transfer pricing regulations or guidelines prior to 1997, reported that many MNEs operating in Brazil employed tax haven affiliates and manipulation of transfer pricing to pay no tax in Brazil. Thuronyi (2003, p. 298) notes that, because of difficulty of determining whether a tax-haven entity is related, some countries apply special transfer pricing rules to any transactions with a party located in a tax haven, deny deductions for such payments, or impose withholding taxes on them.

5. MENDING THE TEARS: ANTI-DEFERRAL RULES AND TAX EVASION

Some would not consider the deferral involved in "simple" tax haven cases described in Section 3 to involve abuse; in that view tax havens simply facilitate the realization of the paradigm described in the section on the international tax system: residence-country taxation of repatriated income and deferral of residence-country tax on income that is not repatriated. Others do not like the results described, perhaps because they advocate capital export neutrality, which requires current home-country taxation of worldwide income, with credits for foreign taxes, and realize that the income in question may never be repatriated and thus never subject to home-country tax.[40] The ability to defer home-country taxation indefinitely may make foreign investment more attractive than domestic investment. By comparison, most would probably consider using tax havens to evade residence-country taxes to involve abuse, especially when it involves domestic funds making a round-trip for investment in the home market disguised as foreign investment.[41] This section focuses on methods used to combat deferral of corporate taxes, but also briefly considers tax evasion

5.1 Basic Features of CFC Rules

Many countries that impose residence-based taxes – and, indeed, some that do not tax foreign-source business income[42] – have enacted controlled foreign corporation (CFC) legislation intended to limit the ability of MNEs to defer or avoid tax on income attributed to tax haven subsidiaries.[43] In terms of Table 1, CFC legislation of countries that tax worldwide income can be seen as shifting income from column (B) to Column (C).[44] Under CFC legislation, certain income of foreign subsidiaries located in low-tax jurisdictions and controlled by domestic parents is treated as if it were distributed currently, and is thus subject to current taxation by the parent's country of residence, rather than being taxed only when repatriated.[45] Arnold and Dibout (2001, p. 40) note:

> The basic function of the CFC rules of every country is to distinguish between acceptable (or good) and unacceptable (or bad) deferral. ... For most countries with CFC rules, the distinction between good and bad deferral is usually drawn on the basis of three factors. In general, deferral is considered to be unacceptable and is eliminated under CFC rules if:
>
> (a) Residents control or have a substantial interest in the foreign corporation;
> (b) The income derived by the CFC is passive investment income or base company income and not genuine business income; and
> (c) The income derived by the CFC is subject to a low rate of foreign tax.

Definitions of control, what constitutes a low-tax regimes, the type of income that is considered "tainted," and the weight placed on the last two factors vary from country-to-country and cannot be described in detail here. (See, however, IFA, 2001b.) All countries that have CFC legislation disallow deferral of tax on income from passive investments (which generally includes interest, dividends, rents, royalties, and capital gains), some extend the definition of "tainted" income to "base company income" (a concept to be described below), and some tax virtually all income earned by subsidiaries located in certain countries. Most countries use "black lists" of tax haven countries, some use white lists, and some use gray lists. Whether a country is on a black list may depend simply on the tax rates in the country in question, but that determination is generally more nuanced. The OECD has recently specified practices that, if continued, will cause a tax haven to be listed as "uncooperative;" see Section 6.

"Base company income" is the term commonly used to describe tainted income other than passive income. The most important kind of base company income is income a CFC derives from selling property or rendering services outside the jurisdiction where the CFC is incorporated or to related parties.

CFC legislation generally is not intended merely to prevent deferral of tax. It represents an attempt to prevent the loss of tax revenue created by combining transfer pricing manipulation with tax havens. Thus Arnold and Dibout (2001, p. 54) state:

> The inclusion of income from related-party transactions in tainted income is usually intended to bolster a country's transfer pricing rules. Transfer pricing rules are intended to prevent the diversion of income to related foreign corporations through the non-arm's length pricing of sales, service, and other transactions. These rules are notoriously difficult to enforce. By treating such income as tainted income for the purposes of CFC rules, countries can avoid the necessity of applying their transfer pricing rules.

Similarly, the OECD (1996, p. 10) states:

> Without CFC legislation, it would be easy for a resident taxpayer in the AL/SA [arm's length/separate accounting] system to avoid domestic taxation on its foreign income (and, indeed, to some extent, even on its domestic income) simply by interposing a foreign corporation in a territory with a lower level of taxation to receive such income instead of remitting ir to the home country (or equivalently, to charge deductible arm's length fees to domestic taxpayers in respect to certain services rendered.

It thus describes CFC legislation as a "back stop" against the difficulty of administering transfer pricing rules.[46] It goes on to note that, "... unless the legislation applies to *all* types of income, active, as well as passive, it will be of limited use in this respect." (OECD, 1996, p. 11)

The United States enacted the world's first CFC legislation in 1962 and by 1986 only five other countries (Canada, Germany, Japan, France, and the United Kingdom) had done so. Since then the practice has spread rapidly, and it is reported that at least 24 countries had adopted CFC legislation by the end of 2000.[47] Not surprisingly, it is primarily the major capital-exporting countries and other members of the OECD that have taken this step. But it seems likely that the list of countries with CFC legislation will grow, perhaps rapidly, in part because of the recent OECD recommendations, to be considered in Section 6. Efforts one country makes to prevent abuse may have repercussions on others, for example, by reducing the benefit of shifting income from a source country to a tax haven.

5.2 Effectiveness of CFC Rules

Arnold (2004) notes that it is difficult to determine the effects of CFC rules; because they are intended to be "prophylactic" (that is, to prevent abuse), their effectiveness "cannot be judged by the amount of revenue that they generate." He suggests, however (Arnold, 2000, p. 17:14), that "CFC rules are reasonably successful in preventing the worst cases of tax haven abuse," situations involving diversion or accumulation of passive income to or in tax havens. He believes, however, that CFC rules are less effective in dealing with foreign base company income. He cites opposition to CFC rules by multinational enterprises as evidence of the "core effectiveness" of the rules.

Unilateral anti-abuse measures are not a panacea, for either developed countries or DTCs. First, without access to information on tax haven activities of their residents, it will be difficult to enforce CFC and similar anti-deferral legislation. For developed countries with close supervision of corporations, gaining information on CFCs owned by domestic parents, especially those that are publicly traded, should, in theory, be relatively easy. In fact, even developed countries find it difficult to enforce CFC rules effectively. For corporations whose owners are resident in DTCs, the problem is likely to be much more daunting

Second, some American multinationals have engaged in "inversion" transactions, in which the parent becomes a foreign corporation and its domestic activities those of a subsidiary.[48] (The ability to do this is predicated on the unusual test the United States employs to determine residence, place of incorporation. Switching to the more common test based on "place of effective management and control" would make this ploy much more costly, as it would require moving management and control to a tax haven.[49]) The result is that CFC legislation becomes irrelevant, except for closely held corporations, and income can be accumulated in the tax haven parent. Inversion of US corporations could have negative effects on the fiscal situation of DTCs, by putting income shifted to tax havens beyond the reach of the US government and thus increasing the benefits of shifting income. Moreover, companies established in DTCs might also be able to engage in inversion transactions, if those countries adopted CFC legislation that started to bite; that would depend on the country's definition of residence.

Finally, CFC legislation generally does not apply when real activity is being conducted in the low-tax jurisdiction. This could become increasingly important, since many e-commerce activities could be lodged in PEs located in low-tax jurisdictions. This topic, which is of greatest relevance for developed countries, is beyond the scope of this paper. (See, however, Cockfield, 2002.)

5.3 DTC Use of CFC Rules

For a variety of reasons, many DTCs have not focused on anti-deferral rules. First, some countries export so little capital that they do not need CFC rules. (Sandler, 1998, pp. 12-13, Table 2, notes that 15 of the 21 countries that earliest adopted CFC legislation were among the 25 jurisdictions with the highest average foreign direct investment outflows between 1990 and 1994.) Where exchange controls exist and are implemented effectively, it is unlikely that the foreign investment required to capitalize a CFC would be allowed. If exchange controls are not effective, it is unlikely that CFC rules could be implemented successfully, either. Increased liberalization of capital markets can be expected to lead to the elimination of exchange controls, greater capital exports, and perhaps the need for CFC legislation.

Second, in many DTCs the limited administrative resources available to deal with international issues should probably be concentrated on administering transfer prices and undercapitalization, rather than CFC legislation, which Sandler (1998, p. 14) has characterized as "notoriously complex and difficult to administer."[50] Arnold (2000, p. 17:14) writes, "[T]he effectiveness of the rules is questionable because of inadequate or non-existent enforcement by tax authorities. Any tax rules that require the computation and verification of the income of foreign entities cause significant enforcement problems for the residence country. Few countries have the tax administration resources to enforce CFC rules effectively at the margin." The scarcity of administrative resources is, of course, vastly worse in most DTCs than in developed countries.

5.4 Developed Country CFC Rules and DTCs

In theory, enforcement of CFC rules by advanced countries could have beneficial effects on DTCs, by making it less advantageous to shift to tax havens income that is properly attributable to DTCs.[51] In fact, it appears that DTCs can expect little assistance from developed country enforcement of CFC rules. Whether CFC rules should apply when it is only foreign taxes that are being avoided (that is, when the taxes of the residence country of the parent are not being avoided) is a controversial issue.[52] Arnold (1986, p. 466) gives the example of a French or US-controlled manufacturing company established in a high-tax foreign country that uses a tax haven affiliate to sell its products, the policy question being whether French or US anti-tax haven rules should apply to the income of the tax haven affiliate, even if the only tax being avoided is that of the country where the manufacturing company is established. The French or US rules may apply in this situation. (Techniques such as contract manufacturing and sales concessionaires can, however, be used to avoid the US rules; see US Department of the Treasury, Chapter 5.) By comparison, most countries apply their CFC rules only if their own taxes are being avoided.[53] (Sweden's CFC rules apply to all income of CFCs, except those in treaty countries.

New Zealand's rules also apply to all income of CFCs, but it has few multinationals.) The more restricted view appears to leave substantial latitude and incentive to shift income from DTCs to tax havens.

It can be argued, of course, that no country has any responsibility "... to act as a fiscal policeman to enforce another country's tax system."[54] (Arnold, 1986, p. 466) Moreover, as Kudrle and Eden argue (2003, p. 61) there are "prisoner's dilemma elements" to the decision to enforce tough anti-abuse rules. "[W]hile all states would benefit from increased vigilance of other home countries in making certain that their subsidiaries do not use havens to avoid paying full taxes due, both special interest politics and perhaps national economic interest suggest that there is less incentive to assiduously police their own firms."

5.5 Tax Evasion in DTCs

In many DTCs tax evasion by individuals is likely to be a more important problem than tax avoidance by corporations. Without the cooperation of tax havens – up to now a forlorn hope – DTCs are unlikely to have the access to the information needed to combat evasion or to enforce CFC rules. This points up the potential importance of the OECD project discussed in Section 6. It is argued there that, while transparency and information exchange may improve in the long run, there is little reason to expect that in the short run tax havens will provide such information to most DTCs. Even if tax havens were willing to provide information, many DTCs probably lack the administrative capacity to utilize potentially available information.

Gaining effective access to the information needed to combat tax evasion requires several steps.[55] First, it is necessary to identify the individual or corporation that is suspected of tax evasion or avoidance, as information will not be supplied in response to "fishing expeditions." This may not be easy, since the name on an account may not be the name of the individual or corporation, and holdings may be routed through several layers of intermediate entities, some of which may be chartered in other tax havens. Second, authorities in the jurisdiction that is being asked to supply the information must be able to obtain the information from the organizations (e.g., banks) that have it. This, in turn, requires that such organizations keep records of the beneficial ownership of accounts they serve.

6. THE OECD INITIATIVE ON HARMFUL TAX COMPETITION[56]

In 1996, responding to a request from Ministers from its member countries, the OECD undertook to "develop measures to counter the distorting effects of harmful tax competition on investment and financing decisions and the consequences for national tax bases,"[57] and in 1998 it issued the first of several reports on what it initially called harmful tax competition.[58] The OECD – often called a "rich man's club" because its 30 members include the most highly industrialized countries in the world (but also Mexico and Slovakia) – was presumably interested primarily in the "consequences for national tax bases" of its members, not those of DTCs. Yet it is quite possible that the OECD project might have the collateral benefit of helping to protect the "national tax bases" of DTCs. Indeed, in 2002, upon the issuance of the OECD's List of Uncooperative Tax Havens, Gabriel Makhlouf, Chair of the OECD's Committee on Fiscal Affairs, stated:

> The ultimate success of this project will benefit all countries: OECD members and non-OECD economies; developing countries and those with economies in transition. The implementation of the commitments to transparency and effective exchange of information will help to protect tax bases and as a result help developing countries ... mobilise their own domestic resources for development.

This section examines whether that outcome is likely.[59]

6.1 The OECD Project in Brief

The 1998 report on the project said that the focus of the first stage of the project was to be on tax regimes intended to attract "geographically mobile activities, such as financial and other service activities, including the provision of intangibles." The OECD said that the project would not initially consider evasion of taxes related to cross-border savings instruments such as bank deposits, because a separate OECD working party was dealing with that issue. (OECD, 1998, pp 6, 12) One might thus surmise that the project's initial objective was combatting corporate tax avoidance. By comparison, the project has thus far focused on improving transparency and increasing effective access to the information that is required for administration of taxes, particularly those of residence countries. In addition to increased and more effective exchange of information, the project has emphasized improved records of ownership of companies and trusts and improved accounting, without which it is difficult to provide access to information in a useful manner. As Easson (2004a, p. 1038) has noted, "...almost the entire discussion of tax havens, and the emphasis on exchange of information, seems to be of more relevance to the evasion of tax on passive investment income than to the avoidance of tax on geographically mobile activities." As explained further below, this switch in emphasis may have important implications.

6.1.1 The purposes of tax havens and preferential tax regimes

In 1998, noting that "Tax havens are appealing to corporate and individual investors," the OECD identified the following "purposes" of tax havens, which preferential tax regimes in OECD members may also further:

> Tax havens serve three main purposes: they provide a location for holding passive investments ('money boxes'); they provide a location where 'paper' profits can be booked; and they enable the affairs of taxpayers, particularly their bank accounts, to be effectively shielded from scrutiny by tax authorities of other countries." (OECD, 1998, p. 49).

These three "purposes" of tax havens (and preferential regimes) further the following types of tax avoidance and evasion:

1. Holding passive investments – evasion of individual income taxes and deferral of corporate income taxes;
2. Booking paper profits – income shifting and deferral of residence-country tax by corporations;
3. Shielding from scrutiny by tax authorities – income tax evasion, especially by individuals, and income shifting by corporations.

6.1.2 Identifying tax havens and preferential tax regimes

The OECD initially used four key factors to identify tax havens and potentially harmful preferential tax regimes found in member nations:

- Little or no tax on the income in question;
- No effective exchange of information;
- Lack of transparency; and
- No need for substantial local activities in the case of tax havens; "ring-fencing" in the case of preferential regimes.[60]

Based on these criteria, in June 2000 the OECD, working through the Forum on Harmful Tax Practices, the group charged with implementing many of the recommendations in the 1998 report, tentatively identified 47 "potentially harmful" preferential tax regimes found in OECD member states and compiled a list of tax havens. Its goal was the voluntary elimination of harmful preferential tax regimes by OECD members and the cooperation of tax havens in eliminating harmful practices.

Two points deserve attention. First, while "little or no tax on the income in question" is a necessary identifying factor, it is not sufficient for the OECD to find that a jurisdiction engages in harmful practices; at least one of the other factors must also be present.[61] Second, in 2001, responding to pressure from the United States, the OECD removed the "substantial activities" test from the list of factors used to determine whether a tax haven is cooperative.[62] In short, lack of transparency and effective exchange of information became the key to determining whether a low- or no-tax jurisdiction was considered to be an uncooperative tax haven and perhaps led to the switch in emphasis mentioned above.[63]

6.1.3 Defensive measures

The OECD noted that tax havens and non-haven countries were likely to respond quite differently to efforts to eliminate preferential tax regimes and tax havens. It argued:

> ... a useful distinction may be made between, on the one hand, countries that are able to finance their public services with no or nominal income taxes and that offer themselves as places to be used by non-residents to escape tax in their country of residence and, on the other hand, countries which raise significant revenues from their income tax but whose tax system has features constituting harmful tax competition.
>
> In the first case, the country has no interest in trying to curb the "race to the bottom" with respect to income tax and is actively contributing to the erosion of income tax revenues in other countries. For that reason, these countries are unlikely to co-operate in curbing harmful tax competition. By contrast, in the second case, a country may have a significant amount of revenues which are at risk from the spread of harmful tax competition and it is therefore more

> likely to agree on concerted action. (OECD, 1998, pp 42-43)

Since the OECD did not expect that all tax havens would respond to moral suasion that had no teeth, it outlined a set of "coordinated defensive measures" that its members might undertake, if necessary, to combat "harmful tax practices."[64] Among these are the following:[65]

- Disallowance of deductions, exemptions, credits, and other allowances for payments made to persons located in jurisdictions engaged in harmful tax practices, except where the taxpayer can establish that the payments are made at arm's length;
- Thin capitalization rules restricting deductions for interest payments made to persons located in jurisdictions engaged in harmful tax practices;
- Requiring that taxpayers report payments, transactions, and ownership involving persons located in jurisdictions engaged in harmful tax practices;
- Taxation of residents on income that benefits from harmful tax practices;
- Denial of exemptions and modification of foreign tax credits for income that is subject to little or no taxation because it arises in a jurisdictions engaged in harmful tax practices;
- Levying withholding taxes on dividends, interest, and royalties made to beneficial owners benefiting from harmful tax practices;
- Coordination of enforcement activities involving entities and transactions related to jurisdictions engaged in harmful tax practices;
- Terminating, avoiding, and limiting treaties with jurisdictions engaged in harmful tax practices.

This list contains measures that could be used to combat both tax evasion by individuals and tax avoidance by corporations.

6.2 Progress to Date

In the 2004 Progress Report on its Project on Harmful Tax Practices the OECD indicated that, of the 47 potentially harmful regimes found in OECD members, 18 have been (or are being) abolished, 14 have been amended to eliminate potentially harmful features, and 13 were found upon further examination not to be harmful. Only two regimes (Switzerland's "50/50 Practice" and Luxembourg's 1929 Holding Company regime) remain, and they are being modified.[66] Moreover, anonymous bank accounts can no longer be opened in any OECD country.[67]

6.2.1 Tax havens: The appearance

Progress in eliminating harmful tax practices of tax havens appears to have been no less impressive, with 33 countries and jurisdictions that might otherwise have been characterized as "uncooperative tax havens" having committed to principles of effective exchange of information and transparency.[68] By early August 2004 only 5 jurisdictions (Andorra, Liberia, Liechtenstein, the Marshall Islands, and Monaco) remained on the list of uncooperative tax havens, and later that month three of these indicated a willingness to undertake measures that may get them removed from the list.[69] This "black list" may eventually disappear, because of the threat that defensive measures will be applied in a coordinated fashion against jurisdictions remaining on the list. If the noose is tight enough, harmful tax practices of tax havens, as defined by the OECD, may follow harmful preferential regimes in OECD members into extinction.

Another important result of the OECD project has been the development of a more inclusive and cooperative approach to the problem of tax havens. It seems fair to say that, before the project, tax havens and non-haven countries did not communicate much, and what communication did occur tended to be hostile, perhaps because havens thought their position to be impregnable.[70] This situation has changed markedly – perhaps because it has become clear to the havens that they are vulnerable to coordinated action and perhaps because the OECD has come to realize that it must be more sympathetic to the interests of tax havens when suggesting that defensive measures be undertaken. The OECD has created a Global Forum consisting of more than 60 members and non-members of the OECD that is intended to achieve "a global level playing field based on transparency and effective exchange of information in tax matters." See OECD (2004c). An important objective of the Global Forum is to see that all financial centers adopt "high standards" for transparency and exchange of information, so that those that do so are not placed at a competitive disadvantage relative to those that do not and thus avoid "the migration of business" to centers that do not cooperate.[71] (See OECD, 2002, p4, 2004c; "G20 Statement on Transparency and Exchange of Information for Tax Purposes," 2004.)

A particularly noteworthy outcome of this more inclusive approach was the drafting of a Model Agreement on Exchange of Information on Tax Matters (OECD, 2002) by a working group consisting of both OECD members and erstwhile tax havens.[72] Article 5 of this model provides a) that, subject to certain safeguards (e.g., for foreseeable relevance, non-disclosure of trade or business secrets, and confidentiality), the country receiving a request for information must provide the information if it is necessary for enforcement of the treaty partner's taxes, even if the requested country does not need the information for its own tax purposes, and b) that its competent authority must have the legal authority to obtain and provide information held, *inter alia*, by banks, other financial institutions, and persons acting in an agency or fiduciary capacity and information on ownership of companies, trusts, etc. These provisions have recently been reflected in Article 26 of the OECD Model Treaty, which previously allowed a country to refuse a request for exchange of information that would not be obtainable in the normal course of tax administration. (See OECD, 2004b.) Moreover, Article 26 now explicitly clarifies that only in "extreme cases" can exchange of information be refused on grounds that it would be "contrary to public policy."[73] These developments suggest that tax havens that have relied on secrecy as their primary marketing feature will, in the future, have to compete for business on the basis of the quality of the services they provide and the strength of their reputations.

6.2.2 Tax havens: The reality

A conclusion that tax havens will cease to exist would be overly optimistic, or at least premature. To see this it is useful to consider corporate tax avoidance and tax evasion by individuals separately.

Corporate tax avoidance. The OECD project accurately describes how preferential tax regimes can be used to attract highly mobile financial and other service activities:

> These regimes generally provide a favorable location for holding passive investments or for booking paper profits. In many cases, the regime may have been designed specifically to act as a conduit for routing capital flows across borders. ... Such tax regimes can be particularly successful if targeted to attract income from base company activities and from passive investment rather than income from active investment. (OECD, 1998, pp. 58, 59)

Preferential regimes are deemed to be harmful when characterized by the features listed in part A of this section. An agreement by all OECD members to eliminate their harmful preferential tax regimes would represent a significant step in the battle against corporate tax avoidance. But the victory may turn out to be meaningless unless similar practices of tax havens are also eliminated.

A commitment to effective exchange of information and transparency is enough to get a jurisdiction removed from the OECD's list of uncooperative tax havens. A jurisdiction can retain the key feature of corporate tax havens – little or no taxation of the income in question – without being on the list. But, as noted earlier, lack of exchange of information and transparency are presumably substantially less important than low tax rates for the use of tax havens by multinational corporations – at least reputable MNCs headquartered in advanced countries – which generally are engaged in tax avoidance, rather than tax evasion.[74] Hines (2004) observes, "the vast majority of the world's tax havens rely on low tax rates and other favorable tax provisions to attract investment, rather than using the prospect of local transactions that will not be reported." Similarly, Easson (2004a, p. 1065) writes, "Some of the activities carried on in tax havens – such as reinsurance or the use of international business companies as vehicles for investment in other countries – are normally not dependent on bank secrecy at all and will not be deterred by any agreement made by their host country to exchange information." (As Devereux, 2002, p. 104, says, "... if the activity is legal there is no reason to hide it.") This implies that corporate tax havens will continue to exist[75] and that enactment and effective enforcement of CFC or other anti-abuse legislation will be required to prevent the use of tax havens to defer home-country corporate tax.

On the other hand, large reputable MNC's are not the only corporate users of tax havens, and the activities of other users may well test the limits of domestic laws and raise questions about economic substance, business purpose, or abuse of law. It remains a feature of international business company (IBC) legislation everywhere that information about IBC activities is protected from foreign tax authorities by strong confidentiality provisions. (See Thuronyi, 2003.) This presumably reflects a demand for corporate vehicles that offer an effective barrier to exchange of information for tax purposes. Corporations that put a high value on confidentiality are likely to find their activities threatened by exchange of information.

Individual tax evasion. Secrecy and lack of access to information are key to the success of tax haven operations that facilitate tax evasion on earnings from passive investments by individuals and closely held corporations. The commitments by "cooperative tax havens" for effective exchange of information may thus appear to constitute a significant victory in the battle against tax evasion. Indeed, noting that Assistant Treasury Secretary Mark Weinberger had said that the US government expects these new TIEAs to be "an invaluable source of information to the IRS," Sharp, *et al*, (2002, p. 193) opine that "The sun is setting on the abusive tax haven industry." But many of these agreements are for "information on demand," rather than automatic exchanges. For example, for the US to obtain information under its TIEAs with the Cayman Islands and the British Virgin Islands, it must identify the taxpayer under investigation, the nature of the information requested, the purpose for which the information is sought, and reasonable grounds for believing that the requested is available in the requested jurisdiction, and, if possible, identify the entity that is believed to have the information. See Sharp, *et al.* (2002, p. 193). Because of these limitations, one observer has concluded (Sullivan, 2004b, p. 904), "it appears that the value of information exchange is primarily limited to confirmation rather than discovery of evasion." Statements by Cayman Islands officials seem to confirm this judgment. See Sullivan (2004b, pp. 903-4).

Moreover, Easson (2004a) has noted a) that tax haven commitments were conditional upon OECD members making equivalent commitments (or else being subject to defensive measures) and b) that OECD members had agreed on exchange of information only for geographically mobile services – that is, not for interest paid to individuals. He concludes:

> This latter point may turn out to be quite important. It suggests that, in the context of the OECD's initiative, bank secrecy and lack of effective exchange of information do not by themselves constitute a harmful tax practice. They do so only if they relate to a preferential tax regime for mobile services. That seems an entirely reasonable proposition, given that *the 1998 report made it quite clear from the outset that it was not concerned with the tax treatment of cross- border savings instruments, particularly bank deposits*, which were the subject of an entirely different study. Assuming that the level-playing-field principle applies, the same should be true for nonmember tax havens. That is to say, the commitment to establish a legal mechanism that allows information to be provided to OECD member countries should relate only to the activities of entities such as international business companies, captive insurers, offshore financial centres, and MNE coordination centres, and not to the tax-evading activities of individual portfolio investors. (Easson, 2004a, pp. 1073-74; emphasis added.)

If this assessment is accurate, it is another reason that the apparent progress on exchange of information and transparency may be much ado about relatively little. To see whether OECD members have made equivalent commitments to exchange information it will be useful to digress briefly to consider the ramifications of the EU savings directive and whether the US will exchange information on interest payments of foreigners.

6.2.2.1 The EU Savings directive

Roughly contemporaneously with the OECD initiative on harmful tax competition, the European Union (EU) set out to tackle the problem of tax evasion on cross-border income from saving by individuals.[76] Initially a "coexistence model" was considered. Under it a Member State could either agree to exchange information or apply a minimum 20 percent withholding tax to interest payments made to individuals resident in other Member States. (See Commission of the European Communities, 1998). Member States that have a tradition of bank secrecy strongly preferred the withholding tax option.

After many years of discussions among its Member States, the EU agreed on the text of a savings directive (European Union, 2003), which calls for automatic exchange of information on interest payments to individuals residing in other Member States. However, three EU members (Austria, Belgium, and Luxembourg) are allowed to levy withholding taxes on such payments, rather than automatically exchanging information, during a transition period that ends only if and when a) the European Community has concluded agreements with Andorra, Liechtenstein, Monaco, San Marino, and Switzerland for exchange of information on request and b) the Council of the EU agrees that the United States is committed to exchange of information on request with respect to interest payments to residents of EU Member States. Moreover, the directive does not go into effect (and the transition period does not begin) until the five non-EU European countries listed above have agreed to apply measures equivalent to those contained in the directive and all dependent or associated territories of the Netherlands and the UK have agreed to either automatic exchange of information or application of withholding taxes.[77]

The five non-EU European jurisdictions listed above have agreed to levy withholding taxes on interest payments at the same rates as those applied by Austria, Belgium, and Luxembourg, beginning on July 1, 2005, at which time the directive would be applied.[78] If, however, four members of the OECD (Austria, Belgium, Luxembourg and Switzerland) do not agree to information exchange, as seems to be likely during at least the transition period for the EU savings directive, it can be expected that the "cooperative" tax havens will point out the lack of a level playing field and perhaps renounce their prior commitments to exchange information regarding bank interest.[79]

While the saving directive would presumably be effective in shutting down much of the evasion related to cross-border bank deposits of individuals, it is likely to be far from water-tight. The EU explains the emphasis on savings of individuals as follows in its "Savings tax proposal: frequently asked questions" (Commission of the European Communities, 2001):

> Q. Why would interest payments made to companies be excluded from the scope of the Directive?
> A. Because there are many more problems of tax evasion in the individual taxation area than in the company tax area. Companies are required to lodge annual tax returns and they are audited or are subject to the possibility of being audited on a regular basis. As far as companies are concerned, non-taxation of interest payments is not the main problem for tax administrations. The issue is more that of tax avoidance through aggressive tax planning.

This answer seems hopelessly naive. EU residents can channel savings through foreign companies, they can establish a residence outside the EU, or they can even establish a non-domiciliary residence in another EU Member State that does not tax foreign-source income of "non-doms." See Langer (2000, pp. 2837-38).

Moreover, at best, the saving directive will apply only to payments of interest to residents of the EU by institutions in the EU and the other five European countries listed above. Financial institutions in those countries would presumably be free not to exchange information with non-EU countries, except as provided by treaty. The playing field would hardly be level if more was expected of tax havens.

6.2.2.2 The United States failure to exchange information on interest payments

As noted above, the Savings Directive does not become fully effective (that is, the transition period does not end) until the European Council is satisfied that the United States is committed to exchange of information on request with respect to interest payments to residents of EU Member States. Whether the US will soon commit to such a policy is doubtful. In January 2001, four days before the Clinton administration left office, the US Internal Revenue Service issued proposed regulations that would have required reporting of all bank interest payments to non-resident aliens, not just those to residents of Canada, as under current law. Interest reporting is, of course, necessary prerequisite for exchange of information.

The proposed regulations met such a firestorm of protest, especially from bankers in Florida, who feared loss of deposits from Latin America, that on August 2, 2002 they were withdrawn and replaced with proposed regulations under which it would only be necessary to report such payments to individuals residing in Australia, Denmark, Finland, France, Germany, Greece, the Netherlands, Ireland, Italy, New Zealand, Norway, Portugal, Spain, Sweden, and the United Kingdom, as well as in Canada. It has not gone without notice that, with the exception of Australia, New Zealand, and Norway, the additional countries listed were all Member States of the EU; Austria, Belgium, and Luxembourg, the only EU Member States that were resisting exchange of information, were not on the list. It was widely assumed that reporting of payment of residents of the other12 EU countries was proposed in order to satisfy the savings directive's requirement that the US exchange information with EU Member States. Indeed, on December 3, 2002 the European Commission made a submission to the ECOFIN Council meeting that explicitly mentioned these developments, noting, "the regulations are due to become effective from 31st December." (See Council of the European Union, 2002).

The August 2002 proposed regulations have also been roundly criticized. (For a highly critical discussion of the IRS action, see Mastromarco and Hunter, 2003). To date (January 2005) the proposed regulations have not been finalized, and it seems unlikely that they will be under the Bush administration.

First, the administration seems to be ideologically opposed to the idea of helping the EU implement the Savings Directive, which has been characterized as a cartel created to protect high-tax EU states from the beneficial forces of tax competition. (See, for example, Mitchell, 2004). An administration spokesman is reported to have said in October 2002 that the White House had no interest in helping the EU implement the savings directive; see Scott (2002).

Second, the timing could not be worse. In 1984 the United States eliminated its withholding tax on portfolio interest in order to assist with the financing of both its growing budget deficit and its balance of payments deficit, as well as to compensate for the closing of the treaty-shopping loophole in its treaty with the Netherlands Antilles, which would otherwise have substantially increased the cost of borrowing for US corporations.[80] Large budget deficits and a weak dollar have re-emerged with the massive tax cuts and the war in Iraq. The collection of information on interest payments to foreigners could trigger capital flight that would lead to higher interest rates, make it more costly to finance the deficit, and put further pressure on the dollar.

Third, the US has implemented its own method of getting information on savings held abroad by its citizens and residents. Under "know your customer" rules, financial institutions outside the United States that are "qualified intermediaries" (QIs) are required to know who the identity of the actual owners of their accounts. If any of an institution's accounts are held by US citizens or resident aliens, the institutions must either file information reports with the IRS or withhold tax from the accounts. This reduces pressures on the US to cooperate with the EU as a means of protecting its own revenues.

It appears that the EU may "fudge" this matter, by certifying that the US is willing to exchange information, despite the fact that the US does not routinely collect information on interest paid to non-residents. On the basis of the European Commission's December 2002 submission mentioned above, the ECOFIN Council concluded at its meeting of 21 January 2003 that the requirement that the United States apply "equivalent measures" to those in the savings directive was "effectively satisfied."[81] (See Council of the European Union, 2003.) Mitchell (2004) has noted, "The EU also has tried to sidestep U.S. opposition by asserting that America already is in compliance – a rather odd claim since interest and capital gains paid to foreigners are neither taxed nor reported."[82]

6.2.2.3 The rest of the world

The OECD project initially focused on identified tax havens and preferential tax regimes in member countries. Only belatedly has it paid much attention to potentially harmful tax practices in other countries.[83] Of course, it would not do much good to eliminate the harmful practices of tax havens if other countries can offer the same tax-evasion services.

6.2.3 Implications for tax evasion

The "vast majority" of the non-OECD jurisdictions that have agreed to transparency and exchange of information have already taken action to immobilize or abolish bearer shares and many have enhanced transparency by regulating providers of trust and company services and ensuring that they maintain information on the ownership of the entities they serve. OECD (2004a, p26). Improvements in transparency such as this will reduce the possibilities of tax evasion by residents of both developed countries and DTCs and place greater pressure on effective exchange of information. Easson (2004a, p. 1074) notes, regarding the contribution of the OECD project, "[I]t is the position adopted by individual OECD member countries that is likely to matter most: What sort of a TIEA [tax information exchange agreement] will be sufficient to prevent the application of countermeasures?" Since the OECD works on the basis of consensus and has no power to compel its members either to apply countermeasures to noncooperative tax havens or to desist from applying them to cooperative ones, he notes, considerable uncertainty exists.

6.2.3.1 Developed countries[84]

OECD members are in a position to exert considerable pressure on any tax haven that refuses to exchange information.[85] Kudrle and Eden (2003, p. 66) describe some of the pressures that could be brought to bear: "The secrecy havens have little option but maximum cooperation because of their vulnerability to action by the OECD. One obvious response to non-cooperation would see the high income countries disallow the cost of debt financing from non-cooperating jurisdictions as a business expense for tax purposes. ... Even more drastic measures are clearly available including the denial of access to the banking systems of the G-7 countries and the severing of transportation links." Also, the US allows deductions for convention expenses only if the tax haven exchanges information. Hishikawa (2002, p. 414) reports that Guernsey and Jersey feared that being labeled uncooperative would harm business confidence.

The Model Agreement on Exchange of Information on Tax Matters has already formed the basis for several recently signed exchange of information agreements between tax havens and developed countries.[86] Such agreements are potentially useful in reducing the possibility that taxpayers resident in signatory developed countries can evade tax by making portfolio investments in or through tax havens – or at least, by increasing the risk of detection, making such investments less attractive. Yet, exchange of information, like CFC legislation, is no panacea. Making it effective will requires concerted administrative efforts, especially since the stakes are so high that enormous resources and ingenuity are devoted to tax evasion.

6.2.3.2 Developing and transition countries

Prospects do not seem even this bright for DTCs. While tax havens may feel compelled to conclude agreements to exchange information with economically and politically powerful developed countries, and perhaps even with a few large DTCs, it is hard to see why they would also feel similar pressure to conclude such agreements with most DTCs, unless pressured to do so by OECD members, something that does not seem to be contemplated.[87] In the absence of such agreements, nothing will have changed, as far as the majority of DTCs is concerned. Indeed, to the extent that tax havens are no longer able to appeal effectively to high-income residents of developed countries who wish to evade taxes, they may redouble efforts to appeal to residents of DTCs.[88] Even with such an agreement in place, tax administration is not self-enforcing; tax administrators must actually request and be able to utilize the available information if they are to combat tax evasion – a tall order for the tax authorities of many DTCs.

Similarly, if DTCs wish to combat the use of tax havens to defer corporate taxes, they will need to rely on CFC or other anti-abuse legislation. But they are unlikely to be able to enforce such legislation without information on tax haven corporations owned by their residents, even if they enact it. More important for the many poor DTCs, for which taxation on out-bound investment may not be much of an issue, without access to information on transactions with tax-haven affiliates of corporations subject to their jurisdiction, DTCs are unlikely to be able to appraise the transfer prices used to value such transactions. As noted, most DTCs are unlikely to be able to conclude treaties that would provide access to the needed information.

Despite this generally gloomy picture, there may be a bit of light. The OECD has compiled a list of defensive measures that both source and residence countries could take to limit the use of tax havens and preferential regimes to avoid taxes. DTCs could invoke these defensive measures (e.g., disallowance of deductions for payments, thin capitalization rules restricting deductions for interest payments, and withholding taxes on dividends, interest, and royalties) against any jurisdiction that imposes "little or no tax on the income in question," even if the jurisdiction does not engage in "harmful tax practices," as defined by the OECD.[89] Such measures may be more effective – and they certainly require fewer administrative resources – than attempting to monitor transfer prices or enforce CFC rules. But this raises a question that this paper has conveniently assumed away and will not address now, whether it is desirable for individual DTCs to adopt such policies, at the risk of deterring direct foreign investment. Given the "prisoner's dilemma" faced by individual countries (mentioned in a different context at the end of Section 5.4), DTCs may undertake this type of action only if they can do so in a coordinated manner – again a tall order. Moreover, it seems unlikely that measures such as these could be used effectively to combat evasion of taxes by individuals.

7. CONCLUDING REMARKS: CAN TAX REFORM MEND THE TEARS?

The following excerpt from the description of the purpose of this conference seems a fitting place to start the conclusion of this exercise:

> [T[he last several decades have seen a dizzying array of different tax reforms around the world. ... However, despite the enormous amounts of time and resources invested in these reform efforts, the lessons from all of this work have

> been very unevenly disseminated, and there are clearly many unresolved issues. It seems unlikely that these issues are going to go away. With the steady advance of such things as globalization, regional integration, and technology, it seems more likely that, if anything, the issues of adapting tax systems to new economic environments and reforming specific taxes will become even more pressing.

The tax reforms that have occurred in DTCs over the last several decades have not dealt adequately with the revenue cracks created by tax havens and transfer pricing. To the extent that tax reform is a unilateral affair, they could not have been expected to do so. At best, source countries could have addressed the administration of transfer pricing and implemented thin capitalization and other anti-abuse rules, and residence countries could have enacted CFC and similar rules. But, as discussed above, it may be unwise for DTCs to implement such rules unilaterally. In some areas progress would have required bilateral cooperation (for example, in administering transfer pricing rules) or multilateral action (particularly in combating tax haven abuses). What bilateral and multilateral action has occurred to date seems more likely to benefit developed countries than to help DTCs mend the tears in their revenue nets. In particular, it seems unlikely that most DTCs will benefit significantly in the short run from the OECD efforts to gain greater exchange of information and transparency from tax havens. The OECD project may have helped marginally to protect the tax bases of DTCs, and may help more in the future. But, for now, it does not seem to have helped much. However, if these efforts are successful and competition between financial centers comes to be based on the quality of services and reputation, rather than on tax secrecy, this may benefit DTCs.

Notes

1. The views expressed here are solely those of the author. He wishes, however, to thank Rosanne Altshuler, Brian Arnold, Arthur Cockfield, Alex Easson, Timothy Goodspeed, Joseph Guttentag, Gary Sprague, Victor Thuronyi, Joann Weiner, Eric Zolt, and participants in the Georgia State conference on The Challenges of Tax Reform in a Global Economy for useful comments on earlier drafts. The paper has not been revised to reflect US enactment of the American Jobs Creation Act of 2004.
2. Where meaning is clear from context, the term "transfer pricing" is sometimes used as a shorthand for "manipulation of transfer prices" to shift income from entities (e.g., parents, subsidiaries, or branches) in high-tax jurisdictions to related entities in low-tax jurisdictions. Of course, transfer prices for transactions between related parties are essential in a tax system based on separate accounting and the arm's length standard, whether they are manipulated or not.

3. One of the pervasive features of the literature on tax havens is the difficulty of defining a tax haven. I consider a tax haven to be a low-tax jurisdiction that actively makes itself available as a vehicle for evasion or avoidance of tax that would otherwise be paid in high-tax jurisdictions. This represents a slight modification of the definition in OECD (1987).
4. Keen and Simone (2004) indicate that in developing countries corporate tax revenues have fallen in recent years, because reductions in corporate tax rates have not been offset by expansion of tax bases, as they have been in developed countries. Although they note the increased use of tax incentives in developing countries, they do not attempt to determine how much this has contributed to the erosion of corporate taxes.
5. I use "tax evasion" to mean the illegal failure to pay taxes that are legally due (for example, by not declaring income earned in a tax haven when the country of resident requires such declaration) and "tax avoidance" to mean minimization of taxes through means that are legal (for example, by deferring residence-country tax on income earned in low or no-tax locations when the country of residence permits such deferral). It can be argued that egregious manipulation of transfer prices involves (illegal) tax evasion, rather than (legal) tax avoidance. The distinction is not important for present purposes. For a discussion of these terms that reaches somewhat different conclusions, see Thuronyi (2003, pp. 154-57). It will generally be convenient for expositional purposes to focus on *evasion* of residence-based individual income taxes and *avoidance* of both source and residence-based corporate income taxes. Under this scheme I lump the use of tax havens to evade residence-based taxes on closely held corporations together with evasion by wealthy individuals, since the same techniques are commonly involved.
6. Kudrle and Eden (2003, p. 50) opine, "... the tax evasion damage to poor countries is almost certainly greater than to richer states." An oft-quoted – and oft-questioned – estimate reported in Oxfam (2000) is that tax havens cost poor countries $50 billion annually in lost revenue. There is no way of knowing the accuracy of such estimates.
7. Kudrle and Eden (2003, p. 66) note, "By any relative measure, most low-incomecountries are hurt more by capital flight and untaxed foreign earnings than are OECD states. Moreover, there is nothing they can effectively do individually or as a group to stanch the outflow. Because most of the capital flow from poorer countries is invested in OECD states, the rich hold the key to taxation reform."
8. These categories, though useful, are not exclusive. For example, Switzerland and the United States, both developed countries, act as tax havens for passive investments. Switzerland is considered a tax haven due to its strict banking secrecy practices. The US arguably became a tax haven for portfolio investment when, in 1984, it abolished its 30 percent withholding tax on interest paid to foreigners. See McLure (1989). This was especially important for residents of countries with which the US does not have tax treaties, as the withholding rate had already been reduced to zero under many treaties. For an indictment of the United States as a tax haven under the criteria of the OECD report on harmful tax competition (OECD, 1998), see Langer (2000). For further discussion, see Avi-Yonah (2000) and references cited there.
9. Avi-Yonah (2000) calls such countries production havens. Countries that levy generally applicable income taxes at low rates (e.g., Ireland) are usually not classified as tax havens. Kudrle and Eden (2003, p. 40) make the useful distinction between activities that take place in a tax haven, activities that are assigned to a haven, and the use of havens to mask reality. They distinguish further (p. 41) between production havens, headquarters havens, sham havens, and secrecy havens. This paper is concerned primarily with the use of transfer pricing to shift income to tax havens and the use of secrecy to mask reality for wealthy investors.
10. See, however, Easson (2004b), the papers in Shah (1995), and Holland and Vann (1998), McLure (1999), Easson (2001a, b) and Zee, Stotsky, and Ley (2002) and references provided therein.

11. Note, however, that the OECD identified "Failure to adhere to international transfer pricing principles" as one of the "other factors" that may assist in identifying harmful tax competition; see section 6.1.2.
12. See, however, Graetz (2001) and references provided there. If all countries levied only source-based taxes and taxed all income, all income earned in a given jurisdiction would be subject to the same tax regime, and capital import neutrality would prevail. By comparison, if all countries levied only residence-based taxes (or if those that levied residence-based taxes granted credits for all source-based foreign income taxes and provided refunds when foreign taxes exceeded domestic taxes) and there were no deferral, all income earned by those residing in a given jurisdiction would be subject to the same tax regime, and capital export neutrality would prevail. Because of deferral and limitations on the foreign tax credit, complete capital export neutrality is not achieved, even for residents of countries that tax worldwide income.
13. See, however, IFA (2000a), OECD (2001b), and McLure (2003b) and references given there. Electronic commerce complicates application of the international system in two ways. First, it brings into question many of the basic concepts underlying that system, including the determination of corporate residence, distinctions between types of income (e.g., income from sale of a product, income from provision of a service, and royalties), the nature of a permanent establishment, and the source of business income guidelines. Second, e-commerce aggravates the problems of transfer pricing and tax havens described below. There are – and increasingly will be – more transactions between related entities, many of them in intangibles for which there are no comparable uncontrolled transactions. Horner and Owens (1996) provides an instructive example of how e-commerce complicates the problem of transfer pricing. Financial transactions and communications – the very lifeblood of tax havens – will be easier and faster. Residence for tax purpose will be more footloose and more difficult to determine. It will thus be easier to locate it in tax havens. Some real activities will also be easier to locate in tax havens.
14. Arnold (1986), US Department of the Treasury (2002), and Goodspeed (2004) provide excellent descriptions of this system. For a description of the economic incentives created by the US version of the international system, including some anti-abuse rules, see Scholes *et al.* (2002). Whereas the United States bases residence on the place of incorporation, most countries define residence in terms of the place of effective management. This distinction is generally ignored here. See, however, the brief reference to corporate inversions in Section 4.2
15. Double source-based taxation or double residence-based taxation could also occur if the sourcing rules or the residence rules of two countries were not consistent.
16. Art. 5 of the OECD Model defines the term "permanent establishment" as "a fixed place of business through which the business of an enterprise is wholly or partly carried on." The OECD Model states that a PE includes a place of management; a branch; an office; a factory; a workshop; and a mine, an oil or gas well, a quarry or any other place of extraction of natural resources. The OECD Model also excludes from the definition of a PE, *inter alia*, "the use of facilities solely for the purpose of storage, display or delivery of goods or merchandise belonging to the enterprise" and "the maintenance of a fixed place of business solely for the purpose of carrying on, for the enterprise, any other activity of a preparatory or auxiliary character." A PE exists where an agent (other than an independent agent) "is acting on behalf of an enterprise and has, and habitually exercises, ... authority to conclude contracts in the name of the enterprise."
17. These are the same conditions under which direct foreign investment is responsive to differences in tax rates in source countries; see Slemrod (1995), Goodspeed (2004), or Gugl and Zodrow (2004) for a clear exposition of these conditions.
18. Whether income is distributed is, of course, under the control of the multinational corporation. Whether or not a given corporation is in an excess credit position may

depend on whether and how its country of residence allows averaging of income and credits across source countries and types of income. It may be possible to circumvent such limits by routing income through an offshore holding company. See Goodspeed (2004). Accumulated (excess and deficit) credits are relevant if credits can be carried forward and back, as is common. Otherwise the only issue is whether credits for current foreign taxes can be utilized to offset residence-based taxation.

19. This is not to imply that nothing else in the international tax area causes tears in revenue systems. Ring (2002) and Kane (2004) discuss tax arbitrage that results from differences in the way different countries treat particular transactions, including double-dip leases (arbitrage resulting from the ability of both the lessor and the lessee to take deductions for accelerated depreciation), dual resident companies (arbitrage resulting from the use of different residency rules in different countries), and hybrid entities (arbitrage resulting from a particular entity being treated as a subsidiary by one country and as a pass-through entity by another, a problem exacerbated by the 1997 US "check-the-box" rules that allow a taxpayer to elect its status). Mintz (2004) discusses how indirect tax-efficient financing routed thorough conduit jurisdictions can be used to accomplish "double-dip" deductions for interest. This paper does not discuss such techniques, which do not rely on manipulation of transfer prices and do not necessarily involve tax havens. Note, however, that hybrid entities may be employed to circumvent the effect of CFC legislation; see US Department of the Treasury (2000, chapter 6), Ring (2002, pp. 96-100) and Kane (2004, pp. 160-65). See also Arnold (2004).

20. The subsidiary in the tax haven generally would pay little or no income tax to the tax haven, because the tax haven either exempts the income or has no income tax. The income may be subject to withholding tax in the source country, but this tax may be lower than the corporate income tax that would be due if the parent reported the income currently. "Treaty shopping" is sometimes used to avoid withholding taxes levied by source countries. Suppose, for example, that a resident of country A that taxes worldwide income wishes to invest in country B, with which A does not have a tax treaty. If the investment is routed through a tax haven that does have a treaty with B, withholding tax can be reduced or eliminated. Most US treaties contain a "Limitation on Benefits" provision intended to prevent treaty shopping; see article 22 of the US Model Treaty and the technical explanation thereof. Since tax havens generally do not have well-developed income tax systems, the US does not generally enter into comprehensive income tax treaties with tax havens but, instead, enters into Tax Information Exchange Agreements (TIEAs).

21. Blum *et al.* (1998, p. 18) describe the advantages of using a corporation to launder money that is equally apt for tax evasion:

> Once the corporation is set up in the offshore jurisdiction, a bank deposit is then made in the haven country in the name of that offshore company, particularly one whose owner's identity is protected by corporate secrecy laws. In that way there is ... one level of bank secrecy, one level of corporate secrecy, and possibly the additional protection of client-attorney privilege if a lawyer in the corporate secrecy haven has been designated to establish and run the company.

The authors note (p. 21) that funds accumulated in an offshore corporation can be repatriated as non-taxable loans, payment of interest on which may be tax-deductible. Of course, such interest deductions may arouse the suspicions of tax administrators. Zagaris (2004), citing criminal proceedings against advisers and clients using phony offshore tax schemes, describes use of tax havens to evade US income taxes, by paying fictitious expenses based on invoices issued by tax haven entities. This form of abuse goes beyond the type described in the text, although it is likely to be accompanied by it.

22. One of these, the Cayman Islands, with assets of just over $1 trillion, has the world's fifth largest international banking sector, which is exceeded only by those of the UK, Germany, the United States, and Japan. (Other "tax-friendly" jurisdictions listed among the top 20 by size of cross-border bank assets are the US, Switzerland, Luxembourg, the Netherlands, Belgium, Singapore, Hong Kong, Jersey, Ireland, the Bahamas, Austria, and Guernsey.) In 2003 US$ 414 billion (up from US$ 172 billion in 1995) of these were non-bank deposits by individuals and non-financial corporations. See Sullivan (2004b). Based on estimates that 70 percent of these originate in the US, Sullivan estimates that US investors hold US$ 290 in Cayman Islands banks, of which an estimated 80 percent or $232 billion, are not reported to the Treasury Department, as required by law. Further assumptions of a 3 percent rate of return and an average marginal tax rate of 35 percent yields an estimate of annual revenue loss of US$ 2.5 billion.
23. In either case the manufacturer acts in an agency capacity. In the first case it does not take title to the materials or goods; in the second case it does take title.
24. Rosenbloom (2000, p. 35.6) notes, "Tax havens ... raise problems ... even if transfer prices in the United States and the other country are identical." For further elementary descriptions of the mechanics of tax havens, see Arnold (1986) and (2001). There may, of course, be other reasons to establish such a corporate structure (or not to do so).

    Figures for the US provide an impression of the magnitude of the problem; in relative terms the problem is likely to be at least as serious in DTCs. Sullivan (2004a, p. 690) reports that in 2001 subsidiaries of US corporations domiciled in four low-tax countries (the Netherlands, Ireland, Bermuda, and Luxembourg) reported 30 percent of all foreign profits of US corporations, despite accounting for only 5 percent of the productive capacity and 3 percent of the employment of foreign subsidiaries of US corporations. He also reports that in 2002 foreign subsidiaries of US corporations domiciled in 18 low tax countries accounted for 58 percent of the foreign profits of US multinationals, "a figure that far exceeds the share of economic activity that multinational conduct in those low-tax countries;" see Sullivan (2004c, p. 1035). Almond and Sullivan (2004b, p. 12) cite an estimate that 237 S&P 500 companies reported unrepatriated foreign profits of $510 billion in 2003 and estimate that 67 US corporations reported more than $352 billion of unrepatriated foreign profits; of this amount, $266 were reported by only 20 corporations.

25. The United Kingdom enacted the world's first transfer pricing rules in 1915. Pagan and Wilkie (1993, p. 16) make the following observations about the historical development of transfer pricing for tax purposes that are worthwhile keeping in mind:

    In 1915 transfer pricing regulation was designed to counteract tax avoidance against a background of relatively straightforward international trade and investment. It applied only to a small percentage of international transactions. ... Today, transfer pricing is about the allocation of income of a MNE between nations. It applies to virtually all international transactions within a MNE group and, because of technological advancements and split functions, a MNE has more international transactions than ever before.

In this earlier period, virtually all trade within MNEs was in commodities, for many of which arm's length prices existed or could be constructed with relative ease and accuracy. Tax administration was involved in detecting deviations from arm's length prices. Today, by comparison, a substantial portion of trade within MNEs involves intangible and other products for which arm's length prices do not exist and cannot be estimated reliably. For further discussion, see Horner and Owens (1996).

26. The true fabric of tax "avoision" that can be woven from the interplay of transfer pricing and tax havens is, of course, far more complex than this simple example suggests. For further descriptions of the mechanics of tax havens, see Gordon (1981), Doggart (1985), Arnold (1986), and OECD (1987). Hampton (1996) discusses the sometimes blurry distinction between tax havens and offshore financial centers. The ability to employ tax havens to reduce or defer taxes is, of course, affected by the anti-abuse legislation considered in the next section.
27. Under one common scheme, the tax haven subsidiary would make a "buy-in" payment to the parent to compensate it for costs of R&D. To the extent that such cost-sharing payments do not reflect anticipated above-normal profits, they are inconsistent with the arm's length standard. See Ballentine (2002) This would seem to be the normal state of affairs, since the cost-sharing rules do not include a "commensurate with income" standard.
28. For an excellent if somewhat critical and dated survey of transfer pricing, see Pagan and Wilkie (1993). They note that although the United Kingdom enacted the first transfer pricing rules in 1915, there was little pressure on such rules until the mid 1960s, when the revival of international trade and investment following World War II began.
29. See OECD (1995), p3.50. O'Connor (1997) describes the application of both traditional and non-traditional methods. See Li (2003, pp. 109-116 and chapters 4-9) for both a summary description of the methods and detailed descriptions of transfer pricing practices in 6 countries (Canada, the United States, Japan, China, Hong Kong, and Singapore). The OECD *Guidelines* explicitly rejects what it calls "global formulary apportionment" – the method used by the US states and the Canadian provinces – to apportion the income of corporations operating in multiple jurisdictions.
30. Moreover, under the "super-royalty" provisions of the 1986 Tax Reform Act, which requires that income attributable to the transfer of an intangible for tax purposes be "commensurate with income attributable to the intangible," taxpayers can be required to adjust the profit rates used to value transfers of technology to reflect the actual income an intangible generates.
31. Ring (2000) describes the history and practice of APAs.
32. As noted earlier, this discussion assumes that the DCT wishes to implement an effective transfer pricing policy. While this is likely to be true for imports of finished products, it is less likely to be true for exports and perhaps for imports of productive inputs, including capital goods. For competitive reasons the country may allow undervaluation of exports. The treatment of imports is clouded by the question of valuation for import tariffs. Lall (1979) emphasizes that some developing countries may take a lax attitude toward transfer pricing in order to present a more positive image to potential investors.
33. See also Lall (1979). Baistrocchi (2004) argues that the problems described here are accentuated by the fact that the ALS is not a precise set of rules, but rather a standard that relies on case law or its functional equivalent for its implementation. Less human capital is required to enforce rules than to implement standards; many transfer pricing

cases are so fact-specific that they defy easy generalization; case law is generally less relevant in developing countries than in developing countries; and standards are more vulnerable to political instability than are rules. Baistrocchi notes that case law plays a minor role in the French tradition of civil law on which many developing countries rely.

34. Even before the United States added non-traditional methods of transfer pricing to Section 482, Schindler and Henderson (1985, p. 1171) noted, "Intercorporate transfer pricing under the scope of Code section 482 is one of the most complex areas of international taxation." Addition of these methods further increases complexity. Ikeda (1992) opined at the time the new OECD guidelines were being considered, "At this stage, there is much uncertainty about the impact that the recent discussions on transfer pricing issues will have on developing countries. Perhaps, as more sophisticated international tax principles are constructed for international income allocation, the problem of insufficient resources in developing countries, will become more serious." Fox and McIntyre (2003) conclude, "The experience in the developing countries since 1995 with the new pricing methods has not been very encouraging."
35. The OECD *Transfer Pricing Guidelines* (OECD, 1995) describe in general terms the kind of economic analysis that is needed under the *Guidelines*. Pagan and Wilkie (1993, chapter 6) describe the role of the transfer pricing economist. The increased prevalence of "large taxpayer units" in some DCTs may tip the scales a bit toward tax administrators.
36. UN (1999, p. 31). The latter figures are presumably percentages of the countries thought to have a problem. This source does not, unfortunately, indicate which countries – or even how many – responded to the survey or thought they had enough evidence to make a judgment. That not all the countries that expressed an opinion thought they had problems may be evidence that some were not paying attention.
37. Under Article 25 of the OECD Model Treaty, competent authorities must endeavor to reach agreement; they are not required to do so. See also Pagan and Wilkie (1993, pp. 214-17). Where competent authorities cannot agree, the taxpayer faces the prospect of choosing between double taxation and litigation.
38. These issues go beyond transfer pricing. Under international conventions a source country can tax business profits only if earned by a permanent establishment (PE) in the country, where such profits are measured by the application of the arm's length standard. E-commerce creates the ability to exploit a market without resort to a PE, and even if a PE were found to exist in the market country, standard transfer-pricing methodologies would not attribute much income to it. For further discussion, see McLure (2003, pp. 303, 305-6) and references cited there, especially to the work of the OECD. Solutions that are conceptually possible, if politically unlikely or technically difficult, might include relaxing or redefining the PE test, so that a significant economic presence implied jurisdiction to tax; including a restricted force of attraction rule in tax treaties; allowing withholding taxes on sales of digital content; and altering the methodology of transfer pricing, perhaps even replacing it with formulary apportionment. See McLure (2003, pp. 306-309) and references cited there.
39. *Report of the Technical Committee on Business Taxation* (1997, p. 6.33) concludes, following Turner (1996), "The existence of penalty provisions and documentation requirements in certain other countries (most notably the United States), combined with aggressive transfer pricing audit procedures in those jurisdictions, poses a threat to the Canadian tax base. In particular, many companies may, in the past, have sought to "overcomply" with tax rules in those jurisdictions, to the detriment of the Canadian tax base." Newlon (2000, pp. 230-31) also notes that there may be an incentive to over-report income in jurisdictions that impose heavy penalties. The use of penalties by DTCs is a two-edged sword. The risk of heavy penalties may discourage investment, more than offsetting any revenu- enhancing effects.
40. Thus Arnold and Dibout (2001, pp. 38-39) write:

> The unlimited deferral of residence country tax on the income of foreign corporations owned by residents is difficult to justify. Deferral encourages residents to divert income, especially passive income, to CFCs in low-tax countries and to accumulate such income in those CFCs rather than repatriate the funds to the parent corporation. It violates the fundamental principles of equity and capital export neutrality on which worldwide taxation are based. Proponents of deferral, however, argue for the preservation of deferral, especially for business income, on grounds of international competitiveness or capital import neutrality. Under this view of neutrality, a multinational enterprise doing business in a country through a subsidiary there should be subject to tax only at the rate applicable in that country so that it can compete equally with other corporations doing business in that country.

> US Department of the Treasury (2000) describes the case for capital export neutrality, along with previous literature. For a critical view of capital export neutrality, see Graetz (2001). Rosenbloom (2001) argues that the US international tax system, including its CFC regimes, should be replaced by a limited exemption system. Evaluation of this and similar proposals is beyond the terms of reference of this paper. See, however, Peroni (2001) and Steines (2001). The former believes (p. 1581) that "the incoherent compromise ... reflected in the absurdly complicated and ineffective subpart F rules is not an acceptable option for the 21st Century.

41. See, however, Mitchell (2004), who treats worldwide taxation as a form of tax harmonization, which he sees as categorically undesirable because "taxpayers are unable to benefit from better tax policy in other nations, and governments are insulated from market discipline." He writes, "Implicit harmonization occurs when governments tax the income their citizens earn in other jurisdictions. This policy of 'worldwide taxation' requires governments to collect financial information on nonresident investors and to share that information with tax collectors from foreign governments."
42. Arnold (2004) writes, "In summary, the CFC problem for countries that tax on a worldwide basis is abuse of the deferral of residence country tax, whereas for countries that tax on a territorial basis, the problem is abuse of the exemption for foreign source income from residence country tax." Thus France employs CFC legislation because it taxes only business income on a territorial basis; it taxes investment income on a worldwide basis. Its CFC legislation is intended to prevent diverting passive income to a tax haven subsidiary and accumulating investment income is such a corporation. Also, in the absence of legislation, passive income received by the tax-haven could be distributed to the parent as tax-free dividends. See Arnold (1986, pp. 134, 201-4). US Department of the Treasury (2000, Introduction, note 17) notes that under a territorial system CFC rules might more accurately be called "anti-exemption rules."
43. CFC legislation is not the only technique used to combat tax haven abuses, but it is the only one considered here. Other anti-abuse techniques include general anti-avoidance provisions and "substance over form" rules. For a comparative discussion of ways to prevent abuse, see Thuronyi (2203, chapter 5). For a brief description of the rationale and functioning of CFC legislation, see Arnold (1986) and (2000), OECD (1996), Sandler (1998), and Arnold and Dibout (2001). The national reports in IFA (2001b) summarize the practices of 30 countries. Much of the following description is based on Arnold and Dibout (2001, especially pp. 30-57.) Sandler focuses on the interaction between CFC rules and tax treaties, which Arnold (2004) also discusses.

> Taylor and Richman (1965, p. 81) describe a pre-1960 scheme used by Colombians to evade tax: forming foreign companies in Panama or Venezuela to do business in Colombia. In theory, if Colombian CFC legislation had existed it would have prevented this ploy; in fact, it is almost certain that it would not have, for administrative reasons. Colombia relied instead on increased withholding taxes on branch profits and dividends. Of course, neither of these would have prevented manipulation of transfer prices to shift income out of the country.

44. Under some circumstances multinational corporations may not want to defer recognition of income. Ault and Bradford (1990, p. 18) note that subpart F income (the term for "tainted" income under US law) may be created in order to take advantage of excess FTCs, without having actually to distribute foreign-source income and thus pay foreign withholding taxes. This corresponds to shifting income from column (B) to column (D) in Table 1.
45. For example, under US law a CFC is a foreign corporation in which more than 50 percent of the voting power or market value of the corporation is owned by US persons each of whom owns at least 10 percent of voting stock. Income of a passive foreign investment company (PFIC) may also be subject to current taxation. A corporation may be classified as a PFIC in any year in which at least 75 percent of its gross income is passive or at least 50 percent of its assets produce passive income.
46. Pagan and Wilkie (1994, p. 18) note that in the 1970s it was realized that there are "simpler and more cost-effective methods of preventing tax avoidance" such as CFC legislation, and transfer pricing was identified as "the final backstop provision." It might be noted that CFC rules and transfer pricing rules are not mutually independent, as transfer pricing could be used to shift income from a subsidiary that is subject to CFC rules to one that is not (or vice versa, if that were more beneficial).
47. Arnold and Dibout (2001) and Arnold (2004) list the following countries with CFC rules in chronological order based on the year in which the rules were adopted: United States, 1962; Canada, 1972; Germany, 1972; Japan, 1978; France, 1980; United Kingdom, 1984; New Zealand, 1988; Australia, 1990; Sweden, 1990; Norway, 1992; Denmark, 1995; Finland, 1995; Indonesia, 1995; Portugal, 1995; Spain, 1995; Hungary, 1997; Mexico, 1997; South Africa, 1997; South Korea, 1997; Argentina, 1999; Venezuela, 1999, Israel, 2000; Italy, 2000; Estonia, 2000. Arnold and Dibout note that the Hungarian CFC rules were so significantly diluted effective 1 January 2001 that it may no longer be appropriate to categorize them as CFC rules. Arnold (2004) reports that Austria, Ecuador, India, and Peru are considering adoption of CFC rules and, citing Thuronyi (2003, p. 297), that Kazakhstan (2001), Tajikistan (1998), Georgia (1997), and Azerbaijan (2000) have adopted anti-tax haven rules that are intended to function like CFC rules.
48. See US Department of the Treasury (2002), Avi-Yonah (2002), Dimon (2002), and Desai and Hines (2002).
49. US legislation enacted in October 2004 includes provisions intended to limit the tax advantages of inversions. Sheppard (2004, p. 394) notes, "The new law, however, leaves in place the elements of current law that make inversions possible. And certainly the effort that went into drafting the inversion rules could have been better directed toward drafting a new definition of residence for a corporation."
50. Thus Arnold and Dibout (2001, p. 28) note, "Other countries, such as Poland, which were subject just a few years ago to a planned economy and which are opening up to the multinationals' activities, are discovering at the same time the complexity of the fiscal questions connected with internationalization of trade and the need for developing appropriate taxation legislation. ... Such countries' concern with protecting their tax base

against international avoidance is expressed more, in the current state of development of their adaptation process, in rules relating to checking transfer prices and undercapitalization than in provisions that are specifically aimed at low-taxation regimes abroad."

51. The OECD noted in its initial report on harmful tax competition (1998, p88), "Residence countries can partly negate the effects of harmful preferential tax regimes in source countries..." While the intended reference was presumably, if implicitly, to adverse revenue effects in the home country of the parent, it seems reasonable to ask whether adverse effects in other source countries could be negated.
52. See Arnold (1986, pp. 134, 466) for further discussion. US Department of the Treasury (2000) discusses this case of "foreign-to-foreign related party transactions."
53. Arnold (1986, pp. 466, 505-6) notes that if both France or the US and the other high-tax country were to apply anti-abuse rules, double taxation might result. Arnold (2004) discusses further the problems that may result from the application of CFC rules to chains of subsidiaries, for example, if a parent is subject to the CFC rules of its nation of residence and its subsidiary is subject to those of the nation where it is resident, but foreign tax credit is not available to the parent for the CFC-related tax paid by the subsidiary.
54. Kingson (2001, pp. 1569-70) distinguishes four situations where US CFC rules apply: 1) interest, dividends, and capital gains from portfolio investment, 2) income from sales or services transactions with related US companies, 3) interest, dividends, and capital gains from non-portfolio investment, and 4) income from sales or services transactions between related foreign companies. Only the first two deter erosion of the US tax base; the other two, he notes, "stem from the idea that subpart F acts as a sort of world tax policeman."
55. For a detailed discussion, see OECD (2000b). Similar steps are required to enforce CFC legislation.
56. This section was published in slightly different form in McLure (2005).
57. Ministerial Communique of May 1996, quoted in OECD (1998, Foreward). At about the same time the European Union began considering a "Tax Package" that included a code of conduct for business taxes and proposed directives on savings and on parent-subsidiaries and dividends. The saving directive is considered briefly below.

    It seems that the OECD made a serious political mistake when it entitled its initial report "Harmful Tax Competition" and referred to that concept repeatedly in its 1998 report. Doing so opened the door to the unfounded charge that it wanted to eliminate all tax competition, not just tax competition that was harmful, and almost scuttled the project. Sheppard (2001) describes efforts to characterize the OECD project as hostile to all tax competition. See also note 61. The OECD now downplays the concept of harmful tax competition and emphasizes "harmful tax practices," which perhaps more accurately describes its concerns – and clearly is more politically acceptable. See the titles of OECD (2000a), 2001a), and (2004a). Also, the OECD initially did not pay enough attention to the devastating effects closing down tax havens would have on the economies of the havens.

58. See OECD (1998). Both Luxembourg and Switzerland abstained from approval of the 1998 Report, so technically they are not bound by its recommendations; see OECD (1998, Annex II) for their statements of dissent. The Swiss dissent includes these points: being restricted to geographically mobile activities, such as financial activities and other services, the report is "partial and unbalanced," it uses low tax rates as a criterion to identify harmful tax regimes, and it disregards withholding as a lower cost alternative to

exchange of information. Peter (2002) provides further explanation of the Swiss position. Luxembourg's dissent states, "the Report gives the impression that its purpose is not so much to counter harmful tax competition where it exists as to abolish bank secrecy."

59. Despite this statement, there is little evidence that helping DCTs was a conscious objective. The few references in project documents to involvement of non-haven non-OECD jurisdictions seem to be concerned primarily with the "cockroach problem," the possibility that harmful tax practices displaced from one non-OECD jurisdiction might be reestablished in another.
60. OECD (1998, pp 52, 59). It is instructive, in the light of the previous discussion of the interplay between transfer pricing and tax havens, to note that "Failure to adhere to international transfer pricing principles" is listed among "other factors" that may assist in identifying harmful tax competition. See OECD (1998, pp 71-72). The idea was that a tax haven might condone the use of artificial transfer prices to shift income to the haven.
61. The OECD reiterated this in the introduction to its 2004 report: "Although a low or zero effective tax rate is a necessary starting point of an examination of a preferential regime, it alone is not sufficient to find harmfulness." (OECD, 2004a, n. 2)
62. See OECD (2001a, pp 27-28). Both Hishikawa (2002, p. 413), which describes deliberations, negotiations, and actions taken up to early 2002, and Easson (2004a, pp. 1043-44), which describes the history of the entire project in greater detail, note that this change was made in order to secure continued US cooperation in the project following the change of administrations in 2001. Sheppard (2001, p. 2023) notes that in February 2001 Treasury Secretary O'Neill confirmed US support for the OECD project, albeit emphasizing that is was "critical to clarify that this project is not about dictating to any country what should be the appropriate level of tax rates." By May 2001O'Niell was saying that he had had cause to "re-evaluate" US participation in the project, suggesting that the project was an attempt to "dictate" countries tax rates and tax systems and "harmonize world tax systems." See US Department of the Treasury, May 10, 2001. Easson (2004a, pp. 1052-59) describes the role Daniel Mitchell and the Center for Freedom and Prosperity played in trying to derail the OECD initiative. Joseph Guttentag, the Deputy Assistant Secretary for International Tax Affairs at the US Treasury department at the time the OECD project was being formulated, commenting on Congressional efforts to deny funding for the OECD if it continued its tax-harmonization agenda, notes that the OECD never had such an agenda and opines, "These lobbyists failed to get the tax havens to break away from the OECD dialogue so they are now attacking the funding of the organization." See Gnaedinger (2004, p. 314).
63. Easson (2004a, p. 1061) states, "The dropping of the 'no substantial activities' criterion effectively meant that a tax haven could be labeled as uncooperative only if it failed the transparency test or refused to exchange information." Devereux (2002, p. 104) makes the same point.
64. Guttentag indicates that these defensive measures were thought necessary because of the initial expectation that tax havens would not cooperate, and would "consider their designation as such to be good advertising which would endear them to their tax-avoidance customers." See Gnaedinger (2004, p. 314).
65. These are from OECD (2004a, p30). This list represents a refinement of the similar list appearing in (OECD (2000a, pp 32-38). See OECD (1998), pp 97-169) for further elaboration of some of these items.
66. OECD (2004a, pp 12, 15). Since both Luxembourg and Switzerland abstained from approval of the 1998 Report, and thus technically are not bound by its recommendations, any action on their part can be viewed as welcome. Switzerland has agreed to effective exchange of information with respect to holding companies in the context of bilateral treaties. Luxembourg has submitted legislation to its Parliament to make its 1929

Holding Company regime consistent with the EU Code of Conduct, but has not addressed effective exchange of information. (p15)

67. OECD (2003b).
68. OECD (2004a, p19) Tax havens could avoid being listed as "uncooperative" by issuing a press release stating their commitment to eliminate harmful tax practices, most easily by becoming a party to the Collective Memorandum of Understanding (OECD 2000c). Progress in achieving greater cooperation and transparency cannot be attributed entirely to the OECD project on harmful tax competition, which is only one of several overlapping international initiatives directed at the offshore financial sector, e.g., efforts to prevent money laundering and the use of secrecy to hide funding of terrorism. Many of these efforts are conducted through the Financial Action Task Force (FATF) on Money Laundering, whose members included tax havens, which are willing to cooperate – or at least want to appear to cooperate – in dealing with non-tax matters such as drug trafficking, organized crime, and terrorism. It is worth noting that, as of late 2004, there was no overlap between the FATF list of non-cooperative countries and territories (Cook Islands, Indonesia, Myanmar, Nauru, Nigeria, and the Philippines) and the OECD list of uncooperative tax havens (Andorra, Liberia, Liechtenstein, the Marshall Islands, and Monaco). For a survey of such non-tax efforts, including the implications of the USA Patriot Act, which prohibits depository institutions and security brokers and dealers operating in the United States from establishing, maintaining, administering, or managing correspondent accounts for many foreign shell banks, see Zagaris (2003), (2004). In an early analysis of the effectiveness of the FATF, Suss, Williams, and Mendis (2002) note that, following the terrorist attacks of September 11, "one of the major competitive factors – increased secrecy from even local supervisors – is no longer a viable option" for offshore financial centers. They also note that jurisdictions that have ignored standards of good governance of their financial sectors are experiencing the discipline of market forces, as shown by difficulty in participating successfully in global financial markets.
69. Andorra, Liechtenstein, and Monaco have agreed to levy withholding taxes on interest payments to EU residents and to exchange information in cases of tax fraud; see the discussion of the EU savings directive below. Easson (2004a, p. 1076) notes that Liberia has been occupied with its civil war and that the reason the Marshall Islands has refused to cooperate is "somewhat obscure."
70. See the account of events in Easson (2004a), as well as the quotation from OECD (1998, p43) at the beginning of the above discussion of defensive measures.
71. OECD (2004a, pp 19, 27). Tax havens have criticized the OECD for not paying more attention to non-haven financial centers such as Hong Kong and Singapore; see Goulder (2004, p. 1192).
72. The non-OECD members of this working group are Aruba, Bermuda, Bahrain, Cayman Islands, Cyprus, the Isle of Man, Malta, Mauritius, the Netherlands Antilles, San Marino, and the Seychelles. The word "erstwhile" modifying "tax havens" should perhaps appears in quotation marks, because, as explained below, it appears that for many purposes, tax havens will not cease to be tax havens. Another working group is charged with developing accounting standards to be used for the maintenance and exchange of information. See OECD (2003b), (2004a, pp 22-27).
73. Some tax havens already agree to exchange information when criminal tax fraud is at issue, but not to prevent tax avoidance.
74. In a similar vein, Arnold (2000, p. 17:20) writes, "If a country imposes no or only nominal taxes, it is a tax haven, even if it is transparent, exchanges information, or requires substantial activities in the country."
75. Powell (2002, p. 232), writing from the perspective of Jersey and Guernsey, predicts, "... both small and large OFCs [offshore financial centers] working to international standards, will continue to find a place in the sun."

76. See also Easson (2004a, pp. 1048-49, 1076). The present discussion considers the savings directive only to the extent necessary to appraise the likely success of the OECD project.
77. Article 17 of the saving directive (European Union, 2003), hardy a model of clarity, which says when the transition period is to begin, does not mention the United States. The European Commission and the Council of Europe sometime seem to interpret prefatory paragraph 24 as requiring that the US also adopt "equivalent measures" before the transition period can begin.
78. The withholding tax rates are to begin at 15 percent, rise to 20 percent at the beginning of 2008, and go to 35 percent on January 1, 2011. The source country of interest payments will be entitled to keep 25 percent of revenues from the withholding tax and will remit the remaining 75 percent to the country of residence of the recipient of interest.
79. A staunch opponent of both the OECD effort to eliminate harmful tax competition and the EU Saving Directive has made the same point: "The OECD did convince many blacklisted jurisdictions to sign so-called commitment letters, which ostensibly obligate low-tax governments to obey OECD dictates, but most of these letters include 'level playing field' clauses stating that the blacklisted nations have no intention of emasculating their tax and privacy laws unless all OECD nations agree to impose the same misguided policies." See Mitchell (2004). For a list of tax havens whose commitment letters contained "level playing field" provisions, see Weiner (2003, p. 237).
80. Avi-Yonah (1998) describes the economic developments that led to elimination of withholding on interest and argued that the time was then ripe to re-introduce interest withholding, which would facilitate the EU's attempt to implement the "coexistence model" version of the Savings Directive.
81. It is unclear why this issue arose. As pointed out in note 75 above, saving directive does not seem to require that the US employ equivalent measure for the transition period to begin.
82. Grob *et al.* (2003) reach a similar conclusion:

    > The USA is considered to already possess equivalent measures. This in itself is an interesting development, since the extent to which exchange of information measures in the USA would be compatible to the new regime in the European Union is questionable. ... Fundamentally, it is probably a decision led by *Realpolitik*. Acquiescence by the USA to the provisions of the Directive would likely have been extremely difficult to achieve in practice.

    OECD 92004c) says regarding participation in its Global Forum:

    > The Sub-Group has initially identified the following countries as examples of significant financial centres that should be included in the process: Andorra, Barbados, *Brunei*, *Costa Rica*, *Dubai*, *Guatemala*, *Hong Kong-China*, Liberia, Liechtenstein, *Macao-China*, *Malaysia (Labuan)*, Marshall Islands, Monaco, *Philippines*, *Singapore*, *Uruguay*.

    > The jurisdictions whose names are italicized were not considered in the project's previous work.

83. For the perspective of tax-haven countries, see the papers in Biswas (2002).

84. See Langer (2002) for a scathing critique of OECD policy that gives erstwhile tax havens nothing in return for signing exchange of information agreements, as well as an historical explanation of the development of tax havens.
85. OECD (2004a, p24). The OECD reports that since 2000, the United States has concluded TIEAs with Antigua and Barbuda, the Bahamas, the British Virgin Islands, the Cayman Islands, Guernsey, Isle of Man, Jersey, and the Netherlands Antilles and that other OECD members such as Germany, Ireland, the Netherlands and Spain are in the process of negotiating similar agreements. See OECD (2003b, p. 19).
86. Bentley (2003, p. 1136) writes, "A country that did not face extreme political or economic reprisals would not otherwise consider signing an agreement based on that model."
87. Of course, once being listed as an uncooperative tax haven has been avoided, there is little incentive to exchange information with DTCs.
88. I am grateful to Lee Burns for this point.
89. The national reports for several countries in IFA (2001b) mention the influence of the OECD project on harmful tax competition in conditioning internal debate on CFC legislation. Thus: "In a general sense, the OECD issues on harmful tax competition were, among others, an important element to be taken into account in introducing legal reforms to the Income Tax Law at the end of 1999." (Argentina, p. 335) Similarly, "[F]ollowing international trends, although it is not a member of the OECD or of the EU, Brazil will closely follow the guidelines established by the OECD as regards controlling operations performed with beneficiaries located in countries with favorable tax treatment." (Brazil, p. 430) Finally, "The Ministry of Finance understands and supports the OECD and EU initiatives against harmful tax competition. Additionally, it should be emphasised that such initiatives indirectly gave the ground and justified the introduction from 2001 of the provisions which require reporting of transactions with entities in low-tax jurisdictions." (Poland (766). By comparison, the national report for Peru (p. 758) says, "The projects of the OECD and EU against harmful tax competition have not necessarily influenced the proposed internal tax norms, which, if approved by Congress, would go into effect starting in 2001." Italy's recently enacted CFC legislation follows the spirit of the OECD project most closely, in that it targets income that flows through tax havens, employing lack of exchange of information as a key determinant of countries on its black list; see Queiroli (2003, p. 1267).

References

Ackerman, Bob and John Hobster (2001), "Transfer Pricing Practices, Perspectives, and Trends in 22 Countries", *Tax Notes International*, Vol. 24, pp. 1151-58.

Ackerman, Bob, *et al.* (2002a), "Global Transfer Pricing Update – July 2002", *Tax Notes International*, Vol. 27, pp. 553- 69.

Ackerman, Bob, *et al.* (2002b), "Global Transfer Pricing Update", *Tax Notes International*, Vol. 28, pp. 357-84.

Ackerman, Bob, *et al.* (2003), "Global Transfer Pricing Update", *Tax Notes International*, Vol. 32, pp. 445-68.

Ackerman, Bob, *et al.* (2004), "Global Transfer Pricing Update", *Tax Notes International*, Vol. 33, pp. 259-65.

Almond, John A. and Martin A. Sullivan (2004), "Economic Analysis: While Congress Dawdles, Trapped Foreign Profits Surge", *Tax Notes*, Vol. 103, pp. 1587-91; Also, *Tax Notes International*, Vol. 35, pp. 11-15.

Altshuler, Rosanne (2004), "Comments" on "Transfer Pricing and Tax Havens: Mending the LDC Revenue Net", by Charles E. McLure, Jr., presented at a conference on The Challenges of Tax Reform in a Global Economy, Stone Mountain, Georgia, May 24-25, 2004.

Altshuler, Rosanne and Harry Grubert (2004), "Taxpayer Responses to Competitive Tax Policies and Tax Policy Responses to Competitive Taxpayers: Recent Evidence", *Tax Notes International*, Vol. 34 (13), pp. 1349-1362.

Arnold, Brian J. (1986), *The Taxation of Controlled Foreign Corporations: An International Comparison,* Toronto:,Canadian Tax Foundation.

Arnold, Brian J. (2000), "Controlled Foreign Corporation Rules, Harmful Tax Competition, and International Taxation", in: *Report of Proceedings of the First World Tax Conference: Taxes without Borders,* 2000 World Tax Conference Report, Toronto: Canadian Tax Foundation.

Arnold, Brian J. (2004), "Controlled Foreign Corporation Rules: Major Features, Recent Developments, and Practical Problems", 4th Annual World Tax Conference, Sydney: Australia, 25-27 February.

Arnold, Brian J. and Patrick Dibout (2001), "Limits on the Use of Low-tax Regimes by Multinational Businesses: Current Measures and Emerging Trends: General Report", chapter 17 in: *Cahiers de Droit Fiscal International,* International Fiscal Association.

Ault, Hugh and David Bradford (1990), "Taxing International Income: An Analysis of the U.S. System and Its Economic Premises", pp. 11-46 in: Assaf Razin and Joel Slemrod, editors, *Taxation in the Global Economy,* Chicago: University of Chicago Press.

Avi-Yonah, Reuven S. (1998), "Memo to Congress: It's Time to Repeal the U.S. Portfolio Interest Exemption", *Tax Notes International,* Vol. 17, pp. 1817-26.

Avi-Yonah, Reuven S. (2000), "Globalization, Tax Competition, and the Fiscal Crisis of the Welfare State", *Harvard Law Review,* Vol. 113(7), pp. 1575-1676.

Avi-Yonah, Reuven S. (2002), "For Haven's Sake: Reflections on Inversion Transactions", *Tax Notes International,* Vol 27, pp. 225-231.

Baistrocchi, Eduardo (2004), "The Arm's Length Standard in the 21st Century: A Proposal for both Developed and Developing Countries", *Tax Notes International,* Vol. 36(3), pp. 241-55.

Ballentine, J. Gregory (2002), "Technology Buy-Ins: Do the Law and the Arm's-Length Standard Conflict?", Paper presented at Tax Counsel Policy Institute Annual Federal Tax Policy Symposium, "The Future of International Transfer Pricing: Practical and Policy Opportunities," February 7 and 8, Washington DC.

Bentley, Duncan (2003), "International Constraints on National Tax Policy", *Tax Notes International,* Vol. 30, pp. 1127-1144.

Biswas, Rajiv (ed.) (2002), *International Tax Competition: Globalisation and Fiscal Sovereignty,* London: Commonwealth Secretariat.

Blessing, Peter H. (2000), "Revisiting the Deferral of Foreign Business Income", chapter 18 in: *Report of Proceedings of the First World Tax Conference: Taxes without Borders,* 2000 World Tax Conference Report, Toronto: Canadian Tax Foundation.

Blum, Jack A., Michael Levi, R. Thomas Naylor, and Phil Williams (1998), *Financial Havens, Banking Secrecy and Money Laundering,* New York: United Nations Office for Drug Control and Crime Prevention, also available at: http://www.cf.ac.uk/socsi/whoswho/levi-laundering.pdf.

Bodner, Paul M., "International Taxation", chapter 39 in: Frederick D. S Choi, editor, *International Accounting and Finance Handbook,* 2nd edition, New York: John Wiley and Sons.

Boskin, Michael J. and Charles E. McLure, Jr. (eds.) (1990), *World Tax Reform: Case Studies of Developed and Developing Countries*, San Francisco: International Center for Economic Growth.

Brumbaugh, David L. (2003), *Tax Exemption for Repatriated Foreign Earnings: Proposals and Analysis*, Congressional Research Service.

Cockfield, Arthur (2002), "Through the Looking Glass: Computer Servers and E-commerce Profit Attribution", *Tax Notes International*, Vol. 25, pp. 269-75.

Commission of the European Communities (1998), "Proposal for a Council Directive to ensure a minimum of effective taxation of savings income in the form of interest payments within the Community," COM 295 final.

Commission of the European Communities (2001, July 18), Savings Tax Proposal: Frequently Asked Questions, *Memo/01/266*, Retrieved from http://europa.eu.int/comm/taxation_customs/publications/official_doc/IP/ip011026/memo01266_en.pdf.

Desai, Mihir A. and James R. Hines, Jr. (2002), *Expectations and Expatriations: Tracing the Causes and Consequences of Corporate Inversion, Working Paper No. 9057*, National Bureau of Economic Research.

Devereux, Michael P. (2002), "The OECD Harmful Tax Competition Initiative," pp.93-107 in: Rajiv Biswas, editor, *International Tax Competition: Globalisation and Fiscal Sovereignty*, London: Commonwealth Secretariat.

Dimon, Samuel J. (2002), "Outbound Inversion Transactions", *Tax Notes*, Vol. 96, pp. 127-49.

Doggart, Caroline (1985), *Tax Havens and Their Uses*, London: Economist Intelligence Unit.

Easson, Alex (2004a), "Harmful Tax Competition: An Evaluation of the OECD Initiative", *Tax Notes International*, Vol. 34, pp. 1037- 77.

Easson, Alex (2004b), *Tax Incentives for Direct Foreign Investment*, The Hague: Kluwer Law International.

Easson, Alex (2001a), "Tax Incentives for Foreign Direct Investment, Part I: Recent Trends and Countertrends", *Bulletin for International Fiscal Documentation*, Vol. 55(7), pp. 266-74.

Easson, Alex (2001b), "Tax Incentives for Foreign Direct Investment, Part II: Design Considerations", *Bulletin for International Fiscal Documentation*, Vol. 55(8), pp. 365-75.

Easson, Alex (1999), "The Tax Competition Controversy", *Tax Notes International*, Vol. 18, pp. 371-

Erich, Peter I. (2002), "Reasonable Limits of Transparency in Global Taxation: Lessons from the Swiss Experience", *Tax Notes International*, Vol. 28, pp. 591-635.

European Council (2002, November 28), Report Concerning Negotiations with Third Countries on Taxation of Savings Income, *Communication from the Commission to the Council SEC (2002) 1287 final*, Retrieved form http://register.consilium.eu.int/pdf/en/02/st14/14909en2.pdf.

European Council (2003, January 21), Council Conclusions on the Tax Package, *Outcome of Proceedings of the ECOFIN Council*, Retrieved from http://register.consilium.eu.int/pdf/en/03/st05/st05566en03.pdf.

European Union, Official Journal of the European Union (2003), "COUNCIL DIRECTIVE 2003/48/EC of 3 June 2003 on taxation of savings income in the form of interest payments." June.

European Union (2004, June 2), Results of Council of Economics and Finance Ministers, Luxembourg, 2nd June 2004 – Taxation, *MEMO/04/134,3rd June*, Retrieved December 29, 2004, from http://europa.eu.int/rapid/pressReleasesAction.do?reference=MEMO/04/134&format=HTML &aged=0&language=EN&guiLanguage=en.

Eden, Lorraine (ed.) (1991), *Retrospectives on Public Finance*, Durham, NC: Duke University Press.

Fox, William F. and Michael J. McIntyre (2003), Globalization and Tax Design in Developing Countries, Retrived from http://www1.worldbank.org/publicsector/tax/AprilMay2003Seminar/FoxMcIntyrePaper.pdf.

G20 Statement on Transparency and Exchange of Information for Tax Purposes. Retrieved 2004, from http://www.g20.org/download/public/20041121_communique_final.pdf.

Gillis, Malcolm (1989), *Tax Reform in Developing Countries*, Durham, NC: Duke University Press.

Gnaedinger, Chuck (2004), "TNI Interview: Joseph H. Guttentag", *Tax Notes International*, Vol. 36, pp. 311-16.

Goodspeed, Timothy J. (2004), *"Taxation and FDI in Developed and Developing Countries," presented at a conference on The Challenges of Tax Reform in a Global Economy*, Stone Mountain, Georgia, May 24-25, 2004.

Gordon, Richard A. (1981), *Tax Havens and Their Use by United States Taxpayers – an Overview*, U.S. Internal Revenue Service, U.S. Department of the Treasury.

Gordon, Roger (1986), "Taxation of Investment and Savings in a World Economy", *American Economic Review*, Vol. 76, pp. 1086–1102.

Gordon, Roger H. and James R. Hines Jr. (2002), "International Taxation," pp. 1935-1995 in: Alan J. Auerbach and Martin Feldstein, editors, *Handbook of Public Economics*, Vol. 4, Amsterdam: North-Holland.

Gordon, Roger and Jeffrey MacKie-Mason (1995), "Why Is There Corporate Taxation In a Small Open Economy? The Role of Transfer Pricing and Income Shifting", pp. 67-91 in: Martin Feldstein, James Hines, Jr., and R. Glenn Hubbard, editors, *The Effects of Taxation on Multinational Corporations*, Chicago: University of Chicago Press.

Goulder, Robert (2004), "TNI Interview: Jeffrey Owens", *Tax Notes International*, Vol. 33, pp. 1189-92.

Graetz, Michael J. (2001), "Taxing International Income: Inadequate Principles, Outdated Concepts, and Unsatisfactory Policies", *Tax Law Review*, Vol. 54, pp. 261- 336; also in *Brooklyn Journal of International Law*, Vol. 26(4), pp. 1357-1448.

Grob, Michael, Paul Gerrits, Stephanie Jarrett, Marnin J. Michaels, and Philip Marcovici (2003, July), The E.U. Saving Directive and Its Impact on the Banking Industry: Part I, *Tax Planning International*, Retrieved from http://subscript.bna.com/samples/TPR.NSF/0/c6f3ac3f629c316d85256d6b0059c999?OpenDocument

Gugl, Elisabeth and George R. Zodrow (2004), *"International Tax Competition and Tax Incentives in Developing Countries", presented at a conference on The Challenges of Tax Reform in a Global Economy*, Stone Mountain, Georgia, May 24-25, 2004.

Hampton, Mark (1996), *The Offshore Interface: Tax Havens in the Global Economy*, New York: St. Martin's Press.

Hines, James R., Jr., National Bureau of Economic Research (2004), *Do Tax Havens Flourish?, NBER Working Paper No. 10936*, November.

Hines, James R., Jr. and Eric M. Rice (1994), "Fiscal Paradise: Foreign Tax Havens and American Business", *Quarterly Journal of Economics*, Vol. 109, pp. 149-82.

Hishikawa, Akiko (2002), "The Death of Tax Havens?", *Boston College International and Comparative Law Review*, Vol. 25(Spring), pp. 389-417.

Holland, David and Richard J. Vann (1998), "Income Tax Incentives for Investment", pp.986-1020 in: Victor Thuronyi, editor, *Tax Law and Drafting*, Vol. 2, Washington: IMF.

Horner, Frances M. and Jeffrey Owens (1996), "Tax and the Web: New Technology, Old Problems", *Bulletin for International Fiscal Documentation*, Vol. 50(11/12), pp. 516-23.

Ikeda, Yuichi (1992), *Treatment of Intercompany Transfer Pricing for Tax Purposes - A Survey of Legislative and Administrative Issues, Working Paper No. 92/77*, IMF.

International Bureau for Fiscal Documentation (looseleaf), *The Tax Treatment of Transfer Pricing*, The Hague: IBFD.

International Fiscal Association (2001a), *Taxation of Income Derived from Electronic Commerce; Cahiers de Droit Fiscal International.*

International Fiscal Association (2001b), *Limits on the Use of Low-tax Regimes by Multinational Businesses: Current Measures and Emerging Trends; Cahiers de Droit Fiscal International.*

International Monetary Fund, Tax Policy Division (1990), *Tax Policy and Reform for Foreign Direct Investment in Developing Countries, Working Paper No. WP/90/70.*

Jovanovich, Juan Martin, *et al.* (2004), "Transfer Pricing in Latin America", *Tax Notes International*, Vol. 34, pp. 495-508.

Kane, Mitchell A. (2004), "Strategy and Cooperation in National Responses to International Tax Arbitrage", *Emory Law Journal*, Vol. 53(Winter), pp. 89-169.

Keen, Michael and Alejandro Simone (2004), "Is Tax Competition Harming Developing Countries More Than Developed?", *Tax Notes International*, Vol. 9, pp. 1317-25.

Kingson, Charles L., "Leonardo da Vinci and the 861 Regulations", *Brooklyn Journal of International Law*, Vol. 26(4), pp. 1565-77.

Kondo, Seiichi (2002), Ending Tax Haven Abuse, Retrieved from http://66.102.7.104/search?q=cache:NzHhz7DLAPwJ:www.oecd.org/dataoecd/60/15/2082521.pdf+seiichi+kondo&hl=en.

Kudrle, Robert T. and Lorraine Eden (2003), "The Campaign Against Tax Havens: Will It Last? Will It Work?", *Stanford Journal of Law, Business & Finance*, Vol 9, pp. 37-67.

Lall, Sanjaya (1979), "Transfer Pricing and Developing Countries: Some Problems of Investigation", *World Development*, Vol. 7, pp. 59-71.

Langer, Marshall J. (2000), "Harmful Tax Competition: Who are the Real Tax Havens?", *Tax Notes International*,Vol. 21, pp. 2831-39.

Langer, Marshall J. (2002), "The Outrageous History of Caribbean Tax Treaties with OECD Member States", *Tax Notes International*, Vol. 26, pp. 1167-1217.

Li, Jinyan (2003), *International Taxation in the Age of Electronic Commerce: A Comparative Study*, Toronto: Canadian tax Foundation,

Makhlouf, Gabriel (2002, April 18), The OECD List of Unco-operative Tax Havens - A statement by the Chair of the OECD's Committee on Fiscal Affairs, Retrieved December 29, 2004, from http://www.oecd.org/document/28/0,2340,en_2649_33745_2082460_1_1_1_1,00.html.

Martinez-Vazquez, Jorge and James Alm (2003), *Public Finance in Developing and Transitional Countries*, Cheltenham, UK: Edward Elgar.

Mastromarco, Dan R. and Lawrence A. Hunter (2003), "The 'U.S. Anti-Savings Directive'", *Tax Notes International*, Vol. 29, pp. 159-76.

McCarten, William J. (1995), "Transfer Pricing", pp.221-25 in: Parthasarathni Shome, editor, *Tax Policy Handbook*, Washington: International Monetary Fund.

McIntyre, Michael J. (2004), "The Use of Combined Reporting by Nation States", *Tax Notes International*, Vol. 35, pp. 917-48.

McLure, Charles E., Jr. (1989), "U.S. Tax Laws and Capital Flight from Latin America", *Inter-American Law Review*, Vol. 20(2), pp. 321-57.

McLure, Charles E., Jr. (1991), "Income Tax Reform in Venezuela: Thirty Years after the Shoup Mission", pp.67-85 in: Lorraine Eden, editor, *Retrospectives on Public Finance*, Durham, NC: Duke University Press.

McLure, Charles E., Jr. (1999), "Tax Holidays and Investment Incentives: A Comparative Analysis", *Bulletin for International Fiscal Documentation*, Vol. 53(8-9), pp. 326-39.

McLure, Charles E., Jr. (2001), "Globalization, Tax Rules and National Sovereignty", *Bulletin for International Fiscal Documentation*, Vol. 55(8), pp. 328-41.

McLure, Charles E., Jr. (2002), "Replacing Separate Entity Accounting and the Arm's Length Standard with Formulary Apportionment", *Bulletin for International Fiscal Documentation*, Vol. 56(12), pp. 586-99.

McLure, Charles E., Jr. (2003), "Taxation of Electronic Commerce in Developing Countries", pp. 283-323 in: James Robert Alm and Jorge Martinez-Vazquez, editors, *Public Finance in Developing and Transition Countries: Essays in Honor of Richard Bird*, Cheltenham, UK: Edward Elgar.

McLure, Charles E., Jr., "Will the OECD Initiative on Harmful Tax Competition Help Developing and Transition Countries?", *Bulletin for International Fiscal Documentation*, Vol. 59(3), pp. 90-98.

McLure, Charles E., Jr., Jack Mutti, Victor Thuronyi, and George R. Zodrow (1990), *The Taxation of Income from Business and Capital in Colombia*, Durham, NC: Duke University Press.

Mintz, Jack (2004), "Conduit Entities: Implications of Indirect Tax-Efficient Financing Structures for Real Investment", *International Tax and Public Finance*, Vol. 11(4).

Mitchell, Daniel J. (2004), "The Economics of Tax Competition: Harmonization vs. Liberalization", chapter 2 in: Marc Miles, *et al.*, editors, *2004 Index of Economic Freedom*, Washington: Heritage Foundation.

Mo, Phyllis Lai Lan (2003), *Tax Avoidance and Anti-avoidance Measures in Major Developing Economies*, Westport, Conn.: Praeger.

Musgrave, Richard A. and Malcolm Gillis (1971), *Fiscal Reform for Colombia: the Final Report and Staff Papers of the Colombian Commission on Tax Reform*, Cambridge, MA: Harvard University International Tax Program.

Newlon, T. Scott (2000), "Transfer Pricing and Income Shifting in Integrating Economies", pp.214-42 in: Sijbren Cnossen, editor, *Taxing Capital Income in the European Union: Issues and Options for Reform*, Oxford: Oxford University Press.

O'Connor, Walter (1997), "International Transfer Pricing", chapter 38 in: Frederick D. S Choi, editor, *International Accounting and Finance Handbook*, 2nd edition, New York: John Wiley and Sons.

OECD (1987), *International Tax Avoidance and Evasion: Four Related Studies,* Paris: OECD.

OECD (1995, as updated), *Transfer Pricing Guidelines*, Paris: OECD.

OECD (1996), *Controlled Foreign Company Legislation*, Paris: OECD.

OECD, Committee on Fiscal Affairs (1998), *Harmful Tax Competition: An Emerging Global Issue*, Paris: OECD.

OECD, Committee on Fiscal Affairs (2000a), Towards Global Tax Co-operation: Progress in Identifying and Eliminating Harmful Tax Practices, Retrieved December 29, 2004 from http://www.oecd.org/dataoecd/9/61/2090192.pdf?channelId=33745&homeChannelId=34897&fileTitle=2000+Report%3A+Towards+Global+Tax+Co-operation%3A+Progress+in+Identifying+and+Eliminating+Harmful+Tax+P+.

OECD, Committee on Fiscal Affairs (2000b), Improving Access to Bank Information for Tax Purposes, Retrieved from http://www.oecd.org/dataoecd/3/7/2497487.pdf.

OECD, Committee on Fiscal Affairs, (2000c), Framework for A Collective Memorandum of Understanding on Eliminating Harmful Tax Practices, Retrieved November 4, 2004, from http://www1.oecd.org/media/MOUrev20novR1.pdf.

OECD (2001a), The OECD's Project on Harmful Tax Practices: the 2001 Progress Report, Retrieved December 29, 2004, from http://www.oecd.org/dataoecd/60/5/2664450.pdf.

OECD (2001b), *Taxation and Electronic Commerce: Implementing the Ottawa Framework Conditions,* Paris: OECD.

OECD (2002), Agreement on Exchange of Information on Tax Matters, Retrieved from http://WWW.OECD.ORG/dataoecd/15/43/2082215.pdf?channelId=33767&homeChannelId=34897&fileTitle=Agreement+on+Exchange+of+Information+on+Tax+Matters.

OECD (2003a), *Model Tax Convention on Income and on Capital*, Paris: OECD.

OECD (2003b), Improving Access to Bank Information for Tax Purposes: The 2003 Progress Report, Retrieved from http://WWW.OECD.ORG/dataoecd/5/0/14943184.pdf?channelId=33767&homeChannelId=34897&fileTitle=Improving+Access+to+Bank+Information+for+Tax+Purposes+-+The+2003+Progress+Report.

OECD (2004a), The OECD's Project on Harmful Tax Practices: the 2004 Progress Report, Retrieved December 29, 2004, from http://WWW.OECD.ORG/dataoecd/60/33/30901115.pdf?channelId=33745&homeChannelId=34897&fileTitle=The+2004+Progress+Report%3A+The+OECD%27s+Project+on+Harmful+Tax+Practices.

OECD (2004b), Changes to the Model Tax Convention, Approved by the Committee on Fiscal Affairs on 1 June 2004, Retrieved from http://www.oecd.org/dataoecd/28/4/33614065.pdf.

OECD (2004c), A Process for Achieving a Global Level Playing Field, Retrieved from http://WWW.OECD.ORG/dataoecd/13/0/31967501.pdf.

Oldman, Oliver, H. David Rosenbloom, and Joan Youngman (1991), "International Aspects of Revisions to the Jamaican Company Tax", pp. 385-413 in: *The Jamaican Tax Reform*, Cambridge, Mass.: Lincoln Institute of Land Policy.

Oxfam (2000), *Tax Havens: Releasing the Hidden Billions for Poverty Eradication.*

Pagan, Jill C. and J. Scott Wilkie (1993), *Transfer Pricing Strategy in a Global Economy*, Amsterdam: IBFD Publications.

Peroni, Robert J. (2001), "The Proper Approach for Taxing the Income of Foreign Controlled Corporations", *Brooklyn Journal of International Law*, Vol. 26(4), pp. 1579-93.

Powell, Colin (2002), "The Five Essential Issues Facing Offshore Financial Centres", pp. 221-32 in: Rajiv Biswas, editor, *International Tax Competition: Globalisation and Fiscal Sovereignty*, London: Commonwealth Secretariat.

Queiroli, Gianluca (2003), "A Comparison of Italian and U.S. CFC Legislation", *Tax Notes International*, Vol. 30, pp. 1265-77.

Razin, Assaf and Efraim Sadka (1991), "International Tax Competition and Gains form Tax Harmonization", *Economic Letters*, Vol. 37(August), pp. 69-76.

Report of the Technical Committee on Business Taxation (1997), Ottawa.

Ring, Diane M. (2000), "On the Frontier of Procedural Innovation: Advance Pricing Agreements and the Struggle to Allocate Income for Cross Border Taxation", *Michigan Journal of International Law*, Vol. 21(winter), pp. 143-234.

Ring, Diane M. (2002), "One Nation Among Many: Policy Implications of Cross-Border Tax Arbitrage", *Boston College Law Review*, Vol. 44(December), pp. 79-175.

Rosenbloom, H. David (2000), "Arbitrage and Transfer Pricing", Chapter 35 in: *Report of Proceedings of the First World Tax Conference: Taxes without Borders, 2000 World Tax Conference Report*, Toronto: Canadian Tax Foundation.

Rosenbloom, H. David (2001), "From the Bottom Up: Taxing the Income of Foreign Controlled Corporations", *Brooklyn Journal of International Law*, Vol. 26(4), pp.1525-54.

Sandler, Daniel (1998), *Tax Treaties and Controlled Foreign Company Legislation: Pushing the Boundaries*, 2nd edition, The Hague: Kluwer Law International.

Schindler, Geunter and David Henderson (1985), "Intercorporate Transfer Pricing: 1985 Survey of Section 482 Audits", *Tax Notes*, Vol. 29, pp. 1171-77.

Scholes, Myron S., Mark A. Wolfson, Merle M. Erickson, Edward L. Maydew, and Terry J. Shevlin (2002), *Taxes and Business Strategy: a Planning Approach*, 2nd edition, Prentice Hall.

Scoon, Iain and Sasha Carter (2003), "News Analysis: Tax Directive: Saved at Last?", *Tax Notes International*, Vol. 30, pp. 1179-84.

Scott, Cordia (2002), "White House Signals Lack of Support for EU Savings Tax Directive", *Tax Notes International*, Vol. 28, pp. 421-22.

Shah, Anwar, (ed.) (1995), *Fiscal Incentives for Investment and Innovation*, New York: Oxford University Press for the World Bank.

Sharp, William M., Sr., William T. Harrison, III, Rachel A. Lunsford, and Scott A. Harty (2002), "U.S. Tax Information Exchange Agreements: a Comparative Analysis, *Tax Notes International*, Vol. 28, pp. 193-206.

Sheppard, Lee A. (2001), "It's the Bank Secrecy, Stupid", *Tax Notes International*, Vol. 22, pp. 2018-24.

Sheppard, Lee A. (2004), "News Analysis: Preventing Corporate Inversions, Part 4: Limitation on Benefits", *Tax Notes International*, Vol. 36, pp. 387-402.

Shoup, Carl S., John F. Die, Lyle C. Fitch, Donald MacDougall, Oliver S. Oldman, and Stanley S. Surrey (1959), *The Fiscal System of Venezuela*, Baltimore: Johns Hopkins Press.

Shoup, Carl S. (1985), "International Arbitration of Transfer pricing Disputes under Income Taxation", pp. 291-315 in: Alan M. Rugman and Lorraine Eden, *Multinationals and Transfer Pricing*, London: Croom Helm.

Slemrod, Joel. (1995), "Tax Policy toward Foreign Direct Investment in Developing Countries in Light of Recent International Tax Changes", pp.289-307 in: Anwar Shah, editor, *Fiscal Incentives for Investment and Innovation*, New York: Oxford University Press for the World Bank.

Slitor, Richard (1971), "Reform of the Business Tax Structure: Analysis of Problems and Alternative Remedial Proposals", pp.463-529 in: Richard A. Musgrave and Malcolm Gillis, *Fiscal Reform for Colombia: the Final Report and Staff Papers of the Colombian Commission on Tax Reform*, Cambridge, MA: Harvard University International Tax Program.

Steines, John P. (2001), "Whether, When, and How to Tax the Profits of Controlled Foreign Corporations", *Brooklyn Journal of International Law*, Vol. 26(4), pp. 1596-1609.

Sullivan, Martin A. (2004a), "Economic Analysis: U.S. Multinationals Move More Profits to Tax Havens", *Tax Notes*, Vol. 102, pp. 690-93.

Sullivan, Martin A. (2004b), "U.S. Citizens Hide Hundreds of Billions in Cayman Accounts", *Tax Notes International*, Vol. 31, pp. 898-906.

Sullivan, Martin A. (2004c), "Economic Analysis: Data Show U.S. Companies Shifting Profits to Tax Havens", *Tax Notes International*, Vol. 35.

Surrey, Stanley S. (1978), "Reflections on the Allocation of Income and Expenses among National Tax Jurisdictions", *Law and Policy in International Business*, Vol. 10, pp. 409-60.

Suss, Esther C., Oral H. Williams, and Chandima Mendis (2002), Caribbean Offshore Financial Centers: Past, Present, and Possibilities for the Future, International Monetary Fund Working Paper No. WP/02/88, Retrieved from http://www.imf.org/external/pubs/ft/wp/2002/wp0288.pdf.

Tanzi, Vito (1995), *Taxation in an Integrating World*, Washington: Brookings Institution.

Tanzi, Vito (1999), "Is There aa Need for a World Tax Organization?", pp. 173-186 in: Assaf Razin and Efraim Sadka, editors, *The Economics of Globalization : Policy Perspectives from Public Economics*, Cambridge: Cambridge University Press.

Taylor, Milton C. and Raymond L. Richman (1965), *Fiscal Survey of Colombia*, Baltimore: Johns Hopkins Press.

Thirsk, Wayne (ed.) (1997), *Tax Reform in Developing Countries*, Washington: World Bank.

Thuronyi, Victor (2001), "Taxation of New Financial Instruments", *Tax Notes International*, Vol. 24, pp. 261-73.

Thuronyi, Victor (2003), *Comparative Tax Law*, Deventer, The Netherlands: Kluwer.

Turner, Robert (1996), *Study of Transfer Pricing, Working paper 96-10*, Ottawa, Canada: Technical Committee on Business Taxation.

United Nations Conference on Trade and Development (1999), *Transfer Pricing*, New York.

United Nations (2001), Report of the High-level Panel on Financing for Development, New York: UN, Retrieved from http://www.un.org/reports/financing/.

US Department of the Treasury (2000), The Deferral of Income Earned Through U.S. Controlled Foreign Corporations: a Policy Study, Retrieved from http://www.ustreas.gov/offices/tax-policy/library/subpartf.pdf.

US Department of the Treasury (2001), Press Release May 10.

US Department of the Treasury (2002), Corporate Inversion Transactions: Tax Policy Implications, Retrieved from www.treas.gov/press/releases/docs/inversion.pdf.

Vann, Richard J. (1998), "International Aspects of Income Tax", pp.718-810 in: Victor Thuronyi, editor, *Tax Law and Drafting*, Vol. 2 (Washington: IMF), pp. 718-810.

Vanistendael, Frans (1996), "Legal Framework for Taxation", pp.15-70 in: Victor Thuronyi, editor, *Tax Law and Drafting*, Vol. 1, Washington: IMF.

Weiner, Joann M. (2003), "OECD Forum on Harmful Tax Practices Marks Fifth Year", *Tax Notes International*, Vol. 31, pp. 233-38.

Whalley, John (1990), "Recent Tax Changes in Canada: Policy Responses to Global and Domestic Pressures", pp.73-91 in: Michael J. Boskin, and Charles E. McLure, Jr., editors, *World Tax Reform: Case Studies of Developed and Developing Countries*, San Francisco: International Center for Economic Growth.

Zagaris, Bruce (2003), "Increasing Cooperation of International Tax Enforcement and Anti-Money-Laundering Enforcement", *Tax Notes International*, Vol. 32, pp. 649-63.

Zagaris, Bruce (2004), "International Tax Enforcement Continues to Increase", *Tax Notes International*, Vol. 35, pp. 759-72.

Zee, Howell H., Janet G. Stotsky and Eduardo Ley (2002), "Tax Incentives for Business Investment: A Primer for Policy Makers in Developing Countries", *World Development*, Vol. 30 (September), pp. 1497-1516.

Appendix

SELECTED TAX REFORM MISSIONS AND TRANSFER PRICING

Since transfer pricing seems to be a potentially important source of revenue cracks in DTCs, it is instructive – or at least interesting – to look back to see what some of the major reports and surveys on tax reform in developing countries have had to say about transfer pricing.

Venezuela: Shoup report. The Shoup mission to Venezuela, in 1958-59, noting that "only those costs or expenditures incurred within the country are deductible," suggested. "In principle, deduction should be allowed for any expense ... which is connected with and properly allocable to income taxable in Venezuela." The report's response to "the administrative problem that is posed by expenses incurred abroad by a business with branches or activities in both Venezuela and other countries," was to propose "the taxpayer's proving both the expense and its allocation in accordance with rules established by the Tax Administration." It continued, in a sentence that seems hopelessly naive by today's standards, "One requirement might appropriately be that the claim for deduction be accompanied by the statement of a certified public accounting firm that the expense ... is connected with and properly allocable to Venezuelan activity under standard ac counting principles, together with an explanation of the method of allocation followed." (Shoup, *et al.*, 1959, pp. 155-156) The report subsequently (p. 173) discussed the need for the tax administration to scrutinize transactions between taxpayers controlled by the same interests to prevent misallocation of income between them and, if necessary, compute the income of each to on the basis of a "fair price." It is not clear whether this discussion is intended to pertain to international transactions, or only domestic ones.

Colombia: Taylor and Musgrave reports. The Taylor mission to Venezuela in the early 1960s expressed the same concern that the expenditures on services rendered abroad were not deductible and reached similar policy conclusions, including reliance on "customary accounting principles" and detailed proof that the claimed deductions are allocable to Colombian income. (Taylor and Richman, 1965, p. 82) A few years later the Musgrave mission reached roughly the same conclusions. (Musgrave, 1971, p. 87; Slitor, 1971, p. 508)

Jamaica, Bahl report. One of the staff papers prepared for the Bahl mission to Jamaica identifies the transfer pricing problem: "An effective review of returns filed by members of an affiliated group requires auditors to verify that prices, compensation, and other aspects of intercorporate transfers are computed on an arm's length basis .... [U]nless transfer prices come under careful administrative scrutiny, their manipulation permits the shift of income to group members taxed at the lowest rates."[1] Although there are no detailed suggestions for the standard to be used in appraising transfer prices, the reference to the provisions of the US-Jamaica tax treaty dealing with associated enterprises and mutual adjustment procedures is instructive.

Comparison. The difference in concerns expressed in the Shoup, Taylor, and Musgrave reports and those expressed in the Bahl report is remarkable. Whereas the first three reports rightly worried that deductions were not being allowed for expenses incurred abroad and expressed faith in outside auditors to certify the appropriateness of transfer prices, the Bahl report, written several decades later, identified clearly the need for "careful administrative scrutiny" of transfer prices.

Comment. It appears that most early tax reform studies in developing countries have had relatively little to say about transfer pricing.[2] It is easy to see why this would be true. First, at the time the earliest studies were done, direct foreign investment and intracorporate trade, especially in intangibles, were nowhere near as important as now. Second, transfer pricing may have been a distinctly second (or third) order problem, because there were "other fish to fry," namely undesirable structural elements in need of fundamental reform. This would certainly seem to be the case in Venezuela more than 40 years ago and in Colombia 35 to 40 years ago. Third, techniques of tax avoidance and evasion were not as well developed or as fully exploited as now.[3] Fourth, it is likely that some of those who undertook tax reform missions, often economists trained in a closed-economy tradition, simply failed to realize the potential importance of transfer pricing.[4] Finally, it should be noted that by the time the Soviet Union dissolved these conditions were no longer true. Considerable attention has been devoted to transfer pricing, especially in resource-rich members of the former Soviet Union.

Note

1. Oldman, Rosenbloom, and Youngman (1991, p. 393). The omitted words are:

> Otherwise, corporations could report, or "characterize," intragroup transactions in whatever manner provided the maximum tax benefit. Payments could be arbitrarily characterized as dividends, interest, royalties, or compensation, depending upon which was subject to the most beneficial source rules, avoided withholding taxes, or permitted a deduction for the payor.

> Unlike the other three reports reviewed here, the Bahl Report also considered th need for thin capitalization rules, see Oldman, Rosenbloom, and Youngman (1991, pp. 393-4)

2. This comment seems also to apply to the papers in Gillis (1989), Boskin and McLure (1990), Eden (1991), Thirsk (1997), and Martinez-Vazquez and Alm (2003).
3. There is another reason for the failure to consider transfer pricing in McLure *et al.* (1990). The explicit assignment was relatively narrow: to consider the need for inflation adjustment in the measurement of capital income in Colombia.
4. Thus, in McLure (1991, p. 73), I observed, "[T]he Shoup mission generally appears to have taken the tax system at face value, without stressing that 'things ain't what they seem' once the lawyers and accountants finish their work. Though the Shoup mission mentioned the difficulties of transfer prices, it did not stress this problem...."

Chapter 5

TAXATION AND FDI IN DEVELOPED AND DEVELOPING COUNTRIES

TIMOTHY GOODSPEED
Hunter College and CUNY Graduate Center

1. INTRODUCTION

From 1980 to 2000, foreign direct investment (FDI) increased substantially in the world. According to statistics from UNCTAD, the world inward stock of FDI was \$0.7 trillion in 1980, \$1.95 trillion in 1990, and \$6.15 trillion in 2000. Corresponding figures for the world outward stock of FDI are \$0.56, \$1.76, and \$5.99 trillion, respectively. Developed countries are the generators of the vast majority of FDI outflows (86% of the world stock in 2000), and the receivers of the vast majority of inflows (65% of the world stock in 2000). However, the shares of developing countries, whose FDI inflows come mainly from developed countries, are increasing. The inward FDI stock of developing countries has risen from 28% of the world stock in 1990 to 33% in 2000, while their share of the world outward stock has risen from 7% to 13% during this period. Some of this increase could be due to an increased use of developing countries as conduits for evasion of taxes.[1]

Table 1 shows that along with an increase in the world share of FDI stock, developing countries have seen a greater real per-capita GDP growth rate than developed countries from 1990 to 2000, in line with economic theory which predicts that capital accumulation is important for growth. The real per-capita GDP growth rate in developing countries was 2.9% from 1990 to 2001, while that for developed countries was 1.7%. However, in spite of their increasing share of FDI and higher real per-capita growth rate, developing countries' corporate tax revenues have fallen as a share of GDP. Keen and Simone (2004) report that developing country corporate tax revenues as a percent of GDP fell from 2.9% in 1992 to 2.3% in 2001. This was partly due to a reduction in statutory tax rates in developing as well as developed countries. Yet developed countries were able to increase their corporate tax revenue as a percent of GDP from 1.9% in 1992 to 2.5% in 2001.

Table 1. Changes in Shares of World FDI Stock, GDP, and Corporate Tax Revenue in Developed and Developing Countries

	Developing Countries	Developed Countries
% change in inwards share of world FDI stock (1990-2000)	+16.9	-9.4
% change in outward share of world FDI stock (1990-2000)	+80.7	-6.9
% change in real per-capita GDP (1990-2001)	+2.9	+1.7
% change in corporate tax revenues as % of GDP (1992-2001)	-20.1	+31.6

Source: UNCTAD (2004) and Keen and Simone (2004).

In this paper, I discuss tax incentives for FDI from both developing and developed country perspectives. I do this by first providing an overview of FDI, noting certain differences between developed and developing countries, differences in the composition of FDI within a country, and differences in the geographic origin of inward FDI. Differences in characteristics such as the industrial and source country mix of FDI will have important impacts on multinational tax incentives due to various aspects of countries' international tax policies. I discuss the role of different tax systems, the computation of foreign tax credits, tax holidays and tax sparing, sector-specific incentives, transfer pricing, and third country conduits, withholding taxes, and tax treaties and exchange of information agreements. I conclude by summarizing the challenges that lie ahead.

2. FDI IN DEVELOPED AND DEVELOPING COUNTRIES

Table 2 lists the 10 largest developing and developed host economies for FDI for 2001, and their inward FDI flows between 1997 and 2001. Among developing economies, China, Mexico, and Brazil had the largest inward flows, while among developed countries, the US, the UK, France, and Belgium and Luxembourg were the largest recipients of FDI flows. In assessing the relationship between taxation and FDI in these diverse countries, it is important to keep in mind several factors concerning FDI.

Table 2. Top Ten Foreign Direct Investment Host Economies in 2001 (Millions of dollars)

Developed Countries	**1997**	**1998**	**1999**	**2000**	**2001**
United Sates	103,398	174,434	283,376	300,912	124,435
United Kingdom	33,229	74,324	87,973	116,552	53,799
France	23,174	30,984	47,070	42,930	52,623
Belgium and Luxemburg	11,998	22,691	133,059	245,561	50,996
Netherlands	11,132	36,964	41,289	52,453	50,471
Germany	12,244	24,593	54,754	195,122	31,833
Canada	11,527	22,809	24,435	66,617	27,465
Spain	7,697	11,797	15,758	37,523	21,781
Italy	3,700	2,635	6,911	13,377	14,873
Sweden	10,968	19,564	60,850	23,367	12,734
Developing Countries					
China	44,237	43,751	40,319	40,772	46,846
Mexico	14,044	11,933	12,534	14,706	24,731
Hong Kong, China	11,368	14,770	24,596	61,938	22,834
Brazil	18,993	28,856	28,578	32,779	22,457
Bermuda	2,928	5,399	9,470	10,980	9,859
Poland	4,908	6,365	7,270	9,342	8,830
Singapore	10,746	6,389	11,803	5,407	8,609
South Africa	3,817	561	1,502	888	6,653
Chile	5,219	4,638	9,221	3,674	5,508
Czech Republic	1,300	3,718	6,324	4,986	4,916

Source: UNCTAD World Investment Report (2002).

First, FDI in the service sector, and particularly in finance, has increased at a greater rate than FDI in manufacturing. According to the World Bank (2003), the world stock of inward FDI increased at an annual rate of 12.2 percent in manufacturing and 13.8 percent in services between 1988 and 1999. In developing countries, the difference in the annual increase in the composition of the inward stock of FDI was even more marked: a 19.6 annual growth rate in manufacturing versus a 28.2 percent annual growth rate in services. The potentially important role of the financial sector is evident in the data for Belgium and Luxembourg in Table 2. While obviously small countries, in 2000 Belgium and Luxembourg overtook Germany and came close to overtaking the US in total FDI inflows.2

Second, the composition of FDI can differ significantly from country to country, sometimes even within regions. Brazil, for instance, has seen greater inflows in the tertiary (service) sector than the secondary (manufacturing) sector in every year from 1996 to 2002. Mexico, while having significant inflows in the tertiary sector, had higher inflows in manufacturing in every year from 1994 to 2000.

Third, FDI inflows are geographically diverse both across host countries and within a given host country. Hence, host countries need to keep in mind different home country tax systems when evaluating the effects of tax policy. For instance, the bulk of FDI inflows into Mexico come from the United States, which has a worldwide tax system. While the US is also a significant provider of FDI in Brazil, a large part of FDI inflows in Brazil have come from Western European countries, which tend to have tax systems that are more territorial than the US. Moreover, the geographic origin of flows into Brazil have changed significantly during the 1990's, with Spain, France, and the Netherlands currently the largest investors from Western Europe.

Fourth, developing countries are usually characterized by greater FDI inflows than outflows, while developed economies' inflows and outflows tend to be closer, with FDI outward stocks often greater than inward stocks. For instance, during the period 1985-1995, developed economies' inflows average \$127.5 billion annually, while annual outflows averaged \$181.7 billion. During this same period, developing economies' inflows averaged \$50.1 billion annually and outflows averaged \$21.5 billion. In 2000, China's inflows were \$40.8 billion while outflows were only \$0.9 billion. In some sense, then, the challenges facing developing and developed economies are different.

Fifth, it is important to recognize at the outset that taxes are only one of many important factors in attracting FDI. A number of studies have shown that an attractive investment climate including factors such as the rule of law and low levels of corruption, good infrastructure, agglomeration economies, as well as geographic proximity, are important factors for attracting capital. Moreover, the reputation of a country is important. Are a country's policies likely to be time consistent – that is, will tax or other incentives granted today be honored in the future, or may a government renege on future promises, perhaps even confiscating a company's assets? Country risk is important and may be endogenously determined by government policies (Eaton and Gersovitz, 1981).[3]

Finally, it should be noted that FDI often has an uneven impact within a country. For instance, NAFTA is generally thought to have impacted Mexico unevenly, increasing incomes more along the wealthier northern border than in the poorer southern states. This can have important political ramifications as those that lose or do not gain as much will tend to be opposed to policies that might benefit the country as a whole.

3. INCENTIVES USED TO ATTRACT FDI IN DEVELOPING AND DEVELOPED COUNTRIES

Developing and developed countries both use certain incentives to try to attract FDI, but the types and frequency of incentives used differs somewhat. Table 3 lists some of the incentives used in 71 developing versus 20 OECD countries. Tax exemption or tax holidays for FDI are used by 55% of developing countries but only 20% of OECD countries. Lower tax rates for FDI are used by 45% of developing countries but only 5% of OECD countries. The types of incentives used more frequently by OECD countries are reduced local taxes and subsidized loans.

Table 3. Types of FDI Incentives in OECD and Developing Countries

FDI Incentive	**% OECD Countries**	**% Developing Countries**
Tax exemption/ holiday	20	55
Lower tax rate	5	45
Reduction in local, municipal taxes/duties	30	18
Subsidized loans	45	18

Source: World Bank (2003) from Bora (2002).

Why do these differences exist? Moran (1998) suggests that developing countries do not have the resources to be able to compete with the large subsidies offered by developed countries, and resort instead to tax holidays and the like. The fact that reduced local taxes is a common subsidy among many OECD countries might be traced to cooperation among national but not sub-national governments. Cooperation typically takes place at the national level and some national governments, particularly the U.S., have little control over subsidies of sub-national governments. More generally, internal political struggles as well as different degrees of power in the world capital market might help explain different tax structures and hence the different incentives adopted in developing and developed countries.

Perhaps more troubling are the deleterious effects developing country incentives can have on their own economies, as well as the negative externalities that can be created for the allocation of world capital. As to the former, Shah (1995) indicates that the use of tax incentives has led to distorted investment decisions in many developing countries because of the lack of any incentive for start-ups that have losses and because of the encouragement of relatively capital intensive production methods. Zee,

Stotsky, and Ley (2002) also emphasize the adverse domestic consequences inefficient tax incentives can have on the economies of developing countries.

4. INVESTMENT INCENTIVES UNDER DIFFERENT SYSTEMS OF INTERNATIONAL TAXATION[4]

The first fact to recognize when thinking about taxation of FDI is that there are generally two distinct types of tax systems used by countries: territorial and worldwide tax systems. The distinction between the income taxed under these two systems is similar to the distinction between gross domestic product (GDP) and gross national product (GNP). Under territorial taxation, and similar to the definition of GDP, a country taxes all income generated within that country whether the taxed entity is foreign or domestic. In the extreme, all income generated outside of the borders of the country is not taxed, as it is deemed to be taxable where it is generated. In contrast, a worldwide system of taxation in principal taxes the income of all residents no matter whether it is generated at home or abroad, similar to the definition of GNP.

Countries that practice worldwide taxation often have a foreign tax credit system to relieve double taxation of foreign earned income. A credit is given for foreign taxes paid, but the credit is usually limited to the tax that would have been paid had the income been earned in the home country. This creates two types of resident taxpaycrs; those that receive full credit for foreign taxes paid and those that do not. The latter group is said to be in "excess credit"; if full credit is received the taxpayer is said to be in "deficit of credit" or "excess limitation."

In practice, most countries do not rely exclusively on the extremes described above. In the first place, most countries have taxes at source on interest, dividends, and royalties, often at different rates. These are called withholding taxes. For instance, an Italian company issuing dividends to its British parent might owe a tax to Italy that would be withheld by the Italian government. The main theoretical rationale for these taxes is to insure that income does not completely escape taxation somewhere. Such tax avoidance is not difficult, particularly if a third country is involved in the transshipment of funds. Generally, these taxes are reduced or eliminated through bilateral treaties, agreements that evolved from recommendations of the League of Nations in 1927. Even if they are not, countries with a foreign tax credit typically grant credit for these taxes subject to the same limitation mentioned above.

Countries practicing worldwide taxation commonly deviate from such a system in many other ways as well. For instance, a U.S. corporation can set up an overseas operation as a controlled foreign corporation (CFC), which is incorporated in the foreign country and for which over 50% of stock is owned by U.S. shareholders. Except for certain types of income taxed currently under sub-part F, the income of a CFC is only subject to U.S. tax when it is repatriated to the U.S. Since a CFC can delay subjecting its income to U.S. tax by not repatriating income, this feature of U.S. international tax law is referred to as "deferral," a common practice among worldwide taxation countries. Yet, at least for the time that income tax is deferred, this makes the U.S. tax system much like a territorial tax system. Nevertheless, countries tend to be classified somewhat loosely as "territorial" or "worldwide" taxation countries.

Whether the U.S. tax system is a truly worldwide tax system is also complicated by other features. For instance, deferral was weakened by the U.S. Revenue Act of 1962 which added Subpart F to the tax code. Subpart F subjects certain types of unrepatriated income of CFCs to U.S. tax currently, as if it had been repatriated as a dividend. Another complication of the U.S. worldwide tax system is that foreign operations can be set up as a branch, which is not separately incorporated. The income (or loss) of a foreign branch is combined with domestic income and taxed currently. The companies that tend to set up foreign operations as branches are concentrated in the banking and petroleum industries. (Goodspeed and Frisch, 1989)

On the other side of the coin, Germany is often thought of as a territorial country. As pointed out in Altshuler and Grubert (2001), Germany actually has a worldwide tax system with foreign tax credits. What distinguishes Germany is that dividend payments from foreign affiliates located in a country that has a tax treaty with Germany are exempt from German tax, effectively creating a territorial system for countries with which Germany has a tax treaty.

Perhaps surprisingly, there is not agreement on the theoretical incentive effects of taxes on FDI coming from tax credit countries. One point of view, laid out by Horst (1977), is that incentives are different for excess credit and deficit of credit firms. The excess credit firm faces the tax rate of the country in which it invests on the margin; the deficit of credit firm faces the tax rate of the home country no matter where it invests. In contrast, Hartman (1985) argues that deferral combined with the fact that mature firms finance investment from retained earnings that are already abroad implies that the foreign tax credit position of the multinational is irrelevant for investment decisions. In Hartman=s view, deferral does not help firms that invest funds that are already abroad and must eventually be repatriated; the return on those funds must eventually absorb the home country tax. Hence, the investment rule for excess-credit and deficit of credit firms is the same: invest abroad if the after-foreign-tax return is higher than the after-domestic-tax return. The Hartman result depends on an unchanging home tax rate among other things. (Altshuler and Fulghieri,1994) Moreover, if investment from tax-credit countries comes mostly from excess credit multinationals, the magnitude of any difference in investment incentives would be small since under either view most foreign earnings would face the host country tax rate on the margin. Furthermore, any difference in investment incentives resulting from territorial versus worldwide would likewise be small in magnitude. This has also been the conclusion of a number of studies (e.g. Altshuler and Grubert, 2001 and Grubert, 2001) examining the hypothetical move towards a territorial system of taxation being contemplated by the U.S.[5]

The empirical evidence on whether tax differences influence the location of FDI is reviewed by Hines (1997), who suggests that taxes have an important impact. Studies looking at the impact of differences in tax systems is mixed, however, possibly due to the fact that any difference that tax systems (worldwide versus territorial) have on FDI arises from firms that are in an excess limitation position under the worldwide system. Firms that are in an excess credit position face the host tax rate on the margin just as under the territorial system. Thus, one might expect it to be difficult to discern any difference. One paper that does find a large effect of territorial versus worldwide tax systems is Hines (1996) who examines locational patterns of inward FDI into the US states that have differing tax rates. One reason that Hines is able to discern some difference between home country tax systems is that he examines a single host country. However, his results probably should not be extended to host countries other than the US.

5. INCENTIVES AND THE COMPUTATION OF FOREIGN TAX CREDITS

One important difference in the computation of foreign tax credits is whether a per-country limitation is used. Some countries treat income earned in each foreign country separately in determining a multinational's foreign tax credit, while others determine the credit on a worldwide basis. Under the former method a per-country limitation on foreign tax credits is computed. Under the latter method, income and taxes from all countries are added to determine whether the limitation applies; thus, the taxpayer will be in excess credit if its (weighted) average foreign tax rate is greater than the home country tax rate.[6] A multinational may be able to reduce its home country tax liability because of the averaging of high and low taxed income, a fact that is important for investment incentives as well as income shifting (discussed later). Consider, for instance, a multinational with a large proportion of income coming from investments in high tax countries and a small proportion of income coming from investments in low tax foreign countries. The multinational will not obtain full credit for foreign taxes paid; that is, it will be in an excess credit position. This firm would then have an incentive (absent under a per-country limitation) to shift income from high tax to low tax foreign countries so that the average foreign tax rate falls.

This is not to say that a per-country limitation eliminates abuse possibilities. Since different types of investments are associated with different effective tax rates, a cause for concern under the per-country limitation is that income may be shifted between income or investment types. To combat this tendency, some countries force multinational companies to make separate credit calculations for particularly high- or low-taxed types of income, sometimes called "baskets" of income. Such categories can substantially increase the compliance costs for multinationals, however.[7]

6. TAX HOLIDAYS AND TAX SPARING AS INVESTMENT INCENTIVES

Many developing countries give multinationals "tax holidays" meaning that they pay no or little taxes for a certain number of years. Such tax breaks only provide incentives for multinationals to invest in the developing country if the multinationals home country taxes on a source basis. If the home country taxes tax on a worldwide basis, tax holidays provide no incentive to locate in the developing country since repatriated income of the multinational will be taxed at the home country rate. Recognizing this, some developed countries that tax on a worldwide basis allow their multinationals credit for such tax holidays; that is, they allow credit for taxes that have not actually been paid. This is often referred to as "tax sparing." Tax sparing provisions are generally written into tax treaties between the developed and developing country.

Although most countries grant tax sparing in treaties with many developing countries, the U.S. does not.[8] There is some evidence that tax sparing does influence the location of Japanese investment (Hines, 2001). Neither tax sparing nor tax holidays benefit start-up companies that have losses in the initial stages, however. And such innovative business ventures might be considered the real engine of economic growth. Moreover, tax sparing and tax holidays tend to encourage transfer pricing abuse. Even if one grants the argument that tax sparing and tax holidays can influence investment location, they may contribute little to growth while reducing host country corporate tax revenue.

7. SECTOR-SPECIFIC INCENTIVES: TAXATION OF FINANCIAL SERVICES

Certain sectors sometimes have a different tax treatment that creates differential incentives relative to other sectors. This sometimes results from elections made by firms in a particular industry (for instance the election to of US petroleum and banking multinational to organize subsidiaries as branches rather than CFCs), but also sometimes results from differential tax treatment of a particular sector by the government. Given the growing importance of FDI in the services sector, particularly in finance, it is useful to consider as an example the taxation of the financial services sector. Financial services are usually taxed somewhat differently than manufacturing companies for reasons that stem from the fact that interest income is a normal course of business in banking. Hence, certain law changes that might not have much effect on the manufacturing sector could have a substantial impact on the financial services sector.

One example of this has been investigated by Altshuler and Hubbard (2001) with respect to the U.S. multinational service sector. They note that Subpart F in the U.S. was greatly broadened by TRA86 to include current taxation of active financial service income. After the law change, a U.S. multinational that does not have excess foreign tax credits would face equal taxation among locations abroad on its financial service income (i.e. it would face the U.S. tax rate on the margin in all locations) and therefore would not respond to tax differences. Using a sample of financial subsidiaries of U.S. corporations, Altshuler and Hubbard find that the location of financial subsidiary assets among foreign countries was sensitive to differential foreign tax rates in 1984, but not in 1992 or 1994. They attribute this to the essential repeal of deferral for these companies after 1986. A host country that recognizes this change and whose FDI in the service sector comes primarily from the U.S. could take advantage of this by increasing its tax rate to the U.S. rate to raise revenue.

8. INCENTIVES TO SHIFT CORPORATE RESIDENCE

One way for a multinational to avoid taxes is to change its place of incorporation to a more tax-favored jurisdiction. This has been dubbed "inversion," and has been alleged to have been a factor in the Daimler-Chrysler merger.[9] US companies have recently come under fire for attempting such re-incorporations. Stanley Works, for instance, first announced it would change its residence to Bermuda, but later reversed its decision in the face of both political and shareholder objections. Interestingly, shareholders objected even thought the company argued that the motivation was to reduce taxes and thereby increase shareholder value. The U.S. objection obviously arose from the blatant avoidance of U.S. tax.

What determines the home country of a multinational corporation? This differs somewhat across countries, but is often triggered by where the parent is incorporated or by the place of the headquarters (regardless of incorporation) that is considered to be the place of management and control. The ability of multinational companies to "invert" is clearly an issue that will impact both home and host country tax revenues from FDI, particularly if a multinational ends up re-incorporating in a tax haven or using a tax haven as an intermediary to avoid taxes.

9. SHIFTING OF INCOME THROUGH TRANSFER PRICES[10]

Transfer prices are the prices attached to transactions that occur between the parent and subsidiary companies within a multinational, such as the sale by a subsidiary of an input that is used in the parent's production process or sale of a trademark by the parent to a subsidiary. Transfer prices are troublesome from a tax policy perspective because they can be used to evade taxes for either the territorial or the worldwide tax system. Abuses under the territorial system are perhaps the most obvious: taxes can be reduced by transferring profits out of the high-tax country and into the low-tax country. A purported advantage of the worldwide system is that this incentive disappears for a multinational that invests in a single foreign country with a tax rate lower than the home country. In this case, income derived from the foreign investment will be taxed at the home country tax rate and the incentive to shift income is eliminated. However, several complications of the tax systems of countries that use the worldwide system of taxation may induce multinationals to use transfer pricing to reduce taxes. For instance, since multinationals typically have investments in a variety of foreign countries, the way in which the credit is computed is important. As mentioned earlier, some countries aggregate income over all foreign countries in determining the limit. In addition, the use of "mixer" companies in countries that use a per-country limitation can also result in income averaging. For these countries, a multinational with a large proportion of income coming from investments in high tax countries and a small proportion of income coming from investments in low tax foreign countries will not obtain full credit for foreign taxes paid. Such a firm would then have an incentive to use transfer prices to shift income from high tax to low tax foreign countries and thereby obtain credit for all foreign taxes paid.

As transfer pricing can be used to evade taxes, governments have naturally developed a set of rules to try to minimize this potential source of tax evasion. The problem is to find an "objective" way of valuing tangible and intangible assets transferred across national boundaries by multinational corporations. The widely accepted international standard is that such transfers be assigned the prices that would have been charged if the transactions had occurred between independent entities. Such prices are referred to as "arm's length" prices - that a transaction between a parent and its subsidiary should be priced as if it had occurred between two unrelated parties in a competitive market. However, arm's length transfer prices are not always easy to calculate because comparable transactions by unrelated parties may not exist. This issue is pervasive for intangible assets because the value of most intangible asset arises from market power generated by the intangible.

When comparable transactions do not exist, the government often provides some guidance in the form of regulations or case law on the range of transfer prices that will be deemed acceptable. Such guidance may include a cost-plus calculation, reference to some industry average such as a rate of return on assets or a margin on sales, or attempts to adjust "inexact" comparables to obtain transfer prices. Profit-based methods (e.g. "comparable profits") as opposed to transactions methods tend to be the most controversial; some countries do not allow comparable profits methods. The U.S. Internal Revenue Service (IRS) has adopted an open approach on the methods used to obtain transfer prices. Multinational companies may now propose a method for determining transfer prices. The IRS examines the proposed method and determines whether or not the methodology is acceptable. If the methodology is acceptable, the IRS enters into an "advanced pricing agreement" (APA) with the multinational. The agreement allows the multinational to use the mutually agreed upon methodology to set transfer prices for the firm; the APA may involve the other countries impacted by the agreed transfer price. APAs are also possible in some other countries (e.g. Germany and The Netherlands).

Transfer pricing abuses are not easy to discover, however, as they are internal to the firm, and, as suggested in Grubert, Goodspeed, and Swenson (1993) there are several reasons other than transfer pricing that might explain lower than average rates of return for foreign-controlled companies. For instance, foreign-owned companies may at first experience a lower than average rate of return because of the start-up costs of a new business (or revaluation of the assets of new acquisitions), but one would expect this to change over time as the firms mature. In addition, unexpected changes in exchange rates can have a large effect on profits at any given time. Effective enforcement of transfer pricing rules requires effective tax administration.

10. THIRD COUNTRY CONDUITS, WITHHOLDING TAXES, TAX TREATIES, AND EXCHANGE OF INFORMATION

The presence of third countries that can be used for transshipment of funds to avoid taxes has been an issue for some time. Recent analyses of transshipment of interest payments through third country conduits – and the tax advantage of deducting such payments in high tax countries - include Mintz (2004) and Mintz and Smart (2004). The traditional focus of transshipment of funds has been the avoidance of withholding taxes, however. As mentioned previously, withholding taxes on interest, dividend, and royalty payments have been used to insure some tax payment, with bilateral tax treaties used to reduce such taxes when warranted. Withholding tax rates can vary widely, however, and this can create incentives to transship funds through a third, low withholding-tax country as the example of Giovannini (1989) clarifies.

Perhaps the most well-known abuse of third country conduits is the use of the Netherlands Antilles to avoid the U.S. withholding tax on interest income, repealed in 1984 in part because of avoidance through the Netherlands Antilles.[11] During the 1960's and 1970's, the U.S. had a withholding tax on interest, but also had a tax treaty with the Netherlands (that included the Netherlands Antilles) which reduced the withholding tax to zero. A typical arrangement was for a U.S. multinational to have a subsidiary in the Netherlands Antilles through which interest was funneled, avoiding the withholding tax.

A recent phenomenon in the U.S. has been the use of a "hybrid" branch of a U.S. controlled foreign corporation.[12] The term hybrid refers to the fact that the branch is recognized as part of the CFC (in a partnership) for U.S. tax purposes but as a separate corporation by the foreign country. If the branch is located in a low-tax country and the CFC makes a loan to the branch which uses the funds to generate passive income, it can reduce taxable income in the resident country of the CFC since it gets to deduct the interest payments. Furthermore, the passive income of the hybrid branch normally would be subject to Sub-part F rules and be taxable currently, but since the U.S. views the two entities as a single CFC, Subpart-F does not apply. Thirdly, the passive income could then be returned to the US parent without additional US tax if the multinational is in an excess credit position.

The use of this vehicle for avoiding U.S. taxes was made easier by a simplification of the way in which taxpayers qualified as partnerships or separate foreign corporations, the so-called "check-the-box" regulations. While useful for simplifying the choice between a partnership and a domestic corporation, the simplification had unforeseen consequences for US-owned foreign corporations. This simplification is widely seen as leading to a proliferation of hybrids.

Among developed countries, modifications to the OECD model tax treaty have largely circumvented the difficulties of accounting for the income of hybrid branches.[13] The commentary (paragraph 8ff) to Article 4 of the model tax treaty now contains language that indicates that the country of source should look at how an entity is treated in the country of residence. In the above example of a hybrid branch, for instance, the OECD model tax treaty now indicates that the country in which the CFC is located should look to how the US views the hybrid branch (rather than its internal law). This in effect would eliminate the hybrid nature of the entity since it would be viewed identically by both source and resident countries. In the above example, the country of residence of the CFC would view the hybrid branch as the U.S. would, as part of the CFC.

Third country conduits that are tax havens pose a serious problem for transactions involving developing countries, however. For instance, Owens (2004) indicates that more than 80% of FDI into China, India, and Russia goes through a tax haven. The OECD's tax competition initiative, clearly discussed in McLure (this volume), is an attempt to control such behavior, and has had some success, though Owens data also indicates that flows through banking centers (measured by foreign bank deposits of non-bank investors) have increased substantially since 1995. This reinforces the importance of understanding the incentives involved in the taxation of the financial services sector, a point made earlier. Moreover, transshipment via transfer prices is unlikely to be solved through the initiative alone because of the hidden nature of such practices. Information exchange agreements, which are meant to reveal otherwise secret information, seems the most promising route with respect to transfer pricing issues.

11. CONCLUSION: CHALLENGES THAT LIE AHEAD

General statements concerning the incentives and revenue resulting from taxation of FDI are difficult to make. This is due to interactions of different country tax systems and the diversity in the geographic origin of FDI across countries, differential taxation across sectors and the diversity of FDI across sectors for different countries, transshipment of funds through tax havens or other conduit countries, and the way that FDI changes over time independently of taxes. To start, host countries need to be aware of the types and origins of FDI, and their different tax treatments in the home countries of different multinationals to be able to design effective incentive systems. The use of third country conduits and changes over time in home country tax systems make the task even more difficult.

Developed countries may find the task of competing for world capital while maintaining corporate tax revenues feasible – some developed countries may even lead the way. But a developing country's lack of resources and expertise put it in a disadvantageous position vis-à-vis developed countries to compete using tax incentives. Even the tax holiday incentive commonly used by developing countries may just give up revenue without getting any additional investment in return to the extent that credit is given for taxes paid abroad, and a foreign tax credit computation that uses country averaging makes it quite difficult to discern the marginal impact of a tax holiday from any given country. Moreover, start-up ventures that generate losses, but are also the foundation of innovation, are disadvantaged relative to other business ventures when developing countries use tax holidays.

The challenges for developing and developed countries would thus seem to be different. Developing countries need foreign capital, but are in a "no-win" situation with respect to attracting FDI by using tax incentives. They seem likely to lose revenue without attracting additional FDI. Developing countries will probably do better by concentrating on improving investment fundamentals rather than using the tax system as the main incentive tool.

Developed countries, on the other hand, have an advantage in using tax incentives to attract FDI. However developed countries might do better by recognizing the benefits of cooperating in certain respects. The challenges for developed countries will likely come in recognizing the increasing need for cooperation in exchange of information to deal with the increasingly important financial sector, the difficult issue of controlling transfer pricing and money laundering, and the need to trace funds through third country conduits. Developed countries may find it in their interest to assist developing countries in monitoring and tax administration as developing countries do not have the expertise to fully monitor transactions. If they do, both developed and developing countries may gain revenue and experience the benefits of a more efficient allocation of capital.

Notes

1. See McLure (this volume).
2. See, for instance, Mintz (this volume) for rankings as a percent of GDP. Belgium-Luxembourg is ranked number one among developed countries.
3. Volatility of FDI, sometimes taken as a measure of country risk, is higher among developing than developed countries.
4. Parts of this section draw on Goodspeed and Witte (2000).
5. The timing of dividend repatriations might be affected, though, as emphasized in Desai, Foley, and Hines (2001).
6. The extent to which countries can be classified on the basis of whether their foreign tax credit systems are per-country or worldwide is sometimes questioned. Usually, the U.S., Japan, and Iceland would be classified as providing credits on a worldwide basis, while Canada, Germany, Greece, Ireland, Italy, the Netherlands, New Zealand, Norway, Portugal, Spain, Turkey, and the United Kingdom would be classified as using a per country limit in determining the foreign tax credit. However, as Ault (1997) notes, this division is somewhat misleading. In the U.K., for instance, the per-country credit limitation can be avoided by routing income through a nonresident holding company. The income going through this Amixer@ company is considered all from one source, and hence averaged and the per-country limitation avoided. Ault suggests that the use of such companies is common.
7. For example, the expansion of baskets under TRA86 has been criticized for unduly increasing the compliance costs of multinationals.
8. However, the U.S. has had a set of rules (contained in Section 936 of the U.S. Internal Revenue Code) that provide tax subsidies for corporations that locate in U.S. Possessions (the primary beneficiary being Puerto Rico), as analyzed in Grubert and Slemrod (1998?) for instance. This subsidy is being eliminated.
9. See Desai and Hines (2002) for an analysis of inversion in general.
10. This section draws on Goodspeed (2002).
11. Papke (2000) gives a good discussion of the history of the Netherlands Antilles case and estimates the impact of withholding tax on interest flows.
12. Hybrids are discussed in IRS notice 98-11, which is summarized in Tax Notes, January 26, 1998, p. 419, as well as in Sullivan (2004) and Altshuler and Grubert (2004).
13. The information in this paragraph is gleaned from discussions with Hugh Ault and Julian Alworth, and subsequent e-mail with Hugh Ault.

References

Altshuler, Rosanne and Fulghieri P. (1994), "Dynamic Effects of Foreign Tax Credits on Multinational Corporations", *The National Tax Journal*, pp.349-361.

Altshuler, and Grubert (2001), "Where will they go if we go Territorial? Dividend exemption and the location decisions of US multinational corporations", *National Tax Journal*, Vol. 54, pp. 787-809.

Altshuler, Rosanne and Harry Grubert (2004), "Taxpayer Responses to Competitive Tax Policies and Tax Policy Responses to Competitive Taxpayers: Recent Evidence", Draft.

Altshuler, Rosanne and R. Glenn Hubbard (2001), "The Effect of the Tax Reform Act of 1986 on the Location of Assets in Financial Service Firms", *Journal of Public Economics*,

Ault, Hugh J. (1997), *Comparative Income Taxation: A Structural Analysis*, Den Haag, The Netherlands: Kluwer Law International.

Bora, Bijit (2002), *Investment distortions and the international policy architecture, WTO Working Paper*, Geneva.

Desai, Mihir, C. Foley, and J. R. Hines (2001), "*Repatriation taxes and dividend distortions*", National Tax Journal, Vol. 54, pp. 829-851.

Desai, Mihir and JR Hines (2002), "*Expectations and Expatriations: Tracing the Causes and Consequences of Corporate Inversions*", National Tax Journal, Vol. (55), pp. 409-440.

Eaton, J. and M. Gersovitz (1981), "*Debt with Potential Repudiation: Theoretical and Empirical Analysis*", Review of Economic Studies, Vol. (48), pp. 289-309.

Giovannini, A. (1989), "*National Tax Systems vs. The European Capital Market*", Economic Policy 9.

Goodspeed, Timothy J. and Ann Witte (2000), "International Taxation", in: B. Bouckaert and G. De Geest, editors, *Encyclopedia of Law and Economics*, London: Edward Elgar.

Goodspeed, Timothy J. (2002), "Transfer Pricing", in: William Lazonick, editor, *IEBM Handbook of Economics*, London: Thomson Business Press.

Goodspeed, Timothy J. and Daniel J. Frisch (1989), *U.S. Tax Policy and the Overseas Activities of U.S. Multinational Corporations: A Quantitative Assessment, Mimeo.*

Grubert, Harry, Timothy J. Goodspeed, and Deborah Swenson (1993), "Explaining the Low Taxable Income of Foreign-Controlled Companies in the United States", pp.237-70 in: Alberto Giovannini, R. Glenn Hubbard, and Joel Slemrod, *Studies in International Taxation*, Chicago: University of Chicago Press.

Grubert, Harry (2001), "*Enacting dividend exemption and tax revenue*", National Tax Journal, Vol. 54, pp. 811-828.

Grubert, Harry and Joel Slemrod (1998), "The Effects of Taxes on Investment and Income Shifting to Puerto Rico", Review of Economics and Statistics.

Horst, T. (1977), "American Taxation of Multinational Firms", *American Economic Review*, Vol. 67, pp. 376-389.

Hartman, D. G. (1984), "Tax Policy and Foreign Direct Investment in the United States", *National Tax Journal*, Vol. 37, pp. 475-487.

Hartman, D. (1985), "Tax Policy and Foreign Direct Investment", *Journal of Public Economics*, Vol. 26, pp. 107-121.

Hines, James R., Jr. (1997), *Tax Policy and the Activities of Multinational Corporations.*

Hines, James R., Jr. (1996). "Altered States: Taxes and the Location of Foreign Direct Investment In America", *American Economic Review*, Vol. 86, pp. 1076-1094.

Hines, James R., Jr. (2001), "Tax Sparing' and direct investment in Developing Countries", pp. 39-66 in: J.R. Hines, editor, *International Taxation and Multinational Activity*, Chicago: University of Chicago Press.

Keen, Michael and Alejandro Simone (2004), "Tax Policy in Developing Countries: Some Lessons from the 1990s, and some Challenges Ahead", in Gupta, S., B. Clements, and G. Inchauste, editors, *Helping Countries Develop: The Role of Fiscal Policy*, (forthcoming).

McLure, Charles (this volume), *Transfer Pricing and Tax Havens: Mending the LDC Revenue Net.*

Mintz, Jack (2004), "Conduit Entities: Implications of Indirect Tax-Efficient Financing Structures for Real Investment", I*nternational Tax and Public Finance*,

Mintz, Jack (this volume), *The changing structure of tax policies for FDI in developing countries.*

Mintz, Jack and Michael Smart (2004), "Income Shifting, Investment, and Tax Competition: Theory and Evidence from Provincial Taxation in Canada", *Journal of Public Economics*, Vol. 88, pp. 1149-1168.

Moran, Theodore (1998), *Foreign Direct Investment and Development: The New Policy Agenda for Developing Countries and Economies in Transition*, Washington: Institute for International Economics.

Owens, Jeffrey (2004), "Promoting International Tax Cooperation", paper presentation at International Institute of Public Finance annual conference, Milan, August 24.

Papke, Leslie (2000), "One-Way Treaty with the World: The U.S. Withholding Tax and the Netherlands Antilles", *International Tax and Public Finance*, Vol. 7, pp. 295-313.

Shah, Anwar (ed.) (1995), *Fiscal Incentives for Investment and Innovation*, New York: Oxford University Press for the World Bank.

Sullivan, Martin (2004), "Data Show Dramatic Shift of Profits to Tax Havens", *Tax Notes*, September 13, pp. 1190-1200.

World Bank (2003), Global Economic Prospects.

Zee, Howell, Janet Stotsky, and Eduardo Ley (2002), "Tax Incentives for Business Investment: A Primer for Policy Makers in Developing Countries", *World Development*, Vol. 30, pp. 1497-1516.

Chapter 6

THE CHANGING STRUCTURE OF TAX POLICIES FOR FOREIGN DIRECT INVESTMENT IN DEVELOPING COUNTRIES

JACK M. MINTZ[1]

J. L. Rotman School of Management, University of Toronto and President and CEO, C. D. Howe Institute, Toronto

1. INTRODUCTION

Developing countries keen to attract foreign direct investment (FDI) have typically used various preferential tax policies to be competitive. Tax holidays have been especially prevalent in the 1980s (Mintz [1990] and Shah [1995]) since they provide new foreign investors a low-tax regime for a qualifying period on the presumption that a company needs time to establish good levels of profitability.

With increased globalization, many developing countries have been incorporating new tax policies for multinationals to establish headquarter, financial and trading operations in their jurisdictions. To attract FDI, while preserving revenue by countering efforts by multinationals to shift profits from high to low tax jurisdictions, many countries have chosen low corporate income tax rates, low or no withholding taxes on income payments to non-residents, or low rates applied to income earned by holding companies. These policies seem to have become common in the past ten years compared to traditional tax holidays incentives.

Picking the top 15 developing countries in terms of the FDI as a proportion of GDP for the 1997-2001 years, I examine their tax regimes to find that special "financing"[2] regimes are commonplace or, alternatively, governments have dramatically lowered general corporate income and withholding tax rates to levels well below those typically found generally. The incentives seem to work. Leaving aside some countries with large natural resources (and therefore high rates of FDI), many developing countries with high levels of inbound investment and, in some instances relatively robust outbound investment, have attractive tax regimes with low rates, especially for finance or trading operations.

From an individual country's perspective, the new tax policy regimes for FDI are less distorting that previous ones, especially compared to tax holidays, which are less popular in some countries. Certainly, only a few countries with the most significant levels of FDI use tax holidays – instead almost half have "financial" regimes that are highly attractive for multinational investment. In contrast, countries with low rates of foreign direct investment tend to have high corporate income tax and withholding tax rates, few incentives for financial and trading income and foreign exchange controls.

Countries with high degrees of FDI continue rely on fast write-offs for capital costs such as accelerated depreciation and investment tax credits, even if corporate income tax rates are kept low.

Below, I shall first review the tax regimes of various developing countries with high levels of investment. I then provide a simple model to explain how income-shifting – the mobility of profits from high to low tax countries – has led to lower corporate income tax rates and less reliance on more traditional incentives. Conclusions follow.

2. THE CHANGING STRUCTURE OF INCENTIVES FOR FDI

Countries hoping to attract FDI have typically used tax policies. FDI is beneficial to capital importing countries by increasing the both the supply of capital as well as introducing improved management and technology transferred from abroad. As studies have shown, several factors influence FDI, including the size of the market, exchange rate controls, infrastructure, the quality of labour, political stability, and taxation. Common tax policies used to attract FDI include corporate income tax reductions, tax holidays, accelerated depreciation (including investment allowances), investment tax credits and preferential treatment of income such as low taxes on earnings from exports. De Mooij and Ederveen [2003] suggest, using meta-analysis, that the elasticity of FDI with respect to the host country tax rate is 3.3. However, most studies only take into account only certain tax incentives such as accelerated depreciation and investment tax credits and rarely examine the impact of tax holidays and certain other incentives that are much more difficult to model and quantify.[3]

To gain some understanding of existing tax regimes used to attract FDI, I analyze those countries that have been most successful in attracting FDI as measured as a proportion of GDP (taken for the years 1997-2002). Table 1 provides information on 15 countries with respect to their world rank among both developed and developing countries in attracting FDI as well as exporting FDI to other jurisdictions. Tax variables are also included such the corporate income tax rate, common withholding tax rates on dividends and interest (especially by treaty), the availability of a special financing regime to attract holding companies in finance and services, tax holidays, capital cost incentives and foreign exchange controls.

As is shown in Table 1, the country with the greatest level of both inbound and outbound FDI – each almost 20% of GDP for 1997-2002 – is Hong Kong (which is no longer a developing country anymore). For many years, it has followed tax policies that tend to encourage holding companies to locate in Hong Kong to serve the Asian market (next to Tokyo, Hong Kong has the largest stock market in Asia). The financial sector, now almost one-half of GDP (Mintz and Richardson [2001]), has been encouraged by tax policies that keep corporate income tax rates (applied to Hong Kong source income only) below international norms as well as avoid levying withholding taxes on payments to non-residents. While Hong Kong has no special financing regime for financial or holding companies, its tax system on the whole has encouraged financial businesses to locate there. Hong Kong steadfastly avoids policies that are targeted to special business activities although it does provide expensing for investments in machinery for many industries.

Hong Kong is an example of what I call a conduit country (Mintz [2004]) with high levels of both inbound and outbound capital flows. Other countries can also be characterized as conduit countries including Belgium-Luxembourg, Netherlands, several Scandinavian countries, Ireland and the United Kingdom. These countries have tax structures that are quite common – relatively low corporate income taxes, averaging 23%, (compared to the average of 31% among industrialized and developing economies (KPMG [2004]), low or no withholding taxes with important treaty partners, exemption of foreign source income earned by affiliates operating abroad and little or no capital gains taxes. Conduit countries are able to attract high levels of FDI because of their low tax rate regimes as well as the absence of foreign exchange controls.

Hong Kong, of course, is not the only successful developing country that has attracted FDI as shown in Table 1. Some countries like Azerbaijan, Bolivia, Kazakhstan, Bahrain and, to a lesser extent, Chile[4], attract FDI to exploit rich natural resources that are a main source of income. Corporate income tax rates and withholding taxes earned from oil or mining production tend to be high and the governments rely less on special preferences like tax holidays and special financing regimes.

Table 1. Top 15 Developing Countries Ranked by Sum of Outbound and Inbound Foreign Direct Investment as a Percentage of GDP (1997-2001)

Developing Country	Rank [1]	Outbound FDI as % of GDP	Inbound FDI as % of GDP	CIT Rate %	Non-resident Withholding Tax (%) [2]	Special Financing Regime [3]	Tax Holiday	Capital Cost Write Offs [4]	Foreign Exchange Controls
Hong Kong	2	19.7	20.9	17.5	none	none	none	Exp	none
Azerbaijan	6	0.0	17.9	25	10	none	none	Acc	yes
Singapore	9	5.4	9.8	22	Div 0 Int 15	yes	Yes (10 yrs)	Acc	none
Malta	12	0.1	12.4	35	none	yes	no	ITC	yes
Chile	13	3.2	7.8	17	Div 18 Int 35	yes	no	Acc	partial
Estonia	14	1.9	8.2	0	Div 0/26 [5] Int 35	n/a	none	none	no
Bolivia	15	0.0	9.9	25/50	12.5	none	none	none	no
Seychelles	18	1.3	7.8	40	Div 0/15 Int 0/10	none	none	PR, Acc	yes
Macedonia	19	0.0	8.9	15	Div 0/15 Int 0/10	no	Yes [6] (3 yrs)	Acc	yes
Aruba	21	0.1	8.4	35	Div 5 Int 0	yes	none	none	Yes
Kazakhstan	23	0.0	8.0	30	15	none	none	Acc	yes
Czech Republic	24	0.1	7.8	28	Div 5/15 Int 0/15	none	yes (10 yrs)	Acc	none
Jamaica	25	1.1	5.8	33.3	Div 0/15 Int 12.5/15	no (except trading)	yes (5-15 yrs)	Acc	none

Table 1. (Continued).

Developing Country	Rank [1]	Outbound FDI as % of GDP	Inbound FDI as % of GDP	CIT Rate %	Non-resident Withholding Tax (%) [2]	Special Financing Regime [3]	Tax Holiday	Capital Cost Write Offs [4]	Foreign Exchange Controls
Malaysia	27	2.0	4.6	28	Div 0 Int. 10/15	yes	yes (10yrs)	Acc	yes
Bahrain	28	1.6	4.9	0	0 (46 for oil income)	none	none	none	none

Source: International Monetary Fund, World Bank, and Ernst and Young (2004).

Notes:

1. Rank is among all developed and developing economies. Of top 10, developed economies include Belgium-Luxembourg (1), Netherlands (3), Sweden (4), Ireland (5), Denmark (7), United Kingdom (8), Finland (10).
2. Withholding taxes apply to both dividends and interest payment unless otherwise noted.
3. Either special regime or much lower tax rate on financial income, headquarter operations, holding companies.
4. Exp: Expensing for qualifying assets.
   Acc: Accelerated depreciation or investment allowance
   ITC: Investment tax credits, including research and development.
   PR: Preferential corporate tax rates for some activities, including export activities.
5. Estonia does not tax income but taxes certain payments made by companies. Dividends are exempt from the 26% tax rate if payments are made to non-residents with at least 20% participation in the Estonian establishment and do not reside in a low tax country.
6. Macedonia's "tax holidays" are generally similar to investment incentives in that income that is exempt is limited to the investments made by the firm.

Several countries besides Hong Kong in Table 1, however, have established financing regime tax policies to attract foreign investment. Singapore, Chile, Malta and Malaysia have created special regimes for financial income or holding companies. In some cases, like Estonia, Macedonia and Bahrain, the low or no corporate income taxes as well as zero withholding taxes encourages FDI as well. Those countries with the most significant outbound investment – Singapore, Chile and Malaysia – have clearly used their special financing regimes to encourage holding and financial companies. However, in the case of Malaysia, stringent currency controls limit its ability to attract FDI.

What is striking about these high-FDI countries is that tax holidays are limited to only one-third of the cases – Singapore, Macedonia[5], Czech Republic, Jamaica and Malaysia, only one-third of the countries involved.[6] Tax holidays, so common among developing countries, are not particularly important to many high-FDI countries. However, the holidays have been important for financial companies operating in some jurisdictions like Singapore.

Most of the high-FDI countries use accelerated depreciation, investment tax credits and other preferential treatment for capital investments. Estonia and Bahrain does not provide fast writeoffs for capital investments since they have no general corporate income tax. Bolivia and Aruba also do not provide incentives for capital investment.

In contrast, the bottom 15 countries (measured as inbound and outbound FDI as a proportion of GDP)[7]:

- Tend to levy relatively high corporate income tax rates (averaging 32% in contrast to 23% for the top 15 countries),
- Levy high withholding taxes on dividends and interest (dividends, interest or royalties are taxed at more than 5 percent) in contrast to the top 15 countries with low withholding taxes (9 countries).
- Apply foreign exchange controls in 10 countries in contrast to the top countries where foreign exchange controls are applied in 7 countries.

The bottom 15 countries use tax holidays (6 countries), accelerated capital cost deductions or investment credits (8 countries), fast write-offs for capital costs (5 countries) and offshore financing or banking regimes (4 countries). In contrast, among the top 15 countries there is somewhat less reliance on tax holidays (5 countries), greater reliance on capital cost write-offs for investment (11 countries) and incentives to attract financing or trading regime, including generally low corporate income and withholding tax rates (10 countries).

3. WHY TAX INCENTIVES ARE BEING RESTRUCTURED?

Tax incentives are intended to increase capital investment and generate economic growth. However, their utility is limited by their effectiveness, complexity and fiscal cost. To capture the notion that tax reforms may be composed of rate reductions rather than accelerated depreciation, investment allowances and tax credits, I will introduce a simple model to analyze the benefits of each type of reform. Tax holidays are left to a discussion below since they are more complicated to consider than simple rate reductions.

3.1 A Simple Income-Shifting Model with Capital Investment

Suppose an economy is composed of two sectors – domestic firms with capital investment equal to k, financed by a fixed supply of savings provided by entrepreneurs, and foreign multinationals with capital investment equal to K. Output produced by a domestic firm is f[k] and by a subsidiary of the multinational F[K], both strictly concave production functions (although given the fixity of k, output in the domestic sector is also fixed).

The multinational finances its capital investments in the capital importing country with offshore debt, D, and equity equal to K-D. In this model, financial transactions are used to shift income out of the jurisdiction, whereby the debt owners (which could be the multinational) are assumed not to pay tax on offshore debt interest that is provided to the subsidiary.[8] The international cost of equity finance is r and the cost of debt finance is i= r+c[D]/D, where c is the total attendant agency and bankruptcy cost of debt provided by the offshore lender (c is a function that is strictly convex in D).

The government taxes both domestic and multinational companies at the same rate, t, on profits net of debt financing costs (domestic firms have no debt finance by assumption). An investment tax credit equal to the rate x is provided to both domestic and multinational firms. Note it is assumed that the capital importer cannot discriminate between domestic and multinational firms under tax policy because treaties prevent it (or alternatively it is not practical to do so in real life).

Domestic and foreign multinational after-tax profits are equal to the following respectively:

(1) $\Pi_d = (1\text{-}t)f[k] + xk$

(2) $\Pi_f = (1\text{-}t)\{F[K]\text{-}iD) + xK$

It is assumed that $0 \le D \le K$ due to financial constraints.

The optimal capital and debt decisions for the multinational are determined as follows (the domestic firm's investment is fixed by supply):

(3) $F'(1\text{-}t) = r$ (investment in K)
(4) $(r+c')(1\text{-}t) = r$ (debt decision)

Note for an interior decision for debt, we require that the tax benefit of interest deductibility to be offset by the marginal resource cost of debt finance. We also note the following comparative static effects:

(5) $\partial K/\partial t = F'/(1\text{-}t)F'' <0$ and $\partial K/\partial x = -1/(1\text{-}t)F'' >0$
(6) $\partial D/\partial t = i/c'' > 0$ and $\partial D\partial/x = 0$

The responsiveness of investment and debt finance depends on the respective second derivatives of the production and debt cost functions as expected. In Mintz and Smart [2004], multinationals can finance capital internally without cost, thereby implying that c"=0 so that the multinational would be either fully debt or equity financed.

The government's revenues from both types of firms are the following:

(7) $T = t\{f[k] + F[K] - iD\} - x(k+K)$

The government is assumed to maximize the weighted average of domestic-owned after-tax profits and tax revenues whereby the latter is multiplied by the (fixed) shadow cost of public funds, λ (>1):

(8) $W = \Pi_d + \lambda T$

The government maximizes welfare choosing t and x. Using the first-order conditions (3 and 4), we obtain the following optimal solutions for the profit tax rate and investment tax credit respectively:

(9) $t =\{(1\text{-}1/\lambda)f+F\text{-}rD\text{-}c\}/\{-(F'+x)\partial K/\partial t +(r+c')\partial D/\partial t\} > 0$
(10) $x = \{(1\text{-}1/\lambda)k+K\}/\{tF'\text{-}1\}\partial K/\partial x < 0$ if $tF'< 1$

The optimal profit rate is positive: the numerator is positive so long as profits are positive and the denominator is also positive given that capital demand declines and leverage rises with profit taxation as shown in the numerator. Clearly, the optimal tax rate is lower the more sensitive the tax base – capital investment and income-shifting through debt responds greater to an increase in the profit rate (the base shrinks with a higher tax rate).

The optimal investment tax credit is negative if the cost of the credit is more than any profits taxes generated by additional capital investment (otherwise the credit would be positive if the converse holds). In other words, the investment tax credit, when negative, is a tax on capital assets.

Optimal tax rates therefore will depend on the elasticity of the tax bases. If debt finance is very sensitive to tax changes (as determined by c"), then the optimal profit tax rate is low due to income-shifting. It would further imply, therefore, that the government would rely on capital taxes to generate revenues from businesses.[9] If capital investment is very sensitive to changes in tax rates, then both the profit tax rate and investment tax credit rate (capital tax rate) will be low.

Note further that the greater the importance of the domestic sector (as indicated by f and k), the higher will be the profit tax rate and investment tax credit.

To sum up, the above simple model comes to the following conclusions:

- Greater income-shifting by multinationals through debt finance pushes corporate tax rate down and reduces the incentive to use investment tax credits (or increase the incentive to use capital taxes).
- Countries with a small multinational sector will be less concerned with income-shifting and thereby less willing to cut corporate taxes.

Some recent evidence has been provided suggesting that income-shifting (whether through financial transactions or transfer pricing), has become increasingly important (Jog and Tang [2001], Mintz and Smart [2004], Grubert and Slemrod [1998] and Hines [1999] and Bartelsman and Beetsma [2000]). Given the significant increase in FDI, particular in the late 1990s, one can understand why governments have become more concerned about income-shifting in general in designing their corporate tax systems.

3.2 What About Tax Holidays?

As discussed above, countries with high levels of FDI do not use tax holidays – yet with a lower profit tax rate for qualifying years at the inception of the project, it would seem the tax holiday would be a popular measure to encourage FDI as well as combat income-shifting since tax rates are kept low.

As sensible this might be – and some countries like Singapore and Malaysia cling to tax holidays – the tax holiday is inferior as an incentive compared to low corporate tax rate regimes provided on a permanent basis. There are several reasons for this as reviewed in Mintz [1990].

First, tax holidays are only given to some firms – new ones entering a market – rather than all companies operating in the jurisdictions. The tax holidays then create a competitive advantage to new companies to the detriment of existing companies that have taken a longer run view of the economy. Governments are pressured to provide other incentives so that non-holiday companies can compete with tax holiday firms. The corporate tax system develops a "Swiss cheese" look over time with more distortions and complexities accompanied by eroding tax revenues. Given the importance of income-shifting, it would seem that a broad-based approach to corporate rate reductions would make more sense.

Second, identifying "new" from older companies can be a mug's game. Companies may close down at the end of the holiday to mysteriously appear as new companies to qualify for new holidays. This leads to not only extending holidays for longer periods of time through churning but heightens the distortions arising from competitive advantages given to holiday companies.

Third, the revenue cost of holidays can be quite substantial without necessarily providing substantial incentives for business investment. If companies must write down capital assets for depreciation purposes and are unable to claim interest deductions, unadjusted for inflation, during the holiday, they could pay quite significant taxes on income earned after a holiday is completed. In the case of Bangladesh and Malaysia in the late 1980s, for example, tax holiday effective tax rates on investments were even above the effective tax rates in the post-holiday period (Mintz [1990]). Further, with debt financing and transfer pricing, companies could shift income from non-holiday to associated holiday companies to shelter income from taxation. The holiday is blunted in its effect by such tax avoidance practices.

Given these problems with tax holidays, it would seem natural for governments to seek other low-rate incentives to encourage foreign direct investment. Some countries, like Bulgaria, Hungary (in the early 1990s) and Macedonia have actually abandoned tax holidays in favour of low corporate tax rate regimes.

4. CONCLUSION

Countries receiving substantial foreign direct investment are relying less on tax holidays than on low corporate tax rate regimes. Although it is still popular to provide accelerated depreciation, investment allowances or other incentives for capital investments, the most innovative incentives in the 1990s have been to lower corporate income tax rates sharply.

Theoretically, sharply reduced corporate tax rates would be predicted from a model in which corporate profit tax bases are more elastic with respect to changes in corporate tax rates. Businesses are able to shift profits easily from high-tax to low-tax jurisdictions without moving people or machines. As shown theoretically, if anything, incentives directed at capital costs would be reduced, or alternatively, countries would rely on asset-based taxes to raise revenues if such taxes are less susceptible to tax avoidance. Empirical work is needed to analyse in more detail the effect of tax incentives on foreign direct investment.

The implications of the changing structure of tax incentives for FDI are important to both domestic and international tax policy.

Domestic policies would need to be adjusted when business tax rates are kept low, in order to ensure that corporate and personal taxes on income are integrated. When the corporate income tax rate is brought below the top personal tax rate, dividend and capital gains taxes paid by individuals are preferentially set so that individuals pay the same tax (corporate and personal) regardless of whether the income derived is in the form of dividends, capital gains or interest and other payments that are deductible from corporate income but fully taxed at the individual level.

On the other hand, international tax policies for a country will be significantly influenced by new low-corporate tax regimes, specifically with respect to the incentive to undertake cross-border investments rather than investing domestically. As discussed in Mintz [2004], the effect of special financing regimes is to provide opportunities for multinationals to invest in foreign jurisdictions with tax-efficient financing compared to domestic companies. Too much cross-border investment is encouraged since international tax regimes are not neutral between domestic and cross-border investments. This creates some difficult issues for international tax co-ordination, which is a subject going beyond the thrust of this paper.

Notes

1. I wish to thank Bob Chirinko for helpful comments.
2. Financing regimes refer more generally to tax policies that apply low rates of corporate tax on international banking centres, holding companies, headquarter operations and trading income.
3. Mintz and Tsiopoulos [1997] found that tax holidays seem to have little effect on foreign direct investment for Mediterranean countries.
4. Chile has a special high tax regime for natural resource industries. See Ernst and Young [2004]. Singapore has a low tax rate of 10% on foreign-source income earned by resident companies.
5. Macedonia tax holidays follow a pattern established by Bulgaria recently in exempting profits up to amounts invested in capital for a limited number of years. In other words, the incentive is more like an investment allowance than a tax holiday.
6. Aruba had tax holidays and offshore financing regimes that were recently abolished, January 1, 2003. The Aruba Exempt Company (AVV) does not pay profit tax.

7. In all cases, inbound and outbound FDI is 2% or less as a share of GDP, using IMF statistics for the period 1997-2001. The developing countries include (ranking of 93 countries is provided in brackets) Philippines (74), Paraguay (75), Russian Federation (77), Ukraine (81), Slovenia (82), Botswana (83), Egypt (84), Uruguay (85), Turkey (86), Pakistan (87), Barbados (89), India (90), Bangladesh (91), Morocco (92), and Kenya (93). The low ranking for Barbados is a bit surprising since as its International Financial Corporation regime has allowed it to be a conduit country for many corporations, especially those from Canada.
8. In principle, the offshore lender could be owned by the multinational. Bankruptcy and agency costs remain relevant to operations.
9. Capital taxes, however, can be avoided by leasing arrangements if the tax is applied only assets owned by companies operating in the jurisdiction.

References

Bartelsman, E. and R. Beetsma (2000), *Why Pay More? Corporate Tax Avoidance through Transfer Pricing Policy, Working Paper 2543*, CEPR.

De Mooij, Ruud A. and Sjef Ederveen (2003), "Taxation and Foreign Direct Investment: A Synthesis of Empirical Research", *International Tax and Public Finance*, Vol. 10(6), pp. 673-694.

Grubert, Harry and Joel Slemrod (1998), "The Effect of Taxes on Investment and Income Shifting to Puerto Rico", *Review of Economics and Statistics*, Vol. 80, pp. 365-73.

Hines, James R. Jr. (1999), "Lessons from Behavioral Responses to International Taxation", *National Tax Journal*, Vol. 52(2), pp. 305-338.

Jog, Vijay and Jianmen Tang (2001), "Tax Reforms, Debt Shifting and Tax Revenues: Multinational Corporations in Canada", *International Tax and Public Finance*, Vol. 8, pp. 5-26.

Mintz, Jack M. (1990), "Corporate Tax Holidays and Investment", *The World Bank Economic Review*, Vol. 4(1), pp. 81-102.

Mintz, Jack M. (2004), "Conduit Entities: Implications of Indirect Tax-Efficient Financing Structures for Real Investment", *International Tax and Public Finance*, Vol. 11(4), pp. 419-434.

Mintz, Jack M. and Michael A. Smart (2004), "Income Shifting, Investment, and Tax Competition: Theory and Evidence from Provincial Taxation in Canada", *Journal of Public Economics*, Vol. 88(6), pp. 1149-1168.

Mintz, Jack M. and Thomas A. Tsiopoulos (1997), "Taxation of Foreign Capital in the Mediterranean Region", *Transnational Corporations*, Vol. 6(2), pp. 51-94.

Shah, Anwar (1995), *Fiscal Incentives for Investment and Innovation*, United Kingdom: Oxford University Press.

Chapter 7

INTERNATIONAL TAX COMPETITION AND TAX INCENTIVES IN DEVELOPING COUNTRIES

ELISABETH GUGL* AND GEORGE R. ZODROW**[1]
**University of Victoria; **Baker Institute for Public Policy, Rice University*

1. INTRODUCTION

Tax policy advisers often counsel the governments of developing countries against using investment incentives under their income taxes.[2] A wide variety of compelling arguments have been offered in support of this position. Investment tax incentives can be costly in revenue terms, generating relatively little new investment per dollar of revenue cost and requiring increases in other distortionary taxes; this is especially problematic if the incentives are general (untargeted), so that they benefit a great deal of inframarginal investments, including those that generate significant economic rents. Non-uniform investment incentives that apply only to certain types of capital assets or firms and thus only to certain business sectors may inefficiently distort the allocation of productive resources and may be perceived as unfair to those entities, especially domestic firms, that do not receive them. Moreover, the econometric evidence on the effectiveness of investment incentives in attracting investment is mixed. The current consensus appears to be that, holding other factors constant, investment does in fact respond positively to reductions in the cost of capital, such as those associated with tax incentives (Cummins, Hassett and Hubbard, 1997; Hassett and Hubbard, 1997). In particular, in their reviews of empirical studies of the effects on taxes on foreign direct investment, Gordon and Hines (2002) and deMooij and Ederveen (2001) conclude that the empirical evidence suggests an elasticity of aggregate foreign direct investment with respect to effective host country tax rates of roughly 0.6-0.7

in absolute value, with the most recent research characterized by substantially larger elasticities. Nevertheless, other observers argue that macroeconomic and other are by far the primary determinant of investment and that tax factors such as investment incentives play a relatively minor role (Chirinko, 1987), with investment responsive, but less sensitive, to cost of capital factors than suggested by the estimates cited above (Chirinko, Fazzari and Meyer, 1999).

Another problem is that investment incentives — especially those that are targeted to minimize revenue cost — can be difficult to administer, as the tax authorities must inevitably draw fine lines in determining which investments meet the specified criteria. Such targeted incentives also create the potential for corruption and for the waste of resources in the form of rent-seeking behavior. Under many incentive schemes, tax administrators must also devote significant resources to ensuring that firms do not use incentives to facilitate tax avoidance and evasion — e.g., using transfer pricing between related or unrelated firms to shift revenues to a tax-favored activity or entity and deductible costs to fully taxed activities or entities or, in the case of temporary incentives such as tax holidays, repeatedly forming "new" firms or subsidiaries to increase the benefits of such preferential tax treatment.

Tax incentive schemes can also be difficult to design effectively and not particularly transparent, again especially if they are highly targeted and/or apply only to incremental investment. For example, it may be difficult to determine the stimulative effects of an incremental investment credit that applies only to investment in excess of an average of investment over several previous years, because current investment will raise average investment in future years and thus lower future credits (Eisner, Albert and Sullivan, 1984). Similarly, the stimulative effects of tax holidays that do not provide for carryforward of depreciation deductions that would normally be taken during the tax holiday period may be relatively small; indeed, such tax holidays can actually increase the cost of capital for longer-lived investments that are subject to sufficiently front-loaded deductions for depreciation and other investment allowances (Mintz, 1995).

Another potentially important consideration in the developing country context is that the effects of investment incentives on the cost of capital may be muted for firms based in countries, such as the United States, that tax their multinationals on a residence basis, subject to a foreign tax credit for taxes paid abroad.[3] In the limiting case in which foreign tax credits are granted contemporaneously and used immediately in the home country, reductions in the effective tax rate in the host country have no effect on investment, since any taxes foregone in the host country are fully offset with home country taxes — the so-called "Treasury transfer" effect. The importance of this often-cited effect, however, is quite limited in many cases. Many capital-exporting countries tax their multinationals on a "territorial" basis and thus impose no home country tax on foreign source earnings, or have entered into treaties that allow "tax sparing" under which fictitious foreign tax credits offset the home country tax liability that would otherwise arise when the host country offers investment incentives. Moreover, given existing home country limitations on the use of foreign tax credits, many multinationals already have more foreign tax credits than they can use (they are in an "excess foreign tax credit position"), so that host country tax incentives are beneficial since host country taxes are reduced while home country taxes are offset using the existing stock of foreign tax credits. Finally, the Treasury transfer argument assumes equal and contemporaneous host country taxes and home country credits. In actuality, the present value of host country taxes, which are paid contemporaneously, typically significantly exceeds the present value of home country tax credits, which are deferred until earnings are repatriated to the parent company. Indeed, under certain circumstances, the home country repatriation tax is irrelevant to investments financed with the retained earnings of the subsidiary, which are affected only by the host country tax (Hartman, 1985). Although the net effect of all these factors depends on the specific circumstances in a country, these qualifications suggest that in many if not most cases the possibility of foregoing a treasury transfer effect does not constitute an important argument against the use of tax incentives (Gordon and Hines, 2002).

Finally, the use of investment incentives is questionable in an environment in which foreign multinationals have considerable discretion in allocating profits among the various countries in which they operate, e.g., through judicious allocation of overhead and interest expenses, and transfer pricing for inputs exchanged between affiliated entities in different countries. Countries with relatively high statutory tax rates will tend to receive a disproportionately large share of deductions and a disproportionately small share of revenues under such schemes. Recent empirical evidence suggests that multinationals do in fact engage in the types of tax accounting manipulations described above (Zodrow, 2004). Under these circumstances, utilizing investment incentives to lower the effective tax rate on mobile capital is inferior to simply reducing statutory corporate tax rates (or lowering withholding rates). Indeed, a lower tax statutory tax rate may have an additional stimulative effect in attracting investment from foreign multinationals because having investments in relatively low-tax countries facilitates such tax avoidance manipulations (Slemrod, 1997).

Nevertheless, despite the various arguments against their use, investment tax incentives are extremely widespread in developing countries (Goodspeed, this volume). Some of this may simply be attributable to the fact that politicians face tremendous pressure to increase investment and spur employment, and tax incentives are a highly visible and relatively flexible means of concrete action toward achieving these goals, regardless of their effectiveness. However, a wide variety of more substantive arguments, with different degrees of validity, have been offered in support of the use of investment tax incentives.

For example, within the context of an income tax, the standard argument for uniform treatment of all types of business assets and all business sectors (and thus against the use of (non-uniform) investment incentives) hinges on a number of assumptions that are unlikely to be fully satisfied in practice. The case for uniformity is strongest within the context of a dynamic model in which labor is taxed optimally over time; if these conditions are not obtained, differential taxation of capital inputs can be desirable (Auerbach, 1989), as in the exceptions that arise to the Diamond and Mirrlees (1971) production efficiency theorem (which precludes taxation of production inputs) when all commodity taxes are not available or not set optimally. Similarly, uniformity requires perfect competition; otherwise, differential taxation designed to offset the effects of market imperfections and to capture economic rents — especially those attributable to foreign owners of capital — will be desirable. However, the likelihood that investment incentives could and would be designed to accurately correct for these market imperfections may be small. Given the administrative and compliance simplicity of uniform rates, especially when coupled with the significant likelihood that any tax differentials enacted will reflect political power rather than optimal tax considerations, the case for using investment incentives to introduce the tax differentials required by optimal taxation must be applied with great caution.

Externalities also potentially provide a rationale for differential capital income taxation. In many cases, such as the generation of pollution, externalities are negative so that, in the absence of the appropriate effluent fees, properly designed investment incentives could encourage activities that do not generate negative externalities. Alternatively, some activities, such as investment in research and development, may generate positive externalities, which would be underprovided in the absence of investment incentives. These arguments provide a rationale for highly targeted incentives that attempt to correct for the externality, but do not support general tax incentives or targeted incentives that are not explicitly tied to the generation of externalities.[4]

Another rationale for investment incentives that is often cited in the developing world is the need to attract highly mobile international capital to increase the returns to local factors and to stimulate growth and technological innovation. The basic line of reasoning is as follows. As is well known (Gordon, 1986; Sadka and Razin, 1991), a country that faces a perfectly elastic supply of internationally mobile capital should avoid using source-based taxes on capital income.[5] In the long run, imposing such a tax will merely drive capital out of the taxing country until the after-tax rate of return returns to the level determined in international capital markets. This migration of capital lowers the productivity of the factors in the taxing jurisdiction that are immobile — land and labor that is relatively immobile. As a result, local factors bear not only the entire burden of the tax but also its "excess burden" — the efficiency cost imposed by the tax-induced out-migration of capital from the taxing jurisdiction.

This efficiency cost or excess burden of taxing mobile capital arises from three sources. First, as noted above, the tax-induced capital outflow lowers the productivity of local factors. Second, use of the capital income tax creates a tax bias favoring production of labor-intensive goods; this effect arises because the tax-induced reduction in wages that occurs as the capital income tax is shifted to labor is less pronounced for goods with a relatively large labor income share, causing an inefficient reallocation of labor to the labor-intensive sector (Gordon and Hines, 2002). Third, as stressed in the tax competition literature (Zodrow and Mieszkowski, 1986; Wilson, 1986), governmental concern about the negative effects of taxing mobile capital may lead to underprovision of public services.[6] These factors imply that, from the viewpoint of the taxing jurisdiction, it is preferable simply to tax the local factors directly, and thus avoid at least the excess burden of the tax on mobile capital.

On the other hand, not all capital is perfectly mobile, at least not in the medium term that is likely to be the focus of most governments. In particular, some capital may earn location-specific rents and thus be relatively immobile, even in the long run. Moreover, once capital is in place, the adjustment costs associated with moving capital in response to a tax increase may preclude either rapid adjustment. Under these circumstances (and abstracting from anticipation effects on future capital accumulation), some source-based taxation of such imperfectly mobile capital may be desirable, especially if foreigners own some of this imperfectly mobile capital so that the tax burden can be exported. Moreover, some form of taxation of business capital is necessary as a backstop to the individual income tax. Otherwise, individuals could incorporate as businesses in order to defer paying tax on their labor income, perhaps indefinitely if income can be withdrawn from the corporation as capital gains that are tax exempt or taxed very lightly (Gordon and Mackie-Mason, 1995). Taxation of domestic capital income at rates approximating those applied to labor income is desirable to limit this form of tax avoidance.

In addition, uniform taxation of foreign and domestic capital is desirable because preferential taxation of foreign source corporate income will encourage avoidance schemes involving domestic capital owners masquerading as owners of foreign capital. Uniform taxation of foreign and domestic corporate income will preclude this avenue of avoidance. Finally uniform taxation of domestic and foreign capital is likely to be a political necessity, and may even be constitutionally required.

This discussion suggests that the problem of capital income taxation facing a developing country that utilizes an income tax can be loosely outlined as follows. Concerns about tax avoidance and the desire to appropriate some economic rents from imperfectly mobile capital (especially if it is foreign owned), often coupled with the political necessity of creating at least the appearance of taxing internationally mobile capital at the same rate as domestic capital, suggest that a uniform tax rate should be applied to all capital income. In contrast, the small open economy argument outlined above, including the tendency for underprovision of critical public services due to concerns about the economic effects of taxing highly mobile capital, suggests that source-based taxation of internationally mobile capital should be reduced or even eliminated. However this result can be achieved in the context of uniform tax rates only by providing such highly mobile capital with the appropriate investment incentives (or some other preferential tax treatment). This is the approach analyzed in this paper — which builds on Zodrow (2003) and Gugl and Zodrow (forthcoming) — as it examines the use of investment incentives in the context of differentiating the tax treatment of perfectly mobile and imperfectly mobile capital when both types of capital are nominally taxed at the same tax rate and international tax competition leads to underprovision of public services financed with taxes on mobile capital. The two types of capital could of course be defined in any reasonable way. The paradigm that we shall employ is that imperfectly mobile capital includes capital already in place in the host country or capital that earns location-specific economic rents, while all other capital, including potential new foreign direct investment, is perfectly mobile.

In order to focus on the question of the use of tax incentives to provide differential tax treatment to perfectly and imperfectly mobile capital, the model abstracts from many other important issues. Most obviously, the analysis focuses solely on the perspective of a single country, and does not consider the general equilibrium implications that would arise if some or all of world's economies acted in a similar fashion. For recent discussions of the general equilibrium effects of both tax incentives as well as constraints on their use, see Janeba and Peters (1999), Keen (2001) and Janeba and Smart (2003).[7] Three additional issues are of special importance. First, the tax system is modeled very simply as the tax rate applied to capital income, neglecting all the complex issues associated with measuring capital income accurately, especially in the presence of inflation. Second, no attempt is made to model potentially beneficial aspects of international tax competition, including the limitations such competition may place on the incentives for overprovision of public services attributable to Leviathan-type tendencies of national politicians and bureaucrats (Brennan and Buchanan, 1980; McLure, 1986; Edwards and Keen, 1996). Third, it is assumed that tax incentives can be accurately targeted to perfectly mobile capital, reducing its effective tax rate. This of course may be difficult to achieve in practice, especially if domestic firms can masquerade as foreign firms that qualify for the tax incentives. Nevertheless, there are many examples of attempts to provide preferential tax treatment only to highly mobile (typically foreign) capital, such as targeted rate reductions and tax holidays or investment credits/deductions that are available only to certain types of capital (e.g., preferences that are "ring-fenced" or not available to domestic taxpayers); such preferences could also be approximated with similar provisions designed to favor only assets that are used disproportionately by internationally mobile capital. The model is thus constructed to analyze in a stylized way the implications of differentially mobile capital for the use of investment incentives when the government is concerned about the efficiency costs, including underprovision of public services, associated with financing such services with source-based taxes on capital income in the presence of international tax competition for perfectly mobile capital.

2. THE MODEL

An outline of the model used to analyze tax incentives for mobile capital following the approach described above is provided in this section; for full details of the model, see Gugl and Zodrow (2004). The model assumes perfectly competitive product and factor markets, with owners of imperfectly mobile capital receiving some economic rents since their factor is only partially mobile. The country whose tax policy is being analyzed is small relative to the international economy and therefore takes the rental rate r of perfectly mobile capital K as given. The country, however, also has a second type of capital, C, which is less than perfectly mobile over the relevant time horizon, and whose inverse supply is given by $w(C)$ with $w'>0$.[8] The country also has an immobile factor, inelastically supplied labor (or the combination of labor and land), L. Profit-maximizing firms produce output with the two types of capital and labor using a constant returns to scale technology and a production function $F(L,C,K)$ that is strictly concave in both types of capital, implying that both types of capital have diminishing marginal products.

Each unit of output is used either as a unit of a numeraire consumption good (X) or is transformed into a unit of a pure public good, denoted as G, that the government provides to its residents.[9] The government finances G with taxes on both types of capital at a uniform tax rate, t, and head taxes on residents, which in the aggregate are denoted as H. In addition, the government can enact tax incentives for perfectly mobile capital, which result in an effective tax rate on perfectly mobile capital of θt, $0 \leq \theta \leq 1$, with values of $\theta < 1$ indicating the presence of such incentives, and $\theta = 0$ indicating that incentives are sufficiently generous to completely eliminate the taxation of perfectly mobile capital.[10]

There are n identical residents of the country, each of whom owns the same share of perfectly mobile capital, which can be invested anywhere in the world economy including the country of residence. Each resident thus has an exogenous amount of income $y \geq 0$ from ownership of a share of perfectly mobile capital. To simplify the analysis while still allowing for the possibility of expropriating rents from foreign owners of imperfectly mobile capital, we assume that such capital is owned entirely by foreigners.[11]

The government is assumed to choose its tax instruments t, H and θ to maximize the aggregate utility of its residents, subject to its balanced budget constraint. Each resident's utility is assumed to depend on the individual share of private consumption and common consumption of the public good, $U(X/n, G)$. As in the tax competition analysis of Zodrow and Mieszkowski (1986), the government recognizes in choosing its tax instruments that an increase in the tax on capital will, in equilibrium, cause an outflow of both types of capital, as profit-maximizing firms facing supplies of both types of capital that are not perfectly inelastic will reduce their demands for both inputs when their prices rise due to an increase in the uniform tax rate on capital, t. Similarly, since a reduction in tax incentives also raises the effective tax rate on perfectly mobile capital and thus its net price to firms, such a reduction also drives out perfectly mobile capital. Finally, the reduction in perfectly mobile capital attributable to either a tax increase or a reduction in incentives reduces the productivity of imperfectly mobile capital (and labor), so that firms also demand less imperfectly mobile capital even though its price is unchanged. Thus, the government, taking the behavior of profit-maximizing firms in its jurisdiction into account, perceives that an increase in the effective tax rate on either type of capital, effected either through a direct tax increase or a reduction in tax incentives, decreases the available amounts of both types of capital.

The following sections discuss solutions to various versions of this optimization problem for the government. We consider first the efficient equilibrium, then the situation in which the government can tax both types of capital but is constrained to tax them at the same rate t (incentives are precluded), and finally the case in which the government is constrained in its use of head taxes but can utilize tax incentives.

Note that in what follows we draw a distinction between efficient provision of the public good and the efficient equilibrium. In the efficient equilibrium, the utility levels of residents are maximized, while efficient provision of the public good does not by itself guarantee that residents cannot be made better off. Efficient provision of the public good implies that the Samuelson condition holds, that is, that the sum of all residents' marginal rates of substitution between the public good and the private good is equal to the price ratio of the public good to private good (which, given our assumptions, simply equals one). However, if the government does not have all its tax instruments available (e.g., incentives are precluded) but can use head taxes to finance an efficient level of public goods, the resulting equilibrium will still be inefficient, as the tax structure will be suboptimal. In this case, it is therefore possible that less efficient provision of the public good might improve the overall welfare of residents by reducing the extent to which the government relies on inefficient tax instruments.

2.1 The Unconstrained Optimum

If head taxes can be imposed and tax incentives are available, then the optimization problem yields the following three results: (1) head taxes H are set so that the Samuelson condition for efficient provision of public goods $nU_G/U_X = 1$ is satisfied, (2) tax incentives for perfectly mobile capital eliminate all taxation of such capital ($\theta = 0$), and (3) the tax rate on imperfectly mobile capital is imposed following a standard inverse elasticity rule ($t = w'C = w/\varepsilon$, where the elasticity of imperfectly mobile capital is $\varepsilon = w/(w'C)$). Thus, the tax on imperfectly mobile capital t will be positive, as the government extracts some rents from (foreign) owners of imperfectly mobile capital, balancing this benefit against the cost of lower productivity of the immobile factor (and perfectly mobile capital) due to the outflow of imperfectly mobile capital that arises from the imposition of the tax. On the other hand, the standard small open economy result holds for perfectly mobile capital — tax incentives should be used to eliminate all taxation of such capital. As noted previously, this result obtains because the price of perfectly mobile capital is fixed internationally so that any positive taxation counterproductively reduces the stock of such capital without capturing any of its returns, while lowering the productivity of local factors by the full amount of both the tax and its excess burden.

2.2 Ban on Tax Incentives with Head Taxes Unconstrained

Suppose next that the government is precluded by law or political considerations from using tax incentives for perfectly mobile capital (θ=1); that is, the effective tax rates on imperfectly and perfectly mobile capital are constrained to be the same. Denote this uniform tax rate, which will be termed the benchmark tax rate, as t_B. Assume that head taxes H are still unconstrained. In this case, the solution to the government's optimization problem implies that (1) public services are still provided efficiently, and (2) the tax rate applied to both types of capital is positive but unambiguously below the rate of w/ε that obtains in the unconstrained case. Thus, the government reduces the extent of capital taxation because it must be applied to perfectly mobile capital as well as imperfectly mobile capital. However, as long as the government of the small open economy is unconstrained in its use of head taxes, the provision of public services is efficient. Moreover, since the results for the unconstrained case established that taxing both types of capital at the same rate is not optimal, using incentives is clearly desirable in this case.

2.3 Constraint on the Use of Head Taxes, with and without Tax Incentives

Suppose now that head taxes cannot be imposed at the efficient level and the government is instead constrained to $H' < H^*$, where H^* denotes the efficient amount of head taxes. As in Zodrow and Mieszkowski (1986), the constraint on head taxes and the resulting use of capital taxation leads to the underprovision of public services as the government reduces public services because it is concerned about driving out mobile capital. Thus, in contrast to the case of efficient provision of public services, the marginal rate of transformation between the private good and the public good is no longer equal to one, and the government can no longer simply maximize residents' income and then choose the level of public goods such that the Samuelson efficiency condition holds. Instead, as soon as the head tax constraint becomes binding and the marginal unit of the public good is financed by capital income taxation, an increase in the public good of one unit implies a decrease of the private good by more than one unit.

Although underprovision of public services in the presence of the constraint on head taxes can be established unambiguously, the results for the optimal tax rate and level of incentives are more complicated. In general, with head taxes constrained below their optimal level, the government must weigh the negative effects of a tax increase (or a reduction in incentives, if available) on the employment of both perfectly and imperfectly mobile capital in the country against the benefit of increased revenue (and thus less underprovision of public services) and the benefit of expropriating rents from foreign owners of imperfectly mobile capital.

To determine the net effect of these factors, suppose initially that no tax incentives for perfectly mobile capital are allowed ($\theta = 1$). Then, relative to the case in which head taxes are set optimally, the tax rate t, applied uniformly to both types of capital, is unambiguously greater than the benchmark tax rate t_B. Indeed, if the constraint is sufficiently binding, t may exceed w/ε, the optimal tax rate applied to imperfectly mobile capital in the unconstrained equilibrium.

Nevertheless, the case for introducing tax incentives in this case is theoretically ambiguous, even in the complete absence of such incentives. Specifically, when $\theta=1$, introducing tax incentives for perfectly mobile capital is desirable only if

$$(nU_G/U_X)(w/\varepsilon) > (nU_G/U_X - 1)[L(F_{KL} - F_{CL})] \; .$$

This condition holds unambiguously when $F_{CL} > F_{KL}$, that is, when imperfectly mobile capital is more complementary with the untaxed factor, labor, since the right hand side of the expression is negative, while the left hand side is positive. In this case, optimal tax considerations in the presence of heterogeneous capital (independent of supply elasticities) do not prescribe uniform taxation and instead call for differentially higher taxation of imperfectly mobile capital (Auerbach, 1979), which is achieved with the introduction of tax incentives for perfectly mobile capital. Note that this effect is amplified if underprovision of public services due to international tax competition is relatively severe, that is, if nU_G/U_X is large relative to one. In addition, tax incentives are relatively more desirable if ε is small, as a relatively inelastic supply of imperfectly mobile capital implies that differentially high taxation of such capital is especially desirable in order to capture the rents enjoyed by foreign capital owners. (If tax-induced underprovision of public goods attributable to international tax competition did not arise ($nU_G = U_X$), this effect would be the only relevant one, and tax incentives for perfectly mobile capital would unambiguously be desirable.)

On the other hand, if $F_{CL} < F_{KL}$, then optimal tax considerations in the presence of heterogeneous capital call for differentially higher taxation of perfectly mobile capital. If this factor is sufficiently important, incentives for perfectly mobile capital can be undesirable even at $\theta=1$, since they create a tax differential in the "wrong direction" from an optimal heterogeneous capital taxation standpoint, even though such incentives will be desirable to tax imperfectly mobile capital at a relatively higher rate. Indeed, it is theoretically possible that differentially higher taxation of perfectly mobile capital (which has been precluded by assumption since $\theta \leq 1$) is desirable in this case.

More generally, as noted in the introduction, the case for incentives may be tempered by concerns regarding resource misallocations attributable to suboptimal tax treatment of specific types of capital. Any such inefficiencies must be weighed against the benefits of lowering the taxation of perfectly mobile capital and reducing the underprovision of public services attributable to the taxation of mobile capital.

Finally, although the case for tax incentives is theoretically ambiguous if the government cannot impose head taxes in the efficient amount, it is possible to show that, in contrast to the case with unconstrained head taxation, full use of tax incentives to completely relieve the tax burden on perfectly mobile capital (θ=0) is never optimal. That is, the second-best optimum always requires a strictly positive θ or smaller tax incentives than are available in the first best optimum. The intuition behind this result is an extension of the results regarding the optimal taxation of heterogeneous capital noted above. Specifically, if head taxes are constrained (and supplementary taxes on labor are not used), the public good will be partially financed with distortionary taxes on the two factors that are complementary to labor, including both perfectly mobile as well as imperfectly mobile capital. Any further increase in the tax on only imperfectly mobile capital moves the tax system further away from the unconstrained optimum. In other words, a small tax-induced increase in the price of both factors is less distortionary than a much larger increase in the tax on a single factor.

These results are sufficiently ambiguous from a theoretical standpoint that some simple simulations of the model may be illustrative in determining the extent to which tax incentives in the presence of international tax competition are desirable in the model. Several such simulations are provided in the following section.

3. SOME SIMPLE SIMULATION RESULTS

As an illustration of the nature of the interactions between the tax rate on capital and investment tax incentives in the model, consider the following numerical example. Suppose the production function is Cobb-Douglas and is given by $F = AL^{1-\alpha-\beta}C^{\alpha}K^{\beta}$, where $\alpha = \beta = .125$; that is, we assume that the total gross income share of capital is 25 percent, and that this share is equally divided between perfectly and imperfectly mobile capital. Assuming that in the unconstrained equilibrium (with H unconstrained and $\theta = 0$), the price of output (p), the return to labor (q), the net returns to perfectly mobile capital (r) and imperfectly mobile capital (w) are all equal to one and that total domestic production and consumption is $F = X+G = 100$, implies that $A = 2.276$, $L = 75$, $K = 12.5$ and $C = 6.25$. Suppose the supply curve for imperfectly mobile capital is linear $w(C) = \gamma C$ (with $\gamma = 0.16$ to be consistent with the value of C in the unconstrained equilibrium), which implies that the supply elasticity is everywhere unitary (ε=1), so that the tax rate in the unconstrained equilibrium is $t = w/\varepsilon = 1$ or $t/(w+t) = 0.5$. The amount of exogenous income (y = 18.75) is set such that it equals total capital income in the unconstrained equilibrium, and the number of residents is normalized to one. The utility function of residents is also assumed to be Cobb-Douglas, and since UNPAN (2004, Table 2) indicates that in 2002 the average share of government consumption in total consumption in developing countries was slightly under 14 percent, the specific form chosen is $U = X^{.86}G^{.14}$, where X denotes the amount of private good and G the amount of public good consumed by the representative resident.

The first set of results examines the effects of constraining head taxes on the tax rate t and tax incentives θ, as well as on various other variables. Table 1 (See appendix) reports in the first column the exogenously specified amount of head taxes (H), followed by columns reporting the equilibrium values of perfectly mobile capital (K), imperfectly mobile capital (C), the tax incentives for perfectly mobile capital (θ) in percentage terms, the amount of public goods (G) and the amount of private goods (X). The seventh column reports "Compensation," the aggregate amount of private good that would be required to compensate residents for the inefficiency attributable to a suboptimal tax structure and underprovision of public goods (measured as a percentage of $X+G$, the total amount of private consumption goods and public goods consumed by residents). The next column shows the extent of underprovision, as expressed by the sum of the marginal rates of substitution of the residents (nU_G/U_X), which equals one if the provision of public goods is efficient. Column nine reports the tax rate on capital expressed as ($t/(w+t)$), and the next two columns show production in the country and the trade balance (which reflects the difference in domestic production and domestic consumption with the latter partially financed by exogenous income y). The last column reports the labor income of residents (qL).

In the unconstrained optimum (the first row), the trade balance by construction equals zero, as the exogenous income y implies that the amount of capital owned by residents equals the sum of imperfectly mobile capital and perfectly mobile capital employed in the country in this efficient (unconstrained) equilibrium. The remaining results in the first half of Table 1 (under "Optimal tax incentives") are consistent with the discussion presented above. Specifically, as an increasingly more binding constraint is placed on the level of head taxation (H' is increasingly less than H^*=7.75 and ultimately declines to zero), (1) a higher tax on capital is required, as the tax rate ($t/(w+t)$) increases from 50 to 58.5 percent, (2) tax incentives decrease as more of the public good needs to be financed by capital taxation, specifically θ increases from zero to 0.33, (3) underprovision of the public good increases, as the sum of the residents' marginal rates of substitution increases from one (indicating efficient provision) to 1.42 (indicating significant underprovision), and (4) the resulting equilibrium is increasingly inefficient, as reflected by higher amounts of required compensation to residents, which ranges from zero (in the efficient equilibrium) to 1.61 percent.

The second half of Table 1 (under "No tax incentives") considers the case in which the government is precluded from utilizing tax incentives (θ is constrained to $\theta = 1$) and thus must tax both types of capital uniformly.[12] The first row of these results, which assumes that head taxes are unconstrained, demonstrates that the residents of the country are better off if the government can utilize tax incentives — as would be expected since the model requires full tax incentives ($\theta = 0$) in the first best optimum. Note that with head taxes unconstrained the amounts of head taxes and public goods are slightly lower if $\theta = 1$ than with $\theta = 0$. The interpretation of this result is that if the country has to tax both types of capital uniformly, raising t will still expropriate rents from foreign owners of imperfectly mobile capital but will also drive out perfectly mobile capital. As proved above, the government will balance these two competing considerations and set a tax rate that is below the tax rate $t=w/\varepsilon$; in our numerical example, $t = 23.1$ percent, less than half of the tax rate in the case where no constraints were placed on the use of tax incentives. With less expropriation of economic rents from foreigners (and lower rents since this capital is imperfectly mobile) and a larger outflow of perfectly mobile capital (and thus lower wages), residents' income is lower in this case and, since both X and G are normal goods, less of both goods is consumed (although these effects are relatively small in the example). Note, however, that because capital taxation is more distortionary, the use of head taxes is even more attractive when incentives are precluded than when $\theta=0$. This is reflected in the facts that (1) the compensation required as head taxes are increasingly constrained is significantly larger for each value of H' when $\theta=1$ than when $\theta=0$ (e.g., when $H'=0$, compensation is 2.74 when $\theta=1$ and 1.61 when $\theta=0$), and (2) a higher percentage of the public good is financed with head taxes if the national government cannot employ tax incentives.[13]

The remaining results in Table 1 under "No tax incentives" are similar to those with "Optimal tax incentives." Specifically, as head taxes are increasingly constrained, underprovision increases to roughly the same extent in both cases, while the increases in the required tax rates are larger without incentives (since these increases in the absence of incentives drive out perfectly mobile capital as well as imperfectly mobile capital) and the required compensation is larger as the tax increases are more distortionary.

Finally, Table 2 (See appendix) reinforces these results from a slightly different perspective. In this case, head taxes are fixed at a suboptimally low level ($H' = 4$), and we examine how the optimal tax on capital changes if the extent to which tax incentives are allowed changes in increments of -0.10. As expected, as the extent of permitted tax incentives increases (θ declines), the tax rate on capital (t) increases, because the cost of using distortionary taxes is lower (that is perfectly mobile capital is taxed to a lesser extent for any given tax rate t). Note that residents are best off (compensation is minimized) if tax incentives are fixed at the 90% level ($\theta = 0.10$) so that the effective tax rate on perfectly mobile capital is 10 percent of the effective tax rate on imperfectly mobile capital. This is of course consistent with the results presented in Table 1, as $\theta = 0.10$ is the closest available option to the reported optimal tax incentive (with H'=4) of $\theta = 0.13$.

4. CONCLUSION

This paper has examined the case for the use of investment tax incentives from the perspective of a developing country in the context of differentiating the tax treatment of perfectly and imperfectly mobile capital when both types of capital are nominally taxed at the same tax rate and international tax competition leads to underprovision of public services financed with taxes on mobile capital. The results of the model utilized in the paper are clear cut when head taxes are available and unconstrained, as head taxes are used to ensure efficient provision of public services and the tax rate on imperfectly mobile capital is set following an inverse elasticity rule while tax incentives are used to eliminate the tax burden on perfectly mobile capital. Once head taxes are constrained and capital taxes are used to replace the lost revenues, underprovision of public services results. Under these circumstances, the case for using investment tax incentives is no longer theoretically unambiguous since, following the literature on the optimal taxation of heterogeneous capital, the efficient tax structure depends on the complementarity of perfectly and imperfectly mobile capital with labor, and it is theoretically possible that tax incentives would move the tax system toward greater inefficiency in the taxation of the two types of capital. Nevertheless, some simulations of the model suggest that investment tax incentives can in some circumstances be quite beneficial in reducing the inefficiencies attributable to the taxation of highly mobile capital, including the underprovision of public services in the presence of international tax competition. These results do not necessarily overturn the traditional presumption against the use of tax incentives by developing countries, as many of the arguments typically marshaled against the use of such incentives, especially the administrative problems and avoidance/evasion opportunities they create, are not considered in the model utilized in this paper. Nevertheless, our results do suggest that the desire to use tax incentives to lower the tax burden on highly mobile (foreign) capital within the context of administratively convenient and politically appealing nominally uniform taxation of both domestic and foreign capital provides a counterargument to the traditional case against the use of such incentives, and may provide a partial explanation for their widespread use.

Appendix

Table 1. Optimal capital taxation with head taxes and/or tax incentives constrained

	Perfectly mobile capital (K)	**Imperfectly mobile capital (C)**	**Price of imperfectly mobile capital (W)**	**Tax Incentives (θ) (%)**	**Public good (G)**	**Private good (X)**
Optimal tax incentives						
H optimal, H=7.75	12.50	6.25	1.00	0	14.00	86.00
H constrained, H=7	12.45	6.16	0.99	2	13.64	86.37
H constrained, H=6	11.66	6.05	0.97	5	13.17	86.81
H constrained, H=5	11.14	5.95	0.95	9	12.69	87.23
H constrained, H=4	10.61	5.85	0.94	13	12.21	87.63
H constrained, H=3	10.06	5.75	0.92	17	11.73	88.00
H constrained, H=2	9.49	5.67	0.91	21	11.23	88.35
H constrained, H=1	8.92	5.59	0.89	27	10.72	88.66
H constrained, H=0	8.33	5.52	0.88	33	10.20	88.95

Table 1. Optimal capital taxation with head taxes and/or tax incentives constrained (Continued)

	Compensation	Sum MRS (>1 implies under-provision)	Tax as % of price of capital (t/(w+t))	Domestic production (F)	Labor balance (qL)
Optimal tax incentives					
H optimal, H=7.75	0.00	1.00	50.00	100.00	75.00
H constrained, H=7	0.00	1.03	50.99	99.49	74.34
H constrained, H=6	0.05	1.07	52.45	98.75	74.12
H constrained, H=5	0.16	1.12	53.88	97.98	73.47
H constrained, H=4	0.31	1.17	54.81	97.18	72.83
H constrained, H=3	0.51	1.22	55.98	96.34	72.26
H constrained, H=2	0.80	1.28	56.87	95.46	71.61
H constrained, H=1	1.17	1.35	57.82	94.55	70.90
H constrained, H=0	1.61	1.42	58.49	93.60	70.16

Table 1. Optimal capital taxation with head taxes and/or tax incentives constrained (Continued)

	Perfectly mobile capital (K)	Imperfectly mobile capital (C)	Price of imperfectly mobile capital (W)	Tax Incen-tives (θ) (%)	Public good (G)	Private good (X)
No tax incentives						
H optimal, H=7.70	9.01	7.70	1.23	100	13.84	84.96
H constrained, H=7	8.75	7.59	1.21	100	13.53	85.26
H constrained, H=6	8.40	7.43	1.19	100	13.08	85.68
H constrained, H=5	8.05	7.26	1.16	100	12.62	86.10
H constrained, H=4	7.72	7.10	1.14	100	12.15	86.50
H constrained, H=3	7.39	6.92	1.11	100	11.66	86.89
H constrained, H=2	7.07	6.75	1.08	100	11.16	87.27
H constrained, H=1	6.76	6.56	1.05	100	10.65	87.63
H constrained, H=0	6.45	6.38	1.02	100	10.12	87.98

Table 1. Optimal capital taxation with head taxes and/or tax incentives constrained (Continued)

	Compensation	**Sum MRS (>1 implies under-provision)**	**Tax as % of price of capital (t/(w+t))**	**Domestic production (F)**	**Labor balance (qL)**
No tax incentives					
H optimal, H=7.70	1.22	1.00	23.13	98.54	73.88
H constrained, H=7	1.23	1.03	24.84	98.01	73.54
H constrained, H=6	1.29	1.07	27.44	97.24	72.87
H constrained, H=5	1.38	1.11	30.12	96.46	72.33
H constrained, H=4	1.53	1.16	32.54	95.67	71.71
H constrained, H=3	1.73	1.21	35.47	94.85	71.05
H constrained, H=2	1.99	1.27	37.93	94.03	70.55
H constrained, H=1	2.33	1.34	40.68	93.18	69.94
H constrained, H=0	2.74	1.42	43.65	92.31	69.22

Table 2. Optimal capital taxation if head taxes are constrained to H' = 4 with various values for tax incentives

	Perfectly mobile capital (K)	Imperfectly mobile capital (C)	Price of imperfectly mobile capital (W)	Capital tax rate (t)	Public good (G)	Private good (X)	Compensation	Sum MRS (>1 implies underprovision)	Tax as % of price of capital (t/(w+t))	Domestic production (F)	Trade balance (F-X-G)	Labor balance (qL)
Constrained tax incentives, H=4												
$\theta = 1$	7.72	7.10	1.14	0.55	12.15	86.50	1.53	1.16	32.6%	95.67	-2.98	71.75
$\theta = 0.9$	7.83	7.01	1.12	0.59	12.24	86.52	1.40	1.15	34.3%	95.69	-3.07	71.77
$\theta = 0.8$	7.97	6.91	1.11	0.63	12.33	86.55	1.26	1.14	36.2%	95.73	-3.15	71.80
$\theta = 0.7$	8.14	6.80	1.09	0.67	12.42	86.59	1.11	1.14	38.2%	95.79	-3.22	71.84
$\theta = 0.6$	8.35	6.68	1.07	0.73	12.49	86.66	0.96	1.13	40.5%	95.88	-3.27	71.91
$\theta = 0.5$	8.61	6.54	1.05	0.79	12.55	86.75	0.80	1.13	43.0%	96.00	-3.30	72.00
$\theta = 0.4$	8.94	6.39	1.02	0.86	12.58	86.88	0.64	1.12	45.7%	96.17	-3.28	72.13
$\theta = 0.3$	9.38	6.21	0.99	0.95	12.55	87.08	0.48	1.13	48.8%	96.42	-3.20	72.31
$\theta = 0.2$	9.99	6.01	0.96	1.05	12.42	87.34	0.35	1.14	52.2%	96.78	-2.98	72.59
$\theta = 0.1$	10.89	5.79	0.93	1.18	12.09	87.77	0.30	1.18	56.0%	97.36	-2.50	73.02
$\theta = 0$	12.31	5.60	0.90	1.30	11.30	88.59	0.47	1.28	59.3%	98.45	-1.43	73.84

Notes

1. We would like to thank Robert Chirinko, Charles McLure and the conference participants for helpful comments. We would also like to thank Don Ferguson for his help with the simulation program.
2. For reviews of the arguments for and against the use of investment incentives, see Hulten and Klayman (1988), Boadway and Shah (1995) and Zee, Stotsky and Ley (2002).
3. For elaboration of this argument, with an application to Colombia, see Echavarría and Zodrow (forthcoming).
4. Investment incentives are also often advocated on macroeconomic grounds as a means of providing short-run stimulus to an economy that is suffering from excessive unemployment or inadequate growth. The validity of the case for incentives on these grounds depends on the reasons for unemployment or inadequate growth. However, the effectiveness of investment incentives in stimulating an economy that is already at excess capacity, as well as the ability of governments to time the use of investment incentives to effectively offset cyclical factors, is open to serious question. The current consensus seems to favor the use of monetary policy over the use of fiscal policy (such as changes in investment incentives) as a stabilization tool. Yet another rationale for investment incentives arises if economies of scale are important in the production of tradable goods, so that investment incentives will increase the scale of operation of domestic firms, lower their costs, and increase their competitiveness in imperfectly competitive international markets. The extent to which national governments can in practice be successful in promoting domestic firms in imperfectly competitive export industries is a subject of ongoing debate.
5. See Zodrow and Mieszkowski (1983) for a similar result in a state and local government context.
6. Of course, tax competition has many other effects, some of which are also efficiency reducing and others that are efficiency enhancing (Wilson, 1999; Zodrow, 2003a; Wildasin and Wilson, 2004). Nevertheless, a central message of this literature is that to the extent that capital is internationally mobile, tax competition puts downward pressure on both capital income tax rates and the public services financed with the associated revenues.
7. These results are mixed, as Janeba and Peters (1999) conclude that tax coordination in the form of eliminating tax preferences for mobile capital are beneficial, Keen (2001) reaches the opposite conclusion, and Janeba and Smart (2003) and Wilson (this volume) construct more general models in which both results can be obtained. Note that these models also generally assume that governments act to maximize revenues, while the approach utilized in this paper assumes that the government acts to maximize the welfare of local residents, taking into account the potential underprovision of public services attributable to concerns about taxing mobile capital. In addition, note that the tax base is perfectly mobile in the Wilson model, while our model focuses on the case in which part of the tax base consists of imperfectly mobile capital.
8. See Gugl and Zodrow (2004) for a discussion of the derivation of the inverse supply function $w(C)$ in the presence of costs of adjusting the capital stock.
9. Note that the issue of using tax incentives to mitigate the effects of tax competition also arises in the context of public services provided to firms; this issue is addressed in Gugl and Zodrow (forthcoming).
10. We do not consider subsidies to perfectly mobile capital, although the model could easily be extended to include them. However, our results show that subsidies in this model are never desirable.

11. This implies the government can ignore the income effects on its residents of taxing imperfectly mobile capital. See Gugl and Zodrow (2004) for a discussion of the implications of domestic ownership of a share of imperfectly mobile capital.
12. For the Cobb-Douglas production function, $F_{CL}>F_{KL}$ if $\alpha K>\beta C$, a condition that is satisfied as long as $(w+t)>r$, that is, as long as the gross price of imperfectly mobile capital exceeds the net price of perfectly mobile capital, a condition that would normally be satisfied (and is satisfied in all of our simulations). In this case, as shown in Section 2, tax incentives will be unambiguously desirable at $\theta = 1$ even if head taxes are constrained to below their efficient level (although full incentives ($\theta = 0$) will never be desirable).
13. It is possible to construct examples where this effect is sufficiently strong that, in contrast to our numerical example, head taxes are higher when tax incentives are precluded than in the unconstrained equilibrium.

References

Bird, Richard M. (1996), *Why Tax Corporations?, Technical Committee on Business Taxation Working Paper 96-2*, Ottawa: Department of Finance.

Brennan, Geoffrey and James Buchanan (1980), *The Power to Tax: Analytical Foundations of a Fiscal Constitution*, New York: Cambridge University Press.

Boadway, Robin W. and Anwar Shah (1995), "Perspectives on the Role of Investment Incentives in Developing Countries", in: Anwar Shah, editor, *Fiscal Incentives for Investment and Innovation*, Oxford: Oxford University Press for the World Bank.

Chirinko, Robert S. (1987), "The Ineffectiveness of Effective Tax Rates on Business Investment: A Critique of Feldstein's Fisher-Schultz Lecture", *Journal of Public Economics*, Vol. 32, pp. 369-387.

Chirinko, Robert S., Steven M. Fazzari and Andrew P. Meyer (1999), "How Responsive Is Business Capital Formation To Its User Cost?: An Exploration With Micro Data", *Journal of Public Economics*, Vol. 74, pp. 53-80.

DeMooij, Ruud and Sjef Ederveen (2003), "Taxation and Foreign Direct Investment: A Synthesis of Empirical Research", *International Tax and Public Finance*, Vol. 10, pp. 673-693.

Diamond, Peter A. and James Mirrlees (1971), "Optimal Taxation and Public Production", *American Economic Review*, Vol. 61, pp. 8-27 and pp. 261-278.

Echavarría, Juan José and George R. Zodrow (forthcoming), "Foreign Direct Investment and the Business Tax in Colombia", in: Richard Bird, James Poterba and Joel Slemrod, editors, *Fiscal Reform in Colombia: Problems and Prospects*, Cambridge MA: MIT Press.

Edwards, Jeremy and Michael Keen (1996), "Tax Competition and Leviathan", *European Economic Review*, Vol. 40, pp. 113-134.

Eisner, Robert, Steven H. Albert and Martin A. Sullivan (1984), "The New Incremental Tax Credit for R&D: Incentive or Disincentive?", *National Tax Journal*, Vol. 37, pp. 171-183.

Garcia-Milà, Teresa and Therese McGuire (2002), "Tax Incentives and the City", *Brookings-Wharton Papers on Urban Affairs*, Vol. 3, pp. 95-132.

Goodspeed, Timothy (this volume).

Gordon, Roger H. (1986), "Taxation of Investment and Savings in the World Economy", *American Economic Review*, Vol. 76, pp. 1086-1102.

Gordon, Roger H. and James R. Hines, Jr. (2002), "International Taxation", in: Alan J. Auerbach and Martin Feldstein, editors, *Handbook of Public Economics Volume IV*, New York: Elsevier.

Gordon, Roger H. and Jeffrey K. MacKie-Mason (1995), "Why is There Corporate Taxation in a Small Open Economy? The Role of Transfer Pricing and Income Shifting", in: Martin Feldstein, James R. Hines, Jr. and R. Glenn Hubbard, editors, *The Effects of Taxation on Multinational Corporations*, Chicago: University of Chicago Press.

Gordon, Roger H. and Lans Bovenberg (1996), "Why is Capital so Immobile Internationally? Possible Explanations and Implications for Capital Income Taxation", *American Economic Review*, Vol. 86, pp. 1057-1075.

Gugl, Elisabeth and George R. Zodrow (2004), "International Tax Competition and Tax Incentives in Developing Countries", Manuscript, Rice University, July 18, 2004.

Gugl, Elisabeth and George R. Zodrow (forthcoming), "Tax Competition and Local Tax Incentives", *Proceedings of the Ninety-Sixth Annual Conference on Taxation*, Washington DC: National Tax Association.

Hartman, David G. (1986), On the Optimal Taxation of Income in the Open Economy, *National Bureau of Economic Research Working Paper 1550*, Cambridge MA: National Bureau of Economic Research.

Hulten, Charles R. and Robert A. Klayman (1988), "Investment Incentives in Theory and Practice", in: Henry J. Aaron, Harvey Galper and Joseph A. Pechman, editors, *Uneasy Compromise: Problems of a Hybrid Income-Consumption Tax*, Washington DC: The Brookings Institution.

Janeba, Eckhard and Michael Smart (2003), "Is Targeted Tax Competition Less Harmful that its Remedies?, *International Tax and Public Finance*, Vol. 10, pp. 259-280.

Janeba, Eckhard and Wolfgang Peters (1999), "Tax Evasion, Tax Competition and the Gains from Nondiscrimination: The Case of Interest Taxation in Europe", *Economic Journal*, Vol. 109, pp. 93-101.

Keen, Michael (2001), "Preferential Regimes Can Make Tax Competition Less Harmful", *National Tax Journal*, Vol. 54, pp. 757-762.

McLure, Charles E., Jr. (1986), "Tax Competition: Is What's Good for the Private Goose Also Good for the Public Gander?", *National Tax Journal*, Vol. 39, pp. 341-348.

Mintz, Jack M. (1995), "Tax Holidays and Investment", in: Anwar Shah, editor, *Fiscal Incentives for Investment and Innovation*, Oxford: Oxford University Press for the World Bank.

Razin, Assaf and Efraim Sadka (1991), "International Tax Competition and Gains from Tax Harmonization", *Economics Letters*, Vol. 37, pp. 69-76.

Slemrod, Joel (1997), "The Taxation of Foreign Direct Investment: Operational Policy Perspectives", in: James M. Poterba, editor, *Borderline Case: International Tax Policy, Corporate Research and Development, and Investment*, Washington DC: National Academy Press.

United Nations Online Network in Public Administration and Finance (UNPAN) (2004), *Basic Data on Government Expenditures and Taxation (1990-2002)*, Retrieved from http://www.unpan.org/statistical_database-publicsector.asp.

Wilson, John D. (1986), "A Theory of Interregional Tax Competition", *Journal of Urban Economics*, Vol. 19, pp. 296-315.

Wilson, John D. (1999), "Theories of Tax Competition", *National Tax Journal*, Vol. 52, pp. 269-304.Also in Wilson, John D. (this volume).

Wilson, John D. and David E. Wildasin (2004), "Capital Tax Competition: Bane or Boon?", *Journal of Public Economics*, Vol. 88, pp. 1065-1091.

Zee, Howell H., Janet G. Stotsky and Eduardo Ley (2002), "Tax Incentives for Business Investment: A Primer for Policy Makers in Developing Countries", *World Development*, Vol. 30, pp. 1497-1516.

Zodrow, George R. (2003), "Reflections on the Economic Theory of Local Tax Incentives", *State Tax Notes*, Vol. 28(10), pp. 891-900.

Zodrow, George R. (2003a), "Tax Competition and Tax Coordination in the European Union", *International Tax and Public Finance*, Vol. 10, pp. 651-671.

Zodrow, George R. (2004), "Capital Mobility and Source-Based Taxation of Capital Income in Small Open Economies", manuscript, Rice University.

Zodrow, George R. and Peter Mieszkowski (1983), "The Incidence of the Property Tax: The Benefit View vs. The New View", in: George R. Zodrow, editor, *Local Provision of Public Services: The Tiebout Model After Twenty-Five Years*, New York: Academic Press.

Zodrow, George R. and Peter Mieszkowski (1986), "Pigou, Tiebout, Property Taxation, and the Underprovision of Local Public Goods", *Journal of Urban Economics*, Vol. 19, pp. 356-370.

Chapter 8

TAX COMPETITION WITH AND WITHOUT PREFERENTIAL TREATMENT OF A HIGHLY-MOBILE TAX BASE

JOHN DOUGLAS WILSON
Department of Economics, Michigan State University

1. THE PROBLEM

With the ongoing integration of the world economy, it is increasingly possible for taxpayers to shift taxable income across countries. This possibility gives rise to the well-known problem of tax competition, whereby governments compete for internationally mobile sources of tax revenue by reducing the rates at which these sources are taxed. The result may be inefficiently low levels of tax revenue. See Wilson (1999) for a review of the tax competition literature.

A number of authors have studied methods for reducing the tax competition problem. But a common limitation of these methods is that they typically require a strong central authority, with the power to alter the incentives facing the governments engaged in tax competition. For example, Wildasin (1989) describes a corrective subsidy on the capital income raised by governments. This subsidy internalizes the "fiscal externality" created by the taxation of mobile capital, whereby an increase in one government's tax causes capital to locate elsewhere, thereby benefiting other regions or countries. For further analysis, see DePater and Myers (1994) and Bucovetsky, Marchand and Pestieau (1998). The latter paper recognizes that the design of a system of corrective subsidies requires information that is difficult for a central government to obtain. Recognizing this information asymmetry, Bucovetsky et al. use agency theory to design an optimal nonlinear subsidy schedule. But the solution again requires a central authority with the ability to levy and finance a system of corrective subsidies.

A less intrusive form of intervention would be an agreement among countries to restrict the manner in which mobile goods and factors are taxed. A number of authors have recently begun to investigate one such restriction: the elimination of "preferential regimes," which allow different tax rates to be imposed on tax bases with different degrees of international mobility. The basic idea is that countries will compete vigorously over the location of highly-mobile bases, measured by the sensitivity of this location to international differences in tax rates. Indeed, if a base is infinitely elastic with respect to tax rates, then countries can be expected to engage in a form of "Bertrand competition," competing tax rates down to zero. In contrast, less mobile bases will be taxed more heavily. If all bases were required to be taxed at the same rate, then governments would no longer face incentives to tax the more-mobile bases at the low levels prevailing under preferential treatment. It is not clear, however, that the non-preferential regime would raise more revenue, because we should expect the uniform tax to lie below the taxes that would be levied on the less-mobile bases if preferential treatment were allowed.

To study this issue, Keen (2001) constructs a model with two identical countries competing over two tax bases with different degrees of mobility. The two countries play a Nash game in their tax rates, with the objective of maximizing tax revenue. He concludes that tax revenue is always higher in the preferential regime. But Janeba and Peters (1999) obtain the opposite result: tax revenue is lower in the preferential regime. Using their terminology, there are gains from nondiscrimination.

These studies differ in three ways. First, Janeba and Peters assume that one of the tax bases is perfectly mobile with respect to differences in tax rates, whereas the other is completely immobile. In contrast, Keen assumes finite levels of mobility for both bases. As previously noted, the two countries will compete the tax on a perfectly-mobile base to zero, if a separate tax is allowed. Second, Janeba and Peters assume that the sizes of the tax bases depend on the rates of taxation where these bases are located, whereas Keen eliminates this dependence. Third, Janeba and Peters depart from Keen by analyzing asymmetric equilibria. The two countries are allowed to differ in the relative importance of their immobile bases as a source of revenue. In the absence of preferential treatment, one government chooses not to compete for the mobile base and instead maximizes revenue from the immobile base. This government prefers a relatively high tax rate because it generates a substantial amount of revenue from the immobile base. The other government is then free to attract the mobile base by choosing a lower rate.

To summarize, Keen shows that the preferential regime is better when countries engage in "head-to-head" competition for the mobile base, whereas Janeba and Peters show that the non-preferential regime wins when one government effectively chooses not to compete. This difference raises the question, Is the difference in results due mainly to the inclusion of country differences in the Janeba-Peters model, or to assumptions about how the tax rates influence the sizes and locations of the tax bases? Janeba and Smart (2003) address this question by generalizing the relation between the tax bases and the rates at which they are taxed. They then generalize Keen's results by showing that restrictions on preferential treatment reduce equilibrium tax revenue if the tax bases do not grow when all governments cut their tax rates, as assumed by Keen. But they also present several cases where restrictions on preferential treatment increase revenue. In particular, if both bases are highly mobile but a coordinated reduction in all tax rates causes them to grow, then restrictions on preferential treatment will increase revenue.

The analysis of "highly mobile" tax bases is incomplete, however, because the Nash equilibria considered in the three papers may fail to exist when one base becomes perfectly mobile, that is, its location is infinitely elastic with respect to tax rate differences between the two countries. Indeed, nonexistence is a necessary outcome in the Keen model, where countries are identical. If both bases are taxed at the same rate (non-preferential treatment), then each country has an incentive to undercut any positive tax imposed by the other country. By offering a slightly lower tax, a country gets all of the tax base, while sacrificing only a small amount of revenue on the less-mobile base. This undercutting occurs until the tax rates both equal zero. But then each country has an incentive to raise its tax rate so that it obtains some revenue from the less-mobile base. Thus, there is no equilibrium in "pure strategies."

This nonexistence result also holds if the perfectly-mobile base is "almost" perfectly mobile. Although the less-than-perfect-mobility assumption eliminates the discontinuous jump in tax revenue in response to "undercutting," a country can still increase its tax revenue considerably by undercutting the other country's tax rate, provided the tax elasticity for the mobile base is sufficiently high. This undercutting may not lead to zero taxes, but it will lead to taxes so low that the each country would then have an incentive to increase its tax rate to capture revenue from the less-mobile base, although it sacrifices the mobile base. As Janeba and Smart explain, the problem is that a country's revenue is no longer a concave function of its tax rate. Each country may desire a high tax rate when the other country's rate is low, while also desiring a low tax rate when the other country's rate is high. The result can be no equilibrium. Janeba and Smart's solution is to impose a concavity assumption, but doing so restricts the degree to which we may assume that one of the two bases is highly mobile, relative to the other. I take an alternative approach.

2. A SOLUTION

There are two solutions to the problem of how to model competition among two identical countries when a pure-strategy equilibrium does not exist in the non-preferential regime. First, instead of assuming that the two countries set their tax rates simultaneously, we could instead model a sequential game, where one country moves first (see Janeba and Peters, 1996). But this approach introduces an asymmetry between the two countries by effectively giving one country a first-mover advantage. Thus, we still do not have an answer to what happens when the two countries compete "head to head."

The second approach is to model the mixed-strategy equilibrium for the simultaneous-move game. This approach produces an equilibrium even in the case of a perfectly-mobile tax base, because it eliminates the non-concavity described above. Each country's strategy now consists of a probability distribution for its chosen tax rates. Under the equilibrium strategy, the country is indifferent among all taxes that receive positive weight in the distribution. The country no longer faces an incentive to "undercut" the other country's tax rate, because there is no single tax rate for the other country. Rather, there is the equilibrium probability distribution of rates. If a country lowers its tax rate, it merely increases the probability that its rate will lie below the tax rate chosen by the other country, thereby increasing the probability that it will obtain the mobile tax base.

The current paper investigates whether the preferential or non-preferential regime raises the most revenue when one base is perfectly mobile, given that a mixed strategy is played in the non-preferential case. Because mixed strategies produce random tax revenue, the comparison involves a comparison between levels of expected revenue. In the next section, I conduct this comparison under the assumption that the other base is completely immobile, as in Janeba-Peters. The two regimes are found to raise the same expected revenue, in contrast to the results of both Keen and Janeba-Peters.

This case is relatively easy to analyze because the model is found to correspond to Varian's famous "Model of Sales" (1980). He assumes stores compete over two types of customers, informed and uninformed, corresponding to the mobile and immobile bases in the current paper. Their objective is to maximize expected profits, corresponding to expected revenue maximization. Customers purchase one or no units of a good, depending on whether the price is greater than a reservation level. With a mixed strategy, each store sells to the constant number of uninformed customers who enter the store, while selling to a fraction of the informed customers that depends on the store's price.

The similarity to the current model is evident. In the same way that a store's mixed strategy is a continuous distribution of prices in Varian's model, a continuous distribution of tax rates describes a country's mixed strategy in the current model. In place of Varian's reservation price, I assume a maximum tax rate at which immobile factor owners are willing to place their supplies on the market; any higher rate would reduce the factor's after-tax return below its opportunity cost. In the same way that a reduction in the store's price raises the fraction of informed customers purchasing a store's product, a reduction in a country's tax rate increases the probability that the mobile tax base locates within the country. The only real difference between the models is that Varian assumes free entry, so that store profits are competed to zero, whereas I assume a fixed number of countries (two), allowing each to benefit from their taxation of the two bases.

After analyzing this case and various generalizations that do not alter the indifference result, I replace the assumption of an immobile base with the assumption of a partially-mobile base, that is, a base that is fixed in supply for the two countries combined, but where the division of this supply between the two countries varies continuously with the difference in the countries' tax rates. I model this mobile base as a factor that is used to produce an output by means of a quadratic technology. My main results agree with Keen: the preferential regime raises more revenue.

Some rough intuition for this result may be provided using reaction curves. Consider first the preferential regime. Under the simplifying assumption that the tax imposed on one base has no impact on the other base (an assumption maintained in all of the papers discussed above), two separate tax games are played: one for the perfectly-mobile base and the other for the partially-mobile base. As previously noted, tax rates get bid down to zero in the first case. For the latter case, the equilibrium occurs where the reaction curves for the "home country" (H) and "foreign country" (F) cross. This equilibrium rate is denoted by T^u in Figure 1. Note that the reaction curves slope up. A rise in foreign's tax induces more of the partially-mobile base to locate in home, and home responds by raising its tax rate.

Moving to the non-preferential regime, the mixed-strategy symmetric equilibrium satisfies a critical property that facilitates comparisons between the regimes: the only way for home to maximize revenue from the partially-mobile base is to increase its tax rate to a level at which it forsakes any chance of attracting the perfectly-mobile base. (Foreign's behavior is the same in this symmetric equilibrium.) Let τ^u denote this revenue-maximizing rate. In equilibrium, home can attract the perfectly-mobile base with a small positive probability by lowering its tax rate slightly below τ^u, but then it sacrifices some revenue from the partially-mobile base. These revenue gains and losses offset each other, so that home is indifferent about reducing its tax rate; otherwise lower tax rates would not receive positive weight in the equilibrium mixed strategy.

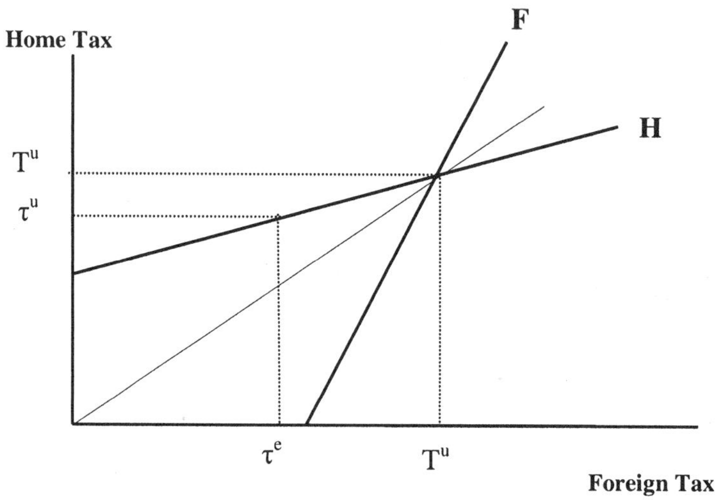

Figure 1.

Under the assumption of a quadratic production function, home cares only about the expected value of foreign's tax rates, denoted τ^e, not on the other properties of the distribution of tax rates. In other words, τ^u would be home's best response to a nonrandom rate τ^e imposed by foreign on the partially-mobile base. Thus, τ^u lies on lies on the reaction curve describing home's best response to foreign's tax rate in the Nash game in pure strategies that the two countries play in the preferential regime. But τ^u exceeds τ^e, since τ^u lies at the high end of the support for the equilibrium distribution of tax rates for the Nash game in mixed-strategies. As shown in Figure 1, this excess of τ^u above τ^e means that these two rates must be below T^u, where the two reaction curves cross. In other words, moving from the preferential regime to the non-preferential regime lowers the expected tax rate facing home (along with randomizing the actual rate), thereby reducing the expected value of its share of the partially-mobile tax base. As a result, home's revenue-maximizing tax rate declines, represented by a move down home's upward-sloping reaction curve in Figure 1 from T^u to τ^u. With τ^u lying below T^u but above τ^e, home is taxing a smaller base more lightly, in comparison to the equilibrium in the preferential regime. Consequently, the expected revenue it obtains by levying τ^u lies below its equilibrium revenue in the preferential regime. Lowering its tax rate to any level τ that receives positive weight under the equilibrium mixed strategy would not change home's expected revenue (given that foreign plays the same equilibrium mixed strategy). Thus, we may conclude that the mixed strategy generates less revenue in an expected value sense than the revenue obtained in the preferential regime. In this sense, the preferential regime is superior to the non-preferential regime, a result that supports Keen.

In the next section, I discuss in detail the model with perfectly-mobile and immobile tax bases. Section 4 replaces the immobile base with a partially-mobile base, thereby obtaining the result just described. Section 5 provides some concluding remarks, including a discussion of how to interpret the mixed strategies considered here.

3. THE MODEL WITH MOBILE AND IMMOBILE TAX BASES

Consider two identical countries, home and foreign, that tax two bases. The two countries compete over a perfectly-mobile tax base, which is fixed in total supply. In particular, this base locates where the unit tax rate is highest. Letting t and t^* denote home and foreign's unit tax rates, the supply of the base to home is given by the function, $b(t - t^*)$, where

$$\begin{aligned} b(t-t^*) &= 0 \quad \text{if } t > t^*; \\ b(t-t^*) &= .5 \quad \text{if } t = t^*; \\ b(t-t^*) &= 1 \quad \text{if } t < t^*. \end{aligned} \tag{1}$$

Thus, the total size of the base is normalized to equal one, and it is split equally between the two countries if they choose the same tax rates. In a similar way, $b(t^* - t)$ describes the supply of the base to foreign. Since foreign and home are treated identically, I may describe the model by focusing on home.

The other tax base is assumed for now to be immobile internationally. Let T and T^* denote the home and foreign tax rates on the immobile base. I assume that this base is inelastically supplied at a level denoted B, if it is taxed at a rate less than or equal to some positive value, T^u. The interpretation here is that there is a fixed opportunity cost to supplying the immobile base, such as the value of its use in non-taxed activities (e.g., developed land versus undeveloped land).

Each country seeks to maximize tax revenue. In the preferential regime, home chooses t and T to maximize $tb(t-t^*) + TB$, subject to $T \leq T^u$, and similarly for foreign. In the non-preferential (or "non-discriminatory") regime, $t = T$ for home and $t^* = T^*$ for foreign. I let τ and τ^* denote these common rates.

The two countries play a Nash game in their available tax instruments. As already noted, the governments engage in a form of Bertrand competition if preferential treatment is allowed, competing t and t^* down to zero. They then raise their tax rates on the immobile base to $T = T^* = T^u$, where the return on the immobile base equals its opportunity cost. As a result, each country's total tax revenue is T^uB in the Nash equilibrium for the preferential regime.

Turning to the non-preferential regime, we have seen that there is no Nash equilibrium in pure strategies. Thus, consider a symmetric Nash equilibrium in mixed strategies. Each country's strategy is now described by a distribution function, $F(\cdot)$, where the argument is τ for home and τ^* for foreign. In particular, $F(\tau)$ gives the probability that home sets its tax rates at τ or lower. Because the tax rates are random, each country faces a random tax base and, therefore, random tax revenue even if it imposes a single tax rate with certainty. If home chooses tax rate τ, its expected revenue is

$$ER(\tau) = \tau[1 - F(\tau)] + \tau B, \qquad (2)$$

assuming $\tau \leq T^u$. In particular, the probability that that home's τ is lower than foreign's chosen tax rate is $1 - F(\tau)$. Since the total value of the mobile base has been normalized to equal one, home's expected revenue from the mobile base is $\tau[1 - F(\tau)]$

The support for this distribution F has $\tau = T^u$ as the top tax rate. No country would set a higher rate, because it would lose all revenue from the immobile tax base. The top tax rate also cannot be less than T^u, because then a country levying this top rate (and therefore having no chance of attracting the mobile base) could increase revenue further by raising its tax rate to T^u.

Noting the correspondence between this model and Varian's model of sales, we know that F will continuously increase from zero to one over an interval of taxes, $[\tau^l, T^u]$. In other words, the density, $f(\tau) = F'(\tau)$, is positive at each τ in this interval. Each of these taxes must yield the same expected revenue; otherwise, the country could do better by shifting density from low-revenue τ's to high-revenue τ's. Thus,

$$\tau[1 - F(\tau)] + \tau B = T^uB \qquad (3)$$

for each τ in $[\tau^l, T^u]$. We may conclude each country's expected revenue equals the revenue it would receive in the preferential regime, where $t = t^* = 0$:

PROPOSITION 1: WITH PERFECTLY-MOBILE AND IMMOBILE TAX BASES, THE REVENUE RAISED IN THE PREFERENTIAL REGIME IS IDENTICAL TO THE EXPECTED REVENUE RAISED IN THE NON-PREFERENTIAL REGIME.

This result supports neither Keen nor Janeba and Peters. Recall that Keen concludes that a preferential regime raises more revenue, whereas Janeba and Peters make the opposite claim. Here the choice between them is a matter of indifference.

To derive the equilibrium $F(\tau)$, solve (3) for $F(\tau)$:

$$F(\tau) = 1 + B - \frac{T^u B}{\tau} \quad for \quad \frac{T^u B}{1+B} \le \tau \le T^u, \qquad (4)$$

where the first inequality is obtained by solving for $F(\tau) = 0$.

Proposition 1 can be generalized in two directions, although doing so eliminates the ability to obtain a simple closed-form solution for the distribution function. First, the total size of the mobile base can be made to depend on the tax rate in the country where the base locates. Specifically, replace $b(t - t^*)$ with the function $b(t - t^*, t^{min})$, where $t^{min} = min\ (t, t^*)$ and b declines with t^{min}. Once again, the tax base locates in the country with the lower tax rate, but now the size of the base depends on this country's tax rate. Given the incentives the countries face to undercut each other's tax rate, a pure-strategy equilibrium again fails to exist in the non-preferential regime. For the mixed-strategy equilibrium, this extra generality will not change the proof of Proposition 1. In particular, the support for the equilibrium distribution of tax rates is again given by an interval, $[\tau^l, T^u]$.

A more ambitious generalization is to assume that the immobile base is also a decreasing function of the country's tax rate: $B = B(T)$, where $B' < 0$ and $TB(T)$ is assumed to be single-peaked. In the preferential regime, each country continues to raise no revenue from the mobile base, instead choosing its taxation of the immobile base to maximize revenue. Let T^u now represent this revenue-maximizing rate. In the non-preferential regime, equilibrium mixed strategies are again described by a distribution function over the interval, $[\tau^l, T^u]$, for some $\tau^l < T^u$. In contrast to (4), however, the density function, $f(\tau) = F'(\tau)$, must converge to zero as τ goes to T^u. The reason is that a marginal drop in τ from T^u has a zero first-order impact on revenue from the immobile base (by the optimality of T^u). For expected revenue to stay fixed, as required under the equilibrium mixed strategy, expected revenue from the mobile base must also be unaffected by the tax reduction, implying that $F'(T^u) = 0$. With all taxes in $[\tau^l, T^u]$ providing each country with the same, expected revenue, $T^u B(T^u)$, given the other country's mixed strategy, we may once again conclude that expected revenue in the non-preferential regime is $T^u B(T^u)$, which is also revenue in the preferential regime (where $t = t^* = 0$).

These extensions correspond to the specification employed by Janeba and Peters. But whereas these authors show that non-preferential regimes are desirable in the case of asymmetric equilibria in pure strategies, the results here show that that the choice is a matter of indifference in the case of a symmetric equilibrium in mixed strategies.

4. PARTIALLY MOBILE CAPITAL

Let us now consider the case studied by Keen, where both tax bases exhibit some degree of mobility. While one base continues to be perfectly mobile, assume that the other base is partially mobile. In particular, increasing home's tax rate above foreign's tax rate reduces home's tax base, but does not eliminate it until the tax difference becomes sufficiently large. For the non-preferential regime, a Nash equilibrium in pure strategies fails to exist, necessitating the use of mixed strategies. For the preferential regime, the tax rate on the perfectly-mobile base is again given driven to zero, leaving the two countries to play a Nash game in their tax rates on the partially-mobile base. I start by examining this game.

Let us interpret the partially-mobile base as internationally-mobile capital, which is used to produce an output. Mobility ensures that its after-tax return, r, is equated across countries. Assume that the production function is quadratic. In particular, the relation between home's output and capital is described by the function, $G(B) = \alpha B - .5B^2$, and the same relation holds for foreign's capital, B^*. (The coefficient .5 is chosen only for algebraic convenience.) With $r + T$ denoting home's before-tax return in a non-preferential regime, profit maximization implies, $\alpha - B = r + T$. Thus, home and foreign's demands for capital are

$$B = \alpha - (r + T) \quad and \quad B^* = \alpha - (r + T^*). \qquad (5)$$

Assume that residents in each country are endowed with $\overline{B}$ units of capital, which they may invest in either country. Then $2\overline{B}$ is the total supply of capital. The market-clearing r is then determined by the condition, $2\overline{B} = 2\alpha - 2r - T - T^*$, or

$$r = \alpha - \overline{B} - \frac{T + T^*}{2}. \qquad (6)$$

Consider now the behavior of home, noting that foreign behaves in a symmetrical way. Substituting the r from (6) into (5) gives

$$B = \overline{B} + \frac{T + T^*}{2}. \qquad (7)$$

This condition defines home's capital demand function, $B = B(T, T^*)$. Setting $r = 0$ in (6) enables us to define a maximum average tax rate, above which no capital is supplied:

$$\frac{T + T^*}{2} = \alpha - \overline{B}. \qquad (8)$$

With taxes t and t^* bid down to zero under preferential treatment, each country maximizes its revenue from the partially-mobile base. In particular, home maximizes $TB(T, T^*)$. With B given by (7), the first-order condition is, $[\overline{B} + .5(T^* - T)] - .5T = 0$, yielding

$$T = \overline{B} + .5T^*. \qquad (9)$$

The positive relation between T and T^* holds because a rise in foreign's tax rate expands home's base, giving home a greater incentive to raise its own tax rate. In the symmetric equilibrium, we set $T = T^*$ in (9) and solve for the common value, again denoted T^u:

$$T^u = 2\overline{B}. \qquad (10)$$

Thus, an individual country's tax revenue is

$$R = 2\overline{B}^2. \qquad (11)$$

Consider now the non-preferential regime, where each country's strategy is given by the distribution function, $F(\tau)$. If home chooses a given τ, then it faces random values of the two tax bases. The expected value of home's partially-mobile tax base, B^e, is given by (7) with τ replacing T, and with the expected tax rate associated with this mixed strategy, τ^e, replacing

T^*: $B = \overline{B} + .5(\tau^e - \tau)$. Expected revenue from tax rate τ may the be written

$$ER(\tau) = \tau(1 - F(\tau)) + \tau[\overline{B} + .5(\tau^e - \tau)]. \qquad (12)$$

Let τ^u denote the tax rate that maximizes revenue from the partially-mobile base. Differentiating the second term in (12) gives the following first-order condition:

$$\tau^u = \overline{B} + .5\tau^e. \qquad (13)$$

Following the arguments from the previous section, $F(\tau)$ increases from 0 to 1 over the interval, $[\tau', \tau^u]$, for some $\tau' < \tau^u$, with each τ in this interval yielding the same expected revenue, $ER(\tau)$. Thus, the expected revenue yielded by the equilibrium mixed strategy is $ER(\tau^u)$. The comparison between $ER(\tau^u)$ and revenue in the preferential regime [given by (11)] then follows the arguments in Section 2. In brief, we know that $\tau^u > \tau^e$, implying that home locates at a point on its reaction curve to the left of the point in Figure 1 where the two reaction curves cross, denoted, (T^u, T^u). Thus, the expected value of home's partially mobile base falls short of the equilibrium value in the preferential regime, and this lower base is taxed at the lower rate, $\tau^u < T^u$. Hence, we obtain—

PROPOSITION 2: WITH PERFECTLY-MOBILE AND PARTIALLY-MOBILE TAX BASES, THE REVENUE RAISED IN THE PREFERENTIAL REGIME IS GREATER THAN THE EXPECTED REVENUE RAISED IN THE NON-PREFERENTIAL REGIME.

5. CONCLUDING REMARKS

This paper has shown that preferential treatment of a highly-mobile tax base can represent a beneficial way of thwarting the revenue-reducing tendencies of tax competition. Without preferential treatment, tax competition erodes not only the revenue from this base, but also the revenue from less-mobile bases.

To prove this result, I had to confront the problems that highly-mobile bases create for the existence of an equilibrium in pure strategies. My solution has been to consider mixed-strategy equilibria, which consist of probability distributions over tax rates. Osborne and Rubinstein (1994) provide several interpretations of such equilibria. One interpretation is that a mixed-strategy equilibrium is a stochastic steady state. Over time, countries choose different tax rates, and each country forms its beliefs about the other countries tax rates by observing the frequencies that these other rates were chosen in the past. A problem with this interpretation is that we should expect chosen tax rates to be correlated over time, in which case individual plays of the game are strategically linked. Another interpretation is that one country's chosen tax rate is based on random private information. It would be useful to pursue this interpretation in a model with alternatives to the objective of revenue maximization. In particular, we might posit potential government decision-makers who differ in the weights they place on government revenue and some measure of resident welfare. Once again, a highly-mobile base can be expected to eliminate the existence of pure strategies in the non-preferential regime, since governments continue to have an incentive to undercut each other in an effort to attract the mobile tax base. But now the realized levels of taxation chosen in the mixed-strategy equilibrium could depend on unobservable preferences of government decision-makers over the relative weights given to revenue and welfare in their objective functions.

By assuming revenue maximization, I have also ignored the possibility that government officials are influenced by special interest groups that are harmed by the taxation of particular bases. This possibility suggests another reason for favoring a non-preferential regime over a preferential regime: allowing tax rates to differ across bases allows government officials to respond to the lobbying efforts of special interest groups in a way that leads to an inefficient tax system from the viewpoint of the given country. But such lobbying need not always imply a less efficient tax system from the viewpoint of the entire system of countries, given the fiscal externalities associated with tax competition. The political economy of tax competition is an important topic for further research.

References

Bucovetsky, Sam, Maurice Marchand, and Pierre Pestieau (1998), "Tax Competition and Revelation of Preferences for Public Expenditure", *Journal of Urban Economics*, Vol. 44, pp. 367-390.

DePater, James A., and Gordon M Myers (1994), "Strategic Capital Tax Competition: A Pecuniary Externality and a Corrective Device", *Journal of Urban Economics*, Vol. 36, pp. 66-78.

Janeba, Eckhard, and Wolfgang Peters (1996), *Efficient Tax Competition and the Gains from Nondiscrimination : The Case of Interest Taxation in Europe, DP 72*, European University Viadrina.

Janeba, Eckhard, and Wolfgang Peters (1999), "Tax Evasion, Tax Competition and the Gains from Nondiscrimination: The Case of Interest Taxation in Europe", *Economic Journal*, Vol. 109, pp. 93-101.

Janeba, Eckhard, and Michael Smart (2003), "Is Targeted Tax Competition Less Harmful Than its Remedies", *International Tax and Public Finance*, Vol. 10, pp. 259-280.

Keen, Michael (2001), "Preferential Regimes Can Make Tax Competition Less Harmful", *National Tax Journal*, Vol. 54, pp. 757-62.

Osborne, Martin J., and Ariel Rubinstein (1994), *A Course in Game Theory*, Cambridge: M.I.T. Press.

Varian, Hal (1980), "A Model of Sales", *American Economic Review*, Vol. 70, pp. 651-659.

Wildasin, David E. (1989), "Interjurisdictional Capital Mobility: Fiscal Externality and a Corrective Subsidy", *Journal of Urban Economics*, Vol. 25, pp. 193-212.

Wilson, John D. (1999), "Theories of Tax Competition", *National Tax Journal*, Vol. 52, pp. 269-304.

DISCUSSANT COMMENTS

ROSANNE ALTSHULER
Rutgers University

McLURE AND GOODSPEED

I found the papers by McLure and Goodspeed interesting, informative, and important to policy makers in both developed and less developed countries. McLure discusses the difficulties host countries face in raising revenue from inward Foreign Direct Investment (FDI) and argues that these problems are particularly complex for less developed countries (LDCs) and countries in transition from socialism (CITS). He paints a fairly gloomy picture of the prospects of these countries mending their "revenue nets." Tax minimization strategies of multinational corporations (MNCs) have become much more sophisticated and complex in the last decade or so. The revenue authorities in LDCs are unable to keep up with these developments and, as a result, often lack the expertise necessary to monitor such activities. It is interesting to learn that the general strategies that McLure is concerned with in his paper – the use of tax havens and transfer pricing - were recognized as being problems for host countries by Stanley Surrey more than twenty-five years ago (Surrey 1978).

Combating revenue losses created by the combination of transfer pricing and tax havens poses even greater problems than transfer pricing or tax havens alone. The problems are in part created by the ability of MNCs to sandwich tax haven affiliates between active affiliates abroad and the home country of the MNC. For example, MNCs are increasingly structuring operations of manufacturing and distribution enterprises with the objective of unbundling functions and placing them in jurisdictions that are compatible with reducing worldwide tax liabilities. McLure has elegantly explained how the use of transfer pricing combined with the ability to structure related operations in tax havens lowers the cost of doing business in host countries and creates tears in host country revenue nets. The next logical question for policy makers in LDCs and CITS to ask is whether MNCs are aggressively using tax havens to lower the tax burden on investment abroad. I believe that there is empirical evidence of this behavior in the data and describe some of it in my comments.

Profits of US MNCs located in tax havens have grown in recent years. Sullivan (2004) reports a dramatic increase in U.S. profits reported in low-tax countries between 1999 and 2004. His analysis received wide coverage in both the U.S. and international press. Sullivan shows that according to surveys of direct investors by the Bureau of Economic Analysis (BEA) in the Department of Commerce, the pre-tax profits of foreign subsidiaries grew from $207 billion in 1999 to $255 billion in 2002. This 23 percent increase in foreign profits was dwarfed by the growth of profits in 18 countries Sullivan denotes as tax havens. Profits in these countries increased 68 percent over the same period from $88 billion in 1999 to $149 billion in 2002. Although this data may suffer from double-counting, they do suggest that the use of havens is growing in significance. McLure points out that this is a problem for both home *and* host countries.

A NBER working paper by Mihir A. Desai, C. Fritz Foley, and James R. Hines, Jr., hereafter DFH, examines the BEA data in more depth and also presents empirical evidence that relates to the McLure paper (Desai, Foley, and Hines 2004). One of the strategies that McLure discusses involves the use of holding companies to minimize tax liabilities through the unbundling of manufacturing and distribution functions. DFH report a significant increase in the number of holding companies in the BEA data, from 722 in 1989 (4 percent of all affiliates) to 369 in 1999 (7 percent of all affiliates). Another important development in the BEA data is the growth in the share of affiliate sales to related parties located in tax havens. Sales to related parties in tax havens increased by 24 percent (30.2 percent to 37.5 percent) while sales to non-havens grew by only 4 percent (17.8 percent to 18.5 percent) between 1989 and 1999.

The empirical evidence reported in DFH suggests that U.S. firms use tax haven affiliates both to reallocate taxable income away from high-tax jurisdictions and to facilitate deferral of repatriation taxes. DFH find that the ownership of tax haven affiliates is associated with reduction in tax payments by nearby non-haven affiliates to the same extent as a 21 percent local tax rate reduction. This phenomenon is exactly the one McLure describes in his paper. DFH develop another interesting and related point in their work: while havens facilitate profit reallocation and deferral of repatriation taxes, they may also lower the cost of capital and, as a result, increase the attractiveness of foreign investment in LDCs and CITS.

DFH uncover another possible positive impact of tax havens on non-havens. The use of tax havens seems to stimulate the growth of MNC activities in non-havens. Work with the BEA data suggests that setting up a tax haven affiliate is associated with greater sales and investment growth in non-havens. This complementary relationship indicates that the presence of tax havens could accrue some benefit to LDCs and CITS. McLure should take this possible relationship into account in his work.

Altshuler and Grubert (2004) provide further empirical evidence that the tax nets of host countries may be unraveling. We study the evolution of the tax burdens of U.S. companies operating abroad from 1992 to 2002. In particular, we focus on the average effective tax rates for manufacturing subsidiaries in 58 countries. Host country average effective tax rates are calculated by dividing the total income taxes paid by U.S. controlled foreign corporations (CFCs) in the manufacturing sector by their total earnings and profits (only CFCs with positive earnings and profits are included in the totals). The global means for each year are presented in table 1 (reproduced here) and represent the average of effective tax rates in all 58 countries weighted by the number of CFCs in each country in 1990. The table demonstrates that the average effective tax rate faced by U.S. manufacturing affiliates abroad has fallen by approximately 57 percent since 1980 (from 33 percent in 1980 to 21 percent in 2000).

Table 1. Average Effective Tax Rates in Manufacturing for 58 Countries (weighted by number of CFCs in each country in 1990)

Year	Average Effective Tax Rate	Standard Deviation
1980	0.33	0.85
1982	0.34	0.98
1984	0.34	1.03
1986	0.32	1.05
1988	0.31	1.09
1990	0.26	0.89
1992	0.25	0.86
1994	0.22	0.72
1996	0.23	0.79
1998	0.24	0.77
2000	0.21	0.67

Source: Altshuler and Grubert (2004).

We investigate whether host country behavior, driven by tax competition, for instance, or company behavior, driven by so-called "self-help techniques," explain the drop in effective tax rates since 1992. We specifically look at the extent to which the use of tax havens can lower the average effective tax rate on investment abroad. The focus is on 1992 onward since researchers have already examined the pre-1992 data (see, for example, Altshuler, Grubert, and Newlon 2001).

How can self-help techniques lower host country effective tax rates? In what follows, I discuss an important self-help strategy that is not addressed in the McLure paper. Companies can use a structure called a "hybrid" or "tax nothing" to lower effective tax rates. Briefly, a hybrid is an entity that is incorporated from the host country's point of view and a branch from the U.S. point of view. The advantage of a hybrid is that it permits companies to avoid the relatively strict anti-abuse rules that apply to CFCs and restrict the use of tax haven subsidiaries. Under these rules, the payment of interest or royalties from one CFC to a tax haven CFC is taxed currently by the U.S. Treasury. A hybrid entity makes this payment invisible to the U.S. because it all occurs within one combined entity. Setting up hybrids has been simplified by the 'check-the-box' regulations announced in December of 1996 and effective January 1, 1997. Table 1 shows a decrease between 1998 and 2000 in average effective tax rates (from 24 percent to 21 percent), which we attribute, in part, to the 'check-the-box' regulations. Hybrids have ripped yet another hole in revenue nets.

The transparent hybrid entity (to the U.S.) could be set-up as a tax haven branch (from the U.S. point of view) of a non-haven affiliate, for example, or alternatively as a non-haven branch (from the U.S. point of view) of a tax haven affiliate. We find evidence for both structures in U.S. Treasury data. For instance, companies incorporated in the Cayman Islands (as CFCs of U.S. manufacturing parents) report real capital on their balance sheets. In fact, the effective tax rate for manufacturing CFCs in the Cayman Islands was almost 6 percent in 2000. And real capital reported in Cayman Island manufacturing CFCs increased by more than 500 percent between 1992 and 2000. Setting up a Cayman Island branch of a German CFC, for example, lowers the effective tax rate in Germany. The point that McLure makes in his paper is that tax planning techniques involving tax havens have consequences for LDCs and CITS trying to attract FDI. LDCs and CITS are competing with Germany, for instance, and even though Germany is a high-tax country, once MNCs have hybrids and other opportunities to lower tax rates faced there, ostensibly high-tax countries may not be that unattractive relative to low-tax LDCs and CITS.

We conclude in Altshuler and Grubert that the decrease in the average effective tax rate between 1992 and 1998 seems to be driven by tax competition (country behavior), but the reduction in average effective rates between 1998 and 2000 was driven by self-help behavior (company behavior). A different dynamic seems to have evolved. Understanding the consequences of this type of dynamic is a goal of McLure's paper. Although McLure focuses on transfer pricing, I believe that hybrids are a significant devise used by MNCs to lower tax burdens abroad that should be explored.

Altshuler and Grubert also present some empirical evidence on inter-company trade that supports the earnings shifting story McLure describes in his contribution to this volume. Data from Treasury files shows that average affiliate sales to all affiliates over total sales and average affiliate purchases from all affiliates over total sales increased dramatically between 1984 and 1992. The share of total sales more than quadrupled over the period (from .049 to .224), and the share of total purchases more than doubled (from .079 to .178). The increase in the importance of these transactions is consistent with the increase in sensitivity of investment to tax considerations. This evidence also demonstrates the growing potential for MNCs to use transfer pricing and earning shifting to transfer profits out of host countries to tax havens. McLure has identified an extremely difficult problem for LDCs and CITS that seek to increase inward FDI.

The combination of the careful and insightful paper by McLure with the empirical evidence I have discussed paint a somewhat gloomy picture for LDCs and CITS. Although McLure points out that many countries recently passed CFC rules, it is my impression that they are less stringent than the U.S. rules and that many countries are using these rules to protect their own revenues and not to create positive spillovers for LDCs and other host countries. While some may hold out hope for these CFC rules, as McLure acknowledges, they are difficult to monitor. And I agree with McLure's argument that the OECD model agreement on exchange of information and the coordinated defense mechanism are crumbs on the table for the LDCs. Maybe the best hope is for the multilateral agreements, but I am not optimistic.

Goodspeed discusses the complicated ways in which FDI incentives are affected by the international tax system of home and host countries. I would like to see Goodspeed model these incentives instead of simply describing them. A theoretical model could show, for example, the hypothetical effective tax rates for simple prototypical investments. This type of model could show clearly how different tax incentives impact effective tax rates in a world in which the use of tax havens and other tax minimizing strategies are available to MNCs. A revision along these lines would be extremely informative to policy makers.

References

Altshuler, Rosanne and Harry Grubert (2004), "Taxpayer Responses to Competitive Tax Policies and Tax Policy Responses to Competitive Taxpayers: Recent Evidence", *Tax Notes International*, Vol. 34 (13), pp. 1349-1362.

Altshuler, Rosanne, Harry Grubert, and T. Scott Newlon (1998), "Has U.S. Investment Abroad Become More Sensitive to Tax Rates?", pp. 9-32 in: James R. Hines, Jr., editor, *International Taxation and Multinational Activity*, Chicago: University of Chicago Press.

Desai, Mihir A., C. Fritz Foley, and James R. Hines, Jr. (2004), *Economic Effects of Regional Tax Havens, NBER Working Paper 10806*, National Bureau of Economic Research, Inc.

Sullivan, Martin (2004), "Economic Analysis: Data Show Dramatic Shift of Profits to Tax Havens", *Tax Notes*, Vol. 104, pp. 1190-1200.

Surrey, Stanley S. (1978), "Reflections on the Allocation of Income and Expenses among National Tax Jurisdictions", *Law and Policy in International Business*, Vol. 10, pp. 409-60.

DISCUSSANT COMMENTS

ROBERT S. CHIRINKO
Emory University and CESifo

GUGL AND ZODROW, MINTZ, AND WILSON

This set of papers examines the potentially constructive role that can be played by preferential tax incentives on mobile capital, an issue that weighs particularly heavily on policymakers in developing countries. The three papers take different but complementary approaches to addressing this issue. Elisabeth Gugl and George Zodrow focus on the tax problem facing a single country, and present analytic and simulation results highlighting the importance of the menu of taxes available to policymakers. While also presenting analytic results, Jay Wilson studies the strategic behavior between two countries competing over the tax base. Jack Mintz returns to a single country analysis in the analytic part of his paper emphasizing the mobility of taxable profits; the empirical part presents interesting evidence on the use of preferential tax incentives in 15 developing countries. While the implications for tax policy differ, these three papers shed much light on preferential tax incentives and important dimensions of the problem facing policymakers.

To place some structure on my discussion of these three different papers, I review each in a common framework: approach, results, concerns and extensions, and remaining issues. Gugl and Zodrow model a single country whose constant returns to scale production function depends on three factors: perfectly mobile capital (K, owned 100% by domestic residents), partially mobile capital (C, owned 100% by foreigners), and perfectly immobile labor (L). A uniform source-based tax is levied on both types of capital at rate t. A preferential tax policy is represented by a parameter, θ, that multiplies t and varies between 0 (no tax on K) and 1 (no preferential treatment of K relative to C). The fiscal authorities also have at their disposal a nondistortionary head tax, H. The rates of return on K and C are r and w, respectively. A key friction in the model is that the supply of C is positively related to its rate of return, and the associated inverse supply curve is w = w[C], w'[C] > 0. This formulation allows for the possibility of rent extraction from foreigners. Lastly, public goods, G, are financed by tax revenues, and enter the utility function.

Four results are derived depending on whether H or θ are constrained or unconstrained. Scenario A assumes H and θ are unconstrained. H is set to deliver the optimal level of G, and θ^A is set to zero (hence K is untaxed). Partially mobile capital is taxed according to an inverse elasticity rule, $t^A = w / \varepsilon[w,C]$, where the fiscal authorities extract rents but are tempered from doing so by the adverse effects on the productivity of the other factors. This scenario provides a very useful benchmark against which to compare the remaining results. Scenario B removes the possibility of preferential incentives ($\theta = 1$). Again, H is set to achieve the optimal level of G. The optimal tax rate, t^B, is positive, but less than t^A because, in this scenario, K is also being adversely affected by the tax rate. These two results based on an unconstrained H are analytically unambiguous and informative.

In the remaining two scenarios, H is no longer set in an unconstrained manner. G is financed by distorting capital taxes, and hence is underprovided. The optimization problem thus becomes more complicated, and no general analytic results emerge. The authors conduct simulations using assumed parameters, and these results suggest that preferential incentives improve welfare.

I like the model for its focus on key issues and illumination of the margins that matter for fiscal decisions. Nonetheless, I would like to mention three concerns. First, the existence and uniqueness of the equilibrium and the role of the curvature in w[C] needs to be studied further, as constant returns in production and the perfect mobility of one type of capital (facing a relatively high tax rate) may cause difficulties. Second, the assumption of immobile labor can be questioned. The huge subsidies paid to East German workers after Reunification and the reluctance in some quarters to expand the EU to low wage countries suggest that the movement of labor is a notable constraint faced by policymakers. Third, G does not influence production. Yet, a few days before this conference was held, one of the largest global competitions was concluded with the awarding of the 2010 World Cup to South Africa, a victory that was due in large part to its superior infrastructure. Thus, I would prefer a production structure in which capital is perfectly mobile, labor (and perhaps a second type of capital) is partially mobile, and public goods are fixed.

The authors' simulations suggest a useful extension that would provide a better treatment of factor mobility that is presently modeled in a static sense in terms of the slope of w[C]. But the degree of mobility depends on the time horizon, from nearly zero (fixed) in the short-run to infinite (perfectly mobile) in the long-run. Bovenberg (1986) and Rosen and Topel (1988) provide useful models in which mobility changes with the time horizon. This extension would complicate the model, but it could then be solved through simulation. Apart from providing natural definitions of the short-run, the medium-run, and the long-run, such simulations would allow for an analysis of the discounted value of welfare changes, would highlight the role of key substitution elasticities and other parameters of taste and technology, and would generate results that align with the planning horizons of policymakers.

Gugl and Zodrow highlight the role of a number of interesting margins, but leave as a remaining issue strategic tax competition among countries, a topic addressed in the paper by Jay Wilson. To place his contribution in perspective, a brief (and necessarily cursory) review of the tax competition literature is warranted. (See Wilson and Wildasin (2004) for a complete review.) Tax competition can be measured in several ways; here we focus on competition among independent governments over a mobile tax base (Wilson and Wildasin, p. 1067). Consideration of interjurisdictional competition begins with the Tiebout model, which suggests that tax competition creates an efficient outcome. Oates (1972) and many other authors have challenged that result, finding that tax competition leads to spillover effects (a fiscal externality) among countries, leading to a "race to the bottom" as mobile capital flees relatively high taxation. The suboptimally low level of tax revenues leads to a suboptimally low level of spending on public goods. Wildasin (1989) proposes a Pigouvian tax to correct the fiscal externality, but this approach relies on a very well-informed and powerful central government. Since the latter assumption is not appropriate in most international situations, recent work has studied the Nash equilibrium between two competing countries each with two tax bases distinguished by their degree of mobility. The results differ widely; Keen (2001) finds that tax revenue is higher when preferential taxes are used, while Janeba and Peters (1999) report the opposite result.

In this paper, Wilson identifies and addresses a problem found in these latter analyses -- the nonexistence of a solution in pure strategies that may arise when one capital base is perfectly (or "almost" perfectly) mobile. He explores a solution in a simultaneous move game where there are two tax bases and each country's strategy is represented by a probability distribution of tax rates. Wilson obtains two results for preferential taxes. When the tax bases are perfectly mobile and perfectly immobile, tax revenues are the same in the preferential or non-preferential tax regimes. However, when the immobile base becomes partially mobile, tax preferences allow a country to obtain higher revenues than in a tax regime where they are not used. The paper contains a nice discussion of the intuition underlying these results.

Nonetheless, three concerns exist. First, the different solutions (obtained when one of the tax bases is perfectly immobile or partially mobile) appear to hinge on the separability of the tax bases. It would be interesting to know how the results change if the factors of production related to the two tax bases interact in a neoclassical production function. Second, the paper refrains from using a sequential game where one country moves first. Yet, such a game would seem to capture the relations between many large and small countries (e.g., the United States and Jamaica). Third and perhaps of most concern is that the connection between a mixed strategy and policy actions is not tightly drawn. Notwithstanding the comments in the concluding section, it would be useful to have more discussion that casts this intellectually interesting technical idea in terms of the constraints and actions relevant to policymaking.

While both the Gugl and Zodrow and the Wilson papers contain many interesting theoretical results, little attention is paid to the empirical facts concerning preferential taxes. Jack Mintz's paper, which has both empirical and analytic parts, nicely fills the gap. He reviews the tax policies in the top 15 developing countries classified by their FDI/GDP ratio for the period 1997 to 2002. Among other findings, the corporate tax rates are generally less than 20%, withholding rates are generally less than 5%, depreciation write-offs tend to be accelerated, and tax holidays are not used frequently, occurring in only one-third of the countries.

This review provides very important information with which to base policy and analytic exercises, though one is then tempted to ask for more. It would be useful to present additional information on a group of countries against which these 15 developing countries can be compared. Additionally, the individual tax parameters in isolation are not sufficient for summarizing investment incentives; reporting explicit costs of capital would also be helpful.

These concerns notwithstanding, the broad conclusions to be drawn from the information in Table 1 are that, in recent years, capital income tax rates are rather low and that tax holidays are not in widespread use. The second part of the Mintz paper explains these two findings. The model highlights the importance of income-shifting through financial transactions. (Transfer pricing is a second avenue by which firms can shift income between jurisdictions.) A high marginal income tax rate attracts debt and interest deductions, and hence lowers the tax base. Since these financial transactions are easy to undertake by multinationals, low income tax rates are optimal. Mintz then argues that tax holidays are inferior to low corporate tax rates for three reasons: 1) newer firms are favored at the expense of older and politically more established older firms; 2) incentive exist to reclassify old firms as new; 3) the investment incentives may be dulled by income-shifting during and after the holiday period.

While the important role of income-shifting is clearly highlighted, several concerns remain. In the model, the cost of debt exceeds the cost of external equity. Yet the well-known Pecking Order model (which is not without its critics) suggests the reverse ordering. Moreover, the cost of internal equity is assumed to be zero, rather than equal to an appropriate opportunity cost. Given the importance of income-shifting in this paper, it would be useful to have more discussion about and evidence on how multinationals shift income between jurisdictions. Finally, the prescription that lowering corporate tax rates is a desirable policy stands in contrast to the traditional view in the tax incidence literature that this policy is an inefficient means for providing investment incentives because the change affects both new and old capital. I do not doubt the finding in this paper, but it would be interesting to know more about the key assumption(s) that overturns the traditional conclusion.

These three papers make several interesting and important contributions to our understanding n not be drawn, the results of Gugl and Zodrow and of Wilson tend to favor of preferential tax incentives. While definitive conclusions ca preferential tax incentives, while the possibility of substantial income-shifting leads Mintz to be cautious about their usefulness. Given the unsettled issues highlighted in these three papers and the potential benefits of preferential tax incentives, the flow of interesting and policy-relevant papers is unlikely to abate soon.

References

Bovenberg, A. Lans (1986), "Capital Income Taxation in Growing Open Economies", *Journal of Public Economics*, Vol.31, pp. 347-376.

Gugl, Elisabeth, and George Zodrow (this volume), *International Tax Competition And Tax Incentives In Developing Countries.*

Keen, Michael (2001), "Preferential Regimes Can Make Tax Competition Less Harmful", *National Tax Journal*, Vol. 54, pp. 757-762.

Janeba, Eckhard, and Wolfgang Peters (1999), "Tax Evasion, Tax Competition and the Gains from Nondiscrimination: The Case of Interest Taxation in Europe", *Economic Journal*, Vol. 109, pp. 93-101.

Mintz, Jack (this volume), *The Changing Structure of Tax Policies for Foreign Direct Investment in Developing Countries?*

Oates, Wallace E. (1972), *Fiscal Federalism*, New York: Harcourt Brace Jovanovich.

Rosen, Sherwin, and Robert Topel (1988), "A Time-Series Model of Housing Investment in the U.S.", *Journal of Political Economy*, Vol. 96, pp. 718-740.

Wildasin, David E. (1989), "Interjurisdictional Capital Mobility: Fiscal Externality and a Corrective Subsidy", *Journal of Urban Economics*, Vol. 25, pp. 193-212.

Wilson, John D. (this volume), *Tax Competition with and without Preferential Treatment of A Highly-Mobile Tax Base.*

Wilson, John D., and David E. Wildasin (2004), "Capital Tax Competition: Bane or Boon", *Journal of Public Economics*, Vol. 88, pp. 1065-1091.

4

TAX STRUCTURE REVISITED

Chapter 9

CAN DEVELOPING COUNTRIES IMPOSE AN INDIVIDUAL INCOME TAX?

JAMES ALM AND SALLY WALLACE[1]
Andrew Young School of Policy Studies, Georgia State University

1. INTRODUCTION

The individual income tax (IIT) is widely used in most all countries around the world, and is often a significant source of revenues for the government. So the short answer to the title question is "of course".

However, the more fundamental issue is the type of IIT that developing countries are in practice able to impose. In particular, will the IIT that emerges in developing countries meet the usual canons of a "good" tax – equity, efficiency, and adequacy? We argue in this paper that it is unlikely that a developing country can actually administer a broad-based, "global" individual income tax, in which income from all sources is aggregated and is subject to a single rate structure after adjustments for personal exemptions and deductions. Instead, we argue that the most suitable form of the IIT that most developing countries are likely to be able to achieve – at least at this point in time – is one characterized by a "schedular" approach to income taxation, in which each of the main types of income flows (e.g., wages and salaries, dividends, interest, rent) is subject to separate rate schedules that are not typically graduated. Such a less ambitious scope for an IIT in developing countries seems better able to achieve the goals of equity, efficiency, and adequacy in the taxation of individual income.

We make this argument by first looking at a framework for thinking about taxes, and then examining the world-wide practice of income taxation over the last several decades. Information from Government Finance Statistics on the shares of individual income taxes in Gross Domestic Product (GDP) indicates a slight upward trend in the importance of the IIT for some – but not all – countries. We then focus on one developing country in particular. The Government of Jamaica has worked hard to reform its individual income tax, and has made significant progress in expanding the base, lowering marginal tax rates, and simplifying the structure of the tax. During this time, the IIT has shifted from a global income tax to one that has important schedular elements. Even so, there is at least suggestive evidence that there remain massive amounts of evasion/avoidance in the Jamaican IIT, that its distribution of tax burdens is much less progressive in fact than in principle, and the tax likely generates significant distortions in behavior. In short, despite the major efforts of the Government of Jamaica in addressing the shortcomings of the IIT, the tax is one that is still plagued by avoidance and evasion and one that still introduces significant inequities and inefficiencies. Nonetheless, we argue that the positive achievements in the Jamaican IIT have come largely as a result of a move toward a more schedular approach to income taxation. We conclude by suggesting that Jamaica should continue its move toward a schedular approach to individual income taxation. More generally, we argue that the individual income tax should remain in most developing countries' tax portfolios, but that a schedular approach to income taxation is likely to be the most appropriate road for developing countries to travel, especially given the emerging forces that reduce the ability of governments to collect income taxes.

2. A FRAMEWORK FOR ANALYSIS: CHARACTERIZING AND IMPLEMENTING A "GOOD" TAX SYSTEM

It is useful at the start to discuss the canons of a "good" tax system because these criteria help frame the discussion of the type of individual income tax that developing countries are able to impose. We have numerous goals for taxes:

- To be fair
- To be nondistorting
- To generate adequate revenues
- To be simple
- To help stabilize the economy
- To promote economic growth.

Still, a careful examination of these factors (Alm 1996) suggests that they mainly involve tradeoffs among three criteria:

- How does the choice affect the distribution of the burden of taxation among individuals, where the burden is defined broadly in terms of the tax burden and the compliance cost burden on taxpayers (***equity***)?
- How does the choice affect the decisions of individuals and firms, where the decisions are defined broadly in terms of the responses of the agents to the entire tax, compliance, and enforcement parameters (***efficiency***)?
- How does the choice of taxes affect the yield of the tax collections, where the yield is defined broadly in terms of the gross collections in excess of administrative and enforcement costs (***adequacy***)?

(Note that we do not define a separate criterion for simplicity. Instead, simplicity is implicitly considered in its effects on the other three dimensions of a desirable tax system.) Consequently, analysis of taxation requires balancing the tradeoffs between equity, efficiency, and adequacy, where each is broadly defined and commonly measured.

Consider the application of each criterion to the individual income tax, beginning with equity. What is a "fair" tax system? There are various notions of a "fair" distribution of taxes:

- Taxes are fair if people pay taxes in accordance with their ability to pay, with those people having equal ability paying the same taxes (or "Horizontal Equity") and those having greater ability paying more taxes (or "Vertical Equity"). This is called the "Ability-to-Pay Principle".
- Taxes are fair if people pay taxes in accordance with the benefits they receive from government expenditures. This is called the "Benefit Principle".

These notions depend on one's own values and these values differ for different people, so there is not much that we can say in general about what is a "fair" tax. Still, it seems obvious that one's notion of a fair tax will depend in some way on how taxes affect the distribution of income; that is, is the distribution of tax burdens progressive, proportional, or regressive?

A second criterion is efficiency. When a tax is imposed, agents respond by changing their behavior to avoid paying the tax. The tax therefore distorts the behavior on both sides of the market by changing the prices faced by economic agents, causing agents to change their behaviors solely because of the tax. This change in behavior is a distortion from the tax, and leads (in most cases) to a loss in efficiency. To minimize these distortions, taxes should be imposed on those agents or activities where any changes in behavior are smaller. Keeping marginal tax rates low, tax bases broad, and taxes simple also reduces distortions.

As for adequacy, a government must generate sufficient revenues from its various tax instruments to pay for the goods and services that it wishes to provide to its citizens. The government must consider the responses of demanders and suppliers when estimating the revenues from the tax. Because most any tax will lead to a lower quantity bought and sold, the revenues will be less than predicted if these responses are not considered. In general, a tax imposed on a responsive base will collect fewer revenues than predicted; similarly, to collect more revenues, taxes should be imposed taxes on agents or activities where responses are lower. Over time, as the economy grows, the tax revenue needs to grow to fulfill increased demands for public goods. Further, on administrative grounds, governments should impose taxes on bases that easily identified and monitored; that is, the costs to the government of collecting taxes need to be considered, and the costs to taxpayers of paying taxes need also to be considered. In this regard, reducing administrative and compliance costs requires doing such things as:

- Keeping taxes simple, because complicated taxes require skilled – and expensive – people to administer
- Collecting taxes from a few "points", because the more agents from which a tax is collected, the more people must be watched and monitored
- Using withholding at source
- Levying only a few taxes
- Exempting low-income households and firms
- Keeping tax structures in place without frequent change
- Using presumptive taxes
- Imposing taxes on a broad base
- Imposing taxes at a low rate.

Achieving adequacy also requires that the tax administration enforce the tax laws (e.g., locate and register taxpayers, use computers where possible, develop adequate audit procedures, enforce penalties, provide services to taxpayers to make it easier for them to comply).

When it comes to the IIT, a classic tax policy question is: "Why have an individual income tax?" There are a variety of ways for the government to raise revenue, with the IIT only one potential type of tax instrument. Proponents of the IIT typically list the following reasons for having the tax:

- It is income elastic; that is, its revenues grow in proportion to income.
- It is progressive in its distribution of tax burdens.
- It can be relatively neutral in its effects on economic decisions, thus reducing distortions in the economy.

Those who are less taken with these virtues of the individual income tax also make strong arguments against the income tax:

- Because it is income elastic, revenues may decline during economic downturns.
- "Bracket creep" due to inflation results in potentially increased tax burdens with no change in real income, and a progressive rate schedule means that taxes will grow faster than real income.
- The tax is often used to give special preferences to certain groups or certain income types, thus disrupting the equity and efficiency advantages of the tax.
- Taxpayers (employers, employees, and self-employed) often feel that compliance with the tax is cumbersome and expensive.
- The tax may require a high level of administration, which imposes costs on the government tax agency.

Even so, the IIT is a staple feature of most tax systems. The next section discusses the practice of income taxation around the world.

3. INDIVIDUAL INCOME TAXATION AROUND THE WORLD

Individual income tax systems can be broadly classified into three main types (Goode 1984). A "global" income tax combines incomes from all sources into a single aggregate measure of income, adjusts this aggregate measure for such items as personal exemptions and deductions, and then applies a single rate or a graduated rate structure to determine the tax liability. In a "schedular" income tax, each of the main sources of income is subject to a separate tax; the tax rates across these different income flows can differ, but are not imposed at graduated rates, and personal exemptions and deductions are typically not allowed. There can also be "mixed" systems, which combine elements of both global and schedular income taxes.

Global systems tend to be found now mainly in developed countries, although in several countries – France, Belgium, and France – global systems have emerged only since the 1950s. The individual income tax systems in developing countries are often driven mainly by colonial history. Global systems tend to be found in former British colonies (e.g., Jamaica), while schedular systems are more common in Francophone Africa and some Latin American countries.

The advantages often claimed for a global system are that a global tax is thought to be most closely in line with the Ability-to-Pay Principle of equity in taxation; that is, a global tax is better able to achieve equity in the distribution of its tax burdens because it is imposed on a comprehensive definition of income that reflects individual circumstances via deductions and exemptions. Further, a global tax on something close to "comprehensive income" is seen as a more neutral tax because a broad-based income tax reduces the incentives for income-shifting activities, thereby reducing the efficiency costs of the tax. Finally, a global income tax imposed on a broad-based definition of income has greater revenue potential than one imposed on a narrower base. A schedular tax is often justified more on the basis of ease of administration. Withholding at source at the main types of income flows – wages and salaries, interest, dividends, rents, and so on – largely eliminates the necessity of individual returns. This administrative advantage comes at the expense of equity and efficiency considerations.[2]

What is the current practice of individual income taxation? Table 1 provides some information on the overall level of taxation in OECD countries and in a selected sample of developing countries for two recent subperiods, 1986-1988 and 1996-1998. As shown there, the overall level of burden, expressed as a share of GDP is roughly double in the OECD countries than in the developing countries in both subperiods. There is also a tendency for the overall level of taxation to rise over time, but this tendency is small for both groups of countries. This evidence is consistent with the notion that higher levels of economic development are associated with higher levels of taxation (Bahl 1971; Tanzi 1987; Tanzi 1992; Burgess and Stern 1993).[3]

Table 1. The Importance of the ITT in Tax Revenues (as percent of GDP)

	1986-1988		**1996-1998**	
	Total Taxes	**Individual Income Taxes**	**Total Taxes**	**Individual Income Taxes**
OECD Countries:	36.8%	11.4%	38.1%	10.9%
America	30.9	11.4	32.8	12.6
Pacific	30.8	13.4	31.9	11.7
Europe	38.6	11.5	40.1	11.0
Developing Countries:	17.7	1.9	18.4	2.5
Africa (10)	19.4	3.1	20.0	4.0
Asia (10)	16.2	2.0	17.7	2.9
Middle East (8)	16.8	1.2	18.1	1.5

Source: Computed by authors from various issues of Government Finance Statistics.

Of more relevance here, the individual income tax is of considerably more importance in tax revenues in developed than in developing countries. For OECD countries, the IIT averages less than 1/3 of total revenues; for developing countries the fraction is closer to 1/9. More generally, taxes on consumption (e.g., value added taxes, sales and excise taxes, taxes on trade) are of much greater relative importance in developing than in developed countries, while taxes on income are more important in the developed world. Even so, the IIT has tended to decline in relative importance in OECD countries, at the same time that it has increased slightly in importance for developing countries. In the United States (as in most developed countries), the individual income tax is a major source of revenues for the central government. The IIT in the U.S. is imposed on income aggregated over all sources of income (e.g., a global income tax). The evidence on the IIT for the U.S. is that:

- The IIT is borne largely by the individual, with a somewhat progressive pattern of incidence.
- The IIT has a number of distorting effects on individual behavior (e.g., labor supply, saving, portfolio choice, tax preferences, tax avoidance/evasion, family structure).
- The IIT imposes significant administrative and compliance costs.
- The vast bulk of the tax is collected from employer withholding at source on wages.

This last observation may be somewhat surprising. Even though the U.S. is widely seen as having the most effective tax administration in the world, as recently as the 1980s well over 90 percent of all IIT collections came from source withholding. This percentage has declined somewhat in the last decade, and has sometimes fallen to roughly 80 percent of IIT revenues. Nevertheless, it remains the case that most individual income tax revenues arise from employer withholding on wage and salary income. At this point, such evidence is merely suggestive that a "scheduler" income tax may be appropriate in countries without the tax collection machinery present in the U.S.

Similar evidence is hard to come by for many other countries. Even so, and despite the predominance of global income tax systems in developed countries, the U.S. General Accounting Office (1996) provides evidence that thirty-four countries employ variants on an individual income tax system in which individuals are not required to file end-of-year returns.[4] Such "no-return" or "final withholding" tax systems vary significantly, but many share some common characteristics. For example, most all countries use employer withholding on wages and salaries. Also, taxes on interest and dividend incomes are exempt or limited; in many cases interest and dividend income is taxed at a flat rate, with the tax withheld by the financial institution or the company. Finally, the unit of taxation is the individual, so that a spouse who elects final withholding must file as an individual rather than jointly. Put differently, there is much evidence of individual income tax systems that have important schedular components. The next section discusses the experiences of one country, Jamaica, that has had the tradition of a global income tax but that has also moved toward a more schedular approach to taxation over the last two decades.

4. THE JAMAICAN EXPERIENCE WITH INDIVIDUAL INCOME TAXATION

The individual income tax in Jamaica has long been one of the major workhorses of the Government of Jamaica revenue system. In fiscal year 2002-2003, the Pay-As-You-Earn (PAYE) portion of the income tax accounted for 21.7 percent of total government tax revenues. Only the general consumption tax (at 27. 4 percent of total tax revenue) is as important a tax revenue source in Jamaica. This general pattern has not changed much since the 1980s.

The individual income tax is governed by the Income Tax Law of Jamaica, which is the same law that covers the corporate income tax and the taxation of interest and dividends. We focus on the income taxes directly accruing to individuals (including sole proprietors and other self-employed individuals), as well as capital income taxation for individuals.

The law granting an income tax was passed in 1919, and the first general income tax took effect in 1920. The tax had a basic threshold (or zero rate), and the rate structure was progressive from 1 to 10 percent of the tax base (Mendes and McLean 2003). The modern income tax was legislated in 1955, and in 1976 the Income Tax Act came into effect. The IIT was subject to a major reform in 1986, when the current flat-rate income tax became effective and numerous credits (e.g., "allowances") were replaced by a standard deduction.

In this section, we discuss the evolution of the IIT in Jamaica over the last two decades. Our basic points are simple. Despite the major efforts of the GOJ in addressing the shortcomings of the IIT – and the successes that these efforts have produced – the tax is one that is still plagued by avoidance and evasion and one that still introduces significant inequities and inefficiencies. Even so, we believe that the positive reform achievements have come largely as a result of a move toward a more schedular approach to income taxation. Further improvements in the IIT will likely require further moves toward schedular taxation.

4.1 The Jamaica Individual Income Tax Prior to the 1986 Reform

At the time that tax reform efforts began in the early 1980s, the individual income tax was the largest and most productive source of revenues for the GOJ and certainly its most visible. In 1983, the IIT was the largest single revenue source, with revenues of 28.9 percent of all government revenues and 7.6 percent of GDP. The IIT had evolved over time, typically by piecemeal changes that had led to increasingly higher tax rates on an increasingly smaller tax base. In theory, the IIT that had emerged was highly progressive, due to its global definition of income, its graduated rate structure, and its use of numerous tax credits that attempted to take into consideration the special circumstances of individual taxpayers. In practice, however, the progressivity was dramatically reduced by many and various loopholes that enabled individuals to avoid and evade taxes on a massive scale. As a result, the tax produced far less revenue than it might have, its impact on the distribution of tax burdens was arbitrary, capricious, and unfair, and it was widely seen as the source of severe distortions in individual behaviors.

These problems eventually led the GOJ to introduce in 1986 a major reform of the income tax. However, before the reform package could be designed, it was essential for the GOJ to have an accurate picture of the workings of the tax. Efforts to inform the tax reform process led to the following picture of the IIT, based largely on information surrounding 1983 and stemming from the work of Alm and Bahl (1985) and Alm, Bahl, and Murray (1991) with the Income Tax Department of the GOJ.

At that time, two types of individuals paid the tax: those with income only from wages and salaries, and those with income from any source in addition to wages and salaries (e.g., interest, rent, dividends). The first group of taxpayers had taxes withheld by their employer under the Pay-As-You-Earn (PAYE) system, and these individuals were not required to file an income tax return unless some error was made in withholding. The second type of income recipient, often referred to as the "self-employed", also had PAYE taxes withheld on wage income, if any such income was earned and if the employer was registered. In addition, these individuals were required to file a tax return upon which all income was totaled and income taxes on total income were paid. In practice, over 90 percent of IIT revenues came from employer withholding. Although the specific features of the base and rate structure of the income tax have changed considerably over time, the broad outline of the tax has remained largely the same.

On paper, the IIT in 1983 was broad-based, with only interest income exempt, and the tax rate structure was high and steeply progressive, rising from a marginal tax rate of 30 percent on the first J$7000 of taxable (or "statutory") income to 57.5 percent on all income above J$14,000.[5] [6] However, in practice the base and progressivity of the IIT were reduced by several factors.

First, an individual's tax liability could be reduced to zero by the application of up to sixteen tax credits of various amounts, for such purposes as personal and child tax credits, alimony, medical expenditures, the employment of household helpers, and participation in savings and life insurance programs. Second, there was a well-entrenched system in which employers provided nontaxable fringe benefits called "allowances" to their employees; among the more popular allowances were those for housing, transportation, utilities, and entertainment. Such allowances were supposed to be included in taxable income under the Income Tax Act. However, in practice no taxes were imposed on the allowances. Indeed, the allowances were often paid simply in cash, with little verification of the actual individual expenditure. Third, income earned from "overtime" activities received preferential treatment. Overtime income was taxed at the lowest marginal tax rate of 30 percent, even if the individual's total income placed him or her in a higher bracket. Fourth, the tax base was reduced by individuals who filed tax returns but who underreported taxable income (termed "underreporters"); the base was also reduced by individuals who simply did not file any tax return ("nonfilers").

Of course, the difficulty here was to quantify the magnitudes of these actual and potential tax bases. The GOJ had little information even on the size of the actual tax base (e.g., the PAYE and the self-employed taxpayers). It had no information on the magnitude of the base erosion via credits, allowances, overtime, underreporting, and nonfiling. To make these estimates, Alm and Bahl (1985) and Alm, Bahl, and Murray (1991) worked with the GOJ to assemble a variety of original data bases that allowed them to estimate the magnitudes of these actual and potential bases.

For example, Alm and Bahl (1985) and Alm, Bahl, and Murray (1991) estimated the size of the actual tax base via several random samples of individual and firm taxpayer records and returns. These returns also allowed them to estimate the extent of base erosion via the use of tax credits and of overtime income. The extent of allowance use was estimated via a special survey of public and private sector employers, conducted by the GOJ.

Estimating tax evasion was much more difficult. The extent of underreporting was estimated using information provided by the Audit Department of the Income Tax Department. All audited tax returns were first collected; these returns gave information both on items reported by the taxpayer, as well as information on post-audit, or "true", return items as determined by the tax auditor. Statistical techniques were then used to estimate the extent of underreporting by all self-employed taxpayers.

As for nonfiling, the extent of nonfiling was estimated in several steps. First, a "master list" of names was compiled for various occupations from various third party sources of information (e.g., telephone directories, trade association lists, firm registration lists from the Small Business Association of Jamaica or from the Ministry of Health). These occupations included service stations, customs brokerages, auto repair, auto parts, hair care, real estate, contractors, transport operators, and spirits outlets; they also included accountants, architects, attorneys, doctors, optometrists, and veterinarians. Second, a stratified random sample of names was drawn from this master list, and these names were then taken to the Income Tax Department to determine whether these individuals filed any tax returns and paid any income taxes. Third, the characteristics of those from the master list who filed returns were used to impute the characteristics of those who did not file any returns.

These procedures should be viewed with some caution. Nevertheless, the picture that emerges from these various estimates is a consistent and plausible one. Tables 2 and 3 give some of the results of these procedures. As shown in Table 2, the statutory distribution of tax burdens appeared on the surface to be quite progressive. The average tax rate rose monotonically (after the first income class), reaching 43.7 percent. When the self-employed and the PAYE taxpayers were examined separately, the progressivity appeared even more apparent. Self-employed taxpayers tended to be higher income than PAYE taxpayers (J$11,012 versus J$7530), and the average tax rates for the self-employed ranged from 0 to 52.2 percent versus 6.9 to 40.0 percent for PAYE taxpayers. This progressivity was also increased by the use of tax credits (Table 2). Tax credits reduced the tax liabilities across all income groups, but lowered them by greater proportionate amounts in lower brackets.

However, avoidance and evasion activities seriously compromised this apparent progressivity. As shown in Table 3, overtime income was calculated to equal J$96.7 million, or nearly 5 percent of statutory income for all PAYE taxpayers. Of more significance, undeclared income of non-filing self-employed individuals was estimated to equal J$583.8 million, or over one-fourth of the official tax base, which resulted in an estimated loss of IIT revenues of J$162 million. Underreported income of self-employed taxpayers was estimated to equal J$112.3, an amount that reduced revenues by over J$50 million. Untaxed allowances were also quite significant, estimated to equal J$246.6 million with an implied revenue loss of J$117 million.

Overall, fully taxed income of self-employed and PAYE taxpayers was roughly J$2.1 billion; total comprehensive income was more than J$1 billion greater. The actual tax base was only two-thirds of its potential, with the major sources of tax base erosion stemming from the failure of many self-employed individuals to file any tax return and from the use by many taxpayers of untaxed allowances. The failure to tax all of these potential bases led to an estimated revenue loss of J$349 million, or an amount equal to 84 percent of the IIT revenues actually collected ($J417). Recall that the tax credits generated another J$325.2 million loss in tax revenues. The total revenue erosion therefore exceeded J$674 million, an amount equivalent to 1.6 times the amount actually collected. Given the patterns of tax base erosion, this revenue loss was essentially a transfer from lower income to higher income individuals.

Table 2. Distribution of Income and Taxes for Taxpayers, 1983 (J$ amounts in thousands of Jamaican dollars)

	Tax Returns	**Statutory Income (J$)**	**Tax Credits (J$)**	**Taxes Paid (J$)**	**Individual Income Taxes**
Under J$ 2,000	26,640	28,023.0	6,863.3	2,083.5	0.074
2,001-4,000	44,365	136,653.1	32,250.5	8,745.4	0.064
4,001-6,000	58,097	293,202.4	60,124.9	27,835.9	0.095
6,001-8,000	49,300	339,036.7	61,033.1	41,459.5	0.122
8,001-10,000	37,469	332,894.5	55,116.6	50,909.0	0.152
10,0001-12,000	28,157	307,933.4	45,206.7	58,170.9	0.189
12,001-14,000	15,922	207,348.7	25,682.5	47,098.6	0.227
14,001-16,000	7,973	119,501.2	12,293.2	31,876.9	0.267
16,001-18,000	5,284	89,643.7	8,163.4	26,061.3	0.290
18,001-20,000	4,411	84,011.8	6,524.2	27,607.6	0.318
20,001-25,000	4,735	104,003.5	7,504.5	36,039.1	0.346
25,001-30,000	1,691	46,153.2	2,118.8	18,728.7	0.405
30,001-50,000	1,243	45,310.4	1,600.9	18,523.3	0.409
Over 50,000	583	47,331.6	716.3	21,883.1	0.437
Total	285,870	2,181,047.2	325,198.9	417,022.8	0.191

Source: Alm, Bahl, and Murray (1991).

The impact of this base erosion on the presumed progressivity of the IIT was even more striking. Recall that the average tax rate on statutory income increased steadily as statutory income increased (Table 2). However, when the average tax rate is calculated by dividing taxes paid by comprehensive income, a very different picture emerges. As seen in Table 3, the average tax rate now rose somewhat in comprehensive income rises initially, but then fell substantially for the top income classes. The IIT therefore changed from an apparently progressive tax to one that was highly regressive, largely because the tax base erosion occurred much more frequently in higher income classes. Hidden in these estimates was substantial variation within income classes in the proportion of income that was fully taxed. For individuals in the PAYE sector, the bulk of their income was fully taxed; individual with equal comprehensive income who were self-employed were much better able to reduce their tax liabilities through nonfiling and underreporting.

In short, tax base erosion reduced tax revenues and introduced substantial horizontal and vertical inequities into the tax system. In combination with the presumed distorting effects of high marginal tax rates on individual behavior, there was a strong case for major reform of the IIT.

4.2 The 1986 Reform

Based in part on these analyses of the individual income tax, the Government of Jamaica introduced in January 1986 a major reform of the income tax. The 1986 reform had several components: all tax credits were eliminated, replaced by a standard deduction of J$8580

- With some exceptions, allowances were made fully taxable under the IIT
- The preferential treatment of overtime income was eliminated
- Interest income (above a threshold level) was made taxable
- A flat rate tax rate of 33 1/3 percent replaced the previous progressive rate structure.

(There were also major reforms of the company income tax and of the system of indirect taxation. See Bahl (1991) for further discussion.)

The impact of these reforms was examined five years later by Bahl et al. (1992). They based their analyses on 1988 wage and allowance information generated from an unbalanced stratified sample of firms, followed by a random selection of employees from each firm and then adjusted to represent the population of employees. For microsimulation analyses of subsequent years, these data were then "aged" to reflect changes in income and in the number of taxpayers over time.

Among other things, Bahl et al. (1992) calculated the average tax rate (or PAYE taxes paid divided by PAYE income) by income class. They found that lower income classes paid zero taxes (due to the threshold), and also that the average tax rate rose steadily above J$10,000 to roughly 25 percent; that is, the statutory tax burden now looked very progressive, in contrast to the pre-reform IIT. However, Bahl et al. (1992) also discovered that, even in the short time frame since the 1986 IIT reform, allowances had crept back into the system, especially allowances for housing, laundry, meals, and uniforms (Table 4). Of perhaps more interest, many (though not all) of these allowances did not have PAYE taxes withheld on them. For example, 96 percent of those individuals receiving the laundry allowance were not taxed on it; in contrast, 97 percent of those receiving the entertainment allowance were taxed on the allowance. Bahl et al. (1992) also found that the average value of allowances generally increased with income, so that higher income individuals benefited more than lower income individuals in their receipt of allowances. This result suggested that the re-emergence of allowances in the IIT was beginning to compromise the presumed progressivity of the tax, similar to the effects of allowances in the pre-reform income tax.

4.3 Further Changes Since 1986

A number of additional changes in the individual income tax have occurred over time, as summarized Box 1.

Box 1. Some Recent Changes to the Jamaica Individual Income Tax

PAYE Threshold Increases:

- Raised to J$10,400 on January 1, 1989
- Raised to J$14,352 on January 1, 1992
- Raised to J$18,408 on January 1, 1993
- Raised to J$22,464 on January 1, 1994
- Raised to J$35,568 on January 1, 1995
- Raised to J$50,544 on January 1 1996
- Raised to J$80,628 on January 1 1997
- Raised to J$100,464 on January 1, 1999
- Raised to J$120,432 on January 1, 2001

Other PAYE Provision Changes:

- Tax on benefits of concessionary loans, beginning January 1, 1992
- Income tax rate reduced from 33 1/3 to 25% beginning January 1, 1993
- An increase in pensioners allowance from $15,000 to $45,000,1994/1995
- An increase in the maximum tax-free lump sum payable from the Superannuation Fund from $50,000 to $120,000, 1994/1995
- Increase in the value of the taxable benefit where a motor vehicle is provided for the use of an employee as of May 1, 1996 Reduction in the personal income tax on dividends for publicly listed companies from 25 percent to 20 percent (January 5, 2001), 20 percent to 10 percent (2001/2002), and 10 percent to 0 (April 2002).

Box 1. Some Recent Changes to the Jamaica Individual Income Tax (Continued)

<u>Other Changes in Individual Taxation:</u>

- Income of service companies treated as income of person who incorporates the company effective July 1, 1995.
- Accommodation for principal member (January 1, 1996). Previously an employee provided with accommodation by the employer the taxable benefit was either the annual value of the accommodation or 15 percent of the value of total emoluments whichever is lower. It was observed that where an employee usually a principal member had other income (e.g., dividends, interest, or income from other companies), it was possible for such a person to receive no emoluments or low emoluments from the company providing the accommodation. In such circumstances, there was a small amount of taxable benefit or no benefit at all. Where the value of accommodation was greater than the total emoluments, it was proposed to apply the 15 percent provision to the average of the sum of the value of accommodation plus the total emoluments.

<u>Changes in Taxation of Interest:</u>

- Implementation of 25 percent withholding tax on interest (1992)
- Income tax of 25 percent on returns from bank type saving/deposits of certain life insurance policies (1993/1994).
- Tax on Interest on certain financial instruments (TB, CD, and similar instruments) to be deducted at source (April 28, 1994).
- Withholding of tax from interest payments at source by stockbrokers, dealers, and other persons registered under the Securities Act, adding them to the list of prescribed persons (April 8, 1998).
- Only 15 percent of tax on interest required to be withheld at source. Additional taxes to be filed are 10 percent for the individual and 18.3 percent for corporations (1999/2000).
- An increase in the withholding tax on interest from 15 percent to 25 percent (2000/2001).

Source: Ministry of Finance and Planning, Taxation Division and Taxpayer Assessment and Audit Department.

Table 3. Actual and Potential Tax Base (J$ amounts in thousands of Jamaican dollars)

	Fully Taxed Income of Self-employed and PAYE Taxpayers	Overtime Income of PAYE Taxpayers	Undeclared Income Of Nonfiling Self-employed Individuals	Underreported Income of Self-employed Taxpayers	Allowances of PAYE Taxpayers	Total: Comprehensive Income	Statutory Income/ Comprehensive Income	Taxes Paid/ Statutory Income	Taxes Paid/ Comprehensive Income
Under J$ 2,000	J$28,023.0	J$0	J$2585.3	J$0	J$1340.8	J$31,949.1	0.877	0.074	0.065
2,001-4,000	136,653.1	0	45,508.2	0	6922.9	189,084.2	0.723	0.064	0.046
4,001-6,000	293,202.4	0	70,744.2	1775.3	17,100.9	382,821.9	0.766	0.095	0.073
6,001-8,000	337,386.1	1650.6	79,868.3	10,538.3	25,099.6	454,543.3	0.742	0.122	0.091
8,001-10,000	323,852.0	9042.5	44,065.4	10,338.0	30,116.4	417,413.9	0.776	0.152	0.122
10,0001-12,000	297,063.4	10,869.8	82,593.8	18,790.6	32,181.9	441,499.8	0.673	0.189	0.132
12,001-14,000	193,234.4	14,114.3	48,940.6	13,463.5	27,452.2	297,204.8	0.650	0.227	0.158
14,001-16,000	110,572.0	8929.2	22,697.4	7580.4	19,486.4	169,675.1	0.652	0.267	0.188
16,001-18,000	79,753.5	9890.2	26,270.4	5405.2	18,051.4	139,370.3	0.572	0.290	0.187
18,001-20,000	77,889.1	6122.7	20572.8	3926.6	17,370.1	125,881.2	0.619	0.318	0.219
20,001-25,000	92,581.3	11,422.2	24,007.6	7149.7	26,525.6	161,686.8	0.573	0.346	0.223
25,001-30,000	42,522.1	3631.1	21,530.8	4715.4	9266.2	81,665.4	0.521	0.405	0.229
30,001-50,000	35,713.9	9596.4	29,436.4	10,942.6	8056.3	93,745.3	0.381	0.409	0.196
Over 50,000	35,900.9	11,430.8	64,941.8	17,696.0	7210.0	137,179.5	0.262	0.437	0.160
Total	2,084,347.4	96,699.8	583,763.2	112,321.6	246.590.2	3,123,720.6	0.668	0.191	0.134

Source: Alm, Bahl, and Murray (1991).

[a] Fully taxed income equals statutory income of self-employed and PAYE taxpayers less overtime income of PAYE taxpayers.

Table 4. Allowances in Jamaica

Type of Allowance	Number of Individuals Receiving Allowance	Average Size of Allowance by Those Receiving Allowance (J$)	Total Amount of Allowance (thousands of J$)
Car	7,465	J$4,697	J$35,062.3
Club	71	13,778	984.85
Credit Card	412	6,363	2,621.8
Education	115	2,987	344.4
Entertainment	134	3,969	530.5
Holiday	425	1,245	529.0
Housing	41,039	6,794	278,826.2
Laundry	74,149	1,517	112,512.9
Meals	35,514	2,641	93,808.3
Travel	13,993	4,619	64,626.6
Uniforms	74,036	1,359	100,613.2
Utility	5,319	2,417	12,851.4

Source: Bahl et al. (1992).

4.4 The Current Jamaica Individual Income Tax

At present, the IIT in Jamaica is levied at a flat rate of 25 percent on wages and emoluments, interest, dividend, pensions, trusts, and annuities; the original flat rate of 33 1/3 percent imposed in 1986 was dropped to 25 percent in 1993.[7] There is a standard deduction (or threshold) for taxation that is applied for each taxpayer, and the current level is J$120, 432, which is about 75 percent of the per capita gross national income of Jamaica in 2002. The tax is relatively simple. There are some allowances and some treatments specific to capital income and self-employed income, but the number of allowances and the extent of specialized treatment are relatively small compared to the pre-1986 reform. Table 5 gives the revenues from the IIT over the last decade. Note that total collections are dominated by PAYE taxes and by interest taxes, both of which stem from source withholding.
The taxable basis of Jamaica's income tax includes emoluments, defined by law to include:

- Wages, salaries, and fees
- Provisions or payments for living accommodation, entertainment, utilities,
- Domestic, or other services
- All other benefits, perquisites, and facilities
- All sums paid to a person by an employer for reimbursable and non-reimbursable expenses

- All annuities, pensions, superannuations, or other allowances payable for past service
- Any payment of money or other consideration made to the holder or past holder of any office or employment related to the termination of that office or employment (other than due to death).

Final tax payments are due by March 15 for the preceding calendar year. Taxpayers make this final declaration using form IT01 for individuals (for self-employed taxpayers), IT03 (for unincorporated bodies other than life assurance), IT04 (for life assurance), and IT05 (for employees with PAYE and other income, pensioners, and the like). Form IT07 is used for making quarterly estimated payments, and form IT06 is used to make final reconciliations of PAYE liabilities of the corporation.

While the Income Tax Law covers all income subject to tax, in practice the tax is more of a schedular tax than a global tax since most tax revenue is received through withholding at source on the different types of income. There are a number of distinct pieces: the PAYE component, the withholding tax on interest, the withholding tax on dividends, the tax on the self-employed, and the tax on other types of income. Wage income is largely withheld at source and remitted directly to the Government by employers. Income taxes on interest and on dividends are withheld at source by financial institutions and companies. The self-employed are required to make final estimated payments quarterly, and also to make a final payment by March 15. The system of flat tax rates and source withholding makes filing a tax return unnecessary for a large portion of the population. Only individuals with multiple sources of income or those who are over-withheld are likely to file a tax return. In fact, there are very few returns filed each year. In addition, it should be noted that allowances are applied against a base of all income and not to separate forms of income.

However, even though the basic structure of the tax is straightforward, the administration of what are effectively separate income taxes tends to complicate the income tax system. The tax is not without other problems as well, as has become evident in a new tax reform effort initiated by the GOJ and for which we are working with the GOJ. The remainder of this section discusses some of the issues and problems that our recent work on this reform effort has uncovered.

Table 5. Individual Income Tax Receipts by Component and by Fiscal Year (J$ amounts in thousands of Jamaican dollars)

	Fiscal Year										
	1992-93	**1993-94**	**1994-95**	**1995-96**	**1996-97**	**1997-98**	**1998-99**	**1999-00**	**2000-01**	**2001-02**	**2002-03**
Individual Income Taxes:											
PAYE Taxes	3,407.5	4,715.7	6,780.7	9,269.1	11,907.3	13,174.7	15,027.9	14,226.0	16,515.4	18,907.2	22,285.6
Tax on Dividends	176.7	218.2	369.8	478.0	483.2	361.7	745.9	1,168.1	853.6	607.9	134.8
Tax on Other Individuals	322.6	423.3	583.1	578.6	630.7	740.7	842.5	836.8	925.8	854.4	1,113.7
Tax on Interest	1,267.6	1,402.2	1,883.6	1,665.6	2,381.9	2,149.7	1,924.9	6,161.3	9,535.1	8,462.8	9,121.5
Total: IIT	5,174.4	6,759.4	9,617.2	11,991.3	15,403.1	16,426.8	18,541.2	22,392.2	27,829.9	28,832.3	32,655.6
Income and Profits Taxes	7,885	10,896	15,377	18,889	21,564	23,297	25,843	29,390	35,457	35,516	40,567
Total Tax Revenues	19,050	28,948	38,072	50,263	55,109	59,224	66,970	75,962	87,074	90,568	102,859
Total Revenues	23,557	33,614	44,596	58,576	63,003	66,426	74,102	90,828	107,692	109,721	118,458

Source: Ministry of Finance and Planning.

Nonfiling and Underreporting. There is much anecdotal evidence of a compliance problem with the self-employed. Indeed, investigative efforts within the Income Tax Department seem if anything to have declined from the already low levels of the 1980s, so that it seems unlikely that either filing or reporting would have improved over time. Recall that failure to tax nonfiling of self-employed individuals and underreporting of self-employed taxpayers resulted in an estimated revenue loss of J$213 million in 1983, relative to total individual income tax collections of $417 million in that year; that is, nonfiling and underreporting led to a loss of roughly one-half of actual income tax collections.[8] If one extrapolates the 1983 estimates of revenue loss to 2002-2003 IIT collections, then nonfiling and underreporting generate a revenue loss of one-half of total IIT collections of J$32,655.6, an amount equal to roughly J$16 billion. Even if one removes the withholding tax on interest (or J$9,121.5 million) from the base estimates on the grounds that it is difficult to evade income taxes on interest, the revenue loss still exceeds J$11 billion. The failure to reduce tax evasion also generates inequalities and inefficiencies in the income tax system.

Allowances and Other Methods of Tax Avoidance. Not all income is legally taxable. In particular, the growth of nontaxable incomes appears to have increased in recent years. There are a number of allowances that have made their way back into the system since the 1986 reform, and these complicate the system and encourage tax evasion and/or avoidance activities. There is a wedge between the corporate and individual income tax rates that may encourage companies to move from corporate to non-corporate status.

Nonindexation. The threshold allowance for individuals is not indexed for inflation, which makes its impact on the equity of the system somewhat arbitrary.

Data Issues. There are also many data issues that make the analysis of the IIT a challenge. To successfully evaluate tax policy and carry out administration, the payment, recording, and auditing systems need to collect and produce accurate data regarding such things as the number of taxpayers, tax liabilities, payments, arrears, interest and penalties, and the like. The starting point of such an information system is often a "Taxpayer Registration Number" (TRN). The TRN number database is developed by taxpayers registering for "something" (e.g., GCT registration, housing benefits, motor vehicle registration, social insurance benefits, incorporation) in the tax system, and includes individuals as well as legal entities such as corporations and sole proprietors. The TRN for individuals begins with a "1" while that for entities begins with a "0." Individuals and representatives of companies are supposed to register at an office of Inland Revenue, and must due so prior to receiving the relevant housing or social insurance benefits, filing a GCT form or income tax return, and so on. Fiscal Services receives the TRN data from Inland Revenue.

However, while new TRNs are often added to the database, it is our understanding that the file is not regularly purged, so that many inactive taxpayers remain on the database; that is, the TRN database does not represent a population of taxpayers but rather a population of taxpayers who were in the system at some point. Obviously, those individuals and companies working outside the tax system often have no TRN. Also, companies may register multiple times if they have multiple branches or subsidiaries. Individuals may register dummy companies in expectation of eventually owning a business. We have even been told that students, as an exercise, may register dummy companies. None of these entries is regularly cleaned off the roles.

The TRN data include a status variable ("Active or Closed"), which is understood to mean whether or not the entity is still operating. However, this variable is not updated unless an entity makes that happen, which we understand is very rare. The data also contain information on the nature of business and the organization type; the former includes a detailed list of industries, and the latter include eight categories (e.g., limited company, partnership, non-profit organization, trust, government, statutory body, other, and sole-proprietor).

For purposes of our work on the ongoing tax reform project, we have been given access to two TRN files. The first contains 180,536 records on all business TRNs, corporations, sole proprietorship, and so on. In the best of circumstances, this file should include only active businesses. Unfortunately, as noted above, this file does not represent the population of businesses because some are not active (and yet not listed as closed), some are dummy companies, and some businesses still fail to register. We have also received a second TRN file that contains TRNs for companies that were registered for GCT purposes only (49,311 observations). Again, a significant number of inactive companies are included, but we cannot determine definitively which are and which are not active.

We have also received a number of micro data files that contain detailed tax information for the individual income tax. Unfortunately, relatively few individuals and even fewer sole proprietorships file tax returns. Additionally, the data cover multiple years, and it is not obvious when the returns are actually filed. Table 6 summarizes some of the information from these files. In total, the information contained in these returns is a fraction of what is reported in the budget even if all years are included. We have also tried matching the TRN files with these Income Tax files, knowing that we did not have the population in the TRN file but had an upper bound. We found some matches, but many returns from the TRN files had no match in the Income Tax files for any year in the file.

Overall Incidence of the Current Income Tax System. Even so, we have been able to use one database, the Emoluments Survey (2001), to estimate the burden of taxation under the current IIT for the year 2001. Table 7 reports these results. Income classes are defined as broadly as possible, and so include all reported wages and salaries, commission, bonus, gratuities and productivity incentives, and all allowances. We include both the in-kind and cash amounts reported for these components of income. We also include two measures of tax liabilities. The first is the actual reported withholding from the Emoluments Survey (2001). The second is calculated using a microsimulation model, which calculates taxable income as the sum of reported cash and in-kind emoluments and then applies the appropriate standard deduction and retiree allowances. We compare the estimated liability to the actual reported withholding.[9] As shown there by the estimated liability burden and the reported liability burden, the average tax rates rise with income, indicating a modestly progressive individual income tax.

However, there is little question that even this progressivity is being compromised by the re-emergence of largely untaxed allowances. Further, the GOJ has made few efforts to bring nonfilers into the tax net, and its audit investigations of those who file tax returns has declined even from the low levels of the 1980s. In short, despite the significant reform achievements of the GOJ in the last two decades, many of the problems with the IIT that prompted the 1986 reform and that are driving the current reform efforts remain unresolved.

5. CONCLUSIONS

What is the form of the IIT that emerges from this perspective? It is risky to make general statements. Indeed, it is certain that tax rules would vary, perhaps significantly, across different countries. Still, we argue that an "optimal" individual income tax in most developing countries would look something like the following:

> The individual income tax should be imposed at constant marginal tax rates on broadly defined, and schedularly defined, tax bases with minimal use of special tax incentives and with similar tax rates imposed on the different schedular bases.

Why? Constant marginal tax rates reduce compliance costs by reducing the incentive to engage in tax shifting schemes; for related reasons, they reduce administrative costs. Broadly defined tax bases allow lower marginal tax rates to generate a given level of revenue, and so reduce the distorting effects of taxes on behavior, including behavior related to noncompliance. Importantly, we argue that income taxes in most developing countries can only be effectively collected by source withholding, thereby lowering compliance and administrative costs and encouraging broad-based coverage. This is most effectively administered by a schedular system of income taxation.

Recent trends and developments also help reinforce this perspective. As emphasized by Tanzi (2000), Alm, Holman, and Neumann (2003), and others, fiscal systems face a wide range of new developments, most of which are related to a broad notion of "globalization" and most of which reduce the ability of tax systems to generate tax revenues. These "fiscal termites" include such factors as:

- The growth of E-commerce, and the corresponding decline in paper trails that allow transactions to be followed
- The substitution of "real" money by electronic money, which also makes it difficult to follow transactions, especially those involved in international transactions
- The growth of transfer pricing within multinational companies, which can lead to grossly understated prices on transactions and which can also make it difficult to trace transactions
- The increasing use of offshore financial centers and of new financial instruments
- The difficulty (and/or the unwillingness) to tax highly mobile financial capital and highly mobile skilled individuals.

These kinds of developments make it increasingly difficult for all countries to tax income on a global basis. They pose a special challenge for countries without a sophisticated tax administration. In the face of these challenges, it seems likely that countries – especially developing countries – will need to find new technologies that can be applied to the ways in which taxes are collected. It also seems likely that countries may be forced, however reluctantly, to a schedular income tax system.[10] As one example, the Government of Jamaica has moved somewhat along this path in the last several decades.

Of course, a schedular tax system leaves self-employed taxpayers largely out of the tax net. However, taxing the self-employed is a major problem for any income tax, regardless of whether the tax is a global or a schedular income tax (Gale and Holtzblatt 1997). Put differently, the special problem of taxing self-employed taxpayers will be present in any individual income tax, and it makes little sense to retain a global income tax solely because of the hope – the vain hope – that a global system will make it easier to tax the self-employed.

Table 6. Results from the Income Tax Files (J$ amounts in thousands of Jamaican dollars)

File	Number of Returns	Dates Covered in File	Wages	Housing Allowances	Interest, Dividends, Annuities	Dividends	Interest	(Net) Tax Payable
IT-01: Self-employed (2001-02)	21,608	1/1999–1/2003	3,097,625,586	31,702,226	242,639,333			704,180,996
IT-05: Individuals (PAYE, Pensioners) (2001-02)	27,811	1/1992– /2003	8,645,880,910	52,942,836		81,077,688	608,513,630	80,410,670

File	Number of Returns	Dates Covered in File	Withholding	Total Employees	(Net) Tax Payable
IT-06: Employer's Declaration PAYE (2001-2002)	9,738	1/1990– 1/2003		195,727	2,600,154,802

Source: Computations by authors.

Table 7. Distribution of Income and Taxes, 2001 Emoluments Survey

Income Class (J$, annual)	**Number of Employees**	**Gross Emoluments (J$ millions)**	**Estimated Tax Liability**	**Reported Tax Withheld**	**Estimated Liability Burden (percent)**	**Reported Liability Burden (percent)**
< $50,000	9,562	J$321	J$0.20	J$0.45	0%	0.14%
50,000-100,000	24,306	1,852	13.0	44.6	0.7	2.4
100,000-120,432	16,257	1,777	0	24.8	0	1.4
120,432-150,000	19,717	2,661	31.9	56.0	1.2	2.1
150,000-250,000	58,827	11,594	798.0	849.0	6.9	7.3
250,000-500,000	76,077	26,897	3,532.0	3,585.0	13.1	13.3
500,000-1,000,000	53,624	36,700	6,174.0	6,190.0	16.8	16.9
1 million – 5 million	26,092	43,839	9,153.0	9,111.0	20.9	20.8
Greater than 5 million	419	2,936	665.0	665.0	22.6	22.6
Total	284,885	128,577	20,375.0	20,526.9	15.8	16.0

Source: Calculated by authors from Emoluments Survey (2001).

In short, for many countries a schedular individual income tax is an imperfect method for taxing individuals. However, other approaches are, we believe, plagued by even more severe problems. As a result, a schedular system may well be the best avenue by which individual incomes can be taxed, now and perhaps sometime into the future.

Notes

1. This research was funded in part by a grant from the Government of Jamaica.
2. For further discussion of global versus schedular income tax systems, see Plasschaert (1976, 1977, 1978, 1980). For more general discussions of the administrative dimension of taxation, see Goode (1981), Bird (1989), and Bird and Casangera de Jantscher (1992).
3. See Wallace and Alm (2004) for information on the practice of individual income taxation in Caribbean countries.
4. According to the General Accounting Office (1996), the countries include: Argentina, Austria, Chile, Colombia, Costa Rica, the Czech Republic, the Dominican Republic, Ecuador, Egypt, Germany, Hungary, Indonesia, Iran, Ireland, Japan, Kenya, the Republic of Korea, Luxembourg, Malawi, Mexico, Morocco, the Netherlands, Nigeria, Panama, Papua New Guinea, Peru, Poland, Romania, the Russian Federation, South Africa, Tanzania, Turkey, Uganda, and the United Kingdom.
5. The exchange rate between Jamaican and U.S. dollars was 1.93 in 1983, 3.94 in 1984, and 5.56 in 1985. The current exchange rate is J$55 = US$1.
6. There was also an extensive system of wage-based payroll taxes and contributions, which in their entirety could increase the marginal tax rate on wage income to well in excess of 70 percent. This system was remained largely unchanged since the 1980s.
7. The tax rate for companies is 33 1/3 percent.
8. This estimate ignores any revenue losses in 1983 from tax credits, overtime, and allowances.
9. Unfortunately, we do not have data to determine whether the actual amount withheld is close to true liability.
10. In fact, there are now calls for even countries like the U.S. to consider a no-return tax system. See Turnier and Little (2004).

References

Alleyne, Dillon (1999), *Taxation and Equity in Jamaica 1985-1992*, Kingston, Jamaica: Canoe Press University of the West Indies and the Consortium Graduate School of Social Sciences.

Alm, James (1996), "What is an 'Optimal' Tax System?", *National Tax Journal*, Vol. 49 (1), pp. 117-133.

Alm, James and Roy Bahl (1985), *Evaluation of the Structure of the Jamaican Individual Income Tax", Jamaican Tax Structure Examination Project, Working Paper No. 15*, Syracuse, NY: Metropolitan Studies Program, Maxwell School, Syracuse University and Kingston, Jamaica: Board of Revenue, Government of Jamaica.

Alm, James, Roy Bahl, and Matthew N. Murray (1991), "Tax Base Erosion in Developing Countries", *Economic Development and Cultural Change*, Vol. 39 (4), pp. 849-872.

Alm, James, Jill Ann Holman, and Rebecca M. Neumann (2003), "Globalization and State/Local Government Finances", pp. 276-298 in: David L. Sjoquist, editor, *State and Local Finance Under Pressure*, Cheltenham, UK and Northampton, MA: Edward Elgar Publishing.

Bahl, Roy W. (1971), "A Regression Approach to Tax Effort and Tax Ratio Analysis", *International Monetary Fund Staff Papers*, Vol. 18 (3), pp. 570-612.

Bahl, Roy, (ed.) (1991), *The Jamaican Tax Reform*, Cambridge, MA: The Lincoln Institute of Land Policy.

Bahl, Roy, Richard Hawkins, Robert E. Moore, and David L. Sjoquist (1992), *Analysis of Jamaican Income Taxes and Allowances, Report No. 1*, Atlanta, GA: Jamaica Tax Review Project, Policy Research Center, Georgia State University

Bird, Richard M. (1989), "The Administrative Dimension of Tax Reform in Developing Countries", pp. 15-346 in: Malcolm Gillis, editor, *Tax Reform in Developing Countries*, Durham, NC: Duke University Press.

Bird, Richard M. and Milka Casangera de Jantscher (eds.) (1992), *Improving Tax Administration in Developing Countries*, Washington, D.C.: International Monetary Fund.

Burgess, Robin and Nicholas Stern (1993), "Taxation and Development", *The Journal of Economic Literature*, Vol. 31 (2), pp. 762-826.

Emoluments Survey (2001), *Taxation Division, Ministry of Finance and Planning*, Government of Jamaica, Kingston, Jamaica.

Gale, William J. and Janet Hotlzblatt (1997), "On the Possibility of a No-return Tax System", *National Tax Journal*, Vol. 50 (3), pp. 475-485.

Goode, Richard (1981), "Some Economic Aspects of Tax Administration", *International Monetary Fund Staff Papers*, Vol. 28 (2), pp. 249-274.

Goode, Richard (1984), *Government Finance in Developing Countries*, Washington, D.C.: The Brookings Institution.

Plasschaert, Sylvain R. F. (1976), *Bulletin for International Fiscal Documentation*, Vol. 30 (1).

Plasschaert, Sylvain R. F. (1977), *Bulletin for International Fiscal Documentation*, Vol. 31 (4).

Plasschaert, Sylvain R. F. (1978), *Bulletin for International Fiscal Documentation*, Vol. 33 (2).

Plasschaert, Sylvain R. F. (1980), *Bulletin for International Fiscal Documentation*, Vol. 34 (3).

Tanzi, Vito (1987), "Quantitative Characteristics of the Tax Systems of Developing Countries", in: David Newberry and Nicholas Stern, editors, *The Theory of Taxation for Developing Countries*, New York, NY: Cambridge University Press.

Tanzi, Vito (1992), "Structural Factors and Tax Revenue in Developing Countries: A Decade of Evidence", in: Ian Goldin and L. Alan Winters, editors, *Open Economies: Structural Adjustment and Agriculture*, New York, NY: Cambridge University Press.

Tanzi, Vito (2000), *Globalization, Technological Developments, and the Work of Fiscal Termites, International Monetary Fund Working Paper 00/181*, Washington, D.C.: International Monetary Fund.

Turnier, William J. and Scott L. Little (2004), "Is It Time for an American PAYE?", *Tax Notes*, May, pp. 559-575.

United States General Accounting Office, *Tax Administration: Alternative Filing Systems*, Washington, D.C.: U.S. General Accounting Office, 1996, GAO/GGD-97-6.

Wallace, Sally and James Alm (2004), *The Jamaican Individual Income Tax, Jamaica Tax Reform Project, Working Paper 5*, Atlanta, GA: Andrew Young School of Policy Studies, Georgia State University.

Chapter 10

A FRESH LOOK AT THE VAT

KELLY D. EDMISTON* AND WILLIAM F. FOX**
**Federal Reserve Bank of Kansas City; **The University of Tennessee*

1. INTRODUCTION

Expected efficiency gains (reduction in efficiency losses) have been an important argument for replacing other taxes, and particularly sales taxes, with the VAT. However, the defense of these gains is often drawn from theoretical analysis of an optimal VAT and from indirect evidence but not from actual VAT practices. For example, Ebril et al (2001, p. 27) partly defend the efficiency gains from replacing a sales tax with a VAT by comparing the gains from sales taxes as they are actually imposed with a uniform consumption tax. But, VATs, like every other tax, are legislated in political environments where the resulting structure contains a series of warts as viewed from the economist's perspective. Administrative practices can further diminish the efficiency gains associated with a VAT. Analysis of both the gains and the consequences of imposing VATs is most usefully accomplished in the context of the taxes as they are actually levied. Then, the efficiency gains that would result from a more efficient structure can also be evaluated, but as the difference between actual practice and the economist's ideal.

Of course, broad based consumption taxation, such as with a VAT, potentially distorts the labor-leisure choice, the savings-consumption choice (for example, depending on the expectations of future tax rates), and other decisions. Exemptions from the VAT base and other structural features that result from the legislative process can impose a series of perverse incentives that distort producer and consumer prices and cause additional efficiency losses. At a minimum, this means that the efficiency gains from moving to an actually implemented VAT are lower than those that would be obtained by moving to an optimal VAT. Obviously, efforts should be made to lessen these additional distortions from implementation of a VAT. Further this could suggest that a VAT is not always the best tax choice given the overall effects of legislating, implementing, and administering the VAT.

The purpose of this paper is to identify and examine some of the key VAT policy issues that have arisen in implementation of the tax. Specifically, the paper examines four issues as examples of the inefficiencies that arise in actual practice with VATs. The first section examines the effect of registration thresholds, normally allowed to lessen administrative burdens, as an example of structural inefficiencies. The second section examines the tariff effects arising from administration of the VAT at border. The third section considers application of the VAT on financial services as an example of exemptions from the tax. Finally, the problem of distributing the revenues of a destination VAT levied at the subnational level is discussed.

2. VAT THRESHOLDS

Nearly every VAT country allows a turnover threshold below which vendors are not required to register as taxpayers. Vendors with turnover above the threshold must register unless they are in an exempt industry. A small number of countries, such as Peru, have no threshold. From there, the range of threshold values is very broad, ranging from relatively low amounts in countries such as Malawi ($1000), Georgia (($1500), and Romania ($7000) to relatively high levels in Cambodia ($125,000), Guinea ($134,000), and Morocco ($200,000).[1] Choice of the threshold level is normally made by comparing the administrative/compliance effects of expanding the number of taxpayers with the revenue gains from a broader tax base. The tax administration in many developing countries is often presumed to be unable to handle large numbers of taxpayers with small turnover and little value added and the threshold frees them from this responsibility. But, developed countries generally have thresholds as well. The incentive effects of a threshold have received relatively little attention and are considered here.

In principle, existence of a threshold need have little effect on business operations if small vendors are selling to registered traders. The tax is simply added later in the production chain, and the only effect is that purchasers receive no credit for VAT implicit in purchases from small firms, allowing for some cascading of the tax. Also, small business sales to non-registered traders are only tax advantaged by the failure to impose tax on the last-stage firm's value added. However, many different transactions occur and in practice the threshold distorts numerous business structure decisions. Among the incentives that are distorted by a threshold are firm size, product mix, and horizontal and vertical integration. An important reason for the distortions is that firms must remit VAT on all of their sales once their turnover exceeds the threshold (of course, after receiving credit for any VAT already paid), and rates are often around 20 percent.[2] As a result, the after tax producer price on all transactions immediately rises by the amount of the tax once the threshold is reached.

The threshold can also influence the types of goods produced by businesses with turnover below the threshold and will affect firm size decisions. Small firms are tax advantaged in some cases vis-à-vis registered traders because they neither bear the compliance costs nor must remit the VAT. The advantage is limited if value added is a small share of revenues for the non-registered trader when selling to other non-registered traders, since the VAT is only avoided on the value added. However, in many sectors, the VAT savings can be a significant component of total business costs. On the other hand, non-registered traders are disadvantaged in sales to registered traders because no credit is provided for tax implicit in purchased inputs, thereby allowing for cascading of the tax. The disadvantage grows with the relative importance of purchased inputs in the non-registered trader's production process. Thus, small businesses are likely to be oriented towards the final consumer market unless they produce goods that have high value added relative to gross receipts.

Keen and Mintz (2004) examine the optimal VAT threshold value based on a tradeoff between administration and revenues and allowing for firm size to respond to effects of the threshold. This model has been used in practical estimates of the appropriate threshold, such as by Edmiston and Bird (2004). Keen and Mintz conclude that thresholds are likely to create discontinuities in firm size[3], which is certainly not surprising since once the threshold is reached the tax is imposed on all sales and not only on the margin above the threshold.[4] Firms can be expected to bunch based on size, either hovering just below the threshold or lying well above it. This should create discontinuities in the expansion process for firms since they will only rise above the threshold once the decision is made to grow significantly. In other words, a vendor below the threshold would only want to consider growing if revenues would rise dramatically (certainly revenues would need to rise more than the tax increase), given that the immediate increase in costs (taxes) at the threshold can be nearly 20 percent of revenues. The marginal incentive to evade taxes is particularly large for firms with revenues near the threshold, likely increasing the extent of underreporting of sales for firms that are above, but close to the threshold.

Another response for some businesses will be to split operations into many small units, each of which lies just below the threshold. Using business splitting to evade taxes is often illegal, but identifying companies where this is taking place could be very difficult for the tax administration, particularly if each individual company is in the name of a different family member, or has a name that is sufficiently distinct so that the tax administration would have difficulty recognizing the relationships. Business splitting imposes the compliance costs of operating multiple firms and potentially the loss of scale or scope economies from operating as a single firm (though the business splitting may be in name only).

Vertical and horizontal integration can also be discouraged since taking advantage of either can increase the chance that firms will exceed the threshold. Discouraging either form of integration means lower profits when the production conditions indicate the potential to take advantage of economies of scale and scope. The effects are probably modest in most circumstances if the threshold is set low, but the small scale of many business operations in developing countries could result in important implications, particularly when combined with the effects of other exemptions.

Kyrgyzstan, where the VAT was only recently extended to agricultural production, provides an illustrative example of how thresholds can influence the agriculture sector and business structure decisions. Individual farmer turnover generally lies below the Kyrgyz threshold, even though the threshold is relatively small on international standards, so extension of the VAT was only expected to impose registration responsibilities on the largest firms. However, the World Bank and other parts of the international community have assisted small farmers in forming cooperatives that will market farm products, among other services. However, the combined activity in each cooperative reaches the threshold and subjects the sales of many very small farmers to a tax of nearly 20 percent on being a member of the cooperative. Initial anecdotal evidence indicates that cooperatives are dissolving because of the tax, potentially resulting in significant efficiency losses in the sector. Imposition of the tax on cooperatives would have had little effect if the tax on food products were otherwise imposed at retail (since the tax would be credited further in the production chain), but there is a strong tendency in Kyrgyzstan for many food products, and particularly those that have no processing, to be sold through small vendors or the informal market where no tax is imposed. Thus, the VAT is being levied for the first time on some agricultural products. Small farmers apparently buy very few inputs on which VAT has been paid, so their ability to obtain credits is of very limited benefit (and indeed, they may not receive credits since the tax is levied on the cooperative).

VAT treatment of agriculture has also influenced vertical integration in Kyrgyzstan. Food processing but not food production was subject to the VAT prior to the recent extension of the tax to agriculture production. The result was a strong incentive to vertically integrate the food industry since the exemption for food production was in practice extended to processing when a single firm performed both. Much of the processed agricultural products were exported so there was no intent to impose VAT anywhere in the chain and no distortion should have occurred. However, domestic production was treated very differently depending on the degree of vertical integration. Processors were discouraged from purchasing from other producers since this signaled imposition of the VAT. In this case, interestingly, the VAT encouraged what is regarded by many as an important efficiency in the agricultural industry, the ability of food processors to guarantee high quality production by producing their own inputs.

The incentives inherent in the VAT may be an important reason for a trend in business structure in Kyrgyzstan. Individual entrepreneurs have grown as a share of employment and value added while small and medium sized enterprises have diminished in importance during the years following adoption of the VAT. Nonetheless, large firms continue to provide a large majority of value added and employment.

3. VAT TARIFF EFFECTS ON EXPORTS

The VAT has often been viewed as export friendly because of the border adjustments that impose the tax on imports and rebate it on exports. However, this is derived from conceptual/theoretical analyses of the tax. In fact, a number of elements of the VAT as actually imposed have a strong potential to discourage international trade and exports, and effectively cause the VAT to operate as a tariff on both imports and exports (though at different rates). First, the effective tax rate on exports is much greater than zero since the tax on inputs used in the production of exports is included until rebates are received. This implies a significant opportunity cost of funds, particularly in developing countries where working capital is often relatively scarce. Further, VAT for which credits are not received (such as when a non-registered trader sells to a registered trader) is included in the producer prices.

Second, rebates for exports are often difficult to obtain. Many countries have made it impossible to obtain cash refunds or have allowed cash refunds for VAT on zero-rated transactions only after a significant delay. Until recently, for example, Kyrgyzstan did not provide for cash rebates of VAT on zero-rated transactions. Cash payments are now allowed but there continue to be long delays. These violations of the conceptual VAT structure have evolved either because of concerns about fraudulent refund claims or to provide short-term increases in tax revenue. Firms that have little if any domestic tax liability against which to use credits, and therefore seek refunds, are particularly affected. Thus, development of a specialized set of exporters is discouraged since they are likely to pay some VAT on the value of exports, but firms that have both domestic sales and exports may bear little VAT on exports because of the ability to take credits against other VAT liabilities.

Many countries also make it difficult to use VAT credits against other tax liabilities (including the VAT). For example, Kyrgyzstan and Romania only allow credits when supported with special invoices. Credits may also be disallowed under audit. Disallowance of legitimate credits results in pyramiding of the VAT. The motivation, as with export rebates, is fear of fraudulent credit claims and pressure on the Tax Administration to increase revenues. These concerns about fraud may be valid, but they come at a potentially high cost in terms of international trade and business structure. Thus, governments must carefully consider alternative means of reducing fraud.

Also, VAT may be imposed at higher effective rates on imports than on domestic production, even though by statute the VAT is to be applied evenly. This occurs if imports can be controlled better than domestic production. Administration of the VAT on imports through the Customs Bureau and on domestic activity through the Tax Administration can also affect the effective tax rate, depending on the practices exercised by each. Higher VAT rates on imports than on domestic production create a tariff that discourages imports. The reduction in imports can reduce exports as trade balances.

Desai and Hines (2002) examine the relationship between reliance on the VAT and exports.[5] They conclude that imposition of a VAT can reduce exports by one-third or more, and that the greatest effects on exports are in the lowest income countries. International trade is also found to decline with the rising role of VAT in the tax mix. Further, US multinational firms are found to reduce their exports from a country by 5 percent for every 10 percent increase in VAT collections. These results do not demonstrate causality, but certainly suggest that VATs are not uniform consumption taxes. Instead, VATs are imposed much more heavily on the international than the domestic sector, and the resulting tariff effects are large and can significantly reduce a country's ability to export.

Appropriately structured free economic zones are one option to allow countries to lessen the tariff effects of VATS. The zones can be used as a means of exporting domestic production because inputs are often imported into the zone without imposition of VAT, and exports are zero-rated. VAT implicit in domestically purchased inputs still needs to be promptly rebated to the zone-based producers if the implicit VAT is to be lowered. Free economic zones are unlikely to assist development of specialized exporters because of production requirements in the zones, though they could be effective for producer/exporters. The zones must be structured to limit sales into the domestic economy to a small share of total production and to impose all relevant taxes on sales into the domestic economy, or domestic production outside the zones will be relatively disadvantaged on both domestic and export production.

4. EXEMPTION OF FINANCIAL SERVICES

Most countries that impose an invoice-credit VAT exempt financial services,[6] meaning that VAT is not levied on the supply of financial services, and credits are not allowed for VAT incurred on inputs (thus, financial institutions pay VAT on purchases of taxable goods and services used in producing the exempted supplies).

As Poddar (2003) notes, the two basic rationales for exemption under a VAT are (1) that the items to be exempted are used disproportionately by low-income people, and therefore exemption makes the VAT less regressive; and (2) the items to be exempted are merit goods, such as medical care and education. Poddar observes that financial services exemptions may make the VAT system more regressive rather than less regressive, and some financial services, such as currency trading, may actually be considered demeritable transactions (because of undesirable speculation). Thus, other rationales must be found if exemption of financial services is to be appropriate. Although financial services generally are exempted from the VAT for practical, administrative reasons, as discussed below, some argue that financial services should be exempted, or zero-rated, for conceptual reasons, even if it were not so difficult to apply the VAT.

4.1 Should Financial Services Be Taxed Under the VAT?

It is not altogether clear that financial intermediation charges should be subject to VAT, even if they can be properly enumerated. For business purchases of financial services, there is a consensus view that they should remain untaxed.[7] The view on consumer purchases is more contentious.

There are two conventional views of the proper tax treatment of purchases of financial services by final consumers, which Boadway and Keen (2003) refer to as a "fallacy" and a "half truth" (60). The fallacy is that financial services should not be taxed because they do not directly enter the consumer's utility function. The half-truth is the opposite conclusion that financial services are a commodity like any other and therefore should be taxed as such.

Grubert and Mackie (2000) argue that financial services used by consumers are not *consumption* goods and therefore should not be in the base of a consumption tax. The basic premise is that consumption goods directly yield utility to the consumer, and financial services do not directly yield utility (see also Chia and Whalley, 1999).[8] Rather, they are properly considered as a business expense, part of the price of an investment. In the future, the consumer sells the "saving good" and uses the proceeds to fund fully taxable consumption, much in the way that a real investment (a machine, say) is not taxed, but rather the future consumption financed by the machine is taxed. Grubert and Mackie argue that any advice one receives in how most profitably to use the machine (or the saving good) represents a part of the machine's total cost, and is properly expensed. Because financial intermediation services are part of the cost of investing, the fees must be exempted in order to avoid distorting the consumer's relative valuation of present and future consumption.[9]

Chia and Whalley (1999), following a similar line of reasoning, conclude from numerical simulations of the U.S. economy that taxing goods alone, and not financial services, yields higher welfare than taxing both goods and financial services at a lower rate with equal yield.

Jack (2000) shows that in the case of implicit, spread-based charges, the finance charge automatically increases proportionately with a tax on final consumption, so taxing it would indeed distort the relative prices of present and future consumption. Consider, as Jack does, the case of an individual who forgoes one unit of current consumption, with price normalized to $1, and faces a VAT rate of 50 percent. By foregoing the one unit of consumption, he saves $1.50, which he deposits at a bank. Suppose further that the market interest rate is 20 percent, which the bank collects on its loans, and that the bank pays 10 percent on deposits, leaving an interest spread (financial intermediation charge) of 10 percent. In the absence of a VAT applied to the financial intermediation charge, the relative price of period 2 consumption and period 1 consumption is $1.50/1.65 \approx 0.91$, the same relative price that would attain in the absence of a VAT (1.0/1.1). Under a VAT applied to the financial intermediation charge, 50 percent is paid on the fee, or $0.075, leaving relative prices of $1.50/1.575 \approx 0.95$. Charging VAT on the intermediation charge has increased the relative price. In this case, where the value-added is proportional to the nominal value of the underlying transfer, financial intermediation services should not be taxed, as asserted by Grubert and Mackie (2000).

Jack notes that application of VAT has different efficiency implications for the two types of financial intermediation *fees* that arise, however. In the case of fixed fees, such as a monthly account fee, it is irrelevant whether the financial service is subject to VAT, as the tax is effectively lump sum and does not affect decisions on the margin (there is only an income effect). In the case of what Jack calls "quasi-fixed fees" (842), however, there is an efficiency argument for applying the VAT. Quasi-fixed fees are charges that are proportional to the *real* value of the underlying transfer, such as fees levied at a fixed amount per transaction (*e.g.*, ATM fees and per-check fees). In this case, in the absence of a VAT, the relative price of period 2 consumption (on the margin) is 1.00/1.05 ≈ 0.95 (20 percent interest on \$1.00 less the \$0.15 transaction fee is \$1.05). With a VAT that exempts financial intermediation charges, the relative price is a lower 1.50/1.65 ≈ 0.91. With the VAT applied to the financial intermediation fee, the relative price is the same as in the no-tax case, 1.50/1.575 ≈ 0.95. In the case of quasi-fixed fees, efficiency calls for the application of VAT to financial intermediation charges.

Fortunately, it is fixed fees and quasi-fixed fees that are easily enumerated, and therefore immune from the more practical difficulties in levying VAT on financial intermediation.

Auerbach and Gordon (2002) would extend Jack's (2000) coverage of the VAT to include taxing financial intermediation charges embedded in financial margins. They argue that Jack implicitly ignores the presence of real inputs in the production of financial services. Using the theoretical equivalence of a VAT and a labor-income tax as a guide in their modeling, they show that both nominal after-tax wage income and nominal consumer prices are the same under a VAT and a labor-income tax. All primary and intermediate inputs used in generating financial transactions should be subject to the VAT to maintain neutrality under this system. Auerbach and Gordon agree with Jack (and also Chia and Whalley, 1999) in that certain transaction costs, such as liquidity and risk premia, do not include real inputs and increase in proportion to the nominal size of the transactions, and thus should not be taxed.

An additional reason for including the financial intermediation charge embedded in financial margins in the tax base, other than the arguments of Auerbach and Gordon (2002), is that the substitutability between forms of consideration (fee or margin) may generate other inefficiencies. If explicit fees are taxable under the VAT, but implicit fees embedded in financial margins are not, there will be an incentive to substitute margin fees for explicit fees. This presumably is the reason why explicit fees generally are exempted from the VAT, even though the conventional view is that financial intermediation charges should be taxed, but are not for practical reasons (Poddar, 2003).

Whether one takes the view that financial services should be taxed fully under the VAT, should be zero-rated under the VAT, or some intermediate view, the normal practice followed by countries of exempting financial transactions is probably not the optimal policy. Under the prevailing view that financial services should be taxed, but it is administratively difficult to do so, exemption likely represents a compromise (between full taxation and zero-rating) (Poddar, 2003). In the case of exempted supplies to final consumers, the effective tax rate generally will be less than the standard rate, but it will not be zero, as is the case when supplies are zero-rated. Because of the lack of input tax credits, exemption allows the collection of some tax on items that would otherwise be untaxable (for practical reasons). Chia and Whalley (1999) and Boadway and Keen (2003) argue that the optimal tax rate on financial services may be some positive rate less than the standard rate. In this sense exemption may be preferred to either zero-rating or taxation at the standard rate. But the fact remains that inputs are taxed under an exemption-based system, and a better choice, conceptually if not practically, would be to tax final purchases at the optimal rate and allow for a deduction of input tax.

Efficiency issues arise with exemption for registered traders that do not arise in the case of full taxation or zero-rating. In the case of exempted supplies to intermediaries, tax cascading can occur because the input tax on exempted supplies will be embedded in the price paid. In some cases, exemption results in a higher tax burden than inclusion (Merrill and Adrion, 1995). Exemption provides an incentive to vertically integrate so as to avoid nonrecoverable VAT costs. Moreover, allocation of input tax credit to taxable and exempted supplies provides additional fodder for distortions and imposes a wasteful administrative and compliance burden. The apportionment system, which varies widely by country, creates incentives for firms to structure financial transactions in such a way as to minimize VAT liability, raising complicated transfer pricing questions (Merrill and Adrion, 1995).

The work of Jack (2000) and Auerbach and Gordon (2002) suggests that financial intermediation services should be taxed under the VAT, including fixed fees, per-transaction fees, and the portion of financial margins that covers financial intermediation. The question then becomes how to tax financial services, especially as it applied to fees embedded in financial margins.

4.2 Practical Issues in Applying VAT to Financial Intermediation

Although some financial intermediation fees, like monthly checking account fees and automatic teller machine (ATM) charges, are explicitly enumerated, most are hidden in other charges. The financial intermediation charge is conceptually and practically difficult to separate from interest rate margins, premiums, and other financial margins charged by financial institutions, from which they derive the large bulk of their revenues. The financial intermediation charge is reflected in a higher interest cost to the borrower and a lower return to the lender.

Under the assumption that charges for financial intermediation should be included in the VAT base, proposals have been offered for ways to get around this thorny problem of separating interest rate margins and risk premiums from financial intermediation. Poddar (2003) argues four principles in doing so. The first principle is that nothing more than the financial intermediation charge should appear in the tax base. *Ad hoc* levies imposed by many developing countries, such as taxes on gross insurance premiums, fail in this regard because the financial intermediation charge is premiums less claims. The second principle is that modifications to the exemption system should reduce the tax on business inputs, therefore eliminating some tax cascading. The third principle is that modifications should lead to a broadening of coverage of financial services, as much of the inefficiencies inherent in the exemption system relate to its narrow base. Finally, modifications to the exemption system should generate administrative and compliance costs and economic distortions that are less burdensome than current practice.

The application of VAT to fixed fees and quasi-fixed fees is straightforward and consistent with Poddar's guidelines. The problem is in including implicit fees; specifically, enumerating that portion of financial margins that is representative of financial intermediation charges. Israel gets around this problem *via* the addition method; that is, they levy tax directly on wages and profits (see Boadway and Keen, 2003). Another option proposed in Canada was the subtraction method (Canadian Department of Finance, 1987): levying the tax on the excess of outputs over inputs. [10] The problem with both of these alternatives is that although they are effective in determining aggregate value-added from financial intermediation, they cannot allocate VAT on a per-transaction basis to taxable consumers and nontaxable businesses (see Boadway and Keen, 2003). The use of formulas in allocating the tax base would likely generate administrative complexities and tax planning opportunities, undermining any efficiency gains in bringing financial services under the VAT umbrella (Merrill and Adrion, 1995).

The preferred approach, considered at length in the European Union, may be to employ a cash flow tax (Institute of Fiscal Studies, 1978; Merrill and Adrion, 1995; Merrill and Edwards, 1996; Boadway and Keen, 2003; Poddar, 2003). Under the cash flow method, all cash inflows (whether in the nature of income or capital) are treated as taxable sales and are subject to tax. This would include the receipt of a loan and interest receipts. All outflows, such as the repayment of loans and interest payments, are treated as taxable purchases and are entitled to rebate. As long as the interest rate available to the government is considered the pure interest rate, the cash-flow method correctly allocates value-added and allows for proper crediting of input tax (Boadway and Keen, 2003).

Boadway and Keen provide a simple example as to how a cash-flow approach would work.[11] They consider a $1,000 loan to a registered trader at 15 percent, which is financed by a $1,000 deposit (from a consumer) earning 5 percent. The VAT rate is 10 percent. The bank must pay $100 tax on the deposit (an inflow), which is offset by a $100 credit when the loan is made (an outflow). When the loan is repaid, it owes tax of $115 (on an inflow of $1,150), and when the deposit is withdrawn, it takes a credit of $105 (on an outflow of $1,050). The net tax paid is $10, exactly 10 percent of the financial intermediation charge given by the 10 percent interest rate spread on a $1,000.

The cash flow approach is not without its own set of problems, however (Merrill and Adrion, 1995; Poddar, 2003). First, borrowers would have to pay tax on the gross amount of their loan, which may constrain liquidity. Second, borrowers, in addition to financial institutions, would have to calculate tax on all financial flows, which may be overly complex and burdensome administratively. Finally, the cash-flow method achieves the theoretically correct amount of tax on financial services only in present value over the course of the financial transaction. Thus, transition would cause windfall gains and losses, as would the changing of VAT rates over the course of the transaction.

The Tax Calculation Account (TCA) system gets around some of the drawbacks associated with the cash-flow method (Poddar, 2003); specifically, solving the liquidity and transition problems. The collection and crediting of tax on inflows and outflows of a capital nature is suspended. The net tax is payable at the end of the transaction and is the applicable tax on interest received minus the interest at the indexing rate (which reflects the pure time value of money) on the deferred tax. Likewise, the net credit is the applicable credit on interest paid plus the interest at the indexing rate on the deferred credit amount.

4.3 Conclusions

While there remains some disagreement in the literature, our feeling is that the sum of the theoretical arguments favors taxing financial intermediation charges, and this should be done if tax administration is sufficiently strong so that financial intermediation charges embedded in financial margins can be taxed, most likely via a cash-flow approach or tax calculation account.

Exemption raises a host of efficiency issues, including the taxation of intermediate inputs, incentives to vertically integrate so as to avoid nonrecoverable VAT costs, and incentives to structure financial transactions so as apportion the maximum amount of input tax to taxable supplies. Even if our view coincided with that of Grubert and Mackie (2000), the view being that financial services should not be taxed, exemption would not be the optimal policy, but rather zero-rating.

In countries where administration is weak, however, exemption may be a reasonable compromise policy. As noted above, the effective tax rate on exempted sales to final consumers will be less than the standard rate, but positive. Exemption therefore allows the collection of some tax on items that would otherwise be untaxable. Moreover, research suggests that the optimal tax rate on financial services may be some positive rate less than the standard rate. In these cases, probably all financial intermediation charges should be exempted, including those, such as fixed fees, that are easily enumerated.

5. ALLOCATING INPUT TAX CREDITS IN A FEDERAL VAT SYSTEM

In a federal system with multiple VATs at differential rates, a destination-based VAT generally is preferred to an origin-based VAT on the grounds of production efficiency.[12] For practical reasons, however, there is cause to consider an origin-based VAT: conventional wisdom used to be that a subnational VAT would have to be imposed on an origin basis to avoid the necessity of border controls (Cnossen and Shoup, 1987; Hill and Rushton, 1993; Bird and Gendron, 2001). Recently there have been several proposals to design a system in which destination-based VATs may be imposed in the absence of border controls. Thus, mechanisms are available for distributing revenues, albeit often with significant administrative costs or limitations on federalism, allowing governments to design destination based subnational VATs. Nonetheless, the result remains that the administrative and compliance costs of allocating subnational VAT revenues on a destination basis must be netted out against the efficiency gains of using a subnational VAT versus other revenue sources. This section briefly discusses these proposals and highlights their relative merits and demerits.

The main issue is the crediting of input tax when there are cross-border sales.[13] Consider two subnational regions A and B, herein referred to as states, with VAT rates of 15 percent and 20 percent, respectively. Firm X in state A exports goods worth 100, produced with 60 worth of inputs, to firm Y in state B. A destination-based system would levy a tax of 20 (20% x 100) to state B, and the exporter would receive a credit of 9 (15% x 60) for taxes paid in A. But it is unreasonable for state B to provide credits for taxes paid in A. The issue is how tax links are to be maintained between traders and input tax appropriately credited.

5.1 Revenue-Sharing

One option is to have a single VAT administered by the central government, with part (or all in the case of Australia) of the proceeds shared among lower level jurisdictions. This is the most common system in place today (Bird and Gendron, 2001). Distribution to subnational jurisdictions is accomplished *via* a formulary approach or on the basis of consumption statistics. This approach has obvious benefits from the perspective of administrative and compliance burdens, but is really no different than a standard fiscal equalization measure (McLure, 2000b; Bird and Gendron, 2001). A revenue sharing system does not give subnational governments revenue autonomy and accountability, which are critical for attaining the full benefits of fiscal federalism, nor is such a system likely to be acceptable to many subnational governments, as was the case with the *National Sales Tax* proposal in Canada that preceded its GST (Hill and Rushton, 1993).[14]

5.2 Independent Subnational VATs

The other extreme, which makes sense only in countries with very well-developed tax administrations at the subnational level, is to allow each jurisdiction to impose its own VAT with its own rates, and perhaps its own base. Input tax crediting would be dealt with *via* a zero-rating/deferred payment or a clearing house approach (Cnossen and Shoup, 1987).

Following the example from above, under a deferred payment approach, currently in place in the European Union (EU), exports are zero-rated and X claims an input tax credit of 9 (15% of 60) from state A. If Y is a registered trader, it does not pay import tax, but rather, pays the VAT on the import when it makes its final sale (because there is no input tax credit). There are some problems with this approach, most notably the possibility that final consumers will evade tax by "masquerading as registered traders" (McLure, 2000b, 303; see also Keen and Smith, 1996), although this can be prevented, or at least mitigated, with effective administration of an overlaid national tax (Bird and Gendron, 1998).

Under a clearinghouse mechanism, the exporter (X) would pay 6 (15% of 100 less input tax of 9) to its state of registration, A. Y would not pay a compensating import tax, would collect 20 percent on sale, and would apply for a credit of 15 from state B, its state of registration. State B would then claim compensation of 15 from state A, which would be handled by a clearinghouse. A major benefit with this system over the zero-rating/deferred payment is that the tax chain is not broken – goods cross the border with tax in tow. But McLure (2000b) notes that this system is "almost certainly too complicated to be practical" (304) and that the importing state has no incentive to carefully audit the claims for credits to be reimbursed by the exporting state.

Bird and Gendron (1998) argue that the dual VAT approach with zero-rating/deferred payment works fairly well in Québec, where the Québec VAT (the Québec Sales Tax, or QST) is applied to the price of goods and services inclusive of the federal Goods and Services Tax (GST). The key difference in Québec and the system of VATs in the EU is the existence of an overriding federal VAT. Bird and Gendron (1998) note that the Québec government, which administers both the QST and GST, has an incentive to monitor the GST because the QST is applied to a GST-inclusive base, and that federal GST audits serve as a crosscheck, to some extent, to ensure that QST has not been evaded.

5.3 Intermediate Options

Two intermediate options have been proposed in recent years: a compensating VAT (CVAT) (McLure, 2000a), and a viable integrated VAT (VIVAT) (Keen and Smith, 1996; Keen, 2000).

The CVAT is in some sense a dual VAT, but only for intrastate sales. Exporters out of state would essentially zero-rate sales, but these sales would be subject to a central CVAT, which is levied at the same rate for all states. Credit is of course allowed for tax on purchases of registered traders, both under the state VAT for intrastate trade and the CVAT for interstate trade. Continuing with our example from above, firm X would zero-rate the sale to Y and would receive a credit of 9 for tax paid on inputs. State B would defer payment of VAT until final sale, but the central government would tax the interstate sale at the CVAT rate. Upon final sale, firm Y would apply for a credit for the CVAT paid. In the case where interstate sales are between registered traders, the end result is the same as in the dual VAT case, and no CVAT is collected on net (it is collected then credited). In the case of interstate sales to unregistered traders or final consumers, the CVAT is a final tax, and the central government would then allocate the revenues to the various states in some systematic way, presumably on the basis of interstate sales to final consumers.

VIVAT is a two-tiered VAT structure. The first tier is a nation-wide tax levied at a uniform rate across states. Sales between registered traders are taxed at this uniform rate, but final sales are taxed at independently determined state rates. The system is equivalent to a uniform base rate applied to the good or service and a system of secondary rates equal to the difference between the state-specific rates and the nationwide uniform rate (Keen, 2000). In our hypothetical case, the VIVAT works in a fashion similar to the CVAT. Assume that the VIVAT uniform rate is 17 percent. Firm X would pay 8 in tax (17 output tax less 9 for input tax). Upon final sale, firm Y would apply the 20 percent rate in state B and take an input tax credit of 17. Again, in the case where interstate sales are between registered traders, the end result is the same as in the dual VAT case, and no central tax is collected on net (it is collected then credited).

5.4 Conclusions

There are trade-offs in each of the various ways of instituting a subnational VAT in a federal system without border controls. The dual VAT is most attractive in the sense of revenue autonomy and accountability in that there is no "central edict" with respect to the state taxes applied to interstate trade, since no such taxes are applied (Bird and Gendron, 2000, 754). States set their own rates under the CVAT and VIVAT schemes, but a uniform rate is applied to interstate sales. In countries where interstate trade is significant, revenue autonomy and accountability are undermined relative to the dual VAT case.

Where the CVAT and VIVAT seem to have an advantage over the dual VAT is in maintaining the tax chain for interstate sales, thereby reducing the vulnerability of the system to fraud. This is especially important in a case where there is no federal VAT, a case for which the VIVAT was especially designed. CVAT would have an advantage in cases where subnational tax administration is relatively weak.

In countries where there is an overlaying federal VAT and subnational tax administrations are very developed, such as Canada, the dual VAT seems like an attractive candidate. The simplicity of the CVAT is a more attractive option for countries with less developed tax administrations. Finally, in cases where subnational tax administrations are well-developed, but no federally administered VAT exists as a cross-check for noncompliance, the VIVAT offers a reasonable approach that balances subnational autonomy in rate setting with a maintenance of a consistent tax chain.

Notes

1. See Ebrill et al (2001).
2. Ebrill et al (2001) provide VAT rates by country. A standard minimum 15 percent rate is applied in the EU. Ten member states impose a standard rate above 20 percent and 14 impose a lower rate. See http://www.eurunion.org/legislat/VATweb.htm#Rates
3. Their model does not directly address other efficiency effects such as whether to produce for final versus intermediate transactions.
4. The obvious response is to impose the VAT only on sales above the threshold. Unfortunately, this creates significant compliance difficulties in providing invoices so

that buyers who are registered traders can obtain credits. Also, significant revenue losses would result from exempting the threshold amount for all registered traders.

5. Desai and Hines also argue the VAT can affect exports as the VAT replaces other taxes that can affect exports and imports and because government tends to be larger in countries that rely on a VAT.
6. As used here, financial services means financial intermediation, the residual component of the cash flow of a financial transaction after principal, consideration for the time value of money, and risk premia are subtracted.
7. Boadway and Keen (2003) discuss some arguments for taxing business purchases.
8. Chia and Whalley (1999) make a somewhat weaker statement. They do not assert that it is inappropriate to tax financial services because they do not directly enter the utility function, but rather that it *may* be inappropriate to tax financial services. They explicitly hold open the possibility that the optimal rate at which to tax financial services may be at a positive rate, albeit somewhat lower than the standard rate (705). See also Boadway and Keen (2003).
9. Whalley (1992) asserts that the same analysis would also apply to nonfinancial services that do not directly enter the utility function, such as transportation, but Grubert and Mackie assert that the extension is not warranted because there is no analogue to a saving good that is sold to finance taxable consumption (see also Rousslang, 2002; Boadway and Keen, 2003).
10. The subtraction method also was suggested as a means of taxing lending activities of banks and similar institutions under the Nunn-Domenici USA Tax in the United States.
11. The example is modified from that presented by Boadway and Keen.
12. There is also the broader issue of whether the preferred sub-national tax should be a sales tax or a VAT. The case is not clear cut as each tax offers some advantages (see Fox and Luna 2002).
13. The problem of cross-border shopping to avoid tax or to take advantage of differential rates also has received a great deal of attention in the discussion of systems of subnational VATs. That issue is not discussed here.
14. Three Maritime Provinces in Canada – Newfoundland, Nova Scotia, and New Brunswick – have accepted a variant of this system under what is referred to as the *Harmonized Sales Tax.* See Bird and Gendron (1998, 2001) for a brief description of this system.

References

Auerbach, Alan J. and Roger H. Gordon (2002), "Taxation of Financial Services under a VAT", *American Economic Review*, Vol. 92(2), pp. 411-416.

Bird, Richard M. and Pierre Pascal Gendron (1998), "Dual VATs and Cross-Border Trade: Two Problems, One Solution?", *International Tax and Public Finance*, Vol. 5, pp. 429-442.

Bird, Richard M. and Pierre Pascal Gendron (2000), "CVAT, VIVAT, and Dual VAT: Vertical 'Sharing' and Interstate Trade", *International Tax and Public Finance*, Vol. 7(6), pp. 753-761.

Bird, Richard M. and Pierre Pascal Gendron (2001), "VATs in Federal States: International Experience and Emerging Possibilities", *International Bulletin of Fiscal Documentation*, Vol. 55, pp. 293-309.

Boadway, Robin and Michael Keen (2003), "Theoretical Perspectives on the Taxation of Capital income and Financial Services", in: Patrick Honohan, editor, *Taxation of*

Financial Intermediation: Theory and Practice for Emerging Economies, Washington, DC: The World Bank.

Canadian Department of Finance (1987), *Tax Reform 1987: Sales Tax Reform*, white paper, June 18.

Chia, Ngee-Choon and John Whalley (1999), "The Tax Treatment of Financial Intermediation", *Journal of Money, Credit, and Banking*, Vol. 31(4), pp. 704-719.

Desai, Mihir A. and James R. Hines Jr. (2002), *Value-Added Taxes and International Trade: The Evidence, Working Paper, November 23.*

Ebrill, Liam et al. (2001), *The Modern VAT*, Washington DC: International Monetary Fund.

Edmiston, Kelly D. and Richard M. Bird (2004), *Taxing Consumption in Jamaica: The GCT and the SCT, Jamaica Tax Reform Project Working Paper 7*, Atlanta, GA.: Andrew Young School of Policy Studies, Georgia State University.

Fox, William F. and LeAnn Luna (2003), "Subnational Taxing Options: Which is Preferred, A Retail Sales Tax or a VAT?", *Journal of State Taxation*, Winter. Also published in *State Tax Notes*, March 10, 2003

Grubert, Harry and James Mackie (2000), "Must Financial Services Be Taxed Under a Consumption Tax?", *National Tax Journal*, Vol. 53(1), pp. 23-40.

Hill, Roderick and Michael Rushton (1993), "Harmonizing Provincial Sales Taxes with GST: The Problem of Interprovincial Trade", *Canadian Tax Journal*, Vol. 41(1), pp. 101-122.

Institute for Fiscal Studies (1978), *The Structure and Reform of Direct Taxation*, London: Allen and Unwin.

Jack, William (2000), "The Treatment of Financial Services under a Broad-Based Consumption Tax", *National Tax Journal*, Vol. 53(4), pp. 841-851.

Keen, Michael (2000), "VIVAT, CVAT and All That: New Forms of Value-Added Tax for Federal Systems", *Canadian Tax Journal*, Vol. 48(2), pp. 409-424.

Keen, Michael and Jack Mintz (2004), "The Optimal Threshold for a Value-Added Tax", *Journal of Public Economics*, Vol. 88, pp. 559-576.

Keen, Michael and Stephen Smith (1996), "The Future of Value-Added Tax in the European Union", *Economic Policy*, Vol. 23, pp. 375-420.

Keen, Michael and Stephen Smith (2000), "Viva VIVAT!", *International Tax and Public Finance*, Vol. 7(6), pp. 741-751.

McLure, Charles E., Jr. (2000a), "Implementing Subnational Value-Added Taxes on Internal trade: The Compensating VAT (CVAT)", *International Tax and Public Finance*", Vol. 7(6), pp. 723-740.

McLure, Charles E., Jr. (2000b), "Implementing a State VAT: Breaking the Logjam in Tax Assignment", *Proceedings of the Ninety-Second Annual Conference 1999*, National Tax Association, pp. 302-309.

Merrill, Peter R. and Harold Adrion (1995), "Treatment of Financial Services Under Consumption-Based Tax Systems", *Tax Notes*, Vol. 68(6), pp. 1496-1500.

Merrill, Peter R. and Chris R. Edwards (1996), "Cash-Flow Taxation of Financial Services", *National Tax Journal*, Vol. 49(3), pp. 487-500.

Poddar, Satya (2003), "Consumption Taxes: The Role of the Value-Added Tax", in: Patrick Honohan, editor, *Taxation of Financial Intermediation: Theory and Practice for Emerging Economies*, Washington, DC: The World Bank.

Rousslang, Donald J. (2002), "Should Financial Services Be Taxed Under a Consumption Tax? Probably", *National Tax Journal*, Vol. 55(2), pp. 281-291.

Whalley, John (1992), "Taxation and the Service Sector", in: Richard Bird and Jack Mintz, editors, *Taxation to 2000 and Beyond, Canadian Tax Paper No. 93*, Canadian Tax Foundation.

Chapter 11

THE PROPERTY TAX IN A NEW ENVIRONMENT: LESSONS FROM TAX REFORM EFFORTS IN TRANSITION ECONOMIES

JOAN YOUNGMAN and JANE MALME
Lincoln Institute of Land Policy, Cambridge, Massachusetts

1. INTRODUCTION

In the past decade, a number of Central and Eastern European nations have introduced new property tax systems or altered existing ones while undertaking enormous changes in their governmental and economic institutions. Against a background of entirely new fiscal policies and approaches to property rights, the political and economic roles of taxes on land and buildings as an adjunct to privatization, restitution and decentralization often have been as significant as their revenue-raising function. These initiatives offer instructive case studies in the design of property tax systems. They give evidence of the varied approaches taken to key elements of transition, including privatization, the development of private property rights, devolution of public decision making and service delivery, and the restructuring of legal and administrative systems. The nations that joined the European Union in 2004, including the Czech and Slovak Republics, Hungary, Poland, Slovenia, and the Baltic countries of Estonia, Latvia and Lithuania, will now begin a new stage of political and economic integration, making this a particularly appropriate point at which to review these countries' experiences in property taxation and to reflect on possible future developments.

2. GENERAL POLICY ISSUES IN PROPERTY TAX DESIGN

All states considering the introduction or reform of taxes on land and buildings face a set of basic policy questions that require clarification of the goals and operation of the tax.

- There are many complexities to the assignment of property tax responsibilities among different levels of government. Usually the basic legislative enactment is a central government function, but local governments may have discretion to set the rate, or to vary the rate within specific limits. Even when the definition of the tax base is contained within central government enabling legislation, local governments may have some ability to grant exemptions or hardship waivers. Administrative functions such as assessment and collection responsibilities need not be assigned to the level of government that receives the ultimate tax revenue. However, such a division can diminish the incentive for efficient collection. All cases require some consideration of the special potential of the property tax as an autonomous revenue source for local or other sub-national levels of government.
- The appropriate base for a tax on real property is a crucial economic and political decision. A market-value base presents administrators with the challenge of maintaining accurate assessments and dealing with the political difficulties of shifts in tax liabilities that reflect changes in relative property values. Non-market tax bases, such as arbitrary amounts assigned per unit of area, may avoid these problems of instability, but they rarely raise significant revenue, for arbitrary levies are politically acceptable only when they remain at nominal levels.
- Advances in property recordkeeping, dissemination of land market information, and computerized assessment and geographic information systems raise new questions as to the role of tax administration and its relationship to other property agencies, such as deed registries and cadastres. New technology offers potential efficiency gains in assessment, administration and collection, but can also be extremely expensive and may yield little additional revenue. Public access to tax and valuation records can enhance understanding of land market developments, but decisions on this point require a balance between open information and taxpayer privacy, particularly for data made available over the internet.
- The legal basis of the tax will serve as the framework for its operation, interpretation and administration. Its statutory construction should

support the goals for the tax and reflect the legal and political culture within which it will function.

- Property taxes are frequently proposed as tools for achieving land policy objectives, from countering land speculation to moderating disruptive fluctuations in land values. These non-revenue functions can be important, but must be approached with caution to avoid unrealistic expectations. The rates of tax that would be required for a direct or dramatic influence on land prices could raise political difficulties of their own.

The transition country experiences of the past decade offer insights into these policy decisions and their practical application.

3. LOCAL GOVERNMENT FINANCE

More than forty years ago, Ursula Hicks concluded, "If local bodies are to play any significant part in economic or social development, they must clearly have access to adequate finance. If they are both to act responsibly and to show initiative, some, not negligible, part of this control over independent, in the sense that the local councils are free to choose the rates (and to some extent the conditions) of their taxes or service charges."[1] The experience of intervening decades has reinforced the validity of this advice, yet it is not easy to identify appropriate autonomous revenue sources for local governments. Geographically small jurisdictions in direct competition for business location are naturally limited in the amount by which they may vary sales or income tax rates from the levels found in neighboring communities. At the same time, international integration through the European Union and other trade zones encourages development of taxes resources must be not subject to international competition.[2] The efficiency loss that accompanies income and sales taxes is compounded when they are utilized by multiple levels of government. Grants and transfers from higher levels of government can be unstable, falling prey to budgetary pressure or political considerations. Around the world, many municipalities that lack a significant source of local revenue must rely upon a patchwork of nuisance taxes, fees and charges that may lead to the worst of all fiscal worlds, imposing high administrative costs, yielding low revenue and contributing to a discouraging business climate.

Land and building taxes can serve as an independent local revenue source even when it is impractical for small jurisdictions to impose or vary the rates of other taxes. Immovable property is unique in this respect, for by definition it cannot be relocated to escape taxation. A jurisdiction seeking to improve its competitive position might well consider a tax on land: a tax object that is immovable and in fixed supply, which cannot be withdrawn from production or reduced in availability in response to the tax. To the extent the tax is capitalized into the price of land, its burden falls on the owner at the time the tax is introduced, and not on future purchasers or businesses considering location or expansion in that jurisdiction. A tax on land does not discourage new construction, renovation, or other improvements.

Partially in response to such considerations, the transition countries of Central and Eastern Europe have all included some form of property taxation in their fiscal reforms. Real estate taxes have been designated as local revenue sources in Hungary, Poland, Romania, Bulgaria, the Czech and Slovak Republics, the Russian Federation, the Baltic nations and Armenia. Although initially some of these nations divided the proceeds between national and local governments, they now assign all property tax revenues to local governments.

This change reflects these countries' recognition of the potential benefits of devolution of powers and responsibilities from central to lower levels of government. Uneasiness with governing bodies perceived to be distant and unaccountable led the Maastricht amendments to the treaty of European Union to recognize "subsidiarity"—assignment of responsibility and authority to the most decentralized level of government feasible for a particular task—as a formal constitutional principle.[3] Far from diminishing the role of local governments, international economic and political integration has heightened attention to the importance of independent, accountable and responsive subnational governments. Sometimes international bodies directly encourage these developments. For example, Armenia joined the Council of Europe in 2001, and pressure from this organization contributed to strengthening local government in the 2002 Law on Local Self-Government.[4] Such developments are by no means limited to transition economies, as illustrated by devolution initiatives within the United Kingdom. The National Assembly for Wales and the Scottish Parliament are the first democratically elected regional bodies to serve the distinct nations of the British Isles.

It is not paradoxical that devolution and integration might proceed in tandem, for the complementary strengths of subnational and international bodies mean that development of one will often highlight the need for the other. A lack of accountability is the greatest political drawback to an international structure such as the European Commission,[5] where the efficiency of centralization must be tempered by political representation and responsiveness.

In transition countries, political decentralization has proceeded more rapidly than its fiscal counterpart. The allocation of tax revenues to local governments has not been matched by local control over tax structure and administration, although some limited local discretion is permitted in Estonia and Poland. Property taxes comprise only a small part of total tax collections[6] and local government revenues, the greater part of which usually derives from distributed shares of central taxes, primarily VAT and personal income tax. The majority of property taxes are paid by business entities rather than by individuals,[7] since housing and land plots owned by individuals are often exempt or taxed at minimal rates, and new construction normally enjoys an initial period of exemption. In the future, greater economic integration, broader employment opportunities, and expansion of the housing market may contribute to a more mobile and competitive environment in which local taxes on immovable property owned by individuals will offer special advantages.

Most post-communist countries are still debating the appropriate size, number, authority and responsibilities of regional and local governments, and the optimal form of intergovernmental fiscal relationships. The number and size of governments affect their capacities for revenue generation, administration and service delivery, an important consideration at a time when a multitude of small towns seek greater independence.[8] All of the new members of the European Union are unitary rather than federal systems, with intermediary levels of government often limited to tasks of administrative coordination. Latvia has begun to increase the decision-making power of regional governments, which formerly served only as agents of the central government. Poland has also taken steps to provide its regional powiats with some self-governing authority, but in both cases the regional bodies are still largely dependent on central government funding.

The Czech and Slovak Republics that began the transition together have diverged in their approaches to fiscal decentralization since their 1993 separation. The Czech Republic contains more than 6,000 local government units, including many with extremely small populations and little administrative capacity. Partly as a result, the country has remained highly centralized and has no purely local taxes, with all tax bases and rates set at the national level. The revenue from taxes on land and on buildings, although assigned to local government, plays a minor role, providing just 3.3 percent of local revenues in 2002, the lowest among the new members of the European Union. In contrast, the Slovak Republic, with 3,000 local governments, has gradually reduced its grant support to municipalities. This has encouraged greater reliance on local sources of revenue, including the property tax, which stood at 12.4 percent of local revenues in 1999 and may well soon equal Poland's 14.3 percent if present trends continue.

4. DEFINING THE TAX BASE

Market value-based taxation is being seriously considered in nearly all transition countries of Central and Eastern Europe, but has been adopted only in Estonia and Latvia, in both cases with regard to land rather than buildings. Estonia developed a value-based tax on land in 1993, followed by Latvia in 1998. Lithuania has introduced market elements in its area-based tax[9] and has developed sophisticated land value maps in anticipation of a new Law on Land Taxation for 2005.

Townships (gmina) in Poland rely more heavily on the area-based Real Estate Tax revenue than do municipalities of other new European Union nations.[10] These jurisdictions have authority to set their own tax rates within maximum limits prescribed by the national government, with rates varying according to property use and adjusted for inflation. The rates per square meter vary considerably by type of use, with business property the most heavily taxed.

The Czech and Slovak Republics each tax land and buildings separately on an area basis that varies according to location and use. A proposal now under consideration by the Czech Ministry of Finance would gradually shift to a value-based land tax administered locally under central government supervision.

Municipal governments in Hungary may choose among a variety of local funding sources that include land parcel taxes, building taxes, communal taxes on individuals and businesses, tourism taxes, local business taxes and any combination of these. Budapest, which raises 35 percent of its revenue from local taxes, does not tax either land or buildings.

With support from the World Bank, Slovenia has developed a property registration system and cadastre. It is preparing to introduce a market value-based tax on real estate to replace its separate land and buildings taxes, with the expectation that the revenues from the new combined tax will offer greater support for local governments.

To further the goals of fiscal decentralization, local governments in these advanced transition countries will need increased authority to decide the rate and level of taxation and to raise sufficient revenues to fund services under local control. Value-based property taxes can enhance the growth capacity of this revenue source without competing with national tax levies.

Russia's experience with property taxation merits special attention. Federal taxes on real property were adopted in 1991 and 1992 as part of a new tax structure at a time of extensive privatization. The Law on the Payment of Land prescribed the amounts per square meter on which the lease, sale and taxation of land would be based. In addition, separate taxes were imposed on the property (buildings, structures and other assets) of enterprises and on the property of individuals. These tax proceeds were shared among federal, oblast and municipal governments until 1999, when 100 percent of the individual property tax revenue was assigned to municipalities. Revenue from the tax on enterprises was equally divided between the oblast and municipality in which its property was located, and only land tax revenue was shared among all three levels of government. Revenues from land and property taxes fell considerably in the late 1990s largely because of inflation. The 1999 Tax Code contemplated that a value-based tax on real estate would replace these three taxes in 2003, but such provisions have not yet been enacted.

In 1997 a USAID-supported pilot project introduced a locally administered real property tax in the cities of Tver and Novgorod Veliky. This project has concluded, and only a few large enterprises that own land and buildings in Novgorod Veliky are currently subject to the tax. These enterprises benefit considerably from this situation, because their movable property and certain other assets are no longer subject to the property portion of the general tax on enterprises. Despite this experiment, tax law and administration remain under the control of the federal government, with little local government autonomy. However, reforms have recently been proposed for the land tax that would introduce cadastral values developed by the Federal Land Cadastre Service as a base for taxation by local governments. Tax rates would be determined locally, within limits set by the Federal law. The land cadastre authorities are developing mass valuation methods within the constraints of limited reliable market data, and have completed the first cadastral valuation of urban land throughout Russia.[11]

Given the many challenges facing the Russian Federation, it is significant that its government is devoting considerable resources and attention to the development of value-based taxes to benefit local governments.

5. VALUE-BASED TAXES AND THEIR ALTERNATIVES

As these examples show, property taxes utilize a wide variety of tax bases, including capital value, annual value, original purchase price, non-value measures such as an area base or parcel taxes, and formulary approaches. Within value-based tax systems, a major distinction concerns annual taxes based on rental value and capital taxes based on sale value. Where the current use of the property is also the most economically profitable use, rental value and capital value will stand in a predictable relationship to one another. The two standards diverge when a prospective purchaser would bid an amount unrelated to current yield in the expectation of a different and more profitable use in the future. The capital-value base has the advantage of more closely approximating a tax on real property wealth and encouraging its most productive or highest and best use. The annual-value base tracks the realized cash income with which owners may expect to pay the tax and exerts less development pressure on unimproved properties. These problems of "cash-poor" taxpayers are a universal political challenge to value-based taxes. Whatever the land use goals, there will always be intense political resistance to tax levels requiring sale or mortgage of family farms, open space and the homes of senior citizens.

A true area-based system that takes no account of differences in land value has the obvious drawback that "residents who own undesirable land must pay at the same effective rate as residents who own highly desirable land in a prime location with access to all services and amenities. This system is unequal in that it effectively requires residents with unequal value assets to pay the same tax per square meter."[12] For this reason, property taxes based on area have generally been replaced by ad valorem measures (as in the Netherlands) or a proliferation of special provisions designed indirectly to recognize some value gradations (as in Tel Aviv). This latter situation negates the simplicity of application that is the prime recommendation for an area-based measure.

Other bases for property taxation include parcel taxes, which impose a set levy for each unit of land and improvements, and acquisition-value taxes, which are based on original purchase price, usually with some modest inflation adjustment. Both have been utilized in California after the Proposition 13 tax revolt of 1978 eliminated the traditional form of taxation at market value. Parcel taxes or flat taxes sometimes find favor on grounds that all property owners should contribute a minimum amount toward the cost of public services. A similar rationale lay behind the short-lived poll tax imposed in Great Britain, which extended this obligation beyond property owners to all adult residents. The state of Victoria in Australia has taken this approach, raising 20 percent of its property tax revenue through a municipal charge on each property and the remainder through an ad valorem levy.

Before the development of widespread land markets, many transition countries utilized area-based measures for land transactions, generally including leases, apartment maintenance charges and tax payments. Area-based systems persist in transition countries' tax systems for a variety of reasons. The lack of well-developed property markets and land registration systems has hindered consideration of value-based taxes in Albania and Belarus. Armenian officials have been unwilling to undertake tax changes that will draw on scarce administrative resources. Although the Czech Republic and Poland have acknowledged potential benefits to value-based taxes during more than a decade of public debate, this change has never commanded sufficient support to overcome doubts as to its political and administrative feasibility. Hungary and Slovakia have not yet entertained formal proposals for ad valorem taxation.

Taxes based on specific property characteristics, including location, provide an intermediate step between systems based on market value and systems that disregard market value. In 1993 Estonia became the first transition country to introduced a tax intended to reflect market value even before sales data were readily available. The tax was initially based on formulas that attempted to take into account such factors as area, location, quality and usage, and it gradually evolved to more sophisticated measures of market value. Other transition countries have taken various steps toward utilizing market-based values in their property taxes. Lithuania has produced land value maps in anticipation of introduction of a value-based tax on land. As mentioned earlier, with World Bank support, Slovenia is preparing a register of land and building values for a tax on real estate that may be implemented in 2005. With USAID assistance, Montenegro and Kosovo also have begun experiments with locally administered ad valorem systems.

Use of a formula to estimate market values can either be an intermediate step towards implementing a value-based system or the final step in a formulary system. For example, in 1998 Latvia introduced a tax based on cadastral values, utilizing officially recorded data as the basis for assessment. Although this has similarities to Estonia's use of land and building characteristics in its valuation formula, there are important distinctions between the two approaches, primarily in the role that official data plays in determining the assessment. Estonia's model resembles a rudimentary form of mass appraisal in which property characteristics help estimate market value. In Latvia, designated property characteristics set the taxable value, whether or not this coincides with market value.

At the extreme, cadastral values may simply replicate the pre-1989 approach. In Armenia, for example, the apartment value based on specific locational and amenity characteristics currently used for tax purposes is nearly the same as the value used to calculate maintenance fees during the Soviet era. An appeal may be made against incorrect attribution of characteristics, such as a mistaken location listing, but not against a final value figure at odds with market value. If characteristics are listed correctly, the fact that two nearly identical units have dramatically different tax values is not a basis for appeal.[13]

6. LEGAL AND ADMINISTRATIVE DESIGN FEATURES

A new structure of property rights requires a legal framework that addresses many fundamental aspects of ownership. Special issues in the area of taxation include the identification of the tax object and the taxpayer, valuation standards and methods, frequency of revaluation, assignment of administrative responsibilities, taxpayer rights and responsibilities, and methods of appeal.

In most transition countries land and buildings were formerly separate legal categories, often with separate owners. Immovable property was often not a significant classification, with non-land "property" defined to include buildings, moveable personal property and motor vehicles. Land and buildings have now begun to be treated as integrated units of real estate for specific purposes. Latvia has introduced an annual "Real Estate Tax" to replace taxes on land and buildings, and similar measures have been proposed in Slovenia and Russia. It is very important that the consolidation of land and buildings into a single parcel for purposes of conveyancing, registration and property law not preclude consideration of imposing different rates of property tax on land and improvements.

The assessment date designates the time as of which all property is to be valued. The fact that property is under construction, unregistered, unoccupied or awaiting occupancy permits may influence its taxable value but should not keep it from the tax rolls. An exemption for incomplete buildings may provide an incentive for deliberate delay in final construction details as a means of tax avoidance.

Tax exemption is commonly provided to religious, charitable and educational property. Estonia has set an admirable example in restricting exemptions by including government-owned property in the tax base. This can be a meaningful intergovernmental transfer of funds and an incentive for appropriate land use when an agency's budget reflects a charge for its property.

The differentiation between legal and physical persons, found in most transition countries, is not necessary for a property tax law, but neither is it an impediment.[14] It is only essential that a taxpayer be identified for each taxable parcel. "In rem" property tax systems define the property itself as the subject of taxation. This can simplify administration and enforcement by avoiding questions of legal title and allowing either the owner, possessor or user of the property to be liable for payment of the tax. To avoid a single property giving rise to multiple taxpayers and divided liability for payment, both of which increase administrative costs and complicate enforcement, taxpayer liability can be established on the assessment date for the full year. A change in ownership during the year does not relieve liability; taxes can be allocated between the parties, and the tax records are not changed until the next tax year. The proceeds of tax payments accrue to the taxing jurisdiction where the real property is located rather than the jurisdiction where the legal owner may reside.

In many transition countries there is a strong official inclination to specify valuation methods and procedures in the tax law in great detail. There are many advantages to specifying only the legal standard and permitting the administrative agency responsible for valuation to specify methods by regulation as administrative resources, market conditions and technical capacity change and develop in the future. The valuation administration should be held responsible for its results, not for adherence to rigid methods and instructions.

Periodic reappraisals are necessary for maintenance of any value-based tax system. Revaluation cycles of three to five years required by law are generally considered reasonable, with interim indexing of values to reflect changes in price levels.

Land and cadastral agencies have contributed to the development of value-based taxation in a number of transition countries. Cadastral agencies in Lithuania, Russia and Slovenia and Land Services in Estonia and Latvia are responsible for developing market-based land valuations for taxation. Professional interest in property value has developed naturally from these agencies' expertise in land and property information systems. In some cases this has been combined with responsibility for recording private property ownership and transfers of property rights. Their data bases and information systems have led naturally to a larger role encompassing valuation as well, both for individual properties and as part of computerized mass valuation systems. Because these agencies are responsible for recording and evaluating sales prices and market data, their employees have reason to investigate property appraisal and mass valuation modeling techniques. As market activity increases, these agencies are in a position to estimate values for taxation as well as for other purposes. These agencies are not precise equivalents to assessing departments or valuation agencies in the United States or Canada, but they have similar goals for professional information processing and political independence.

The Baltic countries have taken bold steps in public posting of valuations, both physically and on the Internet. This encourages the correction of factual errors and the improvement of the overall quality of the assessment list. In most transition countries, the only appeal is directly to a court where a decision may take years. Consequently, it is crucial to establish efficient and impartial forums for administrative review of assessments.

7. PROPERTY TAXATION AND LAND POLICY

Perhaps the most important effect of a property tax is its reservation of a portion of private real estate value, introducing a public element into the basic structure of property rights. For example, an annual tax of 1 percent of market value at a time when property yields rental income of 5 percent effectively makes the public a 20 percent limited partner in the property-owning enterprise—sharing in the proceeds, but not in managerial decisions. This is an ambitious and important step, and it is not surprising that it elicits controversy. A value-based tax establishes a public element in property while retaining private ownership and control. It recognizes that a portion of the growth in property value results from public investment and community growth. This is not an easy argument to convey in a nontechnical manner, but it touches on the most critical aspects of the tax, which extend beyond the fiscal sphere. It is especially relevant to the situation in transition countries, where there is often strong support for retaining a public interest in land as a fixed, nonrenewable element of common heritage—one which, once sold, cannot be reproduced.[15]

The relationships between property taxes and claims of property ownership are complex and sometimes conflicting. A requirement of tax payment can, of course, be a disincentive to registration of ownership, but a tax payment can also be a welcome means of securing evidence of a claim to property at a modest price. This has been particularly true in areas of informal settlement in Africa, Indonesia and Latin America.

As urban centers throughout the world experience rapid inflation in land values, the property tax has received new attention as a potential means of counteracting the disruptive social and economic effects of an uncontrolled rise in land prices. Many questions concerning the actual effect of a land tax on speculation and price levels remain unresolved, including even ambiguity as to the meaning of speculation itself. In particular, for taxes to have a significant impact on land prices, they may need to be imposed at much higher levels than are currently typical.

The difficulty of defining speculation with legal precision has undermined the effectiveness of many anti-speculative measures. For example, in the United States special exemptions from full capital value taxation for land in agricultural use were enacted to counter development pressure upon family farms. In fact, these exemptions have often encouraged speculation by reducing the cost of withholding land from the market in anticipation of future price increases. In many cases, speculators may avoid being taxed on full market value by continuing some nominal amount of agricultural activity in the interim. Various states have attempted, without notable success, to distinguish bona fide farmers from speculators by such criteria as the price paid for property and whether purchasers filed applications for a zoning change. Such efforts are fundamentally flawed insofar as they assume a complete separation of the categories of speculators and bona fide farmers. There is no reason why a bona fide farmer should not consider his property a business asset, capitalizing upon market changes and obtaining the maximum price for it when a sale is appropriate.

All the Baltic countries, with achieving "impressive progress over a decade of transition,"[16] have recognized the importance of regional real estate markets in economic development and fiscal policy. The national land agencies of Estonia, Latvia and Lithuania have published reports on land and real estate sales, prices, taxes and trends in their countries since 2001. Property taxes in these countries respond to both fiscal and land policy objectives, specifically the restitution of property expropriated by the Soviet Union in 1939. Estonia and Latvia had extensive restitution programs, permitting former owners or their heirs, regardless of their present place of residence, to regain their land. A major purpose of the value-based land tax imposed by Estonia was to stimulate more efficient use of this land while not discouraging development by taxing improvements. A tax limited to land did not burden residents in privatized apartments whose cash income bore little relationship to their recently acquired asset.

Lithuania's restitution program was limited to national residents, which reduced the problem of speculation by absentee owners and also eased administration. This land reform effort led to development of an integrated real estate register and cadastre. This in turn produced a state enterprise (The State Enterprise Centre of Registers) with a sophisticated legal and cadastral land record system that is well prepared to implement mass valuation for tax purposes. The Baltic countries view accession to the European Union as likely to increase demand for real estate investment and leasing, and they seek to capture price increases in their tax revenues.

Although the Baltic countries have been in the forefront of those viewing property taxation as an instrument of land policy, property tax proponents in other transition countries also have stressed the nonfiscal benefits of value-based taxation for improved productivity.

8. CONCLUSION

Contemporary property tax reform efforts must identify the appropriate role for a tax on immobile physical assets in an economic era ever more reliant on mobile and intangible factors. The tax can offer a stable revenue source particularly well suited for local government and a valuable adjunct to land policy and property law initiatives. At the same time, it requires administrative capability, legislative support and political acceptance that are often lacking in highly developed and long-established systems, as well as in transition economies. The experience of Central and Eastern European nations in developing new systems of property taxation offers an opportunity to consider new means of dealing with these significant challenges in order to benefit from the tax's potential both as a revenue source and as an adjunct to land policy initiatives.

Notes

1. Ursula Hicks, Development from Below: Local Government and Finance in Developing *Countries of the Commonwealth* (1961), at 277.
2. See Bengt Kjellson, "Taxation of Real Property in Sweden," *Journal of Property Tax Assessment & Administration*, Vol. 1, No. 3 (1995), 93-100, at 99 ("The integration in Europe should also be mentioned. Property taxes are national taxes, in the sense that real property does not move across borders in the same way as capital and people. An increased use of property taxes can be seen as a possible way of generating the necessary tax revenue without touching more 'sensitive' taxes.").
3. See, e.g., Werner F. Ebke, "Company Law and the European Union," 31 *International Lawyer* 961 (1997), at n. 98-99. ("Generally speaking, under the principle of subsidiarity, the Community shall pursue only those objectives which can be better attained by the Community than Member States acting individually....Article 3B(2) provides that in areas which do not fall within the Community's exclusive jurisdiction, the Community shall take action, in accordance with the principle of subsidiarity, only if and in so far as the objectives of the proposed action cannot be sufficiently achieved by the Member States and can therefore, by reason of the scale or effects of the proposed action, be better achieved by the Community.")
4. See Anderson (2004) at 17-18.
5. See, e.g., Emma Tucker, "Culture of Mismanagement Dates Back to the 'Golden Era,'" *Financial Times* (London), March 17, 1999, p. 3.
6. Müller (2003) reports that recurrent property tax revenue as a percentage of total taxes in 1999 was 0.6% in the Czech republic, 1.2% in Estonia, 0.5% in Hungary, 3.5% in Latvia, 2.0% in Lithuania, and 3.1% in Poland. Although these percentages are lower than those found in some developed countries, particularly those with British heritage, they are consistent with figures for many Central European and Nordic nations.
7. This pattern is not limited to transition countries. ".In nearly all OECD countries (France being an extreme exception), however, business property taxes yield much more revenue than residential property taxes." Messere (20002), at 139.
8. See, e.g., Howard (1999) ("Hungary's local government reforms were aimed at making possible local democracy even in the smallest of hamlets.")
9. "Area-based tax" is used here to denote a land or building tax of a specified amount per unit of area.
10. This may in part be due to their recent origin. The Local Self-Government Act of March 1990 "created the gminy (meaning 'commune' or 'municipality'), autonomous local governments responsible for 'all public matters of local significance that are not reserved by law for other units.'" Howard (1999), at 676.
11. The mass valuation process and the reform agenda are described in Overchuk (2004).
12. Sandra Bettger, et al., "The Economic Impact of and Strategy for Implementing an Ad Valorem Property Tax: A Case Study of Krakow," International City/County Management Association Report to the U.S. Agency for International Development (September, 1994), p. 7 (discussing drawbacks of area-based tax in Krakow). Note also that rental value can climb precipitously for owner-occupied residences as market values rise, and the resident taxpayers would not necessarily have increased cash income with which to pay the tax even under an annual value system.
13. Formulary approaches are not limited to transition economies. Chile bases property taxes on the "fiscal value" of land and buildings rather than their market values. On the basis of sale transactions and determinations of soil quality, set values are assigned to specific zones of urban and rural land. Buildings are valued according to specified characteristics and size, adjustments for regional differences in construction costs. In France, dwellings and professional buildings are classified for purposes of the "taxe

foncière sur les propriétés bâties" into eight categories of construction. A specific tax rate developed for each group is applied to the individual property according to its size and other characteristics. A similar approach is taken to the valuation of land under the "taxe foncière sur les propriétés non bâties."

14. The distinction between "legal" or juridical taxpayers and individuals or "physical persons" reflects the basic classification of Russian tax law.
15. "In the case of transition economies the land tax is usually the easiest to administer and it is also often politically less offensive than other forms of real property taxation." Trasberg (2004), at 33.
16. *Baltic States* OECD Economic Survey 2000

References

Almy, Richard (2003), "Modernizing Property Taxes", *The Case Study of Lithuania, Fair & Equitable Magazine*, Vol. 1(12), pp.7-11, International Association of Assessing Officers, Chicago, IL,

Anderson, R. Jerome (2004), "Property Taxation in Armenia: Steps toward Reform and Decentralization", *Journal of Property Tax Assessment and Administration*, Vol. 1(2), pp.15-31.

Bird, Richard M., Robert D. Ebel, Christine I. Wallich (eds.) (1995), *Decentralization of the Socialist State: Intergovernmental Finance in Transition Economies*, Washington, DC: World Bank Regional and Sectoral Studies.

Ebel, Robert D. and Serdar Yilmaz (2002), "On the Measurement and Impact of Fiscal Decentralization", in: Katarina Ott, Anto Bajo and Mihaela Pitarević, editors, *Fiscal Decentralization in Croatia*, Zagreb: Institute of Public Finance-Fiscal Decentralization Initiative.

Estonian Land Board, Land Service of Latvia, State Enterprise Centre of Registers of Lithuania (2001, 2002, 2003), "A Review of the Baltic States Real Estate Markets."

Howard, A.E. Dick (1999), "After Communism: Devolution in Central and Eastern Europe", *South Texas Law Review*, Vol. 40, pp. 661-688.

Malme, Jane H. (2004), "Valuation for Land Taxation in Transitional Economies", *Land Lines*, April, pp 5-6, Cambridge, MA: Lincoln Institute of Land Policy.

Malme, Jane H. and Joan M. Youngman (eds.) (2001), *The Development of Property Taxation in Economies in Transition: Case Studies from Central and Eastern Europe*, Washington D.C.: The World Bank Institute.

Messere, Ken (2000), "Evaluating the Taxing Powers of Sub-Central Governments", *Bulletin for International Fiscal Documentation*, Vol. 54(3), pp. 133-146.

Müller, Anders (2003), "The Importance of Recurrent Property Tax in Public Finance, Tax Policy & Fiscal Decentralization", Institute of Revenues, Rating and Valuation (London), Conference on Property Tax and Land Reform, Tallinn, Estonia.

Oates, Wallace (1972), *Fiscal Federalism*, New York: Harcourt, Brace and Jovanovick.

Oates, Wallace (1999), "Local Property Taxation: An Assessment", *Land Lines*, Vol. 11(3), pp. 1-3.

OECD (2000), "Baltic States", Economic Survey, Paris.

Overchuk, Alexey L., (2004), "Mass Valuation of Land in the Russian Federation", *Land Lines*, April , pp 6-7, Cambridge, MA: Lincoln Institute of Land Policy.

Pallai, Katalin (ed.) (2003), "*The Budapest Model*", Local Government and Public Service Reform Initiative, Open Society Institute, Budapest.

Review of the Baltic States Real Estate Markets, (2001, 2002, 2003), Annual publication, Estonian Land Board, Land Service of Latvia, State Enterprise Centre of Registers of Lithuania.

Sabaliauskas, Kestutis and Albina Aleksiene (2002), "Progress Toward Value-Based Taxation of Real Property in Lithuania", *Land Lines*, October, 11-13, Cambridge, MA: Lincoln Institute of Land Policy.

Swianiewicz, Pawel (2003), "*Foundations of Fiscal Decentralization: Benchmarking Guide for Countries in Transition*", Discussion Paper, Local Government and Public Service Reform Initiative, Open Society Institute, Budapest.

Trasberg, Viktor (2004), "Property and Land Taxation in the Baltic States", *Journal of Property Tax Assessment and Administration*, Vol. 1(2), pp.31-45.

United Nations Economic Commission for Europe (2002), "*Proceedings: Mass Valuation Systems of Land (Real Estate) for Taxation Purposes*", Working Party on Land Administration Workshop, Federal Land Cadastre of Russia, Moscow.

Youngman, Joan M. and Jane H. Malme (1994), *An International Survey of Taxes on Land and Buildings*, Deventer: Kluwer Law and Tax Publishers.

Chapter 12

SOCIETAL INSTITUTIONS AND TAX EFFORT IN DEVELOPING COUNTRIES

RICHARD M. BIRD*, JORGE MARTINEZ-VAZQUEZ**, AND BENNO TORGLER***,[1]

** University of Toronto; ** Andrew Young School of Policy Studies, Georgia State University; ***Yale Center for International and Area Studies, Leitner Progran in International and Comparative Political Economy, and Center for Research in Economics, Management and the Arts (CREMA), Switzerland*

1. INTRODUCTION

"Will underdeveloped countries learn to tax?" asked Nicholas Kaldor (1963), forty years ago. Underlying this question is the assumption that if a country wishes to become 'developed' it needs to collect in taxes an amount greater than the 10-15 percent found in many developing countries.[2] Kaldor's answer to his question was essentially that since even the poorest country had sufficient 'capacity' in both economic and administrative terms to tax more, whether or not a particular country did so depended primarily on its political institutions. Would developing countries be fortunate enough to have those with political power voluntarily give up at least some of their power to block fiscal reform in exchange for social stability? Or would the ruling groups rather wait (in the spirit of *après moi le deluge*) for the revolutionary upheaval that he considered the only alternative (Kaldor, 1963)?

Most of the elements of the discussion of 'tax effort' in developing countries in recent decades are evident in this early discussion:

- Should these countries tax more than they do? Most who have studied this question seem to have assumed, as did Kaldor, that more taxation is just what the doctor ordered.[3]

- Can they tax more than they do? That is, do they have the 'capacity' to collect a relatively larger share of national income in government coffers? Early regression analysis at the IMF launched a flood of empirical studies considering this question, most of which agreed with Kaldor's conclusion that in economic terms such countries can indeed tax more, that is, that their 'capacity' to tax exceeds the 'effort' they make to tax that capacity.[4] Conceptual underpinning for this emphasis on the importance of capacity in determining tax levels – that is, for assessing tax effort in terms of how much a country taxed relative to its measured capacity – was provided by Hinrichs (1963) and Musgrave (1969), who emphasized the importance of 'tax handles' or structural features such as imports which were relatively easy to tap for fiscal purposes.
- Although some literature stresses the limits administrative capacity imposes on taxation in developing countries (Bird, 1989), those who advocate more taxation as an essential ingredient of any lasting solution to underdevelopment have seldom been deterred by such skepticism. In a sense they seem right in ignoring this problem since the evidence appears to suggest that, if the political will to tax is there, the administrative way to do so can be found, if not immediately then shortly.[5]
- Indeed, as again Kaldor (1963) explicitly noted, one of the principal lessons that has been learned from tax reform experience around the world is precisely that 'political will' is the *sine qua non* of any successful tax reform (Bird, 2004) and that a country's tax system reflects its political institutions. In the words of Rodrik, Subramanian, and Trebbi (2002) it appears that "Institutions Rule" in this as in other areas of economic development.

The problem thus seems obvious: if poor countries want to become richer, they need to spend more on public infrastructure, education, and so on. Hence they need to tax more. The main reason they do not do so also seems obvious: it is not in the interest of those who dominate the political institutions of such countries to increase taxes. If this is the story, then economists, who do not readily take to the revolutionary barricades, have a problem in suggesting a viable solution. The emphasis in earlier empirical analysis on 'supply side' factors such as the ready availability of (easily taxed) economic activities such as foreign trade and mining remains important in explaining what countries do, but telling a country that wants to raise its tax levels to find oil is not a particularly promising piece of policy advice. Is the recent political economy literature on the importance of institutions more useful in this respect? Are 'societal institutions' (Alm and

Martinez-Vazquez, 2003) the key to increasing tax effort? What institutions? Can such institutions be modified to produce more 'pro-fiscal' outcomes (assuming for present purposes that this is desirable)? In this paper, we explore some aspects of these broad questions, taking two distinct approaches.[6]

In Section 2 we take a sort of case study approach to the problem, first sketching the broad experience with tax reform in Latin America and the relatively unsuccessful outcomes – if success is defined in terms of increasing the tax-GDP ratio – of these efforts. Some seem surprised by this lackluster performance, but, as did Kaldor (1963), we argue that this outcome is only to be expected since the underlying political conditions in these countries have not, for the most part, changed significantly over this period. We develop this proposition with reference to Mexico's experience over the past few decades.

In contrast, in Section 3 of the paper we take a quite different approach, examining empirically the determinants of tax levels across a broader sample of developing and transition countries. In doing so, we take into account not only the supply factors (tax handles) but also such critical demand factors as institutions, the size of the shadow economy, wealth inequality and 'tax morale' (defined as the intrinsic motivation by citizens to pay taxes, which, it is argued, depends on their attitude toward the state, see, e.g., Frey 1997). If taxpayers perceive that their interests (preferences) are properly represented in political institutions and they receive an increased supply of public goods, their willingness to contribute increases. On the other hand, a state in which corruption is rampant is one in which citizens have little trust in authority and thus a low incentive to cooperate. A more encompassing and legitimate state may be an essential precondition for a more adequate tax system in developing countries. Societal institutions in this sense might be seen as an indicator of the extent to which citizens feel they have a meaningful 'voice' in influencing the state. At the same time, however, the level of taxation can also be expected to be related to the availability of what may be called the 'exit option'[7] of the so-called shadow economy. In general, the larger the shadow economy, the lower we would expect tax effort to be.

In different ways, the distinct approaches taken in Sections 2 and 3 point to the same conclusion, set out briefly in Section 4. A more encompassing and legitimate state is an essential precondition for a more adequate tax system in developing countries. While at first glance giving such advice to poor countries may seem no more helpful than telling them to find oil, it is presumably more feasible for people to improve their governing institutions than to rearrange nature's bounty.[8]

2. THE TAX RATIO AND POLITICAL EQUILIBRIUM

Over the last forty years, most Latin American countries found it difficult to achieve a sustainable policy balance in the face of the often conflicting and frequently changing forces, external and internal, economic and political, that most of them have faced. Both the facts that presumably should govern policy in principle and the intellectual fashions that too often seem to govern it in practice have changed markedly over the last few decades in most countries in the region. It is thus not surprising that their tax policies have also changed considerably -- though less either in level or in structure than might be expected.

2.1 Taxation in Latin America

The data on taxation in Latin America, partial and in many ways unsatisfactory as they are, suggest several interesting conclusions.[9]

- First, over the last few decades taxes have not gone up in Latin America. Some rates have risen, mainly for VAT, but many have declined, mainly for income taxes. Indeed, tax collections as a share of national income have, on average, actually declined a bit. In this sense, the tax effort of most Latin American countries has changed little. Latin American countries continue to be below average in terms of the size of their public sectors relative to their levels of per capita income (IDB, 1998).
- Secondly, those countries that had relatively high taxes at the end of the 1970s were still above the regional average in the 1990s, just as those that depended more on income than on consumption taxes continued on the whole to do so. To take two small examples, in 1980-82 Guatemala's tax ratio (taxes as a percent of GDP) was 9.8 percent, of which only 2.8 percent came from personal income taxes; in 1995-99, the comparable figures were 8.9 percent and 2.2 percent. At the other extreme, although Nicaragua's tax ratio rose from 23.6 percent in 1981-83 to 26.2 percent in 1995-99, the share of taxes on domestic consumption remained dominant, although declining a bit from 49 percent to 46 percent.[10] Of course, tax rates in these countries did not necessarily change in the same way as tax ratios: for example, the VAT rate in Nicaragua rose from 6 to 15 percent over this period.
- Thirdly, although the reality of taxation in Latin America has changed less than our perception of it, as evidenced by the relative constancy in both tax levels and tax structures across and within countries, many changes have taken place in tax policy across this complex region over

the last few decades. Economic and political circumstances have changed dramatically at times in some countries, and sometimes tax systems have changed with them, though not always as one might expect.

In a recent analysis of Mexico, for example, Martinez-Vazquez (2001) notes that one of the most striking features of the various major tax changes that have taken place over the decades has been how very little apparent effect they have had on Mexico's tax-GDP ratio, which has remained almost constant. Tax policy and tax administration reforms over the last two decades have given Mexico a tax structure that is in many ways comparable to that in many developed countries but the tax system has continued to perform poorly in raising adequate revenues.[11]

Mexico's tax effort has not changed significantly for a quarter of a century. Both total federal revenues (which exclude social security funds and subnational governments) and federal tax revenues (which exclude oil and other non-tax revenues) as percent of GDP have moved up and down over the last two decades but have remained relatively stable overall, averaging between 15 and 16 percent for total federal revenues and between 10 and 11 percent for tax revenues. From 1980 to 2003, tax revenues rose only from 10.9 percent to 11.3 percent of GDP, and total federal revenues only went up from 15.3 percent to 16.8 percent.[12]

Given the marked improvements in the tax system over the past three decades (Martinez-Vazquez, 2001), it is surprising that Mexico's tax system has not been able to generate more than 11 percent of GDP in tax revenues particularly since the most common objective of the various tax reforms over this period, including the latest attempted reform by President Vicente Fox at the start of his administration in 2000, has been to increase the revenue adequacy of the tax system in order to be able to improve the quality and quantity of public services.

As discussed below, any country's tax performance can be explained in part by factors common to many other countries. In addition, however, country-specific factors may contribute significantly to explaining revenue performance. One set of country-specific factors, for example, relates to the management of tax policy. The good fundamental structure of Mexico's tax system and its revenue performance has been undermined by numerous ad hoc policy measures. With respect to the tax on enterprise profits, for instance, several economic sectors, including all agriculture and transport, benefited from a special regime in which the tax base was calculated on a cash-flow basis and agriculture and some other sectors also benefited from a tax rate half that applied under the general corporate income tax regime. These and many other exceptions to the supposedly general income and sales taxes added excess burdens, cost revenues, and by undermining the confidence of taxpayers in the fairness of the system probably reduced voluntary compliance.

A second set of country-specific factors has to do with the management of tax enforcement. Tax administration in Mexico has faltered in part because tax policy measures have ignored the ability of the tax administration to enforce complex tax issues and in part because the tax administration has failed to modernize and may in some respects even have gone backwards with respect to some of the institutional improvements achieved in earlier periods. An example of putting the "cart of tax policy" before the "horse of tax administration" is Mexico's liberal use of such complex consolidation rules for dependent enterprises that in effect it wrote almost a blank check for a powerful group of taxpayers (about 350 consolidated groups involving 5,000 separate companies).

Finally, and importantly, despite frequent general pronouncements about the need for higher revenue collections, Mexico seems at times to have pursued a policy – sometimes explicitly -- of keeping the ratio of revenues to GDP relatively constant. A relatively constant tax effort has been achieved in two ways. First, any increase in revenues resulting from economic growth, enlargement of the tax bases, or increased petroleum revenue was generally followed by such discretionary tax policy measures as lower tax rates with the result of keeping actual tax effort more or less constant. During the 1980s, for instance, a reverse or mirror image of revenue movements from petroleum and non-petroleum sources was evident. The chronology of tax concessions parallels periods in which the automatic elasticity of the system would otherwise have produced an increase in revenue effort.[13] Alternatively, at times there has been discretionary relaxation or tightening of tax administration effort. The political economy of taxation in Mexico has long involved periodic discussions and agreements between the government and a more or less willingly compliant compact of large taxpayers whose general tax burden was, in effect, 'negotiated.' The point is not so much that tax enforcement efforts were relaxed when government revenues were up, but more that high concentrated levels of enforcement were launched (in the from of "tax crusades" and so on) only when government revenues were dramatically down due to economic crises and business cycle downturns.

At least in the case of Mexico, then, it appears that reforms in tax structure (1) may have been undermined by unrelated ad hoc measures, or (2) they may have been offset by administrative deterioration, or (3) one or both of the preceding may have occurred less by accident than by intention. Similar relative constancy can be seen in other countries (e.g. Colombia) over the decades despite repeated tax reforms (McLure and Zodrow, 1997).[14] Perhaps, it appears, a 'good' tax reform – one intended to raise more revenue in a more efficient and equitable fashion, for instance -- may be something like a 'good' seat belt law. That is, if everything else stayed the same, lives would be saved (the tax ratio would increase), but things do not stay the same – some people drive faster when they are belted in, so death rates (tax ratios) show little change. In short, countries may tend to achieve an equilibrium position with respect to the size and nature of their fiscal systems that largely reflects the balance of political forces and institutions, and stay at this position until 'shocked' to a new equilibrium.

2.2 Why So Little Change?

Two alternative explanations are obviously possible as to why so much tax 'reform' has had so little effect on tax 'effort.' Either 'supply' ('capacity') factors have altered over the period in such a way as to offset all attempts to raise tax ratios. Or, perhaps more plausibly, ideas as to what the 'proper' tax level should be have altered over time. The two main aims of most tax reforms in the period after the Second World War were first, to raise revenue – and lots of it -- in order to finance the state as the 'engine of development', and, second, to redistribute income and wealth. Since then as now income and wealth were markedly unequally distributed in Latin America, the need for redressing the balance through fiscal means seemed obvious to all, and the ability of taxes to do the job was largely unquestioned. Both goals – revenue and redistribution – could, it was generally thought, be achieved largely by imposing high effective tax rates on income, essentially because the depressing effects of taxes on investment and saving were considered to be small. Indeed, an extra bonus of high rates was sometimes argued to be that they made it easier to lead balky private investors by the visible hand of well-designed fiscal incentives into those channels most needed for developmental purposes.

To exaggerate only a bit, the conventional wisdom at the time was essentially that all developing countries needed to do to solve their fiscal problems was to "learn to tax" (Kaldor, 1963), which to most meant to tax in a properly progressive fashion. Views on the appropriate role and structure of taxation began to change in the 1970s and 1980s, however. By 1990, in contrast to the immediate post-war era, both economists and policy-makers had generally come to believe that high tax rates not only discouraged and distorted economic activity but were largely ineffective in redistributing income and wealth. Reflecting this new view, income tax rates on both persons and corporations were cut sharply and are now almost universally in the 20-30% range in Latin America, as elsewhere in the world (Shome, 1999). On the other hand, reflecting – indeed, to some extent leading – world-wide trends, the VAT is now the mainstay of the revenue system in Latin America (Ebrill et al., 2001). Moreover, the decline of taxes on international trade with liberalization and the WTO as well as increased competition for foreign investment have moved international concerns from the bottom to the top of the tax policy action list in many countries. At the same time, in many countries, a new issue has risen to prominence on the fiscal menu as decentralization made the question of setting up adequate sub-national tax systems an increasing concern, not least in Latin America (IDB, 1997). Life in the tax policy world in Latin America, as elsewhere, was thus very different in many respects at the beginning of this century than it was in the middle of the last century.

2.3 Ideas, Institutions, and Interests

Such ideas matter. As Blyth (2002, p. 274) says, "...neither material resources nor the self-interest of agents can dictate...ends or tell agents what future to construct. Ideas do this." Or, in the more colorful words of John Maynard Keynes (1936, pp. 283-84): "practical men, who believe themselves to be quite free from any intellectual influences, are usually the slaves of some defunct economist...soon or late, it is ideas, not vested interests, which are dangerous for good or evil." Ideas about tax policy have clearly changed. Have institutions and interests also changed?

Some years ago, Michael Best (1976) analyzed Central American tax policy in essentially a 'class' framework, arguing that in principle changes in tax level structure (e.g., the degree of emphasis on income taxation) reflected largely the changing political balance of power between landlords, capitalists, workers, and peasants. Shortly after his article appeared, the Sandinista government – perhaps the most explicitly leftist regime ever to have power in the region (apart from Cuba) -- took over in Nicaragua. What happened to taxes? First, as Best (1976) would have predicted, the tax ratio rose very quickly, from 18 to 32 percent of GDP within the first five years of the Sandinista regime. Secondly, however, almost all the increased tax revenue came from regressive indirect taxes, not the progressive income taxes that one might have expected. Third, and in many ways most interesting, once Nicaragua's tax ratio was increased, it stayed up there even a decade (and three subsequent governments) after the defeat of the Sandinistas.[15]

As this example suggests, politics matters in taxation, but it does not necessarily dominate. Economic and administrative realities, and ideas, also matter. The fiscal reality found in most countries probably reflects a changing mixture of ideas, interests, and institutions. The tax structure that exists seldom seems to have been designed with any particular objective in mind. On the contrary, it often seems, like Topsy, to 'have just growed' in ways shaped by both the changing local environment and the changing external context. In the case of the United States, for example, as Weisman (2002, p. 366) notes, "economic crises and wars helped create a consensus for an income tax that falls most heavily on the wealthiest taxpayers. The consensus [was] forged in the period of 1860 to 1920….." The lengthy debate about taxes that took place over this period was, he says, not really about taxes at all but rather about "what kind of society Americans wanted." Since 1970 or so, the ideas on the relevant balance between taxes and society that were forged over the first half of the 20th century seem to many to have changed; the reality, however, has changed much less and is perhaps not likely to change all that much in the near future.

Recent broader historical and comparative analysis broadly supports this argument.[16] Lindert (2002), for example, suggests that democratic polities do learn from experience, and do, over time, tend to reward more those parties that follow more prudent economic policies. Cheibub (1998) demonstrates that even new democracies have frequently raised taxes. Those who think that populists who promise immediate delivery of the moon to the voters will invariably win should, it seems, consider more carefully the meaning of Abraham Lincoln's famous dictum to the effect that one can fool all of the people some of the time and some of the people all of the time, but that one can never fool all of the people all of the time. Economic history appears to tell us that, at least in societies with the error-correction mechanism that we call "democracy", Lincoln was right, at least to some extent. As Blyth (2002, p. 274) puts essentially the same point: "Political economies …are …evolutionary systems populated by agents who learn and apply those lessons in daily practice."

2.4 How to Tax More

What do such arguments suggest with respect to increasing tax effort in Latin America or in developing countries more generally? Weisman (2002, p.366) concludes with respect to the United States that "…the search for the right balance is an endless process…. The consensus supporting the legitimacy of the income tax is likely to remain undisturbed. But its progressive nature will always be debated as long as we care about reconciling the competing demands of social equity, economic incentives and the need to pay for an expanding government." In Latin America, no real consensus on the 'right balance' appears yet to have been achieved in most countries. The fact that a few developed countries may have, as it were, moved on to a new, less progressive consensus does not imply that it is any less important for Latin America to develop its own viable democratic social consensus on the right balance between equity and efficiency in taxation.

The developed countries have clearly reached different equilibrium positions. Lindert (2003) may be seen in large part as an extended demonstration of the continued viability of the so-called 'welfare state' model in most European countries and a different, lower-tax equilibrium in the U.S. and a few other countries. As Messere, de Kam, and Heady (2003) show, there has been essentially no convergence in either tax levels or structures among OECD countries in recent decades. They argue there is little reason to expect such convergence in the near future. Equally, there is no reason to expect any one balance to be right for all countries developing countries, in Latin America or elsewhere. As always with public policy, no one size fits all. What is right, or at least feasible, in Chile or Brazil, for example, is likely to continue to differ from what may be sustainable in Colombia or Honduras.

What matters is not only how high taxes are (revenue adequacy), but also how the tax level has been chosen, how the taxes are imposed, and how the funds thus raised are used The historical evidence appears to suggest that it is critical to ensure that the linkage between expenditure and revenue decisions is clearly established in the budgetary and political process.[17] As Wicksell (1896) argued over a century ago, allocative decisions in the public sector will be made efficiently only if they are financed efficiently – that is, by benefit taxes, which may be broadly understood in this context as taxes deliberately chosen to finance specific expenditures in the full knowledge of the allocative consequences of both expenditures and taxes. Wicksell further argued that even such good taxes would really only be politically sustainable if the distribution of income and wealth accorded broadly with the politically-acceptable "just" distribution of income – which, as Alesina and Angeletos (2003) demonstrate, may be very different in different countries.

In many ways, then, the central question of tax policy is how to make the "wicksellian connection" (Breton, 1996) operational so that good decisions—that is, decisions that reflect people's real preferences as closely as practically feasible, —are made on both sides of the budget. The key to good fiscal outcomes lies less in any particular budgetary or financing procedure than in implementing a public finance system that, to the extent possible, links specific expenditure and revenue decisions as transparently as possible. The best that can be done to help the relevant decision-makers make the right decision is to ensure that they and all those affected are made as aware as possible of all the relevant consequences. For a country to implement a better tax system – better in the sense of giving the people what they want – it must have a better political system that transmutes citizen preferences into policy decisions as efficiently as possible. "Democracy," as Churchill reportedly once said, "is the worst form of Government except all those other forms that have been tried from time to time."[18]

Of course, taxation is always and everywhere a 'contested concept' (Sabates and Schneider, 2003). Some pay; some don't pay. Some pay more than others. Some receive compensating services; some do not. Such matters are, in democratic states, resolved through political channels. Indeed, history suggests that the need to secure an adequate degree of consensus from the taxed is one of the principal ways in which, over the centuries, democratic institutions have spread. No non-dictatorial government in this age of information and mobility can long stay in power without securing a certain degree of consent from the populace, not least in the area of taxation. State legitimacy thus rests to a considerable extent on citizens' 'quasi-voluntary compliance' (Levi, 1988) with respect to taxation. To secure such compliance, tax systems must, over time, in some sense represent the basic values of at least a minimum supporting coalition of the population (Hettich and Winer, 1999).

No matter how good political institutions may be, however, countries will always encounter difficulties in dealing with distributive issues. How one thinks about taxes and inequality reflects ideas of fairness or social justice, and different people invariably have different beliefs about what is fair – beliefs that may, or may not, have some objective basis. People may have different beliefs for many reasons: because they do not know the truth, because no one knows the truth, because they have been misled about the truth, or just because they see things differently. Successful politicians are those who can manage such conflicts, and one way to do so, as discussed earlier, is by making the wicksellian connection as plausible as possible to most people. Unless this is done satisfactorily, the long-term political sustainability of any tax system remains questionable.

2.5 Latin America Revisited

The central social and economic problem in many Latin American countries is still clearly inequality (de Ferranti et al., 2004). On the other hand, the key, and related, governance problem is lack of accountability. A good tax system is critical to the solution of both problems. Reforms that link taxes and benefits more tightly, such as decentralization and more reliance on user charges, may help accountability. The most important function of the tax system in most countries, however, is simply to provide (non-inflationary) funding for pro-poor and pro-growth spending programs e.g. in improving human capital, and the best way to do so is probably through a broad-based non-distortionary consumption tax, as has long been recognized. It is of course easy to think of ways to tax the rich more effectively, and there are certainly good reasons to do so in countries in which many assets of the wealthy are underutilized and many incomes of the rich may reflect rents secured through political connections or monopolies. Nonetheless, as IDB (1998) stresses, attempts to impose unduly redistributive taxes may backfire, and countries that follow this path may end up with public sectors that are both smaller and less redistributive.[19]

What is actually done will of course be determined in the political arena. Countries vary enormously in the effectiveness and nature of their political systems. Some may be close to 'failed states' in which institutions are so ineffective that it does not matter much what is attempted. It will not work. Others may be 'developmentalist' (as in the early CEPAL model) and want to use their fiscal systems largely as interventionist instruments. Still others may be of a more laissez-faire disposition. Some may be more populist, some more elitist, some more predatory.

The dominant policy *ideas* in different countries – about equity and fairness, efficiency, and growth – like the dominant economic and social *interests* – capital, labor, regional, ethnic, rich, poor -- and the key *institutions* – political (democracy, decentralization, budgetary) and economic (free trade, protectionism, macroeconomic policy, market structure) – all interact in the formulation and implementation of tax policy. This changing interplay of ideas, interests, and institutions over time affects the level of taxation, the structure of taxation, and many of its critical details such as the progressivity of rates.

Indeed, taxation is probably one of the clearest arenas in which to witness the working out of these complex forces. Suppose, for example, that both the public at large and the elite want changes, for different reasons. The elite can always manipulate the state to some extent and may use public concern as 'cover' to achieve its own ends. Consider, for instance, the sad story of property taxation. Once seen as the bulwark of local democracy and accountability, this tax has, over time, come to be considered by the public in the U.S. to be regressive and unfair (Youngman, 2002), thus fostering elite interests in lowering the tax burden on an asset base they disproportionately control. The spillover of anti-property tax rhetoric into more unequal societies to the south has made it even more difficult to institute not only the kinds of specific land taxes that might in principle contribute to land reform (Dorner, 1992)[20], but even the low-rate effective property taxes needed to finance local governments. There remains, of course, a great deal that we do not understand about these complex matters. What seems clear from the work done to date on the political economy of taxation, however, is that while taxes definitely matter in both economic and political terms, they are more driven by than drivers of social and economic conditions.

Viewed from this perspective, Latin America and indeed much of the developing world has yet to experience even the earlier parts of the cycle that produced the (more or less) redistributive and (more or less) growth-facilitating fiscal states, whether of the U.S. or E.U. variety, now found in developed countries – the long preparatory period during which the idea of the desirability, and even necessity, of a larger fiscal system becomes established. Instead, bypassing this 'egalitarian' period, some countries in Latin America seem to have moved directly from the feudal inequality of land-based maldistribution to the modern era of capital-based maldistribution. Doreen Warriner (1969) once said, despairingly, that most Latin Americans did not seem to know what a good land reform means – probably because they had never seen one. Equally, one might perhaps speculate that, in most countries of the region, as Engerman and Sokoloff (2001) almost – but not quite -- say most people may not really know what moderate or justifiable inequality means, since they have never seen it.

Governments in many Latin American countries are in dire straits. Even those that have reached relatively safe harbors politically, and have a certain degree of legitimacy and stability, almost always feel – often correctly – that they are in an economically precarious situation. The budget is politically and economically constrained. Life is difficult. Nothing can be done. All this may be true to some extent, but it is also both too much a counsel of despair and too easy a way out. Even in the most hopeless situations, something usually can be done to improve matters. There will always be dispute over exactly what should be done to improve tax systems. Unless and until an adequate degree of political consensus on what should be done is achieved, however, no significant changes in either tax structure or tax levels seem likely.

As Lledo, Schneider, and Moore (2003, p. 47) stress, the key problem in Latin America is that most countries lack "...an (implicit) social contract between governments and the general populace of the kind that is embedded in taxation and fiscal principles and practices in politically more stable parts of the world." What needs to be added to this bleak but accurate assessment is that history tells us that such principles generally do not become embedded either painlessly or quickly. The specific substantive suggestions that Lledo, Schneider, and Moore (2003) make to improve matters – more use of income taxes, better VAT administration on a broader base, more attention to subnational taxation, more attention to informal activities and environmental aspects of taxation, closer ties to expenditure policy, and so on -- are of course already the stuff of countless existing reports. Who can argue?

The real question is why so little has been done. From this perspective, by far the most important conclusion of Lledo, Schneider, and Moore (2003) -- which is also in many ways the main point of the present section -- is their final recommendation "to improve political institutions in ways that enhance legitimacy and capacity." In other words, there can, so to speak, be no good taxation without good representation. The trouble with this truism is that history suggests that all too many countries have proved unable to achieve either good taxation or good representation without first going through a period of bad taxation which, in Hegelian fashion, called forth forces that in the end improved both representation and taxation. In this perhaps somewhat perverse sense Latin Americans (and those in many developing countries around the world) may be a bit luckier than first appears since they have a lot of bad taxation with which to begin.

3. THE ROLE OF SOCIETAL INSTITUTIONS: CROSS COUNTRY STATISTICAL EVIDENCE

In Section 2, we argued that how much any society collects in taxes to a considerable extent reflects what we called its 'political equilibrium' and that its level of tax effort was not likely to change drastically unless the underlying forces determining that equilibrium level also changed. In this section we probe more deeply into the conditions under which tax effort can be increased by examining empirically the determinants of tax effort across a broad sample of developing and transition countries. We take into account not only 'supply factors' (tax handles) but also critical 'demand factors' such as societal institutions like governance and corruption, and 'framing' institutions such as the size of the shadow economy, inequalities in the distribution of income and 'tax morale.' Our basic working hypothesis is that supply factors matter but that in order to explain international differences in tax ratios we also need to take into account demand factors. In econometric terms, our hypothesis implies that the group of variables representing the role of societal institutions is statistically different from zero. That is, the tax level in any country does not just depend on the ability of its tax administration to collect taxes from the available 'tax handles.' If taxpayers perceive that their interests (preferences) are properly represented in political institutions and consider government to be not wasteful but helpful, their willingness to vote for higher levels of taxation and comply with their tax obligations will increase. 'Societal institutions' are used here as an indicator of the extent to which citizens feel they have a meaningful 'voice' in influencing the state. In general, the greater 'voice,' other things equal, the higher we would expect tax effort to be. At the same time, the larger the shadow economy -- the 'exit option' -- the lower we would expect tax effort to be. An important contribution of this paper is thus to extend the basic tax effort model by establishing the extent to which institutions matter.

A. THE BASIC MODEL: TAX HANDLES AND DETERMINANTS

We begin by re-examining the role of the traditional supply side variables of the tax effort literature. (An overview and summary of this literature is provided in Annex Table 1.) In general, this literature posits the following equation:

$$TE = f(Y, POP, XM, NAGR) \qquad (1)$$

where,

TE: Tax effort
Y: GDP per capita (measured in $US)
POP: rate of population growth
XM: ratio of exports plus imports to GDP
NAGR: non agriculture share of GDP

We measure the dependent variable (Tax Effort) in two different ways: (a) tax revenue as a share of gross domestic product (GDP) -- the traditional measure in the literature -- and (b) current revenues/GDP (excluding grants). Current revenue includes all revenue to the central government from taxes and non-repayable receipts (other than grants), measured as a share of GDP.[21] We call the second measure revenue effort, reserving the label of tax effort for the first measure. The use of the two measures of dependent variable provides for a more robust testing of the model, given different practices and possible mistakes in revenue classification in developing and transitional countries. Data for both measures of the dependent variable comes from the World Development Indicators (WDI) for 2003. Descriptive statistics for the two dependent variables are shown in Annex Table 2. The two measures are highly correlated (r=0.84, statistically significant at the 0.01 level). The model is estimated using cross-section data with mean values for the years 1990 to 1999 for 110 developing and transitional countries. [22] (Data sources and the description of all variables are summarized in Annex Table 3).

The explanatory variables employed in the basic model follow those used in the conventional tax effort literature. Per capita GDP is a proxy for the level of development of a country. A higher level of development goes together with a higher capacity to pay and collect taxes, as well as a higher relative demand for income elastic public goods and services (Chelliah, 1971; Bahl, 1971). In general, we would expect a positive relation between the level of per capita income and the level of tax effort.

Demographic characteristics may also be an important determinant of tax effort. As Bahl (2003, p. 13) points out, in countries with faster growing populations tax systems may lag behind in the ability to capture new taxpayers. This suggests that the rate of population growth is negatively related to the level of tax effort.

The most traditional explanatory variables in the conventional tax effort literature are those controlling for a country's economic structure. These variables reflect the idea that the availability of 'tax handles' should influence the level of tax effort. For example, trade taxes are often a major source of government revenues in less developed countries because they are easier to collect than income taxes. We measure the availability of this tax handle by openness, defined as the sum of exports and imports as a share of GDP. The tax ratio is expected to be positively related to the degree of openness of the economy.

The sectoral composition of domestic product may also affect the ability to tax. A traditional measure signaling the difficulty to tax domestic output is the share of agriculture in GDP. Some argue that the agricultural sector is not much more difficult to tax (Bahl 2003), but the larger its relative importance in a country's economy the lower the need to spend on governmental activities and services, as many public sector activities are city-based (Tanzi 1992). In addition, for political reasons some countries exempt from taxes a large share of agricultural activities. A higher non-agriculture share in GDP should thus produce a higher tax ratio.

Table 1 contains our results for the conventional model. Estimated coefficients for the explanatory variables are in line with predictions for both measures of the dependent variable and largely coincide with previous findings in the literature. A faster rate of population growth leads to a lower tax ratio. A higher share of non-agricultural sector is correlated with a higher tax effort. The coefficient for GDP per capita has the predicted sign in two estimations and is statistically significant in one equation, but again these results are in line with previous studies (see Annex Table 1)[23]. However, openness of the economy is not associated in our results with a higher tax effort.[24]

Interestingly, in Eq. 3a and 3b we observe that Latin American countries have a statistically significant lower tax ratio than other developing and transition countries. This finding gives empirical support to the arguments developed in Section II regarding the unsuccessful outcomes in Latin America.

B. THE EXTENDED MODEL: THE ROLE OF SOCIETAL INSTITUTIONS

The traditional literature on tax effort has ignored the role of demand factors such as societal institutions in explaining relative revenue performance. As noted above, our basic working hypothesis is that while supply factors clearly matter in order to explain international experience we also need to account for citizen attitudes to both their voice and exit options. We thus extend the "basic tax effort model" as:

$$TE = f(Y, POP, XM, NAGR, INSTIT), \qquad (2)$$

where *INSTIT* is a vector of variables representing "demand factors" or societal institutions. Empirically, the additional exploratory variables we use can be grouped as follows:

Table 1. The Traditional Determinants of Tax Effort

Model	**OLS**		**OLS**		**OLS**		**OLS**	
Dependent Variables	***Tax Effort*** Eq. 1a		***Revenue Effort*** Eq. 1b		***Tax Effort*** Eq. 3a		***Revenue Effort*** Eq. 3b	
Independent Variables	***Beta***	***t-Stat.***	***Beta***	***t-Stat.***	***Beta***	***t-Stat.***	***Beta***	***t-Stat.***
a) DEVELOPMENT								
GDP Per Capita	0.075	0.58	0.238**	1.99	-0.278*	-1.89	-0.135	-1.04
Population Growth	-0.435***	-4.10	-0.329***	-3.33	-0.387***	-4.18	-0.251***	-2.92
b) OPENNESS								
(Export + Imports / GDP)	-0.036	-0.38	-0.024	-0.23	-0.057	-0.72	-0.063	-0.84
c) ECONOMIC STRUCTURE								
1- Agriculture / GDP					0.541***	5.39	0.647***	6.15
d) REGION								
Latin America	-0.036	-0.53	-0.111	-1.62	-0.165**	-2.06	-0.274***	-3.36
Observations	109		109		105		105	
Prob > F	0.003		0.000		0.000		0.000	
R – squared	0.196		0.174		0.378		0.413	

Notes: The dependent variables are: TAX EFFORT: tax revenues/GDP, TAX REVENUE: current revenues/GDP.
Significance levels: * $0.05 < p < 0.10$, ** $0.01 < p < 0.05$, *** $p < 0.01$. Regressions with robust standard errors.
In the reference group: OTHER DEVELOPING AND TRANSITION COUNTRIES.

3.1 Quality of Governance Index (See Kaufmann, Kraay, and Mastruzzi (KKM), 2003)

This index reports the mean value of six governance dimensions for the periods 1996, 1998 and 2000. It is based on several hundred variables measuring perceptions of governance and derived from 25 different data sources. KKM (2003) classify the six governance indicators into three groups as follows:

1. Process by which governments are selected, monitored and replaced

- VOICE AND ACCOUNTABILITY: measures the political process, civil liberties, and political rights
- POLITICAL STABILITY AND ABSENCE OF VIOLENCE: measures perceptions of the likelihood that the government will be destabilized/overthrown)

2. Capacity of the government effectively to formulate and implement sound policies

- GOVERNMENT EFFECTIVENESS (inputs required for the government to be able to produce and implement good policies and deliver public goods)
- REGULATORY QUALITY (focuses more on policies, such as incidence of market/unfriendly policies, perceptions of the burdens imposed by excessive regulation)

3. Respect of citizens and the state for the institutions that govern economic and social interactions

- RULE OF LAW (several indicators measuring the degree of agents' confidence in and compliance with the rules of society). According to KKM. (2003, p.4) these indicators "measure the success of a society in developing an environment in which fair and predictable rules form the basis of economic and social interactions"
- CONTROL OF CORRUPTION: measures the perceived corruption (exercise of public power for private gain).

All scores estimated by KKM (2003) lie between –2.5 and 2.5, with higher scores corresponding to better institutions (outcomes). We check the robustness of the statistical results for the governance index by using several combinations of sub-indexes.

3.2 International Country Risk Guide (ICRG) (See Knack 1999)

The ICRG provides an alternative set of data to the Quality of Governance Index, with special emphasis on aspects affecting private foreign investment decisions. The data contain annual values for indicators of the quality of governance, 1982-1997, constructed by Stephen Knack and the IRIS Center, University of Maryland and provided by The PRS Group. Our interest is in the Political Risk Components of the ICGR. We derive an index (mean values) based on a selection of the following components from the Political Risk Components: CORRUPTION IN THE GOVERNMENT, [25] RULE OF LAW ("LAW AND ORDER TRADITION"), [26] BUREAUCRATIC QUALITY,[27] ETHNIC TENSION,[28] REPUDIATION OF GOVERNMENT CONTRACTS, [29] EXPROPRIATION RISK. [30] A higher number of points indicates a lower potential risk. Most values range between 1 and 6 (exceptions: EXPROPRIATION RISK and REPUDIATION OF GOVERNMENT CONTRACTS which range between 1 and 10).

These two variables, the *ICRG Index* and the *Quality of Governance Index* capture some of the 'voice' institutions and, more generally, the quality of the responsiveness of government to citizens' demands. Because of the high correlation (0.72) between the *ICRG* and the *Quality of Governance* variables, we use these two sets of variables in alternate estimations.[31]

3.3 Regulation of Entry

According to public choice theory, regulations can be used by politicians and bureaucrats to pursue their own benefits, as opposed to the interests of the general public. Regulatory discretion enables bureaucrats to create and extract rents. Bribes are collected in exchange for the selective release from regulation. More generally, bureaucrats have an incentive to delay transactions in order to extract higher payments (see Rose-Ackerman, 1997). But, a main problem with rent creation through regulation is that it "...is often inefficient, in part because the policies they pursue to increase the rents from corruption are distortionary" (Djankov et al., 2002, p. 3). There are situations in many developing countries where if people want to open a business, to acquire land or build homes they are confronted with very high transaction costs, and law-breaking may be the only option to survive. Hernando de Soto (2000) tested the seriousness of barriers to entry by creating a new and perfectly legal small business in Lima. His team spent six hours a day at it and was able to register the business 289 days later. The cost of the legal registration was $1,231, or thirty-one times the monthly minimum wage. To obtain the authorization to build a house on state-owned land took six years and 11 months, with 207 administrative steps in 52 government offices and to obtain legal title to that piece of land took 728 steps. Similar experiences have been described in other countries, e.g., Philippines, Egypt, and Haiti.[32] As Frey and Eichenberger (1999, p. 89) argue, many developing countries have both "over-government" and "under-government," that is, a strong combination of interventionism and bureaucracy with property rights that are not sufficiently secured and where there is a high degree of uncertainty. In such an environment there are weak incentives for investment and entry in the formal sector.

We use a new data set provided by Djankov et al. (2002) to measure the degree of regulation of faced by start-up companies. The data are for 1999. Djankov et al. (2002) recorded all officially required procedures that a new entrepreneur must go through in order to enter the formal market sector. To check for robustness, we use two measures of regulation: the number of procedures and the official time required to complete the process. Longer delays and more procedures make entry less attractive, facilitate corruption and may lead to a lower tax ratio. The degree of regulation of entry can be seen as a 'voice' institution in reverse, since it measures how unresponsive the government is to business and citizens' needs and demands. The regulation of entry is also linked to the 'exit' variables presented in the next subsections, as high level of regulation induces a move to work in the informal sector of the economy.

3.4 Tax Morale and the Shadow Economy

A sustainable tax system is based on a fair tax system and responsive government, achieved with a strong connection between tax payments and the supply of public goods. If taxpayers perceive that their preferences are adequately represented and they are supplied with public goods, their identification with the state increases, and thus the willingness to pay taxes rises. We hypothesize that a lower degree of tax morale, defined as the intrinsic motivation to pay taxes, reduces the tax effort in a country. The level of tax effort is also expected to be strongly connected to the 'exit option' -- the decision to conduct, fully or partially, economic activity in the informal sector (the shadow economy). The more taxpayers believe that others work in the shadow economy, the lower the moral costs to them to behave dishonestly and evade taxes by moving their own activities to the shadow economy. In this way the potential intrinsic motivation to comply and contribute to public sector activities gets crowded out. Thus, we hypothesize that a larger shadow economy should lead to a lower level of tax effort. Measures of tax morale and the shadow economy tend to be highly correlated. Several previous studies have shown that low tax morale might be responsible for the rise of shadow economy (see, e.g., Torgler, 2001, 2004; Alm and Torgler, 2004; Alm, Martinez-Vazquez and Torgler, 2004). For these reasons, tax morale and the shadow economy are employed as alternate measures of the "exit option" in our empirical analysis.

The size of the shadow economy is measured as a percentage of official GDP, using data from Schneider and Klinglmair (2003). In line with the observations for the dependent variables, we take the average values for 1990, 1995, and 1999. [33]

Data for the tax morale variable are extracted from several surveys: the Latinobarómetro (1998), the World Values Survey (WVS) 1990-1993, 1995-1997 (see Inglehart et al., 2000) and the European Values Survey 1999-2000 (see European Values Study, 1999). Both surveys investigate socio-cultural and political change and collect comparative data on values and belief systems. Both are based on representative national samples of at least 1000 individuals. The World Values Survey (WVS) is worldwide and covers more than 40 countries, while the Latinobarómetro survey is carried out in 17 Latin American countries. The general questions to assess the level of tax morale in the two surveys are:

> *World Values Survey:*
> *"Please tell me for each of the following statements whether you think it can always be justified, never be justified, or something in between: (...) Cheating on tax if you have the chance (% "never justified" – code 1 from a ten-point scale where 1=never and 10=always)."*
>
> *Latinobarómetro:*
> *On a scale of 1 to 10, where 1 means not at all justifiable and 10 means totally justifiable, how justifiable do you believe it is to: Manage to avoid paying all your tax.*

In both cases the tax morale variable is developed by recoding the ten-point scale into a four-point scale (0 to 3), with the value 3 standing for "never justifiable". The value of 0 is an aggregation of the last 7 scale points, which were rarely chosen.[34] Both surveys cover the period 1990 to 1999.

3.5 Inequality

As discussed in Section 2, inequality in the distribution of wealth and income is strongly connected with public views as to how well the fiscal system addresses social objectives with respect to fairness, social justice and redistribution. If a perceived unfair distribution of tax burdens is thought to be one cause of income inequality, the result may be to lower the level of trust in institutions and eventually to lower tax effort because of widespread tax avoidance and evasion. Highly unequal distributions of income, as in many Latin American countries, can also lead to low levels of solidarity by the elites toward lower income groups. Low levels of tax effort in Central America, for example, are often interpreted as the result of the unwillingness of the richest small percentage of the population to pay more in taxes to provide public services for the masses since the elite can provide their own 'public services' privately, ranging from public safety to education and even roads. Furthermore, income inequality may be associated with political instability. For example, less privileged groups may choose to use undemocratic instruments to improve their situation (Alesina and Perotti 1996). On the other hand, privileged groups may try to maintain their position by illegal means. In summary, more unequal distributions of income and wealth are likely to enhance the exit option for all types of taxpayers. We hypothesize that higher inequality leads to lower levels of tax effort.

To measure the variable income inequality_we use the newest available data set, ESTIMATED HOUSEHOLD INCOME INEQUALITY (EHII), constructed by Galbraith and Kum (2003). This data set combines the information in the Deininger and Squire (1996) and UTIP-UNIDO (average 1990-1999 and average of the whole data set, 1963-1999).[35]

3.6 Fiscal Decentralization

The level of tax effort may also depend on the vertical structure of government, and in particular on the level of fiscal decentralization. Several mechanisms (with opposing impacts) may lead fiscal decentralization to influence tax effort. First, a more decentralized system of government tends to be more responsive and can better meet taxpayers' needs and preferences (Oates 1972). A more efficient and responsive government at all levels may result in an increased willingness to contribute and also in an increased demand for public spending and higher voluntary levels of tax effort. On the other hand, a more decentralized system of government imposes more restrictions on the ability of government to act as a Leviathan exploiting tax bases and increasing public spending since taxpayers may select jurisdictions with lower levels of expenditures and taxes and jurisdictions may compete among themselves to keep taxes and expenditures low (Brennan and Buchanan, 1980). There is some empirical cross-country evidence that higher levels of decentralization lead to lower levels of public expenditure (Arze, Martinez-Vazquez, and McNab, 2004) Furthermore, decentralization may encourage governments to rely more on user charges and fees and less on taxes, so that consumers are more likely to be confronted with the marginal costs of public service delivery (Feld, Kirchgässner and Schaltegger 2003), and such charges and fees may not be recorded as government tax revenues. A greater level of decentralization and autonomy at the local level may thus lead to lower levels of tax effort although this prediction is not unambiguous.

Several other considerations should be mentioned. First, the similarity of some of the explanatory variables and multicollinearity does not allow us to run full specifications including all the potential institutional explanatory variables identified above. Our approach is therefore to run a series of estimations in which some institutional variables are replaced by others, usually from different data sources. One advantage of this approach is that it permits us to check the robustness of the estimated effect of institutions on tax and revenue ratios.

Second, some of the institutional variables may be endogenous. For example, better institutions may lead to better tax performances, but in turn, poor tax performance can reduce the possibilities of establishing or maintaining well functioning institutions in developing and transition countries. To check for the presence of endogeneity, we conduct a Hausman Chi-square test for each estimation. In those cases where exogeneity cannot be rejected, we use a 2SLS approach, as indicated in the tables showing the results.[36]

As data for the institutional variables are derived from different sources, we first present estimations focusing on different institutional factors independently. This approach allows us to look at results for the different variables when we are able to maximize the number of observations. Subsequently, we present the results for fuller specifications. A fuller specification has the obvious advantage of presenting a more balanced view of the role of different institutions (separating the effects of the independent variables) but it has the disadvantage that the number of observations we can utilize is smaller, perhaps resulting in other types of biases.

The empirical results presented in *Tables 2* to *7* suggest strongly that institutions play a significant role in the determination of the level of tax effort of developing and transition countries. Though the conventional supply factors continue to play a robust and significant role throughout the estimations, demand factors clearly matter.

The joint role played by the demand factors can be investigated using a Wald-test for coefficient restrictions to test for *joint* significance. In most cases the F-statistics indicate that the null hypothesis is rejected, meaning that the demand factors play a significant role in the determination of countries' tax performance. The relative role played by demand factors vis-à-vis supply factors is investigated by estimating *beta* or *standardized* regression coefficients. The results in *Tables 2* to *7* show that demand side determinants are highly relevant in explaining tax performance in transition and developing countries. These variables show relatively high beta coefficients, comparable or even higher than the traditional supply factors.

One last general result in Tables *2* to *7* is that Latin American countries show consistently lower tax performance by comparison to other developing and transition countries. This again provides statistical support to our discussion in the previous section of this paper.

Let us now consider the estimates for individual variables. The role of 'voice' institutions as measured by the Quality of Governance and the ICRG variables is explored in Tables 2, 3 and 4 respectively. The main indexes and the sub-indexes have coefficients with the expected sign and are highly significant. Among the selected sub-indexes, corruption and the rule of law seem to play key roles in explaining the level of tax effort. A higher regulated entry also leads to a lower tax/revenue effort. However, we observe a lower impact compared to the other voice variables. In general, these results give support to the hypothesis that societies' willingness to tax themselves depends on the perception that government institutions are honest and responsive and that there is a fair and predictable public sector environment.

The role of 'exit' variables is explored in Table 5 for income inequality, Table 6 for the size of the shadow economy, and Table 7 for tax morale. In most cases, these variables take the expected sign and in many cases the coefficient are statistically significant. Where disparities in the distribution of income are larger, or the size of the shadow economy is bigger, or tax morale is lower, countries tend to show a lower tax effort. However, it seems that the impact is less strong in relation to the 'voice' determinants.

To get a better idea about the strength of the voice and the exit variables, we present in the next two tables fuller specifications with both types of determinants in the same equation. The results are shown in Table 8 (using the shadow economy as the exit variable) and in Table 9 (using tax morale as the exit variable.) These results indicate that both supply (tax handles) and demand variables (institutions) play a significant role in the determination of tax effort.[37] Among the demand side variables, the voice variables *Quality of Governance* and *ICRG* indexes and the regulation of entry variables, take the expected sign and are statistically significant. On the other hand, the exit variables measured by the shadow economy, tax morale and inequality perform less well. Although in some cases coefficients take the right sign and are significant, more often they are statistically insignificant. Thus, it would seem that, overall, voice institutions together with inequality in the distribution of income play a stronger role in the level of tax effort. However, one should be cautious in concluding that exit institutions have only a small effect. For example, exit institutions may mediate the effect of voice institutions in developing countries. Alternatively, causality may run the other way, from voice to exit.[38] The lack of significance of the tax morale variable in *Table 9* may also be partly due to the low number of degrees of freedom.

We summarize the entire set of empirical findings in Table 10. Among the traditional supply side factors, the sectoral composition of a country's economy (non-agriculture share in GDP) has the strongest impact on tax performance. From the side of the demand factors, voice variables, especially for the *Quality of Governance* and *ICRG* indexes, yield the most robust results.

Table 2. The Effects of Institutions on Tax/Revenue Effort (Quality of Governance)

Model	**OLS**		**OLS**		**OLS**		**OLS**		**OLS**	
Dependent Variables	**Tax Effort**		**Revenue Effort**		**Tax Effort**		**Revenue Effort**		**Tax Effort**	
Independent Variables	**Beta**	**t-Stat.**	**Beta**	**t-Stat.**	**Beta**	**t-Stat.**	**Beta**	**t-Stat.**		
a) DEVELOPMENT										
GDP Per Capita	-0.414***	-2.85	-0.262*	-1.93	-0.305**	-2.28	-0.153	-1.60	-0.382**	-2.46
Population Growth	-0.348***	-3.79	-0.211**	-2.54	-0.263**	-2.56	-0.166*	-1.98	-0.324***	-3.28
b) OPENNESS										
(Export + Import)/GDP	-0.085	-1.40	-0.090	-1.53	-0.087	-1.24	-0.084	-1.08	-0.099*	-1.86
c) ECONOMIC STRUCTURE										
1 – Agriculture/GDP	0.418***	3.92	0.533***	5.23	0.421***	4.05	0.567***	5.32	0.453***	4.10
d) REGIONS										
Latin America	-0.195***	-2.64	-0.303***	-3.92	-0.285***	-3.90	-0.355***	-4.05	-0.178**	-2.35
e) INSTITUTIONS										
Index Governance	0.357***	2.95	3.350***	2.97						
Voice and account					0.388***	3.37	0.259**	2.55		
Political Stability									0.303***	2.79
Rule of Law										
Control of Corruption										
F-Test: Institutions	8.72***		8.81***		11.34***		6.48**		7.81***	
Observations	104		104		104		104		104	
Prob > F	0.000		0.000		0.000		0.000		0.000	
R-squared	0.445		0.466		0.499		0.450		449	

Table 2. The Effects of Institutions on Tax/Revenue Effort (Quality of Governance) (Continued)

Model	OLS		OLS		OLS		OLS		OLS	
Dependent Variables	**Revenue Effort**		**Tax Effort**		**Revenue Effort**		**Tax Effort**		**Revenue Effort**	
Independent Variables	**Beta**	**t-Stat.**	**Beta**	**t-Stat.**	**Beta**	**t-Stat.**	**Beta**	**t-Stat.**	**Beta**	**t-Stat.**
a) DEVELOPMENT										
GDP Per Capita	-0.248*	-1.74	-0.436***	-2.77	-0.300**	-2.10	-0.476***	-3.28	-0.350***	-2.71
Population Growth	-1.175*	-1.87	-0.389***	-4.36	-0.250***	-3.12	-0.384***	-4.43	-0.244***	-3.28
b) OPENNESS										
(Export + Import)/GDP	-0.114**	-2.59	-0.068	-1.05	-0.076	-1.26	-0.083	-1.39	-0.093*	-1.70
c) ECONOMIC STRUCTURE										
1 – Agriculture/GDP	0.546***	5.35	0.438***	4.37	0.540***	5.34	0.448***	4.40	0.547***	5.83
d) REGIONS										
Latin America	-0.278***	-3.63	-0.142*	-1.79	-0.252***	-3.14	-0.151**	-2.01	-0.261***	-3.37
e) INSTITUTIONS										
Index Governance										
Voice and account										
Political Stability	0.346***	3.73								
Rule of Law			0.318***	2.85	0.330***	2.94				
Control of Corruption							0.381***	3.35	0.411***	3.99
F-Test: Institutions	13.89***		7.72***		8.66***		11.19***		15.92	
Observations	104		104		104		104		104	
Prob > F	0.000		0.000		0.000		0.000		0.000	
R-squared	0.428		0.428		0.462		0.454		0.497	

Notes: The dependent variables are: TAX EFFORT: tax revenues/GDP, REVENUE EFFORT: current revenues/GDP. Significance levels: * 0.05 < p < 0.10, ** 0.01< p < 0.05, *** p < 0.01. Regressions with robust standard errors. In the reference group: OTHER DEVELOPING AND TRANSITION COUNTRIES. Hausman Chi-square tests fail to detect the presence of simultaneity of the TAX/REVENUE EFFORT and INSTITUTIONS. Thus, only OLS has been estimated. Instrumental variables: voice: ethnic fractionalization, language, catholic; political stability: language, latitude; rule of law: ethnic, language; control of corruption: ethnic, language; index governance: ethnic, language. The F-Test is a statistics on the joint significance of the mentioned variables.

Table 3. The Effects of Institutions on Tax/Revenue Effort (ICRG)

Model	**OLS**		**OLS**		**OLS**		**OLS**		**OLS**	
Dependent Variables	**Tax Effort**		**Revenue Effort**		**Tax Effort**		**Revenue Effort**		**Tax Effort**	
Independent Variables	**Beta**	**t-Stat.**	**Beta**	**t-Stat.**	**Beta**	**t-Stat.**	**Beta**	**t-Stat.**	**Beta**	**t-Stat.**
a) DEVELOPMENT										
GDP Per Capita	-0.489***	-3.19	-0.288*	-1.85	-0.476***	-2.75	-0.295*	-1.87	-0.414**	-2.62
Population Growth	-0.214***	-1.78	-0.151	-1.48	-0.251*	-1.94	-0.160	-1.56	-0.327***	-2.84
b) OPENNESS										
(Export + Import)/GDP	-0.057	-0.94	-0.069	-1.27	-0.078	-1.31	-0.078	-1.54	-0.083	-1.27
c) ECONOMIC STRUCTURE										
1 – Agriculture/GDP	0.271**	2.19	0.455***	3.60	0.377***	3.18	0.521***	4.68	0.345***	2.74
d) REGIONS										
Latin America	-0.136	-1.37	-0.294***	-2.95	-0.062	-0.52	-0.212*	-1.95	-0.063	-0.53
e) INSTITUTIONS										
Index ICRG	-0.504***	3.85	0.408***	3.19						
Rule of Law					0.390***	2.69	0.380***	3.25		
Bureaucratic Quality									0.356***	2.97
Ethnic Tension										
Corruption										
F-Test: Institutions	12.84***		10.18***		7.25***		10.55***		8.80***	
Observations	73		73		73		73		73	
Prob > F	0.000		0.000		0.000		0.000		0.000	
R-squared	0.476		0.500		0.438		0.501		0.436	

Table 3. The Effects of Institutions on Tax/Revenue Effort (ICRG) (Continued)

Model	**OLS**		**OLS**		**OLS**		**OLS**		**OLS**	
Dependent Variables	**Revenue Effort**		**Tax Effort**		**Revenue Effort**		**Tax Effort**		**Revenue Effort**	
Independent Variables	**Beta**	**t-Stat.**	**Beta**	**t-Stat.**	**Beta**	**t-Stat.**	**Beta**	**t-Stat.**	**Beta**	**t-Stat.**
a) DEVELOPMENT										
GDP Per Capita	-0.211	-1.36	-0.409**	-2.32	-0.231	-1.53	-0.378**	-2.60	-0.198***	-3.63
Population Growth	-0.261**	-2.54	-0.305**	-2.45	-0.209**	-2.13	-0.272**	-2.42	-0.209***	-3.29
b) OPENNESS										
(Export + Import)/GDP	-0.107*	-1.68	-0.109*	-1.68	-0.107*	-1.76	-0.013	-0.22	-0.047***	5.04
c) ECONOMIC STRUCTURE										
1 – Agriculture/GDP	0.575***	4.09	0.427***	3.82	0.566***	4.74	0.376***	3.58	0.554***	4.18
d) REGIONS										
Latin America	-0.286**	-2.42	-0.262**	-2.63	-0.412***	-4.12	-0.077	-0.85	-0.259**	-2.58
e) INSTITUTIONS										
Index ICRG										
Rule of Law										
Bureaucratic Quality	0.148	1.45								
Ethnic Tension			0.291***	3.05	0.302***	3.92				
Corruption							0.432***	3.87	2.994***	3.32
F-Test: Institutions	2.10		9.28***		15.35***		15.00***		8.17***	
Observations	73		73		73		73		73	
Prob > F	0.000		0.000		0.000		0.000		0.000	
R-squared	0.433		0.411		0.484		0.495		0.487	

Notes: The dependent variables are: TAX EFFORT: tax revenues/GDP, REVENUE EFFORT: current revenues/GDP. Significance levels: * $0.05 < p < 0.10$, ** $0.01 < p < 0.05$, *** $p < 0.01$. In the reference group: OTHER DEVELOPING AND TRANSITION COUNTRIES. Regressions with robust standard errors. Hausman Chi-square tests fail to detect the presence of simultaneity of the TAX/REVENUE EFFORT and INSTITUTIONS. Thus, only OLS has been estimated. Instrumental variable: latitude. The F-Test is a statistics on the joint significance of the mentioned variables.

Table 4. Tax/Revenue Effort and Regulation of Entry

Model	**OLS**		**OLS**		**OLS**		**OLS**		**OLS**	
Dependent Variables	**Tax Effort**		**Revenue Effort**		**Tax Effort**		**Revenue Effort**		**Tax Effort**	
Independent Variables	**Beta**	**t-Stat.**	**Beta**	**t-Stat.**	**Beta**	**t-Stat.**	**Beta**	**t-Stat.**	**Beta**	**t-Stat.**
a) DEVELOPMENT										
GDP Per Capita	0.247	1.22	0.213	1.01	0.246	1.10	0.210	0.90	-0.150	-0.83
Population Growth	-0.486***	-3.43	-0.384**	-2.54	-0.495***	-3.25	-0.392**	-2.46	-0.413***	-3.44
b) OPENNESS										
(Export + Import)/GDP	-0.043	-0.35	-0.024	-0.17	0.012	0.10	0.037	0.27	-0.074	-0.78
c) ECONOMIC STRUCTURE										
1 – Agriculture/GDP									0.530***	4.06
d) REGIONS										
Latin America	-0.086	-1.04	-0.055	-0.60	-0.138*	-1.71	-0.113	-1.20	-0.249***	-2.81
e) REGULATION OF ENTRY										
Number Of Procedures	-0.242**	-2.15	-0.267**	-2.08	-0.126	-1.34	-0.148	-1.50		
Time									-0.164*	-1.70
F-Test Regulation of Entry	4.63**		4.31**		1.81		2.24		2.90*	
Observations	53		53		53		53		51	
Prob > F	0.000		0.000		0.000		0.000		0.000	
R-squared	0.394		0.299		0.359		0.259		0.522	

Table 4. Tax/Revenue Effort and Regulation of Entry (Continued)

Model	OLS		OLS		OLS	
Dependent Variables	**Revenue Effort**		**Tax Effort**		**Revenue Effort**	
Independent Variables	**Beta**	**t-Stat.**	**Beta**	**t-Stat.**	**Beta**	**t-Stat.**
a) DEVELOPMENT						
GDP Per Capita	-0.228	-1.25	-0.216	-1.08	-0.307	-1.53
Population Growth	-0.286**	-2.33	-0.394***	-3.21	-0.262**	-2.13
b) OPENNESS						
(Export + Import)/GDP	-0.058	-0.54	-0.036	-0.43	-0.015	-0.16
c) ECONOMIC STRUCTURE						
1 – Agriculture/GDP	0.606***	4.35	0.582***	4.72	0.667***	5.25
d) REGIONS						
Latin America	-0.244**	-2.39	-0.300***	-3.89	-0.304***	-3.35
e) REGULATION OF ENTRY						
Number Of Procedures						
Time	-0.191*	-1.73	-0.177	-1.67	-0.213**	-2.02
F-Test Regulation of Entry	3.00*		2.79		4.09**	
Observations	51		51		51	
Prob > F	0.000		0.000		0.000	
R-squared	0.457		0.527		0.466	

Notes: The dependent variables are: TAX EFFORT: tax revenues/GDP, REVENUE EFFORT: current revenues/GDP. Significance levels: * $0.05 < p < 0.10$, ** $0.01 < p < 0.05$, *** $p < 0.01$. In the reference group: OTHER DEVELOPING AND TRANSITION COUNTRIES. Regressions with robust standard errors. Hausman Chi-square tests fail to detect the presence of simultaneity of the TAX/REVENUE EFFORT and THE REGULATION OF ENTRY (instrumental variable: English (legal origin)). Thus, only OLS has been estimated. Instrumental variable: latitude. The F-Test is a statistics on the joint significance of the mentioned variables.

Table 5. Tax/Revenue Effort and Inequality

Model	**OLS**		**OLS**		**OLS**		**OLS**	
Dependent Variables	**Tax Effort**		**Revenue Effort**		**Tax Effort**		**Revenue Effort**	
Independent Variables	**Beta**	**t-Stat.**	**Beta**	**t-Stat.**	**Beta**	**t-Stat.**	**Beta**	**t-Stat.**
a) **DEVELOPMENT**								
GDP Per Capita	-0.043	-0.29	0.250**	2.51	-0.353**	-2.40	-0.074	-0.82
Population Growth	-0.204	-1.44	-0.212*	-1.95	-0.240*	-1.95	-0.224***	-2.74
b) **OPENNESS**								
(Export + Import)/GDP	-0.133**	-2.00	-0.138*	-1.79	-0.119	-1.60	-0.149**	-2.38
c) **ECONOMIC STRUCTURE**								
1 – Agriculture/GDP					0.497***	4.87	0.635***	5.35
d) **REGIONS**								
Latin America	-0.140	-1.50	-0.285***	-3.26	-0.276***	-3.07	-0.459***	-5.07
e) **INSTITUTIONS**								
Inequality I	-0.382**	-2.42	-0.106	-0.98	-0.317**	-2.14	-0.014	-0.17
Inequality II								
F-Test Inequality	5.85**		0.96		4.59**		0.03	
Observations	77		77		74		74	
Prob > F	0.000		0.000		0.000		0.000	
R-squared	0.305		0.248		0.485		0.496	

Table 5. Tax/Revenue Effort and Inequality (Continued)

Model	OLS		OLS		OLS		OLS	
Dependent Variables	**Tax Effort**		**Revenue Effort**		**Tax Effort**		**Revenue Effort**	
Independent Variables	**Beta**	**t-Stat.**	**Beta**	**t-Stat.**	**Beta**	**t-Stat.**	**Beta**	**t-Stat.**
a) DEVELOPMENT								
GDP Per Capita	-0.006	-0.05	0.186	1.54	-0.308**	-2.25	-0.161	-1.160
Population Growth	-0.271*	-1.93	-0.320***	-2.76	-0.255**	-2.02	-0.288***	-2.630
b) OPENNESS								
(Export + Import)/GDP	-0.079	-0.95	-0.064	-0.65	-0.089	-1.13	-0.091	-1.170
c) ECONOMIC STRUCTURE								
1 – Agriculture/GDP					0.490***	4.96	0.614***	5.070
d) REGIONS								
Latin America	-0.044	-0.56	-0.150*	-1.96	-0.186**	-2.03	-0.321***	-3.290
e) INSTITUTIONS								
Inequality I								
Inequality II	-	-2.11	-0.106	-0.90	-0.264	-1.66	-0.018	-0.150
F-Test Inequality	0.336**		0.80		2.74		0.02	
Observations	4.45**		91		88		88	
Prob > F	91		0.000		0.000		0.000	
R-squared	0.000		0.218		0.441		0.430	
	0.286							

Notes: The dependent variables are: TAX EFFORT: tax revenues/GDP, REVENUE EFFORT: current revenues/GDP.INEQUALITY 1: averages 90-99, INEQUALITY II: Averages of the whole data set. Significance levels: * 0.05 < p < 0.10, ** 0.01< p < 0.05, *** p < 0.01. In the reference group: OTHER DEVELOPING AND TRANSITION COUNTRIES. Regressions with robust standard errors. Hausman Chi-square test fail to detect the presence of simultaneity of the TAX/REVENUE EFFORT and INEQUALITY (instrumental variables: ethnic, latitude, English (legal origin). Thus, only OLS has been estimated. F-Test is a statistics on the joint significance of the mentioned variable.

Table 6. Tax/Revenue Effort and the Size of Shadow Economy

Model	**OLS**		**OLS**		**OLS**		**OLS**	
Dependent Variables	**Tax Effort**		**Revenue Effort**		**Tax Effort**		**Revenue Effort**	
Independent Variables	**Beta**	**t-Stat.**	**Beta**	**t-Stat.**	**Beta**	**t-Stat.**	**Beta**	**t-Stat.**
a) **DEVELOPMENT**								
GDP Per Capita	0.171	1.08	-0.267	-1.05	0.166	1.00	-0.357	-1.16
Population Growth	-0.517***	-4.09	-0.708***	-4.58	-0.384***	-2.84	-0.600***	-3.57
b) **OPENNESS**								
(Export + Import)/GDP	-0.155***	-3.31	-0.122	-1.10	-0.139***	-2.88	-0.103	-0.87
c) **ECONOMIC STRUCTURE**								
1 – Agriculture/GDP								
d) **REGIONS**								
Latin America	-0.059	-0.63	0.218	0.84	-0.083	-0.81	0.237	0.78
e) **WILLINGNESS TO PAY**								
Size of Shadow Economy	-0.159	-1.51	-1.404**	-2.18	-0.214**	-2.06	-1.687**	-2.08
F-Test: Size OF Shadow EC.	2.28		4.73**		4.24**		4.33**	
Observations	70		69		70		69	
Prob > F	0.000		0.001		0.000		0.013	
R-squared	0.321				0.232			

Table 6. Tax/Revenue Effort and the Size of Shadow Economy (Continued)

Model	**OLS**		**OLS**		**OLS**		**OLS**	
Dependent Variables	**Tax Effort**		**Revenue Effort**		**Tax Effort**		**Revenue Effort**	
Independent Variables	**Beta**	**t-Stat.**	**Beta**	**t-Stat.**	**Beta**	**t-Stat.**	**Beta**	**t-Stat.**
a) DEVELOPMENT								
GDP Per Capita	-0.158***	-3.620	-0.426**	-2.38	-0.184	-1.09	-0.511**	-2.10
Population Growth	-0.461***	-4.890	-0.673***	-3.98	-0.310**	-2.61	-0.555***	-2.98
b) OPENNESS								
(Export + Import)/GDP	-0.138***	3.330	-0.107	-1.17	-0.123**	-2.23	-0.089	-0.87
c) ECONOMIC STRUCTURE								
1 – Agriculture/GDP	0.461***	4.920	0.2611*	1.24	0.526***	3.97	0.283	1.18
d) REGIONS								
Latin America	-0.184	-1.66	0.129	0.46	-0.233*	-1.90	0.138	0.43
e) WILLINGNESS TO PAY								
Size of Shadow Economy	-0.109	-1.30	-1.223*	-1.90	-0.156*	-1.85	-1.498*	-1.88
F-Test: Size OF Shadow EC.	1.68		3.61*		3.44*		3.55*	
Observations	69		68		69		68	
Prob > F	0.000		0.000		0.000		0.000	
R-squared	0.456				0.387			

Notes: The dependent variables are: TAX EFFORT: tax revenues/GDP, REVENUE EFFORT: current revenues/GDP. Significance levels: * $0.05 < p < 0.10$, ** $0.01 < p < 0.05$, *** $p < 0.01$. In the reference group: OTHER DEVELOPING AND TRANSITION COUNTRIES. Regressions with robust standard errors. Hausman Chi-square test with CONTROL OF CORRUPTION (Kaufmann et al. 2003) as an instrument for SIZE OF SHADOW ECONOMY detected the presence of simultaneity of the TAX/REVENUE EFFORT and the SIZE OF SHADOW ECONOMY. Thus, a 2SLS has been estimated. The F-Test is a statistics on the joint significance of the mentioned variable.

Table 7. Tax/Revenue Effort and Tax Morale

Model	**OLS**		**OLS**		**OLS**		**OLS**	
Dependent Variables	**Tax Effort**		**Revenue Effort**		**Tax Effort**		**Revenue Effort**	
Independent Variables	**Coeff.**	**t-Stat.**	**Coeff.**	**t-Stat.**	**Coeff.**	**t-Stat.**	**Coeff.**	**t-Stat.**
a) DEVELOPMENT								
GDP Per Capita	0.347***	2.80	0.286**	2.09	0.177	1.24	0.087	0.53
Population Growth	-0.262**	-2.05	-0.253*	-1.77	-0.236*	-1.71	--0.224	-1.45
b) OPENNESS								
(Export + Import)/GDP	0.243	1.50	0.199	1.19	0.313*	1.82	0.280	1.56
c) ECONOMIC STRUCTURE								
1 – Agriculture/GDP					0.257	1.26	0.302	1.47
d) REGIONS								
Latin America	-0.403***	-3.45	-0.451***	-2.77	-0.405***	-3.38	-0.453**	-2.69
e) WILLINGNESS TO PAY								
Tax Morale	0.167	1.48	0.260*	1.97	0.164	1.32	0.257*	1.79
F-Test	2.18		3.86*		1.75		3.19*	
Observations	35		35		35		35	
Prob > F	0.000		0.000		0.000		0.000	
R-squared	0.655		0.581		0.686		0.623	

Notes: The dependent variables are: TAX EFFORT: tax revenues/GDP, REVENUE EFFORT: current revenues/GDP. Significance levels: * $0.05 < p < 0.10$, ** $0.01 < p < 0.05$, *** $p < 0.01$. In the reference group: OTHER DEVELOPING AND TRANSITION COUNTRIES. Regressions with robust standard errors. Hausman Chi-square test with LATITUDE as an instrument for TAX MORALE fail to detect the presence of simultaneity of the tax effort and tax morale variable. The F-Test is a statistics on the joint significance of the mentioned variable.

Table 8. Determinants of Tax/Revenue Effort (Fuller Specification with the Size of Shadow Economy)

Model	**OLS**		**OLS**		**OLS**		**OLS**	
Dependent Variables	**Tax Effort**		**Revenue Effort**		**Tax Effort**		**Revenue Effort**	
Independent Variables	**Beta**	**t-Stat.**	**Beta**	**t-Stat.**	**Beta**	**t-Stat.**	**Beta**	**t-Stat.**
a) DEVELOPMENT								
GDP Per Capita	-0.343***	-2.91	-0.423***	-2.38	-0.345**	-2.57	-0.373**	-2.10
Population Growth	-0.349**	-2.36	-0.213	-1.36	-0.181	-1.10	-0.026	-0.17
b) OPENNESS								
(Export + Import)/GDP	-0.172***	-4.70	-0.164	-3.51	-0.090	-1.18	-0.037	-0.47
c) ECONOMIC STRUCTURE								
1 – Agriculture/GDP	0.377***	3.33	0.441***	3.42	0.319**	2.07	0.339**	2.09
d) REGIONS								
Latin America	-0.216*	-1.86	-0.296**	-2.23	-0.175	-1.37	-0.236	-1.77
e) INEQUALITY	-0.185	-0.95	-0.119	-0.60	-0.143	-0.69	-0.061	-0.30
f) WILLINGNESS TO PAY								
Shadow Economy	-0.001	-0.02	-0.041	-0.48	0.111	0.85	0.102	0.74
g) INSTITUTIONS								
Index Governance	0.325**	2.56	0.423***	2.84				
ICRG Index					0.413*	1.99	0.543**	2.48
h) REGULATION OF ENTRY								
Number of Procedures								
Time								
Observations	63		63		55		55	
Prob > F	0.000		0.000		0.000		0.000	
R-squared	0.600		0.530		0.531		0.475	

Table 8. Determinants of Tax/Revenue Effort (Fuller Specification with the Size of Shadow Economy) (Continued)

Model	OLS		OLS		OLS		OLS	
Dependent Variables	**Tax Effort**		**Revenue Effort**		**Tax Effort**		**Revenue Effort**	
Independent Variables	**Beta**	**t-Stat.**	**Beta**	**t-Stat.**	**Beta**	**t-Stat.**	**Beta**	**t-Stat.**
a) DEVELOPMENT								
GDP Per Capita	-0.214	-1.40	-0.346**	-2.22	-0.278	-1.52	-0.438**	-2.36
Population Growth	-0.501**	-2.10	-0.321	-1.22	-0.521**	-2.47	-0.332	-1.48
b) OPENNESS								
(Export + Import)/GDP	-0.142	-1.60	-0.133	-1.40	-0.103	-1.17	-0.083	-0.90
c) ECONOMIC STRUCTURE								
1 – Agriculture/GDP	0.422***	2.77	0.565***	3.51	0.471***	3.20	0.634***	4.14
d) REGIONS								
Latin America	-0.189	-1.19	-0.211	-1.20	-0.276**	-2.07	-0.322**	-2.15
e) INEQUALITY	-0.069	-0.23	-0.104	-0.31	-0.016	-0.06	-0.045	-0.16
f) WILLINGNESS TO PAY								
Shadow Economy	-0.110	-1.15	-0.060	-0.54	-0.122	-1.29	-0.075	-0.65
g) INSTITUTIONS								
Index Governance								
ICRG Index								
h) REGULATION OF ENTRY								
Number of Procedures	-0.199**	-2.01	-0.251**	-2.24				
Time					-0.171	-1.32	-0.244*	-1.81
Observations	39		39		39		39	
Prob > F	0.000		0.000		0.000		0.000	
R-squared	0.686		0.626		0.681		0.629	

Notes: The dependent variables are: TAX EFFORT: tax revenues/GDP, REVENUE EFFORT: current revenues/GDP. INEQUALITY= INEQUALITY II. Significance levels: * $0.05 < p < 0.10$, ** $0.01 < p < 0.05$, *** $p < 0.01$. In the reference group: OTHER DEVELOPING AND TRANSITION COUNTRIES. Regressions with robust standard errors. No 2SLS has been conducted because the standard asymptotic approximations to the distribution of instrumental variables breaks down. The use of weak instruments would produce biases in the 2SLS estimators.

Table 9. Determinants of Tax/Revenue Effort (Fuller Specification with Tax Morale)

Model	**OLS**		**OLS**		**OLS**		**OLS**	
Dependent Variables	**Tax Effort**		**Revenue Effort**		**Tax Effort**		**Revenue Effort**	
Independent Variables	**Beta**	**t-Stat.**	**Beta**	**t-Stat.**	**Beta**	**t-Stat.**	**Beta**	**t-Stat.**
a) DEVELOPMENT								
GDP Per Capita	0.115	0.67	-0.009	-0.05	-0.010	-0.04	-0.109	-0.44
Population Growth	-0.180	-1.06	-0.161	-0.88	-0.245	-1.21	-0.268	-1.31
b) OPENNESS								
(Export + Import)/GDP	0.131	1.01	0.088	0.53	0.303**	2.02	0.311*	1.85
c) ECONOMIC STRUCTURE								
1 – Agriculture/GDP	0.010	0.06	0.035	0.21	0.064	0.26	0.085	0.39
d) REGIONS								
Latin America	-0.304**	-2.45	-0.346**	-2.06	-0.287**	-2.24	-0.358**	-2.37
e) INEQUALITY	-0.284*	-1.76	-0.288	-1.49	0.078	0.28	0.205	0.67
f) WILLINGNESS TO PAY								
Tax Morale	0.064	0.59	0.137	0.99	0.115	0.99	0.204	1.37
g) INSTITUTIONS								
Index Governance	0.249**	2.18	0.310**	2.43				
ICRG Index					0.417**	2.02	0.453*	1.86
h) REGULATION OF ENTRY								
Number of Procedures								
Time								
Observations	32		32		25		25	
Prob > F	0.000		0.000		0.000		0.000	
R-squared	0.785		0.733		0.774		0.744	

Table 9. Determinants of Tax/Revenue Effort (Fuller Specification with Tax Morale) (Continued)

Model	**OLS**		**OLS**		**OLS**		**OLS**	
Dependent Variables	**Tax Effort**		**Revenue Effort**		**Tax Effort**		**Revenue Effort**	
Independent Variables	**Beta**	**t-Stat.**	**Beta**	**t-Stat.**	**Beta**	**t-Stat.**	**Beta**	**t-Stat.**
a) DEVELOPMENT								
GDP Per Capita	0.137	0.88	0.071	0.35	0.170	0.96	0.129	0.58
Population Growth	-0.038	-0.19	-0.017	-0.06	0.051	0.25	0.149	0.59
b) OPENNESS								
(Export + Import)/GDP	0.197	1.36	0.123	0.63	0.198	1.36	0.165	0.84
c) ECONOMIC STRUCTURE								
1 – Agriculture/GDP	0.222	1.36	0.151	0.77	0.212	1.48	0.170	0.94
d) REGIONS								
Latin America	-0.224	-1.01	-0.291	-0.95	-0.247	-1.53	-0.409	-1.64
e) INEQUALITY	-0.452*	-1.76	-0.389	-1.30	-0.466**	-2.08	-0.393	-1.52
f) WILLINGNESS TO PAY								
Tax Morale	-0.104	-0.74	0.052	0.23	-0.146	-0.93	-0.008	-0.03
g) INSTITUTIONS								
Index Governance								
ICRG Index								
h) REGULATION OF ENTRY								
Number of Procedures	-0.012	-0.09	-0.154	-0.98				
Time					-0.113	-0.94	-0.207	-1.68
Observations	23		23		23		23	
Prob > F	0.000		0.000		0.000		0.001	
R-squared	0.835		0.732		0.843		0.747	

Notes: The dependent variables are: TAX EFFORT: tax revenues/GDP, REVENUE EFFORT: current revenues/GDP. INEQUALITY= INEQUALITY II. Significance levels: * $0.05 < p < 0.10$, ** $0.01 < p < 0.05$, *** $p < 0.01$. In the reference group: OTHER DEVELOPING AND TRANSITION COUNTRIES. Regressions with robust standard errors.

Table 10. Summary of the Results

Model	*Estimations without Societal Institutions*		*Estimations with Societal Institutions*		*Fuller Specifications*	
Dependent Variables	**Tax Effort**	**Revenue Effort**	**Tax Effort**	**Revenue Effort**	**Tax Effort**	**Revenue Effort**
Independent Variables						
a) DEVELOPMENT						
GDP Per Capita	(+/-)	(+/-)	(-)	(-)	(-)	-
Population Growth	-	-	(-)	(-)	(-)	(-)
b) OPENNESS						
(Export + Import)/GDP	((-))	((-))	((-))	(-)	(-)	((-))
c) ECONOMIC STRUCTURE						
1 - Agriculture/GDP	+	+	+	+	+	+
d) REGIONS						
Latin America	(-)	(-)	(-)	(-)	(-)	(-)
e) INEQUALITY			(-)	(-)	((-))	((-))
f) WILLINGNESS TO PAY						
Size of Shadow Economy			(-)	-	((-))	((-))
Tax Morale			((+))	+	((-))	((-))
g) INSTITUTIONS						
Governance Variables			+	+	+	+
ICRG Variables			+	+	+	+
h) REGULATION OF ENTRY						
Number of Procedures			(-)	(-)	-	-
Time			(-)	-	((-))	-

Notes: +/-: always significant positive or negative coefficients, (+/-), positive, respectively negative coefficients sign, but not always statistically significant, ((+/-)) positive or negative sign of the coefficients without being statistically significant. The summary about the fuller specifications is based on the results obtained in Table 8 and not Table 9 (exception: tax morale), because of the low number of observations in Table 9.

4. CONCLUSION

The main theme of this paper is that a more legitimate and responsive state appears to be an essential precondition for a more adequate level of tax effort in developing countries. While at first glance giving such advice to poor countries seeking to increase their tax ratios may not seem more helpful than telling them to find oil, it is presumably more feasible for people to improve their governing institutions than to rearrange nature's bounty. Furthermore, improving social institutions, such as enhancing the rule of law and reducing corruption, may not take longer nor be necessarily more difficult than changing the opportunities for tax handles and economic structure, such as the relative share of the non-agriculture sector in the economy or the weight of imports and exports in GDP.

The most important contribution of this paper has been to extend the conventional model of tax effort by showing that not only do supply factors matter, but that societal institutions or demand factors common to all countries also matter quite significantly in the determination of tax effort. Of course, in order to fully understand the performance of any one country one needs to pay close attention to the factors that are particular to that country. To return to where we began, in Kaldor's terms, countries have indeed 'learned to tax'...to the extent that their societal institutions lead them to do so.

Annex Tables

Annex Table 1. Summary of Previous Conventional Studies of Tax Effort

	Bahl (2003) OECD and less developed economies	Alm ,Martinez-Vazquez and Schneider (2004) Developed and Developing countries	Teera (2002) Developed and Developing Countries	Piancastelli (2001) Developed and Developing Countries	Stotsky and WoldeMariam (1997) Sub-Saharan African countries
Dependent Variable	**Ratio of tax revenue to GDP**	**Ratio of total tax revenue to GDP**	**Tax to GDP ratio**	**Total Tax Revenues/GDP**	**Tax share in GDP**
Explanatory Variables	The non-agricultural share of GDP *(positive, statistically significant)*	Agriculture/GNP *(negative, statistically not significant)* Mining/GNP *(positive, statistically significant)*	Ratio of agriculture to GDP *(negative and positive depending on the estimation, strong negative impact for low income countries)* Ratio Manufacturing to GDP *(negative, not statistically significant)*	Agriculture GDP share *(negative and positive, negative and statistically significant in a panel analysis)* Industry GDP share *(positive, statistically significant in a time series analysis)* Service GDP share (positive, not always statistically significant)	The share of agriculture *(negative, statistically significant)* The share of mining *(negative, statistically significant)* Manufacturing share *(positive, negative, not statistically significant)*
	Openness ratio (the sum of the value of exports and imports as a share of GDP) *(positive, statistically significant)*	GNP per capita *(negative, statistically significant)*	GDP per capita *(negative and positive, not always statistically significant)*	GNP per capita *(positive/negative tendency: positive, but not always statistically significant)*	Per capita income *(positive, statistically significant)*

Annex Table 1. Summary of Previous Conventional Studies of Tax Effort (Continued)

	Bahl (2003) OECD and less developed economies	Alm ,Martinez-Vazquez and Schneider (2004) Developed and Developing countries	Teera (2002) Developed and Developing Countries	Piancastelli (2001) Developed and Developing Countries	Stotsky and WoldeMariam (1997) Sub-Saharan African countries
Dependent Variable	**Ratio of tax revenue to GDP**	**Ratio of total tax revenue to GDP**	**Tax to GDP ratio**	**Total Tax Revenues/GDP**	**Tax share in GDP**
Explanatory Variables	The rate of population growth *(positive, statistically significant)*	Taxes on international trade/GNP *(negative, not statistically significant)*	Ratio of exports plus imports to GDP *(negative and positive, not statistically significant, strong positive effect for lower middle income countries)*	Trade/GDP *(positive, statistically significant)*	The share of imports in GDP *(positive/negative, not statistically significant)* The share of exports in GDP *(positive, statistically significant)*
	Simple correlation between tax effort and the size of shadow economy *(negative, but not statistically significant)*	Shadow economy / GDP *(negative, statistically significant)*	Shadow economy *(positive, not always statistically significant, negative and statistically significant in one estimation for OECD countries)*		

Annex Table 1. Summary of Previous Conventional Studies of Tax Effort (Continued)

	Tanzi (1992) Developing countries	Leuhold (1991) African countries	Bahl (1971) Developing countries	Shin (1969) Developed and Developing countries	Lotz and Morss (1967) Developed and Developing countries
Dependent Variable	**Tax share**	**Tax share**	**Taxable capacity**	**Tax Ratio**	**Ratio of tax revenue to GNP**
	The share of agriculture in GDP *(negative, statistically significant)*	The share of agriculture in income *(negative, but not always statistically significant)*	The agricultural share *(negative, statistically significant)*	Per Capita GNP *(positive, statistically significant only for the whole sample and the sub-samples high an low income countries)*	Per capita GNP *(positive, statistically significant for the entire sample and the low income countries, not significant for the high income countries)*
		The share of mining in income *(positive, negative, not statistically significant)*	The mining share *(positive, statistically significant)*		
Explanatory Variables	Per capita income *(positive, but not statistically significant for some years)*	The share of foreign trade *(share of imports and exports in income)* *(positive, statistically significant)*	Per capita income *(positive, not statistically significant)*	Foreign Trade Ratio *(positive, not statistically significant)*	Sum of exports and imports as a percentage of GNP *(positive, statistically significant for the entire sample and the low-income countries, not significant for the high-income countries)*

Annex Table 1. Summary of Previous Conventional Studies of Tax Effort (Continued)

	Tanzi (1992) Developing countries	Leuhold (1991) African countries	Bahl (1971) Developing countries	Shin (1969) Developed and Developing countries	Lotz and Morss (1967) Developed and Developing countries
Dependent Variable	**Tax share**	**Tax share**	**Taxable capacity**	**Tax Ratio**	**Ratio of tax revenue to GNP**
	The share of imports in GDP *(positive, statistically significant)*	The share of foreign grants and loans in income *(positive, statistically significant)*	The export ratio *(positive, but not always statistically significant)*	The agricultural income ratio *(negative, not statistically significant)*	
Explanatory Variables	Level of foreign debt in GDP *(Positive, but not statistically significant in all estimations)*			The rate of change in prices *(positive, only statistically significant for the low income countries)*	

Annex Table 2. Descriptive Statistics for Tax Effort

Variable	Observations	Mean	Min	Max
Total Data Set				
TAX EFFORT	110	17.88	1.09	38.33
REVENUE EFFORT	110	22.27	2.48	46.38
Latin America				
TAX EFFORT	23	17.78	9.98	25.96
REVENUE EFFORT	23	20.95	12.64	29.42

Annex Table 3. Variable Descriptions and Sources

Variables	Description	Source
TAX EFFORT	tax revenue as a share of GDP (average 1990-1999)	WDI (2003)
REVENUE EFFORT	current revenues/GDP (excluding grants, average 1990-1999)	WDI (2003)
GDP PER CAPITA	average 1990-1999	WDI (2003)
POPULATION GROWTH	average 1990-1999	WDI (2003)
(EXPORT + IMPORT)/GDP	average 1990-1999	WDI (2003)
1- AGRICULTURE/GDP	average 1990-1999	WDI (2003)
INEQUALITY	GINI coefficient (average 1990-1999; averages of the whole data set, 1963-1999)	Galbraith and Kum (2003)
SIZE OF SHADOW ECONOMY	shadow economy as a percentage of GDP (average 1990, 1995, 1999)	Schneider and Klinglmair (2003)

Annex Table 3. Variable Descriptions and Sources (Continued)

Variables	Description	Source
TAX MORALE	survey question (average: World Values Survey (WVS) 1990-1993, WVS 1995-1997, European Values Survey 1999-2000, Latinobarómetro 1998)	Inglehart, R. et al. (2000), European Values 199 Survey (1999) and Latinobarómetro (1998)
INDEX GOVERNANCE	covers the mean value of six governance dimensions (periods 1996, 1998 and 2000)	Kaufmann, Kraay, and Mastruzzi (2003)
ICRG INDEX	covers the mean value of six risk dimensions (period: 1990-1997)	Knack (1999)
REGULATION OF ENTRY	Number of procedures and official time required to complete the process	Djankov et al. (2002)

Notes

1. We are grateful to Michael Rushton, our discussant at the conference, and to other conference participants as well as Uri Raich and Francois Vaillancourt for helpful comments on earlier versions of this paper.
2. Kaldor's contemporary, Sir Arthur Lewis (Martin and Lewis, 1956), a few years earlier had similarly argued that..the government of an under-developed country needs to be able to raise revenue of about 17 to 19 percent of G.N.P...in order to give a not better than average standard of service."
3. In recent years, however, influenced perhaps by the growing empirical evidence of the 'costs' of taxation (as reviewed recently in Bird and Zolt, 2003), more analysts have come to share the early skepticism of Bauer (1955) as to the inherent virtues of channeling a larger share of national resources through the public sector. We do not, however, discuss this important question in the present paper.
4. Tanzi (1987) is a good example of such work: for a skeptical appraisal of what can be learned from such studies, see Bird (1976).
5. For example, this is essentially the conclusion drawn in the review by Bird and Casanegra (1992).
6. We do not, however, attempt a formal 'political economy' analysis of the problem: see, for example, Cheibub (1998) and Hettich and Winer (1999).
7. Both the 'exit' and 'voice' options are beautifully set out in Hirschman's (1971) seminal study.
8. We neglect here one obvious alternative way out of this dilemma, namely, military conquest of those more blessed by nature: for a recent exploration of some interesting aspects of this theme, see Teng (2001). We also neglect the obvious fact that many countries rich in natural resources also do not make much tax effort and those that do, often make poor use of the resources thus obtained (Davis, Ossowski, and Fedelino, 2003).
9. For data, and a fuller discussion, see Bird (2003).
10. The figures for the earlier period are from Tanzi (1987); the more recent figures are from Stotsky and WoldeMariam (2002).
11. This statement does not represent a normative judgment of the fiscal performance of Mexico. The share of government in GDP reflects, among other things, the collective preferences of a country for public goods and services vis-à-vis private consumption. From an economic standpoint, these preferences cannot be judged right or wrong. Nonetheless, the general consensus in Mexico is that the current level of revenues is insufficient to support the expenditure programs desired.
12. The overall adequacy of revenues can be further illuminated by examining the behavior of the government budget deficit. The sustained deficits during the 1980s may indicate that Mexico's level of tax effort was too low to cover the level of expenditures desired by the government. The budget imbalance during the 1980s was very pronounced. Closing a deficit of 10 percent of GDP would have required practically doubling the existing level of tax effort. But clearly the same conclusion does not apply to the 1990s. The very small budget deficits since 1993 may suggest either that Mexico has reached some sort of equilibrium vis-à-vis its desired level of tax effort or that other forces have been able to impose fiscal discipline in the federal budget.
13. It has been a common, although not explicitly stated, policy within the Ministry of Finance during much of the last two decades that any increase in revenues should be spent by the Ministry itself in the form of rate reductions or tax expenditures rather than on the expenditure side of the budget by line ministries and other budget units.
14. This phenomenon is by no means confined to Latin America, of course: a striking example elsewhere appears to be India where, after a quick rise in the tax ratio following

liberalization in the early 1990s, matters seem to be settling back to the lower ratio to which the country had long been accustomed.

15. Peacock and Wiseman (1967) many years earlier had explained a similar discrete jump in tax effort and public expenditure in Great Britain as a ´displacement effect´: general perceptions about what is a tolerable level of taxation tend to be quite stable until these perceptions get shocked by social upheavals, and levels of taxation that would have been previously intolerable become acceptable and remain at that level after the social perturbations have disappeared.
16. See Bird (2003) for an extended discussion. One might perhaps question the relevance of historical or even comparative experience in analyzing and understanding the problems of developing countries today. As a recent book notes, however, "Today's industrialized countries were yesterday's developing or transitional economies and for tax policy purposes the demarcation line between them is more likely to be the relative efficiency and integrity of the tax administration, rather than such economic criteria as GDP per capita" (Messere, de Kam, and Heady, 2003, preface). Of course, how a tax administration functions is determined largely by more fundamental political factors.
17. The discussion here focuses on (non-benefit) taxation. To the extent public expenditures are financed from charges, non-tax revenues, and borrowing, other considerations may come into play but these issues cannot be discussed adequately here.
18. As Lindert (2004) shows, this quotation actually had a somewhat different implication in its original context, but it is nonetheless largely right if one is concerned with growth: as Lindert (2004, p.344), concludes, history tells us that "the average democracy has been better for economic growth than the average autocracy…."
19. In any case, as Harberger (2003) shows, even the most redistributive tax will not in itself have any much effect on income redistribution.
20. Although one might rightly be skeptical about the effectiveness of such measures (Bird, 1974).
21. Note that since only central government data are recorded in this source, the tax level may be understated significantly in countries in which subnational governments are important.
22. The use of average values over a period allows maximizing the number of observations.
23. We explored the possibility of a non-linear relationship between GDP per capita and tax effort by adding the square of GDP per capita to the equation. However, the coefficient for the new term was generally not significant.
24. As many countries have proceeded over the past several decades to lower tariff rates as part of their liberalization and economic reforms policies and joining the WTO, the strong link in the past between international trade and revenue collections may have weakened in more recent times.
25. Lower scores indicate "high government officials are likely to demand special payments" and that "illegal payments are generally expected throughout lower levels of government" in the form of "bribes connected with import and export licenses, exchange controls, tax assessment, police protection, or loans."
26. This variable "reflects the degree to which the citizens of a country are willing to accept the established institutions to make and implement laws and adjudicate disputes." Higher scores indicate: "sound political institutions, a strong court system, and provisions for an orderly succession of power." Lower scores indicate: "a tradition of depending on physical force or illegal means to settle claims." Upon changes in government new leaders "may be less likely to accept the obligations of the previous regime."
27. High scores indicate "an established mechanism for recruitment and training," "autonomy from political pressure," and "strength and expertise to govern without drastic changes in policy or interruptions in government services" when governments change."

28. This variable "measures the degree of tension within a country attributable to racial, nationality, or language divisions. Lower ratings are given to countries where racial and nationality tensions are high because opposing groups are intolerant and unwilling to compromise. Higher ratings are given to countries where tensions are minimal, even though such differences may still exist."
29. "This indicator addresses the possibility that foreign businesses, contractors, and consultants face the risk of a modification in a contract taking the form of a repudiation, postponement, or scaling down" due to "an income drop, budget cutbacks, indigenization pressure, a change in government, or a change in government economic and social priorities." Lower scores signify "a greater likelihood that a country will modify or repudiate a contract with a foreign business."
30. This variable evaluates the risk "outright confiscation and forced nationalization" of property. Lower ratings are given to countries where expropriation of private foreign investment is considered likely.
31. There is no fixed rule on how highly correlated two variables have to be before multicollinearity becomes a problem. For example, Allison (1999) points out that values above 0.80 almost certainly are problematic, but there may be difficulties that appear below that value. Because the two sets of variables practically measure the same institutions and we are not testing hypotheses about any specific variable, we find it simpler to use them as alternate measures.
32. Furthermore, de Soto argues that it is nearly as difficult to *stay* legal, as it is to *become* legal. In Venezuela, the share of employees working in legal enterprises decreased from two third in 1976 to less than half in our days. Thus, people have created new business illegally to fill the gaps in the legal economy.
33. See Schneider and Enste (2002) and Alm, Martinez-Vazquez, and Schneider (2004)for a description of the methodologies used in the estimation of the shadow economy.
34. Of the two surveys, the World Values Survey provides more observations. On the other hand, the *Latinobarómetro* allows us to include more Latin American countries in the empirical analysis. Note that the tax morale questions are not identical. Eight Latin American countries (Argentina, Brazil, Chile, Colombia, Mexico, Peru, Uruguay and Venezuela) are available in both data sets. To judge from the average values for the two measures in the two data sets (WVS, 2.215 and Latinobarómetro, 2.113) the variables are almost identical. However, in order to maximize the number of observations, we work with the World Values Survey, which allows us to include other developing and transition countries. The average values for Latin American countries, which can only be constructed from the *Latinobarómetro,* are multiplied by the factor (2.215/2.113) to address some scaling effects. This approach allows us to include a larger number of Latin American countries in the analysis.
35. Galbraith and Kum (2003) estimate gross household income inequality from a regression between the Deiniger and Squire (1996) inequality measures and the UTIP-UNIDO pay inequality measures.
36. In general, as Kaufmann, Mehrez and Gurgur (2002) point out, the choice of an estimator in a small sample situation is still an econometric puzzle: for example, OLS estimators are often found to be close to an instrumental variable technique in many empirical studies. An important problem is that 2SLS produce biased estimators in small samples (see also Green 2000). The choice of adequate instruments for institutions is not extensively addressed in the literature (for corruption see, e.g., Kaufmann, Kraay and Zoido-Lobatón 1999, Bai and Wei 2000, Kaufmann, Mehrez and Gurgur 2002). More recent studies stress the relevance of considering historical and geographic features of the countries as instrumental variables as they influence the outcome through their impact on the institutional and political environment (see, e.g., Hall and Jones 1999, and Acemoglu, Johnson and Robinson, 2001). Recent studies such as the ones of Alesina et al. (2002) or La Porta et al. (1999) offer a broad data set to consider factors such as

latitude, ethnic fractionalization, language, and religion. Taking into consideration that the instruments need to be highly correlated with the regressor for which it is acting as an instrument, our data set indicates that historical and geographic variables perform very well as instruments.

37. We also ran the full specifications with fiscal decentralization as an additional explanatory variable. The results consistently showed the decentralization coefficient to be negative, indicating that more decentralized systems may exert lower tax effort, but the coefficients were never statistically significant.
38. It is difficult to get a clear notion of the causal links among these variables. In most developed countries, for instance, given that good governance and other institutions providing voice have been stable for many years, it might be that if any causality links exists , it may run from voice institutions to exit institutions such as tax morale or the shadow economy, and not the other way round.

References

Acemoglu, D. S. Johnson and J. Robinson (2001), "The Colonial Origins of Comparative Development: An Empirical Investigation", *American Economic Review*, Vol. 91, pp. 1369-1401.

Allison, P. D. (1999), *Multiple Regression: A Primer*, California: The Pine Forge Press

Alm, J. and J. Martinez-Vazquez (2003), "Institutions, Paradigms, and Tax Evasion in Developing and Transition Countries", pp. 146-178 in: J. Martinez-Vazquez and J. Alm (eds.), *Public Finance in Developing and Transitional Countries*, Cheltenham, UK: Edward Elgar.

Alm, J., J. Martinez-Vazquez and Friedich Schneider (2004), 'Sizing' the Problem of the Hard-To-Tax, paper presented at the "Hard to Tax: An International Perspective", in : J.Alm, J. Martinez-Vazquez, and S. Wallace, editors, *Taxing the Hard-to-Tax*, Elsevier: Amsterdam.

Alm, J. and B. Torgler (2004), *Culture Differences and Tax Morale in the United States and in Europe*, *CREMA Working Paper 2004-14*, Basel: Center for Research in Economics, Management and the Arts.

Alm, J., J. Martinez-Vazquez and B. Torgler (2004), "*Tax Morale in Russia*", unpublished manuscript, Georgia State University.

Alesina, A. and G.-M. Angeletos (2003), *Fairness and Redistribution: U.S. versus Europe*, *Working Paper 9502*, Cambridge, MA: National Bureau of Economic Research.

Alesina, A. and R. Perotti (1996), "Income Distribution, Political Instability, and Investment", *European Economic Review*, Vol. 40, pp. 1203-1228.

Alesina, A., A. Devleeschauwer, W. Easterly, S. Kurlat and R. Wacziarg (2002), *Fractionalization*, *NBER Working Paper No. 9411*.

Arze, Javier, Jorge Martinez-Vazquez and Robert Mcnab (2004), *Fiscal Decentralization and the Composition of Public Expenditures*, *ISP Working Paper 0501*, Georgia, USA.: Andrew Young School of Policy Studies, Georgia State University.

Bahl, R. W. (1971), "A Regression Approach to Tax Effort and Tax Ratio Analysis", *International Monetary Fund Staff Paper*, Vol. 18, pp. 570-612.

Bahl, R. W. (2003), Reaching the Hardest to Tax: Consequences and Possibilities, paper presented at the "Hard to Tax: An International Perspective" conference, Andrew Young School of Policy Studies, Georgia State University, May 15-16.

Bai, C.-E. and S-J. Wei (2000), *The Quality of the Bureaucracy and Capital Account Policies, World Bank Working paper 2575.*

Barro, R. J. (1997), *Determinants of Economic Growth: A Cross-Country Empirical Study*, Cambridge, MA: MIT Press.

Bauer, P. (1955), "The Economic Development of Nigeria", *Journal of Political Economy*, Vol. 63, pp. 399-408.

Best, M.H. (1976), "Political Power and Tax Revenues in Central America", *Journal of Development Economics*, Vol. 3, pp. 49-82.

Bird, R.M. (1974), *Taxing Agricultural Land in Developing Countries*, Cambridge, MA: Harvard University Press.

Bird, R.M. (1976), "Assessing Tax Performance in Developing Countries: A Critical Review of the Literature", *Finanzarchiv*, Vol. 34, pp. 244-65.

Bird, R.M. (1989), "The Administrative Dimension of Tax Reform in Developing Countries", in Malcolm Gillis, editor, *Tax Reform in Developing Countries*, Durham: Duke University Press.

Bird, R. M. (2003), *Taxation in Latin America: Reflections on Sustainability and the Balance between Equity and Efficiency, ITP Paper 0306*, Canada: International Tax Program, Joseph L. Rotman School of Management, University of Toronto.

Bird, R.M. (2004), "Managing Tax Reform", *Bulletin for International Fiscal Documentation,* Vol. 58, pp. 42-55.

Bird, R.M. and M.Casanegra de Jantscher (1992), *Improving Tax Administration in Developing Countries*, Washington: International Monetary Fund.

Bird, R.M. and E. Zolt (2003), *Introduction to Tax Policy, World Bank Course on Practical Issues in Tax Policy in Developing Countries.*

Blyth, M (2002), *Great Transformations: Economic Ideas and Institutional Change in the Twentieth Century*, Cambridge: Cambridge University Press.

Brennan, G. and J. M. Buchanan (1980), *The Power to Tax: Analytical Foundations of a Fiscal Constitution*, Cambridge: Cambridge University Press.

Breton, A. (1996), *Competitive Governments*, Cambridge: Cambridge University Press.

Cheibub, J.A. (1998), "Political Regimes and the Extractive Capacity of Governments: Taxation in Democracies and Dictatorships", *World Politics*, Vol. 50, pp. 349-76.

Chelliah, R. J. (1971), "Trends in Taxation in Developing Countries", *International Monetary Fund Staff Papers*, Vol. 18, pp. 254-331.

Davis, J.M., R.J. Ossowski, and A. Fedelino (eds.) (2003), *Fiscal Policy Formulation and Implementation in Oil-Producing Countries*, Washington: International Monetary Fund.

De Ferranti, D. *et al.* (2004), *Inequality in Latin America*, Washington: World Bank.

Deininger, K. and L. Squire (1996), "A New Data Set Measuring Income Inequality", *World Bank Economic Review*, Vol. 10, pp. 565-591.

De Soto, H. (2000), *The Mystery of Capital: Why Capitalism Triumphs in the West and Fails Everywhere Else*, New York: Basic Books.

Dorner, P. (1992), *Latin American Land Reforms in Theory and Practice: A Retrospective Analysis*, Madison: The University of Wisconsin Press.

Djankov, S., R. La Porta, F. Lopez-de-Silanes and A. Shleifer (2002), "The Regulation of Entry", *Quarterly Journal of Economics*, Vol. 117, pp. 1-37.

Ebrill, L. *et al.* (2001), *The Modern VAT*, Washington: International Monetary Fund.

Engerman, S.L. and K.L. Sokoloff (2001), *Inequality, Institutions and Differential Patterns of Growth among New World Economies, National Bureau of Economic Research.*

European Values Study (1999), Questionnaire, Tilburg University.

Feld, L. P., G. Kirchgässner and C. A. Schaltegger (2003), Decentralized Taxation and the Size of Government: Evidence from Swiss State and Local Governments, paper presented at the National Tax Association Conference, Chicago, November.

Frey, B. S. (1997), *Not Just for the Money: An Economic Theory of Personal Motivation*, Cheltenham, UK: Edward Elgar Publishing.

Frey, B. S. and R. Eichenberger (1999), *The New Democratic Federalism for Europe*, Cheltenham, UK: Edward Elgar.

Galbraith, J. K. and H. Kum (2003), *Estimating the Inequality of Household Income: Filling Gaps and Fixing Problems in Deininger & Squire, UTIP Working Paper No. 22.*

Hall, R. and C. Jones (1999), "Why Do Some Countries Produce so Much More per Worker than Others?", *Quarterly Journal of Economics*, Vol. 114, pp. 83-116.

Harberger, A.C. (2003), *Reflections on Distributional Considerations and the Public Finances, Module for World Bank Course on Practical Issues of Tax Policy in Developing Countries.*

Hettich, W. and S.L. Winer (1999), *Democratic Choice and Taxation*, Cambridge: Cambridge University Press.

Hinrichs, H.H. (1966), *A General Theory of Tax Structure Change during Economic Development*, Cambridge, MA: Harvard Law School International Tax Program.

Hirschman, A.O. (1971), *Exit, Voice and Loyalty*, Cambridge, MA: Harvard University Press.

Inter-American Development Bank (IDB) (1997), *Latin America after a Decade of Reforms*, in: Economic and Social Progress in Latin America 1997, Washington.

Inter-American Development Bank (IDB) (1998), *Facing Up to Inequality in Latin America*, in: Economic and Social Progress in Latin America 1998-99, Washington.

Inglehart, R. *et al.* (2000), *Codebook for World Values Survey*, Ann Arbor: Institute for Social Research.

Kaldor, N. (1963), "Will Underdeveloped Countries Learn to Tax?", *Foreign Affairs*, Vol. 41: pp. 410-19.

Kaufmann, D., A. Kraay and P. Zoido-Lobatón (1999), *Governance Matters, World Bank Policy Research Working Paper 2195*.

Kaufmann, D., G. Mehrez and T. Gurgur (2002), "*Voice or Public Sector Management? An Empirical Investigation of Determinants of Public Sector Performance Based on a Survey of Public Officials*", unpublished manuscript, World Bank.

Kaufmann, D., A. Kraay, M. Mastruzzi (2003), *Governance Matters III: Governance Indicators for 1996-2002*, Hashington D.C.: World Bank.

Keynes, J.M. (1936), *The General Theory of Employment, Interest and Money*, London: Macmillan.

Knack, S. (1999), *Aid Dependence and the Quality of Governance, Working Paper*, USA: IRIS Center University of Maryland.

Latinobarómetro (1998), *Codebook 1998*, Chile: Corporación Latinobarómetro.

La Porta, R., F. Lopez-de-Silanes, A. Shleifer, and R. Vishny (1999), "The Quality of Government", *Journal of Law, Economics, & Organization*, Vol.15, pp. 222-278.

Leuthold, J. H. (1991), "Tax Shares in Developing Economies: A Panel Study", *Journal of Development Economics*, Vol. 35, pp. 173-185.

Levi, M. (1988), *Of Rule and Revenue*, Berkeley: University of California Press.

Lindert, P.H. (2002), *Why the Welfare State Looks Like a Free Lunch, Working Paper 02-7*, USA: UC Davis Department of Economics.

Lindert, P.H. (2003), *Growing Public: Social Spending and Economic Growth since the Eighteenth Century*, vol. 1, Cambridge UK: Cambridge University Press.

Lindert, P.H. (2004), "Voice and Growth; Was Churchill Right?", *Journal of Economic History*, Vol. 63 (2), pp. 315-50.

Lledo, V. A.Schneider, and M. Moore (2003), "Pro-poor Tax Reform in Latin America: A Critical Survey and Policy Recommendations", IDS, Sussex.

Lotz, J. R. and E. R. Morss (1967), "Measuring 'Tax Effort' in Developing Countries", *International Monetary Staff Papers*, Vol. 14, pp. 479-497.

Martin, A. and W.A. Lewis (1956), "Patterns of Public Revenue and Expenditure", *Manchester School of Economic and Social Studies*, Vol. 24, pp. 203-44.

Martinez-Vazquez, Jorge (2001), *Mexico: An Evaluation of the Main Features of the Tax System, International Studies Program Working Paper 0112*, Atlanta, Georgia: Andrew Young School of Policy Studies.

McLure, C.E. and G. Zodrow (1997), "Thirty Years of Tax Reform in Colombia", in: W.R. Thirsk, editor, *Tax Reform in Developing Countries*, Washington: World Bank.

Messere, K. F. de Kam, and C.Heady (2003), *Tax Policy: Theory and Practice in OECD Countries*, London: Oxford University Press.

Musgrave, R.A. (1969), *Fiscal Systems*, New Haven: Yale University Press.

Oates, W. E. (1972), *Fiscal Federalism*, New York: Harcourt Brace Jovanovich.

Peacock, A.T. and J. Wiseman (1967), *The Growth of Public Expenditures in the United Kingdom*, London: Allen and Unwin.

Piancastelli, M. (2001), *Measuring the Tax Effort of Developed and Developing Countries. Cross Country Panel Data Analysis / 1985/95, Discussion Paper*, Rio de Janeiro: IPEA.

Rodrik, D., A. Subramanian, and F. Trebbi (2002), *Institutions Rule: The Primacy of Institutions over Geography and Integration in Economic Development, NBER 9305*, Cambridge, MA: National Bureau of Economic Research.

Rose-Ackerman, S. (1997), "The Political Economy of Corruption", pp. 31-60 in: K. A. Elliott, editor, *Corruption and the Global Economy*, Washington D.C.: Institute for International Economics.

Sabates, R. and A.Schneider (2003), *Taxation, Accountability and the Poor, Seminar Report*, U.K.: Institute of Development Studies, University of Sussex.

Schneider, F. and D. H. Enste (2002), *The Shadow Economy*, in: An International Survey, Cambridge: Cambridge University Press.

Schneider, F. and R. Klinglmair (2003), Shadow Economies Around the World: What Do we Know?, paper presented at the Annual Public Choice Conference in Baltimore, March, 2004.

Shin, K. (1969), "International Difference in Tax Ratio", *The Review of Economics and Statistics*, Vol. 51, pp. 213-220.

Shome, P. (1999), *Taxation in Latin America: Structural Trends and Impact of Administration, IMF Working Paper WP/99/19*, Washington, D.C.: IMF.

Stotsky, J. G. and A. WoldeMariam (1997), *Tax Effort in Sub-Saharan Africa, IMF Working Papers No. 97/107*, Washington, D.C.: IMF.

Stotsky, J.G. and A.WoldeMariam (2002), *Central American Tax Reform: Trends and Possibilities, IMF Working Paper WP/02/227*, Washington, D.C.: IMF.

Tanzi, V. (1987), "Quantitative Characteristics of the Tax Systems of Developing Countries", in: David Newbery and Nicholas Stern, editors, *The Theory of Taxation in Developing Countries*, Oxford: Oxford University Press for the World Bank.

Tanzi, V. (1992), "Structural Factors and Tax Revenue in Developing Countries: A Decade of Evidence", pp. 267-281 in: I. Goldin and L. A. Winters, editors, *Open Economies: Structural Adjustment and Agriculture*, Cambridge: Cambridge University Press.

Teera, J. (2002), *Tax Performance: A Comparative Study, Working Paper 01-02*, U.K.: Centre for Public Economics, University of Bath.

Teng, J. (2001), "Endogenous Authoritarian Property Rights", *Journal of Public Economics*, Vol. 77(1), pp. 81-95.

Torgler, B. (2001), "Is Tax Evasion Never Justifiable?", *Journal of Public Finance and Public Choice*, Vol. 19, pp. 143-168.

Torgler, B. (2004), "Tax Morale in Latin America", in: *Public Choice*, forthcoming.

Warriner, D. (1969), *Land Reform in Theory and Practice*, Oxford: Clarendon Press.

Weisman, S.R. (2002), *The Great Tax Wars*, New York: Simon and Schuster.

Wicksell, K. (1896), *Finanztheoretische Untersuchungen nebst Darstellung and Kritik des Steuerwesens Schwedens*, Jena: Gustav Fischer.

Youngman, J. (2002), "Enlarging the Property Tax Debate – Regressivity and Fairness", *State Tax Notes*, October 7, pp. 45-52.

DISCUSSANT COMMENTS

MICHAEL RUSHTON
Andrew Young School of Policy Studies, Georgia State University.

ALM AND WALLACE[1], EDMISTON AND FOX, MALME AND YOUNGMAN, AND BIRD, MARTINEZ-VAZQUEZ, AND TORGLER

This session includes papers on some specific problems, and various methods that have been proposed for dealing with them, for the individual income tax, for the value-added tax (VAT) and the property tax, respectively, and a paper on some of the larger issues surrounding optimal tax effort.

James Alm and Sally Wallace focus on the broad question of the form of the personal income tax should take in developing countries. They advocate a scheduler approach, where each income flow is subject to a separate rate schedule, on a broad base with limited credits and that the tax can be collected at the source to lower compliance and administrative costs.

In Jamaica the individual income tax is characterized by large levels of avoidance and evasion. Taxpayers commonly use allowances, reorganization from corporate to noncorporate, or in the case of self-employed individuals simply do not report or underreport income to minimize their tax burden and the government has implemented few policies to combat these avoidance strategies. In addition, lack of data impedes a systematic and comprehensive analysis of the income tax system: basic information such as the number of taxpayers and tax liabilities is not readily available. The overall effect of these issues is that the current distribution of the tax is difficult to determine, although analysis for past years indicate that it is regressive.

One of the points that Alm and Wallace make is that several Caribbean nations have no income tax which raises the question: why does Jamaica have an individual income tax? Why is an income tax appropriate in this country? Would another revenue source be more appropriate given the challenges inherent in implementing the income tax in Jamaica? Are problems with avoidance and evasion inherent in other taxes also?

Kelly Edmiston and William Fox consider four issues that commonly arise with VATs: how to set the threshold for which traders will be exempt from the system; how to avoid distortions from differential treatment of internationally traded goods; how to tax financial services; and how to administer a VAT in a federation without border controls on internal trade between sub-national jurisdictions.

Although their paper deals specifically with the VAT, each of the four challenging practical issues they raise applies to any system of indirect taxation. The authors are right to say that while the VAT of theory is a beautiful tax, to find its value as an option for developing countries we need to consider the VAT as it can actually be administered. However, this is also true of the alternatives to a VAT, whether a different broad-based sales tax or increased reliance on direct taxes, excises, or other sources of government revenue, and it is to these alternatives that the VAT-in-practice should be compared.

Each of the four VAT issues considered presents in some form the trade-off between which design would, in theory, generate the minimum excess burden, and the administrative and compliance costs of implementing these designs. Administration and compliance costs are very country-specific, and so we would expect different outcomes from solving the trade-off in different countries even if the tax design were optimal in each place.

On each of the issues it would be helpful if we could know more about the magnitudes involved. For example, when setting the threshold for tax-exempt traders, the nature of the efficiency / administrative cost trade-off is well-understood, but for each country the details will be very different. Agriculture in Kyrgyzstan, to take their example, has a unique set of parameters involving the typical size of a single farm and the opportunities for the benefits that arise from forming cooperatives. We are agreed that it is a bad thing to discourage efficient horizontal and vertical integration, but do we know enough about the relevant magnitudes to be able to provide useful advice? On the other hand, for all the between-country differences, there are at least hints that some places have the threshold level wrong. Even without knowing many details of the economic structure of Malawi and of Guinea, it is difficult to imagine they are so different as to justify the threshold for value-added tax in Guinea being 134 times as large as the threshold in Malawi.

The same need for some relevant magnitudes applies to the problems of VAT and international trade. Trade distortions arise not from the VAT of theory but from the VAT of practice where some firms are exempt, where firms are forced to bear a financing cost (often in countries with very imperfect capital markets) due to lack of timely payment by government of input tax credits (sometimes by design rather than by the ordinary time lags from bureaucracy), and where the vigilance of tax enforcement is higher for traded goods. In practice how would a VAT compare to a retail sales tax?

When we turn to the treatment of financial services under a VAT, we find that the issue is complicated by the lack of agreement on what would constitute, even in pure theory absent administrative and compliance costs, an optimal design. Edmiston and Fox, after reviewing the debate amongst economists, recommend that for countries where tax administration is weak, exemption of financial services is the most sensible option. It would be interesting to link the problem of taxing financial services with the issue of setting the firm-size threshold for exemption discussed earlier. How would exemption of financial institutions affect the potential integration between financial and other firms? Furthermore, in an era of expansion of global banking, what are the implications of differential treatment of financial services across countries?

The final issue in the paper is how to run a VAT at the sub-national level that combines some autonomy for sub-national jurisdictions in setting the tax rates and bases with the absence of border controls at sub-national boundaries. The key political questions surround how much fiscal autonomy is desired, or required, for the sub-national jurisdictions, and how those jurisdictions are able to cooperate in administration. On the economic side we need to know the propensity for consumers to travel between jurisdictions in search of lower VAT rates. In addition, if a VAT causes the amount of distortion of international trade that some economists have suggested, will it distort trade patterns within a federation? Consider the Canadian case, as discussed in Hill and Rushton (1993). The VAT introduced at the national level failed to win the (necessary) approval of all provincial governments for a sub-national VAT, in part because the federal government was not willing to entertain variations in rate and base across provinces, and also in part because savvy provincial premiers were not willing to adopt a tax that had proven to be so unpopular with voters nationally. Canada has a population dispersed enough that cross-border shopping by consumers is not a significant issue. But it does have one province, Alberta, that is rich enough from natural resource revenues that it alone among provinces does not apply any sales tax at all. Suppose the other nine provinces all agreed to a VAT system, allowing different rates and bases, and to be administered as a "dual VAT." If most provinces chose a tax rate in the range of 7 percent, but Alberta had none, would inter-provincial trade be distorted, contrary to the neutrality of the VAT in theory? And how would any distortion compare to existing distortions arising from Alberta's neighboring provinces applying retail sales taxes, with not insignificant taxation of business inputs?

The value-added tax looks like something a team of economists might dream up; it is a consumption tax that is designed to minimize excess burden, is not obviously inequitable, and with the credit-invoice method comes with built-in provisions to aid in tax enforcement. The property tax, on the other hand, predates modern microeconomic theory, and as Joan Youngman and Jane Malme tell us, the property tax in all its varieties remains a controversial means of raising revenue.

That the property tax is used in so many places as an important source of local government revenue tells us that there must be something efficient about the choice. Not efficient in George Stigler's (1992) sense that *anything* that lasts as a policy – even subsidy of the sugar industry – is efficient since if it is not it would have been replaced as a policy, nor efficient in the sense of modern optimal tax theory. But efficient in the sense that given the multiple goals of the local tax system - a stable source of revenue with low evasion applied to an immobile factor of production, no obviously large excess burden, a degree of horizontal and vertical equity, visibility, relatively straightforward administration, some degree of taxation according to benefits received from the municipality, and an independent revenue source, and hence some accountability and responsibility for local governments – the property tax is, in layman's terms, pretty good.

Both the paper by Youngman and Malme and the paper by Richard Bird, Jorge Martinez and Benno Torgler describe growing opposition to the property tax in the United States, and the latter paper worries about the anti-property tax rhetoric spilling over into poor countries that could really benefit from an efficient property tax at the local level. But is the situation as bad as all that? Bahl and Linn (1992) warn against the pitfall in urban tax design of aiming at more policy targets than there are arrows in the property tax quiver, but the argument made in this paper is that the targets might be, luckily, quite well aligned.

Youngman and Malme describe the widespread adoption of property taxes for local revenues in transition economies, and this is telling. For all we can say about the efficiency, equity and administrative aspects of different revenue sources, there always remains that hard-to-describe aspect about whether the tax will be accepted by the population at large as an acceptable means of public finance. That so many transition economies, without a long history of property taxation and its relationship to responsible local government, would choose to adopt it as a primary source of local revenues perhaps tells us in North America that for all the problems we might raise about the property tax it is difficult to think of sound alternatives. And in an era when other factors of production are increasingly mobile, taxes on land and buildings become even more attractive as a local tax base.

They note that in the transition countries there is not the degree of local independence in taxation found in North America, and that shares of central taxes are the largest source of local revenue. But with pressures for continued devolution we might expect that to change over time.

The key policy issue for the property tax is how the base should be defined, where the goals are efficiency in land use and investment in improvements, equity, and administrative feasibility. It is interesting to compare the idea that land should be taxed according to the value of its "highest and best use" with the literature on the optimal income tax. The optimal income tax problem begins with the assumption that we cannot possibly observe the value of an individual's highest and best use of time in terms of current potential earnings, much less what might come about from investment in human capital, and so we search for a second-best optimal tax applied to actual earnings. Land does not have the ability humans have to conceal potential value when used optimally, although observation by tax administrators will still be something less than perfect.

The final paper of the session, by Bird, Martinez, and Torgler, serves to remind us that we cannot think of tax policy independently of the uses of the public funds, and the political and legal institutions that will govern how decisions on public finance will be made. The authors confine themselves to positive political economy, recognizing but putting aside the normative question of whether developing countries are under-taxed relative to some optimum.

What determines tax effort? The authors tell us that what we observe across countries is determined at least in part by the "demand" for taxes by a public that evaluates the capabilities of its government to deliver services and redistribution in an effective and fair way, as well as the more traditional "supply" factors such as "tax handles". Of course it is impossible to find measures of the political environment that are easily generalized across countries, and we can likely expect much further research on the issue of the size of government as more data becomes available (see Becker and Mulligan (2003) for a similar analysis but one that highlights competition between political interest groups).

An interesting extension of this line of research will be to see how the tax structure itself is related to the level of tax effort. Suppose we predict that greater reliance on what we would normally consider efficient tax bases will be associated with greater tax effort. If a politically influential segment of the public is concerned that government is a leviathan in waiting, it might prefer an inefficient tax mix in order to restrain the size of government. Would tax-averse voters in the US ever give approval to a VAT at the federal government level, even if at its introduction other taxes, with higher marginal deadweight costs, were reduced an amount designed to provide revenue-neutrality? In practice, tax structure and tax effort are jointly determined.

But given the econometric challenges that anyone working in this area faces, and that we are still not even certain in the profession about the magnitude of deadweight costs of different taxes (Feldstein, 1997), for now our answers to the question of whether institutions are producing a good tax mix and a good level of tax effort, where "good" is defined as being consistent with some reasonable aggregation of citizens' preferences, are going to depend on our intuition regarding whether political institutions are efficient in this "good" sense (see Wittman (1989) for reasons to believe democracies are efficient).

Each of the three papers in this session deals with the effective impact of various taxes as they are implemented in actual bureaucracies, political frameworks, and economic and social institutions. Their value is not only to tax practitioners in developed and developing economies, but also in highlighting what should be fruitful avenues for further economic research.

Notes

1. Dagney Faulk provided these comments on the Alm and Wallace paper.

References

Bahl, Roy W. and Johannes F. Linn (1992), *Urban Public Finance in Developing Countries*, Oxford: Oxford University Press for the World Bank.

Becker, Gary S. and Casey B. Mulligan (2003), "Deadweight Costs and the Size of Government", *Journal of Law and Economics*, Vol. 46, pp. 293-340.

Feldstein, Martin (1997), "How Big Should Government Be?", *National Tax Journal*, Vol. 50, pp. 197-213.

Hill, Roderick and Michael Rushton (1993), "Harmonizing Provincial Sales Taxes with the GST: The Problem of International Trade", *Canadian Tax Journal*, Vol. 41, pp. 101-122.

Stigler, George J. (1992), "Law or Economics?", *Journal of Law and Economics*, Vol. 35, pp. 455-68.

Wittman, Donald (1989), "Why Democracies Produce Efficient Results", *Journal of Political Economy*, Vol. 97, pp. 1395-1424.

5

DOING IT! THE POLITICAL AND ADMINISTRATIVE DIMENSIONS OF TAX REFORM

Chapter 13

EXPLAINING TAX REFORM

WALTER HETTICH* AND STANLEY L. WINER**,[1]
*Department of Economics, California State University at Fullerton; **School of Public Policy and Department of Economics, Carleton University, Ottawa

1. INTRODUCTION

A recent headline in the *Los Angeles Times* warned readers to "beware of the ides of April". The writer, somewhat tongue in cheek, had chosen this title to refer to April 15, the date for filing income tax returns. Although he had misappropriated the Latin term ("the ides" referred to the 15th of March, May, July or October in the ancient Roman calendar), he achieved his intended purpose of linking taxation to a somewhat ominous feeling. There is no doubt that many look on taxation with the kind of foreboding that seems associated with "the ides". (Romans also used the word to refer to the 13th day of all remaining months.)

Economic analysts generally have a more dispassionate attitude toward the subject. They are interested primarily in studying the effects of taxation on individual behavior and market prices, and in describing the distributional effects of tax policies. When the discussion turns to changes in the tax system, however, positive analysis may be replaced by advocacy of particular alternatives. This is illustrated by the frequent use of the word "reform" in the literature, a term usually employed to refer to changes designed to make the system better, where "better" is judged in relation to some ideal standard.

We take a different approach in this paper. It is based on an analysis that views tax policies as equilibrium outcomes of a well specified political and economic system, where information problems for participants are of great importance. As in other areas of economic life, existing equilibria can be disturbed by outside forces. Shocks can upset the existing balance and cause readjustments toward a new solution that is again consistent with all the relevant influences. This leads us to expect a variety of recurring changes and adjustments over time in the ways that individuals and organizations are taxed.

When alterations in tax systems are seen as responses by political decision makers to exogenous shocks, they can be studied and explained in much the same manner as other economic changes or realignments. We can form hypotheses on how and when tax change occurs and can test them empirically with reference to statistical data. Furthermore, a somewhat different terminology from the one generally employed becomes appropriate: it becomes more accurate to talk of *tax change*, rather than *reform,* since the latter word relates primarily to the redesign of tax systems motivated by normative concerns.

Once we start looking for them, we discover that significant alterations in tax systems are a ubiquitous phenomenon, whether we are interested in the distant past or in comparisons across modern countries. For recent examples, we can turn to the websites of major international organizations, where a search will turn up a variety of publications describing recent tax history, in countries as diverse as Switzerland, Poland, Bolivia, Korea and Indonesia.

Although some studies of recent tax 'reform' suggest factors that may have caused the observed policy adjustments, they only rarely use a framework where tax changes are treated as endogenous responses. Political economy models suitable for this task are not used widely as yet in this literature. The present paper tries to move the discussion in this direction. We start by suggesting a descriptive model of tax change that distinguishes among different types of policy responses to outside shocks. We then speculate about the effects of a decline in the costs of international transactions and of international institutional arrangements in this framework. Next, the discussion is expanded to the nature of different constitutional regimes and to their influence on the type and frequency of responses.

We also discuss a second and somewhat different approach to empirical research. This work emphasizes that changes in the tax system must be politically feasible. Since policy proposals will only be adopted and implemented if they have sufficient support by voters and politicians, the research attempts to evaluate whether different 'reform' proposals are consistent with a given or existing political equilibrium.

2. A DESCRIPTIVE MODEL OF IMPLEMENTATION AND REFORM

A good place to begin any discussion of why tax reforms look the way they do is with an understanding of tax systems as equilibrium structures in a political economy, and with the information and coordination problems that face all policy makers in such environments. In confronting these problems, it should be noted, elected officials, bureaucrats and academics are very much alike.

The feasibility of designing and implementing policy plans in the face of information costs are classic questions in social science. The traditional debate was concerned primarily with the choice between central planning and allocation by market forces. Among the most influential ideas in this debate were those of Friedrich Hayek (1945), who argued that only decentralized markets could solve the information problem in a world beset by continual changes in the economic environment. They do this, it was argued, by allowing each economic agent to economize on the information necessary to reach an optimizing decision, while at the same time insuring that in the aggregate, individual plans are consistent and socially efficient.

The historical debate points in a particular direction if one's objective is to construct a framework for understanding how tax systems are in practice chosen and implemented and how they evolve in a competitive political system. The debate suggests that an effective approach for politicians to policy design and implementation will be to decentralize policy making into separate, semi-independent areas. Such segmentation allows specialization in the production of knowledge, and also permits the mobilization of special interests to provide valuable information as part of their attempts to influence policy choices.[2]

In fact, the study of policy making in modern societies indicates that decentralization of policy areas is a common feature of democratic government.[3] While the apparent lack of coordination that results is often decried by economic analysts, this may in fact represent a rational response to information problems associated with the problems of managing complex policy structures. Decisions on taxation and expenditures are taken separately at the political level, and implemented by different administrative bodies, while periodic budget resolutions or politically motivated ministerial or presidential directives are used to maintain broad overall coordination. As far as taxation is concerned, further decentralization of policy making and administration tends to occur in accordance with major tax bases. Moreover, tax commissions and tax reform are usually directed at selected parts of the revenue structure.

To fully understand the nature of tax policy and tax 'reform' in the presence of information costs then, it appears necessary to examine the benefits and costs associated with the segmentation of policy making, and to relate this sort of governance structure to the provision and processing of information necessary for effective policy.

If we go down this path, as we do below, it will be necessary to keep in mind that we are thinking about decision making by governments and politicians engaged in the struggle for political office, and about bureaucrats advising political representatives. Thus the relevant information problems that policy makers face stem from continual change on relevant political as well as economic margins.

A representation of the political calculus when information and coordination costs matter

To begin a more formal discussion, we consider the nature of the equilibrium fiscal system in a competitive political economy. Subsequently we introduce problems of information and coordination that arise in the making of tax and other policies.

In a political equilibrium, the marginal political costs of further reliance on any particular alternative tax source will be equalized across sources, and the common marginal political cost per dollar of revenue will be equal to the marginal political benefit of raising one more dollar and spending it on pubic goods and services (Hettich and Winer, 1988, 1999 chapter 3). Schematically we can illustrate such an equilibrium as follows:

(1) $MPC_i \,/\,)T_i = MPB_G \ , \ i=1,2.....I$ or

(1a) $MPC_i = MPB_G \ X \ )T_i \ , \quad i=1,2.....I$

where MPC_i is the marginal loss of political support (or expected votes) from a small rise in the rate of tax levied on base or activity i, $)T_i$ is the amount of tax revenue that results from this marginal adjustment in tax policy, and MPB_G is the marginal benefit of spending one more dollar on public services. This is a very simple representation of an equilibrium fiscal system, but it will suffice for our purposes.

In order to introduce information and coordination problems in this setting, it is useful to decompose the right and left sides of condition (1a), assuming that it is possible to distinguish impacts of a short-run, distributional nature from the longer-run allocative effects of taxation resulting from tax-induced changes in private behavior. On the left hand side, we may think of a decision to increase reliance on a particular tax base as having three distinct effects on electoral support:

(i) an impact effect on political support, reflecting the short run, primarily distributional consequences for voters of a change in the tax rate, holding the level of all tax bases constant;

(ii) a direct effect on support that results from the consequences of decline in the size of the tax base in question; and

(iii) a general equilibrium or indirect effect on support that depends on the nature and the consequences of substitution towards tax bases not directly subject to the rate increase.

Concerning the right hand side of (1a), we can decompose the change in tax revenue following a small increase in the tax rate into two parts:

(i) a direct effect on tax revenue that occurs when all taxable activities other than the immediately affected base are held constant; and
(ii) a general equilibrium or indirect effect on tax revenue that takes account of the implications for total revenues caused by substitutions away from the activity that is more highly taxed.

Using the above decompositions, condition (1a) can then be re-written as:[4]

(2) *MPC= [impact effect on support+direct effect on support+ indirect effect on support]*

= MPB X [direct effect on tax revenue + indirect effect on tax revenue]

where the second term in square brackets in the second line of (2) is the term [$)T_i$] in equation (1a).

Finally in specifying this simple model, we shall think of the tax instruments for each tax base i (including rates structures, special provisions and the exact definition of taxable activity) as being assigned to a separate group of 'experts' in a Ministry or Treasury. Each group will be assumed to be fully informed about the impact, direct and indirect effects of a change in the instruments under their control, but to have no information about or control over impact, direct and the general equilibrium effects caused by tax instruments assigned to other departments. This stylized framework is intended to represent a situation where decentralization of the policy making process allows specialization in information acquisition, while at the same time creating a problem of coordinating semi-autonomous policy makers.

In a world where information and coordination problems are absent, all the effects represented in the decomposition (2) will be fully taken into account by politicians and their tax officials. In a world where such costs are considerable, however, institutional arrangements will arise within the tax policy process that lead to complete or partial neglect of some of the effects. In that case, the decomposition in (2) provides a useful basis for categorizing the types of tax 'reform' or tax changes that we may expect to observe.

A taxonomy of 'reforms'

In the above framework we can identify different types of reforms, depending on the nature of exogenous shocks and the time frame of our investigation. Reforms in this framework will be of four, and possibly more, distinct types: technical, coordinating, comprehensive and strategic. These reforms are distinguished by the nature of the exogenous shocks that precede them, by the types of information and coordination issues that are involved, and by the time frame involved.

Shocks that are small in magnitude, or which affect only particular activities can be handled by *technical reform*, at least in the short run. This will involve prediction about the impact and direct economic and revenue effects of particular taxes, and can be handled within each tax department without the need for major interdepartmental coordination. Indirect or general equilibrium consequences of taxation are not usually involved.

Technical reform, often implemented by regulation rather than by explicit legislation, will be continual, because minor shocks to the economy are always occurring. Personal income tax codes for example, including the set of regulations that are used to refine the definition of income subject to tax, are in a constant state of flux in all countries where this tax is an important part of revenue structure.

Coordinating reform involves two or more tax bases, and may result from larger shocks that will usually have general equilibrium consequences for support and revenue. Coordinating reform may also result from a series of technical reforms that gradually encroach on the 'territory' of two or more branches of the treasury.

Coordinating reform may also arise as a result of the links between taxation and other policy instruments such as regulation, where other departments controlling the non-tax instrument are involved. Few Americans were surprised, for example, when former President Clinton took credit in 1996 for passing an increase in the minimum wage jointly with a package of tax measures designed to alleviate the impact of higher wages on small business. Voters expect and accept compromises of this sort as a valid expression of the democratic process, regardless of whether they favor or oppose a particular policy. One should note that this example also shows that a full understanding of tax change requires the consideration of how shocks emanating from other parts of government reverberate in the treasury.

The distinction between coordinating reform and *comprehensive reform* is not as tightly drawn as the difference between technical and coordinating reform. A comprehensive reform could also be described as a big coordinating reform. The entire tax system is considered, usually reluctantly in view of the difficulties of compensation that such big policy studies are forced to deal with. As coordinating reform can result from a sequence of technical reforms, so comprehensive reform may emerge over a decade or more from a sequence of coordinating reforms. General equilibrium or indirect effects are of key importance in this type of tax change, which are usually preceded by blue-ribbon panels of experts who work for substantial periods on redesign of major parts of the system.

Finally, it may be worthwhile to single out a type of reform that can be used in the context of international competition for business investment, which we label *strategic reform*. The issue here is not how the tax base is designed or administered so much as the implications of effective rates of tax, however levied, on mobile taxpayers and their capital. It is obvious in this case that a reform of the corporate tax rate is really nothing more than a change in a rate of tax designed to attract activity, and not a 'reform' in any sense that this word is used in the extant normative tax literature such as that reviewed by Hettich and Winer (1999, chapter 5).

Globalization, its associated tax changes and the role of international institutions

It is interesting to consider the effects of a major shock on tax reform using the framework outlined above. Suppose, for example, that the cost of international transaction of various kinds declines substantially, a shock that may be referred to as globalization.

The direct effect of this shock is to make the corporate tax base more elastic. Consistent with the empirical models of tax structure (Hettich and Winer 1984, Becker and Mulligan 1998, Kenny and Winer 2003), we will find tax change occurring as politicians respond by lowering corporate tax rates, and shifting the tax mix towards less mobile bases such as consumption, of course at the political expense of certain distributional and allocative effects that were being pursued before the shock occurred. Since corporate and personal income taxation is linked for high income earners, personal tax rate structures will be flattened in the face of threatened arbitrage between corporate and personal forms of income. Coordinating reform is clearly required.

Lost revenue is partly made up by shifting to less mobile bases such as consumption, as noted earlier. In addition, some base broadening may occur, though the income taxes remain essentially complex. Finally, there may be a net downward pressure on the size of the public sectors depending on the extent to which tax instruments are substitutable in equilibrium.

All of this is born out in what has actually happened over the past two decades in most developed countries (see Profeta 2004 for a recent discussion and similar interpretation of what has happened in E.U. countries). There have been many coordinating reforms over the last twenty years involving both personal and corporate taxation.

It is also interesting in this context to ask why developed countries that have followed this general pattern have done so while maintaining substantial differences in effective corporate rates, as are illustrated in Table 1 from Wilson (2001).

Table 1. Effective Tax Rates (in percent) for Domestic Firms in G-7 Countries, 1996 and 2001

Manufacturing			**Services**	
	1996	**2001**	**1996**	**2001**
Canada	23.5	23.4	29.0	28.3
US	23.8	23.6	25.0	24.8
UK	19.4	17.2	19.2	17.2
Germany	38.0	21.1	37.5	20.8
France	25.3	23.2	27.9	25.8
Italy	31.6	18.1	35.5	21.4
Japan	31.6	22.6	33.1	24.0
Sweden	14.4	14.4	14.2	14.2
Ireland	4.2	4.2	4.2	4.2
(2)			8.7	4.3
(3)			16.2	9.1

Source: Adapted from Table 1 in Wilson (2001).

Notes

1. To single out the tax impact, it is assumed that the interest rate and inflation rate are 6.8% and 1.4% respectively across countries and periods.
2. The Canadian METR for the service sector in 2001 is corresponding, respectively, to the federal CIT rate of 28.12% (including the 4% surtax), combined with the weighted average provincial CIT rate of 14.15%.
3. The German METR for 2001 reflect the federal CIT reduction from the current 40% to 25%, starting in January 2001. The municipal trade tax (16.66% on average) and the solidarity surcharge (5.5%) will still apply.
4. The general CIT rate in Ireland was 32% in 1996, 24% in 2000 and 20% in 2001. A lower rate of 10% is applicable for manufacturing and the international tradable service sector (I.e., financial service sector), to which a corresponding METR of 4.2% is shown in Case (1). Case (2) is for hotel services which is subject to the general CIT rate but enjoys a higher tax depreciation rate of 15% for hotel buildings. Case (3) is for other services which subjects to the general CIT rate and tax depreciation allowance.

Ashworth and Heyndels (2003) also ask this question. They use an index of tax shares from various sources for each of the OECD and European Union countries over the period from 1965 to 1995. Using panel data time series techniques, they look for convergence of tax structures to a system wide average, as might be expected in the face of globalization. They find strong evidence of this convergence as far as reliance on corporate taxation is concerned, but not for personal taxation, and attribute the latter result to the immobility of labor. This work indicates that tax 'reform' can be studied from a positive perspective, and such work bolsters the view we are presenting: that what looks like reform is in most cases a response of a political equilibrium to exogenous shocks.

Reductions in transactions costs that lead to international competition have also lead to reactions by the international community of nations. Institutions such as the WTO are increasingly important in constraining national policy choices so as to manage (that is, to harmonize or to attenuate, depending on one's viewpoint) international competition. This leads to another interesting source of shocks that are exogenous to each country - the international trade ruling. Such rulings may also generate coordinating 'reform', though the countries affected would like a quicker and less painful technical fix if they could get away with it.

An interesting case in point is the recent ruling by the WTO concerning the U.S. tax break for American exporters that establish oversees subsidiaries known as foreign sales corporations, allowing U.S exporters to exclude a portion of foreign sales from the corporate income tax. The WTO ruled in 1999 that this tax provision in the U.S. code is a violation of WTO rules subject to retaliation by the complaining European Union countries. The U.S tried to fix the matter with a technical reform but the revised provision was rejected by the WTO in 2002.(See Vieth, 2003). Now E.U. countries are preparing to levy retaliatory tariffs of substantial magnitude.

As Peter Morici of the University of Maryland reputedly put it, the problem for the U.S now is: "You cannot get rid of [the offending] provision without redesigning the entire corporate tax. Once you get involved in that, it becomes a major piece of legislation." [5] If such legislation were to be drawn up and passed by Congress, should we refer to it as tax reform, or as tax change?

3. INSTITUTIONS AND TAX CHANGE

When outside forces disturb equilibrium, adjustment occurs. The government, or politicians seeking office, will propose policies to redress the imbalance. These may be minor in nature or involve coordinating or even comprehensive reform. Proposals may also have strategic elements related to the political process by which they must be adopted.

Readjustment and policy change occur in an existing institutional framework. Although institutions can be changed if needed, this will require greater effort and call for the creation of a larger consensus. As a result, tax change generally occurs within the channels of existing institutional arrangements and is influenced by current institutional design.

The influence of institutions on “tax reform” can be seen most readily if we study the impact of constitutional restrictions that govern the political process relevant to tax policy. A comparison of tax change in countries that have similar economic structures, but that differ in constitutional design, is particularly instructive in this regard. In this paper, we choose the federal governments of the United States and Canada as objects of comparison, but the major conclusions can be generalized to a variety of countries having arrangements that result either in more centralized or in more diffused decision making power. (For further discussion of the relevant literature, see for example the survey in Kirchgaessner 2002).

We start the description of policy making in Canada, since it has the more direct policy process than the United States, relying on Hartle (1982) and Breton (1996) and others for institutional detail. Proposals are made and passed by the party in power, which generally has a majority in Parliament. They are formulated by a professional cadre of public servants in the Department of Finance and presented by the Minister of Finance to Cabinet, where they must be approved. Policy is subject to tight security over information until relevant legislation is introduced in Parliament. Although some parliamentary committees exist that may review tax proposals, they lack the power to make substantive alterations. All participants in the process are aware that the government's intentions on important matters will prevail. After policy is passed in the House, matters are decided, since the Senate almost never exercises its power of postponement. In fact, tax changes effectively become law at the time they are proposed to Parliament and are rarely changed subsequently, except for technical adjustments or 'reforms'.

The centralized policy process gives the Minister of Finance and his team significant power, allowing him to set the agenda and to select specific policy responses. In designing policies, members of the minister's team will be aware of potential reactions by heads of other departments and will try to anticipate and avoid opposition at the cabinet level. Similarly, they will be aware of likely responses by major interest groups. Nevertheless, the minister and his team of experts have a crucial and determining influence on how tax policy is formulated, chosen and passed.

The decision making process in the United States is much more diffused (see for example, Pechman 1987). Although the President generally sends tax legislation to the House of Representatives, it is expected that his proposals will be altered significantly by Congress. There will be extensive public hearings, and much of the bill will be rewritten in committee before it reaches the floor. After the much revised version of the bill is sent to the Senate, a new set of hearings starts. When passed, the Senate bill may have substantive differences from the one adopted in the House, differences that will have to be reconciled in conference committee. Often, the bill that is sent to the President for signature has only a tenuous similarity to what was originally proposed to Congress by the White House. Moreover, Congress has the power to originate tax bills, a power given by the constitution to the House of Representatives. And even the Senate may enter the game by attaching important tax provisions to bills dealing primarily with other matters and thus become a center where tax policy originates.

Unlike in Canada, where the team of the Minister of Finance and budget secrecy (which makes it difficult for cabinet members to form alliances that challenge the Minister of Finance and the Prime Minister) play central roles, the policy process in the United States allows for participation by many actors. In the executive, the Bureau of the Budget and the Treasury have significant roles in setting the agenda. In Congress, committees have major power to rewrite and influence legislation. During the process, interest groups get the chance to give information and to apply pressure, both in the executive and in Congress, where extensive negotiations on specific details take place. The process is more open than in a parliamentary system, but it is also much more costly in terms of time and of resources. While governments in a parliamentary setting have strong power over legislation between elections, this power is more diffused in presidential systems where power is shared on a more continuing basis over time.

As a result, tax change in the United States system of checks and balances involves much greater transactions costs in terms of lobbying and coordination. We should therefore expect more rapid and frequent change to occur in Canada in the face of similar shocks hitting the two economies. Winer and Hettich (1999, chapter 11) have shown this to be so for a period in the 1970s. There seems no reason why such an investigation could not be extended to encompass other electoral and legislative systems in the European Union for example. Some work surveyed by Kirchgaessner (2002) concerning the financing of budget deficits in divided or fragmented governing coalitions suggests that institutional arrangements do matter in the determination of equilibrium fiscal policy choices. The work of Steinmo (1993) on tax systems in Sweden, the United Kingdom and the United States also confirms the suspicion that institutions matter. But the role of institutions in shaping tax 'reform' has not been studied in much detail so far.

4. THE SUSTAINABILITY OF POLICY REFORMS: AN ALTERNATIVE APPROACH

Existing political arrangements will limit the type of proposals that can be adopted through democratic choice. Another approach to empirical work tries to determine the boundaries of the feasible set of tax changes for given electoral and legislative institutions. One may note that experienced tax policy analysts often make calculations of this nature in an informal manner. We are suggesting that it be done more formally in the tax policy process.

Recent research suggests that such calculations can be formalized and based on explicit models of political equilibrium.

For example, in the field of pension policy Galasso and Profeta (2004) consider the effects of aging on the nature of the social security system in OECD countries. Aging has an economic effect represented by a rising dependency ratio, and a political effect leading to pension systems that are more generous as people generally, and the electorate in particular, become older. Using numerical simulations, they look for policies that are better able to deal with the tension between these forces, and they suggest that increasing the retirement age will be more acceptable to the electorate than a cut in benefits. This is because the former policy mitigates the adverse economic consequences of both the economic and political forces.[6]

Similarly, Uebelmesser (2004) determines the latest point in time when a majority of voters would favor a reform to cut pension generosity. Her calculations indicate that Italy has only a year or two remaining, while Germany and France become what she calls gerontocracies in 2012 and 2014 respectively. In work on female retirement, Buetler (2002) uses data from Swiss referenda to test an empirical model that predicts support for and opposition to the extension of the retirement age.

In earlier work, Rutherford and Winer (1990) suggest different metrics that could be used to measure the 'distance' of a proposed tax policy from that in the existing political equilibrium in a computable equilibrium model. Such metrics are required for a more formal statement concerning the acceptability or democratic feasibility of alternative proposals for change.

5. CONCLUSIONS

Tax systems are best thought of as equilibrium outcomes constrained by a particular governance structure and the nature of the market economy. They can be studied theoretically and empirically as such. Tax reform, or more accurately, tax change, is the natural outcome of shocks in this equilibrium framework. Shocks may have a narrowly political origin, as when the incumbent party loses to the opposition in a polarized political system, or an economic origin. In the latter case, the resulting changes in tax systems will be continual, and of varying magnitude and scope.

We have suggested a way of categorizing the types of tax change that can be observed, beginning with a consideration of the information and coordination problems that all policy makers face. From this perspective, we should expect cycles of reform to occur, proceeding from technical to coordinating to comprehensive reform over a period lasting one or two decades, and depending on the nature of shocks bequeathed by history.

In summary, it is possible to study tax reform or tax change in an evolving political equilibrium as a positive enterprise. Although empirical research in the area is still in its infancy, a sufficient body of work exists to provide guidance and confirmation that such work is worthwhile. Research can be carried out in a formal statistical manner or less formally using historical investigation. Further work on political sustainability and work comparing different institutions and countries appears particularly promising.

Notes

1. Winer wishes to thank the Canada-United States Fulbright Foundation for support, and the Department of Economics and the Center for the Study of Democracy at U.C. Irvine for their hospitality during the Winter and Spring of 2004.
2. Note that even the theory of optimal taxation assumes that policy making is decentralized by separating the theory of taxation from the determination of public expenditures, although this is not usually justified by reference to the information problem.
3. A decentralized tax policy process may also be called a 'piecemeal' process. For an early discussion of the advantages of piecemeal policy making in taxation, see Bird (1970, 455-457).
4. A more complete mathematical derivation of equation (2) is provided in Hettich and Winer (1999, chapter 6).
5. According to the *Los Angeles Times* (Richard Simon, May 12, 2004), the Senate approved corporate tax legislation on May 11, that repealed the export subsidies and replaced them with new tax breaks, primarily for manufacturers. The bill also contained tax concessions to promote energy conservation and production. It remains to be seen whether this legislation, when passed and signed into law, will satisfy the WTO, or whether the trade organization will raise new objections.
6. This paper as well as the one discussed immediately below uses a modified median voter (or median cohort) model, which is likely to be incomplete when a multi-dimensional redistributive issue like pension reform is being discussed. The work is capable of being generalized in this respect.

References

Ashworth, John and Bruno Heyndels (2003), Are Tax Structures Converging in the Long Term, Paper presented at the IIPF Congress, Linz Austria, August 2002, Revised, University of Durham.

Becker, Gary S. and Casey B. Mulligan (1998), *Deadweight Costs and the Size of Government, NBER Working Paper 6789.*

Bird, Richard (1970), "The Tax Kaleidoscope: Perspectives on Tax Reform in Canada", *Canadian Tax Foundation*, Vol 18(5), pp. 444-473.

Breton, Albert (1996), *Competitive Governments: An Economic Theory of Politics and Public Finance*, Cambridge University Press.

Buetler, Monika (2002), "The Political Feasibility of Increasing the Retirement Age: Lessons from a Ballot on the Female Retirement Age", *International Tax and Public Finance*, Vol. 9, pp. 331-348.

Galasso, Vincenzo and Paola Profeta (2004), "Lessons for an Aging Society: The Political Sustainability of Social Security Systems", *Economic Policy*, April, pp. 63-115.

Hartle, Douglas G. (1982), *The Revenue Budget Process of the Government of Canada: Description, Appraisal and Proposals, Tax Paper No. 67*, Toronto: The Canadian Tax Foundation.

Hayek, F.A. (1945), "The Use Of Knowledge in Society", *American Economic Review*, Vol. 35(4).

Hettich, Walter and Stanley L. Winer (1984), "A Positive Model of Tax Structure", *Journal of Public Economics*, Vol. 24(1), pp. 64-87.

Hettich, Walter and Stanley L. Winer (1988), "Economic and Political Foundations of Tax Structure", *American Economic Review*, Vol. 78(4), pp. 701-712.

Hettich, Walter and Winer, Stanley L. (1999), *Democratic Choice and Taxation: A Theoretical and Empirical Analysis*, Cambridge MA: Cambridge University Press.

Kenny, Lawrence W. and Stanley L. Winer (2003), "Tax Systems in the World: An Empirical Investigation into the Importance of Tax Bases, Collection Costs, and Political Regime", Carleton Economic Papers, Retrieved from www.ssrn.com.

Kirchgaessner, Gebhard (2002), "The Effects of Fiscal Institutions on Public Finance: A Survey of the Empirical Evidence", pp. 145-177 in: S. Winer and H. Shibata, editors, *Political Economy and Public Finance: The Role of Political Economy in the Theory and Practice of Public Economics*, Cheltenham U.K.: Edward Elgar Publishers.

Pechman, Joseph A. (1987), *Federal Tax Policy*, 5th Edition, Washington D.C.: The Brookings Institution.

Profeta, Paola (2004), "Public Finance and Political Economics in Tax Design and Reforms", pp. 55-75 in: Luigi Bernardi and Paola Profeta, *Tax Systems and Tax Reforms in Europe*, Routledge.

Rutherford, Thomas and Stanley L. Winer (1990), *Endogenous Policy in a Computational General Equilibrium Framework*, *Research Report 9007*, University of Western Ontario, Also Chapter 12 in: S. Winer, *Political Economy in Federal States: Selected Essays of Stanley L. Winer*, Cheltenham U.K.: Edward Elgar

Simon, Richard (2004), "Senate OK's Corporate Tax Overhaul Bill to Settle Trade Dispute", Los Angeles Times, July 14, 2004.

Steinmo, Sven (1993), *Taxation and Democracy: Swedish, British and American Approaches to Financing the Modern State*, New Haven: Yale University Press.

Uebelmesser, Silke (2004), "Political Feasibility of Pension Reforms", Paper presented at the European Public Choice Meetings, Berlin, April.

Vieth, Warren, "E.U. Imposes 1st Tariff Penalties on U.S. Goods", Los Angeles Times, March 2, 2004.

Wilson, Thomas (2001), "Business Taxes: An Evaluation", Paper presented at the Fraser Institute Conference on Tax Reform in Canada, Toronto, October.

Winer, Stanley L. and Walter Hettich (1999), "Information, Co-ordination and Tax Policy Making", pp. 19-42 in: R. Bird and T. Wilson, editors, *Rationality in Public Policy: Retrospect and Prospect; A Tribute to Douglas Hartle*, Toronto: Canadian Tax Foundation.

Winer, Stanley L. and Walter Hettich (2003), "The Political Economy of Taxation: Positive and Normative Analysis When Collective Choice Matters", in: C. Rowley and F. Schneider, editors, *The Encyclopaedia of Public Choice*, Volume 1, Kluwer Academic Publishers.

Chapter 14

IMPLICATIONS OF TAX ADMINISTRATION FOR TAX DESIGN: A TENTATIVE ASSESSMENT

ARINDAM DAS-GUPTA
Goa Institute of Management, India

1. INTRODUCTION AND OVERVIEW

Richard Bird, recently made the following very perceptive comments about what economists know about tax administration[1]

> "We know very little about tax administration.
> There is no 'one size fits all' policy (OSFA).
> 'The devil is in the details'.
> Implementation is as important as design.
> Political will, support and non-interference in operations are indispensable prerequisites."

If his first observation is taken to mean "we probably know quite a bit about tax administration, but what we know is a small fraction of what we need to know", then these five observations accurately describe the extent of knowledge and the likely scope at present for general propositions in the analysis of tax administration.

The objective of this paper is to discuss major aspects of what is known about how tax administration influences tax design. The discussion draws on both theory and practice. Though empirical evidence is also examined where possible, its rarity in relation to tax administration implies that a lot of what is discussed in this paper is what we *think* we know, rather than what we can confidently say we *do* know. The paper's tone is, therefore, tentative: The discussion in this paper may equally well be seen as suggesting hypotheses as part of an agenda for theoretical research and rigorous empirical testing.

In section 2, working definitions of the terms "tax administration" and "tax design" are proposed. The position taken is inclusive, in that all but a small specified set of activities connected with raising tax revenues are taken to fit into either tax administration or tax design. Benchmarks for judging "good" tax administration and tax design are then briefly described.

This discussion serves as a backdrop to an examination of properties of tax administration and their implications for the design of taxes in section 3. These lessons or conjectures are termed "propositions", though they bear little relation to the rigorous propositions of theoretical economics. After presenting three key insights about the impact of administration on the public budget and tax design, another 27 propositions are presented, and support for them from theory, evidence, and practice (and educated guesswork) are reviewed.

Section 4 draws on the analysis of section 3 to attempt to identify important administrative constraints on the design of four major taxes and two cross-cutting areas of tax policy. In Section 5, bearing in mind Richard Bird's observations on the absence of "one-size-fits-all" administration rules and the importance of finer details, an attempt is made to identify sensible process features in designing administration friendly taxes. Section 6 points to some issues not covered in the paper and concludes with a plea for more research.

The paper focuses on how tax administration influences tax policy: It does not examine how tax administration effectiveness and efficiency can be increased through other institutional, incentive and management reforms. An illustrative selection of such reforms are listed in Annex 2.

2. "TAX ADMINISTRATION" AND "TAX DESIGN": WORKING DEFINITIONS

Imagine that in an economy alternative, economically costless, revenues became available to replace tax revenues. Compared to this situation, in principle all activities, organizations and institutions in the economy that would not exist in the absence of taxes fall within the ambit of what may be termed the economy's *tax system*.

Using this definition, the variety of activities in a modern economy's tax system can conceptually be divided into four sets:

First, defining *normal and penal tax rates*, *tax bases*, *tax concessions*, *taxable entities*, *non-compliance penalties* and

> the *timing of tax payments*. This is what is referred to here as *tax design*. Taxes so designed are formalized as laws of the land in tax laws proper, but also in such things as bilateral tax treaties.
>
> Second, the *institutional process* of translating a tax design into law, or what may be termed tax policy institutions. This covers activities such as public debate and discussion, executive branch tax proposals, legislative debate and legislating tax laws. Tax laws themselves are excluded.
>
> Third, *education and research* related to tax systems, both in general and specific to a particular tax system. Academic research and teaching and expert advice to governments are included here. In the intersection between this and the previous set lie government appointed tax commissions. To prevent overlap with tax administration, educating taxable entities of their specific obligations to comply with tax laws, or what is commonly termed taxpayer education, and training government officials who collect taxes about tax laws and procedures should be excluded.
>
> All other activities within an economy's tax system are taken here to fall within the ambit of *tax administration*. Seen in this way, the scope of tax administration is quite large. A partial list of important components of tax administration is in Table 1.

This brief description of tax systems merits three immediate comments: First, there is much cross-country and historical diversity in each of the activity sets and TA components. Second, several components of tax systems, particularly of tax administration as defined here, have not been adequately analysed and studied. Third, there are no adequate estimates of the social cost of raising tax revenue.

Several properties of TA discussed in this paper will pertain to TDs or "tax administration in the narrow sense", since this area has been most widely examined.

What features can be considered desirable and so used as benchmarks when examining tax design and TA? Ideally, a good tax system will form part of a welfare maximizing public budget. Analysis of TA and tax design using such a framework is, however, limited.[2] The standard optimal tax criterion that the tax system should minimizes the welfare loss associated

Table 1. Important Components of Tax Administration

Institutions and Organizations	Role and Function
The "Tax Ministry"	Monitor, forecast and set targets for tax revenue collection. Formulate administrative law which facilitates the implementation of tax law.
The Tax Department(s) (TDs) or tax administration in the narrow sense	Facilitating and enforcing compliance by taxable entities with legislated tax laws. Key taxpayer related activities include Identification of taxable entities, registration, information collection on tax bases with taxable entities, goods and asset valuation, physical checks and searches, investigation, tax liability determination, ensuring payment of tax dues, facilitating compliance via taxpayer education, taxpayer services and grievance redressal, administrative rulings, representation in tax disputes, enforcing compliance, imposing administrative sanctions in case of non-compliance. Key internal activities include Obtaining and deploying labour, capital and managerial resources, organising and motivating staff to administer tax laws, monitoring staff, appointing and coordinating agents in case of outsourced activities, sanctioning unauthorised conduct, reporting to the Minister, coordinating with other TDs (within the economy and in other economies).
Independent audit, anti-corruption and (usually legislative) oversight bodies.	Ensure that the TD discharges its functions in accordance with the law ("effectively") and at the lowest possible cost to society ("efficiently")
Agents and third parties to whom tax activities are outsourced (e.g. banks, tax withholders, tax farmers, tax form printers)	Performing outsourced activities.
Civil courts, arbitrators, tribunals to the extent that they deal with tax matters	Resolving disputes between TDs and taxpayers or third parties.
Police and the criminal justice system to the extent that they deal with tax matters	Providing protection to TD staff. Legal proceedings and judicial sanctions in non-compliance cases.
Tax practitioners (preparers, accountants, tax lawyers), their associations and their organizations.	Assisting taxpayers in complying with legal tax obligations and minimizing tax dues Representation in case of disputes.
Legally taxable entities (including individuals) and their associations	Complying with tax laws or undertaking activities to facilitate non-compliance. Associations: Coordinating with TDs, tax practitioners and tax policy institutions.

with raising a given amount of revenue is partial, in that it assumes that the expenditure side of the budget, and indeed the mix between tax and non-tax finance is already optimally determined. Since adequate analysis of TA using even this partial framework is not yet available, a number of rules of thumb are perforce used here.[3] Broadly, tax design features that increase the social cost of TA for raising a given amount of revenue (*collection efficiency)* or which constrain the ability of a TA to administer tax laws are identified as administratively undesirable and conversely. Related to the second criterion is the concept of TD *effectiveness.* The two dimensions of *in*effectiveness are the extent to which actual revenue collected by the TD fall short of potential revenue per prevailing tax law (or the *tax gap*) and the extent of inequity across citizens due to TD procedures and administrative law.

3. WHAT WE KNOW OR THINK WE KNOW

Before turning to the impact of the TA on tax design *per se*, its implications for the public budget are first pointed out. To do so, the evaluation framework of Slemrod and Yitzhaki (1996, 1998, 2002) is used. The framework, already useful as an aid to conceptual thinking, has promise as a tool for empirical policy evaluation.

3.1 Tax Administration Costs and the Public Sector

PROPOSITION 1: IF TA COSTS INCREASE, THERE SHOULD BE LESS RELIANCE ON TAX FINANCE, LESS GOVERNMENT EXPENDITURE, OR BOTH.

Intuitively, social costs of different sources of finance in the public budget, including non-tax revenues (user charges, fees, dividends and interest from government assets), debt and money finance, should be equated at the margin to minimize the total cost of financing government provided goods and services. Furthermore, if the tax price of these goods and services increases, the optimal ratio of private goods to public goods should increase as well.[4]

These rules, but only for marginal changes in tax design and administrative procedures, are formalized in Mayshar (1991).[5] A simple exposition of the Mayshar rules is in Slemrod and Yitzhaki (1998): Suppose the welfare function which the government seeks to maximize is $V(U_j(E,w,G))$, where $U_j(.)$ is the indirect utility from private goods of citizen j, $j=1,\ldots,J$, w is the wage rate, G is the quantity of public goods and E is a vector of policy instruments used to raise finance for G. The optimum choice of G and E is given by MBF = MCF_i, where MBF is the social marginal benefit from funds in terms of foregone private consumption and MCF_i is the marginal cost of funds of the ith financing instrument. If distributional effects are neglected, MCF becomes MECF, the marginal efficiency cost of funds. The MECFs incorporate TA costs.[6]

This formula can also be used to examine specific tax design or TD procedures, not just tax and non-tax instruments as a whole. For example, Poapongsakorn et. al. (2000) apply the MECF framework to the evaluation of taxpayer surveys to discover non-filers in Thailand.[7] They compare this to the benchmark alternative of raising income tax rates proportionately to obtain the same revenue.[8]

3.2 The Major Implication for Tax Policy

PROPOSITION 2: WITHOUT TAKING INTO ACCOUNT ADMINISTRATION COSTS, THE EFFICIENCY COST AND THE EQUITY IMPACT OF A REAL WORLD TAX SYSTEM CANNOT BE ASSESSED.

This is uncontroversial. Nevertheless, some examples may clarify the scope of this proposition.

The lump-sum tax, that essential benchmark in economic theory, is subject to lobbying costs. The nearest real-world equivalent, the poll tax, entails TD costs and, as illustrated by the Thatcher tax, additional resource costs stemming from taxpayer resistance and political instability.

In the presence of tax evasion and invoice fraud (evasion reflects imperfect enforcement capacity of a TD), intermediate inputs may continue to bear tax under a VAT so that production efficiency does not obtain.[9] The extent of input taxation is directly dependent on the effectiveness of invoice-matching by the TD.

As discussed below (in the section on tax farming), a taxing scheme which, in theory, greatly reduces TD costs and avoids the excess burden of taxes, may turn out to have little or no impact on TD costs when implemented.

3.3 The Key Tax Administration Insight

PROPOSITION 3: TAX DESIGNS WHICH ECONOMISE ON INFORMATION REQUIREMENTS ARE LEAST COSTLY TO ADMINISTER.[10]

The main functions of a TD and most of TA are concerned with information.[11] While information collection and interpretation are most important and costly for administration, information storage, communication and dissemination is also necessary.[12] Consequently, a leading hypothesis in the literature, that has appeared repeatedly in different guises, is that *tax designs which economise on information requirements are simplest to administer.*[13] The implications of this for tax design, particularly for developing countries, are widely accepted and are part of the standard advice package given to most governments:

"A tax system with *few taxes, a limited number of rates for each tax, limited exemptions*, and *a broad base* has proven, in the context of many developing countries, to be much easier to administer and to result in higher compliance levels than a complex tax system". (Silvani and Baer, 1997, emphasis added).[14]

It is worth examining these design features in relation to their information conserving properties.

Information economies achieved from *few taxes* not only assist TA, but also make *effective tax incidence* on different goods or entities easier to determine and so facilitate tax designs with limited economic efficiency and equity costs in addition to directly lowering TA costs.[15]

Few rates of tax, in the case of taxes on goods, reduce the possibility of non-compliance through misclassification. While no misclassification is possible with a single tax rate, with N tax rates there are $\frac{N(N-1)}{2}$ ways to misclassify goods subject to a high tax rate as goods subject to lower tax rates. This increases the information verification burden of a TD for tax determination.[16]

Few exemptions also limit the number of *effective* tax rates and the need to verify, case-by-case, compliance with the conditions under which exemptions are granted.

The rationale for broad bases comes from the indirect information saving due to lower non-compliance opportunities and incentives. With few exclusions from the tax base, tax evasion or avoidance by claiming to belong to an excluded category becomes harder. Furthermore, for a given revenue requirement, tax rates can be lower than is the case with a narrow tax base.[17] This reduces the incentive not to comply, as expected gains from non-compliance are directly related to the tax thereby saved. Both reduced non-compliance and the likely positive impact on the tax base due to lower economic efficiency costs from low tax rates, lead to secondary, reinforcing, base effects.

Nevertheless, where there is a conflict between information economies and the "standard advice", exceptions arise. For example, for a global income tax, information is needed more to verify the tax base (income), than to verify the applicable tax rate. In fact, when it is possible and cheaper to outsource tax determination and collection via *tax withholding*, information needs of the TD and overall tax collection costs can be reduced by instituting *final withholding taxes.*[18] This fragments the tax base, making it schedular, and goes contrary to the standard advice of few taxes. Furthermore, if gross payments and net income from each source differ, multiple effective rates of tax become likely even with a common withholding tax rate. There is, inevitably, a caveat to this caveat: progressive income tax rates create the incentive to split taxable entities below their economically efficient or least cost size, a problem that arises in the case of unincorporated business firms in some countries.

3.4 Information and Basic Tax Administration

PROPOSITION 4: THERE IS A TRADE-OFF BETWEEN ADMINISTRATIVE SIMPLICITY AND THE EQUITY AND EFFICIENCY OF TAX DESIGN.

As the previous paragraph suggests, the implication of administration cost saving due to information economies is a "pervasive trade-off between accuracy and cost of complexity".[19] The inadequate recognition to date of costly information in optimal tax theory is possibly an important reason for its prescriptions continuing to be, by and large, without practical appeal.

A simple example can vividly illustrate the trade-off between TA simplicity and complex tax design: In simpler times, one can imagine a ruler of a country telling her soldiers "get me as much money or money's worth as you can from my subjects" (the tax design). Soldiers would then do the ruler's bidding (tax administration).

Clearly, neither this tax design nor this tax administration would be acceptable in modern economies, if indeed such a tax system were politically feasible. Problems with this tax system include the absence of a relation between tax revenue and public expenditure, its failure (ex ante) to satisfy Adam Smith's canon of "certainty", its potential inequity, resource allocation distortions including investment distortions, and excessive tax administration discretion facilitating corruption. Nevertheless, the example illustrates how *tax* simplification can be carried too far in the pursuit of *administrative* simplicity.

PROPOSITION 5: TD COSTS DECREASE WITH PRESUMPTIONS.

This follows from the information economies achieved by presumptions and presumptive taxes. Presumptions are pervasive in tax designs even in developed countries, via tax depreciation schedules, fixed schedules for entertainment deductions and ceilings or fixed allowances for other deductions. Alternative minimum tax regimes for corporations (see Tanzi and Sadka, 1993) and turnover based simplified tax regimes in lieu of the VAT for small firms, are other examples.

The selective use of presumptions is unavoidable if taxes are to be administratively feasible. Two criteria can be suggested for replacing "normal" tax laws by presumptions: First, other things equal, presumptions are more likely to be efficient the higher is the TA's (not just TD's) cost of information to determine or verify normal taxes and the lower are the social losses due to equity and efficiency costs. Examples are depreciation schedules, informal or farm sector value added and prices of imports. Second, presumptions that can be used immediately are more likely to be desirable on revenue ground if normal tax determination procedures require information not immediately available and if the TDs future ability to collect tax from the entity is uncertain. Examples are on-the-spot fines and final withholding taxes.

For presumptive taxes which substitute for "normal" taxes, a key design issue is the alternative tax base on which presumptions are to be based: The base(s) for presumptive taxes should ideally be closely correlated with the normal tax base, but should, at the same time, be relatively immutable and not subject to manipulation or concealment from the TD by taxpayers. For example, profession or sector of operation, location, physical business assets and how old the business is can together serve as a joint proxy for income.[20]

PROPOSITION 6: EFFECTIVENESS IN LOW CAPACITY TDS IS INCREASED BY SELECTIVELY EXEMPTING THE HARD-TO-TAX, INCLUDING THE INFORMAL SECTOR, FROM NORMAL TAX COMPLIANCE OBLIGATIONS.

Intuitively, large resource expenditure by the TD chasing after meagre revenue gains if it attempts to verify the, typically unrecorded or poorly recorded, income, sales or other tax base of the hard-to-tax cannot be optimal.[21] Theoretical support for this position is in McLaren (1998).[22] Practical advice to deal with the hard-to-tax suggests the use of presumptive taxes, particularly in less developed countries with large informal sectors.[23] The same is true of self-employed professional, who are among the hard-to-tax in the formal sector.

PROPOSITION 7: INFORMATION CONSERVING TA COLLECTION PROCEDURES (WITHHOLDING AND ADVANCE TAX) CAN INCREASE ADMINISTRATION EFFECTIVENESS AND EFFICIENCY.

Both tax withholding and advance taxes according to a laid down advance tax rate schedule have been found to have revenue benefits, while lowering tax collection costs, and so are to be advocated unless horizontal and inter-sectoral equity violations outweigh TA benefits.

Of different privatized activities, evidence suggests that most important for TA effectiveness is tax withholding.[24] Besides increasing compliance in general, tax withholding may be the only way to collect at least some taxes from small non-resident taxpayers and from "ghosts" who do not file returns and who have not been identified by the TD.

The compliance increasing property of advance tax payments has also found empirically supported in studies of the United States and some European countries.[25]

PROPOSITION 8: TD COSTS DECREASE WITH CONCENTRATION OF THE TAX BASE ACROSS ENTITIES.

Direct evidence for tax base characteristics which reduce TD costs is difficult to come by. Differences in government accounting conventions make TD cost data across jurisdictions non-comparable.[26] Even if cost data could be made comparable, differences in tax mixes and individual tax designs would still pose a problem.[27]

Given common budget accounting rules in Indian states and broadly similar tax structures, data on collection costs and its correlates for the 14 major Indian states for fiscal years 1985/86 to 2000/01 may shed some light on the question.[28] In Figure 1, collection costs as a percentage of own tax revenue of states is graphed against Gross State Domestic Product (GSDP) per capita (different colours are used for different states). The graph suggests a systematic association between the two variables.[29] This accords with intuition, which suggests that administration costs would increase with the number of taxpayers rather than taxes per se, a point made by Lasheras and Herrera (1991).

Other tax base characteristics which should tend to reduce TD collection costs as a ratio of tax collected are population density (or state area and state population), urbanization, literacy, a lower sectoral share of agriculture, and possibly a higher share of manufacturing. In regression experiments, higher literacy rates did not appear to increase collection efficiency. While this preliminary statistical evidence (Annex 1) is not conclusive, all the other variables appear to be statistically associated with increased collection efficiency.[30]

The implications for tax design, if these results can be generalized, is that jurisdictions with higher per capita income will find it less costly to collect a greater proportion of their taxes from income taxes and other direct taxes. In terms of reform, moving to greater reliance on direct taxes with development is likely to be cost efficient. This broadly accords with cross-country evidence on actual tax structures.[31]

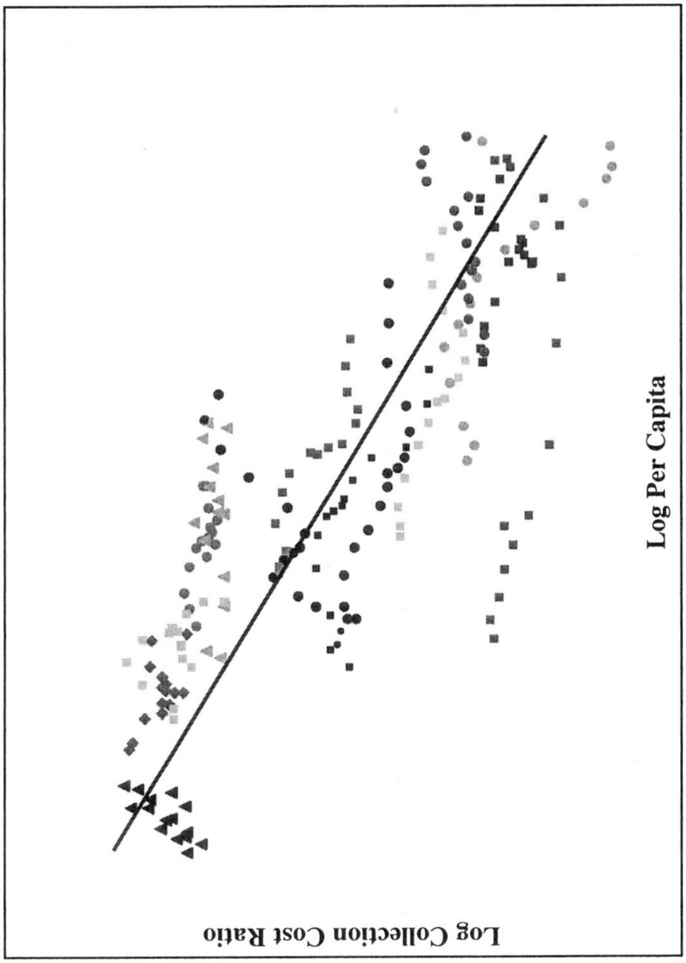

Figure 1. Tax Collection costs and per capita GSDP in major Indian state, 1985/86 – 2001-2002 (3-year moving averages).

PROPOSITION 9: TA COSTS INCREASE WITH COMPLEX TAX BASES.

A precise definition of "complex tax bases" being elusive, a practically useful general discussion is difficult to provide and only preliminary remarks are made here.[32] Nevertheless, some cost increasing features which contribute to complexity figure in the propositions discussed below, with respect to multiple tax entities, international tax bases and non-revenue objectives. Several tax design features leading to complexity are widely accepted and most of these features require more information.[33] In practice, tax provisions having one or more of the following properties can be conjectured to contribute to complexity: (a) they involve greater than average expenditure by the TA (not just the TD) per unit of tax revenue; (b) they lead to frequent tax disputes; (c) the number of pages of tax law, including administrative law and judicial rulings, devoted to qualifications, exceptions or computational instructions is high; and (d) only tax law experts fully understand the provision. Among specific tax design features that are likely to contribute to complexity are: Values (which require both prices and quantities) rather than quantities alone; bases for which a greater number of dates and locations of different events is needed for tax determination; and bases for which a greater number of entities from whom or about whom information is needed for tax determination.

PROPOSITION 10: TD COSTS INCREASE WITH THE NUMBER AND VARIETY OF TAXABLE ENTITIES.

The number of types of entities subject to different taxes, particularly the income tax, tends to be large. Entities are distinguished by residency status, ownership, whether they are incorporated or not, profit or not-for-profit organizations, by the nature of their economic activity (financial sector, trade, production, real estate), by the amount of the tax base in their hands (large taxpayer, small business) and so on. To some extent this is inevitable in modern economies, despite equity violations and the scope for tax avoidance this creates. Nevertheless, since the nature of information for tax determination by the TD typically differs across entities, sometimes because tax design provisions are tailored for particular entities, this increases TD costs. A possible exception to this, especially in low capacity TDs, is targeting TD effort to assess large taxpayers.[34]

The obvious implication for tax design is to reduce the number of tax entities recognized or treated differently in the tax law, though this rule is difficult to apply in practice, especially where more than one tax jurisdiction is involved.

PROPOSITION 11: TD CAPACITY IN CLOSED ECONOMIES INCREASES WITH FINANCIAL DEVELOPMENT.

The extent of adoption of modern accounting methods by business and the extent of use of modern, bank mediated, payment mechanisms (cheques, book-transfers and credit cards) is of importance to the TD. With modern payment technology transactions leave an "audit trail" which permits easier detection and verification of payments in tax investigations by the TD. To encourage adoption of modern accounting and cheque usage, particularly among small traders, taxpayer education and even a cost-based deduction from taxes, could be considered.

On the other hand, as Slemrod (1990) points out, sophisticated financial systems coupled with openness increase the ease with which funds may cross international borders to escape taxes (discussed further below).

Both these observations suggest that appropriate tax designs at different levels of financial development and openness differ. To repeat a now familiar point, design solutions should take account of differences in information availability and economies for the TD.

PROPOSITION 12: IT IS EFFICIENT FOR COUNTRIES WITH LOW LITERACY LEVELS AND UNDERDEVELOPED ACCOUNTING PROFESSIONS TO RELY RELATIVELY MORE ON COMMODITY TAXES.

That reliance on commodity taxes, particularly on international trade in goods (though not services), tends to vary inversely with per capita GDP is a well known empirical regularity. That this is due to the relative ease with which goods can be taxed, particularly at national borders, is also widely accepted. This is well illustrated by customs administration, where border checks continue to be of importance.[35] In contrast, income and value added are intrinsically accounting concepts, especially where there are both receipts and expenses and where these are subject to timing differences. Second, with sales or other payment transactions between citizens that affect tax bases, the information available to the TD from the payment technology in use becomes important. Direct cash or barter payments which do not involve third parties are difficult for a TD to detect. Goods production and sales are least affected by this information constraint.[36] As countries develop, to move smoothly to greater reliance on income taxes, and also the VAT, it is useful for them to focus on developing accountancy capacity and modern payments channels.

3.5 Information Access and the Law

PROPOSITION 13: TD EFFECTIVENESS DECREASES WITH RESTRICTED ACCESS TO INFORMATION (INCLUDING PRIVACY LAWS).

This point is made in Bagchi, Bird and Das-Gupta (1995) who also provide a brief review of restrictions on TD access to information in different countries and their link with widely accepted human rights. As with many of the propositions in the paper, rigorous theoretical analysis and empirical evidence is still lacking on the impact of restricted information access of different kinds. Restrictions apply particularly to financial information from banks and for information that can only be discovered by searches of persons or private records by the TD. Relaxation of privacy laws to increase TD access has costs via violation of human rights and possibly reduced effectiveness of financial intermediation.[37] The implication for tax design is that financial transactions involving banks, unrecorded assets, and transactions involving difficult to verify expenses (e.g. business entertainment) or receipts by individuals or firms should either be excluded from the tax base, or incorporated via presumptions.

With increased information technology and particularly internet penetration, financial development and adoption of modern accounting, information once considered private is increasingly becomes publicly available. So, once again, the efficient tax base will vary with these characteristics of financial development and adoption of information technology. In terms of the tax mix, indirect taxes particularly on cross-border transactions, typically rely less on private information to verify tax compliance and so should be relied on relatively more when privacy laws impede TD effectiveness in collecting income taxes.

PROPOSITION 14: TD COSTS INCREASE AND EFFECTIVENESS DECREASES WITH STRINGENT EVIDENCE STANDARDS.

Related to the previous proposition is the question of standards of evidence. The quality and sufficiency of evidence required by a TD to establish non-compliance is determined by standards of evidence applicable to tax matters in a country.[38] This can range, in legal terminology, between "preponderance of probability" usually adopted in civil cases to "beyond reasonable doubt" applicable in capital crimes. Furthermore, whether the burden of proof is on the TD ("innocent until proven guilty") or on the taxpayer ("guilty until proven innocent") is also relevant for TD costs. Presumptions and presumptive taxes are an extreme example of relaxation of evidence standards. Low standards of evidence increase the likelihood of taxes being only imperfectly related to the designed tax base, and tax offences being only imperfectly related to tax sanctions.[39]

The first general tax design issue is what standards of evidence are appropriate and feasible in different countries given social preferences and the capacity of courts. This will directly affect the revenue potential of the tax system via its impact on TD effectiveness. The second issue is for penalty design which, in turn, depends on the extent to which societies are willing to tolerate wrongful punishment versus letting tax offenders go free.

3.6 Information and TA Organization

PROPOSITION 15: TA COSTS CAN DECREASE WITH SELECTIVE TAX FARMING AND OUTSOURCING.

There are a wide variety of TD functions which can be privatized or outsourced, ranging from producing tax forms, to mandatory financial audits, to tax withholding, to semi-autonomous revenue boards to outright tax farming. Even self-assessment of taxes can be viewed as a form of outsourcing. In terms of tax design, two examples can be given to illustrate the potential for selective privatization to increase TA efficiency or even economic welfare, while giving rise to changed tax designs.

Changing the taxable entity to groups of taxpayers: Such a scheme has been proposed by Ueng and Yang (2000). In the first stage of their scheme, the TD makes a tax demand from a group of taxpayers based on what it knows about the aggregate tax base of the group, leaving contributions by members to be decided within the group. Normal tax assessment and procedures are adopted towards group members by the TD if the group fails to meet the tax demanded by the TD. In their framework, TA effectiveness is increased and the excess burden of tax evasion and taxation is eliminated. Unfortunately, such a scheme may have costs in practice, since within-group coercion is assumed away and the TD's ability to determine taxes in the second stage is assumed to be unimpaired by their lack of knowledge about group members in the first stage. Clearly, both assumptions lack realism, the first in some cases, the second in almost all cases.

Nevertheless the authors give examples of where similar tax farming variants have been used. To take a related example from *non-tax revenue* in India, irrigation charges are recovered in the states of Maharashtra and Andhra Pradesh through local Water Users Associations of farmers, with irrigation departments only billing the entire group. Since association members together have information from direct observation of water use by members, this economizes on additional information needed to assess dues. Furthermore, since associations retain a substantial proportion of dues they collect, for maintenance of local irrigation works and other expenses, they also have the incentive to collect dues.

Substituting auction revenue for excise duty on liquor in India: Several states in India periodically auction local monopoly rights to sell liquor at the retail level instead of levying an excise tax on producers. This can be viewed as a variant of tax farming. The arrangement reduces TD and TA costs, and increases TA effectiveness. Revenue from auctions is also among the most buoyant state revenue sources. Furthermore, efficiency loss from conferring local monopoly rights is not a major issue given that a commodity considered socially undesirable is involved.

Complete privatization of collection of major taxes is clearly not a desirable option, given the potential for harassment and over-assessment of taxes by private agents.[40] Nevertheless, all modern tax systems involve privatization to some degree, via tax withholders, banks as tax collection agents, and in several countries, semi-autonomous revenue authorities.[41] The general principle is to privatize or outsource activities whenever the social costs of doing so, due partly to information economies but also due to collection incentives of the TD versus private agents, are less than the cost of the TD carrying out the activity directly.[42]

3.7 Tax Information and Globalization

PROPOSITION 16: GLOBALLY MOBILE TAX BASES AND ENTITIES REDUCE TD EFFECTIVENESS.

This problem is becoming increasingly serious with globalization. Key areas where cross-border mobility erodes national tax bases include globalization of financial asset markets, multinational corporations, footloose industries, international outsourcing, skilled labour mobility, tax havens and off-shore banking.[43]

Globalization of financial asset markets facilitates evasion or avoidance of interest, dividend income and capital gains taxation. An instructive case of the impact of mobile financial savings on tax design is the German interest tax withholding reform in 1991.[44] A 10 percent withholding tax on interest income introduced in 1991 to curb an estimated 80 percent tax evasion rate, led to a massive outflow of saving and even more evasion. Following a Constitutional Court of Germany ruling, a substantial annual allowance was introduced for interest income. In effect, Germany tacitly admitted its inability to tax this mobile base and introduced a base narrowing tax amendment so as not to decrease the domestic availability of savings. Several countries have, for similar reasons, exempted capital gains while some have also exempted dividends.[45]

The taxation problems associated with transfer pricing by multinational corporations, and continuing international attempts to deal with this issue via legislation based on multilateral models, are widely written about and not discussed here.[46]

Footloose industries, international outsourcing and mobile skilled labour cause tax base erosion under existing tax rules which base taxability on residence rather than nationality (the United States being a major exception). Countries which have nationality based tax bases, on the other hand, must contend with tax evasion and avoidance including via tax havens, which TDs generally find hard to cope with. Several countries have capitulated and introduced lenient tax regimes so as not do drive productive resources away.

By incorporating in a tax haven jurisdiction, or routing transactions through shell entities resident in havens, businesses seek to escape national taxes of their "true" home country.[47] Dealing with tax havens both unilaterally and via multilateral action is emerging as a major battle ground to protect domestic tax bases.[48] So far, despite some progress, the advantage appears to be with tax havens.

There are four important implications of these developments for tax design. First, administratively feasible taxation of capital income and earnings of mobile labour and production will increasingly have to be source rather than residence based. Second, final withholding taxes on interest, dividends and other payments to mobile factors are increasingly being seen as least cost.[49] Third, cooperative tax harmonization will reduce the incentive for cross-border flows.[50] Nevertheless, fourth, given that not all countries have the incentive to enter into tax harmonization agreements – particularly tax havens – concessional taxes on mobile bases relative to immobile factors may be inevitable.

PROPOSITION 17: E-COMMERCE REDUCES TD EFFECTIVENESS.

E-commerce, since it need not leave paper trails, decreases the accessibility of enforcement information TDs have access to in cross-border transactions. The information problem is most serious for cross border sales to final consumers.[51] Nevertheless, only the volume of such transactions is growing and no new issues, relative to, say, mail order sales arise.[52]

To cope with TD ineffectiveness, source and residence definitions and may have to be refined to take account of areas of ambiguity. Without far grater violation of privacy than exists today, systematic taxation of direct sales to final consumers is unlikely to be possible.

PROPOSITION 18: TD EFFECTIVENESS INCREASES WITH INTER-JURISDICTION INFORMATION SHARING AND COOPERATION.

This is a major area of institution building to increase TD and tax system effectiveness in the face of globalization. Given opposing incentives in different countries, globalization is likely to lead to diminished TD effectiveness. Furthermore, while there are exceptions, particularly in the Americas, cooperation between developing countries is more limited than between developed countries.

Cooperation and information sharing are greatly facilitated by common tax definitions (of types of income and other receipts, taxable entities, residence, permanent establishment, sale, and so on).[53] In addition avoidance opportunities are reduced with common tax periods and timing of tax obligations. Therefore, besides tax rate and base harmonization to reduce the incentive for cross-border tax avoidance and evasion, cooperative harmonization of basic tax law categories is of importance.

Not all information cooperation areas relate to sophisticated tax transactions: One basic area of cooperation is to protect tax revenues from leakages associated with cross-border trade in goods. Information exchange between customs authorities on both outbound and inbound shipments (or the possibly less effective alternative of private pre-shipment inspection) can help curb evasion not only of trade taxes but also of the sales tax or VAT. The case of the VAT in the European Union (EU), however, suggests that it is important to distinguish among different types of information in exchange agreements. Using the EU's VAT Information Exchange System (VIES), member countries exchange domestic, tax return and tax invoice based, records of cross-border VAT sales. The system was put in place just prior to removal of physical border checks between member countries in 1993. VIES has not been able to substitute for border-checks. With hindsight, the lesson suggested is that substituting exchange of information that has proved to be of poor quality (i.e. accounts based information) for good quality information (from border checks and control procedures) may not help increase TD effectiveness.[54] What does this have to do with tax design? The discussion in Chang Woon Nam et. al. (2003) points to (a) the weakness of the current, primarily destination based VAT due to abuse of zero-rating of exports but (2) the difficulty in moving to a destination based VAT but with tax collection on the basis of origin as planned. This is due to incentives stemming from the likely change in the shares of different countries in VAT revenue given differing evasion rates. So the planned clearing house mechanism whereby countries collect the VAT on behalf of other members and then redistribute revenues on the basis of destination is being resisted by some member countries. At present, due to these administrative problems, continuation of the present system with re-introduction of border controls appears to be the only way to combat VAT evasion: But this would be a retrograde step in setting up a single market within the EU.[55]

3.8 Tax Information and Non-revenue Objectives

PROPOSITION 19: TA COSTS INCREASE IF THE TAX SYSTEM IS USED TO ACHIEVE NON-REVENUE OBJECTIVES.

This has already been referred to above and is widely accepted. Tax concessions are possibly the major cause of tax base narrowing. Besides redistribution, investment and saving incentives are most common in tax design, [56] though there is a long list of other non-revenue objectives that tax systems have been used for. Besides generally applicable tax provisions, exemptions or concessions for specific groups of taxable entities (end-user provisions) are not uncommon.

Besides base-narrowing, reduced equity, and price distortions, differential treatment of entities greatly increases TA information requirements, increases opportunities for misreporting and complicates tax compliance requirements on taxpayers and third parties. In particular, TD costs can greatly increase if there are new types of activities that have to be verified to ascertain eligibility for concessions: Examples are investment allowances for setting up production units in remote, backward areas, export incentives (requiring information for verification from other countries), installation *and use* of pollution control equipment and tax relief related to the duration or severity of disabilities. In such cases, concessions often end up being poorly targeted and abused: The social return to tax revenue foregone can be low and; at the margin even zero.[57]

It is also important to note that the MECF of other tax instruments, say changing tax rates or an efficiency enhancing reform in TD enforcement procedures, will increase on account of the greater leakage due to tax concessions.

The lesson is clear: Use tax concessions for non-revenue objectives very selectively and only after comparing their effectiveness with alternative, expenditure/subsidy or regulatory instruments which can potentially serve the same objectives.

3.9 Tax Rates and Compliance Incentives

PROPOSITION 20: HIGH MARGINAL AND AVERAGE RATES OF TAX DECREASE TD EFFECTIVENESS.

As discussed, this is an important justification for broad based taxes. This is one proposition for which there is a wealth of empirical evidence and some theoretical support.[58] Though the evidence suggests a negative relation between tax rates and either compliance or revenue, this has a direct implication for TD effectiveness since one of two important dimensions of TD effectiveness are reflected in the tax gap.

Clearly, lower tax rates must ultimately result in low revenue as tax rates move into the positively sloped region of the Laffer curve, so the implied tax design lesson is for moderate rather than zero tax rates!

Five remarks are needed to impart greater precision to this design suggestion. First, tax rates here refer to effective tax rates, taking into account tax concessions, exclusions and the timing of tax payments. Second, both high average and high marginal tax rates for taxpayers have been found to have negative effects on tax revenue and TD effectiveness. Third, however, whether low *expected* effective tax rates, taking into account the extent of tax evasion and the TD's ability to detect evasion and impose penalties, or low effective tax rates *per se* – that would apply to honest taxpayers – increase TD effectiveness, requires further empirical investigation.[59] Nevertheless, since low effective rates of tax reduce the tax burden of all taxpayers, honest or dishonest, these are advisable. Fourth, when combined with the advice to reduce exemptions and concessions, this amounts to suggesting low *nominal* tax rates. Fifth, lowering tax rates, as with most tax structure reforms discussed here, should form part of a package of reforms. For example, as emphasized by Alm, Bahl and Murray (1990), lowering marginal tax rates in the Jamaican case examined by them without simultaneously strengthening the TD could result in lower revenue – despite increased TD effectiveness.

The discussion here leaves open the question of what moderate tax rates, which would maximize TD effectiveness and revenues are. Unfortunately, the no OSFA rule applies to this and there is little information even in cases where systematic empirical work is available.[60] Relevant factors include tax rate effects on economic activity in different economies, the size of the informal sector, the extent of tax withholding and many more. A "seat-of-pants" range for marginal tax rates of a broad- based personal income tax is between 15% and 35% and between 5% and 20% for a broad based VAT.

PROPOSITION 21: IN THE PRESENCE OF TAX EVASION, REDISTRIBUTION AS A GOAL OF THE TAX SYSTEM SHOULD OPTIMALLY BE GIVEN LESS WEIGHT.

This is the prescription emerging from a number of recent papers on optimal tax theory, which incorporate tax evasion.[61] When the TD can commit to an audit strategy in advance, these papers find that the optimal, redistributive, income tax structure is influenced by auditing effectiveness. The broad result is that income taxes should optimally be *regressive*.[62] Though these papers are still too abstract to serve as complete guides to policy, for practical tax design a conservative lesson appears warranted, even at this stage of knowledge: Highly progressive income taxes should not be advocated: besides increasing evasion incentives and reducing TD effectiveness, they are not optimal even from the point of view of redistribution and economic efficiency.

PROPOSITION 22: IN A LOW CAPACITY TD, EFFECTIVENESS MAY NOT INCREASE EITHER WITH AD VALOREM OR SPECIFIC TAX RATES ON GOODS.

Ad valorem taxes on commodities have the potential advantage of being linked to sales value and so are inflation proof and elastic with respect to demand increases. Specific taxes, on the other hand economise on the information needed for base determination and so are considered harder to evade. Both these hypotheses are appealing, but need not hold good in practice as the following example shows.

The state of Maharashtra in India switched over from a regime of specific excise duties on liquor production to an ad valorem regime in 1997. Under this "MRP" (a ceiling or Maximum Retail Price) system, excise duty and MRP are fixed as multiples of the cost of production declared by distilleries and breweries to the Maharashtra Excise Department. Specific floor rates are also fixed for different categories of liquor. The MRP is required to be printed along with the production batch number on all liquor bottle labels and cases. The MRP system led to an immediate increase in excise duty collection which was, however, quickly eroded. Table 2 shows that this increase was eroded even in unit terms, with duty as a percentage of the wholesale price returning to its pre-reform level for two categories within 1 to 5 years and showing a downward trend for the third.

This example suggests a negative lesson for tax design: rate reform, specifically the choice between ad valorem and specific tax rates, may not lead to revenue gains if the TD is unable or unwilling to enforce these rates.

Table 2. The Impact of Maharashtra's Switch from Specific to Ad Valorem Excise Duties on Liquor in 1997

	1996-97 Pre reform	**1997-98**	**1998-00**	**1999-2000**	**2000-01**	**2001-02**
Unit realization of excise duty (Rupees per bulk litre of sale)						
"IndianMade Foreign Liquor	72.63	136.91	131.48	123.43	115.30	101.47
" Country Liquor"	42.88	44.27	45.39	39.81	33.91	29.49
Beer	11.30	20.58	21.56	18.50	19.90	16.87
Index of excise unit realization to All India Wholesale Price Index by product category (1996 - 97 = 100)						
"Indian Made Foreign Liquor"	100.0	175.6	156.6	136.3	122.6	100.4
Country Liquor	100.0	100.4	98.9	86.1	77.8	72.0
Beer	100.0	164.5	156.4	126.9	134.5	114.1

Source: Excise Department, Government of Maharashtra, except Wholesale Price Index: Centre for Monitoring the Indian Economy.

PROPOSITION 23: TA EFFECTIVENESS IS INCREASED IF, WITHOUT GREATLY INCREASED COMPLEXITY, TAX DESIGN AND PROCEDURES TAKE MONEY AMOUNTS AS EQUIVALENT IF THEY ARE EQUAL IN PRESENT VALUE TERMS.

Tax design provisions to prevent inflationary revenue loss are well known and not examined in detail here.[63] The essential principles in highly inflationary situations involve shortening the tax period and ensuring, to the extent possible, that tax laws specify dues in present value terms, that is, include interest provisions. In practice, inflation proofing increases the complexity of the tax code and taxpayer compliance costs, establishing a trade-off between revenue and both economic efficiency costs and TA costs. Thus, the extent of inflation proofing that is advisable will depend on taxpayer sophistication and the rate of inflation, and no OSFA rule is available.[64, 65]

PROPOSITION 24: TA COSTS DECREASE WITH WELL DESIGNED (EFFECTIVE) PENALTIES.

One puzzle is why practical tax designs pay so little attention to the design of penalties for tax non-compliance. A wide ranging discussion of good penalty design is in Oldman (1965). As Bird (forthcoming) puts it:

> "Experience suggests that penalties should increase with (1) the potential revenue loss due to the tax offence; (2) the

difficulty and cost of detecting the offence; (3) the effect of the offence on other taxpayers; (4) the offender's state of mind (a higher penalty should apply if the offence is deliberate and pre-planned); and (5) recidivism."

Other desirable design features of penalties are:

a) In elaboration of Bird's first principle, penalties for lesser degrees of non-compliance should, following the principle of marginal deterrence, be less than the marginal social loss so that taxpayers have the incentive to substitute away from higher levels of non-compliance (Mookherjee and Png, 1994).
b) Penalties for "technical offences" with no direct revenue impact, such as a failure to keep mandatory records or provide information to the TD, should be high enough to reflect both the direct and indirect revenue impact (Das-Gupta and Mookherjee, 1998).
c) Non-monetary penalties, including garnishment, closing of business establishments, public shame and even jail sentences should be selectively employed if culturally permissible.[66]
d) The *procedure* for levy of penalty should be transparent and not subject to TD discretion.
e) Penalties for corruption or inaction by bureaucrats should be high enough to reduce opportunities for non-compliant taxpayers ("gainers") to compensate bureaucrats who are punished ("losers").

PROPOSITION 25: WELL DESIGNED PENALTIES MAY INCLUDE NEGATIVE PENALTIES.[67]

If, after a tax audit by the TD, no non-compliance is detected, then a negative penalty has been found to be optimal in the literature on optimal income taxes. To be practically implementable a precondition must be met: It should be difficult for auditors to falsify the results of audits: else greater bribes and revenue loss will result from negative penalties.

PROPOSITION 26: WELL DESIGNED PENALTIES SHOULD NOT BE TOO HIGH – OR REVENUE MAY DECREASE VIA TAX AVOIDANCE.

This empirical finding in the case of Jamaica by Alm, Bahl and Murray (1990), complements the optimal tax literature which finds non-maximal penalties in the presence of taxpayer and TD mistakes to be optimal (footnote 39).

Further empirical research is required before it will be possible for the exact structure and numerical levels of penalties, as opposed to qualitative results, to draw on existing research.[68]

3.10 The Magnitude of TA Costs

PROPOSITION 27: TD AND TA COSTS ARE NOT ACCURATELY MEASURED – EVEN IN PRINCIPLE.

First consider TD costs. Since government expenditure accounting in developing countries and also many developed countries is cash based, and since there is seldom a system of user charges by one department for goods (e.g. buildings constructed or occupied) or services (e.g. police protection or judicial proceedings, financial audit services by government auditors) provided to other departments, true resource costs of the TD are not captured by government budgets. This is exacerbated by non-market values used to value government assets or asset rentals.

For TA costs, it is probably fair to say that the cost of collecting taxes has not been adequately conceptualised. For example, Slemrod and Yitzhaki (1996) identify five component costs of taxation. They are administrative (TD) costs, deadweight efficiency loss from taxation, the excess burden of tax evasion, avoidance and compliance costs of taxpayers. The latter is a part of TA costs. Even if these cost components are defined as inclusively as possible, the classification at least omits the cost of tax policy institutions, tax education and research. For TA proper, the scope of relevant government activity must be defined to include non-TD activities and third party costs need to be added. In addition, it should be noted that some activities within a tax system may have offsetting benefits so that net cost may differ from gross costs.

The implications for tax policy are firstly, that comparison of different tax design options will, for the time being, continue to be based on experience and seat-of-pants reasoning which may fail to take account of true TA costs.[69] To improve cost estimates, at least for the TD, reform of government accounting is needed, a difficult reform to implement in many developing countries. For example, the move to accrual accounting and partial inter-department charging in Australia, New Zealand and the United Kingdom helps improve the accuracy of TD cost estimates.

PROPOSITION 28: TD COSTS ARE SUBSTITUTES FOR PRIVATE SECTOR COSTS: MEASURED TD COSTS ARE JUST THE TIP OF THE ICEBERG.

Estimates suggest that despite probably understated TD costs due to current government accounting conventions, taxpayer and third party compliance costs are much higher, in some estimates by a factor of 10 to 15, even in developed countries. And these are total costs, not costs at the margin.[70]

For example, Slemrod and Venkatesh (2002) estimate the compliance cost of small and mid-sized business in the United States at around 27 to 28 percent of taxes paid by them, which are around 10 times as high as the compliance cost of large firms with the corporation income tax reported in Slemrod and Blumenthal (1996).[71] In contrast, the cost of collection of taxes by the United States Internal Revenue Service is under 2 percent of taxes collected. For India, recent estimates put the compliance cost of the corporation income tax at between 5.6 percent and 14.5 percent of corporation tax collection compared to imputed administration costs for the corporation income tax of the Indian Income Tax Department of below 1 percent of tax collected. For the individual income tax, Slemrod and Sorum (1984) estimate the compliance costs at between 5 to 7 percent of taxes.[72] Indian tax compliance costs of taxpayers and third parties are estimated, though with a small sample, at a massive 57 percent of taxes compared to administration costs of 2.5 percent. Both in the United States and India compliance costs were found to be regressive for individuals and businesses. Costs were substantially higher for the self-employed, with private compliance costs often exceeding taxes paid in the Indian estimates.[73]

An important feature of tax costs are the substitutability between TD and private sector costs. Extending a point made with respect to outsourcing of tax functions, social cost minimization would dictate that different activities needed to collect the tax be carried out by the TD, private third parties or taxpayers depending on who has the lowest cost.[74] A self-interested preoccupation of TDs and governments with direct TD costs, and the limited attention paid to private compliance costs, makes it more than likely that compliance obligations burden taxpayers more than social cost minimization would dictate. For example, in developing countries, it may be the case that, contrary to prevailing wisdom, self-assessment is more costly than official assessment.[75]

The implications for tax policy are to decrease reliance on high compliance cost taxes and tax provisions. Specific measures that would do this have already been suggested in other propositions: One way is to replace high cost provisions with presumptions, particularly on the self employed. A second is to reduce taxpayer and third party reporting requirements by introducing final withholding taxes. If the results for India are replicated by other developing country studies, which typically have relatively inefficient TDs and unsophisticated taxpayers, then consideration should be given to replacing the individual income tax in similar developing countries with other sources of finance including final withholding taxes. At the very least, the tax threshold should be raised above current levels.

PROPOSITION 29: TA COSTS INCREASE WITH TAX INSTABILITY.[76]

Chattopadhyay and Das-Gupta (2002a) report preliminary willingness-to-pay estimates of the cost of tax instability at around 4 percent of corporation tax paid and 3 percent of individual income tax paid. In contrast, willingness to pay for reduced tax complexity was well under 1 percent of taxes for individuals, while few corporations saw tax complexity as costly. That tax loopholes increase with complexity possibly explains why corporations, who are relatively sophisticated taxpayers, do not find complexity costly.

The policy implication is for fewer tax policy changes particularly administrative (TD or Finance Ministry) notifications and rulings. Pre-announcement of changes and public discussion, while not always possible, is a second measure. Real distortions are also caused, for example in India, by annual budgets since many tax policy changes are announced during budget speeches. Fourth, when policy changes are announced, carefully designed transition procedures should be considered and their benefits weighed against the increased complexity this entails.

PROPOSITION 30: TA COSTS INCREASE WITH TAX AMBIGUITY.

Chattopadhyay and Das-Gupta (2002a) report preliminary willingness-to-pay estimates of the cost of tax ambiguity at around 10 percent of corporation tax paid and 4 percent of individual income tax paid.[77] Tax ambiguity has also been identified as a cause of high compliance costs by Sandford (1994a), Glassberg and Smyth (1995), Kaplow (1996) and James et. al. (1997). Tax ambiguity while facilitated by complex tax concepts, is more directly related to unclear legal definitions and tax provisions. Nevertheless, the battle to define tax concepts unambiguously is likely to be never-ending, if the tax is complex, given sophisticated tax practitioners.[78]

The major implication for tax policy is, once again, reduced complexity.[79] Attempts at clear legal drafting, and simplified tax forms, are likely to reduce ambiguity costs to some degree. Transferring of a part of the compliance burden to administration, for example via official assessment rather than self assessment, also reduces the scope for taxpayer mistakes.[80]

4. ADMINISTRATIVE PROPERTIES OF IMPORTANT TAXES

Drawing on the discussion in the previous section, administrative properties of six taxes or related instruments along with reforms to enable more effective administration are summarized in Table 3 below. It should be noted that only tax structure measures are included in the "reforms" column of the table, omitting administration responses without a tax implication. Note also that the table focuses solely on administrative properties of the taxes and takes no account of efficiency and equity implications. As discussed, there is a trade-off between administration and other desirable features of tax systems.

Table 3. Administration Properties and Reforms

Tax or related policy instrument	**Bases and entities**	**Impediments to administration**	**Reforms or alternative taxes on the same base and entities**
Penalties and evidence standards	All	Penalties not covering all possible tax offences or not aligned with non-compliance incentives. Discretionary penalties. Difficult to prove non-compliance with stringent evidence standards.	Strengthen penalty structure. Streamline penalty imposition procedure.
Concessions to pursue non-revenue objectives	All, particularly income taxes and the VAT.	Increased scope for non-compliance. Greater information needed to verify compliance and eligibility.	Severely limit concessions. Examine relative merits of alternative (expenditure, regulatory) policy instruments
Individual Income Tax	Different types of income all requiring accounting definitions. Different tax provisions needed for entities distinguished by residence. incorporation status. sector of activity.	Overwhelming reliance on paper (or electronic) information not always available on "hard-to-tax" entities and cross-border income or trade flows. Many potential taxpayers. Valuation disputes. Tax avoidance and evasion facilitated by timing differences, understating receipts or overstating deductions, and cross-border activity. Mobile capital and skilled labour income.	Moderate tax rates. Limit tax concessions. Presumptions and presumptive taxes. Schedular withholding taxes. Shortened tax periods in inflationary environments. High tax thresholds in developing countries. Official instead of self-assessment of taxes. International and inter-entity tax harmonization.

Table 3. Administration Properties and Reforms (Continued)

Tax or related policy instrument	Bases and entities	Impediments to administration	Reforms or alternative taxes on the same base and entities
Corporation income tax	As for individual income tax.	Possibility of tax arbitrage between related corporations. Residence determination difficult due to tax havens. Valuation disputes. Tax avoidance and evasion facilitated by timing differences, understating receipts *or* overstating deductions, and cross-border activity. Footloose production activity.	Moderate tax rates. Limit tax concessions. Presumptions. Lenient taxation of mobile factors. Source rather than residence taxation. Multilateral international tax harmonization.
The VAT	Sale of goods and possibly services by firms. Tax rebating of intermediate and possibly capital purchases. Zero-rating of exports. Tax determination dependent on accounting.	Small firms and selected sectors difficult to tax. Retail sector in developing countries difficult to tax. Evasion through misclassification. Evasion possible by under-reporting sales or over-reporting purchases. Evasion of cross-border sales and electronic sales difficult to detect.	Moderate tax rates. Special (non-VAT) simplified regimes for small firms and hard-to-tax sectors using presumptions or presumptive taxes ("forfaits").
Excises	On production of specified goods: usually "sin" commodities, petroleum products.	Smuggling. Understated production. Black markets. Inflation sensitivity with specific rates, valuation problems with ad valorem rates.	Partial privatization. Substituting non-tax revenue (auctioning vending rights). Public monopoly of wholesale trade.
Property taxes	Annual property (land, buildings) value or property sales	Valuation problems and mis-declaration. Non-identification of new properties.	Moderate tax rates. Presumptive valuation. [1]

[1] An alternative to presumptive valuation is self-assessment with pre-emptive acquisition or sale by the TD, proposed four decades ago by Arnold Harberger and earlier by other authors. However, this is not a tax design issue.

5. TAKING ACCOUNT OF TAX ADMINISTRATION IN DESIGNING TAX REFORMS: SUGGESTIONS

The discussion in the paper identifies, however tentatively, a variety of administrative implications for tax design. Many of these conflict with economic equity and efficiency goals which would be considered important for ideal tax systems, absent administrative considerations. Here an attempt is made to provide ten process guidelines for reformers on how to take account of tax administration in designing tax reforms. Inevitably, suggestions are very general. This is a consequence of the absence of OSFA.

1. Before identifying tax reforms plan TD effectiveness and efficiency enhancing reforms (automation, internal capacity and incentive reforms) which can strengthen the TD: Suggestions for this have not been discussed in this paper (but see Annex 2).
2. Identify tax reforms which can make TA more effective without large economic or equity costs and implement these first. This includes penalties, evidence standards, clear laws, and tax stability.
3. Attempt to strengthen international cooperation and information exchange.
4. Identify administrative impediments and costs of the existing tax system, paying special attention to TD and TA information requirements.
5. Examine, if possible estimate, the extent of non-compliance and tax base erosion due to narrow tax bases: Identify scope for rate moderation, base broadening and reducing the number of taxable entities.
6. Examine the nature and extent of legal disputes, dispute resolution procedures and costs. Identify and implement cost reducing reforms to tax provisions and dispute resolution procedures and pricing.
7. Identify and selectively implement reforms which reduce information needs of the TD after weighing their likely efficiency and equity costs.: Presumptions, presumptive taxes, final withholding taxes.
8. Identify privatization opportunities, weigh their costs against costs of the TD carrying out the same activity and selectively implement them.
9. Implement lenient taxation of mobile and hard-to-tax bases which cannot be tackled by final withholding taxes and presumptions.
10. Prospectively take account of likely future trends in economic activity.

6. CONCLUDING COMMENTS

There are at least 3 potentially important ways in which TA affects tax design that are not dealt with in this paper. The first is the link between optimal tax enforcement, particularly tax investigations and audits, and tax design. Recent theoretical work suggests that the two are intrinsically related (see Annex 2). However, further contributions must be awaited as it appears difficult to extract practical lessons from this literature at present. The second is the important issue of bureaucratic inertia as an impediment to tax reform. The problem appears to be related to the issue of political will as a prerequisite for reform, one of Richard Bird's observations noted in the introduction.[81] While there are suggestive pointers in the literature and from experience, I did not feel sufficiently sure of my ground to draw even tentative conclusions about the nature and significance of this impediment. The third issue is the implications of TA for tax assignment and intergovernmental transfers in federations of different types. This topic is inadequately researched. So while several tentative hypotheses can be identified, the issue merits detailed treatment which would greatly expand this already long paper.

How to increase the knowledge base on characteristics of administration that are covered in this paper? How to sharpen our understanding of administrative constraints in the design of taxes?

The emergence of a coherent, information and incentive based, theory of tax administration effectiveness and efficiency will be a great help. Nevertheless, neither the predictions of such a theory, nor informal propositions such as those in this paper can be accepted with any degree of confidence unless rigorous empirical testing is possible. Adequate cross-country or historical information is needed for this: This suggests a crucial role for multi-lateral institutions such as the IMF, the World Bank the OECD and certain UN organs: Only these institutions are in a position to put together a data base which can be used to subject tax administration and its impact on tax policy to rigorous examination.

Annex 1. Regression results for correlates with collection costs in Indian states.

Table A1. Tax collection cost ratio and correlates: Regression Results Data on 14 major Indian states, 1985-86 to 2000-01)

Regression Number	Sign and significance level of regression coefficients (e.g.: "-1" indicates a negative coefficient significant at 1%)								R-square	D-W	Method
	Constant	GSDP per cap	Urban share	Area	Transfer share	Agri share	Manu share	Population			
1. Aggregate regressions											
1A (basic)	-1	-1							0.258	0.076	OLS
1B (full)	-1	**50**	-1	1	1	3	2		0.884	0.701	OLS
1B-a (full excluding sector shares)	-1	9	-1	1	1				0.806	0.450	OLS
1C (full excluding GSDP/pop)	-1		-1	1	1	3	1		0.883	0.691	OLS
1D (significant only)	-1		-1		10				0.991	2.195	WLS, AR1
1E	-5	-5	-1		2	**12**	**60**		0.992	2.054	WLS, AR1-S

Table A1. (Continued)

Regression Number	Sign and significance level of regression coefficients (e.g.: "-1" indicates a negative coefficient significant at 1%)								R-square	D-W	Method
	Constant	GSDP per cap	Urban share	Area	Transfer share	Agri share	Manu share	Population			
1F	**-34**	-1	-1		3				0.991	2.041	WLS, AR1-S
1G	-1		-1	1	6				0.961	2.096	WLS, AR1-S
1H	-1	-1							0.993	2.167	WLS, AR1-S
2. Fixed Effects											
2A (basic)		-1							0.941	0.817	OLS
2B		-3	-3		4				0.943	0.848	OLS
2B-a		-1	-3		3			6	0.944	0.880	OLS
2C			-1		1	4			0.943	0.859	OLS
2D			-1		**16**				0.962	1.965	OLS, AR1
2H		-1							0.993	1.879	WLS, AR1

Table A1. (Continued)

Regression Number	Sign and significance level of regression coefficients (e.g.: "-1" indicates a negative coefficient significant at 1%)								R-square	D-W	Method
	Constant	GSDP per cap	Urban share	Area	Transfer share	Agri share	Manu share	Population			
3. Fixed Effects, State Specific GSDP Effects											
3A (basic)		-ive, <10: 9 +ive, <10: 1 -ive: 2 +ive: 2							0.965	1.352	OLS
3B (full, significant only)		-ive, <10: 8 +ive, <10: 2 -ive: 2 +ive: 2			2				0.966	1.413	OLS
3B-b (full, significant only)		-ive, <10: 6 +ive, <10: 1 -ive: 4 +ive: 3			2				0.992	1.900	WLS, AR1

Notes:

1. In each of the three sets of regressions, the letters A,B,C, etc. identify regressions with the same initial set of included variables. In 1D, 3B and 3C, insignificant variables were then dropped.
2. AR1: First order autoregressive error specification.
3. AR1-S: First order autoregressive error specification allowing for separate processes in each state.
4. Transfer share: Share of Central government transfers in total revenue of the state.
5. Insignificant coefficients are in bold type.
6. Source of Data: The World Bank's data base on state finances in India, used with permission.

Annex 2. Some TA Properties Without Implications for Tax Design

	Proposition	Reform Implication
1	TA effectiveness decreases with administrative corruption[1]	Provide administration with incentives
2	TD effectiveness increases when its goals are aligned with social goals[2]	Provide administration with incentives
3	If the size of a TD is optimal, its marginal budgetary costs will be well below the marginal revenue gain.[3]	Monitor trends in TD cost of collecting taxes and implicitly limit size of the TD in accordance with a cost-revenue benchmark
4	TD audit probabilities and strategy should be jointly determined with optimal taxes (see the discussion below)	Modify audit strategy when tax laws change
5	Long run TD effectiveness is reduced by tax amnesties – as are effective tax rates. Permanent tax amnesties have no offsetting benefits	Declare few, if any, tax amnesties. The scope and duration of the amnesty should be clearly defined
6	TD effectiveness but also TD costs, decrease with sophisticated taxpayers[4]	Selectively educate taxpayers. Regulate tax practitioners
7	TA costs decrease with taxpayer education and assistance	Taxpayer education and assistance are essential TD functions
8	TD effectiveness is increased with explicit performance orientation	Introduce performance orientation (Table A2.1)
9	TD effectiveness decreases with fragmented administration	Consolidate administration
10	TD effectiveness and efficiency are increased, if there are many potential taxpayers, given information technologically enabled intra-TD coordination, with functionally specialized organizations[5]	Automate and organize TDs functionally where there are sufficiently many potential taxpayers
11	TD effectiveness is increased if information from third-parties is selectively used	Selectively introduce third-party reporting requirements

TD audit probabilities and strategy should be jointly determined with optimal taxes.The optimal audit strategy of the TD is still an area in which a consensus is to emerge, despite considerable research effort.[6] One important issue is whether it is empirically reasonable to assume that the TD can commit in advance to an audit strategy or not. Optimal audit strategies, but given a predetermined tax schedule, differ depending on which assumption best approximates practice. Practical advice is typically for a commitment strategy, with "risk-based" selection of taxpayers for audit by computer software serving as a pre-commitment device. If commitment ability is the more realistic approximation, then within a group for which the TD has identical information prior to audit about incomes of group members ("audit class"), audit probabilities should optimally be decreasing in reported income.[7] Thus the observed practice in some countries, of auditing with greater frequency taxpayers who report high incomes, reduces TD effectiveness.[8]

Table A2.1. Institutions for Effective Tax Departments[9]

Objective	Operational Implementation
Clarity of goals	(a) Mission and Vision statements (b) Citizen's Charter (c) Medium range modernization plan
Measure goal achievement or performance	Systems of performance indicators reflecting effectiveness, efficiency and citizen's service quality, to measure Mission achievement and modernization plan progress quantitatively[10]
Enable performance	(a) Operational autonomy for tax departments. (b) Functional organization
Communicate performance	(a) Annual Reports to government on the administration's performance in terms of effectiveness, efficiency and citizen's service quality. (b) Performance reports for individuals, functional units and field offices based on performance indicators Administration budgets linked to performance
Reward and motivate performance	Positive and negative individual and unit performance incentives

Notes to Annex 2:

1. See Mookherjee (1997).
2. See Mookherjee and Png (1985) and Kahn, Silva and Ziliak (2001).
3. See Slemrod and Yitzhaki (1987)
4. See Erard (1993).
5. For example, see McLaren (2003), Silvani and Baer (1997).
6. A balanced review is in Andreoni et. al. (1998).
7. Examples of papers with this result are Cremer and Gavhari (1993, 1996), Mookherjee and Png (1994) and Chander and Wilde (1998). The audit results assume risk neutral taxpayers and, in Chander and Wilde, have a particularly simple form: that the marginal expected tax rate and audit probability functions are identical up to an additive constant. With risk averse taxpayers Mookherjee and Png (1989) show that the audit rule may not be monotonic in reported income. In the case of a corrupt TD and non-compliant taxpayers, Chander and Wilde's results suggest that tax schedules should be even more regressive than in the case of an honest TD.
8. This does not mean that taxpayers who are not observationally identical to the TD must have audit probabilities decreasing in reported income. Two important cases are: If the same tax code applies, less TD effort should be spent on those who are harder to tax. Second, Large Taxpayer Units, widely advocated by policy experts, can increase TD effectiveness, *provided they are identified by characteristics other than reported income.* A theoretical and empirical analysis

for India of the negative impact on TD effectiveness when large taxpayers are in fact identified by reported income is in Das-Gupta, Ghosh and Mookherjee (2004).

9. This is a revised version of a table in Apte and Das-Gupta (2002)
10. For an introduction to and assessment of numerical performance measurement, see Carter (1991). See also Baer, Castro and Vehorn (1997), Febres, et. al. (1998) and Silva (2003).

Notes

1. In his introductory remarks on tax administration in the course " Practical Issues of Tax Policy and Tax Administration in Developing Countries" organized by the World Bank, March 22-25, 2004, New Delhi.
2. See, for example, Atkinson and Stern (1974), Feldstein (1997) and Slemrod and Yitzhaki (1996, 1998, 2002).
3. For example, Adam Smith's canons of taxation of 'Certainty', 'Convenience', 'Economy', and 'Equity'. Note that the first three relate directly or indirectly to TA costs.
4. Though not directly relevant to the rest of this paper, it should be borne in mind that recent attempts to measure the excess burden of taxation suggest that these are much higher than they were earlier thought to be. See Harberger (2004) in this conference and references cited there.
5. See also Atkinson and Stern (1974) and Slemrod and Yitzhaki (2002).
6. Private sector costs and TD costs do not have additive effects on the MECF. The equation derived by Slemrod and Yitzhaki (1996) for the case where distribution is not taken account of is $MECF_i = \frac{\gamma(X_i - MR_i) + C_i + MR_i}{MR_i - A_i}$, where X_i is the potential increase in tax revenue if the tax base remained unchanged after the marginal increase in the ith tax instrument, MR_i is the marginal revenue actually collected: $(X_i - MR_i)$ is therefore termed by them as the "leakage" out of the tax system. γ is a valuation parameter which will be above unity if taxpayer's optimal responses are constrained ("at a corner"), C_i is the marginal private sector compliance cost, and A_i is the marginal administrative cost – so that $MR_i - A_i$ is the net revenue raised. Distributional effects, both on the resource and expenditutre sides are incorporated in Slemrod and Yitzhaki (2002).
7. See also Fortin and Lacroix (1994) who analyse Canadian taxes.
8. It would be of great interest to apply the MECF approach to assess the relative desirability of different financing options from a "public finance" perspective. While usable parameter estimates are not yet available, it is very likely that, in most economies, both administration and compliance costs will be smaller for marginal increases in money or bond finance as compared to, say, revenue from stepped up tax audits.
9. For a theoretical analysis, see Das-Gupta and Gang (2003). The analysis of international experience in Ebrill et. al. (2001) does not find clear evidence of growth benefits from the VAT, though this could be due to data limitations.
10. As illustrated by the administratively simple Thatcher tax, the tax must first have a minimum degree of social acceptability so there is something to administer. I thank Luc Noiset for this point.

11. This hypothesis has been put forward repeatedly in the literature. For a recent example, see Bird (forthcoming). Or consider Slemrod and Yitzhaki (1998): "An important set of generic aspects of income tax structure, non-taxation of imputed rents of consumer durables, taxation of capital gains (if at all) on a realization basis, and pre-set depreciation schedules, are undoubtedly largely driven by practical concerns of administratability."
12. As Lasheras and Herrera (1991) put it, costs increase if more information needs to be collected, used and stored, not if more revenue needs to be collected.
13. This does not justify neglect of necessary information. For example, tax return form simplification achieved by drastically reducing their information content will reduce the accuracy of tax determination by the TD. Nor does this condone the collection of excessive information, usually a much more serious problem (see Bird forthcoming).
14. Or consider Wallschutzky (1989) as quoted in Bird (forthcoming): Keep the tax laws as simple as possible; - Aim for a global tax with few exemptions, credits, rebates, or deductions; - Do not try to use the tax system to achieve too many social and economic goals; - Continually monitor the tax system; - Concentrate on basic tasks such as collection of tax at source and an ID number system; - *Do not collect more information than can be processed; — Actively encourage good record keeping; and — Aim, as a long term goal, for self-assessment*" (emphasis added). Additional references are cited in Bird (forthcoming).
15. A recent government commission in the state of Karnataka in India determined that the number of commodity tax rates on different goods, due to multiple levies and differing bases, was potentially infinite! See Finance Department, Government of Karnataka (2001).
16. For a recent evaluation of the impact of misclassification on customs revenue, see Fisman and Wei (2004).
17. Unless tax rates with a broad base are inefficiently high being beyond the rate(s) at which the Laffer curve peaks.
18. The paper by Alm and Wallace (2004) in this conference reaches broadly the same conclusion based on an examination of Jamaica's tax reform experience.
19. Slemrod and Yitzhaki (1998). Tax complexity is discussed further below.
20. This was the rationale of the Israeli *tahshiv*. See Tanzi and Casanegra de Jantscher (1987) and Rajaraman (1995) for discussion and evaluation of this and other presumptive tax schemes.
21. However, Terpker (2003) points to an inevitable caveat: Resources expended to tax the hard-to-tax may optimally be more than pure revenue and efficiency considerations dictate, if tax morale or compliance by others is adversely affected by the existence of lightly taxed sectors. Such inefficient use of resources is less costly in developed countries which have smaller proportions of hard-to-tax taxpayers according to preliminary evidence in Alm and Martinez-Vazquez (2003).
22. Complete exemption of the informal sector is one of two possible optima for low capacity TDs, due to enforcement costs being intrinsically non-convex in the model of McLaren (1998). He measures TD capacity by the number of audits a tax inspector can conduct.
23. For recent reviews see Alm and Martinez-Vazquez (2003) and Terpker (2003).
24. Evasion of taxes by individuals who have taxes withheld has been found to be lowest among different groups in the Taxpayer Compliance and Monitoring Surveys conducted periodically by the United States Internal Revenue Service. See, for example, Kamdar (1995) and Slemrod and Bakija (1996). For indirect evidence see the discussion of the "balance due effect" in Jouljaian and Rider (1998) and references cited there. For theoretical analysis of withholding, including evasion out of withheld taxes, see Yaniv (1988, 1998) and Das-Gupta (2004).

25. See Yaniv (1999) and the reference cited there. Yaniv (1999) seeks to explain this finding using the prospect theory hypothesis. In particular, non-rational taxpayers who have had to pay advance taxes according to schedules laid down in the tax law are assumed to focus on "out-of-pocket" gains at the time of filing.
26. In the language of production functions, these tax base features can be identified either as productive inputs or components of the "residual", in the spirit of Denison, in a TD production function. Production functions of tax administrations are examined or described in Lasheras and Herrera (1991), Bagchi, Bird and Das-Gupta (1995), Hunter and Nelson (1996), Das-Gupta and Ghosh and Mookherjee (2004) and Bird (forthcoming).
27. Earlier cross-country evidence on collection costs, though not of scale economies, is in Lasheras and Herrera (1991) and Das-Gupta and Mookherjee (1998). The former present data on 10 member countries of The Inter-American Association of Tax Administrations (CIAT) while the latter present data on 19 countries from different sources.
28. Even these data are not fully comparable: Though all states follow the same modified cash accounting system and though major accounting heads are common to all states, local variations in minor accounting heads exist. The data, on "expenditure on collection of taxes and duties" used here, are taken from the World Bank which, in turn, are taken from data compiled by the Reserve Bank of India. Permission from the World Bank to use the data is gratefully acknowledged. For Maharashtra, data have been "cleaned" using government of Maharashtra figures, to remove some transfers to reserve funds booked under the account head. Regarding tax structures, four taxes, the sales tax, stamp duties and registration fees, state excises on liquor and motor vehicle taxes contributed between 72.3 and 99.4 of own tax revenue in different years during this period, with a mean of 90.4 and a coefficient of variation of 0.07.
29. A simple double-log regression has an R-squared of 0.26. This rises to 0.99 on either including other hypothesized determinants or on using weighted least squares and a first order autoregressive error specification.
30. An additional variable, the share of central government transfers to states in their total revenue, proved to be highly significant in most cases, suggesting a negative impact of transfers on state tax collection effort, as reflected in cost efficiency. This is similar to findings for some other countries though the specific channel through TD collection efficiency has not been previously noticed.
31. An OLS regression of the (log) share of "income, profits and capital gains taxes" in total taxes on (log) GDP per capita and dummy variables for oil producing and transition economies, using data on 101 countries from the World Bank's World Development Indicators for 2001, has a positive coefficient, significant at 99% but an R-squared of only 0.288. This is similar to findings of earlier cross-country tax structure studies. Earlier work is in Hinrichs (1966), Bahl (1971), Chelliah et. al. (1975), Tait et. al (1979), Tanzi (1992) and Das-Gupta and Mookherjee (1998). See also Martinez-Vazquez, Bird and Torgler (2004) in this conference.
32. Discussions of complexity are in McClure (1989), Glassberg and Smyth (1995), Kaplow (1996), Slemrod and Bakija (1996), and James, Sawyer and Wallschutzky (1997). According to Bagchi, Bird and Das-Gupta (1995): "Complexity refers to the possibility of the base being wrongly estimated even if all components are fully observable". They point to the measurement of complexity as an important task for research. A recent attempt by Gale and Holtzblatt (2002), who define complexity as the total resource cost of the tax system, partly following an earlier suggestion of Joel Slemrod, is unsatisfactory, as it assumes as true the hypothesis that complexity, and complexity alone, leads to high costs.
33. For example, McClure (1989) identifies five causes of income tax complexity: (a) rules to precisely define real economic income; (b) tax expenditure clauses; (c) provisions to counter abuse of tax concessions or resulting inequity; (d) rules covering the transition between existing and new provisions; and (e) a general lack of logical coherence of the tax law.

34. For example, see Baer (2002) and also McCarten (2004) in this volume. As usual "the devil is in the details": A caveat to this exception is that the *reported* tax base of a taxpayer is not the correct criterion to identify large taxpayers: as with presumptive taxes, characteristics which are easy for the TD to observe and which are hard for the taxpayer to manipulate should instead be used. See Das-Gupta, Ghosh and Mookherjee (2004).
35. The advice to retain border checks is to be found in the context of the VAT by Ebrill et. al. (2001). For example, the removal of border checks in the European Union has resulted in falling VAT revenue from cross-border goods sales (Chang Woon Nam et. al. 2003). For discussion of the case of India, see Das-Gupta (2003).
36. Physical asset sales and ownership also fall into this category. Property and asset taxes are of limited importance in most countries, except for local government finance and some city states (Hong Kong, Singapore) where they can be a major source of revenue. Why an economically efficient base like immobile land is not more heavily taxed is not a question which this paper is competent to deal with. Furthermore, while the logic of the argument being presented here would apply to property and asset taxes, it is difficult to conclude that increased reliance on property taxes is possible or desirable without taking into account alternative potential sources of local government finance. This issue is not pursued further here.
37. For a recent discussion of these issues in the context of tax information exchange treaties see Zagaris (2003).
38. See Bagchi, Bird and Das-Gupta (1995), Bird (forthcoming) and, for the VAT, Das-Gupta and Gang (2003).
39. In case of non-compliance, a Type I error is where a tax offender remains uncaught and a Type II error is where a taxpayer is incorrectly found guilty of a tax offence. Holding constant TD capacity, low standards of evidence increase the incidence of Type II error and stringent standards increase Type I error. The possibility of error is one resolution to the Becker paradox of low penalty rates proposed in the literature (Bolton, 1996, Boadway and Sato, 2000).
40. A general discussion is in Bagchi, Bird and Das-Gupta (1995). See also Ramirez Acuna (1992).
41. Discussion of revenue authorities is in Jenkins (1994), Devas, et. al. (2000) and Talierco (2003).
42. See Toma and Toma (1991). An important issue in outsourcing is the nature of the contract signed between the government and the private agent. A general survey of contract forms is in McAfee and McMillan (1987). For tax farming, the issue is discussed briefly by Toma and Toma (1991). The importance of contract forms in practice is discussed for private pre-shipment inspection services for customs administration by Low (1995). Though not directly related to tax design, the contract form is crucial and largely determines government and social benefits from out-sourcing, both in theory and practice. For related analysis, see Mookherjee and Png (1995), Mookherjee (1997) and Wane (2000).
43. Increased tax competition, another consequence of globalization, does not directly involve tax administration issues. There is a large body of writing on the subject. For example, see McLure (2004) in this conference, Owen (1993), Tanzi and Zee (2000), Lodin (2002), Dwyer (2002) and Zagaris (2001, 2003). The discussion of issues that do concern this paper also draws largely on these papers.
44. This discussion is based on Lodin (2002). See also McClure (2004) in this conference.
45. Three common tax avoidance practices are "double dipping" through different characterizations of cross-border transactions in jurisdictions involved, exploiting differences in entity characterization in host and home countries, and exploiting differences in tax accounting rules in host and home countries. These can, to an extent, be reduced by harmonizing tax laws. See Asian Development Bank Institute (2001).

46. See, for example, Owens (1993), Bagchi, Bird and Das-Gupta (1995) and references cited there, and Muten (2002).
47. Tax havens and off-shore financial centres also facilitate financing and profiting from criminal and terrorist activity and weaken national policing and control efforts.
48. Among the important responses are unilateral Controlled Financial Corporation (CFC) legislation pioneered by the USA, common definitions of "harmful tax competition" and codes of conduct or multilateral action, even coercive action, against tax havens, multilateral guidelines for transparent financial reporting by offshore banks, information exchange or tax collection agreements. See Zagaris (2001, 2003), Lodin (2002) and Muten (2002).
49. Zee (1998) and Lodin (2002).
50. For the inevitable argument against tax harmonization, this time from theory, see Cremer and Gavhari (2000). Also see Fuest and Huber (2001).
51. Asian Development Bank Institute (2001) and Lodin (2002).
52. The major tax design problem arises with apportioning the potential tax base and establishing the jurisdiction which has the right to tax a particular sale or income under either existing source or residence rules (Lodin, 2002). An example from Peha and Strauss (1997) illustrates this: If a doctor from the US gives advice via the internet to a medical team in the UK while on vacation in the Bahamas, where did the transaction take place?
53. Though the main purpose of bilateral tax treaties is to avoid double taxation of income, they help to bring about uniformity of terminology. Furthermore, many treaties also have information exchange clauses.
54. For a description of the VIES see Hutchison (1996) and European Union (2002). Chang Woon Nam, et.al. (2003) estimate VAT evasion in the EU on account of check post abolition. For general conclusions of the desirability of border controls, despite their impeding trade, see Ebrill et. al. (2001).
55. For discussion of clearing house mechanisms and alternatives see Ebrill et. al. (2001), including references to a debate in *International Tax and Public Finance* (2000).
56. An extensive analysis with several country studies is in Shah (1995), though administrative aspects are given limited attention. The studies also provide a comparative assessment of the effectiveness of different types of tax incentives such as tax holidays versus investment allowances.
57. Se for, example, Tanzi and Zee (2000) For a recent Indian example, see Rajaraman et. al. (1999).
58. For example, empirical evidence is in Clotfelter (1983), Alm, Bahl and Murray (1990, 1991), Bahl and Martinez-Vazquez (1992), Das-Gupta, Lahiri and Mookherjee (1995), Joulfaian and Rider (1998) and all nine papers surveyed in De Juan, Lasheras and Mayo (1994). While the basic tax evasion model of Allingham and Sandmo (1972) predicts a *positive* relation between tax rates and tax revenue with penalties proportional to evaded taxes (Yitzhaki, 1974), extensions to allow leakage of the tax base weaken the relation allowing for a "Laffer curve" response.
59. The analysis in Marelli (1982) suggests low effective rates for risk averse taxpayers but low expected rates for risk neutral taxpayers.
60. For example, Alm, Bahl and Murray (1991) report simulations to determine individual income tax rates for Jamaica, but not the results. Das-Gupta, Lahiri and Mookherjee (1995), report results of small perturbations but do not examine large changes in tax rates.
61. See Cremer and Gavhari (1996), Chander and Wilde (1998) and also Boadway and Sato (2000). The relation to tax administration is direct: Tax evasion can only occur if a TD is unable or unwilling to eradicate tax evasion.

62. Furthermore, Cremer and Gavhari (1996) find that a result of earlier general income tax models without tax evasion, that the top marginal tax rate should be zero at a high enough income level, continues to hold.
63. For example, see Casanegre de Jantscher (1992) and Bagchi, Bird and Das-Gupta (1995).
64. Bird (forthcoming) views 30 to 35 percent inflation per year as high.
65. An example from India illustrates how conceptually simple present value adjustments can be viewed as complex by taxpayers even if they are beneficial to the taxpayer: Long term capital gains in India were required to be computed as $S - P(C_S/C_P)$, where S is the sale price in rupees, P is the purchase price in rupees and C_S and C_P are "Cost Inflation Indices" announced for each year in a year-end notification (these merely reproduces a Consumer Price Index) by the Income Tax Department. C_S is for the year of sale and C_P for the year of purchase. This "complicated" system was recently reviewed by an expert committee and its removal has been proposed in the Indian Government's Finance Bill, 2004.
66. Fir an analysis of jail sentences in tax cases see Chu and Jiang (1993), Polinsky and Shavell (2000) and also Garoupa and Gomez-Powar (2000).
67. Mookherjee and Png (1989), Cremer and Gavhari (1996), Chander and Wilde (1998) and Boadway and Sato (2000).
68. Empirical results (reviewed in Andreoni, et. al., 1998) suggest that existing penalties do deter non-compliance. However, discouraging experimental results on the deterrent effect of existing levels of penalties has been obtained by Alm, McKee and Jackson (1992). A theoretical result on the limited deterrent impact of penalties on the hard-to-tax is in Das-Gupta (1994).
69. This is also true of excess burden costs as discussed by Feldstein (1997) and Harberger (2004) in this conference.
70. All compliance cost studies during the past 70 years on which information was found are listed in Chattopadhyay and Das-Gupta (2002, 2002a) along with their main features. Unfortunately, almost all studies to date have been for developed countries.
71. Slemrod and Venkatesh (2002) also estimate that US companies with international operations had compliance costs 143 percent higher than other US companies, which suggests that TD information requirements can act as a hidden cost of openness. It may not be a coincidence that earlier work by Joulfaian (1993) finds that firms with foreign operations, specifically links with tax havens, have significantly lower rates of compliance.
72. Information to express more recent compliance cost estimates for the US in Blumenthal and Slemrod (1992) as a percentage of tax paid was not available.
73. Indian compliance cost estimates are from Chattopadhyay and Das-Gupta (2002, 2002a). The impact of compliance costs on compliance behaviour of individuals and estimates of non-compliance costs of non-filers are examined in Chattopadhyay and Das-Gupta (2002b). Their estimates are preliminary and subject to a large error margin, due to small and biased samples owing to non-response. Nevertheless, estimates for individuals were deliberately biased downward, to reduce the possibility of overestimation, both for individual responses and during aggregation. Various steps taken to do this are described in the studies. Estimates presented here net out bribe costs, since these transfers do not involve additional resource costs. Conversely, tax deductible compliance expenditures are not netted out. The first two studies also attempt to identify "hot spots" or high compliance cost tax provisions and administrative procedures. The estimates do not include "psychic" costs of tax complexity, ambiguity and instability to avoid possible double counting. These are reported separately.
74. Tax deductibility or rebating of costs can, in principle be used to ensure that the compliance burden on individuals and third parties is not excessive. As usual, since this

can make the tax system more complex and open a loophole for inflated deduction claims, general rules are not available.

75. Singapore has official rather than self assessment of the income tax. Taxes for income earned during a year are calculated by the Inland Revenue Authority at the end of the year and paid by taxpayers during the following year in instalments. If there was no income fluctuation, this would merely reduce the tax due in present value terms which could be made good by tax rate adjustment. With fluctuating incomes, the certainty, convenience and taxpayer compliance cost saving this system imparts to tax dues has to be balanced against the risk of high tax dues when there is a negative shock to income. For a relatively recent examination of self-assessment and further references see Sandford (1994).
76. See Bahl and Martinez-Vazquez (1992), Talib (1996), Bardsley (1997) and Chattopadhyay and Das-Gupta (2002 and 2002a).
77. The high willingness-to-pay of corporations, in relation to measured private compliance costs suggests that part of the cost arises from business opportunities which become excessively risky due to tax ambiguity and not just direct compliance activity. While small sample bias is also possible, Chattopadhyay and Das-Gupta provide some case studies of decreased business investment.
78. See Kaplow (1996) and Erard (1993, 1997).
79. Tax complexity and instability also decrease the accuracy of revenue forecasts, making government budget planning harder.
80. Two other important measures, given that tax dispute are inevitable are, first, streamlining of appeals and dispute resolution procedures, though this is not directly a part of tax policy. On the other hand, appeals and court fees of different types need to be aligned with social costs so that taxpayers do not resort to overuse of disputes to delay tax payments or delay tax determination by the TD: These measures seldom receive attention in practice.
81. Complementary discussion on political institutions is in Hettech and Winer (2004) in this conference.

References

Alm James, Betty R. Jackson and Michael McKee (1992), "Estimating the Determinants of Taxpayer Compliance with Experimental Data", *National Tax Journal*, Vol. 45, pp. 107-114.

Alm, James and Jorge Martinex-Vazquez (2003), 'Sizing' the Problem of the Hard-to-tax, Draft paper, Andrew Young School of Policy Studies, Georgia State University.

Alm, James, Roy Bahl and Matthew N. Murray (1991), "Tax Base Erosion in Developing Countries", *Economic Development and Cultural Change*, pp. 849-872.

Alm, James and Sally Wallace (2004), "Can Developing Countries Impose A Personal Income Tax?", paper presented at "The Challenges of Tax Reform in the Global Economy" conference, Andrew Young School of Policy Studies, Georgia State University, May 23-25, 2004.

Andreoni, James, Brian Erard and Jonathan Feinstein (1998), "Tax Compliance", *Journal of Economic Literature*, Vol. 36, pp. 818-860.

Apte, Pradeep and Arindam Das-Gupta (2002), *Improving Maharashtra's Own Revenue Performance, report prepared for the World Bank*, mimeo, Mumbai: Indira Gandhi Institute of Development Research.

Asian Development Bank Institute (2001), *Millennium Tax Conference, 20–29 September 2000, Executive Summary Series No. S33/01*, Tokyo: Asian Development Bank Institute, Retrieved from http://www.adbi.org/PDF/ess/ES33.pdf

Atkinson, Anthony and Nicholas Stern (1974), "Pigou, Taxation, and Public Goods", *Review of Economic Studies*, Vol. 41, pp. 119-128.

Baer, Katharine (2002), *Improving Large Taxpayers' Compliance: A Review of Country Experience, Occasional Paper*, Washington, D.C.: The International Monetary Fund.

Bagchi, Amaresh, Richard M. Bird and Arindam Das Gupta (1995), *An Economic Approach to Tax Administration Reform, Discussion Paper No. 3*, Canada: International Centre for Tax Studies, University of Toronto Faculty of Management.

Bahl, Roy (1971), "A Regression Approach to Tax Effort and Tax Ratio Analysis", *IMF Staff Papers*, Vol. 18, pp. 570-612.

Bahl, Roy and Jorge Martinez-Vazquez (1992), "The Nexus of Tax Administration and Tax Policy in Jamaica and Guatemala" in: Richard M, Bird and Milka Casanegra de Jantsher, editors, *Improving Tax Administration in Developing Countries*, Washington DC: International Monetary Fund.

Barbone, Luca, Arindam Das-Gupta, Luc De Wulf and Anna Hansson (1999), *Reforming tax systems: The World Bank Record in the 1990's, Policy Research Paper WPS 2237*, Washington D.C.: The World Bank.

Bardsley, Peter (1997), "Simplifying the Tax Law: Some Implications for Small Business", *Australian Tax Forum*, Vol. 13, pp. 91-113.

Binh, Tran-Nam, Chris Evans, Michael Walpole and Katherine Ritchie (2000), "Tax Compliance Research: Research Methodology and Empirical Evidence from Australia, *National Tax Journal*, Vol. 53, pp. 229-251.

Bird, Richard M. (1982), "The Costs of Collecting Taxes: Preliminary Reflections on the Uses and Limits of Cost Studies", *Canadian Tax Journal*, Vol. 30, pp. 860-65.

Bird, Richard M. (forthcoming), "Administrative Dimensions of Tax Reform", *Bulletin for International Fiscal Documentation.*

Bird, Richard M. and Milka Casangera de Jantscher (Eds) (1992), *Improving Tax Administration in Developing Countries*, Washington, D.C.: International Monetary Fund.

Blumenthal, Marsha and Joel Slemrod (1992), "The Compliance Cost of the U.S. Individual Income Tax System: A Second Look after Tax Reform", *National Tax Journal*, Vol. 45, pp. 185-202.

Boadway, Robin and Motohiro Sato (2000), "The Optimality of Punishing only the Innocent: The Case of Tax Evasion", *International Tax and Public Finance*, Vol. 7(6), pp. 641-664.

Bolton, Patrick (1987), *The Principle of Maximum Deterrence Revisited, Working paper 8749*, USA: Department of Economics, University of California, Berkeley.

Brown, Karen B. (2003), "U.S. International Tax Administration and Developing Nations: Administrative Policy at the Crossroads", *The George Washington International Law Review*, Vol. 35, pp. 393-399.

Casanegra de Jantscher, Milka, (1990), "Administering a VAT", in: M. Gillis, C.S. Shoup, and G.P. Sicat, editors, *Value Added Taxation in Developing Countries*, Washington, D.C.: The World Bank.

Casanegra de Jantscher, Milka, Isaias Coelho and Arturo Fernandez (1992), "Tax Administration and Inflation", in: Richard M. Bird and Milka Casangera de Jantscher, editors, *Improving Tax Administration in Developing Countries*, Washington, D.C.: International Monetary Fund.

Chander, Parkash and Louis Wilde (1998), "A General Characterization of Optimal Income Taxation and Enforcement", *Review of Economic Studies*, Vol. 65, pp. 165-183.

Chang Woon Nam, Andrea Gebauer and Rüdiger Parsche (2003), *Is the Vompletion of EU Single Market Hindered by VAT Evasion?, Cesifo Working Paper No. 974*, Retrieved from www.CESifo.de.

Chattopadhyay, Saumen and Arindam Das-Gupta (2002), *The Compliance Cost of the Personal Income Tax and its Determinants*, Mimeo, New Delhi: NIPFP, Retrieved from http://www.planingcommission.nic.in/reports.

Chattopadhyay, Saumen and Arindam Das-Gupta (2002a), *The Income Tax Compliance Cost of Indian Corporations*, Mimeo, New Delhi: NIPFP, Retrieved from http://www.planingcommission.nic.in/reports.

Chattopadhyay, Saumen and Arindam Das-Gupta (2002b), *The Personal Income Tax in India: Compliance Costs and Compliance Behaviour of Taxpayers*, Mimeo, New Delhi: NIPFP, Retrieved from http://www.planingcommission.nic.in/reports.

Chelliah, Raja J., Hessel J. Baas and Margaret R. Kelley (1975), "Tax Ratios and Tax Effort in Developing Countries", *IMF Staff Papers*, Vol. 22, pp. 187-205.

Chu, C.Y. Cyrus and Neville Jiang (1993), "Are Fines More Efficient than Imprisonment? ", *Journal of Public Economics*, Vol. 51, pp. 391-413.

Clotfelter, Charles T. (1983), "Tax Evasion and Tax Rates: An Analysis of Individual Returns", *Review of Economics and Statistics*, Vol. 65, pp. 363-373.

Cremer, Helmuth and Firouz Gahvari (1993), "Tax Evasion and Optimal Commodity Taxation", *Journal of Public Economics*, Vol. 50(2), p. 261.

Cremer, Helmuth and Firouz Gahvari (1994), "Tax Evasion, Concealment and the Optimal Linear Income Tax", *The Scandinavian Journal Of Economics*, Vol. 96(2),

Cremer, Helmuth and Firouz Gahvari (1996), "Tax Evasion and the Optimum General Income Tax", *Journal of Public Economics*, Vol. 60(2).

Cremer, Helmuth and Firouz Gahvari (2000), "Tax Evasion, Fiscal Competition and Economic Integration", *European Economic Review*, Vol. 44(9), pp. 1633-1657.

Das-Gupta, A., R. Lahiri and D. Mookherjee (1995), "Income Tax Compliance in India: An Empirical Analysis," *World Development*, Vol. 23, pp. 2051-2068.

Das-Gupta, Arindam (1994), "A Theory of Hard to Tax Groups", *Public Finance*, Vol. 49, (Supplement), pp. 28-39, Proceedings of the 49th Congress of the International Institute of Public Finance, Berlin 1993.

Das-Gupta, Arindam (2003), "Internal Trade Barriers in India: Fiscal Check-posts", Retrieved from http://papers.ssrn.com/paper.taf?abstract_id=436240.

Das-Gupta, Arindam and Dilip Mookherjee (1998), *Incentives and Institutional Reform in Tax Enforcement*, New Delhi: Oxford University Press.

Das-Gupta, Arindam and Ira N. Gang (2003), "Value Added Tax Evasion, Auditing and Transactions Matching", in: John McLaren, editor, *Institutional Elements of Tax Design and Reform*, Technical paper no. 539, Washington, D.C.: The World Bank.

Das-Gupta, Arindam Michael Engelschalk and William Mayville (1999), *An Anticorruption Strategy for Revenue Administration*, PREM Note 33, Washington, D.C.: The World Bank.

Das-Gupta, Arindam, Shanto Ghosh and Dilip Mookherjee (2004), "Tax Administration Reform and Taxpayer Compliance in India", *International Tax and Public Finance*, Vol. 11, (forthcoming).

De Juan, A., M. Lasheras and R. Mayo (1994), "Voluntary Compliance Behaviour of Spanish Taxpayers", *Public Finance/Finances Publiques*, Vol. 49(Supplement), pp. 90-105.

Devas, Nick, Simon Delay and Michael Hubbard (2001), "Revenue Authorities: Are They the Right Vehicle for Improved Tax Administration?", *Public Administration and Development*, Vol. 21, pp. 211-222.

Dwyer, Terry (2002), "'Harmful' Tax Competition and the Future of Offshore Financial Centres", *Journal of Money Laundering Control*, Vol. 5(4), pp. 302-317.

Ebrill, Liam, Michael Keen, Jean-Paul Bodin and Victoria Summers (2001), *The Modern VAT*, Washington D.C: International Monetary Fund.

Erard, Brian (1993), "Taxation with Representation: An Analysis of the Role of Tax Practitioners in Tax Compliance", *Journal of Public Economics*, Vol. 33, pp. 163-197.

Erard, Brian (1997), "Self-selection with Measurement Errors: A Microeconometric Analysis of the Decision to Seek Tax Assistance and its Implications for Tax Compliance", *Journal Of Econometrics*, Vol. 81(2), pp. 319-356.

European Union (2002), "VIES (VAT Information Exchange System) Enquiries", Retrieved from http: //europa.eu.int/comm/taxation_customs/databases/vies_en.htm.

Export-Import Bank of India (1998), *Transactions Costs of Indian Exports: An Analysis, Occasional Paper No. 64*, Bombay: Export-Import Bank of India.

Feldstein, Martin (1997), "How Big should Bovernment Be?", *National Tax Journal*, Vol. 50, pp. 197-213.

Finance Department, Government of Karnataka (2001), *First Report of the Tax Reforms Committee*, Bangalore: Finance Department, Government of Karnataka.

Fisman, Raymond and Shang-Jin Wei (2004), "Tax Rates and Tax Evasion: Evidence from "Missing Imports" in China", *Journal of Political Economy*, Vol. 112(2), pp. 471-496.

Febres, Jorge, Marcio Gomes Da Cruz and Martín Bès (1998), *Management indicators for tax administration in Latin America and the Caribbean*, processed, Washington, D.C: Inter-American Development Bank.

Fortin, Bernard and Guy Lacroix (1994), "Labour Supply, Tax Evasion and the Marginal Cost of Public Funds: An Empirical Investigation", *Journal of Public Economics*, Vol. 55, pp. 407-431.

Fuest, Clemens and Bernd Huber (2001), "Why is there So Little Tax Coordination? The Role of Majority Voting and International Tax Evasion", *Regional Science And Urban Economics,* Vol. 31(2,3), pp. 299-317.

Gale, William G. and Janet Holzblatt (2002), "The Role of Administrative Issues in Tax Reform: Simplicity, Compliance, and Administration", in: Goerge R. Zodrow and Peter Mieszkowski, editors, *United States Tax Reform in the 21st Century*, Cambridge: Cambridge University Press.

Garoupa, Nuno and Fernando Gomez-Pomar (2000), "Punish Once or Punish Twice: A Theory of the Use of Criminal Sanctions in Addition to Regulatory Penalties",

Gill, Jit B.S. (2000), *A Diagnostic Framework for Revenue Administration, Technical Paper No. 472*, Washington, D.C.: The World Bank.

Glassberg, Barry and Christina Smyth (1995), "Tax Compliance Costs: the Problems and the Practice – Inland Revenue", in: Cedric Sandford, editor, *Tax Compliance Costs Measurement and Policy*, Bath, U.K: Fiscal Publications in association with The Institute for Fiscal Studies.

Harberger, Arnold (2004), "Coping with Inequality", paper presented at "The Challenges of Tax Reform in the Global Economy" conference, The Andrew Young School of Policy Studies, Georgia State University, May 23-25, 2004.

Hettich, Walter and Stanley Winer (2004), "Explaining Tax Reform", paper presented at "The Challenges of Tax Reform in the Global Economy" conference, The Andrew Young School of Policy Studies, Georgia State University, May 23-25, 2004.

Hinrichs, Harvey H. (1966), *A General Theory of Tax Structure Change During Economic Development*, Cambridge, Mass: Harvard Law School International Tax Program.

Hite, Peggy A and Adrian J. Sawyer (1997), "A Comparison of Compliance Cost Estimates for the Tax System in the United States and New Zealand", *International Bureau of Fiscal Documentation*, February, pp. 93-97.

Hunter, William J. and Michael A. Nelson (1996), "An IRS Produciton Function", *National Tax Journal*, Vol. 49, pp. 105-115.

Hutchison, Ian (1996), "The Value-added Tax Information Exchange System and Administrative Cooperation between the Tax Authorities of the European Community", in: Glenn P. Jenkins, editor, *Information Technology and Innovation in Tax Administration*, Amsterdam: Kluwer Law International.

International Fiscal Association (1989), *Studies in International Fiscal Law: Administrative and Compliance Costs of Taxation*, Cahiers De Droit Fiscal International, Volume: 74b, Rio de Janeiro: International Fiscal Association.

James, Simon, Adrian Sawyer and Ian Wallschutzky (1997), "Tax Simplification – A Tale of Three Countries", *Bulletin for International Fiscal Documentation,* November, pp. 493-503.

Jenkins, Glen (1994), "Modernizing of Tax Administration: Revenue Boards as An Instrument for Change," *Bulletin for International Fiscal Documentation*, Vol. 48(2),

Joulfaian, David (1993), "Corporate Income Tax Evasion", paper presented at the 49th Congress of the International Institute of Public Finance, Berlin.

Joulfaian, David and Mark Rider (1998), "Differential Taxation and Tax Evasion by Small Business", *National Tax Journal*, Vol. 51, pp. 675-687.

Kahn, Charles, Emilson C.D. Silva and James Ziliak (2001), "Performance-based Wages in Tax Collection: The Brazilian Tax Collection Reform and its Effects", *Economic Journal*, Vol. 111, pp. 118-205.

Kamdar, Nipoli (1995), "Information reporting and tax compliance: An investigation using individual TCMP data", *Atlantic Economic Journal*, Vol. 23(4), pp. 278-292.

Kaplow, Louis (1996), "How Tax Complexity and Enforcement Affect the Equity and Efficiency of the Income Tax", *National Tax Journal*, Vol. 49, pp. 135-150.

Lasheras, Miguel and Carlos Herrera (1991), "Tax Administration and Fiscal System: A Comparative Analysis", processed, Madrid: Instituto de Estudios Fiscales.

Lodin, Sven-Olaf (2002), "What Ought to be Taxed and What Can be Taxed: A New International Dilemma", in: M. Govinda Rao, editor, *Development, Poverty, and Fiscal Policy: Decentralization of Institutions: Essays in honour of Raja J. Chelliah*, New Delhi: Oxford University Press.

Low, Patrick (1995), *Preshipment inspection services, World Bank Discussion Papers 278*, Washington, D.C.: The World Bank.

Marelli, Massimo (1984), "On Indirect Tax Evasion", *Journal of Public Economics*, Vol. 25, pp. 181-196.

Martinez-Vazquez, Jorge, Richard Bird and Benno Torgler (2004), "Increasing Tax Effort in Developing Countries", paper presented at "The Challenges of Tax Reform in the Global Economy" conference, The Andrew Young School of Policy Studies, Georgia State University, May 23-25, 2004.

Mayshar, Joram (1991), "Taxation with Costly Administration", *Scandinavian Journal of Economics*, Vol. 43, pp. 263-89.

McAffee, P.R. and J. McMillan (1987), "Auctions and Bidding", *Journal of Economic Literature*, Vol. 25, pp. 699-738.

McCarten, William (2004), "Large Taxpayer Units and the VAT", paper presented at "The Challenges of Tax Reform in the Global Economy" conference, The Andrew Young School of Policy Studies, Georgia State University, May 23-25, 2004.

McLaren, John (2003), "Corruption and the Organization of Tax Administration: Non-Smithian Benefits from Specialization", in: John McLaren, editor, *Institutional elements of tax design and reform*, Technical Paper No. 539, Washington,D.C.: The World Bank.

McLaren, John (ed.) (2003), *Institutional Elements of Tax Design and Reform, Technical Paper No. 539*, Washington, D.C.: The World Bank.

McLure, Jr., Charles E. (1989), "The Budget Process and Tax Simplification/Complication", *Tax Law Review*, Vol. 45, pp. 25-96.

McLure, Jr., Charles E. (2004), "Transfer Pricing and Tax Havens: Mending the LDC Revenue Net", paper presented at "The Challenges of Tax Reform in the Global Economy" conference, The Andrew Young School of Policy Studies, Georgia State University, May 23-25, 2004.

Mookherjee, Dilip (1997), "Incentive Reform in Developing Country Bureaucracies: Lessons from Tax Administration", *Annual World Bank Conference on Development Economics*, pp. 103-125.

Mookherjee, Dilip and I.P.L. Png (1989), "Optimal Auditing, Insurance and Redistibution", *Quarterly Journal of Economics*, Vol. 104(2), pp. 399-416.

Mookherjee, Dilip and Ivan P.L. Png (1994), "Marginal Deterrence in Enforcement of Law", *Journal of Political Economy*, Vol. 102, pp. 1039-1066.

Mookherjee, Dilip and Ivan P.L. Png (1995), "Corruptible Law Enforcers: How should they be Compensated?", *Economic Journal*, Vol. 105, pp. 145-159.

Muten (2002), "Fiscal relations between rich and poor countries", in: M. Govinda Rao, editor, *Development, Poverty, and Fiscal Policy: Decentralization of Institutions* (Essays in honour of Raja J. Chelliah), New Delhi: Oxford University Press.

Oldman, Oliver (1965), "Controlling Income Tax Evasion", in: *Joint Tax Program, Problems of Tax Administration in Latin America,* Baltimore: Johns Hopkins University Press.

Owens, Jeffrey (1993), "Globalisation: The Implications for Tax Policies", *Fiscal Studies*, Vol. 14(3), pp. 21-44.

Peha, Jon M. and Robert P. Strauss (1997), "A Primer on Changing Information Technology and the Fisc", *National Tax Journal*, Vol. 50(1), pp. 607-621.

Poapongsakorn, Nipon, Kovit Charnvitayapong, Duangmanlee Laovakul and Bev Dahlby (2000), "A Cost Benefit Analysis of the Thailand Taxpayer Survey", *International Tax and Public Finance*, Vol. 7, pp. 63-82.

Polinsky, A.Michael and Steven Shavell (2000), "The Economic Theory of Public Enforcement of Law", *Journal of Economic Literature*, Vol. 38, pp. 45-76.

Pope, Jeff (1994), "Compliance Costs of Taxation: Policy Implications", *Australian Tax Forum*, Vol. 11, pp. 85-121.

Rajaraman, Indira (1995), "Presumptive Direct Taxation: Lessons from Experience in Developing Countries", *Economic and Political Weekly*, Vol. 30, pp. 1103-1124.

Rajaraman, Indira and M. J. Bhende (1998), "A Land Based Agricultural Presumptive Tax Designed for Levy by Panchayats", *Economic and Political Weekly*, Vol. 33, pp. 765-768.

Rajaraman, Indira, Hiranya Mukhopadhyay and Namita Bhatia (1999), *Fiscal Industrial Incentives of the Government of Madhya Pradesh: Costs and Benefits*, New Delhi: National Institute of Public Finance and Policy.

Ramirez Acuna and Luis Fernando (1992), "Privatization of Tax Administration", in: Richard M. Bird and Milka Casangera de Jantscher, editors, *Improving Tax Administration in Developing Countries*, Washington, D.C.: International Monetary Fund.

Rhoades, Shelley C. (1999), "The Impact of Multiple Component Reporting on Tax Compliance and Audit Strategies", *The Accounting Review*, Vol. 74(1), pp. 63-85.

Roy Bahl and Matthew N. Murray (1990), "Tax Structure and Tax Compliance", *The Review of Economics and Statistics*, Vol. 72, pp. 603-613.

Sadka, Efriam and Vito Tanzi (1993), "A Tax on Gross Assets of Enterprises as a Form of Presumptive Taxation", *Bulletin for International Fiscal Documentation*, Vol. 47(2), pp. 66-73.

Sandford, Cedric (1994), "Self Assessment for Income Tax: Another view", *British Tax Review*, Vol. 3, pp. 674-680.

Sandford, Cedric (1994a), "International Comparisons of Administrative and Compliance Costs of Taxation", *Australian Tax Forum*, Vol. 11, pp. 291-309.

Sandford, Cedric, Michael Godwin and Peter Hardwick (1989), *Administrative and Compliance Costs of Taxation*, Bath, UK: Fiscal Publications.

Sandford, Cedric (ed.) (1995), *Tax Compliance Costs: Measurement and Policy,* Bath, UK: Fiscal Publications.

Shah, Anwar (ed.) (1995), *Fiscal Incentives for Investment and Innovation*, Washington D.C.: Oxford University Press.

Silva, Emilson C.D. (2003), "Incentive Effects of Performance-based Rewards in Tax Administration," in: John McLaren, editor, *Institutional Elements of Tax Design and Reform*, Technical paper no. 539, Washington D.C.: The World Bank.

Silvani, Carlos and Katherine Baer (1997), *Designing a tax administration reform strategy: Experiences and guidelines, IMF Working Paper*, Washington, D.C.: International Monetary Fund.

Slemrod Joel (1990), "Optimal Taxation and Optimal Tax Systems", *Journal of Economic Perspectives*, Vol. 4, pp. 157-178.

Slemrod, Joel (1995), "The Simplification Potential of Alternatives to Income Tax", *Tax Note*, Vol. 66, pp. 1331-1340.

Slemrod, Joel and John Bakija (1996), *Taxing Ourselves – A Citizen's Guide to the Great Debate Over Tax Reform*, London: MIT Press.

Slemrod, Joel and Marsha Blumenthal (1996), "The Income Tax Compliance Cost of Big Business", *Public Finance Quarterly*, Vol. 24, pp. 411-438.

Slemrod, Joel and Nikki Sorum (1984), "The Compliance Cost of the U.S. Individual Tax System", *National Tax Journal*, Vol. 37, pp. 461-74.

Slemrod, Joel and Shlomo Yitzhaki (1987), "On the Optimal Size of a Tax Collection Agency", *Scandinavian Journal of Economics*, Vol. 89, pp. 183-92.

Slemrod, Joel and Shlomo Yitzhaki (1996), "The Cost of Taxation and the Marginal Efficiency Cost of Funds, *IMF Staff Papers*, Vol. 43, pp. 172-198.

Slemrod, Joel and Shlomo Yitzhaki (1998), *Tax Avoidance, Evasion and Administration, Working paper*, Ann arbor: University of Michigan, Ann Arbor. Forthcoming in Alan Auerbach and Martin Feldstein (Editors) *Handbook of Public Economics*, Amsterdam: North Holland.

Slemrod, Joel and Shlomo Yitzhaki (2002), *Integrating Expenditure and Tax Decisions: The Marginal Cost of Funds and the Marginal Benefit of Projects, Working paper*, Ann arbor: University of Michigan, Ann Arbor.

Slemrod, Joel and Varsha Venkatesh (2002), T*he Income Tax Compliance Cost of Large and Mid-sized Business, A Report to the IRS LMSB Division*, Ann Arbor: Office of Tax Policy Research, University of Michigan Business School.

Smith, Adam (1776), *An Enquiry into the Nature and Causes of the Wealth of Nations*, (see, e.g., New York, Modern Library, 1937).

Tait, Alan A., Wilfrid L.M. Gratz and Barry J. Eichengreen (1979), "International Comparisons of Taxation for Selected Developing Countries, 1972-76", *IMF Staff Papers*, Vol. 26, pp. 123-156.

Talib, Amin Ali (1996), "The Compliance Costs of Taxation", *Bulletin for International Fiscal Documentation*, Vol. 50, pp. 418-421.

Taliercio, Roberto (2003), *Semi-autonomous Revenue Authorities: Benefits and Costs*, Washington, D.C.: The World Bank.

Tanzi, Vito (1992), "Structural Factors and Tax Revenue in Developing Countries: A Decade of Evidence", in: Ian Goldin and L. Alan Winters, editors, *Open Economies: Structural Adjustment and Agriculture*, Cambridge: Cambridge University Press.

Tanzi, Vito (1977), "Inflation, Lags in Collection, and the Real Value of Tax Revenue", *IMF Staff Papers*, Vol. 24, pp. 154-167.

Tanzi, Vito and Howell H. Zee (2000), *Tax Policy for Emerging Markets: Developing Countries, Working paper*, Washington, D.C.: Fiscal Affairs Department, International Monetary Fund.

Tanzi, Vito and Milka Casanegra de Jantscher (1987), *Presumptive Income Taxation: Administrative, Efficiency and Equity Aspects, IMF Working Paper No. 87/54*, Washington, D.C.: International Monetary Fund

Terpker, Seth, (2003), "Managing Small and Medium-sized Taxpayers in Developing Countries", *Tax Notes International*, Vol. 29, pp. 211-234.

Toma, Eugenia Froedge and Mark Toma (1992), "Tax Collection with Agency Costs: Private Contracting or Government Bureaucrats?", *Economica*, Vol. 59, pp. 107-120.

Ueng, K. L. Glen and C. C. Yang, (2000), "Taxation with Little Administration", *Journal of Public Economics*, Vol. 75(1), pp. 145-156.

Wallschutzsky, Ian (1989), "Achieving Compliance in Developing Countries", *Bulletin for International Fiscal Documentation*, Vol. 45,

Wane, Waly (2000), *Tax Evasion, Corruption, and the Remuneration of Heterogeneous Inspectors*, Washington, D.C.: Development Research Group,The World Bank.

Yaniv, Gideon (1988), "Withholding and Non-withheld Tax Evasion", *Journal of Public Economics*, Vol. 35, pp. 183-204.

Yaniv, Gideon (1999), "Tax Compliance and Advance Tax Payments: A Prospect Theory Analysis", *National Tax Journal*, Vol. 52, pp. 753-764.

Yaniv, Gideon (1998), "Tax Evasion by Misinforming Withholding Agents", *Public Finance Review*, Vol. 26, pp. 362-375.

Yitzhaki, Shlomo (1974), "A Note on Income Tax Evasion: A Theoretical Analysis", *Journal of Public Economics*, Vol. 3, pp. 201-202.

Zagaris, Bruce (2001), "Tax Havens Beware, Fiscal Transparency, and What Else? The Rules are Changing and It's Crazy Out There!", *Journal of International Banking Regulation*, Vol. 3(2), pp. 111–144.

Zagaris, Bruce (2003), "The Procedural Aspects of U.S. Tax Policy Towards Developing Countries: Too Many Sticks and No Carrots?", *The George Washington International Law Review*, Vol. 35(2), pp. 331-370.

Zee, Howell H. (1998), "Taxation of Financial Capital in a Globalized Environment: The Role of Withholding Taxes", *National Tax Journal*, Vol. 51(3), pp. 587-599.

Chapter 15

THE ROLE OF ORGANIZATIONAL DESIGN IN THE REVENUE STRATEGIES OF DEVELOPING COUNTRIES: BENCHMARKING WITH VAT PERFORMANCE

WILLIAM McCARTEN[1]
World Bank

In order to understand the reason for poor performance of the revenue administration, we must first look 'outside the box', beyond the organizational boundaries of the revenue administration, and analysis the impact of important environmental factors on its performance.

Jit Gill, World Bank (2003)...........

1. INTRODUCTION

At the beginning of the 21st century, governments in developing and transition economies continue to search for feasible solutions to the age-old problem of revenue generation. Today, the dominant environmental factors shaping the performance of their revenue administrations are globalization, large informal sectors, and weak administrative capacity linked to corruption. Increasingly, taxpayers, struggling to reduce high compliance costs and shield themselves from arbitrary treatment and corrupt practices, are asking political leaders to improve taxpayer services and embrace an explicit taxpayer service ethos.

In response, tax administrations are exploring a range of strategies to improve taxpayer compliance and achieve their revenue generation goals. However, these strategies are diverse and have different implications for static efficiency and growth. Some countries, as different as Bulgaria,

Jamaica, Latvia, Pakistan, and Tanzania, have embraced multiyear programmatic approaches to reform, involving reorganization of their tax administrations along functional and taxpayer segment lines, reengineering of business processes, and effective utilization of new opportunities in information and communications technology. These programmatic reformers are also benchmarking and monitoring their own performances as a tool for improved managerial effectiveness. The trend towards tax administration organizational reform has been most pronounced in Eastern Europe where, in the space of a decade, transition countries have replaced tax-by-tax frameworks for new functional designs, augmented by special units organized around taxpayer characteristics, such as size of assets or sales. Many governments have seized upon the organizational concept of a large taxpayers' unit (LTU) as a mechanism to introduce new organizational structures and procedures based on voluntary compliance. LTU have spread from Latin America, where it was conceived in the 1970s, to Africa, Asia, and transition countries, where it has piloted administrative reforms in auditing, self-assessment, the functional organization of work, and taxpayer services. Some governments have directed their tax administrations to adopt a taxpayer service ethos, whilst insisting on innovative enforcement measures to boost compliance.

However, scaling up organizational innovations, such as large taxpayers' units, to completely reorganize the tax administration remains an unfinished agenda in many developing countries. Quite a few governments continue to show little interest in modernization processes that involve systemic organizational change allied to a new administrative philosophy. These governments retain a commitment to traditional approaches to revenue generation, whilst accepting organizational and business process modernization only as part of pilot initiatives often required under IMF programs. Many tax authorities reject authentic self-assessment as a general rule for both VAT and corporate income tax and permit it only as a special case. Traditional tax assessment strategies, focused on imposed assessments and negotiation of final tax liability and the neglect of the special needs of small enterprises for simplified procedures, deter enterprises in shifting from the shadow to the formal economy and are inimical to a truly healthy investment climate in the formal sector. Why then, if the path of tax administrative reforms is clearly pro-growth, do only some developing and transition governments follow this path and make a wholehearted commitment to scaling up tax administration pilot reforms?

This paper's motivations are twofold. First, it seeks to shed some light on which organizational models and tax administration reform ingredients contribute most to improving tax compliance, neutrality, and revenue productivity.[2] Additionally, it seeks to explain why administrative reform proposals to achieve these ends are often resisted or adopted in a halfhearted manner, even when governments are sincerely looking for better solutions to their taxation problems. In a nutshell, this is a paper about the logic of scaling up pilot-based organization reforms. It argues that tax administration organizational reforms, along with the self–assessment reforms that it will enable, are the keys to coping with these growth-inhibiting tax distortions. The paper conjectures that the most visible recent innovation in organizational design, the large taxpayers' unit, will have different impacts in different country settings and will require buttressing by key institutional and policy supports, if it is to play its intended role in scaling up administrative reforms.

1.1 Defining the Problem

Globalization, economic dualism, and weak and corrupt tax administration have inspired diverse responses within the set of developing and transition economies. All countries' ability to set and enforce their own taxes is increasingly constrained by globalization, or the deep integration of national economies with the global economy. Contemporaneously, globalization is expanding the number of critical taxpayer services and compliance oversight tools, such as policing transfer pricing practices, which are needed to administer taxes effectively. However, as stressed by Burgess and Stern (1993), taxation in developing countries remains fundamentally different from that in industrial countries. In part, this is because so much economic activity occurs in the informal or shadow economy and thus bypasses taxation. Additionally, the tax administration capacities of developing and transition governments are usually weak and often tinged by corruption.

These forces foster a kind of dualism in tax administration in developing and low-income transition countries, under which administrative practice and policy expectations directed towards large formal sector business units, comprising both export-oriented and import-competing subcomponents, are radically different from those for the small-scale, formal sector businesses. Taxation of economic activity within the formal sector and the incidence of bribery needed to settle assessments are often highly non-neutral in nature.

Over a decade ago Burgess and Stern (1993) warned that by concentration on a few tax handles and the easiest to implement solutions governments in developing countries, with weak administrative capacity, often produce highly distorting tax structures. Berkowitz and Li (1999) report that throughout the 1990s, tax administration policies and practice in transition economies have been capricious and potentially confiscatory, resulting in negotiated tax liabilities. The negotiation of tax liabilities in settings without authentic self-assessment creates a fertile environment for bribery and engenders a business climate that is hostile to new investment and the growth of small business. The relative size of bribe payments, linked to negotiated tax settlements, appears to fall most heavily on small formal sector enterprises both in transition and developing countries. Clarke and Xu (2002) have uncovered a negative relationship between enterprise size and the relative burden of bribes paid. Johnson, Kaufman and Shleifer (1997) contend that high tax and regulatory burdens in post-communist countries drove a significant share of economic activity into the shadow or informal economy during the 1990s. Hostile tax policies and administrative practices lead in turn to static efficiency losses and retard export-led and import competing growth in the fringe formal sector, particularly among small-scale enterprises. This problem is increasingly recognized as a major cause of weak investment growth performance in the developing world, particularly in sub-Saharan Africa. Stiglitz (2004) has proposed that redesigning taxing institutions and policies, including what he calls "corruption resistant tax structures", should be a central concern of fiscal reform for developing countries. However, while the shadow economies of developing countries are characterized by low capital intensities, small scale of operation, traditional technologies, and often wafer thin profit margins, unofficial production in transition economies is more often done in big enterprises with high-capital intensities.

1.2 Recent Government Fiscal Performance

Governments in developing and transition countries vary greatly in terms of their average revenue receipts as a share of GDP, the notional tax base, for a given set of statutory tax rates. Recent compilations by IMF staff of average total tax revenue and total revenue statistics covering developing and transition countries for the early 2000s and the early 1990s, as summarized in Table 1, indicate that, while average government revenue shares grew in the Americas and the North Africa/Middle East zones by between one and two percent, they fell in sub-Saharan Africa, Central Europe, and the countries of the former Soviet Union and the Asia and Pacific region.

In the case of Central Europe and countries of the Former Soviet Union, Mitra and Stern (2003) attribute the fall in tax revenue shares to a major decline in corporate income tax revenue, which was partially offset by domestic indirect tax revenue gains. The reasons for stagnation or declines in sub-Saharan Africa and Asia include not only adjustments to external shocks, such as the external crises of the late 1990s, but also inadequate and inappropriate responses to the challenge of globalization, and increased internal corruption within tax administrations. Aurioll and Warlters (2005) assert that the difference in tax revenue yields, as a percent of GDP, between rich and developing countries is now almost entirely explained by the weakness of direct taxation in the latter. Direct taxation represents only 7 percent of GDP in sub-Saharan Africa versus 22 percent of GDP in industrial countries. Within sub-Saharan Africa, Ghana's performance may be indicative of regional trends. Direct taxes fell sharply in the 1990s during a period of macroeconomic stagnation, which was offset by a strong performance in VAT collection. Stiglitz (2004) warns that for low income developing countries the increasing dependence on VAT collections from large enterprises in the formal sector is reinforcing structural dualism and ultimately discouraging growth by making formal sector participation unattractive.

Table 1. Average Government Revenue by Grouping of Countries (percent of GDP)

	Tax Revenue		**Total Revenue**	
	Early 1990s	Early 2000s	Early 1990s	Early 2000s
Americas	14.9	16.0	18.3	19.7
Sub-Saharan Africa	16.3	15.9	19.3	19.7
Transition countries	27.3	23.4	30.9	26.7
North Africa and Middle East	15.1	17.1	23.3	26.2
Asia and Pacific	13.6	13.2	17.6	16.6
Small Islands	25.5	24.5	33.4	32.0

Source: Clements, Gupta, Pivovarsky, and Tiongson (2004).

2. PRODUCTIVITY OF TAX SYSTEMS: INTERNATIONAL COMPARISONS AND DETERMINANTS

Additional insights into administrative performance can be gleaned by calculating efficiency or productivity indicators of tax revenue systems across countries and by exploring the linkage between corruption and efficiency indicator for the tax system. The value added tax is the logical candidate for the identification of such efficiency indicators because its base, usually equivalent to aggregate private consumption, can be measured from statistical sources that are derived independently from revenue data. As discussed in Ebrill et al. (2002), C-efficiency of the VAT is defined as the ratio of VAT revenue to aggregate private consumption divided by the standard rate of VAT. This measure is described as "both a summary indicator of performance and a useful gauge of the extent to which the VAT bears uniformly upon a broad base." As Figure 1 below indicates, the calculated C-efficiency ratios for 2001 vary dramatically across developing and transition economies, from less that 0.25 for Algeria and the Philippines to over 1.0 for Croatia. This rcsult indicates both that the effective tax revenue burden can vary greatly from the statutory burden and that the scope for improved compliance is massive in countries at the lower end of the distribution.

Econometric estimation can be used to explain the determinants of the dispersal of C-efficiency. Results are reported below, based on data obtained from the IMF's Government Financial Statistic Yearbook and Article IV consultation reports for a sample of 69 developing and transition economies. The White estimator is employed to correct for heteroskedasticity. The approach taken here is to regress the ratio of VAT revenue divided by private consumption on a set of explanatory variables including the standard rate of VAT, the openness of the economy, as measured by the ratio of imports to GDP, and the level of illiteracy. To this list of regressors is added an index for government's capacity to control corruption, recently developed by Kaufman, Kraay and Zoido-Lobaton (2002) and an index, developed by Djankov et al. (2002), which measures the cost of registering a business in the formal sector. This last variable is intended to capture some of the barriers to entry to the formal sector, but it is limited to legal costs and does not include informal payments.

More formally, the equation of interest is:

VAT Rev/Consumption = *f*(SR, imports/GDP, illiteracy, CCI, costentry)

where SR is the VAT standard rate,
CCI is the index for government control of corruption, and
costentry is the cost of registering a business in the formal sector divided by the average wage.

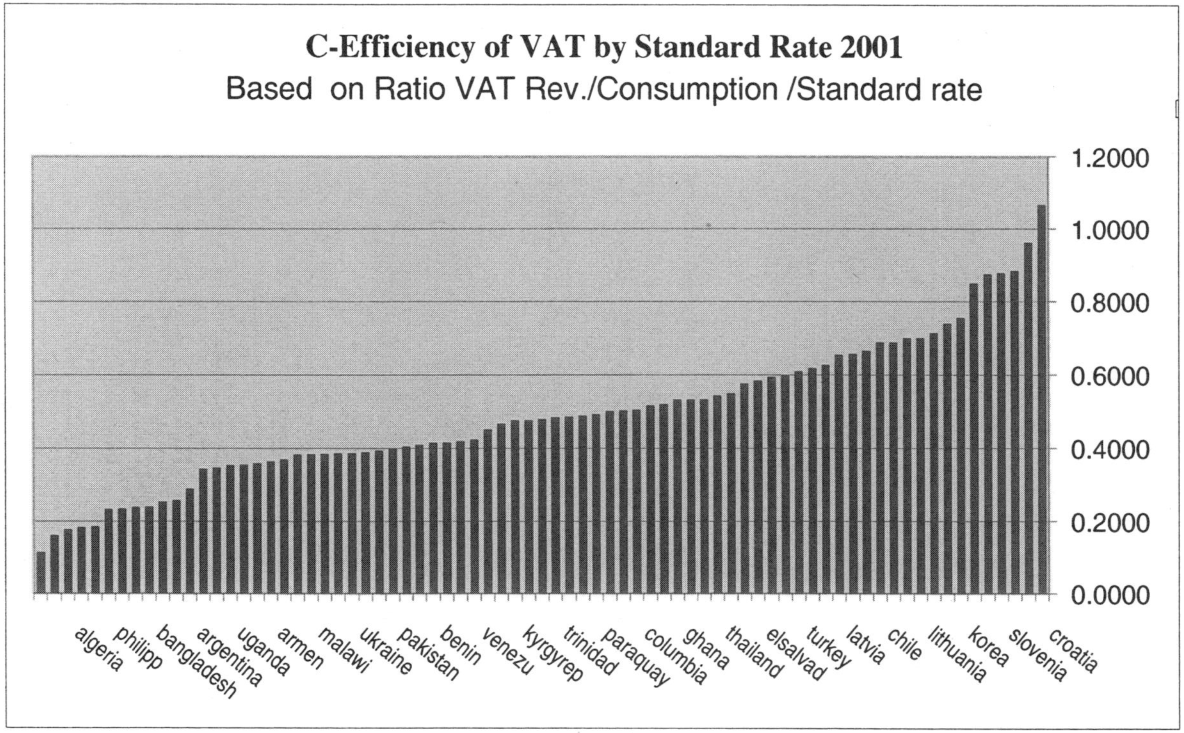

Source: Government Finance Statistics and International Finance Statistics 2003 and 2004 (International Monetary Fund).

Figure 1.

Table 2. Cross Sectional Model of C-Efficiency for VAT Administration Based on 2001 Government Financial Statistic Data

Dependent variable: ceffnum = VAT revenue/ Private Consumption

Variable	*Coefficient*	*Std. Error*	*t-statistic*	*p-value*	
Const	0.152399	0.0211254	7.2140	< 0.00001	***
Lnsr	0.0416384	0.0104857	3.9710	0.000186	***
Imports	0.0459786	0.0206817	2.2232	0.029801	**
Illeteracy	-0.0302823	0.0159709	-1.8961	0.062536	*
Corrcontrol	0.0158922	0.00582424	2.7286	0.008232	***
Costformal	-5.27891e-05	4.56613e-05	-1.1561	0.252006	

Estimation procedure: heteroskedasticity-corrected estimates
Statistics based on the weighted data:
Sum of squared residuals = 291.938
Standard error of residuals = 2.15266
Unadjusted $R^2 = 0.459109$
Adjusted $R^2 = 0.416181$
F-statistic (5, 63) = 10.6949 (p-value < 0.00001)
N = 69 observations
Statistics based on the original data:
Mean of dependent variable = 0.0808495
Standard deviation of dep. var. = 0.0394312

The asterisks in the last column describe the level of significance, with *** referring to the 1 percent level of significance for hypothesis testing, ** referring to the 5 percent level and * referring to the 10 percent level. In terms of the adjusted $\overline{R}^2$, the regressors explain about 41 percent of the variability of the dependent variable, all regressors have the expected sign, and all regressors are significant, except that for the cost of entering the formal sector. This regression result can be interpreting as indicating that improvements in institutions and policies for the general control of corruption will increase the revenue productivity of the VAT *ceteris paribus*.

A bribery variable is not available for the large sample used above, but a smaller transition country sample presents the opportunity to explore whether C-efficiency and the relative level of bribery payments made to government officials are correlated. Based on surveys commissioned by the European Development Bank, Schaffer and Turley (2000) have reported a relationship between the average total bribes paid to all government officials as a percentage of the annual revenues of the surveyed enterprises in CIS and Eastern European countries in the later 1990s and the ratio of the average effective tax rate to the statutory rate. They hypothesize that the relative size of the gap between statutory and effective rates is positively correlated with the relative size of bribes. To test this proposition, the current paper reports two OLS regressions using observations from 17 transition countries: (i) first the C-efficiency of VAT rate is regressed on the bribe "tax" rates as the sole explanatory variable, and (ii) next C-efficiency is regressed on bribes and the imports to GDP ratio, as a second explanatory variable.

$$\underset{}{VATRev/Y/\,t} = \underset{(3.71)}{50.25} - \underset{(-2.51)}{3.70\,(bribe)} \qquad \overline{R}^2 = 0.213$$

where bribe = is the bribe rate as a percent of annual revenue from "firms like yours" from the EBRD Transition Report,

VATTaxRev/GDP/ t = C-efficiency ratio defined in term of GDP for 1997 ,

$$VATRev/Y/\,t = \underset{(3.09)}{34.41} - \underset{(-1.95)}{2.98\,(bribe)} + \underset{(1.90)}{0.243\,(Im/Y)} \qquad \overline{R}^2 = 0.329$$

where bribe = is the bribe rate as a percent of annual revenue for "firms like yours" from the EBRD Transition Report,

Im/Y = imports of goods and services as a % of GDP in 1997

VATRev/GDP/ t = C-efficiency ratio defined in terms of GDP for 1997.

The reported estimates indicate that the bribe rate is a significant explanatory variable with a negative coefficient in determining C -efficiency in transition economies. Therefore, it appears reasonable to conjecture that if similar bribe rate data were available for the larger sample employed in the first regression, it would be found to be a significant determinant of C-efficiency and to have a negative sign. Consequently, tax administrative reforms that can reduce opportunities for and incidence of bribe taking within the tax administration should increase the productivity of the revenue system. When linked to the finding of Clarke and Xu (2002) that the effective burden of bribes falls more heavily on smaller rather than larger enterprises, reducing bribery opportunities through tax administrative reforms would also appear to improve the attractiveness for small enterprises of joining the formal sector and their ability to compete with larger enterprises.

3. REFORM AGENDA

Many developing and transition governments have embarked on ambitious technological and business process transformations of their tax administrations. A typical tax administration reform agenda entails ingredients such as modernizing taxpayer registration, strengthening return processing and payment systems, improving collection enforcement, developing effective audit programs, developing better taxpayer services, introducing automation, implementing unique taxpayer identification numbers, and monitoring large taxpayers. For those countries opting for comprehensive administrative reforms, measures have also included organizational redesign, development of electronic governance capacities, consolidating collection of payroll taxes and pension contributions, increased sophistication of the audit function, extensive access to third party information within and outside the public sector, strengthening of taxpayer services, outreach to key stakeholders, and, most importantly, a commitment to confront corruption.[3] Additional institutional supports have included legal reform covering speedier and less capricious taxpayer dispute resolution mechanisms. As part of the spirit of administrative reform, compliance management is no longer based purely on an enforcement-focused approach, but on a combination of enforcement and taxpayer services.

Quite a few governments have changed the organizational designs of their tax administration, by shifting from a type of tax and geographic focus to some combination of functional or taxpayer segment design elements. More tentative reformers and those with weak administrative capacities have typically implemented pilot projects, such as large taxpayers' units (LTU), and or employed pre-shipment inspection services paralleling national customs operations, as enclaves of reformed practice and, potentially, as organizational stepping stones on the journey to complete organizational transformations.

4. DUALISTIC POLICIES AS A CHALLENGE TO SCALING UP PILOT REFORMS

In this era of globalization, the profiles of taxpayers in developing countries can be categorized broadly into four divergent groups: (i) large taxpayers, who use sophisticated means to minimize their tax burden and interact with the tax authorities both as tax collecting agents of the government and as taxable clients; (ii) medium size enterprises in the formal sector, who maintain weak accounting records of their business activities and ultimately negotiate their assessments, (iii) small traders, particularly in the retail sector; who maintain no accounts and are accordingly subject to arbitrary treatment by tax administrators; and (iv) informal sector businesses, that pay no direct taxes. Major differences in tax burdens imposed on different taxpayer segments map into widely divergent tax burdens and informal payments burdens for different sectors of the economies of developing countries with important consequences for allocative efficiency and the functional incidence of tax burdens.

Aurioll and Warlters (2003) have proposed a model describing why governments might rationally adopt high barriers to entry from the informal to the formal sector in the context of securing adequate revenue, when their tax administration capacity is weak and vulnerable to corruption. Entry barriers impede access to banking credit and legal entitlements associated with formal status. They deter investment and broad-based economic growth, as eloquently explained by de Soto (2001). Nevertheless, Aurioll and Warlters suggest that developing country governments consciously raise barriers to entry into the formal sector in an effort to maximize tax revenue on oligopoly profits without having to improve tax administration capacity. By generating market power, and hence economic rents, for the permitted entrants, high entry fees foster the emergence of large taxpayers. The resulting rents are harvested by the government at a low administrative cost using low-skilled administrative talent through direct taxes on oligopoly profits and even via VAT payments, when the tax burden incidence falls on capital or wages in the formal sector.

Given the strong presumption of high economic rents in the formal sector, even tax administrators with little or no auditing skills, can be confident that their imposed and negotiated assessments can be paid. In developing countries a very few taxpayers often account for a large proportion of total tax collection. For instance, Baer (2002) reports that 0.4 percent of taxpayers account for 61 percent of total domestic tax collection in Kenya and 57 percent in Colombia. The corollary for the informal sector and, perhaps even for the fringe formal sector, is that thin profit margins and weak integration to truncated VAT systems will make it inefficient for tax officials to attempt to collect taxes from this sector.

According to the thesis of Aurioll and Warlters (2005), governments in developing countries internalize the observed degrees of corruption, malfeasance, and general administrative inefficiencies of their tax collecting bureaucracies into policy decisions about which taxes to rely upon and how to achieve their revenue targets. Depending on a rational evaluation of their interests, governments may embark on comprehensive administrative reforms, partial reform packages, or they may accept the administrative status quo, while varying other policies to achieve desired revenue targets.

Table 3. Concentration of Tax Collection in Selected Countries for 2000

	Number of large taxpayers	*% of total*	*% of revenue*
Argentina	3,665	0.1	49.1
Benin	812	1.0	90.0
Bulgaria	842	0.1	51.4
Hungary	369	0.1	42.1
Kenya	600	0.4	61.0
Peru	2,450	0.9	64.9
Philippines	833	0.2	36.0

Source: Bodin (2003).

An evaluation report, prepared by Gray and Chapman (2001) for the UK's Department for International Development, documents the poor collection strategies of many aid recipient countries and expresses puzzlement at the decisions of administrators in some countries, with narrow administrative tax bases, to concentrate excessively on existing taxpayers in order to meet government revenue targets. For example, the Uganda government instructed its Uganda Revenue Authority in 1998 to implement a presumptive income tax on informal enterprises with low turnover. Yet, according to Gloppe and Rakner (2002), the implementation of this process was not taken up with any signs of commitment because enforcing collections from this taxpayer segment was not seen as cost effective.

The production function for tax administration has recently become globalized and undergone a major increase in what economists call technical progress, due to new information and communication technology (ICT) opportunities. Moreover, the diffusion of reform ideas in tax administration is increasingly influenced by the growth of global consulting companies specializing in tax administration modernization and by the increased supply of technical assistance supported by multilateral agencies and bilateral donors.

The potential benefits in increased compliance rates and reduced bribery arising from large scale administrative reforms, linked to automation, are very large. ICT instruments can both support better service delivery and guide the modernization of business processes. See de Wulf and McLinder (2005) for a comprehensive survey of recent ICT applications applied to customs clearance. It is now feasible and cost effective for even the poorest countries to adopt new and proven off-the-self ICT applications for tax administration.[4] Yet the mere fact that the global tax administration production function has shifted will not guarantee that that the new dominant technology will be employed to the full. One of the reasons why administrative reforms used in LTUs and customs units are not universalized is that ultimate government decision-makers do not fully appreciate the potential of these instruments and associated organizational reforms to improve voluntary compliance. Another reason is that in societies where corruption and informal rules are deeply entrenched it is very difficulty for the center of government to unravel the status quo and develop a new ethos and new contractual relations amongst taxpayers, tax officials, and the political leadership of government.

Automation of the tax administration can be a catalyst to organizational and administrative reform and modernization of business procedures. However, Bird (2004) advises that new computer systems have often developed in parallel to continued use of traditional business processes (e. g., Philippines). Failure to scale up and switch tracks can occur, in part, because reform initiatives have not sufficiently recognized the skill constraints of tax officers or the service needs of taxpayers. Vested interests, such as custom clearance brokers, may also resist full implementation of cost-reducing ICT solutions, because such reforms threaten high profits realized under non-transparent and uncertain status quo procedures.

5. ORGANIZATIONAL DESIGN

Tax administrations in any country can be organized broadly: (i) by type of tax (tax-by-tax) with a second tier division by geographic zone; (ii) by function; or (iii) by segment of taxpayers stratified by size of assets or turnover. These categories have parallels in the literature on organizational theory for private enterprise, as described by Mintzberg (1982). The three most common models to structure the organization of private enterprises are: product-based, functional, and client-based. Although most tax administrations can be said to resemble one particular model predominantly, many administrations combine features from all three. See Vehorn and Brondolo (1998),

Table 4. Organizational Design

PRIVATE ORGANIZATION	TAX ADMINISTRATION
Product Base	Type of Tax
Functional	Functional
Client	Client or Taxpayer Segment

Source: Mintzberg (1983).

The schematic framework presented in Figure 2 below encapsulates a story of generic organizational change, reflecting recent international trends, beginning with the type of tax approach and moving to functional and finally a taxpayer segment approach.

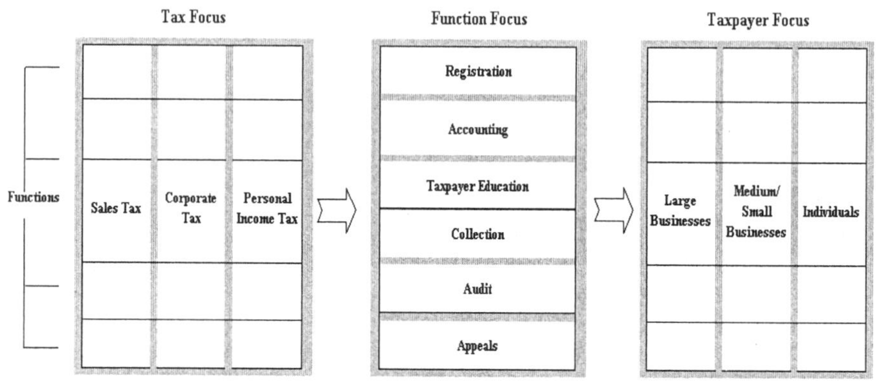

Source: Ebrill, Keen, Bodin, and Summers (2002), p. 135.

Figure 2. The Evolution of Organization Design Ideas for Tax Administration

The type of tax organizational design results in lost efficiency opportunities, through duplication of functions for registration, accounting, audit, collection, training, IT, and human resources. Tax administrations in many developing countries, particularly in South Asia, continuc to bc organized by type of tax with additional tiers determined by geographic zone. This traditional design reflects the belief that close geographic proximity should be maintained between taxpayer and tax collector. Within this framework, tax assessing officers working in small, "circle" offices specialize in acquiring knowledge of the businesses of those taxpayers whose assessments they finalize. Tax assessing work, in such a setting, has low incremental revenue productivity, because of inadequate specialization of tasks and the inability to concentrate resources on the high risk components of the revenue base. The traditional local offices are ill-suited units of administration for effective use of information technology and the introduction of self-assessment with modern auditing. Moreover, excessive direct contract between taxpayers and tax officers exposes the tax administration to an unnecessary risk of corruption.

Under *a functional approach*, responsibilities within a tax administration are divided by major categories of work – taxpayer education and service, registration, audit, enforcement, legal advice, information processing – but staff are involved with all types of taxes. A functional organization allows for tax returns and tax payments to be processed in a single department, rather than in many tax-specific departments.

As countries shift towards a functional model, they are able to improve taxpayer services by providing:

- A single point of access for taxpayer inquiries;
- A common registration function and system with a unique identification number for each taxpayer;
- A single accounting framework, possibly integrated;
- Enforced collection and audit across taxes;
- Dedicated information processing operations; and
- Common support functions such as human resources, ICT, and training.

A functional organization provides a strategic element of cross checking among staff, so that work performed by one function, such as collection and enforcement, acts as a control on other operations, such as auditing and accounting. Such an approach reduces the compliance burden on taxpayers, who only have to deal with a single contact point, and permits greater standardization of work processes across taxes and enhances productivity. Increasingly, the functional approach is being combined with the client or tax segment taxpayer design.

The larger countries of Latin America, notably Chile and Argentina, implemented functional organization reforms, within each major tax group, in the 1960s and 1970s with advice and technical support from the USA's Internal Revenue Service. In the cases of Chile, the modern organizational structures and ethos were absorbed so well that enclaves of administrative excellence have not been required. For the case of Canada, the recent integration of VAT and direct taxes under a functional administration is seen by the business community as having reduced compliance burdens, especially for small business. There is now a single audit in Canada for micro and small businesses. Where previously a number of auditors had visited a company on different schedules to conduct audits on the different taxes, post-integration there is one auditor assessing corporate income tax, value added tax, and any excise duties.

Nevertheless, a pure functional focus also has its disadvantages. It is prone to treat all taxpayers with a one size fits all approach. Management of the functions is complicated by the need to deal with different taxpayer segments, which present different compliance issues and risks, and important non-compliance patterns may get ignored because of a lack of focus on the characteristics of client segments.

Another alternative is the *taxpayer segment approach*, recently adopted by a few developed countries. The rationale for this approach is that each size group of taxpayers, as defined by assets or sales, has different characteristics and tax compliance behaviors. Hence, each presents different risks to the revenue base. According to this organizational philosophy, maximizing voluntary compliance for each taxpayer segment requires delivering a set of strategies that is appropriate to the compliance issues posed by each group. Many developed countries (e.g., Australia, Netherlands, USA) and developing ones (e.g., Pakistan) have gone beyond establishing LTUs and have reorganized administration around different size segments of taxpayers. The extreme heterogeneity of business taxpayers in developing countries makes the cases of exploring this organizational design persuasive.

In 1998 the Internal Revenue Service of the USA embraced the taxpayer segment approach both for auditing. Two years later the USA restructured national and local administrative operations around large and medium sized businesses, small businesses, employees, and exempt organizations. The IRS's Market Segment Specialization Program focuses on developing specialized examiners for a particular market segment. A market segment may be an industry, such as construction or entertainment, a profession, such as attorneys or real estate agents, or a tax preference issue, such as passive activity losses. Its main objectives are to increase the rate of voluntary taxpayer compliance and to make the audit process more efficient and effective. Developing compliance strategies for highly-specialized categories have also been a salient feature of transition country practice, particularly in Russia.

Stiglitz (2004) asserts that "if there were perfect information, corruption would be no problem." If it was possible to observe and document who was bribing tax officials then corruption would be relatively easy to control. Corruption is a problem because it is very hard to observe and document. Hence the limitations on the available information are at the core of the design of corruption resistant tax structures.

One approach to controlling corruption is to enforce a sharp division of labor in dealing with taxpayers and to organize the interaction of tax officials and taxpayers through standardized processes that are easy for internal audit and vigilance agencies to observe. In this context, a powerful organizational concept is the notion of segregating work into front office and back office activities linked to targeted taxpayer surveillance with varying degrees of intensity tied to their revenue compliance risk. This approach is stressed in the work of the CIAT (2001), whose framework is summarized in Table 5 (below). The CIAT has emphasized effective risk management, with improved targeting of activities where the compliance risks are greatest, and use of market segmentation.

Table 5. Schematic Framework for Level of Contact

	Few Contacts	Average Contacts	Intense Contacts
Tax Type Design			
• Value added tax		X	
• Corporate income tax			X
• Individual Income Tax	X		
• Social Security and payroll taxes	X		
• Customs and import taxes	X	X	
Functional Design			
• Returns processing	X		
• Auditing		X	
• Collections		X	
• Appeals			X
• Taxpayer services	X – General		X- Specific
Client Services			
• Individuals	X		
• Small and Medium Companies		X	
• Large Companies			X
Risk Assessment Design			
• Low Risk	X		
• Middle Risk		X	
• High Risk			X

Source: CIAT (2001).

Every tax administration has some characteristics of an organization with a front and a back office design. The front office is the part of the organization where the taxpayer meets the officials of the tax administration. It is the point where the contacts between organization and clients are made. Non-face-to-face contacts with taxpayers via telephone and E-communication channels are front office tasks as well, but they are ones that should be easily monitored. The back office is the part of the organization that operates without personalized contacts with taxpayers. Automation data processing centers such as for processing of returns, collections, and notification of non-filing are good examples of a back office function. As can be seen from Table 5 adoption of a client orientation or client/functional hybrid organizational design will result in a structure with clearly defined division of labor and varying intensities of contact with taxpayers across units.

Some developing counties have adopted a hybrid approach, by actually starting with a large taxpayers' unit to monitor the larges taxpayer segment with work allocated under a functional design. When the large taxpayers' unit is well established and its work methods are reorganized under functional design then these approaches can be introduced for the entire organization.

6. THE LARGE TAXPAYERS' UNIT: ITS RATIONALE AND GROWTH

The classic LTU monitors large taxpayers exclusively through auditing, registration, tax accounting, collections, and taxpayer service provision covering more than one type of tax. Indeed, in some countries, LTUs do only tax auditing. Typically, a LTU will cover VAT, company income tax, and payroll taxes.

The LTU has been described as a potential Trojan horse for administrative reforms in tax administrations which have become seriously dysfunctional or, worse, completely overrun by a malfeasant administrative culture. LTUs have facilitated major tax policy reforms, such as adoption of a VAT, as well as the reform of administrative procedures. Theses include implementation of self-assessment, electronic filing of tax statements, and the functional organization of work by first incubating these changes in a setting where administrative talent and automated resources are concentrated. An LTU can readily pilot the utilization of new revenue management software systems for risk evaluation and audit selection. Related LTU goals are (i) reducing the potential for corruption by automating and restructuring control systems, (ii) strengthening audit skills, (iii) changing attitudes of officials toward taxpayers, and (iv) reducing paper handling through appropriate use of information technology. Other benefits stressed by Bodin (2002) and dos Santos (1994), are to improve the management of arrears, and improve interpretation of the law and consistency in its application. Finally, a somewhat hidden goal of an LTU is to deter revenue officials from negotiating tax liabilities with taxpayers. An indirect impact of establishing an LTU is to improve business climate, particularly for direct foreign investment, by providing sophisticated services, such as advance rulings and to reassure investors that assessment and audits will be dealt with in a fair and transparent manner. As Gill (2003) notes, revenue administration styles that are perceived to be arbitrary or predatory discourage investment.

The business operations of large taxpayers are complex. They have high transaction volumes. They act as withholding agents for the taxes of other taxpayers and they often have non-arm's length transactions with foreign parent corporations. Very often, large taxpayers are branches of foreign enterprises or they themselves own branches abroad leading to issues of how their global profits will be distributed across tax jurisdictions. Large taxpayers employ highly qualified accountants and lawyers and sometimes they use forms of avoidance that are difficult to detect, such as abusive transfer pricing and thin capitalization strategies. Due to the complexity of the business transactions in which large taxpayers engage they also have a legitimate need for advance ruling to clarify the tax consequences of their decisions. These characteristics make it desirable to monitor and service large taxpayers with units having highly specialized personnel with sophisticated accounting and auditing skills.

Strong performance is achieved in the LTU through centralized supervision of operations and the limited number of taxpayers being monitored. In countries with strong government ownership, LTU operations have quickly improved tax revenue performance. The successful reforms incubated in an LTU can demonstrate to the tax administration management, which is often hostile to change, that it is possible and advantageous to modify organizational systems and procedures.

The most important question surrounding the LTU is whether it improves compliance and ultimately revenue productivity by focusing on the few largest taxpayers with the resources of a highly trained and closely-monitored team of tax administrators.[5] By concentrating scarce tax administration resources, particularly auditing skills, where they are most productive, the LTU should be able to permit the adoption of more sophisticated tax administration techniques such as effective auditing of multinational enterprises through competent surveillance of aggressive transfer pricing practices. Work flows in LTUs are usually modified to reduce interaction between tax officials and taxpayers. The access of taxpayers is restricted to the taxpayer service areas and the public is prohibited from entering other offices. Shifting the processing of returns and payments into data processing units that have no public interface will also distance revenue officials from taxpayers.

Self-assessment within the LTU permits the re-deployment of administrative resources to more productive activities and reduces compliance costs for honest taxpayers. By contrast, imposed assessment systems, that distribute the work of completing assessments, in a manner broadly proportional to the number of taxpayers, are wasteful in their use of administrative talent. The IMF emphatically advises that VAT should be administered through self-assessment, but many developing country and transition governments have rejected this advice throughout the last decade and half. See Ebrill et al. (2002). One explanation of this rejection of IMF advice is that these governments continue to be influenced by the strategy described in Aurioll and Warlters (2005), even if they do not have a fully articulated plan. These governments perceive the comprehensive administrative reforms required to make self-assessment viable as too risky a choice, given the need for a fundamental change in organization ethos as well as the need for reengineering business processes impinging on organizational structure and civil service behaviour.

The success of the self-assessment strategy hinges on taxpayer perceptions of the effectiveness of auditing. If taxpayers believe that administrators do not have the capacity to detect tax evasion, or that, even when detection occurs, they can escape punishment through negotiation, political influence, or tax appellate and court processing delays, the compliance rate will fall. It requires initiatives touching almost all aspects of the operations of tax administration departments, including training, new approaches to audit selection, a reorientation of departmental resources, legal changes, and measures to develop a culture of compliance within the broader society. Experiences in many developing countries, such as those reported by Glenday (1997) for Kenya, indicate that scaling up self-assessment may require two years of work by the income tax authorities to prepare forms, information brochures, and procedural internal documents, and to implement personnel reorganization and training requirements.

Pakistan has used the large taxpayers' unit strategy to begin to transform its whole tax administration. Since 2002 Pakistan has been implementing an authentic taxpayer stratified segment approach, with different taxpayer service units focused on the separate needs of small, medium and large taxpayers. Most importantly, Pakistan's bold decision to adopt a universal self-assessment scheme in 2002/2003 for income tax has been the key step in the transition from the pilot stage to universal implementation of functional and segment/client principles. Collection, auditing, returns processing and even specialized services, such as advance rulings, are concentrated in large offices, organized along functional lines. But rather than close its small traditional local offices the Pakistan government has opted to convert these into taxpayer service centers. One indication that the approach is succeeding has been a 14 percent increase in tax revenue during 2004.

The United Kingdom's recent O'Donnell Report (2004) on administrative reform advises that over 60 countries had developed dedicated large taxpayer operations by 2004. This organizational form began in Argentina in the late 1970s and was copied by other Latin American countries, notably Peru, Bolivia and Uruguay, in the early 1980s. With the encouragement of the IMF and some bilateral donors it spread to several smaller African countries in the early 1990s, to transition economies in the mid 1990s,starting with Hungary, and finally to South and East Asia in the first decade of the 21st century.

In the case of Argentina the focus was made more efficient in the early 1990s through the development of a computer-based accounting system, initially for compliance with filing and payment requirements for the 2,000 largest taxpayers. This system was progressively extended to cover 230,000 large and medium size taxpayers, although a single LTU in Buenos Aires continues to monitor the largest 3,700 taxpayers, who account for approximately 50 percent of all revenue generated. The Argentina large taxpayer software was eventually applicable to all taxpayers so that the LTU in this case facilitated scaling up automation and efficiency gains. But, as reported by Baer (2002), the strategy failed to meet the needs of small taxpayer, because of constraints of the tax administration. More recently, the Argentina authorities have attempted to respond by establishing a simplified tax regime for small taxpayers.

Vázquez-Caro (1994) offered an explanation for the motivation of Latin American tax administrations in developing the concept to the LTU during the 1980s. "The rationale for this approach [creating a segmented unit for large taxpayers] was that the individual importance of these taxpayers on total collection made a close monitoring decisive. This focus of collections on a few taxpayers derived not only from the high concentration of taxable income in the country, but also because of the increasing transfer to the private sector of tasks previously handled by tax officials. From having been [simply] large taxpayers, these companies became large collectors of withholding and VAT." Hence, the rise of payroll taxes, and public pension plans in the formal sector, and the increased dependence on VAT in the Latin American revenue mix have turned large companies into the major tax collection agents for government.

However, when administrative reform solutions are implemented only partially, they can fail to achieve their objective and may even accentuate dualistic distortions. Aurioll and Warlters (2005) advocate the use of compensatory discrimination to encourage small entrepreneurs to register under a special status created especially for them. Yet, according to Bird and Wallace (2003), political economy incentives under presumptive tax systems encourage levying taxes lower than those that would be imposed by the regular system. They caution that the net result is likely to be not only to reduce revenues, but also to maintain resources in activities or types of businesses that are more tax efficient than economically efficient.

A side effect of adopting a strong LTU strategy without scaling up organizational reforms combined with special concessional treatment for the fringe formal sector has often been a substantial loss of interest in efforts to achieve an equitable rate of compliance by small and medium size taxpayers. Even at the end of the 1990s, this weak compliance record remained a major issue in Brazil, where, as identified by Tendler (2002), regional politicians ensure a type of informal tax holiday to industrial clusters of small and medium sized enterprises (SME) in order to preserve jobs for their communities. Vázquez-Caro (1994) also cautions that the segmentation of administration based on a taxpayers' size poses an asymmetric information problem in recognizing and sorting taxpayers by their true size. He suggests that the more intense monitoring in Argentina led to efforts by owners to break up large companies.

In a similar vein, Terkper (2003) warns that any program that applies field inspections almost exclusively to large taxpayers will eventually undermine compliance among all taxpayers through its impact on taxpayer morale. The relative success achieved with implementing VAT at the distribution stage in many developing countries, indicates that that many small and medium enterprises can successfully comply under self-assessment programs. Similarly, the results for several African countries, as documented in Terkper (2003), show that semi-skilled staff in many small offices can be upgraded to implement simplified audits.

How do tax administrators achieve the right balance between tax collection from existing known tax-payers and the use of resources to extend the tax base to include those who are currently evading tax? Very different client characteristics of SMEs and borderline informal sector businesses indicate the need to adopt separate approaches with simplified procedures and forms and appropriate changes in the law both to facilitate legal use of specialized windows as well as to ensure that enterprises are classified to the appropriate tax segment. However, adopting presumptive tax regimes, that give substantial discretion to tax authorities and are not well grounded in easily-observable descriptive attributes, should be avoided. The best way forward appears to be to explore simplified reporting and record keeping requirements for the SMEs with regulation being amended to provide well-defined legal underpinnings for simplified processes.

Drawing upon the proceeding discussion Table 6 (below) summarized many of the factors that will influence the probability that proposed scaling up strategies for organizational reform will succeed.

7. ACCOUNTABILITY MECHANISMS AND ORGANIZATIONAL SAFEGUARD FOR GOVERNANCE

A recent literature, emerging from donor-supported tax administration modernization projects, has drawn attention to the inadequate accountability mechanisms between government and taxpayers. This literature, as represented by Moore (2004), advocates building a new social contract to foster a voluntary tax compliance relationship between citizens and government, based on transparency, answerability and controllability.

Table 6. Factors Influencing the Probability that Scaling Up Strategies Will Succeed

Probability determinants	Success	Failure
Aurioll and Warlters (2005) Thesis	Low Barrier to Entry of Formal Sector	High Barrier to Entry of Formal Sector
Revenue Motivation	Low Concentration of Revenue from top ½ of 1% Taxpayer	High Concentration of Revenue from top ½ of 1 % of Taxpayer
Labor Flexibility in Civil Service	High	Low
Assessment Strategy	Commitment to adopt universal Self-assessment for VAT and Company Income Tax	Imposed Assessments
Strong Organizational Checks and Balances and Political Commitment to Combat Corruption	Relatively Robust	Weak
Well-organized Business Stakeholders	High	Low

Such mechanisms have been envisaged by Gloppen and Rakner (2002) as having three components: (i) transparency or the ability of taxpayers to see decision and processes of government are derived and implemented in accordance with known rules and mandate, (ii) answerability or the obligation to provide legitimate reasons for government decisions and (iii) controllability or institutional checks and control to prevent mismanagement and abuse of power and to ensure that corrective measures are adopted when the rule are violated. This accountability approach also stresses the need for developing countries to improve the neutrality of tax administration practice across the three taxpayer segments: large taxpayers, SME taxpayers and small business on the fringe of the informal economy.

To realize the potential benefits of the LTU and client/taxpayer segment approaches, other systems of checks and balance need to be working effectively. One of the most important tasks of the tax administration is to have in place an internal audit and accountability system to detect errors in tax assessments and to police malfeasance. Unfortunately, in many developing countries the vigilance or internal audit responsibilities often remain fragmented and are not used as effective tools of managerial oversight. Precisely because of the great responsibilities given to the staff of the LTU, the managerial center of the tax administration requires a vigilant arm's length oversight capability as a counterweight. A single internal audit unit that would have a vigilance mandate covering all taxes, would report directly to the chief operating officer, and would have some external reporting requirements, such as parallel reporting to an anti-corruption agency, should provide such a counterweight.

A reform plan should fit into a strategic vision of administration, guided by a strong governance framework, and matched to the countries current implementation capacity and business environment. To deal with corruption, Colombia carried out a systematic study of important business processes, resulting in preparation of corruption risk maps to guide procedural changes to reduce opportunities of corruption. Strengthening of internal control systems, including vigilance against corruption has been undertaken in Latvia and Jamaica. Further, changes in tax and customs codes have been made to reduce discretion of revenue officials and simplify procedures. Work flows have been modified in Russia and Latvia to reduce interaction between tax officials and taxpayers. The access of taxpayers is restricted to the taxpayer service areas and they are prohibited from entering other offices. Also moving processing of returns and payments into data processing centers that have no public contact has distanced revenue officials from taxpayers. Other anti-corruption measures enabled by automation include restricting access of employees to scanned copies of original records to prevent tampering and creating audit trails of administrative decisions and changes made to taxpayer current accounts. In 1992 the Inland Revenue Authority of Singapore was established to overcome problems of inefficiency and malfeasance. An integrated, computerized approach to tax administration along functional lines was adopted. A completely new administrative system was introduced step-by-step over the next eight years. By 2002 95 percent of taxpayers in Singapore were satisfied with the performance of the authority.

8. CONCLUSIONS

This paper has argued that changing organizational design is ultimately the key to effective tax administration reform. Tax administration organizational change should aim to consolidate the tax base and improve the tax mix through base-broadening, achieving internal productivity gains that reduce the cost of administration, and encouraging voluntary compliance. These non-incremental organizational reforms, linked to self-assessment with modern auditing capacity, may appear to some developing and transition tax administration authorities to be unproductive or even likely to put the revenue base at risk in the short run, but today they can be justified readily within the context of a longer-term strategic framework that addresses the challenges of economic dualism and the growth of the shadow economy. The arrival of an early 21st century generation of software-based business process systems to guide reengineering of procedures as well as the challenges of deepening globalization indicate that organizational reforms are no longer risky, big bets for governments, if they ever were. Full implementation of tax administration modernization reforms, with fundamental organizational change at their core, can enhance the domestic investment climate, make exports more competitive, improve the trade-off favoring formal sector participation, and strengthen the quality of public governance. Each of these outcomes can boost growth, thereby releasing developing and poor transition economies from their tax administration fetters.

Notes

1 I would like to thank Michael Engelschalk, Graham Glenday, Carlos Ferrira, Esperanza Lasagabaster, Tuan Minh Le, Luc Noiset, Chris Murray, David Sewell, Seth Terkper, and Jaime Vázquez-Caro for advice and helpful comments and to acknowledge the intellectual inspiration of the late Jit Gill.

2 By revenue productivity is meant the tax revenue to tax base ratio adjusted for the rate or statutory tax effort.

3 This list is based on observations contained in Engelschalk (2003), Gill (2003), and Stern and Mitra (2003).

4 By contrast, client-specific ICT software solutions designed for governments have an alarmingly high failure rate.

5 Dos Santos (1994) recommends that "to prevent deterioration in the quality of service, the large taxpayer offices should not control more than about 2,000 taxpayers each".

References

Aurioll, Emmanuelle and Michael Warlters (2005), "Taxation Base in Developing Countries", *Journal of Public Economics*, forthcoming.

Baer, Katherine (2002), *Improving Large Taxpayer Compliance: A Review of Country Experience, Occasional Paper 215*, Washington, D.C.: International Monetary Fund.

Berkowitz, Daniel and Wei Li (2000), "Tax Rights in Transition Economies: A Tragedy of the Commons?", *Journal of Public Economics*, Vol. 76 (3), pp. 369-398.

Bird, Richard (2003), *Administrative Dimensions of Tax Reform*, (mimeo), World Bank Institute.

Bird, Richard and Sally Wallace (2003), *Is It Really so Hard to Tax the Hard-to-Tax? The Context and Role of Presumptive Taxes, Working Papers 0307*, Canada: International Tax Program, Joseph L. Rotman School of Management, University of Toronto.

Bodin, Jean-Paul (2003), *LTU Case studies*, MA.: Harvard Tax Program, Harvard University

Burgess, Robin and Nicholas Stern (1993), "Taxation and Development", *Journal of Economic Literature*, Vol. 31(2), pp. 762-830.

CIAT (2001), *General Design Considerations*, (mimeo), Inter-American Center of Tax Administration.

Clarke, G.R.G., L.C Xu (2002), *Ownership, Competition, and Corruption: Bribe Takers. Versus Bribe Payers, World Bank Woring Paper 2783*, Washongton, D.C.: The World Bank.

Clements, Benedict, Sanjeev Gupta, Alexander Pivovarsky, and Erwin Tiongson (2004), "Foreign Aid: Grants and Loans", *Finance and Development*, Vol. 41.

Das-Gupta, Arindam Michael Engelschalk and William Mayville (1999), *An anticorruption strategy for revenue administration, PREM Note 33*, Washington DC: The World Bank.

Das-Gupta, Arindam and Dilip Mookherjee (1998), *Incentives and Institutional Reform in Tax Enforcement: An Analysis of Developing Country Experience*, New Delhi: Oxford University Press.

de Wulf, Luc and Gerald Mclinder (2005), "The Role of Information Technology in Customs Modernization", in: de Wulf, Luc and Jose B. Sokel, editors, *Customs Modernization Handbook*, Washington, D.C.: The World Bank.

Gray, John and Emma Chapman (2001), *Evaluation of Revenue Projects – Synthesis Report*, London: Department for International Development Evaluation Department.

Djankov S., R. LA Porta, F. Lopez-de-Silanes, and A. Shleifer (2002), "The Regulation of Entry", *Quarterly Journal of Economics*, Vol. 117(1), pp. 1-37.

Dos Santos, Paulo (1994), "*Administration of Large Taxpayers*", (mimeo), International Monetary Fund.

De Soto, Hernando (2000), *The Mystery of Capital*, New York: Basic Books.

Engelschalk, Michael (2003), *Creating a Favorable Tax Environment for Small Business Development in Transition Countries*, Washington, D.C.: The World Bank.

Ebrill, Liam, Michael Keen, Jean-Paul Bodin and Victoria Summers (2002), *The Modern VAT*, Washington: International Monetary Fund.

Fjeldstad, Odd-Helge and Lise Rakner (2002), "Taxation and tax reforms in developing countries: Illustrations from sub-Saharan Africa", *IDS Bulletin*, Vol. 33(3).

Glenday, Graham (1997), "Capacity Building in the Context of the Kenya Tax Modernization Program", in M. Grindle, editor, *Getting Good Government: Capacity Building in the Public Sectors of the Developing Countries*, Cambridge Mass: Harvard Institute for International Development.

Gloppen, Siri, and Lise Rakner (2002), "Accountability through Tax Reform: Reflections from Sub-Saharan Africa", *IDS Bulletin*, Vol. 33 (3).

Gill, Jit (2003), *Nuts and Bolds*, (mimeo), World Bank.

HM Treasury (2004), *Financing Britain's Future: Review of the Revenue Department*, London: U.K. Treasury.

International Monetary Fund (2002), *Government Financial Statistics Yearbook*, Washington, D.C.: International Monetary Fund.

Johnson, Simon, Daniel Kauffman, and Andrei Shleifer. (1997), "The unofficial economy in transition", *Brookings Papers on Economic Activity*, Fall (2), pp. 159-239.

Kaufman, D., A. Kraay, Zoido-Lobaton, P. (1999), *Aggregating Governance Indicators, World Bank Policy Research Paper 2195*, Washington, D.C.: The World Bank.

Kaufmann, Daniel, Aart C. Kraay, Massimo Mastruzzi. (2004), "Governance Matters III: Governance Indicators for 1996-2002", in: *World Bank Economic Review*, Washington, D.C.: The World Bank.

Le, Tuan Minh (2003), *Value Added Taxation: Mechanism, Design, and Policy Issues, paper presented for World Bank Conference Practical Issues of Tax Policy in Developing Countries*, (mimeo), The World Bank.

McCarten, William (1994), "International Transfer Pricing and Taxation", pp 225-228 in: Parthasarathi Shome, editor, *Tax Policy Handbook*, Washington, D.C.: International Monetary Fund.

Mintzberg, H. (1983), *Structure in Fives, Designing Effective Organizations*, New York: Prentice Hall.

Mitra, Pradeep and Nicholas Stern (2003), *Tax Systems in Transition, World Bank Policy Research Working Paper No. 2947*, Washington, D.C.: The World Bank.

Moore, M. (2004), "Revenues, State Formation, and the Quality of Governance in Developing Countries", *International Political Science Review*, Vol. 25(3), pp. 297-319.

Rossotti, Charles O. (1998), "A Concept for Modernizing the IRS", Excerpts from Commissioner Rossotti's Testimony before the Senate Finance Committee", 1/28/1998, Retrieved from www.irs.gov/irs/article/.

Schaffer Mark E. and Gerard Turley (2000), *Effective versus Statutory Taxation: Measuring Effective Tax Administration in Transition Economies, CERT Discussion Papers 0008*, Centre for Economic Reform and Transformation, Heriot Watt University

Stiglitz, Joseph E. (2004), *Development Oriented Tax Policy, Initiative for Policy Dialogue*, Tax Task Force (mimeo), Columbia University.

Taliercio, Robert Jr. (2003), *Designing Performance: The Semi-Autonomous Revenue Authority Model in Africa and Latin America*, Washington, D.C.: The World Bank.

Terkper, Seth (2003), "Managing small and medium-sized taxpayers in developing countries", *Tax Notes International*, Vol. 29, pp. 11-234.

Tendler, Judith (2002), "Small Firms, the Informal Sector and the Devil's Deal", *IDS Bulletin*, Vol. 33(3).

Vazquez-Caro, Jaime (1994), Assessing the Impact of Integrating Functions of Tax Administration on efficiency and effectiveness, Inter-American Center for Tax Administration, Proceeding of Annual Meeting.

Vehorn, Charles and John Brondolo (1999), "Organizational Options for Tax Administration", *Bulletin for International Fiscal Documentation*, Vol. 53, pp. 499- 512.

DISCUSSANT COMMENTS

LUC NOISET
Department of Economics, Kennesaw State University

McCarten, Hettich and Winer, and Das-Gupta

The issue addressed in this session is a difficult one for economists. We are used to using the general principles of economics to help guide us in thinking about tax policy, but we usually leave the details of implementation to others. Economists have developed a great body of work that attempts to describe good tax policy, and I believe there is more agreement than disagreement about what constitutes good *normative* tax policy. The problem is that, as we have tried to spread our message around the world, it turns out that good tax policy depends more on the details of implementation than our normative theories have generally allowed.

The three papers in this session stress that there is more to tax policy than good normative tax theory. McCarten starts off his paper by challenging us to "think outside the box," while Hettich and Winer see tax policy as an equilibrium outcome of prevailing political and institutional arrangements, and Das-Gupta emphasizes that one size does not necessarily fit all. In fact, after thinking about these papers, and thinking of some of my own tax-advising experiences, I am wondering if it might not even be the case that one size only fits one!

Generally, in some countries it looks like there have been attempts to impose a good tax, a VAT, say, or a comprehensive income tax, in a bad tax environment[1] and then trying to change the environment to make the tax work. It turns out that in many cases changing the environment is more difficult than anyone had imagined. Maybe, in some of these cases, instead of trying so hard to make fast and dramatic changes in the tax environment, it would be better to design a tax that fits the environment and letting the entire system evolve at a more measured pace. I think, for example, that the Emran and Stiglitz criticism (which McCarten points out is not new) is not taken seriously enough. The shorthand way that I think of this criticism is this: A badly administered turnover tax may be a better tax then a badly administered VAT.

The Large Taxpayer Units described by McCarten are an example of adapting to a bad tax environment. On one level LTU's make sense because that is where the money is, but every tax administration devotes more resources to monitoring large taxpayers and most do not have LTUs. In the U.S, for example, IRS auditors are permanently on site at the premises of some large taxpayers. When we think about these sorts of innovations in tax administration I think it is important to remember that LTU's have emerged because of failures to get the taxes to work the way they are supposed to. This is not to say that LTUs are a bad idea - there is evidence that they can increase revenues at least in the short-term. The point is simply to note that LTU's are an administrative response to a bad tax environment, another response would be to design a tax that more or less works in the bad tax environment. I don't know what that tax might be (a retail sales tax?), but I do know that "outside of the box" discussions of tax policy for developing countries do not often take place.

McCarten says that LTU's are sometimes thought of as Trojan horses out of which will spring good principles and practices that will spread throughout the rest of the tax administration. This makes a good point, a little learning by doing, but it sounds like the reverse has also happened in some cases, the bad practices and principles of the traditional tax administrations have crept into the LTU's, so the characteristics of the "bad tax environment" have not gone away. McCarten also notes a problem that seems serious and which I doubt can be eliminated. When an elite LTU monitors the largest taxpayers and collects most of the revenue, it is inevitable that there will develop an institutional loss of interest in small and medium size firms. The result will be a higher effective tax rate on large firms and an incentive for large firms to split into smaller firms or for growing firms to stay small and "under the radar." This has been happening in some countries according to McCarten.

The big environmental problem in many countries is of course a culture of corruption and an elite LTU is supposed to help curb corruption. LTU's are organized by function such as collections, auditing, and enforcement. This makes corruption more difficult because one function checks another. But LTU's, will also create more intimate environments and a privileged class of administrators, and this might enable corruption rather than hinder it.

Whether or not LTU's work is an empirical question that has not yet been answered. Anecdotal evidence suggests that they can work. One thing to remember, however, is that even if the results look good in the short-run, if the tax environment is bad it may creep back in again in the long-run.

Das-Gupta is explicit about the point I am stressing here. That is, the characteristics and limitations of a tax administration *should* influence tax policy design. His goal is to outline the lessons we have learned or the stylized facts that can ultimately help to determine what type of tax policy a particular tax administration might be capable of administering. I think the conjecture that drives Das-Gupta's thinking is his proposition 2: Equity and Economic Efficiency the cornerstones of normative tax theory must be traded off against the environment in which the tax system operates. In a more hostile environment equity and economic efficiency should be given less weight.

If the environment is hostile, there are tax policy responses according to Das-Gupta's propositions: keep the tax system stable, minimize complexity, use presumptive taxes. I might add, start with low tax rates so that there can be a period off learning by doing without great incentives to evade and avoid. In 1913, the first year of the U.S. income tax, the marginal rates were between 1% and 7%. In Russia a few years ago the personal income tax rate was wisely lowered to a flat 15%, but unfortunately there still exists a high payroll tax.

It is important to recognize that the capabilities of the tax administration cannot be removed from the culture or environment in which the tax system operates, which makes it difficult to come up with universal propositions. For example, Das-Gupta's proposition 3 says "Tax designs that economize on information requirements are least costly to administer." That sounds simple, straightforward and accurate, but then one thinks of the Thatcher poll tax, which has low information needs, but was very difficult to administer because of a cultural opposition to it.

I believe the approach of Das-Gupta is correct: Generally the correct tax policy must be one that the tax administration is willing and able to administer. But what a tax administration can administer depends on more than the tax administration. In addition to the tax environment variables I have already mentioned, Das-Gupta adds literacy levels, the size and sophistication of the accounting profession and the level of sophistication of the financial system.

For Hettich and Winer tax systems are, "equilibrium outcomes constrained by a particular governance structure." In addition, a change in tax policy is itself an equilibrium of the prevailing political, economic and institutional forces, and they stress that "existing political arrangements will limit the types of proposals that can be adopted through democratic choice."

Hettich and Winer believe that the phrase "tax reform" implies advocacy, which is unseemly for objective economist/scientists, but for me this takes objectivity a bit too far. As I have said, I believe there is more agreement then disagreement among economist on what constitutes good normative tax policy, and if we are in the tax-theory business we must at least hope that what we are proposing will lead to improvement rather than simply a horizontal movement to a different but equally desirable or undesirable equilibrium. Those of us who provide tax policy advice do so because we believe our advice will reform the tax system.

In addition, I believe Hettich and Winer need to be careful not to be tautological when they talk of tax policy changes being the result of exogenous shocks. It is tautological that any new tax policy proposal is initiated for some reason, and that reason can then be considered an exogenous shock, but as tax experts we should be able to judge a proposal on its merits rather than treating all proposals as equivalent exogenous shocks. For example, when new data indicates that some of the most profitable corporations in the country are able to completely avoid tax, a proposal to close loopholes might be thought of as reform; whereas a tax proposal that is initiated solely because of an ideological shift in political power might be judged differently.

Hettich and Winer suggest that economists need to build empirical models of tax policy that take into account political power coalitions, constitutional frameworks, social institutions, and other such variables. These could then be used to help us to understand why tax policy has changed over the years, and more importantly help to determine which among a menu of acceptable tax policies would have the highest likelihood of getting through the political process.

These three papers suggest two important conclusions. First, we can and we should generate empirical work to help us estimate the likelihood that particular tax proposals will be adopted. Second, we can and we should generate empirical work to help us estimate what types of taxes will work best in different types of tax environments. These conclusions are interestingly juxtaposed with the ideas of Martinez, Bird and Torgler in this volume. Those authors consider how one might change some of the undesirable institutions to get a tax system to work better. Another question might be, given that these institutions exist what tax system will work best in their presence.

Notes

1. A bad tax environment includes a dysfunctional tax administration, certain political and institutional arrangement, as Hettich and Winer say, but also as McCarten points out, things such as the lobbying power of the civil service, and the culture of mistrust (I might even say distain) for the government that exists in some countries. See also Martinez, Bird and Torgler in this volume for additional variables one might include as part of the tax environment.

6

LESSONS FOR POLICYMAKERS

Chapter 16

HOW TO APPROACH COMPREHENSIVE TAX REFORM: HAVE THE RULES OF THE GAME CHANGED?

ROY BAHL[1]
Andrew Young School of Policy Studies, Georgia State University

1. INTRODUCTION

Tax reform is not so easily defined. Tax reform could be taken to mean any change in the structure of taxes. These changes could have to do with rate, base, special treatments, etc. One usually does not think of the term "reform" as pejorative in this context, i.e., the fact is that tax reforms can be pretty bad, as well as pretty good. By this definition, every issue of *Tax Notes International* is full of descriptive material on tax reforms.

Comprehensive tax reform is, or should be, a very different concept. It is a term loosely used to refer to bigger tax reforms, and in particular, to tax changes that involve more than one piece of the tax structure.[2] In its broadest form, it might be thought of as a questioning of the existing tax system that

- Puts every piece of the tax structure on the table for review, and puts each at risk in terms of being a candidate for reform,
- Asks how the tax system fits together as a whole to achieve desired objectives vs. subjecting one tax for scrutiny against desirable norms, and
- Includes considerations of administration, implementation and monitoring.

Whether tax reform or comprehensive tax reform, careful study ought to precede recommendation for action. The issue under consideration in this volume, and in this paper, is whether "careful study" means something different now, and whether the questions are different? Should countries be advised to design their comprehensive reform studies in different ways, and should international advisors think differently about how to structure their advice?

Some of the answers to these questions might be found in what has actually happened to taxation around the world over the past 25 years, i.e. have there been marked changes in the level and structure of taxes? Is there something different about the actual tax choices being made by countries? Accordingly, in the first section of this paper, we describe tax change over the past three decades, and attempt to identify its determinants. The focus is on developing countries.

The main objective of this paper, addressed in the second section, is more normative and is pointed toward the issue of whether there are some universal "rules" that might guide the next round of comprehensive tax reform efforts in developing countries. Based on the international experience, a set of propositions about how to do a comprehensive tax reform is offered.

2. HAVE THE LEVEL AND STRUCTURE OF TAXES CHANGED?

There has been almost continuous tax change since the 1970s, all over the world. Most of these were piecemeal changes, probably driven by the need for revenue enhancement. Sometimes these changes were backed up by solid analysis of the reform options, and sometimes they were not. In some cases, these tax changes were the product of truly comprehensive reforms. Arguably some of the best work ever on public finance in developing countries is included in the studies that led to these reforms.[3] What were the results of these two routes to tax reform? Are tax structures, and the claim of taxes on GDP, markedly different now than 25 years ago?

It is not feasible to track through all rate and base changes for every country over a long period of time. And, if a critic argued that this is where the real meat of tax reform lies, he would be right. What we can do is second best. We can examine the pattern of changes in the level and structure of taxes, to indirectly gain a picture of the anatomy of change, and then attempt to identify the country characteristics that are most likely to be associated with such changes. The goal would be to identify the general direction of tax reform over the past quarter-century.

2.1 The Level of Taxation

The most common measure of the level of taxation is the ratio of tax revenue to GDP. This is a simple calculation that reflects the average tax rate in a country. It is meant to answer the question, "what percent of total national output is diverted to government purposes through the tax system." Using data from the IMF's *Government Finance Statistics* (2003), we have computed averages of the ratio of tax revenue to GDP for the 1970s, 1980s and 1990s.[4] The IMF data are the best comparative information available for developing countries, but there are shortcomings in these data. Among these shortcomings are missing data for some years, misclassification of certain revenues, inadequate dis-aggregation by type of tax, and the failure to report all subnational government revenues.

In Table 1, we show the average level of the ratio of taxes to GDP using three groupings of countries: industrialized, developing and transition. Social security taxes are included in this computation. The results for industrialized countries show that there was an increase in the average tax share, from 30 to about 35 percent over this 30 year period. In the case of the developing countries, however, the tax share of output increased only slightly during this period (by about one percent) and since the 1980s has actually declined.[5] In the case of the transition countries, there was the expected decline in the tax share since the 1980s, because of the continuing realignment of public-private expenditure responsibilities. By the end of the century, the tax ratio in industrialized countries was about twice that in developing countries, a larger difference than was the case in the 1970s.

Of course there is a considerable variation across countries in this change in the tax ratio.

Can we find a pattern to this change? A number of hypotheses are plausible to explain why some countries increased their tax ratio more than others.

1. The tax ratio is driven by the growth in per capita GDP which signals both an increase in the capacity to tax and possibly an increase in the demand for public services. Per capita GDP is measured here in the $US.
2. An increased demand for public expenditures to improve the prospects for economic development could drive the increase in the tax ratio, and could spur a tax reform effort that would produce such an increase. In this analysis, we proxy the demand for economic services by the share of government expenditures on economic services.
3. It is plausible that the increase in the tax ratio is determined in significant part by the demand for increased social service expenditures, whose

benefits may accrue heavily to low income families. To measure this effect, we use the share of government expenditures on social services.

4. The tax ratio in developing countries may be driven by a reliance on indirect taxation. In general, tax administration difficulties make the indirect tax system more revenue productive than income taxes in less developed countries. This is true for both the VAT and for some selective excises. The buoyancy of indirect taxes in developing countries has been markedly higher than that for income taxes over the past quarter century. We measure the reliance on indirect taxes in terms of their share of total tax revenues, and expect a positive association with the tax ratio.
5. The tax ratio is dampened by corruption. The null hypothesis is that corruption and taxation are substitutes.

Table 1. Tax Revenues as a Percent of GDP

Country Groups	1970s	1980s	1990s	2000s[a]
Industrialized	30.1 (8.3)	33.7 (8.4)	35.5 (8.5)	33.4 (8.4)
Developing	16.2 (7.6)	17.3 (8.3)	17.0 (7.7)	17.0 (7.9)
Transition		47.7 (9.7)	29.6 (11.0)	29.1 (9.0)
Total	19.8 (9.9)	21.6 (11.3)	22.6 (11.5)	21.8 (10.4)

Source: Government Finance Statistics Yearbook (2003).

Note: Standard deviations are shown in parentheses
a) Only limited data are available.

To test these hypotheses, we estimate the empirical relationship among a number of variables using a (unbalanced) pooled panel of data for up to 166 countries for the 1972-2001 period, estimated with a two-way fixed effects model. The statistical results are presented in Table 2. In all specifications we find that higher levels of per capita GDP drive up the tax ratio. We get this significant result whether the sample is all countries or is limited to less developed countries. The estimated elasticity is stable across different specifications and different sample compositions.

An increasing share of government spending in the economic services is not significantly associated with an increased tax ratio, either for all countries or for developing countries. However, in the LDC sample, an increased share of expenditures for social services is negatively associated with the share of taxes in total output. One implication that might be drawn from this finding is that countries that spend heavily on redistribution services, or even general quality-of-life services, do not get as much support for a higher average tax rate as do countries that do not. Based on these results, we cannot accept the hypothesis that the demand for more spending for social or economic services has been a key determinant of tax level increases in developing countries.

Table 2. Pooled Cross-Section Times Series Estimates[a] of the Determinants of the Ratio of Tax Revenue to GDP: For 1972 – 2001

	Equation 1	Equation 1a	Equation 2	Equation 2a	Equation 3
Constant [b]	1.3780	1.4517	1.3785	1.6756	1.5890
Per capita GDP[c]	0.2433 (8.17)	0.2301 (6.20)	0.2406 (8.05)	0.2381 (6.43)	0.2202 (6.84)
Percent of total expenditures on economic services	-0.0011 (1.62)	-0.0008 (-1.01)	...	...	...
Percent of total expenditure on social services	...		-0.0047 (0.19)	-0.0823 (-2.48)	...
Percent of Taxes Raised form Indirect Taxes	...		...		-0.0016 (-2.02)
$\bar{R}^2$	0.89	0.83	0.89	0.83	0.83
Sample	All Countries	LDCs	All Countries	LDCs	LDCs
Degrees of Freedom	163	116	163	116	128

Note:

a) *t*-values are shown in parentheses below the regression coefficient

b) two-way fixed effects

c) in logarithms

In equation 3, we report the results of a regression of per capita GDP and the share of indirect taxes on the tax ratio. This analysis is carried out for only developing economies. The results show that places with a greater share of indirect taxes in total taxes, cet. par., did not generate a significantly higher tax ratio during the 1972–2001 period. The coefficient in fact is negative when per capita GDP is held constant. This finding is not supportive of the null hypothesis. In any case, we can conclude that the determinants of the size of the tax ratio and its change go much further than simply the level of reliance on the VAT.

We do not have data on corruption for all years in this sample. We do make use of data provided by Transparency International for 1999. To test the corruption hypothesis, we compare the average increase in the tax ratio between the 15 "most corrupt" developing countries for which we have data, and other developing countries. The results show that the tax ratio increased by an average of 2.0 percent in the most corrupt countries and 3.1 percent in the 16 others, in those years for which we have data. The willingness to accept tax increases would appear to be greater in non-corrupt countries.

What we can say from this empirical analysis is that the ratio of taxes to GDP did not increase by very much in the developing countries over the past 30 years. Developing countries that did increase taxes did so largely in response to an increase in GDP. The increased reliance on indirect taxes did not seem to drive this increase, and emphasis on social service spending tended to dampen it. The choice to spend more for economic services did not seem to matter, and there is some support for the argument that corruption and taxation are substitutes.

On average during this period, tax reforms that targeted revenue neutrality with respect to the tax-GDP ratio would have been about on the mark. Though there is much variation across countries, the average developing economy seems to have been content with a level of taxes roughly equivalent to 17 percent of GDP.

2.2 The Structure of Taxation

The average level of taxes in developing economies has not changed much. This leads us to ask whether there has been significant change in the mix of taxes, i.e., structural reform. To measure the structure of taxation, we use the IMF dis-aggregation of taxes. In Table 3 we report the changing share of total taxes attributable to three of these categories, further broken out by industrialized, developing and transition countries, for the period from 1970 to the present.

Table 3. Tax Structure Changes (percent of total taxes)

Income Tax	1970	1980	1990	2000[a]
Industrialized	35.5 (15.1)	37.8 (13.7)	38.6 (10.9)	53.8 (8.1)
Developing	29.6 (19.5)	28.6 (19.1)	27.6 (16.5)	28.3 (17.8)
Transition	12.3 (14.4)	16.5 (13.8)	26.7 (9.6)	23.3 (6.5)
Total	30.7 (18.8)	30.2 (18.5)	29.7 (15.4)	28.5 (16.4)
Indirect Taxes				
Industrialized	27.2 (10.1)	29.4 (9.0)	30.5 (10.1)	19.8 (10.7)
Developing	25.2 (14.3)	29.3 (17.3)	34.9 (17.7)	40.1 (17.8)
Transition	10.5 (11.1)	21.8 (14.4)	37.9 (12.3)	42.1 (9.6)
Total	25.3 (13.5)	28.9 (15.8)	34.2 (15.9)	39.0 (16.4)
Taxes on International Trade				
Industrialized	4.6 (5.8)	2.8 (4.3)	1.0 (2.0)	1.0 (0.6)
Developing	32.4 (18.4)	30.7 (20.2)	25.6 (18.9)	19.0 (18.0)
Transition	7.7 (8.2)	5.2 (3.8)	7.6 (7.3)	5.4 (5.5)
Total	25.2 (20.2)	23.8 (21.4)	18.2 (18.9)	14.1 (16.5)

Source: Government Finance Statistics Yearbook (2003).

Note: Standard deviations are shown in parentheses
a) Only limited data are available.

The results for industrialized countries show an upward drift in reliance on income taxes, mostly due to increase in revenues from the individual income tax and revenues from payroll taxes to finance social security. The corporate income tax share held up during this period, despite significant rate reductions (Keen and Simone, 2004). There was an increase in dependence on indirect taxes, particularly general sales taxes, but a declining reliance on taxes on international trade. The growth of the VAT and trade liberalization explain this pattern. Most of the change in tax structure over this 30 year period appears to be marginal. While there may be major changes in rate and base structure beneath these averages, comprehensive reform that led to big changes in the tax structure does not appear to have been dominant in the industrialized economies in this period. The five point run-up in the ratio of tax revenue to GDP during this period may explain the absence of structural reform.

The tax structure shifts in the developing countries appear to have been more pronounced. The reliance on indirect taxes increased from about 25 percent of total taxes in the 1970s to about 35 percent by the end of the 1990s. Over the same period, the reliance on international trade taxes fell from about 32 percent to about 25 percent. Trade liberalization during the late 20th century was obviously a driving force in tax reform in the developing countries. So was the growing tendency to adopt the value added tax and improve upon its administration. For the developing economies, there was little reported change in the use of income taxes, though there has been a declining reliance on the company income tax. As Keen and Simone (2004) have argued, revenues from the corporate income tax have fallen because of a combination of rate reductions and base narrowing due to incentive polices. More generally with respect to the income tax, the story is the continued inability of the tax administration in less developed countries to assess and collect the income tax base. Apparently, the improved ability to capture information from the public, and the design of new presumptive methods has not been enough to shift emphasis toward income taxes in these countries.

The standard deviations reported in Table 3 suggest a large variation among countries in tax structure choices, especially among developing countries. Is there a pattern to the inter-country variations in these tax structure changes? Three hypotheses might be offered to explain these structure shifts in the less developed countries.

1. The growth in GDP has created more "tax handles." These are primarily in the business sector and are susceptible to capture by the VAT and other general indirect taxes. One would also expect a positive relationship between the growth in income and the share of income taxes in the total revenue mix, because the income tax base is more easily captured as economies modernize. We would expect a negative relationship between GDP and trade taxes, because countries that are modernizing are likely in a mode of reducing tax rates on imports and eliminating taxes on exports.
2. The decline in reliance on taxes on international trade is attributable to trade liberalization. Two factors are at work here. The "openness" ratio (imports plus exports divided by GDP) suggests a broadening of the tax

base on international trade and the possibility of an increased reliance on taxes on international trade. However, increased openness also suggests more pressure to move the taxation of imports to the domestic side and reduce the taxation of international trade.

3. There should be a relationship between tax structure and expenditure structure. If a country is egalitarian in its expenditure choices, e.g., a heavier share of expenditures on social services, then one might expect a similar set of choices on the tax side. That is, one would expect a heavier concentration of income taxes in the revenue structure.[6] By the same token, one might expect that a heavier concentration of expenditures on economic services would be associated with a heavier reliance on the taxes that impose less of a burden on the return of capital and on entrepreneurship. On the other hand, this may be outweighed by a tax base effect, i.e., increased spending on economic services in the longer run may lead to more investment, a stronger company and individual income tax base, and a greater share of income taxes in the revenue mix.

The analysis of the pooled data and the statistical results presented in Table 4 supports some, but not all of these hypotheses. The share of total taxes raised from taxes on international trade fell significantly as income level increased over this period, but it increased with openness, i.e. with increases in the size of the foreign trade sector. The tax handles hypothesis gets strong support in the income tax equation. Per capita GDP is a significant determinant of the income tax share for both developing and developed countries. However, per capita GDP is not significantly related to the growth in the indirect tax share.

Finally, there is only weak evidence that there is a linkage between expenditure structure and revenue structure. The indirect tax share is not related to the share of the budget spent on social services in developing countries. Nor is it significantly related to the share spent on economic services. Neither is the social services spending share related to the reliance on income taxes. These findings seem more consistent with an explanation that the tastes for public expenditures and the tastes for various forms of taxes are independent. There is evidence of an income tax base effect associated with spending for economic services. This is consistent with the hypothesis that countries might, over time, build their income tax base by investing in economic development infrastructure.

In sum, there would appear to be evidence that reforms of tax systems in developing countries have taken place in the past 30 years. The decline of reliance on taxes on international trade can be linked to trade liberalization. We can also attribute the modest growth in income tax shares to GDP growth and to the relatively easier time of assessing and collecting income taxes in modernizing economies. The growth in the indirect tax share – the big change in developing country revenue structures—seems to have taken place independent of either income growth or the growth in the foreign trade sector.

Table 4. Pooled Cross-Section, Times Series Estimates[a] of the Determinants of Tax Structure Change: 1972-2001

	Income Tax Share of Total Taxes		Indirect Tax Share of Total Taxes		Taxes on International Trade as a Share of Total Taxes	
Constant	-3.9059	-3.4959	47.3832	41.6770	69.7286	78.8930
Per apita GDP[c]	7.4278 (7.95)	8.5246 (7.98)	-1.4520 (1.63)	-0.8045 (0.78)	-9.5516 (11.17)	-11.1702 (10.46)
Openness	...	...	...	...	0.0354 (3.13)	0.0378 (2.59)
Percent of expenditures on economic services	0.1104 (5.07)	0.0815 (3.10)	-0.0555 (2.66)	-0.0269 (1.07)	...	...
Percent of Expenditures on Social Services	0.0664 (2.68)	-0.0470 (1.36)	0.0241 (1.02)	0.0119 (0.36)	...	...
R^2	0.89	0.85	0.84	0.85	0.89	0.85
Sample	All Countries	LDCs	All Countries	LDCs	All Countries	LDCs
Degrees of Freedom	163	115	163	115	172	125

Note:

a) *t*-values are shown in parentheses below regression coefficient

b) includes individual income tax, company income tax, payroll tax and social security tax.

c) in logarithms

If the tax structures of developing countries are evolving toward those of industrialized countries, there is substantial structural change in the future for low income countries. The reliance on international trade taxes will continue to fall and the reliance on income taxes will increase as fast as tax administration capabilities will permit. And though it is not shown by these aggregate statistics, there will be significant base broadening. This suggests a future for comprehensive tax reform in developing countries. The question to which we now turn is whether there are some principles or rules that can govern such comprehensive reform in this setting.

3. THE APPROACH TO COMPREHENSIVE TAX REFORM

There are not hard and fast rules about the best way to do a comprehensive reform. Numerous experts and international institutions have led tax reforms and in some cases, the lessons learned have been written down. Examples are Goode (1984), Gillis (1989), Harberger (1989), Bahl (1991), Thirsk (1991), McLure and Zodrow (1997), and World Bank (1991). It should come as no surprise that there is not complete agreement on the best way to do comprehensive tax reform. While the thinking about the elements of good tax structure design has not changed all that much,[7] the setting in which comprehensive tax reform must be packaged has changed quite a lot.

In large part, this volume is about the new setting and this paper is about whether the rules ought to be different because of this new setting. In the discussion below, we offer a set of rules for reform that would seem to fit this new setting.

3.1 The New Setting

The new setting for comprehensive tax reform may cause different thinking about the options for tax reform. There are four factors that will shape tax choices in different ways.

First, the future should hold increases in the average share of taxes in GDP in the developing nations. The more or less constant tax share of about 17 percent of GDP is not likely to hold in the future given the needs for infrastructure and pro-poor services, and the pressures from urbanization and debt repayment. Second, the next round of reform of the value added tax will be much more focused on adjustments in the tax base. This can be a difficult sell. The big revenue hits from the initial introduction of the VAT will not be repeated, as base broadening will be a more slow going strategy for revenue enhancement.[8]

Third, tax reform choices will be more limited because of the new setting. International competition will likely push LDCs away from trying to expand reliance on the company income tax, and in fact, it may push them towards more use of tax incentives. Increased taxes on imports and exports are probably not in the future as a major revenue option. More likely will be continued reduction of the tax rates on imports, the simplification of effective rates of tax on import duties, and revenue reduction from trade taxes as a result of external factors such as compliance with WTO rules and joining trade agreements such as the proposed Free Trade Agreement of the Americas.

Finally, with tax options more limited, LDC tax planners may finally begin to take a closer look at their tax expenditure budgets. The opportunities for revenue enhancement and efficiency gains by moving away from tax preferences are considerable.

In this new context, some of the longstanding ideas about the best route to tax reform might be rethought and possibly some priorities might be changed. The following six propositions are suggestions of this rethinking.

PROPOSITION 1: A COMPREHENSIVE REFORM CAN SUCCEED IN A CRISIS FISCAL SETTING.

The call to do a comprehensive tax reform might be made at a time when bad times have befallen the economy and there is need to adopt bold new actions. Or, it might happen when a new political leadership has taken hold and wants to make a shift in economic policy. Or, it might happen as part of an attempt to resolve a fiscal crisis, e.g., big deficits, a taxpayer revolt and a compliance crisis, or a need to ratchet up (or down) the size of government. In rare cases, it might be prompted by having to make a decision about how to dispose of a significant fiscal surplus. One can think of examples of all of these settings. Rarely will the professional staff have enough influence to call the timing of comprehensive reform. If the timing is not forced by a donor or creditor, it will be determined by a political clock.

One might even question whether comprehensive tax reform should be on the policy menu for developing countries. After all, low income countries are often plagued by budget deficits, significant debt overhangs, inflated public employment rolls and slow growing output. Infrastructure levels are deficient, and poverty levels are often severe, placing pressure on the current budget and forcing government fiscal planners to think only about getting through the current fiscal year. In such a setting, something as high-minded as finding the "right tax structure" which will have only long term payoffs, may seem too costly.

In fact, it might be argued that the best time to do a comprehensive reform of the tax structure is when the economy and the revenue structure are performing poorly (Bahl, 1991). There is a sense that something must be done and tax policy is one area where the government can take aggressive action. The developing country setting might be most appropriate for a comprehensive reform, and policy changes are more likely to be enacted because big changes will be more acceptable. This may be more true now than in the past. There will be more pressure to increase revenue mobilization, a realignment of taxes due to trade liberalization and international competition will be driving government to take another look at their tax structure, and the easy money from a new VAT is a thing of the past for many countries.

To make a good comprehensive reform happen in a developing country, it is necessary to get the key decision-makers thinking beyond the current-year revenue issue to thinking about the overall impact of the tax system on the economy. This is arguably more easily done when the present system is failing. In such times, it is easier to focus the attention of policy makers on the structural problems with the entire tax system and to think through the ways in which the tax system may be retarding economic growth. The same inefficiencies that are so visible when the economy is not going well tend to become invisible in periods of economic growth. Consequently, when the economy is growing, the attention of tax reformers shifts to piecemeal adjustments that are "popular" or that appear to improve vertical equity, and to administrative improvements. The attention of politicians shifts to the expenditure side of the budget during periods of economic growth.

Comprehensive tax reform can be successful if undertaken during a period of fiscal crisis, but only if the goals of the comprehensive reform are kept separate from the goals of the short term revenue fix. Not to keep these separate poses significant risks. As Gillis (1989, p. 506) notes, tax reforms have usually failed when enacted in response to acute fiscal crisis. The fiscal architecture of the deficit reduction reform is built in too much of a hurry, and the fixes are too short term.

The potential pitfall to doing tax reform during a time of poor economic performance is that the government's interest and the energies of the project will be siphoned away to deal with the exigencies of each year's fiscal crisis. A comprehensive reform may be underway precisely because budget deficits are large and growing, but these deficits may be the main impediment to implementing a comprehensive reform. There is great pressure to move the budget toward balance. But quick revenue fixes are often at odds with good structural reform. "Raise the rate" is more often the watchword in revenue enhancement programs than is "broaden the base."

An important but often overlooked issue is that there may be transition costs associated with a structural reform. For example, the reduction in import duty rates in favor of taxing imported goods under the VAT may involve a revenue loss for the period until trade volume increases enough to make up the slack. Or, removing certain deductions from the personal income tax might be a long run revenue winner, but the administration might not be able to capture the new base immediately. So, there are pressures in the early years of a comprehensive reform that might compromise either income distribution objectives or the budget deficit, and these may require interim adjustments.

There clearly are important constraints to trying to build a comprehensive reform during a time of budget crisis. But, these can be managed by separating short term and perhaps temporary fixes from long term structural reforms. Most important is that the comprehensive reform exercise be identified with a long term strategy that is clearly separated from the short term, stop gap measures (Martinez-Vazquez and McNab, 2000). The fact is that the fiscal crisis itself gives the rationale for comprehensive reform and may be a key element of selling any new structural program.

Proposition 2: Comprehensive Tax Reform Should be Designed as Big-Bang vs. Piecemeal.

The conventional wisdom probably favors an incremental approach to tax reform, i.e., it argues that if the existing system is shocked too much, the success of the proposed reform will be compromised. In fact, Goode (1984) made the argument that a reason for the failure of tax reform programs was the insistence by the framers that the entire package of reforms should be accepted as a one off proposition. More recent observers can point to the case of Colombia, where tax reform has been a case study in gradualism over the past two decades (Bird, 2004).

There are good reasons to argue for gradualism. Individuals and businesses have become accustomed to the present system and even to its shortcomings, they understand how it works and how they may comply with its provisions, and they have long since capitalized many of its features. To shock the economy with anything more than an incremental reform will impose significant transition costs as firms, individuals and the government try to adjust to new administrative burdens and to the new distribution of tax burdens. These adjustments will almost certainly lead to political controversy and diminish the probability that the reform will be implemented and/or will succeed. In developing countries, there is the additional hard question of how much the tax administration system can absorb.

The strong counter argument is that comprehensive reform can take place only if the system is shocked. There are two principal supporting arguments. The first is that the reform must bring enough of a change for the taxpayer to see a package of gains and losses. This is opposed to a change in a single tax, where there is a clear division between "winners" and "losers." To illustrate, consider the following:

- A shift from a progressive to a flat rate individual income tax would be more acceptable to working class taxpayers (who would be losers under an equal yield reform program) if it is accompanied by a tightening of the deductions and credit policy that are seen to favor the higher income.
- Elimination of exemptions, holidays and other preferential treatments under the company income tax would be more acceptable if accompanied by an overall rate reduction. Some companies would at the same time win from the lower rate and lose from the withdrawal of preferential tax treatment.
- The elimination of some exempt categories of goods under the VAT would be more acceptable to consumers if the overall VAT rate were reduced.
- A "packaged" tax reform that includes changes in income and consumption taxes produces an outcome where virtually all sectors see an increase in the burden for some taxes and a reduction for others. Such a scenario may be seen by the taxpaying public as coming close to satisfying the maxim of fairness in taxation.

When political leaders can mix and match tax reform components, the prospects for negotiating an acceptable reform package will be enhanced. There should be a little pleasure and a little pain in the new tax package for nearly everyone.

The second supporting argument for a comprehensive approach is that the response of saving, investment, work effort and compliance with a tax rate change may be quite small. Most empirical work in developing countries has found low price elasticities.[9] Therefore, a big change in effective tax rates will be required if there is to be any significant impact on resource allocation. If a driving reason behind the tax reform is to stimulate economic activity by changing the choices made by economic agents, the comprehensive approach would seem preferable to the approach that produces less of a shock to the system.

PROPOSITION 3: THE OBJECTIVE OF VERTICAL EQUITY CANNOT DRIVE A COMPREHENSIVE TAX REFORM.

There is no question but that discussion of the effects of tax reform on the vertical equity of the tax system will be a central part of the debate about the "right" reform package. And, in fact, much of the firestorm around any proposal will center on its regressivity or lack of progressivity. A "burden study" will almost always be part of the comprehensive reform program of background studies.

In truth, policy makers and politicians are not usually so concerned with the impacts on the distribution of effective tax rates across all income groups. The tax burden distributions are often hard to read and understand, and their estimation is often subject to some heroic assumptions and severe data limitations. More likely the focus of policymakers will be on the impacts on particular population groups, e.g., the bottom 20 percent of income earners in the population, or the top 5 percent of income earners.

Some who have done comprehensive reform studies believe that vertical equity cannot be the driving force behind a comprehensive tax reform program in a developing country (Bahl, 1991). In part, this is because developing countries cannot implement progressive tax systems, and in part it is because the costs of moving to a higher level of vertical equity are very high. These costs might include the revenue loss due to exemption of low income families from tax, the efficiency costs associated with the higher rates imposed elsewhere to make up for the revenue loss, and possibly the displacement effects that might result from the introduction of "progressive" measures such as high marginal personal income tax rates.

Tax policy design often mis-steps when it comes to building equity features into the tax structure. The following are features that often find their way into the discussion of comprehensive tax reform, in the name of enhancing vertical equity. As noted, such obvious equity-enhancing measures may not have the desired effects.

- Graduated rate income tax structures have the feel of giving a progressive distribution of burdens, but in fact the level of evasion and avoidance in developing countries often negates this outcome. Moreover, the introduction of progressive rates is often accompanied by the introduction of new deductions and other loopholes for the higher income. Usually, a proportional distribution of burdens is about as good as can be expected.
- Company income taxes are popular measures to place burdens on the wealthy, but the real distribution of burdens may be much less progressive. International competition may lead to a reduction in the tax, and part of the burden may be shifted backward to labor.
- A popular notion is that in the name of progressivity, the property tax on structures should be raised relative to that on land. In fact, this may reduce the progressivity of the distribution of property tax burdens.[10]

Probably the best that can be done in a comprehensive reform program is to argue that the burden on the lowest income classes should not be worsened. Some tax reform programs have been successful in doing this, largely by exempting essential consumption items from indirect taxes (Gillis, 1989). However, such adjustments may be more difficult in good, comprehensive tax reforms in the future. For example, exemptions and zero rating under the existing VAT may be ill advised and pruned out as the next round of VAT reforms is focused on base-broadening. Moreover, the goal of protecting the poor from taxation may have also led to protection of the non-poor, and suggests other targets for reform, e.g., low taxes on petroleum products, low charges for electricity, the exemption of "essential" consumption items, and high individual income tax thresholds.

Some will come to the conclusion that vertical equity can best be handled on the expenditure side of the budget, and that taxation is too blunt an instrument to do much about the distribution of income. Bird (1992, chapter 5) argues that this is too simplistic a conclusion, because too little is known about the impact of either taxes or expenditures on poverty reduction.

PROPOSITION 4: THE EFFECTS OF TAXES ON ECONOMIC DECISIONS WILL PLAY A MORE IMPORTANT ROLE IN THE DESIGN OF COMPREHENSIVE REFORM THAN IN THE PAST.

If there is a new political economy of tax reform, it is mostly about emphasizing the effects of taxes on the economy. Some of this new emphasis is imposed by external factors, e.g., WTO rules or international competition. And some of this is recognition by governments that leveling the playing field for investors is probably the best route to faster economic growth. In most cases, however, developing countries are still in a mode of targeting favored sectors with preferential tax treatments. Some examples of the major preferences that might become under more scrutiny in comprehensive tax reform are the following:

- Exemptions and targeted incentives under the corporation income tax might be replaced by lower tax rates.
- Tariff structures may become more uniform and replace the system of wide variations in effective tariff rates that exists in many developing countries today.
- Extensive lists of exemptions and zero rated goods may be reduced dramatically in the next round of VAT reforms, as may unnecessary rate differentiation.
- As tax administration capabilities improve, this disparity may be reduced.

Perhaps the most difficult selling job to political leadership will be arguing that distortions to economic choices should be removed because they impose an excess burden on the economy.

PROPOSITION 5: FIRST POLICY, THEN ADMINISTRATION.

Most students of taxation recognize that the tax administration in developing countries is a major problem. Most leaders in the fiscal reform movement have recited a major lesson from comprehensive reform studies: policy change without administrative improvement will likely doom a tax reform program to failure. International agencies and bi-lateral donors have ongoing programs of technical assistance to improve tax administration practices and to upgrade the capacity of the staff who administer the tax system. These efforts add value by improving the collection rate and the fairness of the tax system. But still, in the case of comprehensive reform, the question might be raised as to which should come first: an improved tax structure, or an improved tax administration?

A reasonable proposition about the best sequencing of policy and administration is to get the policy right and then deal with the administrative problems. Many will disagree with this. The consumers (and sponsors) of a reform often cannot see beneath a plethora of administrative problems to the real issue, which may well be a badly structured tax. How many times is it said "...what is the sense in creating a new tax structure when the old one is not properly administered?" Too often the call for technical assistance in tax administration from the IRS or from one of the international agencies is premature.

There are two good reasons why it is appropriate for a comprehensive reform to put policy change ahead of administrative overhaul in the sequencing. First, administrative improvements can often generate a quick revenue impact, and of course this may have considerable value. But it may also divert attention away from the real problem which may have to do with structure. Because this may satisfy some of the urgency about revenue needs, the government may lose its enthusiasm about rethinking its tax structure. If the reform goes no further than administration, the government will not even go through the exercise of questioning whether the tax system is affecting the economy in ways that reinforce or offset government objectives.

Second, the true, underlying administrative problem may be with the tax structure. The tax system may be so complicated as to be beyond the capacity of the government to properly administer, or it may be so unfair that payment of taxes will be resisted no matter how much the administration improves. It makes little sense to invest heavily in an administrative infrastructure to assess and collect a tax that is not likely to be in the picture in the long run, at least in its present form. Examples that support this argument include some individual income taxes that are riddled with credits and deductions and would require significant investment to improve administrative practices; or VAT thresholds that are set so low that they require significant administrative effort to capture small taxpayers.

The maxim of "policy first" does not mean that administration improvements cannot begin to march forward until a good structure is in place. Administrative improvements should be a continuing process and there are a wealth of activities that can be undertaken quite independent of structural reform, e.g., training, some basic procedures of audit and assessment, accounting and reporting, and certain EDP improvements.

PROPOSITION 6: FISCAL REFORM IS PROBABLY BETTER THAN TAX REFORM.

Arguably, there are two approaches to comprehensive reform. One is to look only at the tax side of the budget. Usually, the approach is to target a revenue neutral structural reform. The analytic framework is differential incidence, and the expenditure side of the budget is ignored. This approach has the advantage of being manageable in terms of resources required to do the study, and in terms of the time needed to get the work done.

The differential incidence approach, while perhaps the most feasible approach leaves much to be desired. For one thing, it often does not include all elements of financing, e.g., a review of all user charges is rarely part of the study. But more important, it may ignore the fact that Government may be forced to introduce the tax reform at the same time it introduces revenue-enhancing measures to address a revenue shortfall. In short, it leaves out the expenditure side.

It might be the time to ask the broader question about fiscal reform, i.e., one that also includes consideration of the expenditure side of the budget. This would be a more difficult job, would require more resources and time, and will raise many more controversial issues, but it will allow the government to get a better picture of the overall implications of the financing reform under consideration. If one believes the old adage in public finance, that finance follows function, then he or she will be an advocate of the comprehensive fiscal approach.

What would be the advantages of this approach? Certainly it would open the door for a far-ranging analysis and for considering many more reform options. A few examples of the broader questions that might be asked are:

- The vertical equity question could be broadened to consider both tax burdens and expenditure benefits. The differential tax incidence approach to comprehensive reform often leaves the issue at a statement such as "the distributional effects are better corrected on the expenditure side of the budget." The comprehensive fiscal reform would build this directly into the analysis.

- The revenue target of the financing reform could be identified in terms of the projected elasticity of desired expenditures. This would be a far better method of defining "revenue neutrality," which differential incidence analysis usually defines revenue neutrality as the yield of the present system.

4. CONCLUSION: HOW TO GET SUCCESSFUL IMPLEMENTATION

Of course the goal of government is to get its comprehensive reform plan from the bookshelf to implementation. Are there some principles that might be followed to maximize the chances of this happening? Four guidelines might be considered for getting a comprehensive reform program to implementation.

First, the government must see the project as its own and not that of a donor or even that of a technical assistance research team (Bahl 1991; Gillis, 1989). There must be a champion for the reform, and clearly the champion ought to be a power bloc within the government. The advocates should include the Ministry of Finance, and in most cases the final recommendations of the comprehensive reform effort should come from the Ministry. Ideally, the Ministry would be advised by an appointed, representative private sector group that is commissioned to work with the technical team and form its own recommendations. The theory here is for ownership of the program to rest jointly with the government who will impose the tax and bear the political risk, and with the private sector who will ultimately comply with the new tax system. The technical team should assist the government and the private sector commission in developing recommendations, but should not offer independent views.

Second, the technical assistance team should have the right mix of skills and experience, and above all, should have expert credentials. There is something powerful about drawing on the international experience, and the technical assistance team should have the ability to bring this experience to the discussion a relevant way. Most countries have little desire to copy another tax structure, but there is great comfort in getting a thorough assessment of what has worked elsewhere and what has not. The technical assistance team can also bring hard data analysis to the discussion, and in that way, much of the mythology associated with critiques of various components of the tax system can be discredited. Modern tax reforms make use of quantitative tax burden studies based on the modern incidence assumptions, micro-simulation modeling to estimate revenue impacts associated with various rate and base changes, CGE modeling to develop estimates of tax structure change on the economy, etc.

Third, tax reform should not be hurried. It takes time to get the technical proposals properly in place, and the public debate needs time. Comprehensive tax reform often requires new thinking about tax structures. Governments, and the population at large are not good at reacting quickly to such big changes in policy. Sometimes after a debate of several months, what was a radical sounding idea when first introduced becomes a regular part of the discourse. The hope of most tax reformers is that the sequence involves a completed study, then recommendations, then implementation of the reform program shortly thereafter. Usually this does not happen because it takes time for new ideas to be absorbed. The implementation of a major tax structure revision may not take place until years after the initial seeds were planted. It is necessary for a blueprint for comprehensive tax reform to be developed, but political and administrative constraints may mean that it is implemented over a period of time. As Gillis (1989, p. 510) has so properly documented, "Delayed reform is not necessarily lost reform."

While one cannot hurry a comprehensive tax reform, one also cannot dawdle. Governments are not willing to be associated indefinitely with tax reform, even good tax reform. Comprehensive reform tends to be associated with a particular administration and there is need to get on with it while the power is in place and while there is still enthusiasm for the reform program. Even the best of tax reform programs carries unfavorable connotations for most citizens and politicians, and the zeal for even so noble a goal as "getting the prices right" wanes as time goes by and the next election year draws close.

Finally, education about tax reform is important. The staff papers of a reform study should be written in a popular version and should be made available to the interested public. Public hearings also are a good idea, and placing technical material in university and think tank libraries is an important part of selling a tax reform and keeping the ideas in play (McLure and Zodrow, 1997). So too is some education of the press, who are capable of destroying a reform program without fully understanding it. Finally, involving local tax experts as consultants to the program is an important ingredient of local ownership.

Notes

1. Professor of Economics, Andrew Young School of Policy Studies, Georgia State University. Bayar Tumennasan provided valuable research assistance for this paper.
2. Some of the early and very good comprehensive tax reform work in Latin America is Musgrave (1981), Musgrave and Gillis (1971), and Shoup (1959). In the last quarter century, comprehensive reform programs of note include those for Jamaica (Bahl 1991) and Indonesia (Gillis, 1989a).
3. For an interesting review, see Bird (2004).
4. The calculation rule used throughout this paper is to compute the mean value for the ratio for all of those years in a decade for which data are available. In some cases, all years will be available and in others only some years will be available. We ignore those years not available. We report but do not emphasize the results for the 2000s, both because there are only a few years available, and because the number of countries whose data are reported for those years is limited. Only 36 countries were reported for at least one of the years, 2000-2002 in the 2003 data file. These included 5 OECD countries, 19 transition countries, and 12 developing countries.
5. In this comparison, we use an unbalanced sample based on available data (see footnote 2). Keen and Simone (2004a) make a similar comparison using a common sample of countries, and reach the same conclusion.
6. This of course oversimplifies. A more egalitarian set of taxing choices might also involve exemption of essential consumption goods from the VAT, or a high income tax threshold.
7. A useful handbook on tax policy design is Shome (1995) and a good discussion of the issues is in Bird (1992).
8. In their sample of developing countries, Keen and Simone (2004a, page 16) report about 30 percent had a VAT in 1990, but that by 2000 this number had risen to about 75 percent.
9. See, for example, Gandhi (1987), Bahl (1991), and Stepanyan (2003).
10. This happens because the increased tax on structures may discourage investment in housing consumption.

References

Bahl, Roy W. (1991), "The Economics and Politics of the Jamaican Tax Reform", pp. 587-600 in: Roy Bahl, editor, *The Jamaica Tax Reform*, Cambridge, MA: Lincoln Institute of Land Policy.

Bird, Richard (2004), "Managing Tax Reform", *International Bureau of Fiscal Documentation*, February, pp. 42-55.

Bird, Richard (1992), *Tax Policy and Economic Development*, Baltimore: Johns Hopkins Press.

Gandhi, Ved P. (1987), *Supply Side Tax Policy*, Washington, D.C.: International Monetary Fund.

Gillis, Malcolm (1989), "Tax Reform: Lessons from Postwar Experience in Developing Nations", Chapter 14 in: Malcolm Gillis, editor, *Tax Reform in Developing Countries*, Durham: Duke University Press.

Gillis, Malcolm (1989a), "Comprehensive Tax Reform: The Indonesia Experience, 1981-1988", Chapter 4 in: Malcolm Gillis, editor, *Tax Reform in Developing Countries*, Durham: Duke University Press.

Goode, Richard (1984), *Government Finance in Developing Countries*, Washington: The Brookings Institution.

Harberger, Arnold C. (1989), "Lessons of Tax Reform from the Experiences of Uruguay, Indonesia, and Chile", Chapter 2 in: Malcolm Gillis, editor, *Tax Reform in Developing Countries*, Durham: Duke University Press.

International Monetary Fund (2003), *Government Finance Statistics Yearbook*, Washington, D.C.: International Monetary Fund.

Keen, Michael and Alejandro Simone (2004), "Is Tax Harmonization Harming developing Countries more than Developed?", *Tax Notes International*, June, pp. 1317-1329.

Keen, Michael and Alejandro Simone (2004a), "Tax Policy in Developing Countries: Some Lessons from the 1990s, and Some Challenges Ahead", pp. 302-352 in: Sanjeer Gupta, Benedict Clements and Gabriela Inchauste, editors, *Helping Countries Develop: The Role of Fiscal Policy*, Washington, D.C.: International Monetary Fund.

Martinez-Vazquez, Jorge and Robert M. McNab (2000), "The Tax Reform Experiment in Transitional Countries", *National Tax Journal*, June, pp. 273-298.

McLure, Charles and George Zodrow (1997), "Thirty Years of Tax Reform in Colombia", in: Wayne Thirsk, editor, *Tax Reform in Developing Countries*, Washington, D.C.: The World Bank.

Musgrave, R. A. (1981), *Fiscal Reform in Bolivia: Final Report of the Bolivian Mission on Tax*, Cambridge: Harvard Law School.

Musgrave, R. A. and Gillis, M. (eds.) (1971), *Fiscal Reform for Columbia: Final Report of the Colombian Mission on Tax Reform*, Cambridge: Harvard Law School.

Shome, P. (ed.) (1995), *Tax Policy Handbook*, Washington, D.C.: Fiscal Affairs Department, International Monetary Fund.

Shoup, Carl (1959), *The Fiscal System of Venezuela*, Baltimore: Johns Hopkins University Press.

Stepanyan, Vahram (2003), *Reforming Tax Systems: Experience of the Baltics, Russia, and Other Countries of the Former Soviet Union, Fiscal Affairs Department Working Paper/03/173*, Washington, D.C.: International Monetary Fund.

Thirsk, Wayne (1991), "Lessons from Tax Reform: An Overview", pp. 57-70 in: Javad Khalilzadeh-Shirazi and Anwar Shah, editors, *Tax Policy in Developing Countries*, Washington: The World Bank.

World Bank (1991), *Lessons of Tax Reform*, Washington, D.C.: The World Bank.

Index